THE GRAND HUCKSTER

Judge Roy Hofheinz

THE GRAND HUCKSTER

HOUSTON'S JUDGE ROY HOFHEINZ

GENIUS OF THE ASTRODOME

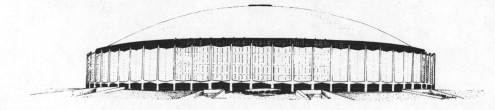

EDGAR W. RAY

MEMPHIS

Memphis State University Press
Memphis, Tennessee

ISBN 0-87870-069-2

To the two wives of Roy Hofheinz, Mary Frances (left) and Dene (right), without whose inspiration the Judge could not have reached unprecedented heights.

And to Maidee, my wife, without whose patience, understanding, keen reading ability, and encouragement, this biography could not have been completed.

TABLE OF CONTENTS

Acknowledgments

During more than two years of research and writing for *The Grand Huckster*, I found it necessary to tape record interviews with more than 150 individuals associated during a half century with Roy Hofheinz. This procedure was necessary because the Judge, handicapped by a stroke in 1970, was not physically able to recall and discuss at length his many accomplishments. Quotations attributed to Hofheinz throughout the book came either from newspaper or magazine stories or from people who recalled what he said and did. So many people helped by providing me with information that I cannot acknowledge all of them here. Their stories and comments, which appear throughout the text, represent an enormous contribution to this biography, and I am deeply grateful to each of them for their generous assistance.

Special thanks I owe to the following:

Mary Frances Hofheinz and her sister, Sally Sullivan, who spent countless hours removing from old files clippings, pictures, and data that, without their help, I could not have utilized. Mary Frances' knowledge of the Judge dates from 1953, and without her many recollections and reviewing of facts only part of the story could have been told. Her assistance was the most valuable I had.

John Easter, now financial officer of Hofheinz Interests, Incorporated, for his keen insight into the character of the Judge and for his sharing of an intimate knowledge of his longtime employer's business affairs.

John J. McMullen, chairman of the Houston Sports Association, and Talbot Smith, chief operations officer of the Houston Astros, for their permission to use copyrighted HSA publications and pictures.

Publishers and editors of the *Houston Chronicle*, which bought the *Houston Press* in 1964, and of the *Houston Post* for their permission to use published stories and photographs from their newspapers. *Chronicle* librarian Sherry Ray and *Post* librarian Kathy Foley were extremely helpful as I sought information about people, many deceased, in Hofheinz's life.

Mr. and Mrs. Harold Israel, of Houston's Gulf Photo, whose cooperation in making available photographs, many in color, went far beyond the call of professional duty.

Mrs. Marjorie R. Terry, of New Smyrna Beach, Florida, my retirement home, whose accurate transcriptions of voices on hundreds of tapes and whose typing of completed chapters expedited my work tremendously.

Mrs. Lyndon Baines Johnson (the lovely Lady Bird) who made it possible for me to have access to the Lyndon B. Johnson Library in Austin, Texas, where I found information, in addition to her own, concerning the long friendship of the late President Johnson and Hofheinz.

Dr. Billy Mac Jones, president of Memphis State University during the writing of this book and a former Texan, whose enthusiasm for the early chapters of the book, sent to him by me as a friend for comment because of his reputation as a historian, led to the signing of a contract for the biography's publication by Memphis State University Press.

Susan Adler Thorp, Vince Vawter, and Joan Hassell of Memphis, whose expertise in condensing some detailed chapters helped the biography reach publication sooner than it could have had I rewritten my own vast research. Mrs. Thorp became a teacher of journalism at Memphis State University after serving as a reporter on the *Memphis Press-Scimitar*. Vawter is news editor of the *Press-Scimitar*. Both were hired as cub reporters by the author when he was managing editor of the *Press-Scimitar*. Miss Hassell's experience as a writer and editor of Memphis publications before she began to free-lance in the field included work for Memphis State University.

Louis M. Hoynes, Jr., New York attorney, and his partner, Bob Kheel, who detailed from court records the chapter concerning Hofheinz's historic recovery of $50 million from Mattel toy corporation for stockholders of Ringling Bros. and Barnum & Bailey Combined Shows, Incorporated.

Ed Ray

1

The Hungry Dreamer

Roy Mark Hofheinz was two years old when his Aunt Deedee enthusiastically forecast her nephew's future to his mother, Nonie Planchard Hofheinz: "Nonie, that boy is going to be a great talker and salesman!" Nonie smiled in appreciation of Deedee's admiration for her only child and watched as her sister took photographs of the boy.

During this conversation Roy sat in his high chair, talking quickly and distinctly and waving his arms for emphasis and attention, just as he usually did during his aunt's almost daily visits with her older sister in Beaumont, Texas. Roy had been born on April 10, 1912, in a Beaumont hospital. He was a "very nice, pretty baby," as Aunt Deedee described him, and all members of the Planchard and Hofheinz families proudly agreed with this assessment.

Roy's mother was a beautiful, energetic, and proud lady of the old school. She did not like her given name, Englena Eliza, and went through life by the name she preferred, Nonie. Of French descent, she had been born in Marksville, Louisiana—"Cajun Country." Records in Louisiana show that the Planchard and Barbin families had immigrated to the French-held territory and had settled on lands granted by Louis XIV. Nonie's mother, Flora Barbin, had married Joseph Planchard, and to them had been born nine children, six of whom survived childhood.

Flora Barbin Planchard died from a heart attack on January 4, 1940, at the age of 89 in Beaumont after attending funeral services for her son-in-law, Alvin A. Valentine, who had passed away three days earlier. Among her papers was found a document showing that her great-grandfather had arrived in Louisiana in 1703 with a commission from Louis XIV to oversee the ammunition and warehouse supplies stored in New Orleans and belonging to the royal government.

The Planchards had given their daughters unusual names. Deedee had been christened Adrian Georgette but never used the names except on legal papers. Later she married Jules Naquin and settled in Port Arthur, Texas, where her husband was in the ice, grain, and restaurant businesses. The oldest Planchard daughter, Judith Josepha, was known as Eta. She married Walter

Mr. and Mrs. Fritz Hofheinz

Bell, who had a long affiliation with the Sun Oil Company and worked in several cities in Texas. A third daughter, Maria Idell, did not mind her name; she married W. Sherman Overstreet, who ran a men's clothing store in Beaumont and later in Shreveport, Louisiana. Another daughter, Loudwenia, also known by her real name, married Alvin A. Valentine, a carpenter in Beaumont, and, after his death, Adolph Lignon, a retired businessman. Nonie's two brothers were Arthur, who worked on an oil rig, and Filmore, a painter.

On his father's side of the family, Roy descended from the Reverend C. Friedrich Hofheinz. Born on April 29, 1840, Friedrich became a Lutheran minister, immigrated from Germany to the United States, and landed at Lockhart, Texas, with 10 cents in his pockets. When his ministerial duties took him to Illinois, he married Emilie Mary Ofrahn, a native of Switzerland but of German descent. The Reverend Mr. Hofheinz and his family then lived at Schiller and Bergheim, Texas (in the vicinity of San Antonio near the town of Boerne). For four years he was grand president of the Order of the Sons of Hermann. To this family were born four sons, among them Fritz, father of Roy. None of Roy Hofheinz's family ever became acquainted with his Hofheinz uncles or had any trace of where they went after leaving southwest Texas.

When Fritz Hofheinz arrived in Beaumont with his family, he found a town in the midst of a boom. Located 20 miles from the Texas-Louisiana border on the tidewater of the Neches River and 50 miles inland from the Gulf of Mexico, the city is a deep-water port thanks to access through Sabine Pass. Basic to the economy of the city in 1900 were lumber, cattle, rice, and other agricultural products natural to the warm, humid, semitropical climate, along with river shipping and railroad transshipments on four major lines. In 1901 the famous Spindletop Oil Field was discovered near Beaumont and became, by the time Roy Mark Hofheinz was born, the oil center of the Lone Star State with 50 producing wells and two refineries.

By 1912 the lumber business, a major factor in the local economy since the Civil War, was declining in importance, although 25 mills were still operating. The seaport brought additional revenue, for the 11-mile channel linking it with the Gulf had been deepened to 25 feet. However, oil was primary in importance to Beaumont's economy, producing $2,750,000 a year in business. Pipelines from most major oil fields in Texas and Louisiana poured black gold into the city's refineries and into seagoing tankers. By 1912 the total investment at Spindletop was $30 million. Beaumont that year thus was a busy city with many good jobs, as well as a city that prided itself on having the best school system in Texas.

However, the prosperity of Beaumont was not evident in the family of Fritz Hofheinz. He received a limited income from employment at Wells Fargo and from occasional work in the shipyards. He could afford only a small, white,

Roy Mark Hofheinz as a child

frame house at 725 Main Street, a block from the shipyards and located in a rough neighborhood of rooming houses. The structure was built on stone props which lifted the floors four feet above the ground and left open gaps through which man and beast could easily crawl.

Nonie never wanted her precocious son to play with the poor "riff-raff children" of the neighborhood; therefore, Roy was frequently forced to play by himself. Under the house proved an ideal place for him to create. With dirt and a small bucket of water, he built mud houses, roads, canals, bridges, office buildings, and, once, after long planning, an entire city subdivision. This was the first of the many creative workshops he would use during his life.

Roy's under-house excursions did not please his mother. Stern, strict, and regal, she believed that cleanliness, in the words of the cliché, "was next to Godliness." She adored her son and wanted him to grow into something "special," and she did not believe that his soiling his clothes and body under the house would allow Roy to become a high-class, proper gentleman; she never forgot that she was descended from the French aristocracy. Nonie preferred to dress her son "like little Lord Fauntleroy, Buster Brown, or something akin to it," Roy later recalled. He would wait until she was busy cleaning house, cooking, washing clothes, or visiting with her sisters and friends in the living room, and then he would quietly slip under the house and get dirty. "My mother kept me immaculate until the minute I could get loose from her," Roy said. "I made a game of evading her apron strings."

Roy worshiped his mother, who never punished him except by tongue-lashings. He wanted to please her, but the urge to crawl under the house to his workshop for activity with his mind and hands was too great for him to heed her warnings and scoldings. Nonie at last realized, after months of washing his dirty clothes, that Roy had unusual creative talent, and she eased up on the fussing about his untidiness. Two or three times Roy was so proud of his under-house creations that he enticed his mother to take a look at them. She was impressed at what she saw, but did not want to admit it. She always stressed to him in her scant leisure time that he should do his best at whatever he tried. She was the intelligent, driving, loving force of his early life. During Roy's life only three other women—his two wives and a daughter—influenced, advised, encouraged, protected, and loved him as had his mother.

His father, Fritz, was gentle and patient with the growing boy. In the few hours he was not working every day, he took Roy to the shipyards, railroads, sawmills, and to other businesses to explain their workings and their importance. Roy readily absorbed information about the community, but it was the city's buildings, streets, parks, land, and government—not the ships, trains, or refineries—that impressed him the most. Roy loved his father deeply and was happy to be alone with him when time permitted. Fritz, in turn, listened as his son showed and told him about his under-house retreat, and he never discouraged the boy's creativity. To his aggressive offspring, he said, "You can make it in life better than your dad if you get a good education, work hard, and be honest in everything you do."

"I'm going to make it!" Roy would exclaim to his Aunt Deedee after telling her of the dreams that inspired him. During this period of his life, he often listened as his mother told her sisters of her desire to own the elaborate, ornate furniture popular during that time. However, there was no money for her to purchase it. Nonie's wish for elegant household furnishings became Roy's, and in future years his taste for the trappings of the 19th- and 20th-century grandeur was never totally satisfied.

Roy Hofheinz did have two cousins, Lee (Bo) and Haas Bell, sons of Nonie's oldest sister Eta and her husband Walter Bell, with whom he played on occasion, but he essentially was a loner—a characteristic evident throughout his career. When he could convince his mother that they should go to the Bell home or else invite Bo and Haas to their home, the three boys did play happily together. The cousins were delighted with Roy's brightness and agility. Together they played tiddlywinks, jacks, and marbles. Roy often got splinters in his fingers playing jacks.

Roy frequently told his mother that he wanted a brother for a playmate, but none came. Bo and Haas had to substitute. Roy's favorite, Bo, would tolerate his cousin's shouts of "That's mine!" when the winner was in doubt as they played "for keeps" in marbles. Roy's possessiveness was evident early in his life, and it was Bo and Haas who gave Roy his first taste of competition. Coca Cola bottle tops usually were used for determining who won or lost at marbles. Roy's urge to win was so great that he practiced shooting marbles for hours until he could hit one 25 feet away. On those occasions when Bo did win all the caps in Roy's prized cigar box, the unhappy lad would go to stores and collect more bottle caps in order to have ammunition with which to win back what he had lost. Preparedness for battle became a lifelong motto for Nonie's "darling."

Bo later recalled that Roy became irritated when he lost but added that, in the long run, his cousin usually came out on top in their contests—as he would do in most of the hectic encounters in his teens and adult life. Roy noted that his mother likewise wanted to win, but she played few games with him because he early learned to outdo her—and she did not like it. However, his father did play games with him and was patient in losing to his rapidly growing, skinny offspring. When Roy entered grammar school in Beaumont, he found himself far ahead of the other pupils because of the teaching he had received from his parents and his own amazing ability to assimilate information.

Nonie Hofheinz was an ardent Catholic, Fritz a Lutheran. They early had agreed that Roy would go to the Catholic Church with his mother. She saw to it that her son gained spiritual training. Roy often questioned the priests about their duties, and they often were amazed at the boy's quest for knowledge and how easily his mind stored facts. In his church studies, as with those at public school, he rarely had to work at home because he listened, questioned, and absorbed everything in class. He was the boy who raised his hand, got the floor, and asked pertinent questions.

Roy worked after school and on weekends, for he learned early the need to have money always on hand both to help out his family and for his own needs. One of these needs was food. The gangling lad was always hungry—not because his body did not get regular, good meals, but because he had a craving for food. Despite his mother's delicious Cajun dishes, which should have filled any normal youngster, Roy constantly wanted more food. In fact, he later recalled frequent dreams about it. Cajun oyster-and-rice dressing, beans and rice, and waxy pecan cakes were his favorites. Nonie's recipe for cakes was passed to his Aunt Deedee, and for the next 60 years no one else had it. Deedee would make the cakes for Roy and send them to him at Christmas or on other special occasions.

Before he entered grammar school, the eager lad had learned to count and value money. Because of this Nonie began sending him to the grocery store when she had small orders. As the months rolled by, he became so adept at making these purchases that Nonie gradually began giving him longer lists, and eventually he took over the buying of all the family's food. He had an eye for a bargain and stretched the few dollars available in his purchases at the farmers' market two blocks away.

One day when he was there, Roy noticed a produce farmer pulling off the brown outside leaves on heads of lettuce he was stacking in his booth; he obviously did not want the discolored leaves to detract from the greenness which customers wanted. The lad asked the produce man if the brown leaves were edible, to which the seller replied, "Yes, but customers won't buy with brown showing, or they want a big reduction in price." Roy excitedly asked if he could have the brown leaves free both then and in the future. The man agreed, for this would reduce the amount of garbage he had to carry out. "Mother made the best salads from those lettuce leaves," Roy would recall later. "We learned that those brownish outside leaves were the most nutritious. We were happy to get them for nothing, for we were poor and needed all we could get honestly for our money."

Years later, at a party he hosted for friends, employees, and prospective business associates, Roy noticed someone pulling the outside leaves from heads of lettuce. "Don't do that!" he exclaimed. "Those brown leaves are the best part of lettuce!" By then Roy Hofheinz was known as an outstanding chef who received great pleasure from preparing food, for he combined his mother's Cajun recipes with his own special taste to produce unusual and sumptuous dishes of heavily spiced foods. Friends called him "Roy the Gourmet." His love of food eventually became his worst enemy—and defeated him after he had won the greatest physical victory of his life.

On weekends and after school, Roy, as a lad, sold the two local Beaumont newspapers. In a loud, clear voice he hawked these publications which he also eagerly read and digested each day. In addition he sold magazine subscriptions and did odd jobs. When he was nine, he applied at a grocery store for any type of part-time position, telling his prospective employer that he was good at math, could read instructions, and was willing to work hard. His well-prepared "pitch" got him the job. Already he was showing the sales ability he was to demonstrate as an adult.

On his first afternoon at work at the grocery, the manager told him to put 14 ounces of beans in each bag marked one pound. Roy protested that this was dishonest, but did as he was told for the rest of the day. That evening at home he told his father what the manager had ordered him to do. Fritz Hofheinz counseled him never to do anything dishonest. The next day at work Roy told the grocer that he would fill each bag with one pound of beans but would not shortchange the customers, who were neighbors, with only 14 ounces of beans. "You do as I say, or you won't have a job," the grocer responded. Thus Roy was fired with only one afternoon's meager pay. When he told his father and mother that evening about losing his job, they said they were proud of him. Although he would have a long career in politics, business, and promotions, Roy Hofheinz would never be accused, even by his enemies, of straying from a strict code of honesty.

Another thing Roy learned as a child was how to coin slogans to aid his sales efforts. One example was his effort to sell soda pop. This was the age of national prohibition, but Fritz Hofheinz liked his beer and made it at home. Occasionally these bottles of homemade beer would explode at night, awakening Roy and frightening him, but eventually he learned to recognize the noise without fear. And from it he got an idea for his soda pop stand. To attract customers he printed a large, colorful sign which stated, "NEAR BEER SOLD HERE. BUT NO BEER SOLD NEAR HERE."

As he grew, Roy developed a lively interest in and love for school athletics, professional and sandlot baseball, road shows, and animals. He petted and cared for a collie dog his parents gave him, and they went many places together when he had time to loaf. During his life Roy would have so many dogs that he could not remember the name of the first pet, but he would remember his anger when anyone mistreated the animal. A love of animals and a willingness to try to improve their lot would be a characteristic of his adult life.

This youth of many moods also joined the knot hole gang of the professional baseball team in Beaumont. This enabled him to attend their games free. He was not as interested in the techniques of the game as in the crowd's reaction. His cousin Bo said Roy had a good knuckle ball on the mound. Occasionally he tried tennis. In athletic competition of any type he wanted to win, once commenting, "Who in the hell wants to play to lose anything? I wanted to win, win, win in anything I undertook."

One year the newspapers announced that the Ringling Bros. and Barnum & Bailey Circus was coming to Beaumont. Roy wanted to see the show and begged his parents to take him, but there was not sufficient money for three to attend. However, his parents did buy a general admission ticket in the end zone of the big tent for him, escorted him to the gate, and told him they would meet him after it was over. Roy later recalled that seat: "It was a damned narrow board I sat on during that show. I could see only one of the three rings, but I loved every minute of the animal acts and the Wild West Show." From that time forward he was an avid fan of the circus and rodeo, and as an adult he collected circus artifacts, equipped circus rooms in two of his homes, created a circus display room in one wing of the Astrodome, and—finally—bought financial control of that same circus from John Ringling North. Moreover, remembering that hard seat at this first circus, he saw to it that seats in the Astrodome were extremely comfortable.

Grammar school proved easy for Roy Hofheinz. He loved math, literature, and grammar and was a top student in all three. His teachers allowed him to skip two of the first five grades, and his name always was on the honor roll. Each year he participated in spelling bees and won first place consistently. However, there was no state or national competition for him to enter at that time. He also was excellent at debate and believed that he could solve any problem by reasoning and speaking. One day, however, when he saw two casual friends fighting in the neighborhood, he learned that such was not always the case. Disliking violence, he ran over and begged the two boys to stop. They did not listen as he continued to talk. Finally, irritated at Roy's intervention in their quarrel, the two fighters stopped, told Roy to mind his own business, and threatened to beat him up if he persisted. He kept arguing for them to stop. Suddenly the two boys turned and began swinging at him, but they missed because he had sensed their intent. Roy turned and outran them to his house, then stuck his head out a window to shout, "Cowards! Cowards!"

During visits to the home of his cousins Bo and Haas Bell, Roy often met a young woman, Mary Poye, who proved to be a lifelong friend—and of particular help to him as a teenager. She and Nonie had a friendship that lasted until Nonie's death. Although Mary was not a relative, she felt like a member of the Bell, Planchard, and Hofheinz families. "They took me in," she recalled. Nonie's mother and father lived across the street from the Bells. There on College Street, Mrs. Planchard ran a rooming house and cared for her ailing husband. The Bells rented apartments, and the Poye family lived in one of them.

Mary Poye's most vivid memory of Roy Hofheinz's childhood years resulted from her marriage to Matt Spolyar, which took place in the Bell home. "My family was poor and couldn't afford to give us a real wedding send-off," Mary recalled. "All the Planchards, Hofheinzes, and Bells got together and gave us a happy wedding breakfast and inexpensive but useful gifts. Roy was seven. Dressed in white, he was a lively figure, his brightness adding to the fun. We all sang, and he joined in loudly, even if his singing was nothing to brag about." Roy's "Aunt Mary," as he called her, was a constant watchdog and influence in his years as a teenager and when he was a young adult in Houston, where she moved after her marriage. The Spolyars bought a motel, Holiday House, on South Main in Houston and operated it for years. Roy never forgot her kindness, especially the good food she provided him when he was hungry in Beaumont and Houston. Her brother Leo, who was about Roy's age, occasionally would play marbles with him and the Bell boys. Years later, when he was a businessman in Houston, Leo asked his sister, "Where's he [Roy] getting his marbles from now? He got all of mine."

During World War I, Roy Hofheinz watched the feverish activities at the

Port of Beaumont, a center for ships about to leave for Europe. Between 1912 and 1922 Beaumont grew from a population of 28,198 to 44,255. The land-locked port handled up to three million tons of freight for world markets. An average of four vessels a day was tied up at local wharves each year in the early 1920s. Free from tidal waves and Gulf hurricanes, the port prospered because its channel had been dredged from 25 to 44 feet to handle big ships. Oil, grain, cotton, sulphur, and many other commodities flowed through the city. Howev-er, the prosperity associated with the war and the postwar boom did not touch the Hofheinz family. Fritz continued to work for Wells Fargo for a meager salary which the inflation of that era eroded drastically.

Desiring a better life for his family, Fritz, in 1923, after consulting with Nonie, decided to move his family to Corsicana, Texas, a city which was located south of Dallas and was smaller than Beaumont. There he established a clean-ing and pressing business, using Nonie and Roy in the work to cut down on overhead and thereby increasing his profits. Roy entered the seventh grade in Corsicana. At age 11 he was younger than his classmates, but he quickly demonstrated that he was an outstanding pupil. His English teacher was so impressed with his work that she entered one of his essays in a statewide competition that attracted hundreds of entrants. It won first place.

Unfortunately the cleaning and pressing business in Corsicana failed to prosper as Fritz Hofheinz had hoped. He was advised by friends and members of his wife's family to move to Houston, which reportedly offered greater opportunity, for no city in the state could match its growth. When school ended in May of 1924, with Roy completing seven of the 11 grades then required for graduation from high school, the family left Corsicana in a battered 1918 Oldsmobile. Roy had just reached his 12th birthday. The trip proved difficult, for rains had made the road a shambles. "We got stuck in mud three times during the trip, and the car had to be pulled out by mule teams," Roy would recall. "People helped—for money. Each time my father was charged $10, and that was hard, tough cash for him to put out. We had received enough from selling the Corsicana business for emergencies and to rent a home and start a new business in Houston, but that $30 gave us a setback for our arrival in Houston." Neither Fritz nor Nonie Hofheinz dreamed that Houston would prove a magic city of opportunity for their gangling, aggressive, brilliant, and eager son.

2

Teenage Scholar and Promoter

When Nonie, Fritz, and Roy Hofheinz moved into a modest home at 1612 Jefferson Street, near downtown Houston, to open a family cleaning business, they had high hopes. Little did they care that writers of the day pictured the Bayou City as dirty, hot, humid, and rain-plagued, a place of overflowing bayous, poor sanitation, and ever-present mosquitoes and insects. Despite these drawbacks, however, Houston was prospering and its population was growing each year. The census of 1910 showed 78,800 residents, making it the 73rd largest city in the nation, while Harris County had a population of 138,276. By 1920 Houston had jumped to 45th largest city in the country with 115,693 residents and 186,667 people in Harris County. World War I had brought a rush of workers to a city whose leaders had convinced local voters and the federal government to finance the digging of a 50-mile ship channel south to the open waters of the Gulf. Port Houston thereby became almost unique in the world.

When World War I ended, Houston became a center for shipping, oil, gas, and finance. Big corporations, especially petroleum firms, began building office structures downtown, and word spread through the economic world that here was a city overcoming its semitropical drawbacks and its difficult living conditions. Between 1924, when the Hofheinzes arrived, and the Depression which began in 1929, Houston continued to boom.

That summer of 1924 the Hofheinz cleaning business got off to a hot, slow start. Fritz, Nonie, and Roy worked 12 hours a day trying to make the enterprise pay. Roy's major tasks were to operate the machine which squeezed clothes dry and to help his father with deliveries in an old, used truck. While riding with his father, Roy studied the city's streets, buildings, and general terrain, thereby gaining a background that would enable him later to analyze the city's needs and to understand its people.

In September that year he entered South End Junior High as an eighth grader. The following year South End would become San Jacinto High School (and ultimately Houston Junior College). Roy was tall for his age, growing toward an eventual six feet in height, and he entered school activities with enthusiasm. He knew that, as in elementary school, he would have to learn his lessons in the classroom in order to work at the family business in the afternoons, evenings, and weekends. Ben Sewell, who became an attorney in Houston and who was a year behind Roy in junior high, later recalled, "Most of us in junior high had gone to school together from the first grammar grade. Coming from outside of Houston, Roy wasn't part of the regular native gang of buddies. Roy sensed he didn't 'belong,' but soon everybody on the campus knew who he was. He made a point to impress them. He didn't take part in a lot of the junior high social activities. There were some pretty affluent students in school. They had cars, and they'd spend a lot of time at Gables Drug Store on Main Street. Houston was a pretty small town then, and students from high school and college would ride up and down Main Street looking for diversion."

Harry Holmes, Jr., in 1978 a wealthy lawyer in Houston, was a Hofheinz classmate who lived on Alabama Street near the home on Winbern (off Alabama) to which the Hofheinzes moved. He recalled, "I was in the 8th grade when he entered junior high. I remember Roy attracted attention as a 9th grader by competing to be a cheerleader. He and Bo Wynn were picked as the yell leaders because they were the ugliest guys in school. Roy was a leader in raising money to build a fence around the junior high. A carnival night was scheduled. Roy decided to put on 'The Greatest Holdup Ever Performed' in his booth. Roy dressed in tight red pants and a red-and-white striped coat and a Katie straw hat, and he stood outside as the huckster for students to pay 25 cents to see his show. When customers got in the booth, all they saw was a pair of red suspenders holding up a pair of pants, but Roy's concession made more money than any others."

Holmes also recalled Roy's working at his father's cleaning business: "Roy came to junior high in the old truck which had a black box on the back. He'd pick up everybody's dirty pants in the morning, take them to his father, and come back to school. The following day he would bring them back to school, being sure to collect before turning over the pants."

During this period Roy's physical hunger increased. His mother had a rule that no matter what she put on the table he had to eat all he put on his plate. This was no problem, for the meals often included only small portions. Roy vowed then that when he grew up and acquired money he would always have, both at home and at work, a bountiful supply of food to satisfy his own appetite and that of his family and friends. Fortunately for him, his Aunt Mary Spolyar and her husband moved from Beaumont to Houston where they opened a simple steam table restaurant at 622 Travis Street. It was patronized by many workers of the city's three newspapers and by businessmen. Roy proved a frequent visitor, for Aunt Mary's home cooking at the restaurant and her warm words of encouragement induced him to come around frequently. "Roy sometimes would slip up on me, pick me up from behind and hug me tightly," she recalled. "I loved the lad and was happy I could give him a break from the hard grind of school and work."

Despite the hardships Roy endured, he completed junior high with top honors just after he turned 13. He had no close teenage friends, but he had become casually acquainted with a wide variety of people. In Houston he first became aware of the problem of racial and economic discrimination, and he felt sorry for blacks and Chicanos as well as poor whites who eked out a living not nearly as good as that of his own family. He asked himself, "Why do I have to go to school where blacks are barred? Why do tan, brown, and black skins create prejudice among the economically dominant whites? Why am I hearing and reading of a rebirth of the Ku Klux Klan of Reconstruction Days in my new home town?" He resolved that he always would be on the side of the poor and the disadvantaged.

After a year in Houston, the Hofheinzes gave up the cleaning business, and Roy's father took a job as the driver of a Shepherd's Laundry truck. This freed Roy to use his own initiative in making money. And there was another change for the family, for it moved to 1619 Winbern Street (later renamed MacGregor); theirs was a modest home, but it was in an area that included many old, turn-of-the-century mansions on Lovett Boulevard and Montrose and Riverside streets, then the wealthiest part of the city. Thus Roy, like some other poor children, found himself mixing with the sons and daughters of descendants of pioneer families and with those of "silk stocking" residents.

It was here that he came to know Harry Holmes, Jr., and also where he met and came to respect the man who later would become one of the wealthiest oilmen in Texas, Hugh Roy Cullen. The Holmes family lived next door to the Cullens. Harry, Jr., later would recall: "Mr. Cullen and Daddy had a garden together. . . . Roy lived around the block, and he visited with me and Mr. Cullen often." Although Roy and Harry Holmes, Jr., competed in many ways all their lives—and many would think they were enemies from their teenaged days—the two were friends. Perhaps they were not close friends, but, in a showdown, *friends*. Moreover, Roy's youthful friendship with Cullen led to many joint associations and civic endeavors at a later date.

The principal at San Jacinto High School when Roy began there was T. H. Rogers, a tall, thin, elegant man, while E. C. Gates, the assistant principal, was scholarly and well-proportioned physically. Both men were finger-pointing disciplinarians that students respected. Roy went out of his way to make himself known to them. His favorite teacher was J. P. Barber, who taught English and speech. A tall, thin man who looked more like a cowboy than a master of language, Barber set a record of producing outstanding debaters. During his 10 years at San Jacinto, he coached boys' debate teams which won the city and district championship seven times and the state title four times. Roy learned that Barber listened both to students' ambitions and woes—in short, that he was a regular fellow.

"Mr. Barber was the teacher whom I admired most as I got my education," Hofheinz later recalled. "He gave me public speaking lessons I never forgot. I am grateful for the many extra hours he gave me, stressing the important points of reaching an audience. I was two years younger than most of my classmates, and I guess he thought I was a little unusual and so gave me extra attention."

Barber, a graduate of Southern Methodist University, owned a small ranch in Bellaire, an incorporated town southwest of Houston. Students called him "horse trader" because he usually had daily information for them about his 15 mounts. "Horses and students are pretty much alike," Barber commented during an interview after four of his students had won state debating honors one year. "Teaching my students, I merely hold the reins, allowing them to find themselves. Anyone with ordinary ability can develop into a good speaker if he will watch his own possibilities and stay within his bounds." Barber's good humor, his ability to relate meaningful anecdotes, and his eloquent voice provided daily inspiration for young Roy Hofheinz, who, in time, became San Jacinto's top extemporaneous debater.

In 1925 there were five public high schools for whites in Houston—Sam Houston, John Reagan, Jefferson Davis, Charles Milby, and San Jacinto. Competition among them was highly spirited in all athletic and academic fields. Because of his age, Roy did not feel physically able to compete in athletics with older and more mature youths; he decided to stick to cheerleading. His eloquent pep talks about the glory of San Jacinto, his winning smile, and his agile movements kept him in the cheerleader task he learned in junior high. "I always made a hell of a lot of noise," he recalled. Roy soon discovered that no printed programs were offered spectators at football games. He went to Principal Rogers and asked if he could produce and sell programs for all games. The principal said there was no money available.

"If you will give approval and let me handle getting up the programs by myself, can I have any profits?" Roy asked. Rogers appreciated Roy's eagerness to furnish the service and agreed, but he emphasized the school could give him no help. Salesman Roy went to merchants, sold advertising space and laid out programs, making sure names, positions, numbers, and lineups were accurate. He did not sell ads by pleading with merchants to "help out good old San Jacinto." Instead, he figured what attendance might be for each game from school records and made his sales pitch on what the ads could do in sales for the businessmen. He was so convincing that he had little trouble making enough to pay for printing with some profit for himself. He sold each program for 10 cents and kept the money for himself and his mother. Roy sold out of programs each game, for he carefully calculated how many people might be present. Fans appreciated the service never before offered at San Jacinto games.

The boldness and penetrating jives of Roy the cheerleader often irritated athletes on rival teams while entertaining supporters of San Jacinto. Verbal exchanges of students often led to after-game fights. E. A. "Squatty" Lyons, short, muscular co-captain of the Reagan team, recalled his introduction to the lively Hofheinz boy:

> Arnold Krichamer, our football coach, knew that after games some players had beaten up rival enthusiasts. He heard some talking about getting that Hofheinz kid. He called me aside and told me to get some of our boys together and guide Roy to his car outside the playing field. I commandeered Roy by the arm and started taking him through a mob on the steps of Reagan. I got a dozen other boys to walk beside us. We almost had to fight our way to Roy's car, but we got him there and nobody got hurt.
>
> When Roy was safely in his outrageously decorated Model T, he thanked me and we shook hands. He was a very smart young fellow, perhaps 13 or 14 years old. I kinda took a liking to the guy and watched him from then on. He was very active in debating. I heard him on several occasions and I think he won every time. I considered Roy a friend after that rescue.

Lyons later would vote as a Harris County commissioner to call bond elections to build the Astrodome.

Roy's Model T was a conversation piece of downtown Houston. He bought the car for eight dollars and spent $15 repairing it in the workshop he had built behind his house. Houston's Main Street saw it often as teenager Hofheinz became a successful dance promoter and radio personality.

Hermon Lloyd, one of the architects of the Astrodome, was a Rice University student when Roy attended San Jacinto. "Halloween used to be a big holiday in Houston," he recalled. "Almost everybody, and particularly high school and college students, would swarm to Main Street downtown. Boys would pop girls on their butts with rubber balls and they would play tricks on each other. Rivalries were emphasized in chatter, and fights often broke out. The most vivid recollection I have of Roy," Lloyd recalled, "came when I saw him running down Texas Avenue toward the Rice Hotel from the City Auditorium with practically half of the Reagan football team after him. He was running for his life, it seemed. Roy apparently had been very articulate again with the Reagan boys, who had missed getting him once before, I was later told. He looked like he should have been on the track team because he reached the Rice Hotel and its safety well ahead of his would-be tormentors."

Making top grades in classes, leading cheers, selling programs, winning debates, and helping at home did not take up all of the teenager's time. He went to bed late and arose early, a lifetime habit. A few hours of sleep would revive his body.

Small parties in homes, movies, and athletic events were the main leisure activities of young people. Radio was just beginning to make its way, and television was yet to emerge. Roy's keen sense of the wants of young people caused him to begin two types of enterprises to make more money. It was the era of the big dance bands, and top music makers attracted adults to Kensington Hall, End of Main Hall, and the University Club downtown. The first two could hold up to 2000 couples. Roy decided to promote, on his own, Friday night dances for teenagers. He also felt he could become a radio announcer because of his gift of gab.

Roy observed the adult dances and got to know the hall managers. He told them his plans: he would rent their places from time to time, do his own advertising, book his bands, and be responsible for all bills. Although skeptical that a 14-year-old could be his own promoter, they agreed to rent if young Hofheinz produced the rent money in advance. They also stipulated Roy would have to clean up after dances, there would be no alcoholic drinks allowed, and they would keep the proceeds from concession stands. "I was an independent operator and manager, I emphasized," Roy recalled.

Young Hofheinz went to the manager of Radio Station KTLC and asked if he could buy time for a weekly night amateur hour. He said he would sell the advertising, round up talent, and do the emceeing. The station manager also was amazed that a lad could be so ambitious, but the idea sounded good and he agreed if Roy would provide the money in advance.

Roy promoted several dances, from eight to midnight, at $1.10 a couple, but he decided to gamble on two big events he called the "Pom Pom" and "Yo Yo" extravaganzas. Each would start at eight and end at 4:00 A.M., with two to four orchestras alternately furnishing music. He increased the price per couple to $2.20. He drove his Model T covered with ads on Main Street and near schools to call attention, and he used his radio show to mention upcoming events.

Clark Nealon, retired sports editor of the *Houston Post,* who watched Hofheinz closely after he first became affiliated with the Houston Sports Association, National League franchise winner, recalled when he first observed the then young promoter-politician: "On Sunday nights when I was a young sports writer, Roy would come up to the office and he always looked the dude. I remember one particular ensemble—white flannel pants, blue sports coat, and skimmer straw hat. Roy would bring his own neatly typewritten stories to the city desk and I'd watch him convince the editor of the news value."

Squatty Lyons recalled: "For his 'Yo Yo' dance, Roy employed two orchestras, one white, one black. The blacks were led by then little-known Louis 'Satchmo' Armstrong of New Orleans. The whites played the first four hours, and then Satchmo came on and played like mad until 4:00 A.M. He was a big hit and only a few left, although the dance floor was so crowded couples could hardly move." Lyons also remembered that "Roy didn't miss a bet in advertising that dance. I recall being at a wrestling match at the auditorium when all of a sudden something dropped down and there was a wire megaphone—with Roy Hofheinz's voice announcing his 'Yo Yo' dance. I had to take my hat off to a guy like that."

Having attended several of Roy's dances, Lyons asked his friend why prices per couple were 10 cents extra on the dollar when there was no city or state tax levied. "That's Hofheinz tax," Roy answered with a grin. Dealing with taxes would occupy a great deal of Hofheinz's time when he became a controversial but successful political leader. The "Yo Yo" and "Pom Pom" dances, the latter at Kensington Hall, broke all attendance records for such events up to that time.

A. Linton Batjer, Jr., a classmate of Roy's, who later was a teacher, said at the 50th anniversary celebration of the 1928 San Jacinto graduating class: "I remember one dance at Kensington where the advertising said 'from eight 'til?, three orchestras, and no intermissions.' When I left about 3:00 A.M., there were still about 300 couples on the floor. I believe the success of Roy's dances was caused by two things: one, they were advertised well, and, two, they were good dances due to good orchestras and good people attending. Roy would have his advertising posters well-prepared and would go downtown, advertising with his car, and would also ask various merchants if they would place posters in their windows. Few refused because he was quite a salesman."

Walter F. "Buster" Hackney was a Hofheinz classmate for four years. He and his older brother, Joseph Charles, were great admirers of the student promoter. Their family supported the budding promoter-politician throughout his career. Buster became a professional baseball player, Marine combat correspondent, and writer. He was president of the Professional Baseball Association of Houston which, in 1969, honored Roy Hofheinz for his great baseball achievements. "I went to most of Roy's dances," said Buster. "I remember how he used to push and roll chairs to prepare for them. I also remember how he cleaned up before and after dances—he was good with a pushbroom. I was always impressed with his advertising signs, usually red and white placards announcing coming events. He never failed to walk between dancing couples holding up a sign advertising the next event. He policed the dancers, and, if he saw anyone trying to imbibe, he'd chase them off, for he promised the hall manager there would be no drinking. High class young people from all walks of life enjoyed those shindigs. There was no fighting, no trouble, just fun."

Harry Holmes, Jr., remembered one phase of Roy's advertising of the big "Yo Yo" dance: "Roy stood in front of the Gulf Building downtown, then the tallest, wearing a clown suit and holding rein on a billy goat. He also had taken two garbage can tops and welded them together for a big yo-yo. He stood out there spouting off about the big dance coming up."

At dusk the night of the "Yo Yo" dance, the front wheel of Roy's Model T collapsed at Main and McGowen, one of the busiest corners in town. Beyond it, out South Main, was an esplanade which was the main route for people in growing suburbs to go home. Roy got out of his car, pasted more posters on it, and thumbed a ride to the End of Main Hall. The car was removed early the morning after the dance, Roy's biggest success until that point. Two of Roy's classmates doubted that Roy's car had broken down. They laughed and said they thought he took the wheel off, not once, but several times at that intersection so that his advertising would be effective in attracting last-minute diversion seekers. For his biggest dances, Roy arranged for special buses to take students without cars to and from the gala events.

Harry Holmes, Jr., also told how he and Roy competed in summer with soda water stands on corners near San Jacinto High. "The school corner at Holman and Austin was the best, and we had some fights about it. The first guy who got his stand there had first claim to it." The competition was fierce. Roy recalled Harry gave away drinks one day to cut down on his rival's business. There was price-cutting, no doubt, to sell cold drinks. The city's transportation jitneys were Model T Fords with little strips on the doors, Holmes recalled. "When the back seat was filled, they put people on those little strips on the doors. People would come out Austin Street and make a turn at Holman—in jitneys and their own cars—and then start back to town. Roy fought to keep his stand at the 'end of the run' so he could get business from those who paused there."

Extremely tired after the "Yo Yo" event, Roy went home and found Nonie waiting. He dumped $1500 into her lap. "Aren't you proud of me?" he asked. "No," she answered. "I expected it of you." She could always bring him down to earth.

That he was not allowed any cut from dance hall concessions made an impact on Roy. "It was regrettable for me," he said when discussing concessions at the Astrodome one day. "It taught me the value of those things. Baseball is your best concession sport. It's the only event where customers have to get rid of one and take one" (meaning visits to restrooms and drink stands).

With profits from his dances, Roy paid for radio time. Before he began his amateur hour—10 years before the famous Major Edward Bowes became a national success with green entertainers—young Hofheinz figured how many people the air show might attract—he was ahead of Nielsen statisticians—and sold supporting advertising. One day, San Jacinto Assistant Principal Gates met Roy in the school hall. Roy asked Gates to listen to his show that evening because he planned something of interest for the principal. Gates said that he listened to the show regularly and would be sure to dial in that night. Intrigued, Gates invited several teachers to visit his home for refreshments and to listen to the show. The amateur hour moved along smoothly. Roy's voice suddenly boomed out that he was going to dedicate the next musical selection to Mr. E. C. Gates, the assistant principal of his school. Then came the song, popular at that time: *I'll Be Glad When You're Dead, You Rascal You!* Gates said his friends ribbed him unmercifully, but all had good laughs.

The next day at school, Gates saw Roy in the hall, but the student's eyes were glued to the floor, for he had seen the assistant principal walking toward him. Gates stopped him to talk. Knowing that Roy thought he was going to be thrown out of school or punished in some way, Gates then laughed heartily, relating to his venturesome young friend finally that he and the others at his home had enjoyed the dedication. The relieved juvenile promoter grinned with joy. Gates and his teachers particularly congratulated Roy on his radio commentaries. They were bright and his delivery of commercials convincing, they said.

Having learned to appreciate the educational value of newspapers when he sold them on Beaumont streets, Roy carefully read the *Press,* the *Post,* and the *Chronicle,* Houston's highly competitive dailies. He became particularly interested in politics and politicians, proceedings in court, and administrative bodies. When he visited Aunt Mary's restaurant, he left for the courthouse, a short distance away, to introduce himself to officials, ask questions, and listen to lawyers argue cases in civil and criminal courts. Most of them took an interest in the youngster, for his debating ability had already been publicized in high school and occasionally in the dailies. The lad was an intriguing figure to all who dealt with public business.

Walter Embree Monteith's reputation for honesty impressed Roy. Monteith was Harris County judge for four years, judge of the 61st Judicial District of Texas for 10 years, and mayor of Houston for four years. Monteith was the first officeholder Roy supported. Political aspirants in those days held rallies as their prime means of winning votes. Impressed with Roy's ability to debate, Monteith asked the high schooler if he would talk for him. Roy eagerly agreed, for nothing suited him better than to expound before groups. The lad was a hit from the beginning, for nobody in Houston had previously seen a youngster on the stump speaking extemporaneously. The political fever in Roy grew as he made the rounds, and the experience brought a decision in his junior year to study law after he finished high school. Politics was dominated by men of legal training.

Despite his busy schedule, Roy did not neglect eyeing pretty girls in his classes. Younger than most of his female classmates, he nevertheless pursued a few. He was persistent in his attentions when he decided he liked a particular girl. Annie Beth Towles, now Mrs. Carr Robinson of Dallas, was Roy's first date. The five-foot, 100-pound beauty, with light brown-blond hair, was an excellent dancer, having attended special classes. She was on the beauty page of the 1927 school annual. She went with Roy to two or three of his dances, and, because she was popular, did not have to be a wallflower while her date attended to chores connected with his promotion. She said it was remarkable that Roy could line up capable high school and college musicians for his regular dances, but she particularly remembered the big "Yo Yo" and "Pom Pom" affairs when he hired top professional musicians.

Another beauty, brunette "Boots" Martel, got Roy's attention. In 1969, Frank E. Mann, Houston city councilman, wrote Hofheinz a letter enclosing a picture of Boots, her sister, and Roy taken at the old Foley Apartments near the Saint Agnes Academy in 1926. The letter read: "Boots is still one of your big boosters. I don't guess you have changed your ways as she mentioned to me that you were quite persistent in seeking her attention. She tells me that you would come by her home, driving your Model T, to visit. She especially remembers that on one occasion when she would not come to the door you later appeared at her home, honking your horn, and finally leaving a box of candy on her front lawn. She remembers waiting a short while after you had driven away to make sure the coast was clear. When she went out to get the candy, lo and behold, 'The Judge to be' appeared out of nowhere and got in his visit." Roy may have taken a few other girls to dances but no longer recalls all their names. He usually was too busy to "fool around."

Roy became acquainted with newspaper reporters and editors as he visited his Aunt Mary and the courthouse. After he began producing programs for athletics, he felt the daily newspapers did not cover high school sports as well as they should, so he went to the *Chronicle,* which published afternoons and Sundays, and asked for a job as San Jacinto correspondent for sports. He would get in his copy by midnight, after games, he promised. This led to a high school sports column written by Roy for which he was paid 10 cents a printed inch. He then included in his ambitions owning a newspaper, but the nearest he would get to that was during his political campaigns when he published his own tabloid political flyer called *Justice.*

Roy continued his essay writing and participation in debates during his senior year in high school. "Success Comes in Cans, not Can'ts" won him the school and state essay championships. The manuscript essentially was a lecture on people who know what they want in life and go all-out to get it and about those who alibi their ambitions with "I just can't do it." As a junior, Roy had been the only Houstonian who qualified for the debating finals of the Texas Inter-scholastic League's competition in Austin. He won third place.

Roy had a great disappointment in his senior year when he and three other members of the San Jacinto debating team won their way to the state finals at the Texas capital. He lost to Emeline Lovellette of Denison High School, his only defeat as an extemporaneous speaker that year. The five-foot-two, auburn-haired, brown-eyed, bespectacled, slim, elegantly dressed daughter of a wealthy Denison couple brilliantly matched wits with the pride of San Jacinto. It took the judges a long time to decide the winner. Dejected, Roy went home to prepare for graduation and took much kidding from classmates for losing to a female. He was long-faced for several days, according to Assistant Principal Gates. The judges told Barber after the decision that Roy's speech was "too perfect" and must have been memorized, which was against the rules. It was not. After that Roy Hofheinz never underestimated the abilities of women.

The June of 1928 yearbook of the San Jacinto graduating class pictured Roy as a charter member of The Rostrum, a club devoted to public speaking. Roy also was shown as a member of the Hi-Y Club, organized "to create, maintain and extend, through the school and community, high standards of Christian character." Roy was treasurer—he always wanted to know where the money was or was coming from. Yell leaders displayed with Roy were Farnsworth "Flip" Calhoun and Harold Clark. Hofheinz also was a member of the Boys Booster Club "to accumulate money to help pay for bleachers on the football field." Its motto was "Always ready, always faithful."

Two months after he was 16, Roy Hofheinz graduated with highest honors. He had spent all the money he made to help his family and to buy clothes and attend social functions accompanying graduation days. When he got his diploma, his card of academic credits was withheld because he still owed $3.70 for fees. Shortly, however, he received great news from the University of Texas Board of Regents: an offer of two scholarships to the growing seat of higher learning in Austin because of his San Jacinto academic standing and public speaking ability. By the middle of July he remembered he needed his official list of grades and was able to get it by paying the $3.70 from profits of door-to-door sales of quality aluminum pots and pans.

During the spring of 1928, the newspapers daily printed stories about the candidates and delegates coming to the National Democratic Convention to be held July 26-29 in Houston. No one was more interested than Roy Hofheinz. He wanted to see the proceedings and learn how delegates reacted to various speeches. The biggest delegation would come from New York to back Governor Alfred E. Smith, but there was some doubt "The Happy Warrior" would win because he was Catholic. Before the formal convention proceedings began, Roy cornered some New York delegates and told them they would certainly need an active and interested page to carry messages and run errands. He picked New York because he hoped to see and talk with Smith, but the candidate did not appear, much to the youngster's disappointment. Roy sold himself and got the job. His tall, skinny frame—he had grown to six feet—was constantly on the move during the speeches and voting of the convention. The excitement of the four days increased Roy's desire to get into politics.

At the convention was 20-year-old Lyndon Baines Johnson, a student at Southwest Texas State at San Marcos. Son of southwest Texas State Legislator Sam Johnson, Lyndon had political fever. He asked a friend at college who had a car to go with him and their girl friends to the Democrats' show at Houston.

They reached the convention site, Sam Houston Hall, in time for speeches and roll calls, but Lyndon had no credentials, and doorkeepers would not let the party into the hall. Johnson screamed to be allowed to see convention officers. His demand was granted, partly to calm him. Johnson then waved copies of the *College Star,* his campus newspaper, before officials and said he was a reporter for the paper. Hearing a hot barrage of words from Johnson, the officers, probably in defense of peace, accredited Lyndon as a working reporter and gave gallery passes to his friends.

It was on the convention floor that Roy and Lyndon first met. They were to become lifelong friends. Both had politics in their eyes. The convention was the first big political thrill for each. They saw Franklin D. Roosevelt, an active floor manager despite his paralysis, nominate Smith for president. Both Hofheinz and Johnson heard talk that if Smith were nominated by the convention, many Texas delegates and politicians would support Republican Herbert Hoover. The speculation later became truth.

While serving the New York delegation as page, Hofheinz visited the Texas delegation, which included John Garner, future vice-president; Sam Rayburn, longtime and powerful speaker of the United States House; Tom Connally, who was running for the U.S. Senate, a seat he later would win, against KKK incumbent Earl B. Mayfield; and other state politicos with whom Roy was to deal. Roosevelt, Garner, and Rayburn impressed both Roy and Lyndon. Little did these youths dream that they ultimately would have strong ties with the Democratic leaders of New York and Texas.

The expected fight to keep Smith off the ticket did not develop. Smith and Joseph T. Robinson of Arkansas were nominated on the first ballot with more than two-thirds of the votes. During the Smith-Hoover campaign, the Catholic-trained Hofheinz boy did his bit for the whole Democratic ticket. He was greatly disappointed the following November when Herbert Hoover won 444 electoral and 21,392,190 popular votes to 87 and 15,016,443 for Smith.

Tragedy struck the Hofheinz family on August 12, 1928, when Fritz Joseph Hofheinz's laundry truck was struck by a car on Heights Boulevard. He died August 15 in Baptist Hospital of a fractured skull, never regaining consciousness. Nonie and Roy had little cash on hand, but there was sufficient insurance to pay for funeral costs, and there was the hope of collecting damages. The death settlement finally provided $5000 which Roy told his mother to put aside for a rainy day because he was taking over, at 16, as the family breadwinner and would take care of her.

Within a month, *Houston Kiwanis Magazine* carried a tribute to Roy Hofheinz because of the death of his father. It said, "Roy has been one of the most interested and loyal of the boys associated with Kiwanis boys' civic activities. He has considerable talent for public speaking—at the command, not only of our Boy Builders, but of Kiwanis Club members. For the first time in his life,

Roy is facing deep sorrow and serious responsiblity. There is little that can be said or done for him. But we have faith in him and the strength and resiliency of his character. After the first crushing impact of bereavement, he will gather himself together, and out of sorrow and bitterness, he will win the strength and courage and understanding, the bittersweet compensations for struggle and suffering." Roy Hofheinz had traveled often to various towns in the Houston area to speak to boys' groups. "Be Different" was his usual subject as he emphasized the many problems boys would be required to face when they finished school.

Feeling he had to stay home with his mother, Hofheinz turned down the scholarships at the University of Texas and applied to Rice Institute because he knew that, if accepted, he would have no tuition to pay. William Marsh Rice, founder of the university which opened in 1912 with beautiful grounds near where the Astrodome later was built, stipulated in his bequest that only students of top quality be accepted and that they pay no tuition. Roy was so outstanding academically that Rice immediately agreed to enroll him in its prelaw school.

To support his mother, Hofheinz decided to expand his promotion of dances outside Houston. From 1508 Francis Street, where he and his mother moved, he booked halls in various towns from Houston to Lake Charles, Louisiana. Just after Rice opened in September of 1928, Roy began staging college dances. A picture in the *Houston Post* helped publicize one of these affairs. It showed Howard Calvin, Frank Mendell, Malcolm Bennett, and Hofheinz clad in pajamas atop Roy's Model T on downtown Main Street. "There's no reason we can't wear pajamas downtown, at parties or anywhere else," Hofheinz was quoted as saying. The picture revealed the Model T equipped with a baby-sized parasol, a water bucket labeled "For Shame," and a variety of pithy sayings. The pajama boys and the car did the job—people chuckled and spread the word of the unusual advertising.

The last dance Roy promoted as a Rice freshman was held on May 29, 1929. The *Houston Post* carried this notice: "A burlesque entertainment, 'Corruption of the Modern Youth,' will be one of the features of the final ball of the Rice Institute Pre-Law Association in the Rice Hotel June 6." Frank Mendell joined Hofheinz in the promotion. Because of his letters seeking bands, Hofheinz became acquainted with many in the entertainment field. He soon led them into a national organization called "Music Bookers of America," which provided information on the quality and cost of entertainers.

Classes at Rice were held during the day; therefore, at the end of the school year in June of 1929, Roy decided he should transfer to Houston Junior College, established in the building of his high school, so that he could attend night classes and work on his promotions during the day. His dawn-to-midnight operations continued as he excelled in classes and continued debate training at the junior college. The market crash in October did not upset Roy

Roy and his Model T as pictured in 1928 newspaper ad. Reproduction of *Houston Post* photograph by Carol Gregg, MSU Art Services.

and his mother too much, for she carefully had hoarded the money awarded for her husband's accidental death and Roy had regular work. In addition to his promotions, he was assistant announcer on the radio station which earlier had allowed him to start an amateur hour.

Well established in the Harris County Courthouse, still in use today as the county's Civil Courts Building, was the private Houston Law School which boasted it was the largest in the South and the oldest in south Texas. Captain Jesse E. Moseley and Captain Ewing Werlein, veterans of World War I, had developed the school which, in the fall of 1930, had 220 freshmen in its enrollment of 440. One of the freshmen was Roy Hofheinz, who had been awarded the first free scholarship by the school because of "his public speaking ability and other possibilities." Announcement of the scholarship was made in the *Houston Post* on August 22, 1930. A two-column picture of the 18-year-old Hofheinz sitting in his outlandish Model T carried the caption, "A budding Demosthenes."

Law School President Moseley and Dean Werlein were attracted to Hofheinz when he was a member of the junior college debating team with Willard Nesmith as his partner. Werlein was so impressed with Roy that he and Moseley gave the scholarship worth $300. Chester Bryan, a former county judge and a friend of the youth, heard about the scholarship and paid about $100 for all books Roy needed. The law school leaders knew that Roy had been involved in a variety of activities at San Jacinto, Rice, and Houston Junior College, and that he desired to become a lawyer. They wanted the rising scholar to be enrolled in their school.

Entering the 1929 freshman law class was Irene Cafcalas, born on January 10, 1912, and known as Dene. She was a black-haired beauty, daughter of James George Cafcalas, a native of Greece, and Ethel Van Zandt of Wheelock, Texas. Cafcalas had emigrated to Galveston, Texas, when he was nine years old to live with an uncle. Family problems in Greece had caused his relatives to send him to the United States. Ethel came from a family of farmers. The Cafcalases had four children. A son did not survive childhood, but three daughters, Irene, Mary, and Lucille, grew up in Houston where their parents worked before marriage. As the girls matured, they helped their parents in restaurant businesses. Mary married Russell Rau, later connected with Braniff Airways. Lucille married Harold Bales, a salesman for the *Houston Chronicle* circulation department. The younger sisters watched as the romance between Dene and Roy developed and led to marriage. The Cafcalas daughters' skin and hair reflected their Greek heritage.

Dene was popular in high school and junior college. Rice and Houston Law School students often dated her. When she helped her father as a cashier in his restaurant, she continually turned down requests for dates from admirers. She, like Roy, was always busy with school and part-time work. She was a great listener, a ready wit, and compassionate with those who might want to share their problems with her.

When the first assembly of the law class was called on September 11, 1930, a newspaper photographer took a picture of the 220 freshmen students in a small auditorium. The first floor was crowded. Standing prominently in the balcony—all alone—was Roy Hofheinz, getting a good view of all his new classmates and unimpeded in listening to instructions by being herded with the others. Among law school lecturers were Langston King, judge of the Criminal District Court; Bennett B. Patterson of the prominent firm of Cole, Cole, Patterson, and Kemper; Claude Pollard, former Texas attorney general; Judge C. A. Teagle, president of the Harris County Bar Association; and Representative Daniel E. Garrett, member of the U.S. House from Houston.

In October of 1930 Lyndon Johnson, a June graduate of Southwest Texas State, got a job as teacher of debate and public speaking at Sam Houston High School with a salary of $1600 for nine months. His uncle, George Johnson, a bachelor teacher at Sam Houston, had sold E. E. Oberholtzer, Houston school superintendent, on the abilities of his nephew. On arriving in Houston, Johnson found the atmosphere and sights different from the 1928 convention scene. Thousands of unemployed men stood against walls and sat on ledges in the downtown area. On some streets there were Depression bread lines and soup kitchens for ,loitering, unhappy men and women. Stores had few customers.

Sam Houston Principal William Moise gave Lyndon a free hand in developing school debaters among the 1700 students. Johnson soon renewed his friendship with Roy Hofheinz, who then was in his second year of law school. Roy was speaker for his freshman class at the annual banquet of the Houston Law School on September 10, 1930, and Johnson had heard about it. Hofheinz and 27 classmates had organized the law school's Lambda Phi Debating Society during his freshman year. Roy became secretary-treasurer. He and Kenneth McCalla, a few years his senior, were chosen chief debaters. McCalla later became an outstanding state prosecutor and judge.

The society learned that the National Student Federation of America was sponsoring a visit of a two-man team from English universities to debate with teams of 25 American colleges and universities. Secretary Hofheinz wrote Virginia Loomis, debate secretary of the federation in New York, asking if Houston Law School could be included in the visitors' schedule and what the fee might be. At first the federation secretary hedged, saying the schedule of the English team was full, but added that the visitors might squeeze in a trip to Houston as their last stop in the United States on December 19. Roy and McCalla agreed they would be willing to debate just six days before Christmas, and the Englishmen, anxious to see for themselves something of fabulous Texas, accepted the extra date after having won all decisions from American opponents. The fee was $85.

Newspapers widely publicized the "First Houston Intercollegiate International Debate—All English Universities versus Houston Law School." Lyndon Johnson and his team of debaters at Sam Houston were among the 500 people who crowded into Sidney Lanier Junior High School Auditorium for the positive and negative orations on the issue, "Resolved: That the Principle of Democracy Has Been Tried and Found Wanting." The Depression had brought that question to the minds of many in the nation. The *Houston Press* reported the debate on December 20:

> Two young Englishmen who had marched triumphantly through a series of debates in this country were defeated when they met two Houston Law School students. In 25 debates in the United States, it was the first time that an audience voted against the Britishers. The Houston Law School students were Kenneth McCalla and Roy Hofheinz. Opponents were B. J. Crehan of the University of Liverpool and D. Hope Elletson of Oxford University. They were sent to the United States as the most brilliant forensic talents produced in Great

Britain by an exhaustive series of examinations. The vote was 259 for the Houston pair and 241 for the visitors. McCalla and Hofheinz had the negative of the motion.

Hofheinz booked Louis Armstrong to play for a dance at Lake Charles Country Club. He got word a few days before the dance that Armstrong could not appear. He was committed to pay rent to the country club and therefore decided to find black musicians in Houston who could substitute. He jumped into his Model T and drove to Houston's Dowling Street where he interviewed various black musicians. He picked 14 and named them the "Birmingham Blues Blowers." He gave them dance music sheets and had them practice for several hours. Having no uniforms available, he went to a variety store and bought 15 pairs of broadcloth pajamas at $15 each. Half were red with white stripes and the other half white with red stripes. A tailor helped fit the "uniforms" to the sizes of the new band. Roy and his new group then went by bus to Lake Charles. Those who bought tickets to hear Louis Armstrong at first were disappointed to learn of the substitution, but when the night was over, the dancers had no complaint; the pinch-hitting band made the evening a success.

Those uniforms, however, proved troublesome. As the musicians played in the hot clubroom, they perspired, and the pajamas stuck to them. At intermissions, those in white with red stripes could not leave the bandstand, for to do so would have been to expose contours of the body taboo in public in those days. An unexpected feature of the band's performance was the urge of the trombonist to do solos. He spoke to the leader and got his chances—much to the delight of Roy and the dancers. The "Birmingham Blues Blowers" were such a success that they played together for years. Hofheinz and others booked them in Houston and in many east Texas towns.

Edwin L. Bruhl, Houston certified public accountant, who audited Hofheinz's books for a quarter of a century, shared this recollection:

> My first personal view of Roy came when he was going to law school. He and Dene were there, and they were pointed out to me several times. In fact, they didn't have to point Roy out to me because he pointed himself out very well in class. He was probably the man who displayed the most interest in what he was learning than anybody else. He was usually asking questions and holding up his hand. At the end of each session, he talked with instructors, and I never did quite learn whether he was instructing them or they were instructing him.

So quickly did Hofheinz learn the basics of law that he decided to go to court and have his disabilities as a minor removed so he could take the Texas bar examination before graduation from law school. At 19, two years before he normally would legally be an adult, Roy passed the bar examination, got his license, and opened a law office. He would continue to go to law classes at night, for he wanted his degree. While practicing law, continuing his promotions, and courting Dene, he plotted his future.

3

Early Law Practice
and Marriage

Roy Hofheinz opened his law office on Capitol Avenue, a block from the Harris County Courthouse and jail, where the original *Houston Press* Building stood. He continued his study of law although he already was a member of the bar. The Depression was at its worst in 1931. Lawyers, like everyone else, had to scratch to live. The legal neophyte Hofheinz shared a $17-a-month office with Charles Mayer, who knew the loopholes in the law and handled divorces for bargain fees. Hofheinz remained a loner—he did not enter into a partnership, but the two lawyers did have a big sign showing both names hanging so low over the sidewalk that unobservant pedestrians bumped their heads.

Then competing with Hofheinz for any kind of criminal law practice were Percy Foreman, a new Houston resident who was older than Hofheinz; Frank Mann, later a city councilman; and others whose names became prominent in Houston and Harris County law practice and politics. Foreman ultimately became one of the nation's outstanding lawyers. It was he who, examining the evidence, advised James Earl Ray to plead guilty to the murder of Dr. Martin Luther King, Jr., in Memphis. The reputations of Hofheinz and Foreman for winning cases spread throughout Harris County. Their brilliance and victories brought them a steady increase of clients.

Because small fees from defendants were insufficient for Roy to support his mother, study law, and court Dene Cafcalas, he continued booking bands for dances in Houston and east Texas. He also worked as a disc jockey on the radio station which had allowed him to initiate an amateur hour.

Hofheinz's legal studies would have suffered had it not been for Dene. A brilliant student, she made complete notes of lectures by distinguished lawyers in the courthouse, and, when Roy was not present because of some case or other activity, she allowed him to read or copy what she had written. One of Dene's humorous complaints later in life was that she attended all the classes, yet, after Roy's photographic mind had studied her notes, he got better grades than she did.

Theirs was a vacillating romance. Occasionally they found time to go to movies. They discussed legal points, Dene then feeling she one day would have her own career at the bar. It was natural that these two sharp minds would clash, but beneath their discussions was a growing love.

Frank Mann kiddingly accused Roy of going with Dene because she was a free meal ticket. If that was the case, Jim Cafcalas got his reward, for after he retired from the restaurant business, he worked for and was a small stockholder in one of his son-in-law's businesses, Houston Slag Materials Company.

In those trying days of the Depression a "blue plate" vegetable meal cost 15 cents at Foley's. "If we got meat with the vegetables, it was 10 cents extra," Mann recalled. "Chili was 10 cents for a big bowl. We'd buy chili and fill the bowl with a half bottle of ketchup and crackers, and that would satisfy our hunger. Word got around about the chili deal, and the manager finally had to put up a sign reading 'Crackers and Ketchup a nickel extra.' "

Hofheinz did go to jails and made friends of officials, but he never went to cells and unethically solicited business. The young lawyer's personality was so dynamic and his reputation as a high school and college debater so widespread that his name quickly popped up when court officials were asked by accused people what lawyer to call. A year after handling many small criminal cases, Hofheinz moved into a second-floor office in the State National Bank Building. Sharing offices with him—but not a partnership—was Kenneth Aynesworth.

Mann recalled one case he witnessed when Hofheinz almost was held in contempt of court. "It was a theft case," he said. "Roy represented a black man. In those days, if a black man stole from another black, the jury didn't pay much attention, but if a black stole from a white, it was a different can of worms. The accuser of the black was white. I remember Roy standing before the jury making his argument. Facing Tom Harris, a tough and vigorous, sometimes vicious, chief prosecutor for the state, and the jury, Roy said, 'Gentlemen of the Jury, every iota of testimony Mr. Harris has presented to you today is as false as the hair on his head. I dare him to take off his toupee.' Harris' face turned red, and Judge Langston King rapped for the bailiff to lead the jury from the courtroom. King severely dressed down Roy for the remark, but fell short of citing him for contempt. When the jury came back to the courtroom, its members and spectators were still chuckling about Roy's remark. Prosecutor Harris left the courtroom and sent an assistant in his place because I think he could not stand the embarrassment of wearing a toupee, not popular then. Roy won the case."

Hofheinz and Mann once jointly had a case involving a black client accused of stealing a chicken. They discussed their procedure and came up with an idea based on the corpus delecti rule in a murder where, if the state could not produce the body, there could be no conviction of the accused. The case was in Justice of the Peace J. M. Ray's court. When the state got through with its evidence, Hofheinz and Mann agreed Frank would make technical motions and Roy would argue before the jury.

"I asked for a dismissal because the state had failed to produce the corpus delecti of the crime," Mann said. "The judge asked me what I meant by corpus delecti of the crime, and I answered, 'That is the article the defendant is supposed to have stolen. Nobody knows if it ever existed unless the article is recovered.' The state's attorney said he did not know what happened to the article, but he had a strong suspicion that our client ate the evidence. Judge Ray dismissed the case because the state didn't produce the corpus delecti. That was one Roy didn't have to argue, but he argued in hundreds of others and won consistently. It was amazing how quickly that 20-year-old grasped fine points of criminal law."

Hofheinz handled several murder and rape cases. Not a single person he defended in a capital case ever went to the penitentiary, he recalled. "I found the facts, and they were presented as best I could, and I won every time in the big trials."

The young lawyer maintained his interest in politics. Having seen Franklin Delano Roosevelt in action at the 1928 Democratic Convention in Houston, Hofheinz became an enthusiastic supporter of the crippled New Yorker. He read of Roosevelt's achievements as governor of New York and hoped the squire of Hyde Park could capture the 1932 Democratic nomination and then oust Herbert Hoover from the White House. Change had to come, Hofheinz felt, for the Depression was ruining the country.

When William G. McAdoo, the Alabamian who missed in his presidential nomination bids, threw his support, pledged to Texan John Nance Garner, to Roosevelt on the floor of the 1932 party convention in Chicago, the New Yorker was nominated, and Garner was named to run with him to form a North-South ticket. Hofheinz crowded in speaking engagements for the Democratic ticket with his law practice and promotions. He was elated and felt a new day was dawning for the United States when Roosevelt overwhelmed Hoover. Throughout his long tenure, Roosevelt would have the support of the young Houston liberal.

Although Roy Hofheinz often ate at Foley's with Dene and visited Aunt Mary's for in-between and other meals, he remained skinny and almost emaciated for his six feet. Frank Mann recalled, "Roy was very skinny and thin, and one time in court he was trying to put in evidence to which the state's attorney objected—to no avail. Roy quipped—and he was good at that—to the prosecutor, 'You're not only trying to hang my client, but you're trying to hang me.' Judge A. C. Winborn, also sharp and witty, looked up from the bench and said, 'Roy, your ass is not heavy enough to break your neck.' We had lots of fun those days in courtrooms."

Two women often watched Hofheinz in action: Dene, his girl friend, and

Mother Nonie, who told friends the young man who supported her was on his way to greatness. Dene's main purpose was to give Roy notes for the lectures he had missed—and to have a little time with him at lunch at her father's restaurant.

Although he was making ends meet financially and had good prospects ahead, Roy Hofheinz had one case which caused him to abandon his criminal practice. A white man was accused of rape and incest involving his stepdaughter. Hofheinz carefully assembled data and testimony about the family. He kept the jury and spectators intensely interested with his flair for pertinent questions and cross examination. He put the stepfather on the stand and led him through the story of the family differences as told to him by his client. It was a dramatic trial for the curious. The jury debated only a short time before it returned a verdict of "not guilty." Spectators applauded and some congratulated Hofheinz on his skillful handling of the case and for freeing an "innocent man." Outside the courtroom, the relieved stepfather shook hands with Roy and with a serious look on his face said, "I can assure you that I have learned my lesson. I will never do that to my stepdaughter again."

Hofheinz was shocked by the revelation that he had worked to free a guilty man. He immediately made up his mind to abandon criminal practice. He brooded for days because there was nothing he could do to change the verdict, and it weighed on his conscience. Never a man to ponder decisions, he made them quickly and stuck by them adamantly.

Learning Hofheinz was going into civil practice, the International Association of Oil Field, Gas Well and Refinery Workers of America, with 3400 members at the time, engaged him as counsel. It was a coalition of working people which was to support Roy Hofheinz and later his son, Fred, in their Houston political battles.

During these years, Roy continued to drive his Model T, dressed flamboyantly in white suits and shoes, wore flowing black ties, and topped his thick black hair with big white Panama hats. He never skipped a chance to eat at his favorite restaurants in between the meals his mother cooked from a well-stocked pantry.

The Cafcalas family lived at 4501 Harrisburg Boulevard. Roy visited there often, and Dene's younger sisters, Mary and Lucille, also became fond of him. Hofheinz loved to visit Galveston Bay and often took Dene and the sisters along on fishing trips. He went duck hunting occasionally, and his pleasure in the joys of the outdoors grew.

Nonie and Aunt Mary watched Roy's romance closely. Once when he and Dene broke off their friendship, he told them, "It's just as well. I am not going to have any Greek children." He was hurt—and deeply in love—when he said it. The estrangement of Roy and Dene lasted nearly six months. Both had won their bachelor of law degrees with honors in the 1933 graduating class of

Houston Law School. Dene and Roy avoided each other during graduation. On July 18, 1933, they unexpectedly entered the same elevator, Roy heading for his office and Dene for an interview which she hoped would land her a job as a clerk in a successful lawyer's office. Roy asked her if he could see her early the next day at her home. She agreed, and both smiled at the thought that their former close relationship might resume.

Hofheinz arrived at the Cafcalas house as promised. Wearing a gingham dress, Dene greeted him at the door. He said he did not want to enter, just to take her for a ride. She did not hesitate. They rode around town in his old Ford and finally stopped for lunch. After a discussion of their differences, Roy proposed marriage and Dene agreed. They got back in the car, and, instead of driving his love back to her home, he headed north on the old Beaumont Highway. "We're going to get married today before you change your mind," he said, and she laughed happily. They drove as fast as the old car would permit to Shreveport, Louisiana, where Roy's uncle and aunt, Mr. and Mrs. W. S. Overstreet, lived. They got there in time to get a license. With the Overstreets as witnesses, they were married before a justice of the peace on July 19, 1933. Dene did not have time to change her gingham dress.

Families in Houston were informed, but were not surprised. Dene bought a few clothes the day after the wedding, and she and her husband had a four-day honeymoon in the Louisiana city before returning home. Dene's father urged them to stay in his home until they were more independent financially, and the couple accepted. Dene talked of going ahead with her job plans, but Roy told her he wanted her to be his wife, not a career woman. She promised not to seek a job, but to help him with his cases at home, if needed, and to back him up in whatever he wanted to do. Dene knew her husband was politically ambitious and that 1934 would be a political year with various offices up for grabs. If Roy was going to get into politics, she said she would participate with him.

Happy months followed in a duplex the Hofheinzes rented at 1401 Blodgett. Dene served as cashier as Roy put on a few more dances. Roy's civil law practice brought in enough to pay for their modest needs and to support his mother, but his mind was alert to political offices he might seek. He began smoking big cigars, perhaps anticipating passing them out if he and Dene had a boy. A cigar in his hand or the corner of his mouth was from then on a daily addition to the Roy Hofheinz picture. One of Roy's many diversions was taking pictures at his new home, some with an old movie camera he had acquired. Visitors often were startled when flashbulbs popped as they entered the house.

Dene appeared with Roy as he made speeches. When she felt he was saying too much or overdoing it, she told him. He listened but, when he explained why he did things in the Hofheinz way, she went along, proud of his ability to command attention by his logic and eloquence. His way was to be hers all her

Roy and Dene Hofheinz. **Photograph courtesy the *Houston Post.*

life. She was proud to be the wife of a promising young lawyer and pledged she would be the homemaker and, she hoped, the mother of several children.

When Nonie and Aunt Deedee asked Roy, after marriage and children, why he had changed his mind about not having any Greek children, he laughed and said, "Dene provided the Greek blood, I didn't." The happy Hofheinz couple was usually short of money, and Jim Cafcalas came to the rescue occasionally. Roy and Dene were 21 years old and knew that if Roy was to get into politics they should not go in debt for a house until finances were better.

Because they had been reared Catholics in different traditions, Roman and Greek, Roy and Dene decided to join the St. Luke's Methodist Church. They attended regularly. He also joined the Fraternal Order of Eagles, which quickly named him publicity chairman because of his newspaper and radio experience.

The Texas legislature, Roy decided, should be the first political goal. When Rolland Bradley, incumbent in position two of the Harris County legislative delegation, announced he would not seek reelection in May of 1934, Hofheinz—22 in April—decided that seat would be his target. Dene agreed, and together they stepped up their study of the city and county so that he would be ready to announce and campaign.

Hofheinz and seven others qualified as candidates for the House seat in the Democratic primary in July of 1934. Some thought Hofheinz got into the race just to publicize his law practice, but they were wrong. He had planned his course and he was going to use every legitimate promotional means to win—with the help of his beautiful wife.

4

Boy Wonder Legislator

Standing in front of the Gulf Building, Roy Hofheinz began his campaign for the Texas legislature. He wore a stiff celluloid collar, a black ribbon tie, a white suit and shirt, and a white Panama hat to touch off his flashy style. He shook hands with everybody he could stop, and he talked about his candidacy. The *Press, Chronicle,* and *Post* briefly reported that Hofheinz had entered the legislative race. Roy scraped up enough money to buy a few radio commercials, but his main campaign weapon was his eloquence at rallies.

Fred Hartman, longtime editor of *The Baytown Sun,* a daily in suburban Houston, was a steadfast Hofheinz political ally from 1934 on. Looking back at Roy's first campaign, he reported:

> I can never forget the first time I ever saw Roy in the summer of 1934. . . . We staged an old-fashioned political rally downtown at the corner of Peters and Commerce streets. . . . We conceived the idea of having a special political edition of our newspaper. We advised all candidates they could speak at the rally we arranged if they would buy ads in that edition. If one bought a $10 ad, he could speak 10 minutes and $5, five minutes. . . . A huge crowd turned out for the event. It was rather remarkable how the official list of candidates coincided with the names of those who bought ads. The name of Roy Hofheinz was not on our ad list. I'm sure the reason was he didn't have $5. We introduced various candidates and after several hours of oratory, I was at the microphone ready to say goodnight to everybody. I felt a tug at my coat and I looked back, and there was the skinniest little guy I believe I had ever seen. He wore a tight seersucker suit and introduced himself as Roy Hofheinz. He said he knew the rally was over, but asked if I minded if he said a few words over the mike before we turned it off. Well, I was caught with my hair kinda short, for we really had produced a commercial rally. Just as he influenced so many other people down through the years, Roy influenced me that minute.
>
> I announced we hadn't reached the end of the rally, that the final speaker was Roy Hofheinz, seeking one of the five state representative posts in Harris County. In all my life, I have never heard such a political speech. You would have thought he was speaking before the Democratic National Committee or United States Supreme Court. It was a personal speech. He told how he had

Roy campaigning for legislative seat. Photograph courtesy the *Houston Post.*

fought his way up, had a wife, and just enough money to keep his britches from being patched. He didn't attack his seven opponents—he just wanted to sell himself. I apparently wasn't the only one under his spell, for he swept the Tri-Cities boxes in the primaries. It was his eloquence which grabbed us.

Dene Hofheinz was as busy as her husband. They went separate ways, knocking on doors and shaking hands on the streets with men and women. They seemed tireless, working from early morning to midnight. The Cafcalas family joined in, too. Money was found for cards and some posters, but essentially it was a person-to-person battle for votes. No section of the county was missed as Hofheinz, his family, and friends sought support.

Backers of candidates in those days heckled opponents of their favorites at rallies. Hofheinz was a victim one day and interrupted his speech, made without notes, to say, "I do not propose now or ever to pay attention to paid agitators who wear red ties and have closed minds. I have neither respect nor appreciation for any man of any color who has for his purpose the stomping of the American flag under his feet. I believe Communists are my hecklers." Daughters of the American Revolution read Hofheinz's statement about the flag and pledged to support his candidacy.

Hofheinz received 11,000 votes to qualify him for a runoff with Harvey Draper, who previously had unsuccessfully sought the legislative seat. All three Houston newspapers endorsed Draper. Roy felt he had to have his own printed media to tell his story so he created a tabloid named *Justice*. His first issue gave his platform:

> I feel that qualifications and not platforms are the means by which candidates for the state legislature should be judged; however, in order that my position might be clear on matters which are of pertinent nature at this time, I declare myself in favor of the following measures: Ratification of the Child Labor Amendment to prevent the exploitation of child labor in factories and sweat shops. Textbooks must be printed in Texas instead of by Eastern concerns. This alone will mean the expenditure of approximately three million dollars yearly with the press men of this state. I favor legislation which has for its purpose the furtherance and upbuilding of the school system of this state, and I will urge a scholastic appropriation of $17.50 per capita. I favor the submission of the repeal of Prohibition to a vote of the people of Texas to the end that this question might be forever eliminated from our political horizons. I favor the creation of an adequate statewide police system as a means to curb organized crime in this state. I favor the exemption of the homestead up to a valuation of $3000 from all types of taxation. I am in favor of a reduction of ad valorem tax rates where the same is plausible or feasible. If elected, I will dedicate myself to the task of conscientiously representing the people of my district day-in and day-out during the sessions of the legislature.

In a newspaper interview, Hofheinz added to his platform "the right of labor to bargain collectively with employer without interference and old age pensions to supplant the 'deplorable conditions of poor houses in this state.' "

The next issue of *Justice* carried the headline "Attorney Exposes Fake Statements." The story read:

> Roy Hofheinz has exposed, by the statements of his opponent wherein he calls himself "real estate broker," that his opponent is in reality only a building manager for S. H. Kress & Co's five and ten cent chain store, and as a representative of such company, had sought election to the legislature for the past eight years and has never been elected. The condemnation does not lie primarily in his connection as Kress representative, but in the fact that Mr. Hofheinz's opponent is trying to fool the people of Harris County and to camouflage and distort his actual chain store connection. . . . Mr. Hofheinz says there is but one major issue in the campaign—whether the people desire a chain store lobbyist and representative to serve them or a capable and qualified attorney who has only the interest of the people at heart.

The fiery young campaigner first took up baseball terminology in attacking

Draper: "He has been at bat three times—no runs, no hits, and the public has made no errors."

The Fraternal Order of Eagles endorsed Hofheinz. Pat Henderson, an opponent in the first primary, endorsed Roy, who began calling his opponent "Ten Cents Draper." The black-oriented *Texas World* called Hofheinz a great candidate. "He has extreme youth," the newspaper said, "but he is a 'comer' in politics." The *Houston Labor Journal* maintained the support it had given Hofheinz in the first primary.

Final vote in the race was Hofheinz 21,244, Draper 20,270. The *Houston Chronicle* commented that Hofheinz should not have been elected over the more experienced and proven Draper. However, the *Post* and *Press* complimented Hofheinz on his "phenomenal victory" and wished him well. Roy was the youngest legislator ever elected in Texas and perhaps in the nation at that time.

In postelection interviews before he was to leave for Austin, Hofheinz said he would propose a "fence law to curb thievery and another bill to throw out racing bookies." He explained that an anti-bookie bill could "throw out the crooks in the business around town and elsewhere." He said that he would rather have pari-mutuel betting than legal bookmaking but really wanted neither.

James V. Allred of Wichita Falls was elected governor in 1934 by defeating Tom F. Hunter of the same city in a runoff Democratic primary, which was tantamount to election. Hofheinz had no Republican opposition on the Harris County general election ballot. Considered by some a liberal by contemporary Texas standards, Allred campaigned with promises to help eliminate causes of the Depression and to put the state on a progressive, prosperous course through legislation to end the many evils evident in state government. Hofheinz met and liked Allred and voted for him. He felt he would have an ally at the top when he battled on the floor of the House for legislation he believed the state needed.

Robert W. Calvert of Hillsboro, ultimately chief justice of the Texas Supreme Court, was a candidate for Speaker of the House for the 1935 session beginning in January. He recalled, "One humorous incident occurred during my campaign. Roy came to Austin for a brief visit, and I had him as a dinner guest at one of the local hotels. He ordered a regular dinner from the menu and then directed the waitress to bring his dessert first. Noting our astonishment, he explained that when he was a child he always wanted, but could not have, his dessert first; that he made up his mind then that when he became independent of parental control, dessert was going to come first." Roy could not always follow that desire in the years ahead, but it never changed.

Harry McLeary Wurzbach of Seguin, Texas, representing the Fourth Congressional District, including San Antonio, had died on November 6, 1931, and Richard Kleberg, son of the owner of the vast King Ranch in south Texas, announced his candidacy to fill the vacancy. Lyndon B. Johnson, 23, wanted a political job. He had used school teaching only as an interim occupation until he could get into politics. He supported Kleberg, and, after the congressman's victory, he asked the wealthy ranch man for a job in Washington. On November 29, 1931, Kleberg notified Johnson he would hire him as an assistant. Hofheinz read the news and was not surprised. He congratulated Johnson and kept in touch with him. When Johnson heard that Hofheinz had won his way into the legislature, he sent his congratulations, for he felt the law school debater he had heard and talked with in Texas' largest city was capable of going far in politics. Johnson early in 1934 had married Claudia "Lady Bird" Taylor, an Alabama beauty, who joined him in complimenting Hofheinz, whom she hardly knew.

Living in Liberty, Texas, 45 miles east of Houston, was another budding politician, Price Daniel, who was to become legislator, governor, U.S. senator, aide to President Johnson, and finally a Texas Supreme Court justice. He recalled, "We got the Houston newspapers in Liberty and I read about the young man who had startled the public with his victory at 22. I met him soon after his election at a meeting of Young Democrats of Texas. I was elected president of this organization and Roy supported me, along with the rest of the Houston delegation." Daniel said that Hofheinz was an excellent speaker at Democratic meetings and was "one of the best young statesmen."

Roy and Dene Hofheinz knew that legislative pay was poor with few expenses allowed, but a steady flow of legal clients gave them sufficient money to make ends meet for a while after his victory. They decided to buy a new, yellow car so that trips to and from Austin, 190 miles away, would be easier during the 120-day session scheduled at the capitol for January of 1935. Dene loved that car and proudly practiced driving it before the move to Austin when the new year began.

The couple found a room in Austin, but they quickly learned their expenses would put a strain on their bank account. "I did not seek any help or loans from any lobbyist," Roy said. "They knew, by my reputation, they would get a rough rebuff from me if they even hinted they wanted to 'help' me. Not one payoff was ever offered me, and I was proud that my honesty was well-established." It was a rough beginning for a 22-year-old legislator in Austin, but Roy Hofheinz was determined to make his imprint on the older and experienced legislators who felt no qualms about taking the favors and support of lobbyists for big interests.

Hofheinz continued his reputation for unusual attire despite the money pinch. Allan Shivers of Port Arthur, later governor and the leader of a revolt which brought many conservative Texans into the Republican Party, was in the Texas Senate when Representative Hofheinz of Harris County arrived at the state capitol building. "Roy was the only person in the entire capitol in those

Depression days who could wear a different suit each day and sometimes two or three on the same day," he recalled. Shivers and Hofheinz were never political friends because Roy stuck steadfastly to the liberal Democratic line, thus placing the two men far apart in their philosophies.

The first legislation Hofheinz offered was a bill to give Harris County's juvenile board control of institutions for juvenile delinquents and dependents. Both houses passed it, and Governor Allred signed it. A new supervisory board for the juvenile system thus could be appointed. The measure paved the way for Hofheinz ultimately to become a celebrated authority on errant and unfortunate juveniles.

The Harris County legislator captured statewide attention when he led a fight to prevent advertising by dentists. During debate he said, "A dentist told me that if I opposed the attempt to strike the advertising section from the dental bill, he would give me hell. He was a gentleman from California, L. M. Hamman. I said to him, 'If there is any hell to be given, I'll give mine first.'" Hofheinz then pointed out Hamman, who was sitting in the gallery, and the dental lobbyist arose and bowed, waving at Roy.

"I resent the activities of these advertising dentists—and their women lobbyists!" Hofheinz shouted. "If a man is damaged by some of these dentists, he can't sue because they operate chains and live away where you can't get service. I say to Representative Duval, if he does represent Hamman legally, he has an easy job because nobody can get service on him in order to sue him. I see a blond-headed lady sitting up there who has considerable success with the older, bald-headed members of the House."

Representative W. E. Pope, Corpus Christi, dean of the House members and nearly bald, walked to the speaking stand. "Were you talking about me?" he asked Hofheinz. "Oh, no, Uncle Elmer, I didn't mean you," Roy replied to one of the most influential veterans of the House, with a reputation of supporting big business. Hofheinz continued: "There are advertising dentists who tell us what they are going to do to us. Let's get our crack at them now. Let's not be dictated to by a chain dentist from California." In those days, mail order advertising for dentures and other dental work was widespread in the nation. The House got rid of the advertising section of the regulatory bill in a hurry.

Hofheinz introduced a civil service bill for Houston and Harris County employees, arguing that it would save them from political abuse. It was an early "Hatch Act" (a federal law which now protects federal employees from political coercion). Governor Allred vetoed the measure, and both houses upheld him. It was one of the few times the governor disagreed with his thunderous young supporter from Harris County.

Debate over the bill for repeal of Prohibition took up much of the legislators' time. Hofheinz joined those who fought against a proposal for a state monopoly on the sale of alcoholic beverages, and they won. During debate,

Hofheinz said, "I am one of those who has to nurse the drys when they fall over in a coma from too much liquor. I never touch hard alcoholic beverages, but I believe that the man who wants to drink has a right to one." In later years, Hofheinz always had liquor available for his friends and guests, but seldom had more than one or two drinks. He had little respect for people who actually got drunk.

State old age pensions also were a hot topic for the legislature. Hofheinz said he would withhold pensions from persons with $360 a year income. Thirty dollars a month then would go a long way and could keep people out of poor houses. He made his position on old age pensions clear:

> Claims have been advanced that old age pensions would devour the savings of the thrifty, that we would soon become penniless paying for this aid. This argument is an old fraud. It is like the scarecrow left too long in the strawberry patch, its tattered rags having lost the power to alarm. Walk up and examine its stuffings with me. What actually does it cost California and New York and Montana and other states paying pensions to care for their aged outside the poor houses? The surest answer is to ascertain how much you and I should have to pay each year toward that aid. The cost per capita per year ranges as low as six cents in Maryland and Kentucky and $1.80 a year in Nevada. A maximum of 15 cents per month per capita. How do these amounts compare with what we are paying for other functions of government? We have been paying the bill for some big businesses that won't pay as they go. . . . The time has come when we should provide a few dollars and close up the highway to the poor house.

Hofheinz's mastery of facts and figures amazed all who heard him speak. The press gallery was particularly intrigued, and stories of the Harris County orator's activities brought him the title "Boy Wonder of the Legislature." He introduced a bill for the regulation of public utilities, and that brought a horde of lobbyists to the capital. All sorts of legislative delaying tactics were used by lobbyists' friends to prevent passage, but in the 1937 session of the legislature, an almost identical bill was approved. Roy then weighed 140 pounds and was one of the most personable, best-dressed men in the House. His sporty dress was the subject of much kidding. He was popular with fellow members, even when engaging them in rough and tumble debate.

When a bill to tax the gross receipts of newspapers came to the floor, Hofheinz vehemently opposed it. "All three newspapers in Houston were against me," he said, "but I am against this punitive tax. Newspapers have done a great service in fighting the Depression and all the things that go along with Depression." The bill was defeated. Hofheinz was equally steadfast in opposition to a state sales tax. In a spectacular fight on the floor, he arose time and time again to denounce, in biting, ringing terms, the proposed tax which he called "inequitable, unfair, and a burden upon poverty." He always had a quick

John B. Connally, Jr.
Photograph courtesy
Read-Poland, Incorporated.

retort or a reasonable rebuttal when tax advocates tried to sway his colleagues.

John Bowden Connally, Jr., the Texas governor wounded in the same car when President John F. Kennedy was assassinated by Lee Harvey Oswald in Dallas on November 22, 1963, was a student at the University of Texas when Hofheinz served in the legislature. The handsome native of Floresville in southwest Texas was almost five years younger than Hofheinz. When they first met, Connally already had heard of the Harris representative's eloquence. Interested in politics from his early teens, Connally often sat in the capitol gallery to listen to debates as part of his academic work. In 1978, when he was seeking the Republican presidential nomination after a long career as a Democrat and an aide and close adviser to Presidents Johnson and Nixon, Connally recalled the beginning of a friendship and political association which lasted beyond his break with Democrats:

> I met Roy in the capitol and watched him during the regular and two special sessions over a two-year period. Roy, as the youngest legislator in Texas history, was an extremely impressive figure to me and the other students who

watched the sessions. Roy was handsome, articulate and aggressive. He showed great courage in tackling problems of the state. He had great mobility, mentally and physically, which I think was characteristic of him all his life.

Connally and Hofheinz had no idea in 1936 that they would become national figures as they pursued politics, law, and business. Their paths would cross often.

Reporters often cornered the Harris County legislator, 23 in April of 1935, to ask personal questions. They learned he was an avid reader of newspapers, wrote for and studied the text of speeches by men he admired, and each week eagerly awaited the arrival of *Time* and the *Literary Digest* on newstands.

Money became short one month and Hofheinz could not make the payment on the yellow Pontiac. "Dene, then pregnant, broke down and cried when that happened," Roy recalled. "She was a brave woman, but she loved that car, and it hurt her to lose it. Oh, I could have gone to lobbyists and gotten help, but I didn't."

Dene gave birth to Roy Mark Hofheinz, Jr., at 3:00 A.M. on December 18, 1935, at Memorial Hospital in Houston. The Christmas season for the Hofheinz and Cafcalas families was one of great joy and pride. Dene and the baby returned to an apartment at 2413 Barbee, rented after the duplex no longer suited their needs. The Cafcalases told all who asked that Roy's first son closely resembled his Greek grandfather (and Roy, Jr., the adult, did). The new father passed out many boxes of cigars to celebrate the birth of his seven-pound, six-ounce son.

Roy could look back that Christmas to a spectacular beginning as a politician although he was deeply in debt when the year closed. A clipping from the *Houston Press* on his desk said, "At the age of 23, Hofheinz now stands as one of Texas' most energetic and effective zealots. Serving his first term, he already has the unique distinction of carrying out every major promise he made to the electorate. Today, 10 and a half months after taking office, Hofheinz has seen the establishment of the Public Safety Department for which he fought, the repeal of Prohibition, the passage of an old age pension law, and has led fights against a state sales tax and income tax. Hard work and courage have filled his 23 years. His record of active legislative work and political courage has made political observers mark him down in their future book as up and coming."

5

The Youngest County Judge

Suave, judicious, and supported by the Harris County political "establishment," W. Henry Ward, 56, sat securely, he thought, in the office of county judge at the beginning of 1936. For 54 years he had been a Houston resident. He had graduated from the University of Texas Law School at Austin and had married Hortense W. Malch, a practicing attorney. He presided over the Commissioners Court, ruling body of county government, and Probate, Lunacy, and Juvenile courts of Texas' largest county, now grown to more than 350,000 people. Commissioners Court decided how millions of taxpayers' dollars would be spent each year, aside from the outlays of the mayor and City Council of Houston and other municipalities and districts in the county.

Because his law practice had suffered his first year as a legislator and he had a wife and baby son to support, Hofheinz began considering, after New Year's Day, what political office he might seek in the 1936 Democratic primary. He wanted to stay in Houston, not continue to make round trips to Austin. The county judge's job paid $7500 a year and was a stepping stone to higher political office. He and Dene decided the judgeship would be his second target. In the 1935 legislative session he learned much about the needs of juvenile delinquents, the plight of the mentally ill in jails, and the needy and elderly people whom he had helped get small state pensions. He also had stored in his computer-like mind facts about state, county, and city governments and how they were run. His beliefs were strong—he wanted efficient and honest handling of the taxpayers' business. He felt qualified to run for the office.

Roy and Dene at night checked the record of Judge Ward after Roy handled cases in court and made speeches to various organizations. He was much in demand for his patriotic talks and eloquent insight into the problems of government.

On May 2, the eager young politician finished drafting his announcement. He personally carried it to the three Houston and other newspapers and radio stations in the county. In his announcement, he pledged not to practice law while in office, not to campaign for any county commissioners, to promote humane treatment of the mentally ill, and to get fair treatment for those charged with lunacy. The candidate also pledged to help juvenile delinquents and to expedite probate business in a fair and judicious manner. Finally, he vowed to work hard and to save taxpayers' money where possible.

Hofheinz's announcement startled Harris County political circles. Most had felt that, if Hofheinz stayed in politics, he would run for the legislature again. After all, he had just turned 24 years old in April. The *Press, Chronicle,* and *Post* all had supported Judge Ward when he was reelected county judge in 1932, and it appeared, from editorial comment they had published during his tenure, that they would continue to do so. But newspapers and politicians were unfamiliar with Hofheinz's ability to find his target and shoot for it. His announcement indicated he had done his homework on how to attack Judge Ward.

The *Sun,* a Goose Creek county newspaper friendly to Ward, noted, "Roy Hofheinz has proved himself the outstanding showman in the campaign. Hofheinz has turned many otherwise dull and uninteresting political rallies into good shows. But, does any of this prove that this young man has the qualifications to make a successful county judge? The office of county judge requires a man who has a wide experience of several sorts—one whose judgement is based on sound reasoning." The *Sun* observed that Judge Ward had the required experience and had proved his ability.

Judge Ward paid little attention to his challenger in the beginning. He avoided rallies, sending friends to speak for his candidacy. He felt safe and shrugged off suggestions that a callow youth could unseat him. An article by Ed Kilman in the *Houston Post* caused Ward to reconsider, however. Kilman observed that Hofheinz's oratory had been effective and that he had continually challenged Ward to appear at political rallies with him. Ward thus realized he would have to fight, for Hofheinz's oratory and challenges had caused voters to wonder if all was well with his administration.

Endorsing Hofheinz were the Magnolia Lodge #7, Sons of Hermann; the Independent 100, an Italian organization; oil and refinery unions; the Texas-American Citizens Labor Club of Magnolia Park; and Chicano and black organizations. The Legislative Institute put out a political recommendation with a working man's ticket. It listed, besides Hofheinz, Kenneth McCalla, Roy's former debating partner and legislative colleague, for district attorney, and Albert Thomas for the Eighth Congressional District. A coalition of voters outside the "establishment" supported them and was showing muscle.

John H. Crooker, for many years one of Houston's leading attorneys and the son-in-law of Judge Ward, was alarmed by the gains Hofheinz was making. He took to the stump for his father-in-law as did his 21-year-old son, John H. Crooker, Jr. The senior Crooker charged that Hofheinz's claims in his campaign talks that he had worked his way through college and made his way up on his own were untrue. Rather, the money Nonie Hofheinz had received because of her husband's accidental death had paid for Roy's education. This attack inflamed Dene Hofheinz.

Roy's doctor had ordered him to take a rest; he had lost 19 pounds because of his hectic campaign schedule of meeting oil and refinery workers at 4:00 A.M. when shifts changed and of shaking hands with people at filling stations, stores, and on the streets until late at night. Dene took over for her husband on the stump and in meeting voters. In her first talk at a Magnolia Park rally, she lashed at the "unfair and unjustified attacks leveled at my husband's personal record. The county judge's son-in-law attempted to attack my husband's conduct toward his mother," she said angrily. "Having gone with my husband four years before we were married, I know that he did work day and night to support his mother while obtaining a higher education. I do know that every penny received on account of his father's death was given to his mother for her own benefit." Reviewing Roy's work in the legislature, Dene added, "I know he is entitled to a promotion. I spent every day at the legislature with my husband. I know that he worked hard day and night for all the people of Harris County."

Dene's irritation grew when Judge Ward, finally on the stump, kept saying, "I ask you who honor your mother what you think of a man who parades his mother through a political campaign in order to get votes?" Yet, his personal attacks on Hofheinz hurt Ward. The rank-and-file voters of Harris County knew how hard Roy, the teenage promoter, had worked because it had been well-recorded in the press and on radio.

The major turning point in the campaign came when Judge Ward got word that Hofheinz was going to attack the incumbent's handling of the R. E. Brooks estate in Probate Court. Called a "grand old man," Brooks had been, in public life, a judge, real estate investor, and leader in the community. When he died in 1929, his estate was valued at between $3 and $5 million, with $3 million listed as debts. Ward took over jurisdiction of the estate when elected in 1932. Not knowing what Hofheinz might say about his administration, Ward took the offensive. The *Houston Chronicle* carried a headline: "Ward Beats Hofheinz to Draw, Replies to Charge Not Yet Made on the Handling of Estates." Ward's vigorous defense of his handling of the Brooks estate was countered by Hofheinz with charges that Ward had used the case to favor friends and that he did not act in the best interest of Brooks' widow. Mrs. Brooks supported Hofheinz's contention in a letter published in the *Press*. In his political tabloid, *Justice*, Hofheinz carried more details and charges against the incumbent. He also bought radio time and spread charges of mismanagement by Ward.

The *Houston Chronicle* continued to defend the integrity of Judge Ward, but the *Press* and the *Post*, which previously had supported him, changed to Hofheinz. The *Press* said, "In our opinion, Roy Hofheinz has shown intelligence and unusual ability in the legislature and during this campaign. While he has conducted a severe campaign against Judge Ward, we believe it has been

Roy, elected Harris County Judge at the age of 24, with Dene and Roy, Jr.

justified by the facts he has uncovered in Judge Ward's record. We consider Hofheinz's age no valid objection to his election." The *Post* observed that Hofheinz had been an outstanding legislator and an excellent lawyer, adding that Hofheinz had "ideas about handling estates, lunacy cases, and juvenile delinquency matters which are sound and wholesome." The *Post* believed that "his career will carry him far up the ladder of political success, that he will prove one of the outstanding public officials of Harris County. We say the voters will make no mistake in naming Roy Hofheinz their county judge."

Jack Valenti, a Houston native who later became president of Motion Pictures and TV Producers, Incorporated, was 14 years old when Hofheinz campaigned for county judge. Valenti's father at the time was employed by the Houston city government, so politics intrigued Jack at an early age. He recalled, "I became enchanted with Roy when he challenged Judge Ward. Roy's sole weapons were his voice and his brass, which he took to the stump and radio. Reams of newspaper copy were written about 'the beardless wonder,' 'the boy orator,' and the 'bayou buffalo' whose extraordinarily articulate voice caught the fancy of the people. He had command of language and logic, total discipline over the linking of brain and tongue, as well as the uncanny ability to get his message and personality across on radio—television later."

Valenti also observed that "there was more than just oratory. Roy's brain was a peculiar instrument. It stored facts and, on command from his mind, could . . . spit out the information he needed at the precise moment he needed it. I was entranced by Hofheinz." Apparently so were the voters. In the July 24 primary, tantamount to election, Hofheinz overwhelmed Ward 44,195 to 18,726. Kenneth McCalla won the district attorney's race, and Albert Thomas won the nomination for Congress. It would not be long before Hofheinz and his debating partner, McCalla, would occupy offices in the courthouse close to each other. Newspapers took pictures of the Hofheinz and McCalla families celebrating together.

Hofheinz, in his victory statement to voters, said, "I will strive sincerely to conduct myself as county judge so that I may prove worthy of the vote of confidence and the support of citizens. I reiterate my campaign pledge that my office will be conducted in such a manner that the finger of suspicion will never be pointed toward me."

The *Houston Chronicle,* big paper loser, said it regretted the defeat of Judge Ward, but was "entirely friendly toward Hofheinz who has been so singularly honored by voters. The *Chronicle* hopes he will rise to the great opportunity now given him and knows he will try to do so." The *Goose Creek Sun* congratulated Hofheinz, saying it was a "bit red-faced" because of its support of Ward.

Happy but worn to exhaustion by his campaign, Hofheinz after his victory left for Mexico for a hunting trip with Skelly Skelton, Gene Whitehead, Red McDonald, and Dick Young of Houston, and Dan Fagan of Tulsa, Oklahoma. They shot six bucks their first stop and went deeper into the Mexican interior to hunt ducks. Hofheinz sent pictures home and to the press to show the party would not be lying about its successful shooting of wildlife.

Roy and Dene went to a Democratic rally in Dallas on September 15. Vice-President John Nance Garner was there. Having met Hofheinz at the 1928 Democratic national convention in Houston, Garner quickly found and congratulated the county judge-elect. The vice-president, Hofheinz, Governor Allred, and Colonel Paul A. Wakefield, Allred's military aide, were pictured in the *Houston Post.* When reminded Hofheinz was only 24, Garner observed, "At that age, too, I became county judge, but I was appointed and can't dispute Roy was the youngest county judge ever elected in the nation."

The Hofheinzes came home, but Roy quickly took another vacation by going on a fishing trip to Port Aransas with B. J. Thigpen and George Carmany. Again to prove the party had good luck, Hofheinz took pictures of kingfish and mackerel catches and sent them to newspapers.

His nomination as county judge did not end Hofheinz's legislative work. Governor Allred called another special session of the legislature after the July primaries. Hofheinz got the floor, talked about conditions in the state hospital for the insane, and demanded an investigation. He repeated that many insane

*Roy with Vice-President
John Nance Garner*

people had been kept in jails because there was no room for them in state hospitals. He said 105 insane persons were in the Harris County jail in July, many of them sleeping on dirty floors.

It was then that he and Allred had another disagreement. The governor wanted to take $3 million from highway funds to support the pension fund for Confederate veterans. Money for veterans previously had been taken from highways with none paid back. "It strikes me," Hofheinz said in debate, "as rather foolish business for the governor on one hand to talk about a $5 million fund to advertise Texas, and then on the other hand urge taking away $3 million from the fund with which to build roads for tourists." Hofheinz spoke again on hospital conditions and declared to legislators, "You had Communism investigated, but when someone tries to do something for humanity, I find opposition. The asylums have nobody to lobby for them, and the legislature ought to present their case for them." He won his point. The legislature agreed to look into the unhappy plight of the mentally ill in institutions and jails. Roy came home to check again on conditions of the insane in Harris County so that he would be ready to move locally when he took office.

Hofheinz also was disturbed about charges that Harris County's appointed relief board and its administrator, W. W. Whitson, had not carried out their duties properly. He unveiled a study showing that, of several hundred cases investigated, more than 300 were unworthy of aid. That put Whitson under fire. At the same time, the judge-elect attacked the Community Chest, asking why it should not participate in direct relief. He said the Chest was giving $2500 a month for salaries of its employees, but nothing for direct relief. William Straus, chairman, and others on the relief board resigned. At a hearing, Hofheinz told Straus that he did not want to ruffle feathers of the men who had served on the board, but that he needed facts from Straus and the board so taxpayers would know how relief money was being spent. Straus walked out of the hearing room, indignant that he and board members should be called to accounting. A new city-county relief board was named on December 31, temporarily composed of Houston Councilmen Walter Pearson and George Waters, County Commissioner R. H. Spencer, E. L. Crain and N. S. Leach of the Community Chest, and Hofheinz. They represented the beginning of a new era for Harris relief efforts.

Newspapers, especially the *Press,* commended the judge-elect for bringing the relief situation into focus. They also applauded when Hofheinz announced on December 16, 1936, that he would ban secret sessions of Commissioners Court, often held in past years despite protests by the press. Hofheinz said the people had the right to know everything about their business. In his attack on the Community Chest, Hofheinz had charged that relief rolls were padded and that the Chest really was not doing anything to straighten out the situation except paying salaries for workers. In a key speech in December before a group of businessmen, Hofheinz said he wanted all property in the county reappraised by capable people so that taxes could be equalized. Little did Hofheinz or his listeners realize that this attitude would soon bring him into a battle with Jesse Jones and one of his biggest real estate properties.

Just before Christmas Judge Ward met with the juvenile board with Hofheinz present. After the session, Ward walked up to Hofheinz and said, "When you get time, come over and spend a few days with me. I'll be glad to help you in any way I can." Hofheinz thanked his July adversary and said that he would. In the next few days, the county judge-elect got a close look at how the busy office operated.

As Dene watched, beaming and holding her year-old son, "Butch," Hofheinz was sworn in as county judge on January 1, 1937. Commissioners taking office at the same time were Beatrice Massey, Tom A. Graham, R. H. Spencer, and William Tautenhahn. From then on, throughout his life, Roy Hofheinz was know as "the Judge."

6

The Whirlwind of 1937

Harris County residents in 1937 experienced a continuing political whirlwind—progressive motion at all levels—named Hofheinz. In his inaugural speech, Judge Hofheinz pledged as his major aims the strict, fair, honest, and open management of the taxpayers' money with a tax increase only as a last resort for essential services; full-time devotion to his position; conservation of assets of heirs and estates in Probate Court; a firm but compassionate approach to juvenile deliquency; and a full investigation and a humanitarian approach to lunacy cases. The Hofheinz program, said the *Post,* was "progressive and enlightening." The 24-year-old judge, the newspaper added, "is a man of action. The people have reason to look forward to two years of constructive achievement." The *Post* was right.

In Hofheinz's first session as presiding officer of Commissioners Court on January 5, bids for shell for county roads were up for approval. After glancing at them, Hofheinz quickly asked, "How is it that the bids are all alike?" H. J. Lahrssen, county purchasing agent, replied that all shell producers got together before bidding. "Isn't that a violation of anti-trust laws?" the Judge asked. Commissioner Tom Graham observed that "shell producers must have forgotten that the National Recovery Administration [which had set some prices when President Roosevelt was getting the country out of the Depression] no longer exists. Unit prices are not legal." The purchasing agent added that deals in shell, typewriters, nails, automobile tires, and other items bought by the county also had been submitted with identical figures. Hofheinz told Lahrssen he wanted to be informed quickly when instances of identical bidding occurred. He said that he believed that shell prices in Harris County were the highest in the state and that he would investigate while holding up the bids before him. The Judge asked County Auditor Harry L. Washburn to prepare a list of shell prices bid and purchased over a period of years. He also asked for specifications for buying materials. Experience in operating the $4 million county road program had convinced County Engineer Charles R. Haile that when a ton of shell was bought for a railroad car, 15 percent was salt water—a $37,000 loss. Specifications showed a ton to be 2000 pounds. Haile recommended that the weight figure per ton should be increased to 2400 pounds to offset the water content. The court agreed to the new specifications.

A week later, Parker Brothers, one of the shell producers, agreed to a 2400-pound specification which, in effect, would give the county 20 percent more for its money. Lawrence Fuqua, secretary of the Texas Shell Producers Association, did not like Parker's decision and told the commissioners he would tell members of the association that specifications should be 2200 pounds per ton not exceeding 15 percent water. "Your new ton specification is unfair," Fuqua shouted. Hofheinz countered by declaring he would go to State Attorney General William McGraw and ask him to invoke the anti-trust law against the producers and any other bidders who would flaunt a new competitive policy of bidding. The commissioners did not vote but tacitly agreed to follow Hofheinz's thinking.

Having studied the shell monopoly for a week, the Judge asked Fuqua at the next meeting which type of road lasted longer, one of gravel or one of shell. Fuqua answered, "The gravel itself will last longer, but the binder will disappear quicker." Washburn interrupted to say the initial cost of gravel road was greater, but maintenance lower. Hofheinz had learned that the county had owned a 100-acre gravel pit near Fayetteville for 20 years, but that it was not in use. "Why did the price of shell drop from $150 to $106 when the county bought the gravel pit?" the Judge asked Fuqua, who replied he did not know whether the figures were true or not, but "maybe it was to keep gravel out."

Hofheinz and Fuqua then were on their feet, angry. "How much does the shell cost the producers?" the Judge asked. Fuqua replied, "The shell producers dredge the materials from Galveston Bay, pay a five percent tax to the county, and charge 90 cents per cubic yard at the unloading dock." Hofheinz retorted, "It seems curious to me that you get shell for nothing and charge 90 cents." Fuqua began talking about the investment of shell companies in dredging equipment. "We're not worrying about academic questions," Hofheinz interrupted. "The commissioners and I want to save the county money. You're engaging in restraint of trade when you go to your members and say they have to be bound by association prices. What business has the association in telling Captain Bill Parker for Parker Brothers, for instance, how to do business? We conduct our business with individuals, not associations." Engineer Haile was instructed to telephone Parker to see if he still agreed to the 2400-pound specification. A few minutes later Haile reported that Parker was standing firm. The court then declared an emergency and asked that new bids on new specifications be produced the next week.

To Hofheinz's consternation, Parker Brothers, W. L. Jones Company, and Horton and Horton bid on the 2400-pound basis, but increased the price 10 percent. "Mr. Parker told us he would bid at the old price," Hofheinz said, adding, "Fuqua told us he would not recommend the new ton specification without a price increase. He made a threat a week ago, and he made it good. If that isn't collusion, I don't know what it is. If we could throw some of these bids in the jug for a day or two, I'd be in favor of doing it." He argued against acceptance of any bids, but Commissioner William Tautenhahn, for whose district the shell was sought, said he had an emergency condition on several roads that demanded immediate attention. "Rather than let those people flim flam the county," the Judge said, "I'd be in favor of advertising for gravel and, if necessary, pay a higher price for it." Commissioners Spencer and Tautenhahn said acceptance of one bid would not prejudice the county's case against producers. A contract for 350 cubic yards was awarded to Horton and Horton with a motion approved saying, "Commissioners protest the fact that bids were the second set of identical bids on the same deal."

Hofheinz proposed at the third meeting that the commissioners go into the shell business to save money. "We could purchase a tugboat, barges, and build a landing place as an adjunct to our road building program," he argued. "I'm told Corpus Christi pays 65 cents per cubic yard for shell while we pay $1.25 or more. I believe Harris County could produce its own shell for 35 to 50 cents per cubic yard. The cost of getting started, I figure, would be around $75,000." Commissioner Beatrice Massey said she thought the Judge's investment figure was too low. "What if it costs $100,000 or even $150,000?" asked Commissioner Graham. "Wouldn't it be worth it?" Mrs. Massey said Graham's figure was more likely, but the investment still might pay. The court then agreed to limit shell purchases to emergency requirements while a plan for the county to dredge its own shell was studied.

Texas State Auditor Tom King and Assistant Attorney General Victor Bouldin left Austin immediately to check into the Harris County shell situation as a result of Hofheinz's plea. The state officials also had read that the Texas County Judges' Association, meeting at Wharton, had voted, after hearing a speech by Hofheinz at its convention, a resolution endorsing competitive bidding.

Hofheinz gained an ally in the shell fight in Houston Mayor R. H. Fonville, who said he felt the city would be glad to join the county in an effort to beat down shell prices. At his request, the City Council voted to join in the shell investigation. The next bids of shell producers for county needs varied from five to 21 cents a cubic yard. The amount of material needed by commissioners, however, was reduced after bids were opened, members of the court agreeing to buy only quantities absolutely needed pending negotiations of Hofheinz with producers. The next day, Hofheinz asked producers to open their books for study, but they refused.

Commissioners fired their heaviest shot at the shell men on February 2 when they voted to ask for bids on 50,000 cubic yards to allow independent producers outside Harris County to participate. Assurances that the city would

*Houston Mayor
R. H. Fonville.* Photograph
courtesy the *Houston Chronicle*.

be an ally in this maneuver were given by Mayor Fonville, Hofheinz reported. He added that the city was expected to advertise for bids on a similar large amount of shell or gravel. Hofheinz asked that gravel bids be requested by the county despite the fact that he expected the material could not compete with shell on price. "If we find that gravel cannot compete with shell as far as price is concerned, then because of the great expense, we will have concrete evidence to lay before the Texas Railroad Commission in asking for a special reduction in freight rates for gravel. If we can get the rates reduced from about 90 to 60 cents, we'll be able to have competition between the two materials." He thus laid the groundwork for a trip to the state regulatory agency.

The wishes of Mayor Fonville were overridden on February 10 by City Councilmen S. A. Starkey, Oscar Holcombe, and Walter Pearson after the mayor and Hofheinz pleaded with them to delay buying 30,000 cubic yards of shell for about $35,000. Starkey sought to justify the action by arguing that streets were in terrible condition because of recent rains and "any saving we might effect by delay will be more than offset with the loss we will suffer." Hofheinz disagreed, pleading, "Stay with the county and advertise as we're doing today for 50,000 cubic yards of shell. You will save the city thousands of dollars with competitive bidding."

Councilmen disregarded Hofheinz and Fonville, but taxpayers read with satisfaction about their efforts to save money. The result that day was the City Council's awarding of contracts to Parker Brothers, Haden Company, Horton and Horton, and the John Young Company to supply 7000 cubic yards each at $1.15 a ton on loaded cars and to W. L. Jones for 2000 cubic yards at $1.25 through the hopper. All five companies had submitted identical bids on 30,000 yards—the flat rate, on cars and by cubic yards through hoppers. Each got a part of the total order. Fonville regretted the council's action, saying a delay could have saved money. The *Press* said the council's action was a "shellacking for taxpayers." "The Harris County Taxpayers' Association," said E. A. Calvin, president, was "getting tired of such stuff at City Hall. The shell producers are making dupes out of some members of City Council." There also was talk of recall action against the three councilmen if they continued such business.

Mayor Fonville refused to sign the council's 30,000-ton award. Trying to appease, the five successful shell bidders announced they had agreed the city might cancel any remaining part of the order if and when the council believed it advantageous for the city to do so. This proviso allowed Fonville an out to sign the order.

As a result of Hofheinz's campaign, a Corpus Christi firm, Heldenfels Brothers, offered to deliver shell at 10 cents a cubic yard cheaper than paid to the Harris County monopoly. Bids had been asked on 50,000 cubic yards. Submitting were Parker Brothers, the Haden Company, the John Young Company, and W. L. Jones Company. After argument about the ability of Heldenfels to make good on its bid, Commissioners Graham, Spencer, and Massey lined up against Hofheinz when he attempted to get approval of the Heldenfels' low bid. Hofheinz threatened court action if the bid was not accepted. That day, February 27, the shell war nearly blew the dome from the courthouse. Arguments were so furious it was difficult to follow them. Because of Hofheinz's court threat, the four commissioners finally decided they would go to Corpus Christi to look at Heldenfels' operation and elsewhere to see how shell was produced. That stopped contract awarding that day. The next day the commissioners read in newspapers that Hofheinz was "nobly fighting the taxpayers' battle."

The commissioners went to Corpus Christi and on March 3 reversed themselves, voting to accept Heldenfels' low bid. It was the first time in more than a decade that an "outside firm" had won a shell bid. County Engineer Haile said the county would save at least $6000 on this one order. The new vote did not deter Hofheinz from going to Austin again to urge the railroad commission to reduce gravel freight rates. Heldenfels, however, had problems. He found it politically difficult to get a permit to dredge in Galveston Bay and had to seek other places to buy shell so that he could fulfill his contract. On March 5, the Corpus Christi firm did produce its first delivery just before a time limit imposed by commissioners was to expire.

Hofheinz won on another front. On April 12, the railroad commission dropped freight rates on gravel by 24 percent—99 to 66 cents—effective May 1. Now Harris County could bring in its own gravel from Fayetteville, if necessary, to compete with shell. But city councilmen did not change in their deals with the shell producers. This caused the *Press* to say, "It is hard for the city to get a break when some city councilmen are involved in price juggling going on in the purchase of shell. Under the pressure of independent competition of Heldenfels Brothers against the big four shell producers here, and aided by the effective campaigning of Judge Hofheinz in the courthouse, the price of shell to the county has been hammered down to a low of 77 cents. Compare that with the $1.45 price paid by the city on the recent airport shell deal engineered through council by Commissioner S. A. 'Tobe' Starkey." Heldenfels had offered shell for the airport at $1.15.

To head off Heldenfels, the council inserted in its next bid some specifications which the Corpus Christi firm said would subject it to confiscation; and it therefore refused to bid. Thus the big Harris producers still had the field to itself in dealing with the city. The *Press* observed, "Starkey might just as well be working for the shell producers instead of in the employ of the taxpayers supposedly safeguarding and furthering their interests."

Despite all some councilmen could do to help the shell monopoly, competition in shell bids was reestablished and, over a two-year period, the average price paid was greatly reduced. Gravel also started coming into use again.

The shell fight was just one of many for Judge Hofheinz in his first year in office. Working from before dawn to midnight, he required his two secretaries, Jessie Traynor and Evelyn Johnson, and later Edna Dato Harling, to stay on the job from 7:30 A.M. to 7:30 P.M. during the first three months he was in office.

Hofheinz was a whirlwind on other fronts as well. In other progressive action Hofheinz *initiated a plan for Harris County flood control.* The county had experienced water disasters at least once a decade. Hofheinz went to the legislature and asked for a Harris County flood control authority and for a return to the county by the state of some of the state ad valorem tax money it had collected so that drainage could begin. The Judge's leadership in changing Harris County from a Venice-like area took several years (and will be fully detailed subsequently). He *spent much time at the county's Bayland School for Boys,* where he studied problems and began a program, at the penitentiary-like institution and in Juvenile Court, which would be hailed nationwide. The Judge *nudged the Houston Community Chest into giving $3000 to direct relief instead of spending all its money on administration.* There were 850 persons, most of them heads of families with from one to 10 dependents, needing help. He also caused reexamination of the relief roll families and their needs. Some, he felt, did not deserve aid. Hofheinz *fought to keep the county tax rate the same as in 1936 despite an increase of $207,760 in the budget.* He insisted that vigorous collection of delinquent taxes would more than balance the budget and charged that 40 percent of Harris County property, in addition, was unrendered by owners. He began a drive to get tax valuations up to date, demanding that experts be hired to check properties and help the assessor-collector. This thinking brought him into conflict the next year with Jesse Jones' real estate interests. He *successfully lobbied with state officials to get most of the insane in Harris County jails into hospitals or homes where they could live under decent conditions.* To finance this, he won an appeal to get state pensions for aged inmates, 60 or older, in the psychopathic ward so that they could support themselves privately.

The Judge *successfully invited independent east Texas oil and gas companies to come into Harris County in competition with major companies headquartered in Houston to bid on the county's gas and oil needs.* He *lobbied through the legislature a constitutional amendment applying only to Harris County which would allow Harris to adopt a pay-as-you-go program for building roads instead of paying high interest rates on bonds.* He traveled 3800 miles to all parts of the state campaigning for an amendment applying only to one county. Statewide approval was necessary. As he traveled, newspapers hailed his eloquence and gave support to his idea. The voters approved the amendment in October. He *demanded a franchise tax on Harris County utilities, then unregulated by the state, which he said were not paying their fair share of the cost of county government.* He immediately got into a running battle with telephone and other utility companies. *Through facts he released to newspapers,* Hofheinz *broke up fee-grabbing of specially appointed sheriff's and constable's deputies in Harris and bordering counties.* These part-time officials could make money only by making arrests for fees, many of them on flimsy allegations.

Looking ahead to statewide development of highways which could lead to Houston, he *went to the Texas Highway Commission to support southwest Texas residents in their bid for a major highway from Laredo, on the Mexican border, to George West;* it would cut the road distance to Houston by 56 miles. Although this highway did not directly connect Houston with Laredo, Hofheinz felt an ultimate diagonal route from Laredo to Houston would be beneficial. The new road would be through Freer and Duval counties. The road from Houston to Beeville was improved to George West. The short-cut extension would be off Highway 202 from Three Rivers in Live Oak County to Laredo, traversing McMullin, Duval, and Webb counties. The highway commission approved the plan before the year was over. The Judge *made trips to support new highway links from Houston to Dallas, Fort Worth, San Antonio, and Beaumont.* He helped begin the major network of highways going into Houston today. He *spoke to civic and business groups in various parts of the state on his program for juvenile delinquency. Remaining active in the Democratic Party,* he *was the roundly applauded principal speaker at the 1937 Texas Young Democrats Convention in Houston;* his friend, Price Daniel, presided. *As an official observer of the important Houston Port Commission,* Hofheinz *successfully demanded that meetings be open to the press.* He had to fill any vacancy on the commission; when H. C. Cockburn resigned, the county judge appointed

W. W. Strong, a respected labor leader, to give the working man a voice in the port's affairs.

The Judge *appointed, as his first decision in Probate Court, C. E. Gates as administrator of the Brooks estate.* Hofheinz said "the milking" of the estate had put it in bad shape. He told Gates, succeeding Sewall Myer, to get the estate in order in a hurry and without undue expense. He also lifted any bond requirements for Mrs. Brooks to appeal decisions made by Judge Ward. His campaign promises of cleaning up estate mismanagement were beginning. He *became upset again when commissioners let a year's contract for light bulbs.* There were 10 identical bidders. "I think you are damaging any effort to do anything about identical bids by letting this contract to one of the bidders," the Judge said vehemently. He *found time to check cemetery conditions for paupers.* "I am advised," Hofheinz wrote Dr. J. Herbert Page, county health officer, "that during the last few years pauper burials have been conducted in a most haphazard manner. Few records have been kept, and in only a few instances head markers have been placed on graves. Investigation shows that in some instances coffins have not been completely buried and many of them only barely covered. Unquestionable, definite records should be kept. In fairness to all concerned, I must say that responsibility for this cannot be placed upon any one department." He demanded action in setting up new burial conditions and got it. *Lawyers were summoned to his courts for hearings almost at any hour.* They gathered often at 7:00 A.M. and 7:00 P.M. to clear dockets; he did not conclude some hearings before midnight.

Serving on the Harris County Juvenile Board as well as presiding in Juvenile Court, Hofheinz *asked the legislature to pass a bill allowing him to earn $2000 annually extra for that work.* All members except Hofheinz were paid $200 a month for their time-consuming decisions. The law was passed, and the Judge's income for 18 or more hours of work each day was increased to $9500 annually. Traveling expenses on official business were reimbursed. He *ruffled the feathers of many officials and employees in the courthouse with his demands for efficient work and quick action.* When the Judge would tell Dene whose toes he had stepped on, the compassionate lady would go to offended people and mend fences. Dene Hofheinz carried out this role for her brilliant husband all her life. She knew he was essentially a kind man, but also that he was impatient and sharp with inefficient, slow-thinking, or lazy workers, or those who alibied they could not get a job done. Hofheinz *was disturbed by the fact that workers who had to use county ferries south of the Houston ship channel were inconvenienced in going to and from their homes north of the channel.* A plan for a tunnel under the channel to help the workers began growing in his mind, and later he had a tough fight to win a tunnel free from fares. *While helping with temporary relief measures for the Harris County insane, he demanded the state put a hospital in Houston.* Newspapers supported him and editorialized about his efforts to bring about humane treatment of the insane. He *led the way by September 4 for Commissioners Court to add $297,500 to the tax valuation of Southwestern Bell Telephone System by slashing depreciation allowances.* Increases in other valuations followed so that by September 8 a total of $1,285,800 in valuations had been added to the tax rolls.

Hofheinz's busy year contained one pleasant interlude, a visit by President Roosevelt to Houston on May 2. The Judge, clad in his best white suit and panama hat, was one of the official greeters, and a picture of him next to FDR was carried by the *Press*. The president had not forgotten the page boy of the 1928 convention and congratulated him on his quick rise to county judge. Hofheinz was not invited to board the Navy vessel on which Roosevelt fished the next day in Pork Aransas, but he had a binocular view of what the president and his party were doing. Roy and some friends engaged a fishing boat and stayed near the president. "There was too much Navy surrounding the president's ship to make good fishing possible for him," Hofheinz told newspapermen. "I looked through binoculars at the presidential party and saw a number of fancy naval officers. I don't know what classification were the ships surrounding the president's, but they seemed like battleships. No wonder fish were scared away. I made movies of the president every time I could get close enough." Word came down that Roosevelt had landed two small mackerel and his son, Elliott, two tarpon. Hofheinz said his party did better—four tarpon over a two-day period, the same time the president had relaxed in the bay aboard ship.

Texas' leading political figures were in Houston for the Roosevelt visit. Hofheinz had met most of them during his nearly three years of political activity. They had written him congratulations on his successes. In the months and years to come, most of them would have political or business associations with the phenomenon named Roy Hofheinz. His polite but firm, honest, and progressive demeanor began winning the Judge many professional friends and admirers. One of them was Leon Jaworski, son of a Waco, Texas, Baptist preacher and seven years Roy's senior. As a brilliant attorney in a big law firm, Jaworski had watched at a distance as Hofheinz was elected legislator and county judge. He recalled, "I first came to know Roy personally when he was county judge. He was presiding over Probate Court. Having been rather active in the probate field with will contests, both representing opponents and contestants, I sat down and talked with Roy quite often. He was very young, tremendously able and very articulate—beyond his years in every respect."

As Hofheinz spoke and attended many civic functions and parties as county judge in 1937, he met William F. "Bill" Bennett, who had taken over as vice-president and commercial manager of Radio Station KXYZ, owned by Tilford Jones, nephew of tycoon Jesse Jones. Hofheinz's interest in radio had not diminished since his amateur host days, and he kept in touch with developments by talking with Bennett and others and reading radio publications when he had a few minutes free. A calm, affable, and energetic salesman, Bennett liked the progressiveness of the Judge and admired his radio speeches. Their mutual admiration was to lead to a close business relationship when Hofheinz left the county judge's office at the end of 1944.

Hofheinz kept open house at his Barbee Street home for friends. Dene always had extra food handy at home and made certain that her husband had good supplies in his office, for Roy's passion for food never changed. She never knew how many people the Judge might bring home for dinner at any hour. Nonie often was at the home, and she and Dene advised the Judge when he brought up questions. He delighted in his toddling son, Roy, Jr., whom he had dubbed "Butch," and played with him as much as time permitted, especially on Sundays.

Roy continued relaxing by fishing and hunting. He induced a few of his friends to help him build a rustic place on Galveston Bay and called it "Ship Shack." Newspapers kiddingly reported that Roy's friends walked down the street after excursions to the retreat showing blisters and cuts from the work they had done there. Even then, Hofheinz knew how to coax and lead friends into tasks which he enjoyed supervising and which he paid for with food and good fellowship.

Christmas of 1937 proved another extremely happy time for the Hofheinz and Cafcalas families. As the political whirlwind slowed for Yule festivities and the year's accomplishments were reviewed, Dene and Roy were happy that she was pregnant again.

7

A Friend of Juveniles

Hundreds of law-abiding citizens of Harris County, Texas, today still voice their thanks for the philosophy and official actions Roy Hofheinz took as county judge from 1937 through 1944. During this period he could give only part of his time to juveniles, for the law provided that he not only preside over the court's judging of errant young people, but also over three other important courts and two boards. Because of the Judge, each of those citizens who had erred as juveniles, had an opportunity—and often a second one—to reform.

The handling of juvenile delinquents in Harris County was a political hodge-podge until after Hofheinz, as a Harris legislator in 1935, pushed a bill through the Texas legislature creating a nonpolitical Harris County Juvenile Board whose members would be the county judge and the judges of district courts; they had the authority to make rules and oversee the financing of the important task of saving boys and girls from the wrong way of life. County and city money would be appropriated for the program.

When he took office at age 24, Hofheinz remembered the charges during the political campaign that he was too young to understand and judge juveniles. He had overwhelmingly convinced voters that he could do the job better than the man he defeated, W. Henry Ward, and that the time had come for him to produce. "I consider the problems of youngsters as of much more importance than punishment or confinement in an institution," he said as he began his work. "I want citizens in all walks of life to get involved in juvenile work through a parole system so that a sound, humanitarian approach can be made to helping young people."

He recommended to the juvenile board that W. E. Robertson be named supervising director of the juvenile system, including investigation and paroles. He knew that Robertson understood young people. District Judge Ewing Boyd was concerned that Hofheinz and Robertson would not get all money needed because the city government in the past had not contributed what was considered its fair share. "Well," responded Hofheinz, "we have a ray of hope in Mayor Fonville. He always has had the interest of youngsters at heart." Fonville did convince the City Council to help finance the juvenile program.

Judge Hofheinz dictates letter to his secretary, Evelyn Johnson.

Speaking to the Lions Club of Brenham on January 20—Hofheinz was in constant demand as a speaker—the Judge made clear his philosophy about juvenile delinquency. He emphasized that most delinquencies were attributed to broken families and undesirable home conditions. In another talk before the Optimist Club in Houston, he said, "It is the aim of the Harris County Probation Office to seek to build up the family ties first, and if this is impossible, to place the delinquent child in custody of persons rather than commit him or her to some institution."

Hofheinz normally reserved Sunday for his own family, but in his first week of office he went to the Bayland Home for Boys at Clear Lake, where delinquent and dependent boys lived, to mix with the youngsters and study their institutional life. He saw a group of boys playing baseball and found they lacked essential equipment. The next day he went to an Elks Lodge, where he was a member, and got the money for equipment. David H. Hudson, Elks leader and a realtor by profession, helped the Judge raise the money. They went together to the school to present the equipment and to participate in a baseball game. Hofheinz commented, "Mr. Hudson and I both believe that good times and clean sport are important in building these boys into normal kids with an even chance in life."

On his 25th birthday, Hofheinz wrote a letter to the Texas Probation Board in Austin protesting a new rule which would send to the penitentiary youths from 17 to 21 who had violated probation. "To send these youths to the penitentiary instead of youth institutions would be to place a stigma of convict on them while there was still hope for reforming them. I am sure the records are full of instances of youths, after reaching 17, having been committed to the state reform school instead of the penitentiary, having been released as law-abiding young men." The board softened the rule so that the discretion of a county judge could be involved.

On August 16 Judge Hofheinz sentenced a 16-year-old youth who had taken part in a holdup to go to church every Sunday and report to Officer Robertson at the probation office at 8:00 A.M. the next morning until he was 21. The young man also had to tell the probation officer what the minister discussed in the pulpit, Hofheinz ruled. On August 30, the lad, in working clothes and a lunch bag in hand, made his first report. He said the minister talked about "God's condemnation of intemperance and the punishment given for ungodly intemperance—excessive eating, drinking, and vices of different nature. The sermon was why all are not saved." He felt chastened by the sermon, the boy said, and then went to school.

Of Judge Hofheinz's prediction that "Sentencing a delinquent youth to attend church and Sunday school while on parole probably will become a fixed policy of juvenile court," the *Press* commented: "He is to be commended." Letters poured into the Judge's office. One minister wrote, "In my opinion, it is one of the most constructive steps yet advanced toward the reformation of juvenile delinquents." On September 4 the *Post* reported, "Sunday school attendance and passing grades in school were made conditions in paroles given 10 boys who appeared before Judge Hofheinz." The *Press* reported on September 17 that "a little boy who was sent to reform school when he was nine and killed his brother before he was 12, went back to his lessons today with a date to go fishing with Judge Hofheinz. Convinced that the youngster could be rehabilitated, the Judge sent him to Bayland with a promise to visit and take him fishing. This is but one more example of his compassion for young people."

The first boy Hofheinz sentenced to church was brought back into court three weeks later on a charge of attempting to hold up a grocery store, much to the regret of the probation officer and Hofheinz. But when a Houston businessman appeared and offered to give the boy a job and the pastor of the church he attended offered to look after him, Hofheinz paused and said, "I'm going to do something perhaps I shouldn't. I'm going to let these men help you. Do you think you can do as they tell you?" The boy agreed that he would walk the line from then on—his second chance. He was the first of about 25 boys ultimately ordered to attend Sunday school as a condition of parole.

Newspapers printed stories about juvenile court all through 1937 without using the names of the boys and girls charged. Hofheinz cooperated, for he felt stories about the problems of young people in the press—without giving names—would educate the public to the growing problem of juvenile delinquency.

When Governor Allred addressed the Houston Junior Chamber of Commerce at a banquet January 23, 1938, he opened with a eulogy of Hofheinz. "Roy Hofheinz typifies for me the work of this organization. I rather envy him his outlook on life. I rather envy him the forward-looking, enthusiastic, and compassionate manner in which he is performing his duties as county judge, especially in the juvenile field. If some more of us had his enthusiasm and willingness to work, we'd be doing a lot better in our efforts to improve our communities."

Judge Hofheinz wanted women as well as men to get into juvenile work. At the annual convention of the Texas Federation of Women's Clubs at Laredo, he said, "Women in this group have the opportunity of accomplishing a real task in the prevention of juvenile delinquency. I am convinced that it is far better to pay $10 of the taxpayer's money to rehabilitate a youngster in a home than to spend one dollar on him in a penal institution." He stressed the home and church as agencies which must be considered in dealing with the problems of youth in crime. His new plan of attempting to adjust young people by placing them in natural surroundings had failed in only five of 60 cases in which he was personally interested since he took office, he told the clubwomen.

Hofheinz's feeling as a responsible young parent doubled when on March 15, 1938, Dene Hofheinz gave birth to a second son, James Fred, immediately dubbed "Spud." A cigar smoker since before the birth of his first son, Butch, the young judge was generous in passing out stogies to commemorate the event. Little did Roy and Dene imagine then that it would be Spud who would grow up to be much like his father in temperament and follow many of the footsteps the Judge would indelibly stamp on Houston and Harris County.

In addition to Bayland Home, there was a juvenile ward in the Harris County jail where delinquents were kept until the time juvenile court disposed of their cases. The matron was appointed by the juvenile board. Hofheinz and the juvenile board were informed by Officer Robertson that she repeatedly punished adolescents in her charge by keeping them all night in dark cells little more than a yard square and that she had refused to allow new beds, mattresses, sheets, and pillow cases to be placed in the boys' section. "I don't want to tolerate that practice in the sheriff's jurisdiction any longer," said Hofheinz. Judges on the board agreed and ordered that the juvenile ward of the jail be a separate institution in the custody of a new matron outside the jurisdiction of the sheriff.

On the night of October 5, 1938, Judge Hofheinz had a great deal of fun kidding his wife about her role as the driver of a getaway car for two juvenile delinquents. "How am I going to keep young boys in custody if you're going to help them escape?" he asked, as he entered his home. The "prisoners" were the two youngest boys at Bayland, 10 and 11. Having decided to run away from Webster public school where all at Bayland attended, they stopped outside the little town on the highway and waved arms for a lift. Along came a nice-looking young woman driving a Ford. "Please, ma'am," they yelled, "can we have a ride?" The woman stopped, picked them up and let them out at suburban Harrisburg. Meanwhile, the Webster principal had phoned Bayland superintendent Murray about the runaways. Murray found them in Harrisburg trudging toward Houston. "Such a nice lady picked us up and brought us to town," the boys told Murray. "She said she was Mrs. Hofheinz, the county judge's wife. We thought that was kinda funny cause he sent us to the home a few weeks ago, but we didn't say anything to her about that." To hide her red face as her husband kidded her, Dene sighed, "And such nice, polite little boys, too."

At the beginning of his third year as juvenile judge, Hofheinz was confronted with a situation which the United States Supreme Court outlawed many years later. Houston and Harris County police officers often offered signed confessions as quick evidence of the guilt of arrested persons. F. G. Richardson, publisher of the *Houston Defender,* a black newspaper, had written Hofheinz that signed confessions were not always an indication of the confessors' guilt, that many of them were obtained by officers through the medium of the third degree. Two black boys in Hofheinz's court two weeks earlier had repudiated signed "confessions." They told the court that they were forced to make them by police officers, and that they did not burglarize a residence as charged. Their straightforward and earnest statements made an impression on Hofheinz, and he postponed judgment until a thorough investigation could be conducted. A week later police officers apprehended another black boy who admitted the burglary and led them to the loot, which was recovered. Consequently, the other two black boys were exonerated and released.

Editorialized the *Defender,* "As we have so often stated in past years, many Negroes who are guiltless and know nothing about the crimes with which they were charged and who were forced to sign 'confessions,' have been sentenced to state prisons, or the electric chair, or hangman's noose as a result of the barbaric and inhuman third degree methods employed by police officers. Judge Hofheinz has rendered a mighty fine service to the Negro race and social order by the unusual, yet courageous, if not Solomonic, position he assumed in behalf of these two colored boys. He deserves special commendation for his attitude and action."

Hofheinz believed that institutional treatment of juvenile delinquency would almost disappear within the next two decades if wisdom prevailed. In a speech to Rotary, April 14, 1939, he said, "I haven't had a single boy out of 2000 in my court who has had anything like a normal home life. There is just no exception." On this fact he based his espousal of the foster home, a relatively new method in Texas. "I believe that anything which approaches a home environment is better than any institutional care," he added. "I say that with the institutions being the best or the worst administered." The one exception to eventual elimination of the institution, Hofheinz added, would be "one semi-correctional state institution for juveniles hardened to crime." He concluded that the number of such youths would be reduced as juvenile agencies learned how to reach them early in their misconduct. The next week, Hofheinz carried the foster home idea to San Antonio where he addressed the Texas Conference on Social Welfare.

Some of the reports carried by Houston newspapers on Hofheinz's handling of juveniles were relayed across the nation by wire services and recognized in magazines devoted to juveniles. On June 6, 1939, he received an invitation to address a joint meeting of the National Association of Juvenile Judges of America and the National Probation Association during the annual National Conference on Social Welfare in Buffalo, New York, scheduled June 17. It was the first time a southern juvenile court judge had ever been invited to address the conference, and it was the first time the youngest elected juvenile judge had been so honored. "Naturally, I consider it an honor to be invited," Hofheinz told newsmen, "but the compliment really belongs to Harris County and Texas."

While preparing for his trip, Hofheinz was reminded by a secretary that all lawyers in Texas had to register with the clerk of the Texas Supreme Court under a new state law providing no attorney could practice unless he was a member of the State Bar Association with a membership fee of four dollars a year. He mailed a letter to the clerk and said, "Enclosed is my check for $4. This will cover my dues in our new union. Please advise me whether we are affiliated with the AFL or CIO." He received no answer.

His long debate training prepared Hofheinz for his first national exposure in Buffalo. "Newspaper publicity is an aid to the administration of justice by juvenile court," he told the National Probation Association. "I am not unmindful of theories that the juvenile court and all its decisions should be removed from public print, but I cannot concur in that view," he said, adding, "The cooperation of the press and radio of Texas has done more to educate the public about the juvenile court, its functions and results, than any other factor." Judge Hofheinz emphasized, however, that names of juvenile defendants and delinquents should not be made public. "During the last two and a half years, the people in Harris County have learned much more from human interest stories of conduct of boys and girls in our program than in any similar period in the history of the county," he said. "Milestones were the development of the Harris County Juvenile Board, the probation department removed from political influence, and careful attention to problems confronting the juvenile judge." A United Press dispatch noted, "Hofheinz urged growth of the concept that in juvenile court the state act in the child's behalf instead of his prosecutor, increased means of thorough investigations of the backgrounds of each youngster in trouble, and development of a foster home program to remove as many children as possible from institutional environment."

The packed convention of officials from northern and eastern cities, some who had spent 40 years in developing their juvenile probation departments, listened with remarkable attention as Hofheinz told the story, without notes, of rapid progress in Houston and Harris County. Reporters had to work hard to keep up with his swift oratory. They were accustomed at such conventions to having written texts of speeches handed out by convention officials. The delegates were particularly interested in Hofheinz's recommendation that juvenile authorities solicit cooperation of newspapers and radio stations to educate the public. Numerous questions were informally directed to him by delegates after his speech, and several requested clippings of the type of stories carried by Houston newspapers. "Freedom from political interference and freedom from the atmosphere of the court are two of the essentials of any successfully operated juvenile court," Hofheinz told one colleague. "We have those freedoms in Harris County." Stop any "hush-hush policy" if you have it, he told another questioner. The *Buffalo Times* carried a picture of Hofheinz that day labeled "Baby Jurist."

In his zeal for anti-institution climates for juvenile delinquents, Judge Hofheinz did not lose sight of the fact that some boys could not be cared for in the way he wished. Two delinquents had to be sent to the state training school at Gatesville. "There just doesn't seem anything else to do with them," he remarked about sentencing the two boys, 16 and 15. The records of the boys, who had been in his court before, included runaways, car thefts, burglaries and other infractions.

Because he always wanted to know the facts—all the facts—and paid no attention to hearsay, Judge Hofheinz decided after the Buffalo trip to visit the state school for boys at Gatesville, for girls at Gainesville, and the school for the feeble-minded at the psychopathic hospital in Austin (his duties included handling Lunacy Court). He came home to demand that the state program for reclaiming delinquent boys and girls should be strengthened through accelerated efforts to find foster homes and jobs for the youths when they were eligible for paroles. "I find that 65 percent of these boys and girls who land in our state schools come from broken homes, many of them unfit for children," he said. "It is our duty to them to lend a hand when they are eligible for parole. Harris County boys will be taken care of as soon as possible."

At that time the state cared for more than 1000 delinquent boys and girls on the farms at Gatesville and Gainesville, spending $250,000 annually for their maintenance and education. "The boys' school," said Hofheinz, "is not as much of a prison as it used to be, but it still is a pretty strict regime. They've taken down the high fence and supervisors no longer carry guns. Boys are forced to leave their clothes downstairs when they go to bed upstairs so if they run away, it will be in the raw. They still keep bloodhounds to track runaways. Whippings, which they call 'buntings,' are pretty frequent. Most of the boys say they deserve them, however. There are two menus, with employees getting better food than the boys. In the girls' school, everybody eats the the same food." He added that he was pleased with the girls' school. "All but two of the girls told me they felt they had benefited by their time there," the Judge said. "I noticed a big improvement in the attitude of most of them since they were in my court. The girls live in cottages and have a self-government system. Half of their time is spent in vocational training and the rest in work about the school. Courses in typing and other subjects which will help the girls get jobs are stressed."

Hofheinz often was irritated by failures of the Houston Police Department to get all information possible about a juvenile brought into court. He asked Houston's police chief if he could appear at the police station and talk with all officers, and an agreement was reached that he could appear before each of the three shifts as they reported for work. He was a great teacher, one of the officers recalled, as he outlined how the Judge gave instructions, step by step, in compiling information about youths and their families. "It is not the prerogative of the police department to withhold information from Juvenile Court," Hofheinz said. "It is not fair, either, to the court or the boy, to judge a case with only half of the information available." He referred to a case where a boy had stolen a car, but the record did not show he had done so before.

Hofheinz's national reputation was given another boost when the U.S. Junior Chamber of Commerce's monthly publication carried an article entitled, "Today's Young Man." The article disclosed a few intimate details of Hofheinz's home life, beginning with the nicknames of his two sons, "Butch" and "Spud," and continuing with an account of his carpentry and brick masonry achievements at his new home on West Oaks Street. The story detailed the Judge's hobbies of hunting, fishing, and photography. "All of this is to let you know," said *Future*, the official Jaycee publication, "that it isn't necessary to give up any of the joys of living to be the man who handles the largest volume of cases of any judge in Texas. It's all in knowing how. His probate system has been copied by three large counties in the last two years, and he addressed the National Probation Association because of the national attention his record attracted."

Another invitation to speak came to Hofheinz from the National Juvenile Agencies Association convening in New York in October, and along with it came a request that he appear on the national "We the People" radio program during his visit. He was told the radio show would be unrehearsed and that Al Smith, the former governor of New York who had lost his presidential bid at the 1928 Democratic convention in Houston, would be introduced and talk with him.

On October 20, 1939, at the convention, Judge Hofheinz repeated his views about juveniles in institutions. Again he was the first southern judge ever to address this specific and important group of juvenile officials and workers. He received, as he did in Buffalo, a standing ovation for his advanced thinking.

In introducing Hofheinz October 24 on the radio show, Al Smith praised the Judge for his juvenile work and added, "He is doing something I've always wanted to do." Hofheinz spoke briefly, outlining his work and explaining a merit system in effect at the Bayland Home. Walter Winchell, Broadway columnist, who was read daily all over the nation and abroad, wrote on October 31, 1939, "A 27-year-old officeholder from Texas topped Al Smith during their dialogue on 'We the People.' This stripling had more poise and was faster on his cue."

The February of 1940 issue of the *National Probation Association Magazine* carried an article entitled "Telling the Public" written by Hofheinz. It outlined his whole program for juvenile delinquency but emphasized his open-door policy of allowing newspaper and radio reporters to tell the stories of youths in trouble. Commenting on the role of the media, Hofheinz wrote, "Let us resolve to give America light on the problems of juvenile court, and I have confidence that citizens themselves will utlimately find a way to retard delinquency and assist the court."

Olen W. Clements, Associated Press reporter, wrote on April 11, 1940, one day after Hofheinz had reached the age of 28, this story:

> Harris County Judge Roy Hofheinz made a special trip to New York to tell the National Conference of Juvenile Agencies about the reformation of what was once a prison for juveniles. So successful was he that he was invited to tell his story on a national radio network. Three years ago he looked over the Harris County house of correction and saw weary youngsters working in the fields, cultivating foodstuffs, raising cattle and producing dairy products. He decided the lads needed a home, not a workshop. Figuratively, he threw the key to the place away right that minute. He proposed to the Juvenile Board that Bill Murray, a red-haired former football coach at Judge Hofheinz's old high school, be put in charge of the home. . . .
>
> Bill Murray went to work. He found an institution of 60 to 90 boys between the ages of 9 and 16. They had marched lockstep from their dormitories. Their windows and doors had been barred. They had slept under the watchful eyes of an armed guard. It was an institution that placed emphasis upon the proper raising of cattle and foodstuff. That era ended. Murray and Hofheinz evolved a merit system. Youngsters were paid salaries competitively for their labor and play. Each merit was worth a figurative penny and a "bank" handled the merits with the youngsters as bankers, passing on financial matters after careful study. The place was changed to resemble a home under normal circumstances. Each youngster was given an equal opportunity. Bayland Home became a unit of juvenile democracy. Each boy had to earn 750 merits a week because that is about what it costs to keep him in the institution. He is paid 125 merits a day,

plus what he can earn on the side which ranges from 24 to 250 merits a week, depending upon the job he performs. The merits are good at the commissary. Five merits will purchase an ice cream cone or a piece of candy, but a youngster must have these merits above the 750 a week he earns.

The institution has certain work that is handled by contract only. Youngsters bid for the work—cleaning drainage ditches, washing windows and keeping the athletic field in proper shape. Shrewd boys between 10 and 12 bid on these contracts and hire boys to do the labor. Whatever profit is made by the contractor is placed to his credit in the merit bank. Now and then a lad loses money and can't pay his employees. He is promptly sued in the home's court and the matter is adjudicated according to civil law.

By the end of the 1930s Hofheinz had become a community leader. With others, he recognized that Houston was a great industrial complex, an arsenal for Europe's Allied leaders who had appeased their way into World War II. A program for complete cooperation with the national defense effort was under way early. When the Chamber of Commerce took stock at the end of 1939, it found the Port of Houston second only to New York in tonnage and that the area was gaining increasing recognition as a desirable location for industries and distribution facilities. A survey had shown that 62 percent of the city's population was more or less directly dependent upon the petroleum industry and related businesses. Houston was ready, its leaders decided, if the United States was drawn into the conflict. It no longer was a frontier town. While it still had youth and vigor and while it had more than its share of vision and resolution, it was beginning to have the problems of maturity. Industry was becoming a significant factor in the economy, but there was need for greater diversification in Houston's economic base. Having weathered the depths of the Depression better than most American cities, Houston, in 1940, was ready to meet its challenge.

The 1940 census showed Houston with a population of 385,514, Harris County with 526,961, and the Houston-Galveston area with 728,042. Pouring into the city were farm workers, mostly of Mexican descent, and blacks looking for jobs.

All Houston newspapers continued to carry gripping stories about cases in juvenile court during 1941. There was uneasiness in many families that year because the clouds of World War II hovered over the nation. The lend-lease assistance President Roosevelt and the Congress had given European allies, many felt, would ultimately draw the country into its second world conflict. That happened abruptly when Japan attacked the American naval base at Pearl Harbor on December 7, 1941. The Hofheinz family learned of this event while on a hunting trip.

The agony and the uncertainty of Americans at the beginning of the war upset more households as youngsters wondered when they would be called for duty. The atmosphere produced more cases and problems in juvenile court, but Judge Hofheinz patiently followed the course he had charted for three years.

On April 11, 1942, one day after his 30th birthday, the Judge was invited to Washington to join with other federal and community leaders to find and promote healthful influences for servicemen who were swarming into military camps. He related his long experiences with young people, and his advice to the military and civilians helped set up guidelines for the military and for communities which had to cope with the training on their outskirts of thousands of young men and women.

After military camps near Houston began receiving trainees, many young girls sought out young men for adventure. Hofheinz sent several to the Mary Burnett Girls' School when authorities arrested them for sexual advances. The probation department kept working on plans to remove some of them from the school and get them into home atmospheres again. Hofheinz sent one girl to her sister at College Station rather than back to her mother, who had been found unfit to supervise the girl. This was but one example of how the Judge and the probation department continued to work to salvage young people.

The beginning of the end for the famous Bayland Home came on April 12, 1941, two days after Hofheinz's 29th birthday. Webster School District trustees notified the juvenile board that they would accept no more Bayland boys because 50 were already enrolled at their school; only 31 of the dependent and delinquent boys were acceptable, and they wanted no more. On the 15th Hofheinz and Robertson secured a tentative compromise: two teachers would be sent by the district to Bayland to teach elementary classes, and 12 youths of high school age would be accepted at Webster if they were put into Webster foster homes. The trustees claimed that many of the boys came from Houston and that their educational costs should be paid by the city. The juvenile board deferred this plan pending a further study of the situation by a committee composed of Hofheinz, Robertson, and Judge Boyd.

On July 15, 1941, the board and Webster's trustees agreed that Webster would provide two regular teachers and one manual training instructor at Bayland. Hofheinz said two teachers would be inadequate for the job of covering grades one through six. After further discussions, the Houston School Board provided $2000 of the $5000 needed to help pay for teaching 60 to 65 boys at Bayland in the third through the ninth grades. A few boys of high school age, including the junior class vice-president, would be allowed to finish at Webster. The new plan for the Bayland boys was tried until April 1, 1942, when the Houston School Board decided it would not grant any more money to Bayland. Webster, after a year's experience, again said it would accept only eight or nine of the Bayland boys.

World War II brought an outbreak of "gang fever" in underprivileged areas in many American cities, and Houston was no exception. "Black Shirts,"

"Snakes," and other gangs, mostly made up of boys of Mexican or black descent and a few from poor Anglo neighborhoods, joined to commit all types of crimes ranging from theft to murder as they sought both money and diversion. Some residents of Webster never liked having the Bayland Home in their midst, and reports of "gang fever" caused them to fear what might happen to their children because of minor incidents involving them and Bayland inmates.

On June 12, 1942, when the question of schooling the Bayland boys again was being debated, Judge Frank Williford, who had grand jury jurisdiction, ordered an investigation of Bayland. He said he had complaints from about 100 "substantial people" about the administration and behavior of the Bayland boys. The first 12 witnesses called were from Webster and nearby LaPorte. They testified that Bayland lads were given too much freedom and not enough supervision, and they wanted the institution moved away from them. After deliberation, the grand jury presented a report of its findings to Judge Williford, who said its contents would be kept secret for the moment.

Bayland superintendent Murray was brokenhearted by this turn of events and resigned after four and a half years of diligent leadership to become personnel officer of the Kuhn Paint Company. Shortly after that, main points of the grand jury report became known. It recommended separation of the dependents and delinquents at Bayland, sterner discipline, and supervision of the school by the juvenile board. "Take the bad boys out," said the jury.

On August 3, 1942, the jury's proposal to limit Bayland to dependents only and to send delinquents to Gatesville was brought before the juvenile board, but action was delayed until August 6. Hofheinz protested the plan, saying, "No man who has sat where I have for five years and judged these boys could think this community should abandon all responsibility to give temporary institutional care to the youngsters who have taken the wrong turn. Don't put the stigma of Gatesville on every boy who won't fit immediately into a foster home. Put the dependents in an expanded foster home program in connection with Faith Home. They'll fit. The 'bad boys' won't without some help from us first. We've never sent our delinquent girls directly to Gainesville without some help from us first. You're putting a stigma on the dependent boys you've had in Bayland together with the delinquents."

The next day the board named Hollis Clark, a probation department worker, to be temporary successor as Bayland superintendent. It then voted to limit Bayland to dependents only. The board instructed Clark to grade and discipline those left, to attend all board meetings, and to report on what was going on. Before the vote, Hofheinz made another eloquent plea, but finally he had to accept defeat.

The juvenile court judge then rushed to Gatesville to check conditions there before he sent the 22 delinquent boys still at Bayland to the state school. He returned saying there was some hope because the legislature had provided more funds, but it was not the best solution. He then got busy trying to find a new county institution for delinquent boys. The board of the Bayland Home Association, which supervised the Meyer trust, agreed to give the county the old Bayland Home Building on Richmond Road for the purpose. Hofheinz obtained promises from county auditor Washburn, the Houston School Board, and trustees of emergency relief agencies to refurbish and operate the old Bayland home until the end of the year, but the juvenile board tabled action, preferring Gatesville for delinquents.

Hofheinz was determined to keep as many as possible of the 22 delinquents left at Bayland from going to Gatesville. He took two boys, 12 and 14, to his home to be with Butch and Spud temporarily. He had learned that the boys' father and stepmother refused to have anything to do with them. Hofheinz found a middle-aged couple on a farm who promised to love and handle them with watchful discipline. The boys left Hofheinz's home in tears, but they were happy they were not going to Gatesville. Ultimately, only two of the 22 went to the reform school. Others either were sent back to their own homes or else placed in foster homes. "If I had my way, you'd stay at Bayland," he told all of them.

Margaret Davis, a great reporter for Houston newspapers for half a century, was a witness to the closing of "Boys' Town," as she termed it, by the county. In a tear-jerking story describing accomplishments there, she wrote, " 'Why?' begged the youths who found only happiness there." She saw the lads carrying small treasures in bundles and holding their sugar rationing cards ready for transfer elsewhere. It was ironic at that time that Mary Dale in her national advice column told an inquirer to write to Judge Hofheinz if she wanted the best answers to juvenile delinquency.

Hofheinz's campaign for foster homes so that he would not have to commit delinquents to Gatesville continued in speeches. He told the Lions' women's auxiliary in Houston on May 7, 1943, "No greater service can be performed by a man or woman than the molding of the life of a boy or girl. It means the youngsters will come back better children. Thirty-five percent sent to state institutions either wind up in the same institution or the penitentiary. No institution, from Boys' Town, U.S.A., on down, can provide a normal, happy life for a youngster or create a home environment so vital to his development at a time when he or she needs it most. No youngster is born mean. There is some good in all kids and lots of good in most of them. When they go bad, it is because you and I thought responsibility to the community ended with our responsibilities to our own children. The first is the foster home. Taking a boy out of circulation is no solution to the growing problem of juvenile delinquency. Records clearly reveal that long institutional care does not mean the youngsters will come back better children. You can keep a delinquent child in your home—not for an indefinite period—for $29 a month. The county pays it."

The "gang fever" among juveniles during World War II caused the Judge to change some of his thinking about delinquents. Until then, he and the probation department had dealt mainly with individuals, but when groups started plaguing some parts of Houston, Hofheinz said to one gang brought before him, "I'm getting fed up with gangs, no matter what you call them." He decided to consider them collectively because they had put fear into other youngsters and had attacked many adults. The gangs of Europe, as Hitler and Mussolini came to power in the 1930s, were brought home sharply to the Judge's mind because of the new development in his home city. Criminal gangs might plague his country, too, he felt, and he decided to get tougher.

The record showed that in 1942, 4268 juveniles between 13 and 16 were involved in crime in Houston and Harris County. Hofheinz complained to the city's Crime Prevention Bureau that it should give more time to prevention of juvenile delinquency than to apprehension after crimes. This led to a shakeup of the bureau and transfer of its work to the County Probation Department.

Once he removed five girls from a gang, sending two to the Convent of the Good Shepherd, three to relatives. Four of them had been married at young ages to gang members and, in fear of their husbands, had been forced to steal. He had no hesitation in sending more than 50 gang leaders and followers to Gatesville. He said, "Gang fever was like an outbreak of typhus, such as Los Angeles and other cities were experiencing."

On July 1, 1943, a new law enacted by the legislature, one long sought by Hofheinz and Robertson, went into effect. The law provided that civil courts or juvenile courts designated by the juvenile boards, would handle juvenile delinquency cases. The purpose of the law was to change the method of handling delinquent children from criminal procedure to guardianship as wards of the state. The Harris County Juvenile Board designated Hofheinz to handle cases for the next six months, to the end of 1943, after he reminded the board that "continuous jurisdiction of juveniles was needed." The board then ordered a juvenile detention ward in the old Jefferson Davis Hospital as a temporary site for holding all juveniles for at least two months—until their cases were decided. Hofheinz's jurisdiction was continued the next two years.

Hofheinz also tried to get a detention home for Negro girls in Harris County. He had 60 to 75 under his jurisdiction with no place he could send them despite the seriousness of their delinquencies, including murder. By February of 1944, the county decided to build a $30,000 institution for delinquent black girls.

Famous Father Flanagan of Boys' Town visited Houston on April 20, 1944, to help Hofheinz continue his battle for saving youths. He said it was "cheap politics" for judges to be forced to send kids to institutions and praised the continuing work of Hofheinz, who was 32 on April 10, 1944.

With dance halls and nightclubs filled with military trainees in Houston, high school students petitioned the Houston School Board that year to allow "tune-in" dance clubs to operate at schools in the afternoons after classes. The school board refused, which gave Hofheinz an opportunity to sound off before the Harris County Grand Jury Association in a speech: "Dancing should be included in diversions in city schools in continuing the fight against worsening juvenile delinquency." He knew that in his teenage days his dances had provided happy, supervised outlets for the energies of young people.

Hofheinz did not let up on his battle for businessmen and women and others to get into the battle against juvenile delinquency. He remained disgusted by gangs and kept sending most members to Gatesville. He forced the trial of several members who were older than 17 into criminal courts, where they could be sent to the penitentiary. When his jurisdiction over juvenile offenders ended in 1944, he left a record many felt was unsurpassed in the nation.

In Probate Court, where he spent many long days and nights during his county judge years, Hofheinz also had to deal with many juveniles, heirs to small and large estates, until they became of legal age. One was William Louis Young, Jr., son of a Houston policeman, whose father died in 1942 leaving a small insurance estate. His mother had died earlier. His grandfather had been chief of police of Houston at one time. Young was 14 when he first went to the probate office to see Hofheinz about money he thought he needed. "The Judge became my guardian and confidant and was like a father," he recalled in 1978. "I had to go to the Judge every time I wanted something, and I soon learned he was a wonderful man. My father didn't leave much money, and the Judge wanted to see it spent on the right things. I'd go to his office wanting something, but when I left, I couldn't imagine why I ever wanted it in the first place. He had explained why I didn't need most of the things I asked. He actually appointed my sister, Janet Richey, as my guardian, but he knew what to do and what not to do, really, and she let the Judge handle me. He told me to get an education and work hard. Sometimes I was lonely, and I'd go to his office to talk, and sometimes we listened to baseball games on the radio and other times just carried on conversations."

It was at Austin High that Young asked Mary Frances McMurtry, a slim, vivacious brunette, for his first date, and she said yes. Mary Frances was one of three daughters of Mr. and Mrs. Drew L. McMurtry. Her sister, Sally, was to become Mrs. El Roy Sullivan, and sister Patricia, Mrs. Charles W. Semands. Years later, Mary Frances—after a divorce from Milton Gougenheim—was to become, following the death of Dene Hofheinz, the wife of Roy Hofheinz.

On his dates with Mary Frances, Young told her of the benevolent judge who handled his affairs. Both were 16 years younger than Hofheinz. Through Young's stories of the Judge, Mary Frances began following newspaper stories of Hofheinz's activities. She did not dream that more than 10 years later she would be secretary to Mayor Hofheinz of Houston and finally his second wife. She never met Hofheinz until he walked into the mayor's office after his election.

Hofheinz arranged a scholarship for Young to go back to Allen Academy where he played football, basketball, and baseball, although he weighed only 140 pounds and stood five feet, ten inches tall. He was such a good athlete the coached asked him to stay an extra year, although he had credits for graduation. Young went into the service in World War II, came home, and Hofheinz helped him get a job with Brown and Root. He did accounting work. Young would today be the first to tell anyone that Roy Hofheinz "has done as much, if not more, for Houston than any other single individual."

8

The Hofheinz-
Jesse Jones Battle

Mounted on a panel inside the door to one of the bathrooms in Roy Hofheinz's "Huckster House" on Galveston Bay was an enlarged editorial cartoon depicting Jesse H. Jones as an octopus, his eight muscular arms enfolding the business, civic, professional, and political lives of Houston. When Jones died in 1956, Hofheinz, in respect, moved the satirical drawing away from the eyes of celebrities and visitors to his retreat.

Millionaire Jones' *Houston Chronicle* did not support Hofheinz when he ran for the legislature and county judgeship—"too young," it editorialized. Hofheinz was not bitter; he often said Houston's three newspapers did a good job of reporting, and he believed in freedom of the press. He also had cultivated—from his teenage experience in writing high school sports for the *Chronicle* and promoting dances and from his political campaigns—respect from many of the people working for Jones' paper, as well as reporters and editors on the *Press* and *Post*.

Hofheinz took office as county judge just as the nation began to emerge from the Depression. He had campaigned on a promise to keep the county's financial affairs sound, to seek equalization of the tax burden so all would pay a fair share, and to follow a "pay-as-you-go" philosophy in funding needed roads. He did his homework on county taxes and was ready with his first major proposal on February 1, 1937, a month after he took office. He announced to the four commissioners that he wanted a plan to force all owners to place stocks, bonds, and all other properties on the county's rendered tax roll. He said that the tax rate could be stabilized and several million dollars added to the county's coffers if J. W. Hall, tax assessor-collector, had help in bringing tax valuations up to date. "The law makes it mandatory that everyone asked by the assessor render his property," the Judge said. "The penalty for refusal is a fine of $20 to $1000. If this provision of the law is carried out, it will prevent owners from concealing property which the assessor knows nothing about." Hofheinz had found that many corporations and other private businesses had not followed the law. He believed about 40 percent of properties in the county were unrendered.

With time for tax rate consideration coming up, Hofheinz announced on May 16, in a speech before the American Legion and carried by Radio KPRC, that property values would be "readjusted this year as they never have been adjusted in former years. The necessity for equalization can no longer be avoided." Under the law, Commissioners Court turned into an equalization board when the assessor completed tax rolls. Two days later he rejected many departmental money requests, arguing that a sound budget could not accommodate them.

To help the assessor, Hofheinz went to Austin and looked up corporate records in the secretary of state's office. Certain corporate incomes, he told commissioners, indicated a vast difference between the worth of the corporation on state and county records. Publication of his finding immediately brought representatives of 20 corporations into the assessor's offices to render increased valuations, and others followed. Most protested, but the tough guy in the county judge's seat who would speak his mind caused them to act—nervously.

The real tax valuation battle began on January 7, 1938, when the Commissioners Court voted to ask for bids by private experts to revalue all Harris County property. Howls from many quarters were sounded in the press. When bids were opened, Hofheinz cast the deciding vote rejecting the bids, explaining that he was not certain the bids were right and wanted bidders to reconsider. On February 25, new bids came in, and the court awarded a contract to a Fort Worth firm, Freese and Nichols, for $135,000. Commissioner Spencer was the only dissenter and threatened to file suit to block the contract. He said he felt it was an improper delegation of authority by the court. Hofheinz and Spencer engaged in a heated debate, the Judge arguing that the new low bid was $22,000 under the previous low and that expert help was needed for equalization.

The Harris County Taxpayers' Association on April 7 asked District Judge Ewing Boyd for an injunction against the revaluation contract. Boyd denied the plea, but the association said it would appeal. The Fort Worth firm had gone to work, and Commissioner Spencer did not like its methods. He told Hofheinz in another stormy exchange on May 8: "You fellows [commissioners] are not trying to be fair. You are not interested in taxpayers." Hofheinz rejoined: "We're interested in 90 percent of the taxpayers and you in just 10 percent!" The Texas Court of Civil Appeals on May 12 granted the taxpayers' association a temporary injunction against the revaluation program. Commissioners immediately voted to appeal to the Texas Supreme Court.

The first revaluation explosion came on June 23 when commissioners, sitting as an equalization board with figures supplied by the Fort Worth firm, multiplied the taxable value of the Burlington and Rock Island rolling stock by 500 percent. A 400 percent raise for two Missouri Pacific subsidiary lines was met with the company's refusal "to pay a dime of the new assessment." The same day, the Texas high court granted the taxpayers' association an injunction against the contract, saying, "The contract for evaluation of the entire tax structure of Harris County necessarily supersedes the powers, duties and function of the tax collector and assessor. Since these duties are devolved the assessor by law, attempted deployment of other persons to perform such duties is an expenditure of public funds for unauthorized purposes."

Hofheinz and Washburn did not comment, but after studying the decision, Hofheinz said the high court's opinion actually was a go-ahead signal for revaluation. With new information already in hand, the equalization board continued hearings, but also voted to ask the supreme court for a rehearing on the injunction ruling. That move kept the Fort Worth firm on the job.

Houston Belt and Terminal Railway was next to get a higher valuation. Shell Refining Company, on July 11, accepted an increase of $2,348,735, or almost 100 percent, precipitating the comment by Judge Hofheinz: "Representatives of Shell told me that if it and a few other large companies had been singled out for raises, it would have fought them to the last, but since the county is engaged in a conscientious effort to put all taxable property on the rolls at fair and equal valuations, officials of Shell said they were willing to pay their share. Shell's increase would add $24,000 a year to its county tax bill." Sinclair Refining Company was raised $1,286,633 over its 1937 assessment.

A tax strike was threatened on August 16 by 50 downtown property owners. The next day Hofheinz invited them to hold an across-the-table conference before hearings were completed on valuable Main Street property, much of which was owned or controlled by Jesse H. Jones, then in Washington serving in President Roosevelt's cabinet. During their mass protest, some of the merchants threatened to help defeat a $3,100,000 bond issue scheduled for property holders' approval on August 27. Hofheinz and the four commissioners had decided to call the bond election because they felt it would be a bargain for the court to make an exception to the "pay-as-you-go" program on road bonds and for a new courthouse because they had been assured the Public Works Administration in Washington would pay 45 percent of the $5,500,000 estimated cost. In other words, PWA would give the county $1,300,000 for the badly needed courthouse and $1,100,000 for county roads if Harris County would vote bonds for the rest of the money. Getting the projects at 55 percent of cost was reason enough, the court figured, to bypass the constitutional amendment applying only to Harris County which Hofheinz had sponsored and won approval for in the legislature and in a state election in 1937.

Tobias Sakowitz and W. B. Bates represented the protesting downtowners at a special meeting with Hofheinz in his office. Hofheinz told them that members of the court and the real estate men who set downtown valuations would sit at the other side of the table if the merchants would meet with them. "We'll go over every factor," Hofheinz said. "I think we can have a meeting of the minds." Sakowitz replied, "I think so, too." The two men went back to the merchants who immediately picked a committee to sit with the equalization board. On the committee were George Hamman, John T. Scott, T. H. Monroe, Milby Dow, Oscar Weyrich, Ben Taub, Gus A. Brandt, E. A. Hudson, William Sutherland, Ed Dupree, Ernest Hester, and Sakowitz. Across-the-table discussions followed.

After many other firms accepted new valuations, the downtown taxpayers asked that revaluation of their property be delayed until 1939, but Hofheinz and the commissioners turned them down. Revaluation would not be done if there should be such a wait, Hofheinz said, taking full responsibility for the program. "I feel certain," he added, "that people at large and most of the downtown property owners will be convinced in time that the county's revaluation board honestly has sought to equalize values." Commissioner Spencer disagreed and branded the revaluation methods "unheard of and unprecedented." He advocated halting the whole program.

On August 21, the *Houston Chronicle* editorialized strongly against the revaluation program. The *Chronicle* was joined in opposition by the *Press* and the *Post*. Hofheinz responded by going on radio that night to fight for revaluation and the upcoming bond issue approval. He had time to place an ad in the *Houston Press* that day saying, "Hear Judge Hofheinz discuss Jesse Jones vs. the people at 7:45 P.M. on KTRH and KXYZ." Jones, of course, was the owner of the *Chronicle*. During his speech, Hofheinz noted that the *Chronicle* earlier had supported the bond issue, but had changed its views when Jones "realized that the commissioners court would definitely compel him and all other taxpayers to pay a fair and proportionate tax in this county. . . . But now, my friends, when they find Mr. Jesse H. Jones' Bankers Mortgage Building property, Mr. Jesse Jones' Gulf Building, Mr. Jesse Jones' Rice Hotel, Mr. Jesse Jones' Lamar Hotel, Mr. Jesse Jones' Texas State Hotel, and all the other vast properties of Mr. Jesse Jones will have the value set in public before the board of equalization, and before all the newspapers in Harris County, and not have them set behind closed doors or by a quiet rendition of the Tax Assessor's office, then they find that . . . the bonds should not be voted."

Hofheinz argued that "the constitution does not say that Mr. Jesse Jones shall pay on 30 percent of the value of his property and Sam and Sally Smith on 60 percent of the value of their home." He then discussed current valuations on many Jones properties and how they should be revalued. He also discussed the need for passing the bond issue and asserted that taxes would be equalized whether the bonds passed or not. "When that happens," Hofheinz added, "you small folks who have borne the burden while Mr. Jones is eating the plums, will have your property reduced in proportion by the amount of which Mr. Jones and other tax escapers have been able to refrain from paying."

The atmosphere was tense the next day when the equalization board met.

An injunction suit to stop revaluation was filed by Helen Oischewske and her husband, William; H. C. Houst; J. E. Burkhart; Dick Young; H. O. Southerland; R. Mack Chall; Pearl Ross Wright; J. B. Ross; and M. A. Stewart. The latter three were executors of the estate of the late Mrs. Ellen B. Ross. That added fire to the hearing. Hofheinz and Commissioner Spencer leaped to their feet in anger and hurled wads of paper at each other during a row over a plant operator's refusal to give tax investigators access to his place of business. "Judge Spencer," shouted Hofheinz, "will you be quiet?" Reddening, Spencer rose again and threw a crumpled sheet of paper at Hofheinz, striking him in the face. "Judge Spencer, you will get out of the courtroom and keep quiet," he shouted. Hofheinz threw a paper wad of his own in Spencer's direction. Quiet followed.

Columnist "Soapy Joe" (M. E. Walter, known as Emmet) answered Hofheinz's radio blast at Jesse Jones in the *Chronicle* the next afternoon. He was joined by the *Post*, which also blasted Hofheinz editorially. Hofheinz and the three supporting commissioners knew then the battle was fully joined because of the attacks by the *Chronicle* and the *Post*. Hofheinz again bought radio time and went on the air a second night. During his talk, he asserted:

> Somehow Jesse Jones always buys property in the path of the public improvements growth of Houston. If we don't tax a man who has a million dollars as well as the one that has a hundred dollars in proportion, it is manifestly unfair. . . . You men who are employed in refineries and whose owners have come in and agreed on a fair income on their property, you men who work in the oil fields whose owners have agreed to fair increases on their property, you merchants in Houston who have already agreed to increases on your stocks or merchandise or decreases as the case may be, you employees of the public utilities who have in this fight agreed to a fair value, get behind this program to be fair to everybody and don't let one pay on a 40% basis and Jesse Jones' Houston papers and Houston interests on 30%. This is a people's fight. Jesse Jones cannot wrap the minds of thinking men and women around his fingers by distorted facts in his own papers. You want these bonds. It is your and our job to carry them.

At the next equalization board meeting on August 24, Hofheinz stated that the 37-story Gulf Building owned by Jesse Jones had been escaping taxation on county rolls. A few minutes before making the statement, he wired the Federal Communications Commission urging an immediate government investigation of the operating methods of Radio Station KTRH, as well as KXYZ and KPRC, because he had been refused permission to discuss the Gulf Building tax rendition in his radio address the night before. Hofheinz then read to the court the part of his speech that he was supposed to have made and which he said was censored. He asserted that the "largest building in the Southwest was not taxed at all! . . . I challenge Jesse Jones to come clean with the people and admit in the columns of the newspapers he has failed, neglected, or maliciously refused to submit the Gulf Building, the largest building in the South, for taxation in Harris County."

Completing his reading of the censored part of the speech, Hofheinz wired the Federal Communications Commission and said, "Because Jesse H. Jones is opposed to paying his fair share of local taxes, his interests are combined against the local revaluation and tax equalization program. . . . In order to present the facts," he said, "it has been necessary to use the radio stations on a commercial basis but we must submit script to the lawyers of Jesse Jones before we are able to discuss Jesse Jones' real estate interests. Jesse Jones' lawyers have deleted, I believe without justification, parts of my address last evening and refused to permit me to quote from deeds of Harris County or from the rendered rolls of Harris County, which rendition was made by Mr. Jones' tax men." Hofheinz then requested a full investigation "of the monopoly of Jesse Jones, of the newspapers and the radio stations in Houston. We feel that even Mr. Jesse Jones should not be permitted to stifle the public press and then refuse anyone who disagrees with him to cite the facts for the record over the radio."

The equalization hearings continued. Finally Hofheinz thumbed through papers before him and announced that, in connection with the Gulf Building rendition, he would read an order which he would ask Commissioners Court to pass. The order had the effect of ordering the National Bank of Commerce of Houston to appear before the commissioners to prove that the bank owned the building rather than the Gulf Building Corporation. The building, presently shown as part of the capital stock of the bank, was thus not subject to taxation. Unless the bank could prove ownership, the Gulf Building Corporation would be deemed the owner and would be subject to a stiff tax bill. Judge Hofheinz called for a motion and Commissioner Graham made it; Commissioner Tautenhahn seconded the motion, whereupon Commissioner Spencer rose to say, "I don't think this court ought to accuse any taxpayer, big or little, of dealing with the county fraudulently without a hearing. I don't think this court should be guilty of ex-parte proceedings. I think that the representatives of the bank should be invited to come in and make an explanation. I would not otherwise take part in such a serious accusation as you have made." Judge Hofheinz made no comment. He called for a vote. Spencer was the only one to vote no.

At this point a letter from E. S. Pritchard of Pritchard and Abbott, which had the subcontract for equalizing values on real estate, was delivered. Hofheinz read it to the court. "Mr. Backlund [M. A. Backlund, assistant auditor for the Commerce Company, Bankers Mortgage Company] telephoned the office of Pritchard and Abbott yesterday afternoon about four o'clock or four thirty and instructed that we list the Gulf Building in Block 81 under the names of the Jones properties. This information was received by Miss Ellen Petitsils and given to me this morning. This for your information." Hofheinz commented that the telephone call was received in the office of Pritchard and Abbott after the copy of his radio address was submitted to the radio station for approval and after the deletion of that portion of his speech dealing with the Gulf Building had been made. The motion, passed by the board, was made to read so that it directed Bank of Commerce representatives to appear before the board on Friday.

The *Chronicle*, in its report of Hofheinz and the deleted speech, stated that immediately after the motion was passed "L. J. Fourney, chief clerk in the tax assessor's office, introduced a letter which he requested Judge Hofheinz to read. Hofheinz refused, however. This letter, which was written by R. P. Doherty, vice-president of the National Bank of Commerce, June, 1937, notified the tax assessor that the Gulf Building had transferred the building to the National Bank of Commerce which thereupon became the owner. Apparently," the *Chronicle* continued, "Judge Hofheinz had checked the deed records and found the building still in the name of the Gulf Building Corporation, as the deed transferring it to the bank had not yet been recorded. If he had conferred with the tax department, he would have found that it had known since June, 1937, of the transfer, and was in possession of Mr. Doherty's letter announcing the transfer. It was on the basis of this information that the tax department has been assessing the building in the name of the National Bank of Commerce. Doherty said that the property has been assessed and the tax paid each year in the ordinary manner, and the tax department is in possession of these facts and they can be verified by any one interested."

In a subsequent *Chronicle* story on the Gulf Building, the public was told, "Lawrence F. Fourney, chief of the assessing department of the county tax office, said there'd been on file in the county tax office since June, 1937, a letter showing transfer of ownership of the Gulf Building Corporation to the National Bank of Commerce. He said he would gladly have shown the letter to Judge Hofheinz if he had known the judge was going to make such a charge." Fourney observed, "This letter from Doherty has been in the file of the tax office since June, 1937, and an inspection of it by Judge Hofheinz would have been welcome at any time."

Max H. Jacobs, associate editor of the *Post* who later became a radio business partner of Hofheinz, apparently was furious with the county judge's charges that Jesse Jones had ordered his newspaper to reverse its stand on tax revaluation and the bond issue. He spoke over Radio Station KPRC on August 26, and the text was printed by the *Post*. Jacobs defended his integrity as a journalist and stated that Jones had no editorial power over the paper. Moreover, he accused Hofheinz of being a rank political opportunist. Recalling he first knew Hofheinz as a political candidate, Jacobs said:

He thought then and he has told me so a dozen times that we were veritable Horace Greeleys and Joseph Pulitzers. We were then courageous, high-minded journalists who were working for the welfare and advancement of Houston and Harris County and the people. Then Judge Hofheinz took office. He had been county judge now for a year and a half. During that time many public issues had arisen which called for editorial comment. The *Post* generally has agreed with Judge Hofheinz. We supported him whole-heartedly. We stated in our editorial columns that we were proud of him and the accomplishments of his administration.

What goes on in a newspaper office as a rule is strictly confidential, but Roy Hofheinz has raised this issue and I am going to tell you the truth about a few matters. Roy Hofheinz himself has asked me for a favorable editorial comment on his acts as county judge, not once, but on many occasions. Because his requests were proper, we commented favorably. I wrote the editorials and Governor Hobby approved them. I say to you that at no time during Judge Hofheinz's campaign and at no time since that campaign, and at no time during the last few days up until this good hour, has the *Houston Post* or anyone connected with it asked for any tax concessions for anybody or even for the *Post*. If anybody intimates or says that the *Houston Post* asked Roy Hofheinz for tax concessions from his administration, that intimation or that statement is not true. I don't know how we could state it any plainer. On the other hand, he has asked the *Post* for assistance and he has received that assistance. I say to you further that this friendly relationship between the *Houston Post* and County Judge Roy Hofheinz still existed about 10 days ago when the *Post* endorsed $3,100,000 in county road bonds and bonds for modernization of the court-house in an editorial which Judge Hofheinz has read to you proudly over the air. Ten days ago, Roy Hofheinz did not say Jesse Jones owned the *Post*. He still fought with the great, high-minded Jones. Last night and tonight you heard what he said about the *Post*. He charged that we changed our attitude about the county bond issues because we received word from Jesse H. Jones to change our attitude. He charged that Jesse H. Jones owns the *Houston Post* and dictates its policy. Let me tell you the truth about these charges. On the masthead of the *Houston Post* you will see that J. E. Josey is the chairman of the board and W. P. Hobby is president of the *Post*. The *Post*, in a statement over the signature of these two men, published an ad saying that they and they alone were the owners and the publishers of the *Post*. Now you can believe the statements of these two men or you can believe what our youthful county judge tells you. Two years from now he will be running for a state office. I will tell you exactly why Roy Hofheinz is raising this Jesse Jones issue. As a matter of practical politics—it is considered good practice to aim at the lion in the forest, though one shot strikes down the lowly sparrow on the bush.

Attorneys for the National Bank of Commerce on August 27 filed their answer to the order of the county board of equalization citing the bank to appear for a hearing on its assessment. They asserted that the bank "on and long prior to December 31, 1937, and all time since that date . . . has been the sole legal and lawful owner in fee simple of the property commonly known as the Gulf Building, and in exclusive possession of the property. That such ownership has at all times been open and well known, and the time of the making of that order and the wholly unnecessary and baseless slurs and innuendoes set forth therein, such ownership was either well known by this court or could have been definitely ascertained by the court upon the slightest inquiry." The bank's attorneys also argued that the court had acted beyond its jurisdiction and that the bank "should have been accorded a hearing before any action was taken by this court, undertaken to affect its rights or to reflect upon its good faith, good name and integrity of its officers and directors. Accordingly, the National Bank of Commerce of Houston will respectfully ask this court that you enter an order finding that the charges insinuated in your formal order were unfortunate and untrue and that such order be revoked and stricken from the minutes of this court."

Hofheinz bought radio time on August 26 for one more speech before voters went to the polls the next day. He again accused the bank and Jones' Gulf Building Corporation of collusion to avoid payment of taxes on the Gulf Building. He wondered why the deed on the building had not been recorded. "Why hide it from the people? From whom were they hiding it? I invite the National Bank of Commerce to answer these questions on the front page of the *Chronicle*. . . . I say again that on records of the tax assessor's office for 1938, had it not been for our equalization program, if it had not been for our hiring men of integrity who would not be bulldozed by even a power so mighty as Jesse H. Jones, we could not have put that $1,216,000 on the tax rolls. . . ."

The *Post* countered Hofheinz's speech by reporting on August 27 that Hofheinz had declined to state under oath the charge he made that the National Bank of Commerce had resorted to subterfuge to escape taxation. Hofheinz reportedly was challenged by Frank A. Liddell, attorney for the bank to make the statement under oath. "I dare you to swear it!" Mr. Liddell shouted. Judge Hofheinz was silent for a time, then he said it was "a conclusion" of his.

All during the hectic election week, revaluation continued by the equalization board. Humble Oil and Refining Company, the county's largest taxpayer, agreed to an increase of about $7,500,000 over its 1937 assessment. H. L. Stone, representing Humble, appeared before the board. "What is the attitude of the Humble Company on this increase?" asked J. L. Abbott of the revaluation team. Stone replied, "I think you have fair figures on the new yardstick although it is a rather long yardstick, but as long as it is used for everybody, we think it is fair."

"Does the Humble Company object to public improvements?" Hofheinz asked.

"For any improvements the public is willing to vote," Stone answered, "the Humble Company will pay its share." Stone added that Humble would pay $112,000 more state and county taxes in 1938 than in 1937.

An increase of $105,000 was agreed to by the production department of the Gulf Oil Corporation, and Anderson-Clayton Company agreed to an increase of $176,219. Hughes Tool Company agreed to an increase of $160,000, but the Gulf Brewing Company got a reduction of $4000.

Hofheinz's oratory on the radio could not match the fear of "higher taxes" implanted by the *Post*, the *Chronicle*, and by many owners of property. Perhaps Jesse Jones' power indeed was too great. The bond issues were defeated, and down the drain went 45 percent of the money promised by the Public Works Administration. Also defeated was Commissioner Massey, who had supported Hofheinz. Judge Hofheinz took the election results gracefully, noting that he had "never found fault with the result of any election. I wanted to give the people a chance to say whether or not they wanted needed improvements at 55 percent of cost. The people have spoken and I shall not complain."

The *Press* editorially observed that "youthful Judge Hofheinz made a desperately bold fight to carry the bond issues over powerful opposition engendered by the ill-considered increases in assessments which the county's revaluation experts proposed to levy against a large number of taxpayers. The fact that this campaign was futile was no discredit to him. He was up against overwhelming and invincible odds." W. W. Edwards, writing in the *Houston Labor Journal* after Hofheinz's radio campaign, wondered why, if Jesse Jones did not own the *Post*, "it invariably out-chronicles the *Chronicle* in playing him up in the most favorable light. And why are the studios of KPRC [the *Post* station] located in one of Mr. Jones' hotels while the downtown office of the *Post* is located in another of them? Is it customary for competitors to favor each other in that sort of way?"

Soon after the election, the suit by nine taxpayers against the Fort Worth contract, filed in District Judge Roy Campbell's court, was called up for arguments. The court recessed on September 3 after Commissioner Spencer testified about his opposition because lawyers for both sides felt that an agreement could be reached. Ernest A. Knipp, attorney representing the equalization board, went to Austin for conferences with the attorney general and comptroller because the state had a major interest in the outcome of the case. They agreed on terms of settlement of the suit.

Albert J. DeLange, attorney for the nine taxpayers, also was eager for a compromise, and he and Knipp worked diligently to reach an agreement. On September 9 all litigation over revaluation ended with Judge Campbell's approval. The court directed that Freese and Nichols, the valuation team, be paid $87,500 from delinquent tax collections and end their work. All involved said they were happy with the settlement. The county's pending Supreme Court appeal also was dropped in Austin. Hofheinz and his three supporting commissioners said tax equalization would not stop. A mass of records, maps, 270,000 valuation cards, and recommendations were inherited by the board from the discharged appraisers.

Before quitting, S. W. Freese said the county received an extra $108,000

Jesse H. Jones (left) and his nephew, John T. Jones, Jr. **Photographs courtesy the** *Houston Chronicle.*

annually in taxes as a result of his work. The equalization board immediately sent regular notices to about 3000 persons whose renditions were not in accord with values. Hall's staff began revising and changing hundreds of valuations placed on property by Hall. With a general idea that valuations would be concluded with about $320,000,000 on the rolls, commissioners had to vote on a tax rate. A new rate of 97 cents, compared to $1.01 for 1937, was approved on September 15 by the court.

The *Press* pointed out on September 17: "The county's equalization program bore fruit for the great masses of taxpayers. Commissioners ordered a four-cent reduction in the combined county-navigation district tax. Despite this reduction, the combined rate, less an expected delinquency of 12.5 percent, will produce $288,838 more for the two units of government than the old and higher rate. . . . The equalization program is credited with adding around $20 million to the rolls. It is significant, as County Judge Hofheinz points out, that not one home owner's value was raised. . . . It should be perfectly clear that the equalization program has worked to the little taxpayer's interest."

In subsequent years, great attention was given to equalization of assessments by elected assessors and their staffs to keep tax rates at relatively low levels. Hofheinz and three commissioners had paved the way to end favoritism and slipshod methods in tax valuations. In 1978, looking back after a television business association, along with involvement in civic work and political campaigns with Roy Hofheinz, John T. Jones, Jr., nephew of Jesse Jones and publisher of the *Chronicle* from 1950 to 1966 when he resigned, said, "This is an assumption on my part, but I feel Roy used what was then known as the Jones interests as a sort of foil. . . . Roy picked the biggest, most visible dragon in town—Jesse Jones. As a political technique, that was, I think, quite logical. Certainly, I think it worked for Roy. He was able to use it as a tool along with his very, very obvious speaking ability and his—not quite so obvious but particularly important—organizational ability to become the youngest county judge Harris County ever had—and I think his record still stands. He used his techniques while in the legislature. He used them, ultimately, to get radio stations and part ownership in a television station. I don't think I'm the first person to say there's a touch of flamboyance in Roy Hofheinz. . . . As the years went by, I found him to be a man of his word. Sometimes his word wasn't what you wanted to hear, but he is a man of his word."

9

Catalyst for
Public Improvements

Houston's unprecedented growth as one of the world's great cities cannot be attributed to any one man or organization. It was the magic of many minds—imaginative, competitive, unselfishly civic—whose determined spirit of achievement thrust the former bayou town into a thriving metropolis as the 21st century approached. Historians long will debate the importance of individuals—Roy Hofheinz, Jesse H. Jones, Hugh Roy Cullen, J. S. Abercrombie, W. B. Bates, George R. Brown, J. A. Elkins, Leon Jaworski, Glenn McCarthy, Albert Thomas, William P. and Oveta Culp Hobby, and R. E. "Bob" Smith—who gave of their time and substance to the city's development. But it was Roy Hofheinz who is credited with having an unparalleled record as the leading public servant and promoter of public improvements for Harris County.

Hofheinz was the principal catalyst for major development beginning in 1935 during his service as a legislator. He should be ranked as the most oratorical, imaginative, competitive, humane, controversial, tempestuous, colorful, and self-confident person in the parade of Houston's great leaders. His two years as a legislator, eight years as county judge, and three years as mayor of Houston catapulted him into a postion of leadership unexcelled by any other individual, bringing a better way of life to the people of Harris County. Hofheinz excelled in many areas of public service. However, the most memorable include the countless number of hours he devoted to modernizing Harris County's flood control and transportation systems.

When Houston was young, the Buffalo Bayou, which now passes through the heart of the city, was simply an artery of commerce. Little money was expended on its improvement. As the 20th century began, however, a group of farsighted citizens showed interest in improving the channel, especially since it played an important role in the settlement of Harris County. In 1911 the Harris County-Houston Ship Channel Navigation District was created, and within two years the Houston ship channel to Galveston Bay was completed. Recurrent storms, however, silted the channel, and the cost of its operation and maintenance became exorbitant. Then in May of 1929 the first major flood of the 20th century hit Houston. Lives were lost, property was destroyed, and many of the enterprises along the channel were lost. Despite this "storm warning," nothing was done to remedy the situation. Then in December of 1935 a second and more devastating storm flooded the area. Demands for immediate action swiftly followed on the heels of that catastrophe. Houston was described by "Soapy Joe" of the *Chronicle* as "the Venice of Texas with streets becoming swimmin' holes after rains." In his campaign in 1936 for county judge, Roy Hofheinz promised to make flood control a major goal of his administration.

As his first step to fulfilling that promise, Judge Hofheinz paved the way for drainage of Buffalo Bayou and its tributaries to end the public's fear of storms and hurricanes. In January of 1937, Hofheinz went to the state legislature seeking legislation for a comprehensive county flood control authority and the return to Harris County of ad valorem tax monies so that the drainage job could begin. Just out of the legislature himself, Hofheinz won support for his request from both the Texas Senate and House. But he ran into a major obstacle when his longtime friend, Governor Allred, threatened to kill the bill because of his policy of never returning to a county money that had been paid to the state. Despite heavy public pressure favoring Hofheinz's plan, Allred vetoed the legislation.

Not to be defeated, the newly elected county judge persuaded the legislature to pass a bill creating his proposed Harris County Flood Control Authority. This time a state tax remission was not included in the measure. On August 4, 1937, the new authority launched a $7 million, five-year flood control plan, aware that federal money then was flowing into public works projects across the nation. With Hofheinz in the lead, the authority named auditor H. L. Washburn as coordinator of countywide drainage plans.

The following year failed to bring flood control construction to Harris County despite the untiring efforts of Hofheinz to get Army engineers to help secure $9 million from the federal government for improvement of the ship channel and tributary system. However, 1939 brought hope in Houston's struggle for flood control. Early that year, the Harris County Flood Control Committee petitioned the Commissioners Court for a $500,000 bond issue; the WPA earlier had assured the county of $1,500,000 if the bond funds were provided. Hofheinz immediately began campaigning for the bond issue, saying "It's the most outstanding improvement that you've been offered in years." Hofheinz stressed that if the joint county-WPA program was approved, there would be no increase in taxpayers' bills. "This is a bargain no drainage district can afford to neglect," Hofheinz said.

Hofheinz soon returned to Austin, again seeking passage of a tax remission bill for Harris County. This time, Governor Allred was out of office. Hofheinz argued that the new bill would permit half of Harris County's state ad valorem taxes for 10 years to be returned for flood control. He estimated that this money would bring $3,500,000 into the county. Hofheinz told the legislators, "The bond election and the WPA grant will only be an inaugural for the big flood control project. That money will be far from enough." Harris County deserved tax remission, he said, because "the Port of Houston has brought reduced freight rates for all Texas, and it has proved to be one of the greatest investments the people of Texas have. Its continued growth insures the welfare of every nook and cranny in Texas." The legislature passed the bill and Governor O'Daniel signed it on May 8, 1939.

Harris County property holders followed suit and approved the bond issue. Hofheinz immediately began pressing WPA officials to supply the promised federal funds for flood control. Army engineers gave their approval to the project by July 13—the day after a torrential rain poured more than nine inches of water on Harris County in three and a half days causing tens of thousands of dollars in damage to streets, homes, and businesses. On November 7, the reality of flood control came a step closer when General Schley announced that the Army engineers' plan for flood control in Harris County would be ready within one week. The flood control authority then called for public hearings on tentative plans for $32,525,700 to do the entire flood control project.

Meanwhile, Hofheinz's flood control proposal continued to face problems. The state attorney general ruled that the Harris County tax remission bill was unconstitutional. Hofheinz vowed to appeal Attorney General Gerald Mann's ruling all the way to the Supreme Court. The entire local financing of flood control would have been stopped by Mann's opinion. Next, concerned citizens and property owners began to worry publicly about the erection of flood control works—a new system of dykes and levies—and how it would affect private property and their personal lives. On November 30, property owners west of Houston scheduled a meeting to protest the flood control project and to urge the Commissioners Court to reject the engineers' vast program. In vain, Hofheinz attempted to stop the protest meeting, arguing that the Army engineers were entitled to explain their project in detail before protest meetings were held. The citizens would not listen to Hofheinz's pleas, however, and the protest meeting fostered a new wave of doubt about flood control in Harris County.

Again, however, Hofheinz was not to be defeated. Although progress on implementing his dreams for flood control were slow, Hofheinz set out for Washington, D. C., in March of 1940 seeking action. He returned home to Houston optimistic. In June the Texas Supreme Court bolstered Hofheinz's hope for the project. It ruled that the Harris County tax remission bill was constitutional, a decision which required Attorney General Mann to approve a county bond issue for the project.

The Commissioners Court decided on July 2 that it would offer tax remission money to Army engineers to start work on the master flood control plan. Acquisition of right-of-way for the project was initiated by Hofheinz and the

Commissioners Court, which served as a flood control district. The plan's accompanying WPA project, comprised of a countywide drainage program, got underway on July 24. The flood control project moved into high gear in 1941. County auditor Washburn, who had served as coordinator and chairman of committees seeking construction, received great praise for his detailed work, but the public knew it was Roy Hofheinz who was the catalyst, eloquent spokesman, and hard worker who was making good his campaign promise.

Judge Hofheinz's contributions in improving public services for the people of Harris County continued at an unfaltering pace, and his efforts on many major projects frequently overlapped each other. The Houston ship channel often was involved in his projects. Today, beneath the ship channel, is a no-toll tunnel which serves as a free transportation passageway for Harris County residents. When Roy Hofheinz was elected county judge in 1936, residents of the county's Baytown area had been trying to get a tunnel dug under the channel to save time and transportation costs for its working residents. The earliest problems concerning the proposed tunnel, according to Fred Hartman, editor of the *Baytown Sun,* included where to put the tunnel under the channel and which population centers the tunnel should connect. Hartman said:

> There was a man who owned much land . . . actually about where the present south terminal of the tunnel is located. His name was H. C. Cockburn, a wealthy Houston oil man with tremendous oil and real estate holdings. He came forward with a plan to put a toll tunnel at that point. We went to see Judge Hofheinz because the Cockburn toll plan already been put before the County Court.

But Hofheinz was opposed to a toll tunnel. During his campaign for a third term as county judge, Hofheinz spoke at a rally held under a beautiful group of trees between old Pelly and old Goose Creek, two small communities which comprised Baytown. Hartman reflected: "Here again Roy reached oratorical heights that I'd never heard before. His adversary in debate was the city attorney, Shannon L. Morris, who was behind the toll tunnel."

Everyone at the rally appeared to be in favor of the toll tunnel. But after the Judge finished his speech, he had won the crowd over. The people were willing to put their eggs in Hofheinz's basket. Hofheinz was against a toll tunnel, and soon everyone else was, too. "That was the last I ever heard of a toll tunnel," Hartman said. "I don't know what would have happened, and we might have had a toll tunnel there all these years if he had not gotten on the platform that day."

Meanwhile, three ferry boats that operated without charge plied the channel transporting workers from Baytown to Pasadena and Galena Park, from Lynchburg to the San Jacinto battleground area, and from Morgan's Point between the Point and Baytown. Hofheinz conceived the idea of having the Texas Highway Department take over the Morgan's Point ferry when a delegation of businessmen from East Harris County visited him on April 18, 1939. Headed by H. W. Kilpatrick and Baird Felton, the delegation also requested that another ferry be bought to expedite transportation because motorists often were forced to wait up to three hours to cross the channel during rush hours.

On May 22 Hofheinz was accompanied by other county officials on a trip to Austin to the highway commission where Hofheinz requested that the state assume operation of the ferry at Morgan's Point. To convince commission officials, Hofheinz presented them with an elaborate brief, which included photographs showing the congested conditions at the ferry landings. Two months later the state highway department agreed to take over Morgan's Point ferry, an agreement which meant an annual $25,000 for the county road and bridge department.

Hofheinz's strong opposition to a toll tunnel under the Houston ship channel remained alive, and the issue again was rekindled when Cockburn proposed to the Commissioners Court in November of 1939 that he be granted a franchise to build a private toll tunnel under the channel. The commissioners delayed action on Cockburn's proposal, allowing time for others also interested in building a tunnel to submit proposals. Although the commissioners favored construction of a tunnel, they said that a franchise which took precedence over the free ferry service would not be considered. This was the beginning of a long fight between Hofheinz and Cockburn.

Cockburn's plan involved construction of a tunnel entirely with private funds, a toll tunnel with fees collected from the vehicles which used it. The tunnel would cross under the ship channel at a point about a mile and half above the Morgan's Point ferry crossing. Hofheinz already had made up his mind to oppose a toll tunnel. And when he opposed a needed public project, he usually came up with an alternative. On March 28, 1940, the *Chronicle* reported, "Harris County may build its own vehicular toll tunnel under the ship channel financed through WPA aid and the issuance of revenue bonds at no cost to the taxpayers, County Judge Hofheinz disclosed. The plan appears feasible, he said, and Colonel F. C. Harrington, national WPA administrator, had assured him he would look with favor on such a project."

Hofheinz and Cockburn became public adversaries and often clashed over the commissioners' delay in deciding on the proposed tunnel and who should build it. "I'd like to know something one way or the other by Monday," Cockburn said in an appearance before the commissioners. "I don't want to sit here while the whole world is out calculating against me."

Hofheinz replied, "Well, we want the world to calculate against you. We want all the information we can get on this tunnel proposition."

On April 25, 1940, a plan to build the tunnel with public funds was presented to the commissioners by Wayne F. Palmer, a Mobile contractor, who told Hofheinz he intended to bid for the project. On the same day, city unions and Associated General Contractors let the court know they opposed using WPA labor to build the tunnel. Hofheinz's delays of the toll tunnel were injected into his campaign as he sought a third term for county judge. Houston attorney, Charles T. Pritchard, was his Democratic primary opponent.

Tunnel promoter Cockburn was a friend of Nat Terrence, tabloid editor of *Houstonian,* which steadily had opposed and criticized Hofheinz. The *Houstonian* headline on Friday, July 19, 1940, said, "Von Hofheinz Tunnel Blockade Keeping Hundreds Out of Work." A sub-headline added, "County Fuehrer Roy Hofheinz of the Firm of Hitler, Hamburger, Himmler, Hofheinz, Hess and Hohenzollern, Unlimited, Reminds Us Too Much of Hitler Who We Greatly Despise and Hate." The story reviewed the Judge's career, implying that he had acted as a dictator, "which would have been expected from someone with a German name!" Referring to the Judge as Baron von Hofheinz, as Herr Hofheinz, and as Fuehrer Hofheinz, the paper concluded, "The voters who do not have Nazi names will most certainly vote for Charles T. Pritchard, Jr., who possesses a good, old-fashioned, British, Anglo-Saxon name." In that same sheet of July 19 was another story, the headline stating, "Cockburn Says America Should Not Elect Officials Like Hofheinz Who Have Arrogant and Dictatorial Attitudes and Who Do Not Respect the Feelings of Their Fellow Men." Cockburn defended his tunnel project and lambasted "von Hofheinz" for his "dictatorial" conduct in office.

This vicious attack was answered by the *Houston Post* in an editorial. Similar editorials appeared in the *Press,* the *City Digest of Houston,* the *Rural News-Tribune,* and the *Goose Creek Sun,* July 12, 1940, entitled "Brilliant Record in Office Recommends Judge Hofheinz." Despite smear tactics employed against Hofheinz by the editor of the tabloid, *Houstonian,* Hofheinz received renomination support from the *Houston Press,* the *City Digest of Houston,* the *Rural News-Tribune,* the *Goose Creek Sun,* and the *Houston Post.* Hofheinz's primary victory over Pritchard, who had been a classmate at San Jacinto High, was more impressive than his defeat of Judge Ward four years earlier. He won by more than a two-to-one majority: 50,588 to 21,415.

The *Press* editorially backed Hofheinz's determination not to let private interests build a tunnel under the ship channel. It said the tunnel should be a publicly owned enterprise. Cockburn's plan was rejected by the Commissioners Court on July 19, 1940.

The plan for a tunnel under the channel became dormant when federal aid was not forthcoming because of World War II. But on July 24, 1941, Hofheinz reiterated that he wanted a tunnel—free to traffic—and would oppose efforts of "any self-serving individual to build a private tunnel." On August 4, Congressman Albert Thomas said a federal survey should be made to fix the site of a tunnel because of controversy regarding its ultimate location. Then, on May 26, 1943, when a five-county master plan for the Houston area to get $125,000,000 for roads was unveiled, two tunnels under the ship channel were included with Hofheinz's support.

Meanwhile, traffic on the Pasadena ship channel ferry was so great, with war priorities preventing a bridge or a tunnel, that Hofheinz and the Commissioners Court decided to find another ferry to speed workers to their jobs. On a trip to New York, Hofheinz and Commissioner H. A. May found a 40-foot car-ferry boat anchored at Kingston, 100 miles up the Hudson River, suitable for the Pasadena crossing. After a 39-day, 3400-mile trip from New York—a voyage made "nightmarish" by storms, sleet, and snow, the ferry finally arrived in Houston. Hofheinz told the crowds greeting the ferry's arrival that the roads leading to the new ferry landing would be improved and that the county would build new slips while the *Kingston* was being reconditioned and renamed the *Hugh May,* honoring the commissioner who made the trip from New York aboard her.

Not until April 26, 1945, four months after he left office and 16 days after his 33rd birthday, did Hofheinz's long fight for free tunnels come to a happy and important climax for Houston. The new County Judge Glenn Perry and the Commissioners Court unanimously voted to hire an engineering firm to plan for two tunnels—one at Pasadena and the other at Spillman Island—at a cost of $10 million. Hofheinz's role in the tunnel development was recognized when he was selected to give the principal address at the dedication of the Washburn Tunnel in 1950.

The development of county, state, and federal highways as major transportation arteries into and out of Harris County and the simplification of vehicular travel throughout Houston were other interests of Roy Hofheinz as county judge and later during his years as mayor of Houston. Hofheinz was an admirer of William P. Hobby, publisher of the *Houston Post,* who served as governor of Texas from 1917 to 1921. Hobby headed the Houston Chamber of Commerce's Highway Committee during Hofheinz's early political career. The young county judge became the most active spokesman for Houston-area highway improvement proposals endorsed by the chamber committee, the Commissioners Court, and the City Council. Not only did these groups successfully seek a closer route from Mexico through Laredo to Houston, but also they fought for new arteries to San Antonio in the west, Fort Worth and Dallas to the north, Beaumont to the east, and Galveston to the south.

Hofheinz joined officials of Bexar, Tarrant, Jefferson, and Dallas counties in backing a resolution for a constitutional amendment to provide a direct road building tax. The idea was to have the state win the right to divert a cent or more in gasoline taxes for the construction of major state roads. This was to be an addition to the "pay-as-you-go" amendment Harris County already enjoyed. In his fight for the amendment, Hofheinz argued that the proposal would not "cost any other county or any other voter in Texas one single red cent. We

The Washburn Tunnel.
Photograph courtesy
the *Houston Chronicle.*

propose this amendment because it will mean a savings of $500,000 to Harris County annually in interest charged. No one ever could accuse Hofheinz, as county judge, of not seeking every means possible to save taxpayers money from operating expenses and in building public works.

Throughout his public career, Hofheinz was an instrumental force behind the construction of Houston's modern highway system, with the major concentration of his work condensed into three short years. Those three years proved to be difficult and busy for Hofheinz because road construction money was hard to get due to the nation's overriding wartime needs.

Hofheinz's efforts were highlighted during those years by his push for developing these road improvements: *January 7, 1938*—Hofheinz encouraged the construction of a proposed highway from Houston to Fort Worth; *July 26, 1938*—Hofheinz agreed to favor construction of a super highway to Galveston; *February 10, 1938*—Hofheinz promised full cooperation to obtain right-of-way for the construction of an eight-mile link for Highway 75, bringing it to Houston over North Shepherd Drive; *August 26, 1940*—Hofheinz encouraged the state highway commission to take over a county-owned concrete highway linking "the greatest historical shrine in Texas, the San Jacinto battleground" with U.S. Highway 90.

By 1939 seven years had elapsed since the state gasoline tax had gone into effect, and a surplus of $9 million had been accumulated. One of Judge Hofheinz's plans would extend the debt relief to bonds issued on roads still under county jurisdiction.

William P. Hobby. Photograph
courtesy the *Houston Post.*

His quest to improve land transportation in the area continued. On September 5, 1940, he announced that Harris County had interested the highway department in a plan to construct a 60-mile local highway within a 12-mile radius of Houston. Hofheinz said he had been assured that the highway commission was in favor of a circular highway around Houston and would send engineers to survey the proposed route. Hofheinz went to Austin to lobby for the needed state funds. There he was joined by Governor Hobby and Houston's Mayor Oscar Holcombe. Hofheinz's persistence in seeking state road aid was spotlighted on September 2, 1940, when the *Chronicle* reported from Austin, " 'The time has come when we're going to do more for the cities,' said Brady P. Gentry of Tyler, to a Houston delegation led by Hofheinz."

On September 28, the department decided to allocate several million dollars worth of street and highway improvements for Houston and Harris County, now the state's biggest city and county. Three state highway commissioners immediately toured the city to inspect bottlenecks at underpasses and deadends. It was Hofheinz who explained the problems as they toured. But it was on October 18, 1940, when Hofheinz's untiring efforts thrust Houston's highway system into the modern half of the 20th century. Plans then were announced for a new "circle highway" to surround the city's outskirts from Hempstead Highway on the northwest to Almeda Road south of Houston.

Four main highways would be intersected by the proposed circle route, which also would serve as a defense belt should the city need it.

Throughout the war years, Hofheinz struggled to promote continued development of Harris County's roads. Sparked by the salesmanship of Roy Hofheinz, the end of the war brought renewed and speedy construction of a super highway network leading to Houston, a highway system which helped make it one of the great cities of the world.

10

Bonanza for
Rice University

Events in Harris County Probate Court during the fall of 1942 involving Rice Institute (now University) should be recorded in gold ink in the history of that outstanding private institution of higher learning in Houston. It was then that Judge Roy Hofheinz brought to a climax the settlement of the largest estate in Texas history with Rice a prime beneficiary. With an investment of $1 million cash and assumption of $4,274,833 in debts, Rice trustees bought 29/64ths of the Rincon Oil Field in Starr County, Texas. By the fall of 1979, this business venture had brought $42 million to he university's endowment fund—with more to come.

W. R. Davis, spectacular multimillionaire oil operator who had homes in Houston and New York, died in New York City in 1940. An international and glamorous figure, Davis had vast holdings, principally in Texas, and, under law, his estate had to be settled in Harris County Probate Court because most of his property was in Texas. Original probate papers were filed in New York, but jurisdiction was transferred to Judge Hofheinz, who faced a monumental task of bringing order and solvency to the estate against which were many claims— among them loans by four big banks and delinquent federal income taxes.

Hofheinz appointed James Lee Kauffman of New York City as ancillary administrator of the estate on March 9, 1942. When the estate finally was put in order by the end of the year, Kauffman gave credit to Hofheinz "for consummating a deal which older heads had first considered just a crazy dream of a young and ambitious judge." Rice was one of three centers of learning Hofheinz had attended, and Kauffman said the Judge "was actuated by a keen desire to do something of lasting benefit for an educational foundation. He was the sole promoter of the deal, interested all parties connected with it, and supervised the entire procedure, including the sale of property."

Hofheinz and Kauffman went to Washington two weeks after Kauffman's appointment to meet with representatives of banks holding Davis' loans: First National Bank of Boston, Bank of Manhattan in New York, Harris Savings and Trust of Chicago, and First National Bank of Oklahoma City. They also went to the Internal Revenue Department to discuss income taxes Davis owed. Discussion centered around the $5 million government claim. The problem was to avoid foreclosure by the banks holding first and second mortgages against all Davis properties and to see that any valid claim of the government be paid. Hofheinz had learned that no major company would consider buying the Davis properties until some provision was made with the government on taxes which, under federal decisions, took precedence over the loans. It was calculated at the conferences that the total sale price of the properites would not permit the liquidation of the estate.

Hofheinz won his pleas—an agreement was reached that the banks would not foreclose and the government would release its lien so that a fair sale might be negotiated. Several major oil companies investigated the properites at Hofheinz's invitation, and the highest bid to the court was $5 million. The Judge rejected all bids because none would permit any net realization for the estate after payment of indebtedness. Hofheinz called another meeting of bank officials in Chicago, and he and Kauffman sold them on the idea of setting up a separate corporation to purchase Davis properties at the highest figure bid by the oil companies. The Rincon Corporation was organized after a hearing in probate court on September 30. It immediately purchased the 29/64ths of the working interest in the rich Rincon field. The new corporation paid $297,000 cash and assumed liens totaling about $5 million. It also agreed to a multimillion-dollar oil payment.

Realizing that major oil companies were eliminated as purchasers of Rincon because of tax liabilities, Hofheinz conceived the idea of selling the property to Rice, which would have to pay no taxes. He figured that the institute could pay, from oil revenues, the banks and other creditors 100 percent of all income and wipe out indebtedness in from three to five years. Knowing that Rice could not dig too deeply into the money William Marsh Rice had given to establish the institute in 1912, or other contributions to the foundation which paid expenses of the institution, Hofheinz sought to find men who could give Rice financial help. He went to Harry Wiess, Humble Oil and Refining Company president; George R. Brown, shipbuilder and contractor; H. R. Cullen, oil millionaire; and Harry Hanszen, administrator of the Hermann and M. D. Anderson estates, to urge them to give and raise money to help the institute buy the property. Hofheinz's facts and figures from Davis records about the possibilities of Rincon—and his sales eloquence—convinced these outstanding men that Rice had a great opportunity.

The Judge then went to Rice trustees to tell them of his plan. On the institute's board were John T. Scott, Harry C. Hanszen, W. M. Rice, B. B. Rice, A. S. Cleveland, and Edgar O'Dell Lovett, institute president. In discussions were Tom M. Davis and Palmer Hutcheson, attorneys from the firm of Baker, Botts, Andrews and Wharton. The trustees agreed that, Rice's will permitting, if $500,000 could be raised, they would put up another $500,000 from the foundation treasury and assume the Rincon indebtedness. They filed a plea in District Judge Norman Atkinson's court for a judgment concerning their authority. The state of Texas was made a "friendly" defendant in the case. Attorney General Gerald C. Mann and his assistant, Harold McCracken, testi-fied in favor of Rice. C. A. Dwyer, Rice business manager, testified that the institute's total resources in 1936 were valued at about $13 million. He said the original Rice endowment of $5,784,884.38 and other gifts of $990,387.97 had resulted in $6,775,272.35 in capital at the time. Founder Rice had stipulated that 10 percent of each year's income from his gift be added to capital invest-ment. Dwyer said that because of war conditions which cut the money market, the income from Rice investments had dropped, and that there was only enough income to assure operating expenses but none for much-needed ex-pansion, including a library building. L. T. "Slim" Barrow, vice-president of Humble in charge of the geological department, testified he estimated the Rincon field would ultimately produce 56,750,000 barrels of oil and that net income of the portion of the property to be acquired by Rice would, over a period of years, total $18,600,000. In his estimate before Judge Atkinson, Hofheinz figured the investment would bring Rice at least $12,750,000. That figure would double Rice's resources, he said.

Judge Atkinson ruled that the trustees did have the right to make the deal—a down payment of $1 million and assumption of $4,274,833 in debts to be paid off with oil revenues. In making a final announcement to the public of the Rincon transaction on December 18, the Rice trustees said, "Special thanks go to County Judge Roy Hofheinz, who conceived the idea that these properties would be a valuable acquisition for Rice and through whose efforts the interest of George R. Brown, Harry C. Wiess and others was enlisted. . . ." The deal, said the trustees, "involved a novel scheme of financing heavily encumbered and rich oil properties for the benefit of a tax-free educational institution which is expected to set a national precedent. It started as a problem for Judge Hofheinz, but he worked it out with great imagination."

The M. D. Anderson Foundation, whose cancer hospital in Houston today has worldwide fame, gave $300,000 of the $500,000 needed by the trustees. In exchange, the trustees agreed to construct a building on the campus to be named for Anderson, an early Houston philanthropist. The trustees also gave credit to these persons for raising money: John Q. Weatherly, Perry Olcott, L. T. Barrow, Morgan Davis, John R. Suman, John H. Freeman, W. B. Bates, H. M. Wilkins, J. A. Elkins, I. M. Wilford, Warren Dale, John V. Boyce, Palmer Hutcheson, Tom M. Davis, Alfred H. Fulbright, J. A. McNeese, H. I. Wilhelm, Attorney General Mann, and his assistant, Harold McCracken.

Properties involved were the Alice, Texas, Recyling Plant and oil prop-erties in the Rio Grande Valley and in the Garwoods Oil Field in Louisiana. In court, the properties were estimated to be worth about $10 million when Davis died. Revenues from Rincon paid off the indebtedness and then tax-free cash poured into the institute's treasury. The other half of the working interest in the Davis properties obtained by Rice was held by Continental Oil Company, which had been operating the fields and continued to do so after the sale to the institute. The fields had 135 producing wells.

When the Rice deal was finally recorded on December 23, 1942, Douglas McGregor, U.S. District Attorney, said the government had no objections to the transaction but suggested that a line be added to the contract reading "funds remain intact until all tax questions are settled." Hofheinz, however, named City National Bank of Houston the depository.

"That is not according to my instructions," said McGregor.

Hofheinz replied, "Your instructions have been changed. The Washington office agrees with me that since this court holds current jurisdiction over these funds and since I am responsible for them, I'm certainly not going to place them in banks outside the jurisdiction of this court."

McGregor said, "I then withdraw the approval of the deal in my appearance in court."

Hofheinz replied, "You've already appeared and approved and the sale is made." McGregor left the courtroom, and the last obstacle to the sale was removed.

Hofheinz and his family celebrated Christmas in 1942 with special thanks that the Judge had accomplished for Rice a deal nobody thought could be made except Hofheinz himself. He and Dene also could look back to Christmas of 1941, when they also had given thanks that a big campaign promise made in 1936 by Hofheinz had been fulfilled. He had told the public when first running for election that he would see that the Brooks estate would be settled with no more questionable actions in Probate Court. On Saturday, November 1, 1941, the *Chronicle* had run a news story headlined, "$504,577 Brooks Estate Check Delivered as Climax to Unusual Halloween Party." The story read: "Undoubtedly the most unusual Halloween party in the nation ended just before midnight Friday in the office of Guardian Trust Company as Judge Roy Hofheinz, some 20 attorneys and officials of three taxing agencies completed a two-week probate hearing and divided more than $500,000 in assets of the R. E. Brooks Estate. By paying $58,272 in back taxes to Harris County and the Channelview and Galena Park independent school districts before midnight of October 31, the Brooks Estate saved some $800,000 in penalties and costs. After the Halloween party, it was learned, however, that the deadline on the amnesty provision did not actually come until midnight November 1, and the matter could have waited until today."

What actually happened that Halloween was the delivery of a check for $504,577 by E. A. Kelly, special United States attorney, to H. L. Nicholson, Brooks administrator, and the division of money among creditors of the estate and tax agencies, to the county for court costs, and to the administrator and attorneys for services. The check was in payment of 1506.2 acres of Brooks ship channel property which the government had bought as part of the site for the San Jacinto Ordinance Depot for use in the war. The party was not the conclusion of the Brooks estate, which had been in litigation since the death of Judge Brooks 12 years before, but it was the biggest sale of estate property and the biggest lump sum payment yet made to claimants.

The largest check issued by Administrator Nicholson went to the heirs of J. J. and Mary Ann Sweeney—$361,952.60. For his services as administrator, Nicholson received $25,228.85, and numerous small claims were paid also. The Massachusetts Bonding and Insurance Company was paid $2037.34 for a premium on a $1,010,000 surety bond for Nicholson. Hofheinz said that the probate proceedings were the longest in the history of the county, that they represented the largest sale of land ever approved by Harris Probate Court, that total delinquent taxes paid were the largest ever authorized by the court, and that Nicholson's bond was the largest ever authorized by the court.

The cause of the extended hearings was the conflicting interests of some second- and third-class claimants. The question of allocation of proceeds from the sale brought the most discussion. One of the many unusual problems encountered was the discovery that an elderly man and his wife were still living in an old, ramshackle house on the property sold to the government. They refused to move. Attorney Kelly, representing the government, declined to deliver the check consummating the deal until some way of removing the couple was discovered. Although they had no title to the property, the couple refused to move because they said they had no place to go. To solve the problem, Judge Hofheinz called relief director W. B. Collier who, accompanied by government officials, went to the couple and found them to be infirm and in need. Collier arranged with the Old Age Assistance Commission for an increase in the couple's pension and found them a house near Almeda which was within their means. Judge Hofheinz arranged for an Army truck to move the couple's meager belongings. "President Roosevelt and God must have answered our prayers and come to take care of us," the old squatter told Judge Hofheinz as he moved into his new home.

There were other complications before the Halloween party ended successfully. It was discovered at 5:00 P.M. that amounts allocated to various claimants did not add up properly. Hofheinz called on assessor-collector Jim H. Glass for assistance, and he brought a comptometer and an operator to the probate courtroom to refigure. By 9:00 P.M. second-class claims had been corrected. It was then discovered that claimants wanted cashiers' checks for their payments. Hofheinz called C. M. Malone and Brown Baker of the Guardian Trust Company, and the two bankers opened their offices. While Halloween enthusiasts celebrated outside, the men made out the checks, which were distributed there to end negotiations at 11:45 P.M.

Fond as he was of dogs, Hofheinz on April 27, 1943, had to refuse for probate a will which left $6000 to two English setters. E. B. Stewart, eccentric recluse, had lived alone on a five-acre tract near Seabrook for 16 years before his death in February of 1942. This estate included seven rental houses in Houston. In his handwritten will, Stewart stipulated the net income of the estate should be used by the executor, Dr. F. J. Mock of LaPorte, his physician, for the support of "my dogs." He provided that "Big Boy" and "Snapper" should always be allowed to sleep in his house and that the Clear Lake house ultimately should be converted into a hospital for dogs. The will was contested by two sisters, Mrs. J. L. Walters and Mrs. F. C. Schuller, and a brother, Dave D. Bartell. J. L. Burns, who lived on a tract adjoining Stewart's Clear Lake property, and Ray Larrebee, who had lived in Seabrook, both knew Stewart and testified for the contestants that Stewart was mentally incompetent. They convinced Hofheinz and he ruled in favor of the relatives, but he gained promises that the dogs would be properly cared for until their deaths.

Another unusual case came before Hofheinz on May 4, 1943. A contested codicil to the will of Captain Carl Strongren, a Sinclair tanker skipper, was admitted to probate by Judge Hofheinz. A brother sought to invalidate the codicil as it was not signed by two witnesses. Hofheinz ruled that under Texas Statutes, Article 8290, a man "at sea" did not have to fulfill the requirements of a regular will. Although Captain Strongren was in Marcus Hook, Pennsylvania, when he wrote the will and codicil, his boat was preparing to leave. Therefore, Judge Hofheinz ruled, the captain was in sea service and not obliged to have two witnesses. The brother decided to appeal to district court, but Hofheinz was upheld. The *Texas Bar Association Journal* ran a special article about Hofheinz's "at sea" decision.

Hofheinz had two opponents in his race for a fourth term in July of 1942. Edmond J. DeCoux, attorney, and Jim M. Heflin, attorney and legislator for eight years, waged bitter campaigns seeking to unseat the 30-year-old judge. Attacks were made on Hofheinz's "absenteeism" in Washington and other cities, conditions at the Bayland Home for Boys, how he delegated the signing of some papers to assistants, and his opposition to a toll tunnel.

When DeCoux attacked Hofheinz's probate court work, the Judge took to the air on July 22 to reply, "Criticism of Harris County Probate Court has been coming from a political opponent who has never handled a single, solitary probate case, and I doubt if he even knows in what part of the courthouse the court is located." Moreover, Hofheinz asserted, "I think an interesting highlight of this campaign is that one candidate who now professes to be the great protector of estates and a great probate lawyer, actually has never tried a single, solitary case in Probate Court. I still feel, as I felt five and a half years ago, that an estate should be administered in a manner that would please the widows and orphans and keep property for them without trying to please promising, non-performing politicians and their satellites."

A political ad in the *Post* on July 24 was captioned in bold black letters, "Widows and Orphans Speak." A letter from Mrs. R. E. Brooks told about the "wonderful job" Hofheinz had done. Another ad from heirs to the Rhodes estate came from Mrs. W. S. Rhodes, the widow. She said, "All heirs are grateful for the way Judge Hofheinz has handled our estate." Leading lawyers came out with stories and ads supporting Hofheinz. On July 26 the voters spoke. Hofheinz received 34,680 votes to 17,758 for Heflin and 5942 for DeCoux. Hofheinz was assured of office until January 1, 1945. For the fourth straight time when Hofheinz was in a contested election, Dene Hofheinz had served as his campaign manager. She, as well as her husband, knew where the votes were, and they got them.

In his eight years as judge of Harris County Lunacy Court, Hofheinz never relented in his campaign to get insane persons out of the Harris County jail psychopathic ward into state hospitals or to assure their freedom to live in private institutions and homes through state pensions. In addition, he gained national attention by challenging the governors of Illinois and other states to quit "dumping" mentally ill persons in Texas. Welfare workers brought to him several cases involving persons who had been "shipped" to Houston so that the burden of caring for them would be off the hands of other states. "Through the efforts of Judge Hofheinz and the staff and the fine cooperation we've been receiving from the superintendents of state hospitals and the Texas Board of Control, we have eliminated the disgraceful conditions which existed in our psychopathic ward a few years ago," reported W. E. Robertson, director of county institutions two years after Hofheinz's election. "Two years ago, the horrible psychopathic ward population was more than 100 and now it is only 26. Capacity is 60 and those left live under better conditions, although all should be removed."

Newspapers did not report lunacy cases regularly in deference to family sorrows. Hofheinz handled many mentally ill cases with delicacy and, as the *Press* said editorially, with "great compassion." In his campaigns for reelection, no candidate could find fault with Hofheinz's original pledge to get the insane out of "dungeons with disgraceful conditions."

11

"All The Way With LBJ" in 1941

> If I could prepare and deliver my speeches as well as Roy Hofheinz, I could be the President of the United States.
>
> Lyndon B. Johnson
> June 27, 1941

When U.S. Representative J. P. Buchanan of the Texas 10th Congressional District died of a heart attack in Washington on February 22, 1937, Lyndon B. Johnson, Texas director of the National Youth Administration, who had quit his position as aide to Congressman Kleberg, was in Houston on business. He spent that night with his Uncle George Johnson, who earlier had helped him get a teaching position in Houston's Sam Houston High School. Young Lyndon read in the *Houston Post* the next morning of the death. Uncle George quickly suggested that his nephew should get into the upcoming special election to fill the vacancy. LBJ also was encouraged by his younger friend, Roy Hofheinz, who had just begun his first term as Harris County judge.

Johnson entered the race and with a whirlwind campaign, in which he was dubbed the "Blanco [County] Blitz," he won a plurality (no runoff necessary then) over eight opponents on April 10. The closest candidate to Johnson was Williamson County Judge Sam Stone. Johnson got only 27 percent of the votes cast, but his victory had special significance for Texas because it launched LBJ into the national political picture. He had been the one candidate who expressed all-out support for President Roosevelt and his policies.

Roy Hofheinz was celebrating his 25th birthday when he heard of his friend's victory. He realized that, as head of the largest county government in the state, he would have another special friend in Washington on whom he could call for help, advice, and federal assistance in the problems of his home area. When Hofheinz went to Washington on county business, he seldom failed to call or see Johnson. Their friendship blossomed. Hofheinz also became a good friend of John Connally, LBJ's aide who first had watched Roy in action in the legislature when he was a student at the University of Texas. As a congressman, Johnson accompanied President Roosevelt to Galveston on one of his fishing trips to Texas and Hofheinz was one of the main greeters along with Governor Allred.

The Harris County judge's success was watched closely by Johnson and his aides, and when LBJ decided to seek the U.S. senate seat left vacant by the death of Morris Sheppard on April 9, 1941, he immediately called Hofheinz to help organize a statewide campaign for the senate term ending in December of 1942. Governor "Pappy" O'Daniel called a special election for June 28, hedging on whether he would get into the race himself. Hofheinz visited Johnson in Austin on April 25. The next day, Texas newspapers carried the announcement that the Harris County judge would be Johnson's manager in 26 southeast Texas counties. Hofheinz praised Johnson's leadership, noted the candidate's support of President Roosevelt, and proclaimed that Texas needed "experienced leadership, real statesmen, and not politicians seeking promotions. I am offering my unqualified support to the man best qualified to represent Texas in the Senate."

Johnson opened his campaign on May 4 at San Marcos, the home of his alma mater. Hofheinz was there along with many Houston and southeast Texas supporters. Having earlier contacted campaign managers in each of the counties assigned to him, Hofheinz planned a big motorcade of more than 50 cars and a 37-passenger bus to travel 125 miles from Houston to San Marcos. Johnson called the night before and suggested that the motorcade might create traffic problems on the poor highway and urged Hofheinz and his campaigners to drive individually to the rally. Hofheinz commented, "We had planned the motorcade to show the folks the strength and solidarity of the Johnson-for-Senator movement in southeast Texas, but we would not be willing to offer any hazard to traffic safety."

By then Dene Hofheinz had gotten into her usual role of helping her husband politically, although this time it was for a friend. She did much of the office organizational work as her husband carried on his official duties. The Judge took time late in afternoons and at night to work for Johnson. Dene, as well as her husband, knew where Hofheinz had great strength in Harris County and had become acquainted with political leaders in other counties in the area.

Meanwhile, Governor O'Daniel had caused an outcry of indignation when he announced in a speech at a memorial service at San Jacinto Battleground outside Houston on April 21 that he would appoint Andrew Jackson Houston, 86, sick and senile, as interim senator pending the upcoming special election. O'Daniel visited the son of the legendary Texan, Sam Houston, for 10 minutes at his LaPorte home to tell him he would name him senator as a special honor. Andrew Jackson Houston actually was a Republican and had run unsuccessfully for governor three times. Critics said O'Daniel chose the son of the Texas hero because he knew that the elderly man would not oppose him in June if he sought the seat himself. Houston took the oath in Washington on June 2, despite doctors' warnings against the trip. It was 95 years after his father had undergone a similar ceremony in 1846. Houston became ill shortly after the swearing-in and was rushed to Johns Hopkins Hospital. He underwent an operation for a pancreas malignancy and died on June 26, two days before the special election to fill the Texas senate seat.

Paying $100 fees to campaign in the special, non-partisan election for the senate seat were 29 persons—Democrats, Republicans, and a Communist. Attorney General Gerald Mann of Sulphur Springs, with whom Hofheinz had several legal battles; U.S. Representative Martin Dies of Orange, 40-year-old son of a former congressman whose name was cursed by liberals when he headed the House Committee on Un-American Activities; and Johnson received the most coverage. But O'Daniel finally got into the race, and one of the most unusual political battles in Texas history was underway.

The "Big Four" were listed by the Belden Survey of Public Opinion as O'Daniel, Mann, Dies, and Johnson—in that order. LBJ, the poll showed, had less than 10 percent of the vote of those who expressed early opinions. Johnson workers throughout the state then redoubled efforts to get support for the only candidate who voiced all-out backing of President Roosevelt. The president made it clear he wanted the young congressman promoted to the senate.

LBJ campaigned across the state in a small private plane. Indefatigable Lady Bird accompanied him. The Texas heat was so intense Johnson lost weight and began feeling ill. Lady Bird worked just as hard as her husband. Believing her husband was making history, she took with her a movie camera. Johnson landed in Houston for his first campaign visit on May 9. Hofheinz had arranged for all city and county employees to shake hands with him at City Hall and the courthouse, and escorted him to say hello to leading business and professional people in Houston. Lady Bird Johnson recalled in 1978: I remember walking around the streets of Houston with Dene Hofheinz. We began at the Rice Hotel and she introduced me to many people within two blocks—everyone from shoeshine boys to managers of stores. She really knew them all from previous campaigns. It was obvious how much she shared and understood Roy's interest in politics." Mrs. Johnson also remembered that the Hofheinzes had great influence with black voters and "made it possible for people in homes for the elderly and in nursing homes to register and vote. Those people were some of his many interests."

Hofheinz organized hundreds of teachers from surrounding counties to form a motorcade to hear Johnson speak that night. Johnson said Hitler would write any "war ticket" and the nation should stand ready for anything he did.

John Connally was on the road with Johnson. He recalled that LBJ became "quite ill, a fever turning his face white," at Happy Hollow Lane. Dr. Arthur Scott came to see him and said Johnson should go to a hospital. "Naturally, Mr. Johnson protested," said Connally, "because he had speaking engagements all

Roy campaigning for LBJ in Houston. **Photograph courtesy the LBJ Library.**

over the state, particularly in east Texas. But he felt so poorly he ultimately did go to a hospital." Connally and Gordon Fulcher, who was handling publicity for Johnson while on leave of absence from the Austin *Statesman-American,* which was owned by Charles Marsh, LBJ's longtime political friend and advisor, jointly told Johnson: "We'll put out a statement that you're ill and must cancel your speaking engagements. We have two people, Roy Hofheinz and Everett Looney [Austin lawyer], who can fill in for you." Running a high fever, Johnson "wasn't rational then," recalled Connally, "because he insisted that we not say anything about his going to the hospital. We said to him, 'Well, you can't go to the hospital and cancel a bunch of engagements and get surrogate speakers like Hofheinz and Looney and people not know about it.' We left him and called Hofheinz and Looney. Just before Mr. Johnson went to the hospital, he ordered us out of his house—he was just absolutely furious because we had let out the news."

Connally did leave, and the campaign went on with two substitutes filling the candidate's engagements. Hofheinz, speaking on May 20 in behalf of Johnson, went on a state radio network. He branded Governor O'Daniel an anti-Roosevelt candidate and added, "The one issue in this race is are we for

President Roosevelt or are we against him?" Hofheinz said that at no time had O'Daniel supported Roosevelt. The Judge eloquently railed at O'Daniel, now in front of the race because of his position as governor, for his radio talk two nights previously in which O'Daniel had "ridiculed our president." Noting that the governor reportedly had not voted for Roosevelt, Hofheinz asserted, "If we want to present a united, effective front to Hitler and Mussolini, then we, as loyal Texans and true Americans should unite in electing Lyndon Johnson, for he is the longtime friend and choice of the president of the United States."

Radio broadcasts for the state were in Hofheinz's hands as well as the organizing of counties assigned to him. Remembering the impact of his *Justice* tabloid in his own campaign, Hofheinz supervised production of an issue supporting Johnson. It carried a price tag of five cents, and thousands of copies were sent to various LBJ headquarters for distribution.

There was no doubt of the truth of the big front-page headline: "Lyndon Johnson Sweeps Ahead in U.S. Senate Race." LBJ's handshaking tour, his radio talks, and those of many friends such as Hofheinz had captured the attention of voters, and up went LBJ in the Belden poll. *Justice* carried a front-page picture of Johnson and President Roosevelt shaking hands, captioned, "The Friend of President Roosevelt." Another headline outlining Johnson's meteoric career was entitled, "From Farm Boy to Right Hand of President—Lyndon Johnson Earned Education." LBJ's record was carefully written, year-by-year, and a big, front-page box listed LBJ's platform.

A special Hofheinz touch in *Justice* was a big picture of two little boys shaking hands with Johnson. It was captioned "Johnson is Little Fellows' Friend." Wearing shirts with that slogan printed on the backs were Hofheinz's two sons, Roy, Jr., and Fred. *Justice* said that when Johnson saw the picture he thought it such a "great human interest photograph" that he autographed it, sent it to President Roosevelt, and later found it in a place of honor in the president's study. Another picture showed Lady Bird and Mrs. Rebecca Baines Johnson, LBJ's mother, on the campaign trail. A huge cartoon on an inside page was captioned "Which Side Will Texas Be On?" On one side of the drawing, showing a rope-pulling, were caricatures of Johnson and Roosevelt and on the other side Charles Lindbergh and Senator Burton Wheeler and the "me, too, boys." The inference was that Johnson and Roosevelt were faced with accused apologists for Hitler. A double-page series of cartoons in the center of *Justice* showed Johnson "From Farm Boy to the Right Hand of the President." The last page carried a big footline: "A Vote for Johnson is a Vote for National Defense." This issue of *Justice* was a great selling "pitch-kit," a forerunner of many Hofheinz was to use in his future business life.

Hofheinz's efforts caused Johnson to halt before his illness to write to the Judge, "In spite of the fact that I have been constantly on the go since announcing my candidacy, I must take a few minutes to express to you my gratitude for your efforts in behalf of my campaign. The fact that you are taking such an active part greatly encourages me. When I am elected, I will never forget your assistance which will make possible that election. You may be sure that your confidence urges me and causes me to give the best that I have."

Hofheinz enlisted highly respected State District Judge Allan B. Hannay as Harris County chairman of the southeast Texas campaign. He made the announcement as he listed other Houston leaders who had joined Johnson's campaign in a speech to campaign workers on Radio Station KPRC. Plans were also announced for the recuperating Johnson to speak in the southeast Texas counties. Two thousand persons on June 20 ate barbecue at Miller Memorial Theatre in Houston's Hermann Park; they were there to hear John Snell, president of the Harris County Young Democratic Club, praise Johnson and announce that he was suspending himself from the presidency of the organization for the remainder of the campaign to work for LBJ.

The next day Hofheinz turned his speaking power against Attorney General Mann, who had been quoted as saying Johnson did not vote in the House for full parity for farmers and stockmen. "I want to know," he said, "and all Texas wants to know, who is the individual who is pushing dangerous and false words into the mouth of the attorney general who didn't bother to check. I refer to General Mann's retraction of a statement that Johnson had voted against full parity payments. I score the attorney general for being so little acquainted with the congressional procedure that he cannot tell you the yeas from the nays on the roll call."

Johnson went to Houston again on June 26, and Hofheinz had a motor parade ready to greet the candidate at 10:00 A.M. prior to his final rally that night before a capacity crowd of 15,000 at Sam Houston Coliseum. Cars stretched for a mile as Johnson rode through the streets waving to friends. Bands, sound trucks, automobile horns, and loud greetings heralded his entry into the city. Newspapers reported that in the last week of the campaign Johnson had jumped from fourth to first place in the polls. Enthusiasm in Big Houston was at a peak.

In his final talk, Johnson said: "I will continue steadfastly my policy of going all the way with Roosevelt. They have called me a 'yes man' because of my announced loyalty to the president in this critical period. It doesn't matter, the issues are too great and the times too critical for name calling. We must not repeat the tragedy of France." In introducing Johnson at the final rally, Hofheinz sensed victory for LBJ, predicting he would get 45 percent of the total vote cast. "We've been getting reports from all over the state," he said, "which reflect victory."

When Texas newspaper headlines said the morning after the election that Johnson was the front-runner in vote counting, Carter W. Wesley, general manager of *The Informer,* a black-oriented Houston newspaper, wrote Johnson at his Austin headquarters, informing him that many blacks had voted for him. Moreover, he said that many people "voted for you simply because they thought you were the best man for the job. There was a great number of us who expected nothing in return, but voted for the pleasure of supporting a man whom we thought would do justice to a large job. I think the major portion of the credit should go to Judge Roy Hofheinz. I never knew Judge Hofheinz before this campaign, but I am very much impressed with his forthright method and his intelligent, sensible radio talks. I like men who do what they think ought to be done and don't sit around waiting for somebody to help them or to show them how, and he seems to be that type of person."

Five hours after the polls closed, Johnson was leading by 3000 votes in the unofficial count by the Texas Election Bureau, which got its figures from newspapers throughout the state relayed by wire services. Dallas, Houston, and other newspapers said Johnson had 167,276 votes, O'Daniel 162,124, Mann 134,870, and Dies 71,275—96 percent of the votes. Johnson would win "barring a miracle," said Bob Johnson, manager of the election bureau. Johnson began making senate plans, but O'Daniel refused to concede. Finally, late returns and "corrected counts" gave the election to O'Daniel by 1311. The circumstances surrounding the tallying of votes were suspicious.

On July 3, 1941, the Texas senate voted to permit its investigating committee to examine the peculiar election returns, but Johnson's longtime political advisor, Sam Wirtz, told him not to join in a contest, and LBJ decided to get his affairs in order and go back to Washington as a congressman. When Johnson went to see Roosevelt, the president growled at him and said, "Next time, sit on the ballot boxes." Little did the president realize that seven years later Johnson would really be involved in another battle of ballot boxes. All counties under Hofheinz's campaign jurisdiction had given pluralities to Johnson.

Lady Bird Johnson said in 1978 that she remembered the campaign of 1941 vividly. She also commented on the "enormous vitality" of Hofheinz. "He had native intelligence, drive, industry, and a passionate belief in his philosophy and goals," she said. "I would have expected something daring and innovative from him in whatever endeavors he got into."

John Connally recalled in 1978 when discussing the 1941 campaign:

> Roy was a tremendous speaker and advocate. I watched him all during that campaign. He was always a controversial figure, largely because he was an activist. He had tremendous imagination. He was a bit of everything—an unusual man. He had the versatility very few people have in life. He was in politics for himself and for other people as well. He was a great story teller— bon vivante. He fancied himself, at least, a gourmet cook and I think he was. He had the imagination, really, and the showmanship of a Billy Rose or P. T. Barnum. At the same time he had the stability of any good businessman, or any

good lawyer, in the country. He really was and is a remarkable fellow and I have never been one of his critics.

I understand why people might or might not like him, but I have always, perhaps, been more understanding and tolerant than most people because I always thought he was so much more than the average person that it was only the jealous who envied him and were critical. And that's probably an overstatement, but Roy is just a remarkable man because of the variety of things that he has done in his life and the excellence with which he's done them.

Connally left LBJ and became a naval officer in 1942 just after World War II began. In the fall, he had a leave and wanted to stop in Houston on his way to his home in southwest Texas. He remembered:

I called Roy and told him I was going to come through Houston. "That's great," Roy said, "we'll go duck shooting." I said I didn't have any guns or any equipment. Roy answered, "I've got the guns, the waders, the decoys—I've got everything you need. Come, I've got the best duck blind, the best shooting on the whole Gulf Coast. Come go shooting with me."

So I went out to a little farm house he owned. It was primitive, even by my standards, and they're pretty primitive. We went out in an old Ford, his hunting car. We slept on cots, as I remember it, and during the night it rained, the roof leaked and we got wet. I was miserable. We got up at 4 o'clock in the morning to go into the duck blind and the old Ford wouldn't start. The ground was of black, mucky soil and was slick. It was dark, cold, raining, miserable. We put on all the gear Roy had assembled and got into the car. It wouldn't start, so we walked down the slick road about a quarter of a mile, found a farmer taking his milk into town. He brought us back to the Ford and pushed us off. We drove as far as we could, then started walking into a thicket. We were in waders, jackets, hats and carrying those decoys, guns and shells, and it was like a torture course to me—an obstacle course. We crashed through matted wild roses. It was really a jungle of brush and thorns. We had to stoop to get through, sometimes with our noses about six inches above water. We finally got to the blind. Roy told me what a great blind it was and how great the shooting was going to be. We got in the blind, finally, by 5 or 5:30—before daylight. We then caught our breaths and got settled.

We finally left there about 11 A.M. after never having fired a shot and I thought: "Man alive, is this duck shooting? If it is, I don't want any more of it!" I kidded Roy a long time about this unfruitful trip because he had said—he was always expansive and very proud of what he had—"I've got the best duck blind on the Gulf Coast." He alibied about our failure that he had never been out there before that he didn't get his limit. His attitude was just incredible.

From January until August of 1942, Lady Bird Johnson worked in her husband's Washington office and took a refresher course in typing, shorthand, and business accounting at night. "After Lyndon's loss, we moved into a Buckingham apartment with Nellie Connally (John was away in service) to save

Lyndon Baines Johnson and the Judge in 1941.

money. Nellie and I used to have friends for dinner and we would do the cooking. We'd rush home from Lyndon's office to prepare meals. Roy Hofheinz came to Washington on business and we invited him out to dinner. He came, but it turned out he cooked the dinner himself." Neither she nor Nellie could recall just what he cooked, but it was generally conceded it was a highly seasoned combination of Cajun and Texas ingredients. Lady Bird wrote Roy in Houston, "Thank you for coming and for cooking us dinner. You're the kind of guest that always is welcome, particularly after a hard day at the office."

On the last day of 1942, Lyndon Johnson performed a personal service for Dene and Roy Hofheinz they never forgot. In early October, Mrs. Hofheinz fell ill, and a doctor thought she had uremic poisoning. She was taken to Memorial Hospital and after an examination, Dr. Ed S. Crocker, family physician, said, "Why Mrs. Hofheinz, you are pregnant!"

Dene and Roy were stunned, they later told their only daughter, "Little Dene," because she thought she had already undergone menopause. She actually was two months pregnant, but did not know it. With two lively boys already in the family, the couple nevertheless was happy a third child was on the way and hoped it would be a girl. Mrs. Hofheinz went back to her West Oaks home to prepare for another member of the family.

Judge Hofheinz was out of the home all of the day before New Year's. Mrs.

Hofheinz felt ill and tried to reach him. She thought a miscarriage might be coming, she later told friends. She went to Memorial Hospital without her husband, but sent word to the Judge's office. Aides called and could not find him. One called Congressman Johnson in Washington for help. Quickly LBJ called postmasters and state police to search for the Judge. He was found and rushed to the hospital just before Mrs. Hofheinz gave birth to Dene, a tiny, premature baby, at 10:00 P.M.

On January 1, 1943, the *Press* reported: "County Judge Roy Hofheinz was celebrating his biggest New Year's Day today. He became the father of a tiny but sturdy five-pound baby daughter in Memorial Hospital. Mrs. Hofheinz, while not yet allowed visitors, was in satisfactory condition, hospital attendants reported. The baby will be named Dene, after her mother, and if she has any middle name, her mother will pick it, the Judge said firmly. Dene's mother's name actually was Irene, but over the years all but her sisters called her Dene, so the daughter's will be Dene legally, not Irene."

For a while doctors did not know whether mother and child would survive. Hofheinz took time out from the hospital to go to the courthouse to be sworn in for a fourth term as county judge, but returned to check hourly on the condition of his wife and daughter. "Little Dene," or "Little Doll" as her father called her, was told she was taken home before her mother, who had trouble shaking off the effects of the premature birth.

When she was sufficiently well to write, Mrs. Hofheinz sent Lyndon Johnson a postcard, still preserved in the LBJ Library in Austin, which said, "Dearest Lyndon: Outside of the office, you were the first to know about our baby girl and approximately when she would arrive. She will thrill at the story about your sending postmasters and state police to find her daddy who did arrive on time. I am deeply grateful to you for that and also the lovely flowers which are helping me to recover. Give my love to Bird and hoping to make you acquainted with my daughter soon, I am sincerely your friend, Dene Hofheinz (Mrs. Roy)."

Johnson replied on January 11, "I enjoyed your note, and it made me happy to know that you are feeling well enough to write. Talked to Roy last night and got an up-to-date report on you and the young lady. I have already been selecting a dress for her, and I am going to have her ready for a uniform just as we suited up Butch and Spud during the last-go-round [election]. Hurry up and get out of there because I know you are missed a lot. Love. Lyndon B. Johnson."

In the years to come, "Little Dene" and the two daughters of the Lyndon Johnsons, Lynda Bird and Luci Baines Johnson, were to have fun together at "Huckster House," at the LBJ Ranch, and in Washington.

12

Early Homes, Family, and Civic Life

Modernistic, ship shape, bayfront home on sloping bluff, 24 feet above water, on only sand beach section of Galveston Bay in Bayview. Splendid neighbors, all utilities, five full lots, solid slab foundation, asphalt tile floors, sun deck, built-in modern furniture, completely furnished including stove and Frigidaire. All-weather lighted tennis court, two-car garage, servants' quarters, 310-foot pier, conveniently located near Kemah and Texas City industries. Immediate occupancy. Price, complete, $5750. Phone L 5888.

Open today first time, lovely rambling California colonial style white brick fireproof home, on acre tract in exclusive West Oaks just beyond River Oaks. Furnishings optional. Winding ravine, 53 huge oaks, eight pines, leather-paneled modern master bedroom, three bedrooms, two baths, herringbone inlaid oak floors, carrara glass-walled baths, lifetime standing-seamed copper roof, copper gutters and downspouts. Double brick walls with plaster canvassed and painted interiors. Beautiful character oak paneled den, 10 x 30 screened porch, steel casement windows, four overall rugs, two huge porches, central heating plant, attic ventilation. House completely repainted and reconditioned. Two-car garage, large hobby woodworking shop, mahogany panel playroom, photography dark room, servants' quarters, St. Augustine lawn. House built and for sale by owner. Price $16,000. For appointment, phone L 5888.

For sale ads in Sunday classified sections of Houston Chronicle *and* Houston Post, *July 11, 1943.*

Stuart Young, Bailey A. Swenson, Leon Green, and many other Houstonians read those advertisements with a bit of sadness that hot Sunday, for they had helped build and enjoyed many hours of recreation in the two homes Roy Hofheinz developed after he was elected judge. They knew the places would sell easily for they were different—just as was the creator whose conviviality, imagination, and drive had led them into giving of their time and labor during construction. Although in the 1930s he first was a politician with legal brilliance, Hofheinz had a passion for building, as he demonstrated when a boy in the dirt

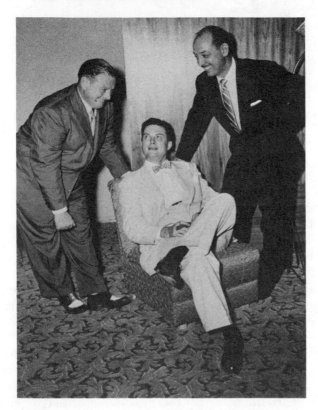

Left to right: Leon Green, Roy Hofheinz, and Bailey Swenson

under his Beaumont home. It never abated. Just as he did when he became the builder of the Astrodome, the multi-talented judge utilized the brains, brawn, and friendship of many people in making his ideas come true. Swenson and Young were among the first side-kicks who enjoyed—and sometimes were irritated by—the thinking, humor, and companionship of Hofheinz.

Swenson, a Houston native who, although older, knew Hofheinz in his high school days, was a Rice graduate in architecture. He won safety poster and home building contests as a teenager at San Jacinto High School and attracted attention with a three-dimensional subdivision plan for which he was paid by a builder. "I could draw anything—either mechanically or free hand and could paint and sketch—and that got me into Rice," Swenson recalled in 1978. He graduated from Rice in 1932 and set up an architectural office. When World War II came, he was commissioned a commander in the Navy. He came home, started again in architecture and, as a sideline, became part owner of radio stations. Today he owns an art gallery in Houston, still is in the radio business, and is a man of means.

Young, a native of York, Pennsylvania, looked to the South after high school graduation, drifted to Atlanta with other job-seeking friends, worked, and went to Georgia Tech at night. He learned to become an expert pattern

Stuart Young

maker and put finishing touches on his inherent ability to create—with his mind and hands—masterpieces of carpentry. The Depression caused him to leave Atlanta and seek better opportunities in Houston. Beginning in 1935, it was he who read the creative mind, listened to the fast, imaginative talk of Hofheinz, and built models, furniture, and hundreds of other beautiful objects for use by his friend. Although he had many opportunities to go into business for himself, Young never left Hofheinz's influence and demands until his death.

"Ship Shack" was the first house in the two listed advertisements. Swenson recalled that Hofheinz was in the legislature when they met on a Main Street sidewalk and talked about earlier days:

> Roy talked and talked to me, and I couldn't figure out why he wanted to gab so long, but finally he invited me to his office. I went the next day and got bored sitting around waiting. He'd send word through his secretary that he'd be through with business at hand shortly. I sat there two or three hours. Roy had a way of holding people, but he always had a reason for seeing any person he went after. I finally found out what he wanted. He had bought a lot on Galveston Bay, and he wanted to get a group together to build a house on it as a recreation center. I was interested because I was an architect and I had an instinctive admiration for Roy.

I met Stuart Young when he came to Houston seeking a job. I found him to be one of the finest craftsmen of any type I'd ever seen. I introduced him to Roy and their compatibility was evident from the beginning. It wasn't long before Roy helped Stuart get a job with the county—close to him. Stuart was delighted to join in building "Ship Shack."

I also introduced Roy to Leon Green, son of a native of Russia, who was trying to learn the building business in association with real estate man David Hudson, who sometimes helped us. Green latched onto me because I was an architect and I got him some work. He later became an investment builder and had his own motels and apartment houses. Roy was wary of Leon at first, but he finally asked the eager immigrant to help with "Ship Shack." They became lifelong friends.

We were the four who did most of the work on "Ship Shack," but from time to time others would join in what we considered fun although it was often hard work. Newspaper reporters—Fred Hartman of Baytown and Douglas Hicks, city editor of the *Press*—were among those who went to the bay site ostensibly to help but mostly to enjoy outings. Evelyn Johnson, Roy's secretary and later wife of newsman Hicks, joined us at times.

We designed "Ship Shack" in marine style. I was interested in naval matters and that influenced Roy. The house was one story built on a slab and had a heavy pipe railing around the top. It was built C-shaped with one corner a private bedroom. The other part sticking out of the C was the kitchen and bathroom and the rest was just one big room. Dene was pregnant when we got the house finished and the bedroom was to be for her and Roy. The rest of us slept, when the house was finished, in the big room—sometimes 30 at a time.

"Ship Shack" did not go up in a hurry because Saturday afternoons, Sundays, and holidays were the only hours the "construction gang" could get together. Fun, poker, and storytelling, eating Hofheinz's gourmet specialties, and boat excursions took away much from their building labors. Cold weather did not deter the weekend erection of the retreat. "I had a small boat called 'Why Knot,' and Roy had an outboard speedboat named 'Knots 2 U,'" Swenson recalled. "We did a lot of fishing and shrimping during and after completion of the house. We'd even dig out raw oysters and eat them out there in the mud. Roy did Cajun cooking—hot and spicy—and it went great with cold beer."

Although Hofheinz owned the house and land, he told those who helped him they would always have free use of it. The Judge was never happier than when there was a big crowd around. "Ship Shack" was just 38 miles from the Harris County Courthouse, between Kemah and Clifton, and just southeast of the Corinthian Yacht Club. A small creek ran by the land into the bay.

Hofheinz's duck hunting leases were elsewhere because the "quacks" which flew over Galveston Bay near "Ship Shack" were not considered large enough to shoot and eat. Swenson's and Hofheinz's goose hunting parties had to "drive all over the country to try to anticipate where geese would land. Geese didn't flock to swamplands." Swenson said one duck hunting place was "some kind of an alligator bog down south, a horrible place. I once went down there and there was supposed to be a large crowd, but it turned out only former Governor Allred, Roy, and I dared the freezing weather. We sat in a small van. I was in the middle of the seat and caught hell if I swung my gun toward Roy and caught more hell when I swung it toward Allred. We killed two ducks over the limit and I was the guy who had to bury them because I had no political job. Both of them were known as law enforcement people so I had to be the culprit. I didn't have much fun on that trip." The site of that excursion was "somewhere near Edna."

Poker was one of Hofheinz's great pastimes. Swenson recalled, "Roy would win everybody's money with one exception, as I remember. His passion to win was never curbed. If he couldn't win in one way, he'd change the game and win that way. But then, generously, he'd give us all our money back because he didn't really like to take from friends. The exception came one night when I won all the cash. I gave back only 10 percent because I wanted to keep proof I didn't lose again."

Alita Holman, a native of Columbia, South Carolina, met Stuart Young when he was a student at Georgia Tech. She renewed acquaintances with him on a visit to Houston in 1935 and met the Hofheinzes who then had baby Butch. Her long-distance courtship with Young continued, and they were married in 1941. Mrs. Young immediately joined the Hofheinzes' inner circle. "Stuart told me how he, Roy, Leon, and Bailey camped at 'Ship Shack' and built it with a little help from others," she recalled in 1978. "I went there first when Dene was in the process of moving in for a three-month summer vacation. She became my best friend—a great one. Our families were close from then on." Alita Young was one of the volunteers who tried to help elect Lyndon Johnson senator in 1941.

"We just did things spontaneously," recalled Bailey Swenson in discussing the close relationship of the builders of "Ship Shack."

> One night in 1939, we were sitting around talking at Roy's West Oaks home and the subject of the World's Fair in New York came up. Only Leon Green, Dene, Roy, and I were there, but all of us said we wanted to see the big show. In 45 minutes, we were packed, dressed, and ready to take off in Roy's black limousine for New York. We threw a lot of blankets in the car. We took turns of one person sleeping on the floor in the back and one on the seat in the back, one driving, and one to keep the driver from going to sleep. We didn't spend a single night anywhere. We stopped in places to eat like Antoine's in New Orleans, where we had pompano in paper, and other various places which appealed to Roy's appetite. Except for food and visits to toilets, we went straight through the country. I had the wheel when we entered New York over the Pulaski Skyway. I studied a map and I came down one block from the Taft

Hotel where we had reservations. The Taft was favored by Texans because we could get large rooms and all kinds of service.

On our first visit to the fair, Leon Green fell and hurt his ankle and we spent only a few hours there. The rest of the time we just toured New York. On the way back we stopped in Washington and decided to go to see the Washington Senators play baseball. That was long before Roy ever thought of going into professional baseball. Roy began talking to fans at the ticket gate about the Senators' team, and Dene went to the ticket office to buy seats. A bunch of kids gathered around Dene and when she came back to us, the kids followed her and one said, "Oh, lady, please talk some more. We like your accent."

Friends did not contribute as much labor to the Hofheinz's West Oaks home as they did to "Ship Shack." Stuart Young, however, was the master carpenter who was paid to carry out building ideas Hofheinz supplied. The "For Sale" advertisement adequately described the physical features of the rambling structure which served not only as a comfortable and unusual home for the family, but as a meeting place for political and social activities connected with Hofheinz's career. Dene never knew how many people her husband would bring home to dinner without notifying her, but Roy kept her pantry and refrigerator well stocked. Often the Judge would do the cooking himself when he brought home friends and political associates.

The large woodworking shop was the scene of many happy evenings when Hofheinz and Young got together to put together ideas for the home and furniture and for additions to the house. Butch and Spud often watched the two men in action. "Everywhere we lived Dad had a shop," recalled Fred Hofheinz. "Dad would get great pleasure out of not doing building himself, but in seeing it done—the cabinets, furniture, and gimmicks. He was his own general contractor, and the kind of things that he would build were the unusual and the interesting—the things people would talk about." Most of the internal furniture, fixings, and trappings in places the Hofheinzes lived came from Roy Hofheinz's ideas and Stuart Young's hands. They were different, but just what Hofheinz wanted, and they were conversation pieces in Houston for many years.

Before the sale of his two homes, for which he received his advertised price, Hofheinz carefully studied property throughout Houston. He learned that a plot of 67.5 acres fronting on Yorktown Drive, a half-mile west of Post Oak Road, was for sale by Sidney S. McClendon. The Judge bought the undeveloped land for $18,000 on August 15, 1943, one week after he sold his West Oaks home. On January 21, 1944, he bought 10 acres adjoining the Yorktown tract from Mrs. W. Coltser of Galveston County and Mr. and Mrs. J. DeLong of Harris County for $400 an acre. Later he bought other small tracts to give him about 80 acres for a new homestead called "Yorktown."

The Hofheinz family had to move out of the West Oaks home before a garage apartment the Judge and Young had begun at Yorktown was completed. Roy Hofheinz, Jr., recalled: "We moved to a little shack at Spring Branch owned by Dave Hudson, our builder friend. It had no running water and we had to use an outhouse. Mother drove Fred and me to school. Little Dene was with us but not in school. We were miserable for about six weeks."

The family moved into the Yorktown apartment when it was nearly completed. "It was a hot little place," said the junior Hofheinz. "In the garage there was room for a washing machine and a workshop. Stairs led up to two bedrooms and a screened porch. Fred and I shared the porch, Mother and Dad one bedroom, and my little sister had the other. They were cramped quarters—no air conditioning." Yorktown became the property anchor for Roy Hofheinz to become a millionaire. The garage apartment was but the beginning of an unusual new home that ultimately was the scene of great activity and entertainment, including a party for the King and Queen of Greece. The sale of "Ship Shack" did not end Hofheinz's desire for a Galveston Bay retreat. He soon acquired an old home overlooking Galveston Bay which was to become his famous "Huckster House."

Gifted, ambitious, self-confident men, especially those who grow up in poverty, never are satisfied fully with their accomplishments. They must go from one achievement to another to continue proving their abilities, responding to inner urges striving from greatness. Roy Hofheinz, experienced in law, the judicious handling of and leading people, radio selling and announcing, public speaking, and hard-nosed politics, decided in his second term as judge that he could never be a wealthy man in climbing the political ladder without a high personal income. He would not accept under-the-table, illegal financial benefits as many in political life have done through the years.

Hofheinz's experience with radio as a teenager and as a means of helping him get elected to the legislature and as county judge led him to plot a course for acquiring a station which he hoped would bring him the financial security which later would allow him to seek higher political office, beholden to none.

On October 23, 1940, Hofheinz and three wealthy oil operators of Houston—J. R. Parten, Hugh Roy Cullen, and W. N. "Dick" Hooper—were granted a charter by the Texas secretary of state for the Texas Star Broadcasting Company. Hofheinz immediately announced he would go to Washington to file an application with the Federal Communications Commission for a license to broadcast. The capital stock of the company was listed as $100,000, fully subscribed.

Cullen, Hofheinz's neighbor during his teenage days and an associate in promoting the University of Houston, was president of Quintana Petroleum Company. Parten was president of the Woodley Petroleum Company, and Hooper was an independent operator. All three men had watched Hofheinz during his outstanding political career and had confidence the Judge could become a successful businessman. They knew of his career as a radio salesman and promoter during his teenage days and of his great use of radio in his political campaigns.

Two other corporations applied for the same radio frequency for which Texas Star Broadcasting asked. Scripps-Howard Radio, Incorporated, sparked by Jack R. Howard, son of Roy Howard, great developer of Scripps-Howard newspapers, and Greater Houston Broadcasting Company, backed by leading Houston businessmen, were the competitors. The *Press* in Houston was one of Scripps-Howard's papers and regularly supported Hofheinz in politics. On April 23, 1941, the FCC said it would call hearings on the applications. Hofheinz appeared in Washington on October 16, 1941, and told the commission that if it would grant his company a license, he would sever his connection with public office. No action was taken by the commission. With the entrance of the United States into World War II, the FCC decided that applications for frequencies would be frozen, preventing new construction of stations except in cases where there was no primary service or unless applications had equipment on hand. That stopped all Houston frequency applicants—temporarily. They would have to wait. Hofheinz was never one to give up; he was determined to get that radio license in one way or another despite the war, and he carefully planned how he would be ready if another hearing were called by the FCC. As the war turned more favorably toward the United States, Hofheinz felt the FCC would call another hearing. When the FCC announced in the summer of 1943 that it would reopen the Houston case in May of 1944, Hofheinz decided to consolidate his assets to be ready financially to win the radio frequency. That was why he decided to sell "Ship Shack" and West Oaks and some smaller pieces of property he had bought at bargains: to get cash in hand for radio.

Hofheinz used only a little of the cash he assembled to buy Yorktown, which he acquired with a small down payment and a mortgage, arranged with a banker who later would have a big part in backing Hofheinz business ventures, James A. Elkins of the City National Bank. As probate judge, Hofheinz had appointed this bank as administrator in some estates. He also became a close friend of Judge Elkins as they sat next to each other when the Houston Buffs of the Texas League played professional baseball.

During these years, the Judge enjoyed his family tremendously. The junior Hofheinz said the relationship between his mother and father never changed from the beginning of their marriage. "Mother was a great supporter of Dad," he recalled. "She urged him to do what he wanted to do. It was a very close relationship, and she encouraged him, bowed to his will on most things, and then went right on about her business, gave up her own career to rear us children. She was a wonderful person."

Twenty-seven months younger than his brother Roy, Fred Hofheinz recalled a "close relationship between my mother and father. The impression I had then was that they were very involved together in all projects. From the very beginning of my memory, they always acted in tandem. Mother was never one who went off on her own. She always did her thing while Dad did his thing. They worked together. Mother was always sweeping up behind him and involved in his political activities, while at the same time she took care of us kids. In their private life, he was very much dominant in their relationship—he the leader and she the follower, almost to the point of being obsequious, although that's a strong word. I think her underlying motive was to help her husband— very normal for that period."

Fred said his mother was ill most of her adult life, but few people knew it as she carried on without complaint. In her 20s, she developed acromegalia, known as "giant's disease." She had a tumor on her brain that grew into the pituitary cavity, pressed on the pituitary gland, and caused it to exude growth hormone and develop bones beyond their usual size. The tumor proved benign, but it caused Dene to have fierce headaches. The family physician, Dr. Crocker, watched the condition for years and said it was inactive much of the time.

All the ideas of women's liberation were completely foreign to his mother, Fred said. "She was content to be a mother and a housewife and to support her husband. She had no other interests. When she got involved in the American Cancer Society once, I think her underlying motive was to help her husband with his political and public ambitions." The second Hofheinz son said there was never any inclination to spare the rod "when we were young, but it wasn't over-used, either—a normal situation." In fact, he added, the whole family situation was normal except for his Dad's public exposure. "We were always put right on the pinnacle and we learned by that," he added, "with both positive and negative aspects of early childhood exposure."

When three, Fred remembered, "Dad hauled me duck hunting with him, so you can imagine how much I got out of the duck hunt—very little—but the point is, he hauled us everywhere—growing up with Dad the whole way. He worked hard, but we were welcome to join him at any point and we frequently did."

Roy Hofheinz's reputation in Texas as a public speaker was unexcelled during his judgeship days, and his ability to hold a crowd spellbound brought him more invitations than he could accept. Dene and the boys often were with him as he talked about juvenile delinquency, care of the insane, the need for efficient government, and, during World War II years, patriotism.

Aunt Mary Spolyar told how Hofheinz perfected his speaking ability as a teenager. "I often saw him practice speaking by looking into a mirror and observing his own actions. He would ask me, 'What do you think of that?' and I'd tell him what I liked or didn't. He'd also ask me about people and say, 'Should I shake hands with this man or not?' and I told him I didn't know, he'd just have to make up his mind by instinct—and he did it to perfection. While practicing, he'd often tell me the latest jokes and he kept me in stitches." After he married, Roy put marbles in his mouth and rolled them around while practicing speaking to strengthen his pronunciation and vocal muscles. Roy used his speaking skills to promote national defense both before and during World War II. For example, a year before Pearl Harbor, Hofheinz spoke at the annual Navy Day banquet sponsored by the Theodore Roosevelt Post 391 of the American Legion at the Texas State Hotel in Houston. He said, "The people of Harris County must assume responsibility in our national defense, just as our youths are doing in giving a portion of their lives in making America first in the world on land and sea."

Hofheinz not only invested Probate Court trust money in war bonds, he also spoke often to groups selling them. Movie star Dorothy Lamour was invited to Houston to speak in behalf of war bond sales, and Hofheinz gave her an eloquent introduction. Show business personalities fascinated the Judge, and in the years to come he would know and enjoy the company of many of them.

The need for safety measures during World War II caused the formation of an Affiliated Safety Council in 14 Harris County communities. Hofheinz was a prime spokesman. He also assisted his friend, Robert Everett "Bob" Smith, who served as volunteer director of the Harris County civil defense effort. Smith, ultimately one of the richest Texas oil, cattle, and land tycoons, had become a Hofheinz friend during the frenzied war days. Their association in patriotic causes led to political, civic, and business ventures. Their final accomplishment as a team would be the building of the Astrodome, completed two decades after they first became associated.

Conventions always attracted Hofheinz, for there he had opportunities to speak to and learn about people from many walks of life. His experiences in them paved the way for his leadership in making Houston, after 1965, one of the world's great convention centers. In 1939 Hofheinz successfully invited the National Association of County Officers to hold its 1940 convention in Houston. The magazine, *County Officer,* in May of 1940 carried a picture of Hofheinz and other county officials attending the Houston convention and noted, "We who attended the convention in April owe a great deal more than a vote of thanks to Judge Roy Hofheinz and his local committees. Our laurels to Houston and Harris County and the State of Texas."

Hofheinz also became involved in the movement to promote the University of Houston during this period. Houston Junior College had expanded into a four-year institution a short time after Hofheinz spent a year there. The old San Jacinto High School was not large enough for the increasing number of local students at the new private university. When Houston leaders decided on a $1 million campaign to raise funds for four new buildings for the university, Hugh Roy Cullen was named general chairman, Hofheinz chairman of the alumni division, and editor Oveta Culp Hobby chairman of the public division.

Pappy Lee O'Daniel campaigning for governor of Texas. Photograph courtesy the *Houston Chronicle.*

Millionaire Cullen gave $269,000 to start the drive, observing that he and his wife "became interested in the University of Houston because its enrolled students strive for self help. The university gives the same advantages to the poor as the rich." The campaign began February 2, 1938, and by March 31, 1938, the money was raised and work on the first building started. Cullen turned the first spade of dirt. Although Hofheinz's personal gift to UH was as much as his family budget would allow, his enthusiasm for the university caused other young struggling alumni to give nearly $20,000. In time, Roy Hofheinz would be one of the greatest financial contributors to this community-oriented institution of higher learning.

In his 1942 campaign for reelection, Hofheinz had special shirts made for his two sons which bore this message on the back: "Please vote for my daddy, Roy Hofheinz." The Judge told the *Press,* "My wife is all ready to handle my campaign ably as office manager and planner. My two boys are able card pushers at afternoon rallies and picnics."

"We feel a good husband and a good daddy should have our help, especially since he has been such a good public official," Mrs. Hofheinz said in a press conference in behalf of her husband.

Bailey Swenson traveled over Texas with Roy during the Judge's campaign for the "pay-as-you-go" tax amendment for Harris County. The architect was keenly interested in politics and had been a page, as had Hofheinz, for the New York delegation during the 1928 Democratic Convention. "One time we went to Amarillo for a teacher's convention with Roy as the principal speaker," Swenson said. "He was given a nice room in a hotel. Later the manager of the hotel came to Roy and apologetically said there was a woman who didn't have a nice room and wondered if he wouldn't mind trading with her. Here he was, the principal speaker, and yet a woman came first. They then put us in a room where our knees almost touched the wall when we sat on the side of the bed. It was a horrible night with the two of us in one bed. It was the damndest, most uncomfortable trip we ever took. We returned in a blizzard and dust storm—all in 24 hours."

The trip occurred when "Pappy" Lee O'Daniel was running for governor. Swenson said that every morning O'Daniel talked to the women of Texas on a radio hookup. Roy listened and quickly came to the conclusion that radio was going to be important in any political campaign. The men running against O'Daniel did not use air time regularly and they lost, proving political writers wrong in their belief that O'Daniel did not have a chance.

Hofheinz would win reelection but would suffer a great loss, for World War II caused Stuart Young to leave county employment and join Brown Shipbuilding Company. He did well and designed the *U.S.S. Ellis*. Fortunately, this separation was temporary. "Brown wanted him to stay after the war," Mrs. Young said, "but he decided to go back to scheming, designing, and working for Roy because he knew his friend would get out of politics one day and become a builder." No person, other than his two wives, contributed more to Hofheinz's success in the years ahead than Stuart Young.

13

Ole Country Boy's
Radio License

The Federal Communications Commission ruled, after World War II began, that applications for another Houston radio frequency were frozen unless the three corporations seeking it could show they had the equipment to operate. Roy Hofheinz thereupon rented a warehouse and began filling it with new and used paraphernalia, which could be put together for a station operation. His teenage experience as an announcer and time salesman had brought him some knowledge of what was needed. He studied the equipment of operating stations and made inquiries throughout the country where he might buy necessary items. Little by little, despite wartime strategic materials restrictions, he assembled everything blueprints showed would be necessary. His two opponents apparently made no such effort—they were waiting until granted a frequency.

The FCC also required that an applicant for a frequency file reports on the broadcasting behavior of other stations in the market. There were three Houston stations operating: KXYZ with the ABC network, operated by Tilford Jones, nephew of Jesse Jones; KPRC with the NBC network owned by the *Post*; and KTRH with the CBS network owned by a group of business executives. Hofheinz had no money to commission surveys for the FCC, but he and Dene had enthusiastic manpower in their families, and they called on their relatives to help get the facts. Roy Hofheinz, Jr., remembered how data was gathered: "The names of the programs of all radio stations had to be catalogued. Dad had all our relatives doing checks in their homes. We were too poor to pay people, so Dad depended on his own folks to get the raw material and then he would put it together—well-prepared statistical facts. I, and others, sometimes spent from dawn until midnight at a table listening to a station and making notes."

His visits to Washington in behalf of Harris County federal business—and in 1941 to the unprecedented third-term inauguration of President Roosevelt—not only kept Hofheinz's friendships with elected and appointed officials active, but brought into his life a man who became known as the nearest to a brother Roy ever had—W. Ervin "Red" James. James would be helpful to the Judge in obtaining his radio station. A native of Montgomery, Alabama, from a family of seven children, James was more than a year older than Hofheinz. After high school, he journeyed to Washington, got a job in the Commerce Department, and went to George Washington University at night, including summers, for seven years, winning his law degree in 1941. The stocky, red-haired, eager, and eloquent Alabamian was regarded as a comer in the federal bureaucracy.

"I met Roy in Washington in 1939," recalled James. He recounted Hofheinz's disappointment in 1941 when, despite a favorable ruling from a federal examiner, the Harris County judge did not win his original radio application because of the equipment ruling. He said Hofheinz left Washington determined to meet the FCC's new requirement. Hofheinz and James developed a close if long-distance friendship during the months the Judge planned his final "pitch" for the radio frequency. Said James:

> When the FCC modified its ruling to say that if an applicant already had equipment on hand it would consider licensing, here comes Hofheinz to a new hearing. Roy then had 75 percent of the stock in Texas Star. H. R. Cullen and J. R. Parten lost interest in the station and sold to Roy after the first application failed. That left only Dick Hooper as a 25-percent partner.
>
> Hooper was a very interesting fellow. His father was a doctor in Conroe, near Houston, and developed the Doctor Hooper Oil Fields in and around Conroe, so he was of a wealthy family. In his early days, Dick had an unfortunate accident on a hunting trip when he shot off his left arm. He got on a horse and went into town and a doctor saved his life. He was a determined man. He went to the University of Texas and played baseball with one arm. I'd say he was a unique and outstanding athlete despite his handicap. He and Roy had many common interests—hunting, baseball, politics—and full confidence in each other as they went to Washington for the hearing.

James was not in Washington in May of 1944 at the final FCC hearing because he had joined the Navy, but he prepared Hofheinz with what to expect. James told Hofheinz that after the first unsuccessful hearing, FCC Chairman Fly had called him into his office and said, "Red, you're not helping yourself any going up and down the halls of this commission with that young Hofheinz from Houston because he's not going to get a radio station." James said he replied, "Mr. Chairman, he should because he's qualified. You modified the rule on strategic materials, but that's your problem. I stood up to him the best I could and left." James sent the warning of Fly's opposition to his new Houston friend. "I don't know why Fly was opposed to Roy," James said, "but I have some surmises which I don't care to put on the record." There were powerful Houstonians in Washington who did not like Hofheinz.

On the first day of the hearings, Fly personally examined and cross-examined Hofheinz, who acted as his own lawyer, after examiners for the commission had put documents into the record. Much was made of Hofheinz's failure to resign as county judge when he put in his application. Factually,

W. Ervin "Red" James (left) and Dick Hooper. James photograph courtesy the *Houston Chronicle.*

Hofheinz said he would resign if he got the license, but not before. "Roy told me later he felt Fly had made mincemeat out of him that first day," James said. "He said he felt sure Fly's influence would kill his application." Hofheinz actually was so depressed that night he telephoned Dene and said, "We're wiped out. There's no way we can make it with the commission." He told his wife about Fly's attitude and recalled how they had sold their properties to get money for the station—all for naught. Dene replied in her normal, consoling fashion, "Well, Honey, we didn't have anything to start with. You come on home and we'll start all over again." Overhearing the conversation was Hooper who said later, "That's the first time I ever felt sorry for Hofheinz." Hooper was a scrapper like Hofheinz. He was not as depressed as his partner. He asked Hofheinz what it would cost to appeal an unfavorable ruling if it came. "Oh, Dick," Hofheinz replied, "it's too much money, it would probably cost $25,000." Hooper asked, "If we lost in an appeals court, how much would it take to go to the Supreme Court?" The Judge replied, "Another $50,000." "Well, I'm good for that much and more," Hooper said. "Now, son, you get some iron in your backbone and go back over there and stand up to 'em—and we'll take this thing all the way to the Supreme Court, if necessary."

When Chairman Fly finished questioning Hofheinz the next morning, he asked, "Do any commissioners have questions?" One of the commissioners was Cliff Durr, a Rhodes scholar at Oxford and a brilliant lawyer. He was a close friend of Red James who, in the interim between the first and second hearings, had given the commissioner detailed information about Hofheinz. While Fly tore down Hofheinz the first day, Durr quietly took copious notes. "I have a few questions," he replied to Fly. It took Durr two days to review the Judge's outstanding political record, his reputation for honesty, his support from Hooper, who was on the board of the First City National Bank with Hofheinz's fatherly counselor, Judge Elkins, and then to emphasize that Roy was the only applicant who had fulfilled the commission's requirement for equipment. Observers said Durr made sure that there was no way Fly, on the basis of the record, could vote against the Judge's application unless "to make himself look like anything except a damned fool." Two days later, on May 23, the FCC voted unanimously to grant frequency 1230—250 kilowatts—to Hofheinz and Hooper with call letters KTHT (Keep Talking Houston Texas).

Hofheinz listed the names of U. S. Representatives Lyndon B. Johnson and Albert Thomas and other Texas political figures as references in his application, but he said he did not call on them to put pressure on the FCC. No evidence was developed that they did.

Jack Howard, president of Scripps-Howard Radio which lost in the application battle with Hofheinz, gave a different version of how the Judge won: "Roy would arrive at the 1941 hearing each day wearing one of those peanut-sized Stetsons, lugging a bulging, richly-embossed Mexican leather briefcase and—breathless. His act—a most effective one—was the simple little ole country boy against the rich corporation. The hearing concluded without decision. Time slowly dragged along in the FCC bureaucracy. Jim Hanrahan and I had been actively involved in the first hearing, but were soon off to the wars. Months later—Jim was with the Army in Italy and I with the Navy in the Pacific—I received a notice in the mail from the FCC to the effect that the Houston hearing had been reactivated. Acknowledgement was requested within 60 days. By the time I received the legal notice, eight months had gone by. Well, as you may have guessed, because Scripps-Howard Radio failed to reply to the notice or take action to retain its place in line, Roy was granted the license by default."

Red James was at Fort Scuyler in New York's Bronx taking Navy officer indoctrination when he received a letter from Hofheinz—"one of the few he ever wrote in his life"—telling him about the license grant. "He called me the greatest friend he ever had—blah, blah, blah," said James. "It was a real jewel of a letter. And, hell, I just tossed it in the trash—it was all in a day's work. Wish I had saved it." The Hofheinz-James association grew closer in the years ahead, with James becoming a resident of Houston and Hofheinz's law partner as well as his stormy counselor. They had many verbal battles, as do many brothers, but their personal ties remained strong. James in 1978 was a Houston State District

Court judge and regularly visited with his retired friend at 2929 Lazy Lane, River Oaks.

Had he not received his radio station license, Hofheinz felt he would have to file for a fifth term as county judge—insurance for his family's security; therefore, on May 16, he had routinely announced as a candidate for reelection in the July Democratic primary. He was at a crossroads, not certain which direction he should go. Glenn A. Perry, 38, a native of Iowa whose family had moved to Houston in 1911 when he was a boy, decided to seek the county judgeship as speculation grew early in 1944 that Hofheinz would step out. A lawyer, he became secretary of the Harris County Democratic Executive Committee in 1937 and held the non-salaried post until the time of his announcement for the judgeship. Perry was well-acquainted with Hofheinz's political acumen, as they had worked together for party candidates, and began campaigning early so that he would have a head start. Hofheinz hopefully planned for a new career, and Dene made no effort to line up the Judge's normal coalition of labor, Chicanos, blacks, and the underprivileged. The Judge really intended to take his name off the ballot when he returned from Washington with the favorable decision for a radio station, but he was shocked when he read a Washington news story saying that Chairman Fly and the FCC might reopen the Houston case because the Harris County judge had not actually resigned. In some Washington circles and in Houston powerful opposition to Hofheinz's owning a radio station had not diminished.

For two weeks Hofheinz went back to the stump, but it was not the type of campaign he ordinarily waged. He was upset by one situation which led him to believe Houston city government was trying to help Perry win. There was no inclination on the part of city councilmen and other officials to help Hofheinz, for in his official county capacity he often had chastised them verbally for various actions affecting the welfare of Houston and Harris County. The incident involved two of Hofheinz's supporters who received a water bill on joint rental property. The bill had a campaign card for Perry attached. It appeared that the city was supporting Hofheinz's opponent by enclosing campaign literature to its 75,000 customers. According to the *Post*, "The judge lost his usual self-composure and practically blew up." Investigation by the city manager revealed that the card was enclosed as a joke on the two Hofheinz partisans. Fred Hofheinz recalled the brief 1944 campaign:

> As a child, I remember the race was played down and the decision to run was a last-minute decision. The campaign was minimal. I remember, however, at the very last minute, Dad hustled hard and went to rallies. The most effective way in those days to win votes was to shake everyone's hand. Dad made a big rush to try to get in touch with everybody at the last minute, but his heart really wasn't in it. The radio frequencies in Houston at that time were owned by rather influential people, particularly in the Democratic administration, and it

was not altogether certain that Dad would actually get that license. For instance, two of the frequencies were owned by the *Chronicle* and the *Post*, so he stayed in the race. When Dad finally got his license, we were still living in that garage apartment at Yorktown which was cold in winter and hot in the summer.

Voters were unsure about Hofheinz's intentions. That and the Judge's late, halfhearted campaign caused in July his first political defeat by a narrow margin. The loss eliminated any further argument by Washington opponents, and nothing came of the FCC threat to reopen the Houston case.

On January 15, 1944, Hofheinz decided that, because he was planning to give up the judgeship for radio, he should set up a law office as a sideline to the business activities he plotted. Joining the "Law Offices of Roy Hofheinz" were Richard W. Fairchild of Austin, who had been assistant state attorney general for five years, and Irvin Keppler Boarnet, a former high school classmate who had served as assistant to the Judge since 1941. Hofheinz's role in this and later law firms was to be that of legal expert who advised rather than handled actual cases. His two years as a legislator and nearly eight years as a judge handling thousands of cases gave him the knowledge necessary to be top man and signal-caller in a law firm.

With no further obstacle in the way of opening his radio station, Hofheinz offered his resignation in October of 1944 to Commissioners Court. The commissioners refused to accept it, issuing a statement that they needed the Judge's advice on many pending projects he had initiated. Hofheinz finished his term on January 1, 1945. His political career thus was sidetracked until he could reach his goal of becoming financially secure. At 32, he could look back with great satisfaction on his record of service to the people of Harris County. No other man of his young years had ever provided the leadership, vision, determination, and political action which contributed so greatly to the growth and success of Houston and Harris County. It would be eight years—during which time he would become a millionaire—before the force of Roy Hofheinz's political progressiveness would be felt again in the city which provided him the opportunities to show his genius.

14

Little Known Financial
Nest Egg

"I am not going into politics again until I am a millionaire," Roy Hofheinz told his family when he left the county judge's office. In January of 1945, he already had a start toward his goal—two partnerships with wealthy men who believed in his integrity and sales genius. The least-known partnership, when formed—and today—was on a handshake basis with George Mattison, Jr., of Birmingham. His 50 percent interest in the Houston company they formed was a financial nest egg for Hofheinz the rest of his life.

When Sheffield Steel (now Armco) established a plant in Houston, under federal Defense Plant Corporation authority just before World War II, Hofheinz learned that one of the corporation's problems was disposal of waste from furnaces. Hofheinz went to visit Ralph Gray, president of Sheffield, in Kansas City. Gray said he would be glad to give the waste, or slag, to anyone with the means of taking it away from the plant. Already planning to leave politics and enter business, Hofheinz said he wanted it and went back home; then, on county business later in Washington, he went to the trade office of the National Slag Association to get information on the uses of the steel waste.

He was told that Mattison, president of Mattison Slag Association in Birmingham, was the best slag expert in the country with experience since 1919. "My first vision of Roy came when he walked into my office in Birmingham late in 1943 and said he was interested in the uses of blast furnace waste," Mattison recalled in 1978. "After discussions of the market and uses of the waste, we felt an immediate promotional kinship, although I wasn't sure about the young judge's business ability. Roy was never much at writing letters, but we had many visits, climaxed with a conference with the president of Sheffield, Ralph Gray."

Gray occasionally had dealt with Hofheinz on county road and legal matters involving the establishment of the steel plant and had respect for the ability of the young man who ran Harris County government. The future of Houston Slag Materials Company was assured when Gray visited Houston to talk with Mattison and Hofheinz at the Texas State Hotel. Hofheinz told Mattison on arrival that Gray wanted them to have breakfast with him in his suite the next

George Mattison, Jr., (left) and George Lanier. **Mattison photograph courtesy the** *Birmingham Post Herald.*

morning. With breakfast and casual talk out of the way, they got down to business. "If I were going to come to Houston to go into the slag business," Mattison quoted Gray, "I would be interested in approaching Roy Hofheinz so he could help me get started. He knows the people and the ways of Houston. Roy would have no business trying to go into the business unless he had as his associate someone like you, George, who knows the ins and outs of slag." Mattison thus was convinced that Hofheinz should go into business with him. He asked Gray to excuse them, and the two went into the hotel hall.

"Hi, partner," Mattison said. "We've got to work together or both of us will be out of consideration." Hofheinz replied, "That sounds all right to me." They shook hands on a partnership. Each beamed as he walked back into Gray's suite. Mattison told the steel chief, "You have just seen develop the youngest partnership in the state of Texas." Hofheinz proposed Houston Slag Materials Company as the name. "What's the need for the lengthy title?" Mattison asked. Hofheinz replied, "They use the word materials in the Houston area, and I'd like to put it in our title." Mattison agreed.

Mattison said another Houstonian wanted to get Sheffield's waste and had been to the Defense Plant Corporation office in Washington to make an

Judge James A. Elkins. **Photograph** courtesy the *Houston Chronicle.*

application after Houston Slag had proposed a contract. Mattison heard of the possible competitor and called Hofheinz quickly, finally finding him in Washington. He told the Judge that a friend of the other bidder, an official high in DPC, had pigeonholed Houston Slag's contract. "I think the DPC man wanted to get into the business himself," said Mattison. Hofheinz immediately called Representative Lyndon Johnson and, after telling his influential friend of the problem developing, the two went to DPC to inquire about the contract holdup. The next day the DPC official sent the contract to Houston to George Lanier, a nephew of Mattison chosen by the partners as operating head of the new company.

A quiet, studious man with a sharp business mind and with the contract in hand, Lanier told Mattison and Hofheinz he would need $15,000 to get the business under way. Mattison offered to put up the money, but Hofheinz said that was not necessary; he could arrange a loan. Judge Elkins of City National Bank had confidence in Hofheinz and approved the loan. "We borrowed no more than $10,000 after that first loan," Lanier said. "The business then carried itself." Houston Slag cleaned out all slag produced prior to and during World War II by Sheffield. Lanier said another contract was negotiated with Sheffield in August of 1947, when Sheffield bought another blast furnace from DPC to increase its output. That contract still is in operation with Armco, which took over Sheffield in a merger.

Houston Slag began producing its product, analogous to crushed stone, on July 1, 1945. Fifty percent of the steel waste had been used as ballast for railroads until Lanier and Mattison began marketing their material, which could be used with concrete or asphaltic macadam in buildings and on highway construction. Slag by itself makes a hard, clear road, Mattison said. "There's no comparison of oyster shell with slag. Blast furnace slag is angular, cubicled, and has enough spaces between its layers that cement or asphaltic mix can intermingle and hold the pieces together. Either of these combinations makes a solid, very good highway, roadway, or building."

In late 1944, when Lanier and Mattison began planning the company's program, Hofheinz specified no effort should be made by them to make contracts with Harris County until he left office. He wanted no charges of conflict of interest thrown at him in campaigns should he seek political office again.

"We had a terrific job breaking into the market where shell dominated," Lanier said, adding that Hofheinz's experiences with the price-fixing shell monopoly and the negotiating of county road contracts gave him expert knowledge. "In the beginning we needed all help possible in having slag accepted by engineers and contractors of Harris and other counties, and the Judge was most helpful, after he left office, in selling our product," Lanier added. The Houston area proved a good market for the new company. "We have been very successful, very fortunate," Lanier said in looking back in 1978.

Commented Mattison in 1978, after he sold his company in Birmingham to Pellican Materials Company and retired, "I never saw a better salesman than Roy Hofheinz. It just depended on what the product was as to what line his approach would be. He was strictly a salesman from the word go. He worked up for us in the beginning something you hardly see anymore—a 'pitch-kit' as he called it. It was a box-like thing, and it contained a lot of flip-over slides. He would set that thing in front of a prospect—no matter what he was selling—and he'd flip over the slides and talk about his subject. Usually he got the business."

After Houston Slag got its start, Hofheinz left to Lanier, who got occasional advice from his uncle, the job of running the plant and marketing. Lanier said wryly, "Of course, Roy was glad to accept a check now and then as half owner of the business." Mattison said he and Hofheinz never had an argument during more than three decades of partnership. The Birmingham partner stipulated in the beginning that Hofheinz could not pledge his share of the company for any loan or other business venture. When money for his family's needs became short, Hofheinz always could touch Houston Slag for "bread and butter." Lanier knew when Hofheinz called and asked, "How are you fixed for blades?"—an advertising commercial once popular in newspapers and on radio—the company checking account would have to be reduced. The longtime success of Houston Slag alone could have made Mattison and Hofheinz wealthy men. Ultimately the partners formed Hurock, Incorporated, which took over part of the business of Houston Slag. Hurock now sells in many parts of Texas.

Ed Bruhl, 10 years Hofheinz's senior, who had casually observed Roy when he was in Houston Law School, came into the Judge's active life after returning from service in World War II. A CPA, Bruhl joined the F. G. Masquelette Company. "My first business contact with Roy came when one of the vice-presidents of City National Bank, Bill Menasco, called and said he had a client for the then immense sum of $15,000, and the bank wanted someone to give the young fellow regular financial advice. He asked if I would consider working with him. I'd been out of the Army only a year and needed clients. The young fellow turned out to be Roy Hofheinz, who needed funds. Hofheinz and Judge Elkins were already good friends because of Roy's assignments of estates in Probate Court—all legally proper—to the bank, and their personal compatability. Judge Elkins no doubt asked Menasco to call me."

Bruhl and Hofheinz became business friends, but Masquelette and Bruhl decided to assign another young CPA, Vernon Bain, to do the field work on the Judge's ventures. Bain and Bruhl, over more than three decades, audited Hofheinz's accounts, saw that his income taxes were paid properly, although they were contested by Internal Revenue Service almost every year, and advised him constantly on financial deals. "We had one firm instruction from Roy over the years—never try to cheat Uncle Sam," both auditors said. "Sometimes Roy overpaid, but we got him refunds, the last in 1978 for about $100,000," said Bruhl.

Hofheinz over the years offered Mattison opportunities to go into real estate and other businesses with him in Houston, and the Birmingham partner agreed, including one major joint enterprise—the purchase of a radio station in Birmingham when Hofheinz was developing a chain. The story of that station, WILD, is part of a bigger one—Hofheinz's lightning-like advance as one of the nation's most innovative and daring investors in and developer of communications. It was in radio Hofheinz had another millionaire as a handshake partner.

Another important individual in Hofheinz's financial development was Hugh Roy Cullen. Although their political philosophies were far apart, Cullen and Hofheinz had great respect for each other after they were neighbors when the Judge was a teenage promoter. Cullen was a big financial backer of the Dixiecrats who nominated Strom Thurmond of South Carolina for president in a breakaway from the Democratic party, while Hofheinz was always steadfast in his loyalty to the regular party.

The Judge knew Houston and Harris County real estate because of his experience in checking assessments and taxes during his years as county judge. In his salaried political days, he invested his extra dollars, and later he bought small pieces of property, often with 10 to 25 percent down. He treasured the advice of Cullen and often sought it as once poor-boy Cullen became a

Ed Bruhl. Photograph courtesy the *Houston Chronicle.*

multimillionaire through oil and real estate. The two men also had a common interest in the development of the University of Houston. After he became wealthy, Hofheinz followed in Cullen's footsteps in giving of his substance to the university.

Cullen encouraged Hofheinz in real estate ventures and often, as a partner, furnished money for Roy to buy. The public did not know which man bought what because deals were usually completed in the names of trustees. One transaction which did go on the record in Hofheinz's name was his purchase on January 29, 1949, of 8.15 acres near the Houston YMCA for $326,500. The tract was irregularly shaped with 260 feet of frontage on Jefferson Street. The Houston Independent School District trustees decided to sell the land, which had been a school playground, because they felt they would get nothing for it if the state took it through condemnation for expressway purposes. Hofheinz borrowed most of the money. When he was in a squeeze in financing radio, he sold the tract to Cullen. Cullen developed the property into Cullen Center, now a business center in downtown Houston.

Asked about how Hofheinz financed his real estate buying, auditor Bain said, "A down payment each time of 25 percent would have been high. Roy pyramided. He would buy a piece of property and he might pay $5000 and put down 10 percent, or $500; then he would have the property revalued later and the figure would come out to maybe $10,000. He then would put that asset with real estate buy number two and buy another piece. He'd use the same process in buying real estate number three and on and on." Bain knew that Hofheinz was gambling, but he felt the Judge knew property well and could borrow money so quickly that he eventually would be a winner. Short-term notes were the Judge's specialty. As they came due, he would find ways to pay interest, refinance, or pay off by the sale of some property which had increased in value. After his early pyramiding, however, the Judge became more and more reluctant to sell anything he owned.

Conservative Cullen did not like pyramiding. He had cash for what he wanted to buy. Hofheinz did not. As the Judge piled one real estate transaction atop another, Cullen finally dropped out of the partnership. When Hofheinz approached Cullen and asked that he help finance new radio station permits the Judge had acquired, Cullen wrote that he was not interested, for "in my opinion you are assuming a great responsibility and skating on very thin ice." Hofheinz did not give up and sought to see Cullen again. On July 14, 1949, the Judge received another letter from Cullen. The oilman observed that Hofheinz had "been trying to see me for some time and I haven't given you an appointment for the reason that your high-pressure sales talk runs up one's blood pressure." Cullen counseled the Judge to "convert your assets into cash—all except your immediate home—and place 50 percent to 75 percent of it aside for your wife and children and gamble the balance of it. It would be a most sensible thing to do." Hofheinz did not take Cullen's advice, for he was never a conservative in handling money.

Discussing relationships of Hofheinz with his financial partners (there were three principal wealthy men assisting the Judge as his assets grew—Mattison, Cullen, and, beginning in the 1950s, Robert E. "Bob" Smith), Bain said, "Despite his pyramiding policy and his idiosyncracy with respect to handling money furnished by other people, I never found the Judge failing to account for what he did in partnerships. We, including chief auditor Ed Bruhl, always were in contact with accountants and treasurers of his partners, some of whom didn't know what was going on until the bills came in. Despite his peculiar trait of going ahead without permission from his partners at times, he never minded anybody who had been associated with him knowing all about his business. His was an open book. He never argued with accountants with respect to how to treat him in tax returns. So if there were any mistakes made, they were made by people who prepared his financial statements and tax returns. I don't know of any partner who ever suffered financially because of partnership with Roy." Auditor Bruhl added, "I can certify that no person who ever performed any service for Judge Hofheinz didn't get paid well. He was not a freeloader, but there were an awful lot of freeloaders on the Judge during his career. A few should have been prosecuted, but Roy wouldn't do that."

Bain said he felt the Judge's attitude was that, when partners turned money over to him for investment, no particular accounting was due the financiers until "such time as Roy saw fit to render that accounting or to sell property and give a final accounting. The Judge trusted investors because he thought they went along with him due to his operating ability, and he felt investors should trust him as the operator and means of making their investments pay."

William F. "Bill" Bennett, veteran Houston radio sales manager who started with one of Jesse Jones' stations, joined Hofheinz in 1948 as sales manager of KTHT, the Judge's first station, when it changed its frequency to become more powerful. In 1978 Bennett gave a picture of the Judge's handling of station finances: "The Judge didn't keep too much cash on hand. Two or three times he barely had enough to meet a payroll. . . ." Bennett had to devise a method for keeping sufficient cash on hand to pay bills and meet the payroll. "Auditors and I worked out the problem," Bennett recalled. "When a $10,000 payroll was coming up, I'd tell the bookkeeper to hold out $10,000 in checks sent us by advertisers. The bookkeeper would go in to get the Judge to sign checks—he wouldn't let anybody else sign checks in the beginning of my employment. The Judge would look up and say, 'Hell, I don't think we have that kind of money in the bank.' The bookkeeper then would say, routinely, that he had just received a bunch of checks that morning; actually he may have had them for a week. The Judge never caught on. If he did, he never said anything." Bennett emphasized that the Judge was generous almost to a fault with his employees, entertained them often, kept their confidence, and, in his own unusual way, successfully continued toward his goal of becoming a millionaire.

Ben G. McGuire, Houston mortgage banking and investments expert, met Hofheinz through Leon Green in the late 1940s, and they became close friends. Looking back in 1978, McGuire said he remarked in the early days of their friendship that television ultimately would ruin radio. At that time, Hofheinz was prepared to add TV broadcasting; he already had plans and some equipment for it. Quickly the Judge replied, according to McGuire, "TV is not going to ruin radio. TV will make radio better. People will still be listening to radios in their automobiles and out-of-the-way places when they don't have television sets on. Radio's going to get hurt, but it's going to be good. You're wrong, Ben." He has been proven correct.

15

A Radio Whirlwind

In less than a month after he got his license for KTHT in mid-1944, and with the financial backing of W. N. "Dick" Hooper, Hofheinz flashed his 250-watt, 1230 signal on the air from modest, second-story offices in the old Southern Building at 700 Main. Hooper thought so much of Hofheinz that he, like George Mattison, Jr., required only a handshake when the two men decided to go into business together—Hofheinz serving as the station's operator and Hooper as the financier. Hooper's credentials were the best. He was on the board of directors of the City National Bank and could furnish a financial statement in the millions.

Broadcasters' Engineering Service, headed by W. E. Antony and O. S. Drake, came from Shreveport, Louisiana, to install the Western Electric equipment Hofheinz had gathered and stored in a warehouse near Buffalo Bayou during World War II. Louis Jelly, in 1979 a radio engineer with KULF in Houston, took the job of keeping the equipment functioning properly. "It was modest but adequate equipment for the start of a small station," Jelly recalled. He said Hofheinz "picked his brains" and those of everyone around who knew anything about radio until he became an expert on every phase of radio operations in a short time. The Judge named Ted Hills his first manager, but it was Hofheinz who ran the show. KTHT soon joined Mutual, a national radio network.

The signal of KTHT—"Keep Talking Houston Texas" or "Kome to Houston Texas"—was weaker than rival stations. In his battle to get his first radio license, Hofheinz had argued that his three competitive stations were owned by a monopoly controlled by Houston newspaper-real estate tycoon, Jesse Jones. Hofheinz felt his long delay in getting a license was because of Jones' influence in Washington. It was then that Hofheinz made up his mind he would later get a stronger position on the dial.

Jim Cafcalas, Hofheinz's father-in-law who owned a restaurant in the basement of Foley's Department Store, was the first to buy advertising time on KTHT, but many others followed. Hofheinz had sales ability and could create promotional gimmicks his staff successfully carried out. At an annual em-

The staff of KTHT at their annual Christmas party in 1945.

ployees' Christmas party, Hofheinz was given a whip as a present because of his ability to drive employees toward his goal of "getting ahead" with his station. Hofheinz had fun whirling the whip, and he gently tapped a few with it while laughing and joking and thanking his aides for their help. KTHT used a news-music-public service formula for attracting listeners, but on-the-scene news coverage was its big weapon to secure early attention. In late 1944, the Judge learned that General Electric was producing an experimental wire recorder, predecessor of today's tape recorders. He soon convinced GE's president to allow him to try a model in KTHT's new coverage. That wire recorder, perhaps the first used by a small radio station, proved to be the needed ingredient which brought Hofheinz local and national attention. Each recorder played for 30 minutes during direct transmission to the station from remote areas of the city, or its contents could be transferred to discs for later broadcasting. After experimenting with the first recorder, Hofheinz equipped a truck for instant news relay to his station; announcers for competing radio stations relied heavily on the telephone to broadcast reports away from their stations. Although each wire recorder weighed more than 25 pounds and was a burden for anyone to carry, the new equipment brought the results that Hofheinz had envisioned.

It was unprecedented in 1945 for a small station to cover big national or international events, for each depended on its national network for such news. When it was announced that the organizational meeting for United Nations would be held April 25-June 26, 1945, the Judge decided to put KTHT into the news spotlight by attending the conference and sending reports back home.

Needing a break from his hard work in establishing the station, Hofheinz, his wife Dene, and their two sons, Roy, Jr., and Fred, took off on the 20th Century Limited for San Francisco; there they made their headquarters at the Sir Francis Drake Hotel. The Judge joined the press corps and was kidded about his bulky recorder by network engineers and announcers. But, as usual, Hofheinz knew what he was doing. His charming eloquence and story-telling abilities attracted the attention of attaches of Vijachclav Mikhailovich Molotov, spokesman for Joseph Stalin of the Soviet Union. Molotov was the key man in international war deals for Stalin—the ill-fated Nazi-Soviet Pact of 1939, the Teheran conference in 1943, Yalta in 1945, Potsdam in 1945, and at the United Nations kickoff. The wire recorder would certify that nothing Molotov might say would be distorted, Hofheinz said.

Broadcasting, the weekly radio news magazine, reported on May 28, 1945, that "News beats are being scored at the conference against wire correspondents of the networks at San Francisco by a protocol-busting Texan, president of a new, small independent station, himself still in the 'cub' stage. Through the medium of a wire recorder and a direct circuit, Roy Hofheinz has been supplying his station, KTHT, Houston, with one of the most comprehensive jobs of coverage of the United Nations Conference on International Organization of any independent." Hofheinz had purchased a direct line for an hour a day, Monday through Friday, from San Francisco. He delivered a 15-minute show daily over it, expanding to a half-hour if the news warranted. He used the remaining time to conduct station business.

"Undeterred by State Department frowns," *Broadcasting* reported, "Hofheinz has recorded many of the important press conferences. When U.S. press chief Michael McDermott tried to bar him from those sessions, the Texan protested that he was doing exactly the same thing as newspaper reporters— they made verbatim notes, he recorded. He carefully shut off the recorder when off-the-record or background material was being given. The State Department also tried to bar him from the news meetings of other nations. However, he threw protocol for a loss by getting permission directly from the delegations involved."

Drew Pearson, in his "Washington Merry-Go-Round" column, reported to the nation on Hofheinz's activities at the conference. He noted that several hundred of the recorders had been ordered by foreign governments before the Judge had left San Francisco. Hofheinz's trip established his station as an enterprising news media, and General Electric had made a profitable experimental deal with the right man.

The second big event which endeared the Judge's station to a growing audience came when a devastating Gulf hurricane struck the Texas coast area on August 26 and 27, 1945. Advance warnings of the hurricane, which killed three, injured many, and caused $20,133,000 in damages, spurred Hofheinz to assemble his staff hurriedly to plan coverage. Where the advancing hurricane would hit was not definite, but if high winds and rain struck the Houston area, Hofheinz wanted to be prepared.

Throwing out the regular schedule, KTHT concentrated on the storm. About 600,000 persons followed the coverage with nervous, almost breathless, interest. KTHT did what no Houston competitor attempted to do and what no radio station had ever done: it gave the people of the Houston area a first-hand account of riding out a tropical hurricane with winds blowing at 100 miles per hour.

Throughout the afternoon and night, KTHT broadcast emergency announcements. These included those from the Red Cross, the Harris County Volunteer Emergency Services, bulletins on streets that were impassable or dangerous, announcements by the city police, and bulletins from the highway patrol where announcer Von Reece was stationed. Max Jacobs, Hofheinz's longtime friend, and in 1945 a public relations counsel, radio commentator, and news correspondent, was recruited to supervise the coverage and to interview officials from stricken areas. Dick Altman, program director, covered reports from throughout the Houston area. In shirt sleeves, Hofheinz for 16 consecutive hours directed the staff, arranged special lines and broadcasts, and interviewed officials and civic leaders of stricken areas. Francis Gilbert made 23 broadcasts directly from the Weather Bureau. Ross Smitherman interviewed refugees of the storm and made them feel at home at Houston's Sam Houston Coliseum. Evelyn Cotner and Lillian Killough remained all night at the switchboard to give special information to callers, who jammed trunk lines for 12 hours. John Pace, KTHT salesman, and others of the staff spent the day advising Houston merchants of the storm's progress. Louis Jelly and Jayne McCorkle operated controls as KTHT broadcast the only storm report direct from Houston. The reports were carried on the Texas State Network, which Hofheinz had joined.

Hofheinz later received numerous letters praising the station's coverage of the storm. The nation's radio editors, in their annual poll, cited KTHT for public service. KTHT's unparalleled coverage of the storm was acclaimed also by officials of governmental agencies and civic leaders of Houston as an outstanding public service.

The third big news event which made KTHT a leader in its field came in April of 1947 when disaster struck Texas City, a port next to Galveston, 50 miles south of Houston. The French ship, *Grandcamp*, which had arrived at the pier across from the Monsanto Chemical Company, had exploded. When news of the explosion reached Houston, Ben Kaplan, KTHT's news editor, Bill Guy, an announcer, and O. B. Johnson were sent to Texas City. The station manager called Hofheinz in Washington to tell him of the disaster. The Judge, in the capital seeking other radio permits, flew home and commanded the weeklong coverage. All radio commercials were cancelled, and the station remained on the air 24 hours a day, giving graphic details of the continuing holocaust in which 461 persons died, 115 were reported missing, and 4000 injured. Property damage to the surrounding area was estimated to be $67 million. Engineer Johnson recalled the scene vividly:

> There was a lot of confusion. I don't remember any single thing outstanding except the big thing—shrapnel was falling, just like it did on Saipan. A steel propellor shaft landed near us. It came from the second ship that exploded. There were huge pieces of metal flying, parts of the hull of the vessel. Shrapnel just came down all around us in the lot beside us. I didn't get hurt. I was used to hitting the deck and I knew when to do it when I heard that second explosion. Ben Kaplan was going out to where he could look at the lit-up scenery. I pulled him down. I said, "Stand by for shrapnel," and it came. Right there—just bing, bing, bing, all around us.

KTHT's play-by-play reporting of the disaster gave Houstonians a front seat in a theater of death. Hofheinz personally went to the scene to do some announcing, and he appealed for money to aid disaster victims. KTHT raised more than $85,000 of the $689,000 contributed by various sources during the next month for relief work in the stricken city. "Roy was a tremendous innovator of news coverage," Kaplan recalled in 1979 after a long career in reporting and public relations.

Nonie Hofheinz traveled between Houston, Beaumont, and Port Arthur during her son's years as county judge. He continued her support. She was stricken at the Yorktown home and taken to Greenwood Sanitorium in Houston where she died July 17, 1945, of a cerebral hemorrhage at age 59. The Judge's grief was great, but his plunge into radio ownership kept him from dwelling on memories of the first woman who told him he was on the road to greatness.

Although pleased with his outstanding achievements in radio in such a short time, Hofheinz continued to look to the future. To obtain a signal as strong as his competitors, Hofheinz applied to the FCC for frequency 790 and 5000 watts of power and for a license for a frequency modulation (FM) station. Some engineers felt FM would revolutionize radio because it gave a clearer signal than AM. Meanwhile, the Judge suggested to his cronies that, since he was applying for a new frequency, it might be well for them to apply for 1230 which he would have to abandon if he moved his station down the dial. Leon Green, Bailey Swenson, Max Jacobs, Douglas Hicks, and Fred Harling took his advice. Hofheinz's application for 790 was immediately opposed by two applicants from Lubbock, Texas, the Lubbock County Broadcasting Company and Plains Radio Broadcasting Company. The Lubbock County Broadcasting Company was composed of G. H. Nelson, Wendell Mayes, and C. C. Woodson. Mayes was a former mayor of Brownwood, Texas, and owner of Station KBWD there, and was part owner of WACO in Waco and WNOW in Austin. Woodson was publisher of the *Brownwood Bulletin*. Nelson was a former district attorney and state auditor in Lubbock. The other applicant, Plains Radio Broadcasting Company of Amarillo, owned KFYO in Lubbock and KGNC in Amarillo and principally was owned by Globe Publishing Company of Amarillo. Principals were Gene Howe, president of the Amarillo *Globe News*; Parker Prouty, manager of the Lubbock *Avalance* and *Journal*; and O. L. "Ted" Taylor, executive manager of KFYO, KGNC, and KTSA in San Antonio, KRGV, Weslaco, Texas, KTOK in Oklahoma City, and KANS in Wichita, Kansas. Taylor also was one-third partner in Taylor Howe Snowden Radio Sales Representatives. There also was a competing Houston applicant, Lee Segall, an advertising man and creator of radio's "Dr. I.Q.," who already had a license for KIXL in Dallas. Still other competing applicants were WEAU in Eau Claire, Wisconsin, controlled by Morgan Murphy, owner of WEBC, Duluth; MDFG, Hibbing, Minnesota; WRLB, Virginia, Minnesota; WDGL, Superior, Wisconsin; and KVOL in Lafayette, Louisiana.

Hofheinz filed one of the most extensive and impressive documents ever seen by the FCC. The application, rather than the typed-in printed form filed by the average applicant, was a mammoth 300-page volume bound in saddle leather, hand-sewn, and engraved in 14-carat gold. It was the greatest "pitch-kit" Hofheinz had designed until that time. During the proceedings before the FCC, Hofheinz served as his own counsel, unlike most applicants who usually hired one of the many professional radio attorneys practicing in Washington. Hofheinz was determined to wage his own battle, a move which was so unusual and dramatic that it caused the FCC to delay a decision on the case for one year. It was in May of 1947 that KTHT was granted 790 kilocycles with 5000 watts. The FCC also granted Hofheinz's cronies a permit to operate on 1230.

American Broadcasting Company, which owned and operated KECA in Los Angeles, filed a petition in the U.S. Court of Appeals for the District of Columbia alleging that permission by FCC for KTHT to operate on 5000 watts at night would set up interference in Los Angeles to KECA, which also operated on 5000 watts with the same frequency. ABC was represented by a battery of three highly paid Washington attorneys, while Hofheinz represented himself, working from a coffee table in a Washington hotel room. After one of the biggest "paper wars" in the history of the Appelate Court, the court upheld Hofheinz. It was February of 1948 when all barriers to KTHT 790 were shattered.

When KTHT switched from 1230 to 790 and his friends took over 1230 as Station KNUZ, Hofheinz received permission from the FCC, through Red James, to operate both stations for 24 hours. KNUZ announcers told all listeners "to switch your dial to 790 if you want to continue hearing programs which have been on this channel." James said the new KNUZ operators temporarily "were furious that KTHT was permitted to try to carry its ready-made audience to another channel."

While the KTHT 790 case was being fought through the FCC and the Appeals Court, Hofheinz, as an aside, had been pushing through a permit for the construction of a new 468,000-watt frequency modulation station in Houston. FM had come to the fore just before World War II, during which it was developed for military use. After several months of engineering revisions and modifications to solve newly developed conditions, the permit finally was granted in early 1946. Equipment for FM stations was practically nonexistent. There was a copper shortage. No manufacturer had a tried, tested, ready transmitter available. It was a new field plagued by scarcities. Nevertheless, Hofheinz made up his mind to have the first FM station in Texas. He started a little late. Seven other applicants scattered across the state already had had permits for more than a year. The Judge plunged into a "first FM" fight. Running up an $800 telephone bill in a few days in coast-to-coast efforts to locate scarce items, Hofheinz resolutely piled up needed pieces of equipment. In just 15 days, he had an FM station on the air. On August 21, 1946, KTHT-FM changed its call letters to KOPY and inaugurated daily service from 3:00 P.M. to 9:00 P.M. Initially, public reaction to FM was mixed. There was enthusiasm over the clear reception, especially for musical programs.

Hofheinz quickly rose to national prominence in FM radio when he was elected president of the newly organized Frequency Modulation Association at its convention in Washington in January of 1947. The association established offices in Washington and had about 200 members while Hofheinz served in this post for two years. "KTHT-FM will be on a self-sustaining basis from the first minute on the air," Hofheinz told a *Broadcasting* reporter. "We intend to prove that FM broadcasting can be a profitable venture." Once again, future years would prove Hofheinz correct.

In March of 1946, Hofheinz hired an assistant, John Stephen, to help him with his plans for a chain of radio stations. While in Austin, Stephen was co-founder of "Radio House," the university's original student broadcast facility. He also taught radio broadcasting in the school of arts and sciences and was news editor of the old Texas Broadcasting System. John Connally, a classmate of Stephen, recommended that Hofheinz hire Stephen when he returned from Navy service in the Pacific. "With my background, Roy and I were meant for each other," Stephen said in 1979. "I was originally assistant to the president, later variously a secretary, vice-president, and was in other corporate capacities in the various radio companies Roy was to acquire. I also was general manager of KOPY. In 1950 we formed the law partnership of Hofheinz and Stephen, which functioned until 1954. I was executive assistant to Mayor Hofheinz from

1953 to 1956 and also special counsel to the City of Houston during the same period." Hofheinz and Stephen fought many radio and city government battles together.

Hofheinz continued to innovate in the world of radio. When the national Republican and Democratic nominating conventions were scheduled for Philadelphia during the summer of 1948, Hofheinz moved to prove again that an independent local station could do more than play recorded music and rebroadcast network programs. With the assistance of a staff which included an expert cabinetmaker, Stuart Young, an architect, Bailey Swenson, and two professional engineers, he designed a special "cruising radio studio." The unit, costing $25,000, was a complete radio station on wheels. With the unit, it was possible to proceed into an emergency area, and its unique weather station was licensed by the U.S. Weather Bureau to report official weather and to broadcast continuously without electrical connections, telephone lines, or other aids. The unit also was prepared to house and sleep its operators. Hofheinz first used the mobile studio to cover the 1948 Republican National Convention, parking the curious facility near Independence Hall in Philadelphia. "As the convention moved along, the Judge had runners going in and out of the hall with news to be broadcast back home," O. B. Johnson recalled. "We kept a pretty hot line. The unit attracted great attention, for it was unprecedented for a little radio station to be broadcasting as well as the networks."

After the opening convention, the KTHT entourage went to New York and parked at Radio City for a week. Radio industry officials and curious New Yorkers were amazed at the mobile unit. After the Democratic convention was covered on the return to Philadelphia, Hofheinz took his unique studio to Washington where members of the Federal Communications Commission and federal officials inspected it—and enjoyed the taste of top Texas food furnished by Hofheinz.

In early 1947 Hofheinz began expanding his ownership of radio stations by looking toward the vast Rio Grande Valley. Hofheinz's interest in the area dated back to his days as a county judge when he frequently traveled to Brownsville and other points to talk about problems of juvenile delinquency. At this time, the Valley did not have much radio service, and the Judge knew it. There were small stations in Brownsville, Weslaco, and Harlingen, but none of them served the entire Valley. Even the high-powered regional stations in San Antonio and Corpus Christi did not broadcast clearly into the Valley, and Mexican stations were heard only sporadically and weakly. What was needed, reasoned Hofheinz, was a station which would serve the function of an All-Valley voice.

When Hofheinz filed an application for a new 50,000-watt radio station located at Harlingen, radio professionals were astounded. Harlingen then was a small, sleepy Texas town of 15,000 people. Never in the history of broadcasting had there been a 50,000-watt station in a city of less than 100,000 people. But Hofheinz was determined to get his station. When confronted by amazed industry representatives, he supported his position by saying, "I believe in Texas. And I believe in Texas' Rio Grande Valley. It is one of the last frontiers in this country for free enterprise and development. The Valley needs a station which will serve its entire length—from Brownsville to Mission. I propose to give it that station."

Old and skeptical station operators shook their heads. Not many seasoned observers conceded Hofheinz had any chance for favorable commission action. Hofheinz at last had filed an application which was not met with an immediate rash of competing applications. No one wanted to compete for this one. Despite the fact that the application was unopposed, more than a year elapsed before the FCC decided to approve the application. The fight, which had not developed on application for the station, promptly developed when Hofheinz's application in Harlingen was granted.

Shortly after the grant of the application was announced by the FCC, an opposing petition was filed by L. B. Wilson, Incorporated, licensee of Station WCKY in Cincinnati. The powerful station, heard in 34 states and specializing in late-night musical shows, claimed that the operation of the new Harlingen station would interfere with its signal in Oklahoma, Missouri, and Iowa. Rather than endure another long procedure of a court appeal, with its attendant waste of time, Hofheinz acceded to the demands of WCKY and changed the night power of his proposed station to 10,000 watts. Practically this offered no great loss to Hofheinz's plans, for the same area still would be covered by the Harlingen station with a signal stronger than any other station in the Valley. The skirmish with WCKY, however, had consumed another year of Hofheinz's time. Not until February of 1949 were all objections finally removed and approval of Hofheinz's application finalized.

Even with the grant in his pocket, Hofheinz still faced a hard struggle to get his station on the air. He wanted a new, modern studio and office in Harlingen. A large tract of land on a heavily traveled thoroughfare was purchased, and plans were drawn by Bailey Swenson. But those plans hinged on the Harlingen City Council and Hofheinz's ability to convince them to abandon construction of a street across the selected property. Because of state legal requirements, the street had not been built and Hofheinz prepared to argue successfully the case. During the council meeting, Hofheinz was making his strongest argument favoring his proposed building when one councilman asked if it was true that the street had been put through the property. Most positively not, Hofheinz replied, telling the council that the street was not within four blocks of the property. Much to Hofheinz's surprise, however, the councilman was right. Sometime between Hofheinz's visit to the property the day before and that night, the street had been built. Hofheinz had spent two and one half years to clear the way for a station which had no competing application. But he was beaten by a bulldozer. Another location was selected.

Hofheinz was not set back by the defeat in Harlingen. His radio operations spread into Alabama in a short time. Birmingham millionaire, Thomas N. Beach, a prominent mortgage banker, started station WTNB in 1946. A stranger to the broadcasting business, Beach cast about for a partner who knew the game. He did not know Hofheinz, but in the course of his inquiries among radio men, he met with a single answer: the man with the magic radio touch was the Judge. Hofheinz accepted Beach's offer, and soon the two men formed the Pilot Broadcasting Corporation. Eventually, Beach tired of the radio business, and Hofheinz, with George Mattison, his Birmingham business associate, bought control of WTNB and changed its name to WILD. While in Birmingham establishing sales techniques for the WILD staff, Hofheinz met and hired radio announcer Loel Passe, who became one of his closest and most loyal employees for more than a quarter century.

Following the success of their first radio enterprise, KTHT, Hofheinz and Dick Hooper also won permits from the FCC to construct powerful stations in New Orleans and Dallas. It took the men four years to get the New Orleans permit and two years to get one for Dallas, battling powerful radio and business interests along the way. Jesse Jones fought the permit requested for the Dallas station, and Louisiana interests confronted Hofheinz in New Orleans. Hofheinz derived great satisfaction from gaining the Dallas permit because in so doing he defeated the powerful Jones.

Dating back to the early days when Hofheinz had tried to break up the Houston radio monopoly Jones enjoyed, Hofheinz and the *Chronicle* owner had battled. Having failed to keep him out of Houston's radio world, the former Secretary of Commerce had "put screws on in every possible way to stymie my radio operations," Hofheinz said. KTRH, Jones' powerful 50,000-watt station in Houston, operated on the 740 signal broadcasting an east-west signal. Hofheinz's crew, however, found that frequency 740 in Dallas was open for development and Hofheinz set out to show his most formidable adversary, Jones, he could get it. Faced with numerous FCC applications for the 740 frequency, Jones slipped into the picture, proposing that the FCC allow him to revamp the daytime operation of KTRH in Houston, a move which would end the Dallas efforts of Hofheinz. Hofheinz and Jones were set for a head-on collision. Before the FCC hearing, Hofheinz used skillful legal maneuvers to prove that the KTRH proposal meant a loss of broadcast service to 83,000 persons to the west of Houston. Consequently, the KTRH case against Hofheinz went up in thin smoke.

One other radio station, KSEO of Durant, Oklahoma, also opposed Hofheinz's application, but the defeat of KSEO came more easily for Hofheinz than the challenge posed by Jones. KSEO claimed Hofheinz's proposed Dallas operation would seriously interfere with its broadcasts and ruin its operation. When the Oklahoma station argued that it was entitled to protection of the Texas area that received its signal, Hofheinz proved it wrong. He convinced the FCC that his proposed station would serve Texas listeners, something the station did not attempt to do. Hofheinz made his point, and the FCC once again granted another Hofheinz request.

Because of mounting financial needs, he ultimately gave up his permits for Dallas and New Orleans stations. Meanwhile, Hofheinz continued to improve the operation of KTHT. Because its quarters at the Southern Building were too small for AM and FM stations, the Judge set up an office in the old South End Christian Church on South Main Street which eventually was renovated into a modern radio center. Hofheinz again called on the expertise of his friends, Stuart Young and Bailey Swenson, to carry out his remodeling ideas. Swenson recalled, "Roy called me out to the old church one morning and said he wanted to start work. Roy, as usual, wanted to do the job in a hurry. So, I had to draw on a piece of sheet rock with a stick of black crayon details of how to build control room windows with three layers of glass with jams to prevent vibration. I didn't help Roy much on assembling what equipment he needed for remodeling. He did that on his own."

With Hofheinz's guidance, Young and Swenson built "by ear" as the new radio home was developed out of that old church. Finally, in January of 1950, Hofheinz was ready to show off his remodeled studios. Frank White, president of the Mutual Broadcasting System, came to Houston to dedicate the new station. Pete Johnson, vice-president in charge of engineering for Mutual, observed that Hofheinz "not only has made proper use of 200 different shades of paint and paper, but has made a superb use of sound technical principles to achieve the maximum fidelity of acoustical reproduction which is a goal of every good broadcaster."

In January of 1950, after only five years in the radio business, with real estate and slag investments—and only 37 years old—Roy Hofheinz was a millionaire. Regardless of his business enterprises and financial status, he never lost his interest in politics and public service. In 1950, however, he was not quite ready to return to the political arena. Television was beginning to capture the nation's attention, and Hofheinz wanted to be a part of that.

16

Yorktown and
"Huckster House"

In a letter to Hofheinz in October of 1943, Lieutenant Leon Green wrote from Alaska: "Had a letter from one of our mutual friends stating that you bought a large farm. Although I don't like milk much, I still would like to taste a glass of milk, especially one that you yourself milked. With a farm, pigs, and chickens, I'll bet you are plenty busy these days." Green was referring to the Yorktown tract west of downtown Houston which Hofheinz bought when he sold his "Ship Shack" on Galveston Bay and his home on West Oaks. This proved a valuable homestead. Hofheinz figured that the undeveloped area about 10 miles from Harris County Courthouse ultimately would be one of the most valuable tracts in the fast-growing city. Again he was right. Yorktown today is off Westheimer Road in the heart of what is known as the "Magic Circle Galleria Area." The famous galleria is only a few blocks from the place where Dene and Roy nurtured their three children and entertained hundreds of friends, business associates, and political colleagues. Yorktown's value grew so fast that it became the strongest spoke in the various financial wheels the Judge was to spin.

From the garage apartment in which the family first lived rather uncomfortably, Yorktown became an elegant two-story residence, gradually built beginning during World War II, when materials were scarce, and continuing into the late 1940s. Stuart Young and Bailey Swenson helped Hofheinz plan the house, which ultimately had a living room, an entertaining room decorated with circus artifacts, dining room and kitchen, bathroom, hall and a glassed-in, octagonal-shaped breakfast room downstairs, and six bedrooms and four baths upstairs. A swimming pool was the last feature added. Today the pool still can be seen near apartment houses on Yorktown Road. The residence was torn down when 82 acres of the property were sold in 1969 for $6,471,233.40

Behind the living quarters, an inevitable big workshop was built. There Hofheinz planned and Stuart Young built furniture and anything else wanted for the Judge's home, office, and hunting, fishing, and recreation retreats. Yorktown also was an exhibit for the radio age. Aside from a radio in every

Roy and Roy, Jr., in the workshop at Yorktown

room and three television sets, there was a complete short-wave transmitter on which the Judge and his sons could "ham talk" around the globe. Built into the walls was a complete industrial-type, factory intercommunication system with microphones in every room, telephone connections, and radio plugs. Even the bathrooms had microphones. When Leon Green returned from the war, he did not find the farm he had envisioned.

Albert Lopez, a native of Mexico who first went to Detroit to work, but wound up in Houston as a young man, married and the father of three children in 1947, worked for the Hofheinz family the longest of any domestic employee, and he was still by the Judge's side in 1979. He saw the Yorktown home grow from a garage apartment (later torn down) to a center visited by outstanding men and women from all parts of the United States and foreign countries. "After I left Detroit, I went to Houston with my family looking for a job," Lopez recalled. "I lived in a little place in the Yorktown area. . . . One day a lady drove up and stopped by my mailbox and began talking to me. It was Mrs. Dene Hofheinz, who introduced herself. . . . She suggested that if I wanted extra work I could come to Yorktown and help develop the yard. I told my wife and she said, 'You don't know those Hofheinzes; get the job you want.' But the applications didn't bring me a job. The next time I met Mrs. Hofheinz at the mailbox, I told her my situation and she said for me to come to the house and start mowing grass. . . . I went to work the next day and to show I wasn't lazy, I really pushed myself cutting that big yard." The Judge was impressed, for he hired Albert on a regular basis.

At first, Lopez worked Saturdays and Sundays while doing odd jobs for others during the week. "One day the Judge stopped his car near where I was working," he said, "and asked if I was getting anything to eat and if I weren't, I could go to the kitchen and get what I wanted. . . . He started making me sandwiches—for himself and me. He used to like beer. 'Don't you like beer?' he asked me one day. I said 'No.' I didn't want to show him then that I did drink beer, but later I began accepting his offers." Lopez said he watched the family grow, and the members had a busy but good life. "There wasn't a sweeter lady in the world than Mrs. Dene Hofheinz," he recalled. "If you needed help, she would help, but you had to tell her the truth."

Hofheinz built a small house near his own Yorktown home for Mr. and Mrs. Lopez and their three children. As the family grew to include seven children, the Judge added rooms to their abode. The Hofheinz and Lopez children played together. Lopez recalled that many other offspring of Hofheinz friends often visited Roy, Jr., Fred, and little Dene, who in later years called herself Dene II.

As Hofheinz bought retreats, Albert Lopez developed the grounds, and he was there when blinds for duck hunting were built. Lopez became a horticultural artist and in 1979 was kept busy outside the Hofheinz River Oaks mansion and at the Galveston Bay "Huckster House." When Dene II and Fred first had homes in Houston, he did their yard work, also. "The Judge has been good to me and my family," Lopez said. "He and Mrs. Dene Hofheinz gave my children good clothes, presents, and included us in on Thanksgiving, Christmas, and other special occasions. There never was anything pretentious about them. They paid me well and encouraged us to be good citizens and treated us almost like their own family. They appreciated anyone willing to work and do it well, and I did my best. When my son, Adam, married, Fred Hofheinz was present as recognition of the friendship of the Hofheinzes and Lopezes."

The most dramatic story involving the friendship of the two men came in September of 1978 when the Judge was in retirement at his River Oaks home. Recalled Lopez:

> I have a brother, Leon, who likes to go to Mexico every chance he gets. He and his wife went to a little town, and their car and another were involved in a bad accident. My brother was taken to a little hospital, and after an operation there, the doctors said he was going to die if he didn't get further expert medical attention somewhere. The Mexican doctors said they'd try to operate

Albert Lopez

again, but weren't sure of success—my brother might die in four hours. They said the best thing to do was to fly him to the United States in a plane with oxygen. I was called in Houston by my brother's wife, and I drove across the border in a hurry. I found my brother in bad, bad shape. I tried Mexico City, Monterrey, and Guadalajara on the phone seeking airplane help, but no luck. My wife said, "Albert, you've never bothered the Judge for one penny. You call him and tell him the situation you're in." Instead I called my daughter, Martha, who works at Diagnostic Hospital, and asked her to call the Judge. She reached him—it was on Saturday about 3:00 P.M. She called us back about 3:45 P.M. and said, "Wait there for a jet from Houston to pick up your brother. The Judge is sending one!" I almost fell over with joy. The jet came from Houston, picked up my brother, and had him in the Diagnostic Hospital by 7:00 P.M. He stayed in the hospital under expert care for a month and a half.

Lopez felt he should make arrangements to pay for the jet flight which saved his brother's life. "In late October after my brother was on his feet again," he said, "I went to talk with the Judge about the expense. He listened and then waited before saying anything. Finally, he said, gruffly, 'Don't be expecting any Christmas bonus this year. You've got yours.' You know how the Judge talks— tough, but he has a big heart. I just went up to the Judge as he sat unsmiling in his wheelchair and gave him a big kiss. He had saved my brother's life and didn't want any repayment for what he had spent."

Roy Hofheinz's affection for his three children and his wife constantly was evident. Although the Judge was tied up with business from early morning until midnight, he found time, especially on weekends, to be with them. Preserved in the Hofheinz files is a letter Roy, Jr.—Butch—wrote. Dated December 2, 1941, and written in block letters, it said:

> Dear Santa:
> Please send my brother and me some house slippers, cowboy boots, tinker-toys, tool chests, and Snippie electric scissors. We would also like to have paint sets, clay modeling sets, a blackboard, and some Victrola records. Spud [Fred] wants an English tricycle, and I want a scooter, also a coal bin for my electric train. A Merry Christmas and a Happy New Year to you.
>
> Butch Hofheinz

The family was living in the West Oaks home then. Judge Hofheinz wrote the postmaster at Santa Claus, Indiana, and asked him to mail the following letter:

> North Pole
> December 11, 1941
>
> Dear Butch Hofheinz:
> Your long letter came to me today. My little book shows that you have been a pretty good boy, but there is some room for improvement. Your brother, Spud, has been a pretty good boy, but he, too, can be better between now and Christmas.
> You and your brother certainly do want plenty. I do not know that I will have enough toys to go around to everybody and still give you everything you want, but if you and your brother continue to be good boys and get no black marks between now and Christmas, I will do my best to bring you what you want. If you are good boys, you will know that you have been on Christmas morning when you wake up, and if you are not real good boys you will find that out, too.
> Your friend and the friend of all good little boys.
>
> Santa Claus

The brothers got almost everything they wanted. They were not docile—just active, normal boys with a father who was continually before the public and eager to have his sons get into the spotlight with him. Hofheinz's desire to give them and their younger sister the best was one motive for his leaving politics at the end of 1944 for eight years.

The three children were outstanding, but they needed the daily discipline of Dene to keep them in line. They could have made their way well without parental help, but time proved that the Judge's ability to earn would also put them in the wealthy class as adults. Fred Hofheinz recalled that "Dad was always a great sports fan. I remember virtually every Rice Institute football game we attended. It was a regular Saturday affair for the family. . . . Dad loved the excitement of baseball, too. He used to take me to games. . . . Dad taught me football and baseball, and he gave me a sports-minded bent. . . ." Fred also recalled that his older brother "got all the lessons. By the time it got to me, it had all been filtered through and was all rather general. . . . I remember the encouragement he gave my brother to learn how to speak and think on his feet. . . . He pressed me and my brother hard on debate and speech and on those things he thought were important parts of education. He used to say, 'It's more important how you say something than what you say.' "

Little Dene in 1979 recalled when she was the baby of the family at Yorktown: "I was reared on cigar smoke, and the first band I ever had put on my finger was a paper cigar band from Dad's cigar. It sort of became a ritual with us when he'd undo a new cigar. . . . I was the baby of the family, and I guess there's just no way around it. I was in every way treated like a baby. . . . I enjoyed being the daughter of Dene and Roy Hofheinz. It would almost be hard to say which I enjoyed being the most, but Father was bigger than life to me." Of the three children, it was Dene II who stayed closest to her father in the year following her mother's death.

After he sold "Ship Shack" on Galveston Bay, Hofheinz looked for another place he could buy as a retreat for his family and friends and for entertaining his mounting list of radio advertisers and real estate developers. He did not like to give cocktail parties, luncheons, and dinners at Houston hotels and restaurants for business purposes. He preferred a place where he could cook, entertain informally, and show off the joys of boating, fishing, and bathing in his pool and in Galveston Bay.

In June of 1950, he found an old house on the highest ridge in Galveston overlooking the bay. He paid $4500 down and gave a note for $8000 for the property. It became "Huckster House," and within a few years, the Judge had spent more than $100,000 in developing it into a showplace for entertaining political, civic, and business figures from throughout the country. He and Dene furnished it with antiques and circus artifacts gathered from around the world, worth more than the property itself. Built about 1894 and loaded with gingerbread popular during that period, it is one of the oldest houses on the bay, having withstood the ravages of the severe hurricanes of 1900, 1915, and 1941 and the extremely high lashing tides of "Carla" in 1961. From the bay side it looks like a fairy tale house with a porch wrapping around that side. On one end of the porch is a big gazebo with an onion-shaped roof going up to a point, and on the other end is a Victorian-looking turret soaring to the sky. Spoolly fretwork banisters and decorations are everywhere. When finished, "Huckster House" was a Shangri La for Roy's and Dene's friends and business associates to enjoy. The huge, triple, front and back doors can be pushed aside so that the Gulf breeze blows through the house.

On the bay side is a big room called the "South Seas Lounge." Its island decor features strawpaper and bamboo on one wall and a jungle print paper with lemons, oranges, and bananas on another. Rattan sofas are covered in a specially printed matching fabric. Great old shutters that have been in the house all along are painted bright yellow, and the window frames are bright orange, picking up the colors in the wallpaper. AstroTurf covers the floor. Dividing this room from the "Gallery" is a big planter which is one of the Judge's creations. Built of driftwood and cholly cactus and containing artificial plants which grow to the ceiling, the planter was one of Hofheinz's projects when he needed something to do with his hands.

From the "Gallery" one walks through an ornate fretwork arch into what the Judge calls the "Circus Room." It has a red and white striped circus tent for a ceiling, clowns and balloons on the walls, and a big sign over the triple door which reads "The Greatest Show on Earth." One wall is covered with priceless circus posters displayed in a montage style. There is a grand old Seeburg player piano with an art glass front. Antique arcade machines include an old baseball game, a Davy Crockett rifle gallery, a William Super Star baseball pinball machine, and a "Test Your Sex Appeal" machine. There is a Seeburg nickelodeon which holds all the old "big band" favorites from the 1940s, 1950s, and 1960s, as well as hit records written by "Little Dene." There are three old organs formerly used by organ grinders. On one side of the room is a complete soda fountain which was built by Stuart Young. To the side of that and on the wall is a giant antique roulette wheel. The light fixtures hanging from the ceiling are big white glass balls painted with circus clown faces.

Adjacent to the "Circus Room" is a bathroom named "The Hofheinz Opera House" which boasts a seating capacity of one. Old theater handbills decorate the walls, and there is a "show-biz" mirror encircled by lights. Another bathroom off the "Circus Room" is named "Tin Pan Alley" and is decorated with old sheet music; it features musical notes for door pulls, and a banjo, a violin, and other musical instruments are displayed on one wall there.

There are four bedrooms downstairs. The "French Room" has a massive, ornate French bed of hammered brass and is covered with a purple quilted bedspread. There is a gold lamé cornice board over the bed with a crown in the center and purple fringe along the bottom. On one wall is a hand-painted scene of Paris. Colors in this room are tones of green and purple, and windows sport white, lacy curtains. The "Gay Nineties Room" has a wonderful old brass bed, and antique valentines in ornate frames fill the wall behind it. The wicker sofa, dressing table and mirror, table, and dressmaker form—the base of a lamp— are all antiqued white. The entire front wall, which takes the shape of a gazebo porch outside, is covered with the house's original shutters; they are painted mint green. Pastel butterflies dance on the wallpaper in back of the bed and cover the ceiling. Pastel candystripe wallpaper covers the other two walls, and the floor is carpeted in lavender. The "Harem Room" is done in red and black and has a giant, carved wooden bed lacquered black with gold leaf accents. The border around the room is designed from softly draped fabric sprinkled with glitter and displaying harem boy faces. The "Caribbean Room" has bamboo and straw on the wall in back of the twin beds. The ceilng is hand-blocked native print panels, and the beds have spreads which also are of a native print. Tigers peek out from the jungle print on the walls. On one wall is a mural showing a young man lounging on a crate with his feet up on a rum barrel, on which is painted "Trader Roy's Fine Old Rum," and there is also a topless native girl. The light fixture hanging from the middle of the ceiling fan looks like a small keg and says "Roy's Rum." All of the bedrooms still have their original ceiling fans.

Through the triple doors and down two steps is a huge screened-in dining and recreation area with a brick floor. It overlooks the swimming pool. At one end of the room is a brick fireplace, a big barbecue pit with a stainless steel cover designed by the Judge, and a large charcoal broiler. At the other end of the room and up the steps is a wall painted bright green with yellow stripes and big circus-style block lettering of "Huckster House" over the passageway to the kitchen. Yellow formica-topped picnic tables, and yellow, green, and red rattan chairs are there for eating, playing games, or just daydreaming. Groups of up to 200 people have been fed and entertained here. Above the fireplace is a fiberglass caricature of Roy Hofheinz in his huckster days; he is wearing a red and white sport coat and a Katy straw hat, while smoking a big cigar and waving a cane. It is surrounded by "show-biz" lights. As one enters the house from the screened porch, he sees a sign reading "Welcome to Huckster House, Friends. If there's something you'd like but don't see, keep looking. Roy Hofheinz." Real baseballs are the pulls for the brightly painted green drawers surrounding the wet bar and barbecue pit.

Upstairs, the first room one enters is the "Temple of Chance" with a convertible round pool and poker table in the center of the room. On the ceiling is wallpaper featuring kings, queens, and jokers of playing cards. A big gold horseshoe adorns one wall and painted on it is the message "Dame Fortune is a Cockeyed Wench Who Looks Not Where She Aims." On another wall hangs a sign which reads "21 Delightful Ways to Commit Suicide." There is a beautiful turn-of-the-century Regina music changer with an art glass front. Another table-model Regina sits on a table, along with an old Royal Victrola. An antique barber's chair is covered in red velvet and sits near the door of a small bathroom called the "Artistic Tonsorial Saloon."

One of the large bedrooms upstairs is named the "Brag Room." The walls are pecky cypress, and the wild west decorations in the room include ropes, horseshoes, branding irons, an old wagon wheel, an old skull, and a big brass lighting fixture. On the wooden headboards for the queen-size beds are carved "Here Lies Billy the Kid" and "Here Lies Jesse James." Draped over one headboard is a western saddle, over the other boots and lariat. The bedside tables are made from old powder kegs and the lamps from hubs of wagon wheels. At one end of the room sits a great old gun table, which was a gift from Ben McGuire, Hofheinz's financial consultant. Under each of the four legs is a little shelf on which players could place their guns in order to discourage access to them in case of an argument. On one wall is the original old fireplace from the living room of the house, now moved upstairs and painted to look like an old saloon. Above is a sign which reads "Last Chance Saloon." A painted sign on one side of the mantle shows a piece of cheese with a little rat sitting on top and says "Free Lunch." On the other side is a sign showing a mug of beer; it says "Five Cents."

The long bedroom on the other side of the house is called the "Buccaneer Room." One long wall is painted with the rolling sea and pirate ships. Also on display are a huge, leering pirate's face, a treasure map, and a treasure chest overloaded with jewels. The walls are painted light turquoise, and sisal rope carpets cover the floor. Going up into the turret is a ship's ladder of rope. There is a small door at one end of the room. Its window has bars and is marked "The Brig." This room is painted to give the impression of stone walls. There are four bunk beds hanging down on chains and they have blue and white striped canvas covers which look like bare mattresses. This room is the favorite of almost all children visiting "Huckster House."

17

Super Salesman and Political Enthusiast

Roy Hofheinz's record from the summer of 1944 until 1951, when he was firmly establishing himself as a wealthy citizen, proved him a business phenomenon unsmirched by family or financial scandal. Hofheinz's confidence in himself grew with each success. He was going to run any business in which he was involved, and he would brook no interference. He was arrogant, some thought, in his headlong pursuit of money and fame; ruthless and egotistical, others said, because he would allow no obstacle to block him as he pursued goals; and a genius, his friends said, because he was far ahead of most people in his thinking.

World War II had not ended when Hofheinz got KTHT on the air. Much of the station's time was devoted to military recruiting, defense, and the war effort. Hofheinz sent announcers to the *USS Houston* when a new war bond drive was on. The drive was broadcast direct from the ship at its Houston dock. A memorial plaque honoring the men who lost their lives on the original cruiser *Houston* was unveiled as part of the ceremony marking KTHT's kickoff of the bond rally. KTHT announcers went to defense workers at Houston's largest shipyard for broadcasts to promote the war effort. A shipyard workers' orchestra provided music for the broadcast. Congressman Albert Thomas appeared at that event to talk about Washington's financial needs to prosecute the war. When Houston shipyard workers finished the 300th warship completed in the Houston area, thousands gathered to witness KTHT's ceremonial broadcast of the ship's launching.

On November 14, 1944, just after KTHT began, a special war bond promotion involved giving scarce nylons to women calling in requests for musical selections. The first 20 women to call would receive the much-desired hosiery. In an 18-hour broadcast, KTHT established a new record in bond-buying by this telephone predecessor of today's fund-raising telethons. The war finance committee arranged for a battery of telephones and for 75 Office of Civilian Defense workers to answer calls—plus hundreds in a motor corps organized to pick up pledges and deliver bonds to KTHT listeners. Churches, schools, and fraternal, civic, labor, and political organizations helped KTHT in selling bonds. The result was a $1.2 million sale.

Remembering his tireless work with youth as county judge, Hofheinz placed special focus on girls and boys in KTHT programs. He established "Teen Time" to gain the reputation of "favorite station" among Houston's young people. For example, to focus the attention of teenagers on law enforcement, Hofheinz seized upon human-interest events in the news and built special broadcasts around them. With the cooperation of the Houston Police Department, the station made formal awards of wrist watches to two "junior policemen." Ceremonies honoring them were broadcast. Hofheinz also had local school musical units broadcast to encourage local talent. Teenage style shows, activities of Sea Scouts, Boy Scouts, and Cub Scouts with youngsters participating, amateur hours for young would-be entertainers, Easter egg hunts at Playland Park financed by the station, University of Houston Frontier Days celebrations which involved the "best beard competition" and how participants grew them, battles of high school bands, play-by-play broadcasts of high school football games, auditions for potential entertainment stars, coverage of school spelling bees, journalism discussions by high school editors and reporters—all were part of building a growing audience for the station.

"KTHT Builds a GI House" was a series of 200 programs broadcast twice daily from March 19, 1946, from the site of a test home for returning World War II veterans which KTHT designed and built. Besides endeavoring to build a listening audience, the promotion campaign intended to focus the attention of the entire community on what the mayor and City Council had designated as "Houston's Number 1 Problem in 1946—housing"; to help prospective veteran homebuilders by uncovering and making known to them the home building shortages, black markets, and general construction problems which existed under inflated post-war conditions; and to make a positive contribution to the solution of housing problems by giving all homebuilders and homebuilding associations "laboratory tested" data on home costs and problems. In carrying out the promotion campaign, Hofheinz used every channel of publicity at his disposal—newspapers, magazines, syndicated columns, spot announcements, broadsides, signboards, and tie-ins with veterans' organizations and homebuilding associations. He first made plans for the project with Stephen Tully, director of the Houston office of the Office of Price Administration.

The plan for the "GI House" included a living room, dinette, and kitchen on one side, and two bedrooms and a bath on the other, with a single-car garage and storage room. The house was to be constructed on a $7000 budget in 30 days, if possible, as a practical demonstration to the community of the problems in attempting to secure economical housing quickly. It was not to be a "model home," but rather one which actually reflected inflated costs, material shortages, and other typical problems confronting a prospective GI builder. At no

KTHT's "GI House" was constructed in 42 days at a cost of $7250.

time were black markets patronized. All materials were purchased on the open market by "John Doe" to avoid using the station's influence in acquiring scarce items. Construction throughout was carried out in a manner that a typical home builder would have to rely on.

KTHT purchased a lot at 3818 Rice Boulevard. Veterans' organizations participated in a stake-driving ceremony on March 22, 1946. Dick Altman was key special events reporter for the promotion. Daily broadcasts brought hundreds to watch. David Lucas, commander of the Houston post of the American Legion, took a special interest in the building. On May 27 the house was completed. Due to shortages of materials and labor difficulties, the actual time of construction was 42 days and the total cost $7250, instead of 30 days and $7000. The modest house was opened to public inspection on May 28. More than 5000 visited the home, and thousands more acknowledged the value of information disseminated by the broadcasts and by abstracts of costs and construction data which were given freely to the public.

For this service to his community, Hofheinz was saluted as Houston's "Big Little American" by Morton Downey's "Coca-Cola Club" program on Mutual.

C. Lupton Thomason, Houston manager of Coca-Cola, presented Hofheinz with a scroll at a ceremony in the KTHT studios during the Downey broadcast. Jesse Jones' *Chronicle,* as well as the *Post* and *Press,* found the "GI House" so newsworthy that they carried reports. Homebuilding for veterans in Houston was greatly stimulated. Finally, the City College of New York gave an award of merit to KTHT "for the most effective promotion of a public service radio program for 1946."

Hofheinz's radio station also promoted the Houston Fat Stock Show. His enthusiasm for the show grew year by year, and it later found a home in Astrohall, next to the Astrodome, as a result of a building deal with the Judge. He had only been in the radio business eight months when KTHT began daily special broadcasts of the event. In the 1946 show, Hofheinz bought the champion 4-H Club and Future Farmers' barrow. In the 1947 show, he entered "KTHT Midnight" in the show, and it was a prize winner. Hofheinz saw to the steer's growth and kept it at a friend's farm. Singer Gene Autry, who ultimately got into major league baseball, as did Hofheinz, was hired to appear at one of KTHT's five daily broadcasts during the run of the show.

Openings of new businesses fascinated the Judge, and he sent announcers to tell about them. He did not skip benefit performances of any kind and met comedian Jerry Colonna, who was interviewed at one of them. Later when KTHT's new auditorium was available, Hofheinz put on a "Theater Time Celebrity" series. Movie star Marie McDonald was among the personalities who appeared.

Hofheinz also involved the station in the local political process, setting aside 10 hours of prime time for political broadcasts at no charge to candidates. The Judge, out of office for only a year and a half, announced in June of 1946 that KTHT would sponsor five great radio rallies as a public service for the people of Houston and 10 southeast Texas counties. He said that outdoor rallies would be held every Saturday night in different parts of Houston, and that two of Houston's best-known bands would provide music—with expenses to be borne by KTHT. All 140 candidates responded quickly because all were scrambling for time on the radio to tell their stories. Hofheinz was giving them opportunities for free exposure on important night hours. Price Daniel was a candidate for attorney general, and he showed up to speak at a rally, but Pat Neff, his opponent sent a transcription to be broadcast instead of appearing in person. Representative Albert Thomas, a candidate seeking reelection, also opted for the latter approach. Hundreds turned out for the rallies and thousands listened at home. Hofheinz followed up with special studio broadcasts with runoff candidates debating—at no charge.

Following the rallies, Hofheinz made arrangements with the *Houston Press* to broadcast results of the November general election. He hired students to man precincts. The *Press* did the same. Working out of the *Press* newsroom from 10:00 A.M., the students received early results from various precincts. A leased wire to the Texas Election Bureau in Dallas brought in state results. Mutual's network commentators were advertised as coverage participants. Hofheinz worked for 18 hours giving political sidelights and analyzing the trends of voting. He knew every precinct and he could quickly determine who was winning. American General Insurance Company and City National Bank sponsored the election returns as a public service. There was no doubt that KTHT won the greatest audience that night. Quick local and state returns set a pattern many local stations and newspapers were to follow in the years ahead. KTHT then was still on 1230, but its public service election efforts no doubt were partly responsible for the later decision to go to 790 and become more powerful.

Hofheinz also took the lead in live baseball broadcasting in 1951 by offering play-by-play action from the Texas League. Bill Bennett recalled that "the Judge worked his way into the top brass of both the AFL and CIO unions and obtained permission to go to their meetings in an effort to sell the rank-and-file on the idea of sponsoring baseball. He said the press always printed 'bad things' unions did, seldom said anything good about them. After every presentation to the various unions, the Judge actually got standing ovations for his eloquent talk and new ideas. It would cost the unions, the Judge figured, $85,000 to $100,000 a year to sponsor half of Mutual's major league game-of-the-week output." The unions signed the contracts, much to the surprise of Hofheinz's assistant, John Stephen.

Later the Judge discovered that Ford Motor Company and the Houston area Ford Dealers Association had money for advertising which they were saving until the market became more competitive. Hofheinz learned that these funds would become taxable in certain parts of the country. Thus he was able to make a good case for the Ford dealers' spending the money. "At that time," Bennett recalled, "both KLEE and KATL stations carried delayed play-by-play telegraphic reports of Houston Buffs games at night. With Mutual's game of the day on in the afternoons, we felt that we could make our audience even more baseball-minded by carrying the night Buffs contests live, which would put us ahead of the other stations and certainly would give us more lively accounts. Because the other stations had beer sponsors for their games, the Judge told the Ford dealers' committee, with members from Houston to Corpus Christi and the Valley, that families at night would rather listen to broadcasts sponsored by Ford than by beer companies. He convinced every member of the Ford dealers to vote for live night baseball sponsorship. As soon as we went on the air with live broadcasts and Loel Passe adding 'home town enthusiasm' to his accounts, the other stations tried to follow suit, but they were too late. We had the audience, and they finally dropped baseball." When KSOX in Harlingen began operating, the baseball broadcasts were carried there, too.

In the summer of 1948, Joe Louis Holiday graduated from high school and applied to KTHT for a job. Black, intelligent, and ambitious, he impressed the Judge with his speech and manners and was hired to be a "Man Friday" to the station owner. "The Judge and I hit it off pretty good from the beginning," Holiday recalled in 1978 after he left the Hofheinz entourage following more than a quarter of a century of service. "He couldn't work without a 'pitch-kit.' So, if he was selling a Budweiser sponsor, I put Budweiser in his office refrigerator. When he brought Budweiser people in, I opened the refrigerator and they saw nothing but their beer. An hour later he might have Falstaff people in. I'd do a quick-change and when the refrigerator opened, there was nothing but Falstaff there. I didn't dare be late with anything he wanted. He was a perfectionist."

Throughout his radio, mayoral, Astrodome, and Astrodomain years, Hofheinz had Holiday on call, day and night, sometimes 18 hours at a time. Holiday, like Albert Lopez, the Hofheinz home maintenance man, became a member of the trusted inner circle of Hofheinz associates. No one dared turn up his eyebrows when Joe accompanied Hofheinz to any business, civic, or social function in Houston and on foreign trips. Theirs was a sad business farewell in 1973 when Holiday and another Hofheinz trusty clashed. However, even after his retirement to River Oaks, one of the Judge's most frequent visitors was Joe, who bought Yellow Cabs and made good money to add to the home and savings Hofheinz had helped him gain during his long service.

Holiday's admiration for Dene Hofheinz was as great as that for the Judge. One day in 1948, she drove to KTHT in a new Cadillac. "The Judge rushed out to her," Holiday recalled, "and told her to get out and let him have the car—he had to go to Harlingen in a hurry. 'Get a way home,' he said, and off he went. I took her home. She wasn't upset at being so abruptly treated—she knew her husband. I never saw Mrs. Dene upset in my whole life. She was the only one who could really handle him then."

Hofheinz visited Harlingen frequently when KSOX was under construction. He first set up an old quonset hut on barren, sandy land and often got into work clothes as he and engineers worked on directional problems so that his station could get a signal across the valley. When he finally was ready to open the station, he hired a pilot with a monoplane to fly all over the area dropping little socks with "Listen to KSOX" imprinted on them.

When Representative Lyndon Johnson decided in the spring of 1948 to run for the United States Senate a second time, he again appointed Hofheinz his south Texas manager. Hofheinz had helped carry Harris County in 1941. Johnson trailed Coke Stevenson, a former governor, in the first primary and faced an uphill battle to win the runoff scheduled in August. Although he had to observe FCC rules about time on the air for political opponents, Hofheinz had the KTHT auditorium, which was an ideal spot for Johnson rallies. Again

Hofheinz spoke eloquently for his longtime Washington friend and said he had been cheated out of the senate seat in 1941 by illegal east Texas last-minute votes. Johnson often was in Hofheinz's home and the KTHT offices during that hectic campaign.

When Hofheinz went to Philadelphia with his special studio on wheels to broadcast Democratic convention proceedings that summer, he was able, inadvertently, to give a big Texas radio plug for Johnson. Recalling it, Red James, who had bird-dogged political leaders for Hofheinz interviews, said that he cornered his political friend, Senator Lister Hill of Alabama, who had nominated Franklin Delano Roosevelt for his third term in 1940. Hill also was a good friend of Lyndon Johnson. James said, "Lister asked me if he could get in a good plug for Lyndon when Roy interviewed him. I said 'Sure, put it right in your talk.' Roy's banker friend, Judge Elkins, and his radio partner, Dick Hooper, were supporters of Coke Stevenson. They listened in Houston as Hofheinz brought out Senator Hill's roles in the party. Toward the last three minutes, Lister looked at me and I nodded. He suddenly said, 'I hope the good people down in Texas will elect my dear friend, Lyndon Johnson, to the United States Senate. Senator Johnson would be a tower of strength for them in the Senate with me.' "

Judge Elkins sent Hofheinz a telegram blistering him because it was the bank's money which sponsored the broadcast. Bill Bennett, KTHT's general manager in Houston, got a call from Hooper asking what was going on. Bennett said he thought it was just a gratuitous circumstance. James was told Hooper replied to him, "No, I tell you what it was, by God; it was that Red James who planted it." James admits that "he guessed right, for Roy really didn't know that Hill was going to boost Johnson." Hofheinz chuckled about it later when explanations partly cooled off Elkins and Hooper.

Bill Bennett recalled that when Hofheinz got through introducing Johnson at rallies, "Roy got the applause because he could talk rings around LBJ. Johnson was slow drawn and Hofheinz rapid fire, and when the two got through a rally, you'd swear it was the Judge running for office and not the man who became president. Roy could get a crowd into a real lather. He just told listeners what a great man Johnson was, and you'd think it was the Second Coming. I think the Judge really got Johnson elected with his big vote in Harris County."

Houston Chronicle editor Everett Collier had vivid recollections of the 1948 Stevenson-Johnson campaign. Jesse Jones' paper threw its support to Stevenson and assigned Collier to cover the campaign for the newspaper and its radio station, KTRH. "I remember at the outset," he said, "that Johnson, in Roy Hofheinz's presence at the Rice Hotel, stuck his nose next to mine, as he was wont to do, and told me that he got cheated out of the 1941 race and never again would he let himself be cheated out because he felt he had honestly won in 1941.

I think that sentiment had a lot to do with what Roy and Johnson did in 1948."

When 2000 Texas Democratic Convention delegates met at the Will Rogers Auditorium in Fort Worth after Johnson had been declared an 87-vote winner over Stevenson in unofficial Texas Election Bureau figures, Collier and Hofheinz were there as reporters eager to broadcast whether disputed figures from Boss Archie Parr's Duval County would be counted to give Johnson official victory. Party chairman Robert W. Calvert, ultimately a Texas chief justice, appointed a subcommittee to recommend to the executive committee which course to follow. When the subcommittee's report favoring Johnson went to the full executive committee, the vote to send it to the convention floor was tied 28-28 when Calvert, presiding, refused to vote and Mrs. Seth Derbandt of Conroe changed her vote from Johnson to "present." Suddenly a member of the committee who had been absent during debate rushed into the committee room and shouted: "I'm Charlie Gibson from Amarillo, and I vote for Johnson." That did it. Convention delegates adopted the executive committee's findings and ordered Johnson's name on the November ballot as the Democratic nominee. The Texas Supreme Court upheld the convention's action when Stevenson appealed the convention verdict, but Federal District Judge T. Whitfield Davidson of Dallas granted a temporary restraining order asked by Stevenson, preventing ballot printing. Johnson forces went to Chief Justice J. C. Hutcheson of the U. S. Fifth Circuit Court of Appeals asking him to overrule Davidson. When Hutcheson said he would get other members of the court together in October for a hearing, Johnson forces were panicky because the deadline for ballot printing was September 17. Abe Fortas, a Memphis native turned Washington attorney and friend of Johnson, had been SEC attorney, general counsel of PWA, and Undersecretary of the Interior. He was asked by Johnson's attorneys about bypassing Hutcheson and going directly to the U.S. Supreme Court. Fortas recommended they apply to Justice Hugo Black. On September 28—election ballots had been held up—Black issued an order setting aside Davidson's ruling, saying federal courts had no constitutional authority to intervene in state elections. Thus the case reverted to the Texas Supreme Court's decision allowing Johnson's name to go on the ballot. Stevenson's legal battles thus ended. In November Johnson beat Republican Jack Porter of Houston by 350,000 votes. No one followed the legal proceedings in behalf of Johnson—and offered advice—more anxiously than Hofheinz. He gave a whoop of joy when Black's order was announced. After all, Johnson had won in 1941, he felt, and deserved the 1948 decision.

By the time of the campaign of 1948, KTHT was on its feet financially. This allowed Roy and Dene to begin collecting circus artifacts, antiques, and other valuable furnishings for their home and for "Huckster House." Roy, Jr., recalled that "Dad developed a good relationship with Frank Arnold and Raymond Rogers, interior decorators, who helped him put together the pieces which made the remodeled KTHT studios attractive. Arnold and Rogers were great fans of New York collections. They showed Dad old posters and clippings and things to use in lieu of wallpaper. Dad began to get an enthusiastic feeling for artifacts and gew-gaws about 1947. 'Huckster House' was decorated with some of the stuff left over from KTHT which Arnold and Rogers found. Dad also did a lot of buying through Houston dealers. They'd go and look for things for him, and occasionally he would go himself to various places. Mother and Dad, on trips to Europe after he made money, also bought many antiques, music boxes, and other things now collectors' items."

When financier Hooper ultimately saw the bills piling up for the expansion of KTHT and KSOX in Harlingen—he owned 25 percent of both stations—he squirmed and began questioning auditors and KTHT employees about the reasons for expenditures. Although he had no complaint about Hofheinz's ultimate accounting, he apparently wanted more to say about operations. What he and Hofheinz said to each other in the early 1950s was not made public, but on May 25, 1950, Hofheinz applied to the FCC for permission to buy out his partner. For the record, he said the buyout was for "taxation purposes." The FCC approved, and Hofheinz thereby became the owner of all the Houston and Harlingen stock and 49 percent of WILD in Birmingham. Hooper, however, did not withdraw from joint bid with Hofheinz for a television station.

When the United States Supreme Court ruled in 1954 that segregation in public schools must end "with all deliberate speed," it ignited legal action which resulted in bitterness, the busing of students with billions in extra costs, a rush of hundreds of thousands to private schools, and political debates which continued more than 25 years later. Two and a half years before that historic decision, Judge Roy Hofheinz became nationally known as a champion of public schools. In the fall of 1951, R. C. Hoiles, owner of seven "Freedom Newspapers" in California, bought the three major dailies in Texas' vast Rio Grande Valley, which was citrus country where legal Mexican-American citizens and thousands of illegal migrant workers from south of the border constituted a great majority of the population. The *Valley Morning Star* in Harlingen, the *Monitor* in McAllen, and the *Brownsville Herald*—all dominant newspapers in the area under the direction of Hoiles—quickly become editorial vehicles for denouncing public schools and school teachers.

Hofheinz opened KSOX in Harlingen a month after Hoiles took over the three newspapers. A product of the public schools, a great believer in equal opportunity for all Americans, regardless of color, and still a major Texas political figure, the Judge read newspaper attacks on the educational system. He decided on a major course of action: he personally would deliver KSOX talks on prime time combatting the reactionary ideas Hoiles' papers fostered constantly. Taking as his theme "Must the Valley be Run According to Hoiles?" Hofheinz began his counterattack on December 7, 1951, and he followed up almost nightly with new information and challenges to Hoiles to meet him in a public debate. The Hoiles organization fired a number of executives and employees of the newspapers when it took over, and Hofheinz seized upon that, too, in his radio talk. The Valley was stirred by the newspaper-Hofheinz fight so greatly that the Associated Press, United Press, *Time* magazine, and *Editor and Publisher* (the weekly newspaper national magazine) told the nation about the conflict.

Hoiles came to the Valley from California to defend his position when advertisers and school patrons swamped him with complaints about his philosophy. He announced he would accept the challenge to debate, but there was delay in setting a time and place. Hofheinz issued a public statement, "Mr. Hoiles is backing out. I have wired him as follows: 'Many interpret your statement to mean you have accepted my challenge to debate. I have some questions. I think they deserve an honest yes or no answer. First, are you willing to debate publicly your stand on the school issue? I will be willing to debate under any recognized set of rules. I will not accept you as chairman of the meeting and a participant in the debate, too.' " Hofheinz then noted that the newspapers for 10 days had abandoned referring to school teachers as "immoral and un-American." *Time* magazine described Hoiles as "ill-tempered," in favor of "child-labor," and traced his career in acquiring newspapers. Hoiles finally could stand Hofheinz's heat no longer, and two debates were arranged in February of 1952 in McAllen, both to be broadcast over KSOX. Crowds estimated by United Press at 5000 each night attended the debates and thousands listened on radio.

Bill Patterson, McAllen attorney, was moderator, and Philip Bowie of the McAllen Citizens' League was timekeeper. In introductory remarks, Patterson said, "The statement of the subject tonight has been selected by Mr. Roy Hofheinz—the statement of the subject for tomorrow night has been selected by Mr. R. C. Hoiles. . . . The subject tonight—for the benefit of the radio audience—is 'Resolved, that the tax-suported school system should be abolished. . . .' " Hoiles spoke first, arguing for the affirmative position. Referring to public schools as "government schools," Hoiles held that public schools were both the cause and effect of what he envisioned as the nation's drift toward socialism and Communism. He quoted the Declaration of Independence and the Communist Manifesto to advance his stand. He asserted that the graduated income tax and the federal reserve system both were Communist-inspired and promoted by the public schools. Hoiles concluded, "Communism and Americanism are compatible. Communism and government schools are *compatible*."

Hofheinz answered Hoiles eloquently, arguing that the public schools had made it possible for the children of the poor to have a chance to elevate themselves through education. He noted that equality of opportunity was a basic element of American principles. Moreover, he noted that "the two opposite poles on this platform clearly demonstrate that there is no indoctrination of a fixed code or the preservation of a cult's idea . . . in the minds of any youngster in our public schools. Why? Because the publisher of 10 newspapers from California and the radio operator from Texas, though many years separate us in ages, find both of ourselves products of the public school system of America. If there had been any effort either to indoctrinate me or to indoctrinate him on one side or the other, the school teachers certainly missed something somewhere down the line." Throughout that evening and the debate of the following night, Hofheinz effectively defended public education. The Judge did not change the policy of "Freedom Newspapers" which today have expanded into many cities, but he caused them to explain again and again that their news columns were "clean of bias" and reported news factually and honestly, but had a right to continue opinions on editorial pages.

The popularity of Hofheinz and KSOX with the masses of people in the Valley skyrocketed. Going on the stump always brought a sense of exhilaration to the Judge. His friends felt if Hofheinz ever chose to run for statewide office, he had built-in votes in the Valley. From an economic standpoint, the debates caused KSOX to gain business quickly. With his wealth, Hoiles could absorb any economic jolts to the Valley newspapers, and did. They still operate today.

18

Sam Rayburn's Rebuff

When Texas Governor Buford Jester died suddenly on July 11, 1951, Lieutenant Governor Allan Shivers moved into the chief executive's mansion in Austin, causing political realignments which shook the state. As operator of two Texas radio stations and often their political commentator, Roy Hofheinz watched and reported the changing scene with enterprise and enthusiasm. Because politics was his first professional love, he spent more money than any other independent radio operator in personally guaranteeing through 1952 that his audience got stories centering around Shivers, billionaire Sid Richardson of Dallas, U.S. House Speaker Sam Rayburn, Adlai Stevenson, and General Dwight D. Eisenhower.

President Harry S. Truman started it when he instructed his attorney general, Herbert Brownell, to tell a U.S. Senate committee that the oil wealth off the shores of Texas, Louisiana, and California—the Tidelands—belonged to the nation and not to the three states bordered by the submerged oil lands. A bill declaring the Tidelands to be national property passed Congress and was upheld by the United States Supreme Court. The decision infuriated legions of oil operators in the three states. Richardson took the lead in fighting to gain states' rights to the undersea black gold. In February of 1952, Richardson flew to London with George Allen, President Truman's close friend but also an Eisenhower partner in a downtown Washington restaurant. Richardson was among the first who pleaded with Eisenhower to seek the Republican nomination in 1952 and fight "Trumanism," meaning the president's stand on the Tidelands. Richardson promised support if Eisenhower would run. At the same time, leading Democrats urged the World War II hero to seek the Democratic nomination.

Shivers, looking ahead to 1952 when he would have to run for a full term as governor, was an outspoken critic of the court's Tidelands decision. With his hand-picked Texas Democratic executive committee, Shivers controlled the state Democratic Convention in September of 1951. About 3500 of the 4000 delegates were behind him. When the convention was over and a platform

Sam Rayburn.
Photograph courtesy
the *Houston Chronicle.*

calling for return of the Tidelands had been adopted, Shivers was asked if he would support Rayburn, the longtime Texas power in Washington, for the Democratic presidential nomination. Shivers replied sharply: "I would like to know what his views are." Texas Congressman Wright Patman was quoted by the press as answering for Rayburn, "Sam Rayburn's views were well known long before Shivers was born." Neither Rayburn nor Senator Lyndon Johnson appeared at the convention—they could not publicly join hands with Shivers.

Hofheinz took his mobile equipment to the state convention and gave excellent insights into the split of the "Shivercrats" and the party loyalists. He also covered the Texas Republican convention, split between supporters of Senator Robert Taft, the front-runner of GOP regulars, and Eisenhower. Early in the spring of 1952, Eisenhower enthusiasts invaded Republican precincts in every county. Pressure was applied and political promises were made by Richardson and his supporters as the Taft regulars sought to hold on, but Eisenhower's strength grew. The result was two Texas delegations, after bitter conventions, going to Chicago, one pledged to Taft and one to Eisenhower.

Hofheinz did not take his mobile unit to Chicago for the two national party conclaves in July as he had to Philadelphia four years earlier. The Judge, sons Roy, Jr., and Fred, wife Dene, chief KTHT engineer O. B. Johnson, and another technician drove to the windy city in station wagons and cars. "I drove up much of the way myself," the junior Hofheinz recalled. "The fight between Taft and Eisenhower factions over the platform (including the Tidelands issue—Taft supported nationally owned submerged lands) was so intense that the platform committee decided to hold secret sessions so that the general public wouldn't know the bitterness involved." Hofheinz had his son Roy suspend a wire microphone in the conference room, but the wire was discovered and cut. The Judge then managed to secure a prototype of a wireless microphone. Some of the platform committee's deliberations were captured for broadcast using this first wireless microphone in the United States.

Hofheinz was among the first to report how Eisenhower strategists decided to defeat Taft's delegates. The route chosen was to prevent the seating of Taft supporters. As a test case, Texas became a crucial state. Closed-door dealings led to the credentials committee's voting to seat the disputed Eisenhower delegations from Texas and Georgia. That began the Eisenhower victory parade. Taft thought he would have as many as 600 delegates on the first ballot, but the first count showed the senator trailing Ike by 590 to 500. Before a second ballot began, a shift of Minnesota's 19 votes to the general gave him the nomination. Senator Richard Nixon was named his running mate.

At the Democratic Convention, Hofheinz added buttonhole wireless mikes to his equipment. His friend John Connally helped round up party leaders for interviews. Senator Lyndon Johnson and Connally wanted Sam Rayburn to win the nomination, but Adlai Stevenson and a platform supporting national ownership of the Tidelands won. Senator John Sparkman of Alabama was chosen as Stevenson's running mate. The liberal Democrats of the party outvoted Shivercrats and the other conservatives. Hofheinz interviewed Shivers, Tom Connally, and others, and a big Texas audience got an unhappy reaction to the Democratic ticket.

Hofheinz went to the State Democratic Convention in Amarillo in September when Shivers—whose forces had been required, before they were seated, to say at the national convention that they would support the party nominee—changed his pledge and denounced the Stevenson-Sparkman ticket. The division of the Texas Democratic Party was complete. Shivers and the Democratic nominee for attorney general, Price Daniel, said good Democrats could support Eisenhower and still be real Democrats. However, Roy Hofheinz never wavered from the liberal Democratic line. He decided to help Stevenson as much as possible, and he had plenty of know-how, attested by his successes in leading two Johnson senate campaigns. When he got home from the convention, he said publicly he would support Stevenson despite pressures to use his influence for Eisenhower who, it was argued, was acceptable to both parties.

After making a major speech in Houston in support of Stevenson, Hofheinz and Gould Beech journeyed to Dallas and went to Stevenson headquarters. Speaker Rayburn was handling the campaign. Beech recalled, "We finally went into his suite and talked to Rayburn. Hofheinz said that he was ready to do whatever needed to be done and added, 'Here's Beech. He's an experienced ghost and script writer and he's available. I am personally prepared to give the maximum of $5000 to the campaign.' Rayburn responded, 'If there's anything we need done, we'll let you know.' That really deflated us."

Rayburn did want the $5000, and Hofheinz sent it. Yet he was at loose ends, having volunteered his services without receiving a positive response. Ready for political involvement, Hofheinz turned to Beech on the plane returning to Houston and said, "What do you think of my running for mayor?" Beech said, "Well, you made a helluva beginning—a speech for Stevenson in an Eisenhower town." Beech recalled that he and Hofheinz:

> decided when we got to Houston we'd send up a trial balloon and see what happened. I called Ben Kaplan at the *Press* and said, "Roy Hofheinz is thinking about running for mayor." Ben had a speculative story on the front page of the *Press* the next day. The situation then was that Councilman Louie Welch from the north side had declared for mayor. He was really gutting Mayor Oscar Holcombe and our feeling was, after talking it over, that they'd be cutting each other and Hofheinz would run his own race and would beat them. Immediately after Kaplan's story appeared, the switchboard at KTHT literally lit up like a Christmas tree. It was just an immediate, spontaneous response. Many people called and said, "Yeah, get in there, get in there!" It was only a few days before the filing deadline. The mayor's race was held simultaneously with the presidential race in November. The *Press* story caused the "fathers of the town" to sit up and take notice. At that time there were kingmakers—Jesse Jones, Governor Hobby, the Brown brothers of Brown and Root, and Judge Elkins among them. Normally they would have been for Holcombe. They called Hofheinz in and talked with him. They had decided, apparently, that Holcombe was through, for the time being at least, and it would be better to have Hofheinz than Welch. Holcombe had already printed material planning to run, although he had said early in the year he might not. On the final day—the deadline—the morning paper reported "Holcombe Bows Out." Holcombe said something to the effect that "Now there is a good man running, Hofheinz, and I won't run."
>
> At this meeting of the kingmakers, incidentally, Emmet Walter, *Chronicle* editor, represented Jesse Jones. He later told me, "When I told Mr. Jones about the decision that they should support Hofheinz, Jones said, 'Dammit, Emmet, that guy's got my picture in his john.'" So Jones couldn't have been too keen about Hofheinz. Thus the situation dramatically changed because the kingmakers had come to Hofheinz—he didn't go to them. Holcombe just dropped out. Well, immediately Welch charged that Hofheinz was going to be a puppet of Jesse Jones and Oscar Holcombe. Holcombe, out of vanity or whatnot, had announced openly that he was going to support Hofheinz.

Before Hofheinz made it official that he was in the mayor's race, he called on Leon Jaworski to seek his advice and help. Jaworski had not been a supporter of Holcombe as mayor, and the Judge wanted the lawyer's nod going his way instead of Welch's. Jaworski recalled that their conversation started with Hofheinz saying, "You know, I have a difficult name. Suppose you ran for office, Leon, the biggest handicap you would have would be your name."

"I think," Jaworski said, "he was just saying we had something in common. I said to him: 'Roy, you know I'm a great believer in the fact that while the name on the ballot can have some appeal, or lack of appeal, I just believe that an individual can overcome whatever his name may be. It's like the old saying—what's in a name?' " Jaworski said he saw in Hofheinz great possibilities for new Houston leadership and told him he would help his campaign as much as his time permitted.

When the October 5 deadline for entering the race came, there were four seeking the mayor's office: Hofheinz, Welch, W. Gail Reeves, who had run unsuccessfully in 1950, and Sam C. Johnson, a former newspaperman and assistant to Holcombe for six years. Newspapers reported the next day that Hofheinz's three opponents held a secret meeting to discuss campaign tactics against the Judge. "I don't care if they gang up," said Hofheinz. "I'm going to be elected. Politics is like a football game. You can tell who has the ball and is headed for a touchdown because all other candidates are trying to tackle him." In the drawing, Hofheinz got the first position on the ballot.

Jack Valenti enlisted with Hofheinz's campaign team. The future motion picture czar then was partner in a public relations firm which worked with Beech, John Stephen, and others in preparing promotional material. Millionaire Bob Smith joined Dene Hofheinz on the "campaign board" and brought with him Welcome Wilson, a real estate investment youngster who had helped the oil nabob when he was civilian defense director during World War II. All of them would be involved in Hofheinz's administration as mayor. Hofheinz named an acting manager for KSOX in Harlingen and asked Beech to stay with him in Houston. "As I stayed in the Texas State Hotel day and night for about six weeks, I became political strategist, planner, and key interviewer for the Judge," Beech said. "I had put together a liberal coalition in Montgomery when Red James ran for Congress, and I immediately sought to do the same for Hofheinz. I knew he had labor and black support."

Roy's "Man Friday," Joe Louis Holiday, sat in on conferences as he helped round up the leaders of the Harris County Council of Organizations, a black entity. Holiday came from a family of school teachers. Hobart Taylor, taxicab company owner, and Carter Wesley, newspaperman, were among the black leaders Holiday knew well. Holiday said that Hofheinz's record of fairness and friendship with blacks was all he needed for support. Hofheinz, incidentally, was the first owner of a "white" radio station who employed a black disc jockey. Jax beer wanted a market in the black community and thought a black deejay could help sales. Auditions were held for a number of men and Cesta Ayers was chosen. He had been emcee for dance promoter Don Robie. "We called Ayers Dr. Daddy-O," said Holiday. "He and I worked together. I was the engineer." Holiday said the white-black relationship in Houston then was such that Hofheinz actually did not have to be openly fair with blacks, but the Judge did not mind if he was criticized for going after their help. "Never did the Judge try in any way to buy the black vote," Holiday recalled. "If he had," he added, "we would not have worked for him." Beech and Holiday got word from the black council leaders that they had endorsed Hofheinz. They worked for him, and on election day their vote for the Judge was overwhelming.

Early in the race the question whether Hofheinz was a legal resident of Houston was aired. Opponents said Yorktown had not been annexed until 1951 and there was a law requiring a candidate for mayor to have lived in the city five years. Hofheinz talked to lawyers, refused to worry about it, and went on campaigning. When newspapers asked Hofheinz for a statement about his finances after he announced, he listed a "conservative" net worth of $825,531.82. This included 100 percent ownership of KTHT, 50 percent partnership in Houston Slag, 100 percent ownership of Harlingen's KSOX, 49 percent partnership in Birmingham's WILD, income producing properties—Settegast lot, $500; Walkarte property, $15,000; Whitty Street lots, $7500; Birmingham land, $23,100; ship channel land, $20,000—and furniture, fixtures, and library. He listed his total liabilities at $981,031.83.

Television then was coming into its own, and Hofheinz knew it. He bought time for a number of dramatic appearances. He said in his first talk he wanted to rid the city of ratridden areas, improve sewer lines and drainage, blacktop streets everywhere, and move forward with a business approach. "Let's look to the future with boldness and vision," he said. "It means investing in order to take advantage of great opportunities which lie ahead. Our city will grow and citizens as stockholders will benefit." He promised competitive bidding, an open book of planning, employees of top ability and integrity, and the same employment policy for people of all races. He reviewed his accomplishments as county judge—the Rincon oil deal for Rice, flood control, end of star chamber sessions of the County Court, competitive bidding, initiation of the largest road bond issue ever concerned by a Texas county, and a successful fight to block a toll tunnel and to get plans moving for two tunnels under the ship channel—"making East Harris County one great industrial area." He said he had a "progressive, constructive, and intelligent program for Houston."

The *Chronicle* and the *Post* endorsed Hofheinz, but the *Press* stuck with Welch. *Press* editor Carmack liked Councilman Welch's blistering attacks on "Holcombeism" and the machine he had built over a long period. The *Press* and Holcombe were often at odds because of reporter Ernest Bailey's stories of corruption in the administration.

After the mayor's race concluded, national television publications said

Hofheinz was a pioneer in attracting voters through the tube. In his appearance on October 14, he introduced his family. Showing off his wife, sons, and daughter, Hofheinz also reviewed his record and his lifelong career as a salesman for Houston. The *Chronicle* reported that the Judge concluded his broadcast by answering "the charge hurled at him by opponents suggesting that he was the 'hand-picked' candidate of certain groups and interests. He said he had always been an independent official and had never been dictated to, as the record would show. 'I'm too old to start joining any clique now,' he said in a ringing voice that carried conviction." Hofheinz said in one speech—he went on radio as well as television—"Houston is a business which has $50 million a year income, 7000 employees, and 650,000 customers. The customers look to this business to supply water, fire protection, health protection, and police services. The customers also look to this business to build and maintain streets and thoroughfares and to enforce laws aimed at making streets safe." He added that Houston, like any business, was suffering from growing pains. "I ask the customers to consider what the responsibilities of the business of Houston would be in a few years when for every 10 homes now there will be 15—when for every 10 cars now there will be 15—when for every 10 children now there will be 15."

"Will Houston," he asked, "unlike the nine other major cities, continue to be a city of individual homes or will it be a city of tenements and crowded apartments? To keep abreast of growth, the city must have an administration that will push ahead with improvement projects for which the people have already voted bonds. We should be fair to every section of the city, but give priority to those sections in greatest need. Your approval of bond issues shows that you want your business conducted on a farsighted basis." In 1979, Houston had more automobiles per capita and a faster population growth than any other major American city. No Houston prophet was more accurate than the Judge.

Working as a receptionist in the office of Mayor Holcombe during his last two terms in office was 24-year-old Mrs. Milton Gougenheim, the former Mary Frances McMurtry, who long had been told by her school friend, William L. Young, once a ward of Hofheinz in Juvenile Court, that Judge Roy Hofheinz was "just about a saint." The young lady would be exposed during the campaign to her future husband—Roy Hofheinz. "In early October, 1952, after Mayor Holcombe did not announce for reelection, I read in the papers 'Hofheinz to run for Mayor,' " Mary Frances recalled. "His picture was of a friendly man with a huge smile. I thought to myself, remembering all the wonderful things Bill Young told me: 'Oh boy, I've got a candidate!' A couple of weeks later, Ann Craig and Ruth Johnson, who worked in the mayor's office, asked me if I would like to go with them that evening to a political rally at Berry School on the north side of Houston because Judge Hofheinz was to speak there. When Judge Hofheinz took the platform, I thought to myself how young he looked—it seemed to me that he had been county judge all my life. He gave a wonderful, rousing speech that had the big crowd cheering when he finished. I remember that I clapped until my hands actually hurt. He won me as one of his faithful followers from that day forward. He was absolutely magnetic. I could hardly wait to get out and campaign for him."

The campaign was vicious at times. An anonymous circular was distributed saying Hofheinz did not want anybody to vote for him unless he or she cast a vote for Adlai Stevenson. The Judge's three opponents denied printing the circular. Hofheinz told newspapermen he did not know the source, but added: "General Eisenhower has earned his position as one of the great men of history. He is above stooping to meddling in petty local politics." Just before election day, November 4, two "over-zealous workers" for Welch admitted they had ordered the circulars distributed hoping to hurt Hofheinz. They worked for C. E. King, a realtor who was a Welch financial backer. The two publicly said they were trying to connect the Judge with "Trumanism," not Eisenhower. Welch apologized for the workers.

Beech told of another big effort to discredit Hofheinz. He said:

> Two Sundays before the election, there began to appear church ads in the newspapers for people to "Come and Hear About The Danger Houston Is In." Someone had made a fake recording in which Hofheinz was alleged to have said to liquor people: "You can be sure I'll open up the town to gambling and whiskey." One of the opposition had gotten a preacher to enlist other preachers in listening to the recording with the admonition "We think you ought to know this." Some of the ministers did tell of the recording during sermons. Our headquarters almost panicked when some of the black preachers were asked to go for the fakery, but it didn't phase them at all. They had sense enough not to believe any such recording. The voice on the record was not Hofheinz's. Hofheinz went to the Reverend John Knowles who had said something in his pulpit about the record. The Judge had known Knowles' father. "What in the world is happening about the record?" the Judge asked. Knowles replied, "Well, Roy, you know my father and I've known you, but when it comes to corrupting this town and its morals, I just couldn't stand by and let you do it." It was then we found out fully about the record. Hofheinz told Knowles he had been taken in. Knowles came out and publicly disavowed the whole business. The Church of Christ minister went on radio and television to expose the fakery. So, to some extent, the thing backlashed on the opposition. The technique of the record producers was to get a few ministers together in a room and say, "Of course, this is a violation of the law to have this recording, but we want you to hear it." Some of them just bought it hook, line and sinker. Both white and black preachers were involved.

Billy Graham said in his 1952 Houston crusade that the city was "the most corrupt in America." Beech said this comment, plus the truth that a number of scandals in the Holcombe administration had been uncovered by the press and grand juries, had to be faced. "I remember stories about a rookie policeman having a stable of call girls," said Beech. "Policemen also had been caught robbing freight cars. There were gambling and political payoffs at different levels. The numbers racket flourished." Beech added, that "near the Harris County Courthouse were horse parlors with radios blaring out on the street various sporting deals. There was evidence of much corruption during the Holcombe regime. The Judge's opponents wanted to plant the idea Hofheinz would allow such conditions to continue." Hofheinz said he would close the town and would take steps to clean up any corruption in the police department. The Judge had a hard job convincing some people he was sincere because Holcombe cronies and veteran employees under Holcombe actually did campaign for Hofheinz. When the police rookie with a call-girl list was exposed and charged, the officer said, "Hell, everybody in the Police Department has some outside source of income." That was an overstatement, but there was plenty of corruption.

Candidate Johnson was the first to make personal attacks in his opening television appearance. He said of his opponents: "Mr. Welch has a faculty of putting his foot in his mouth. . . . Mr. Hofheinz was truly a traveling county judge. . . . Mr. Reeves is just a real estate salesman." Candidate Reeves came back on TV with: "Candidate Johnson did practically nothing about public health during his six years as Holcombe's assistant. . . . Hofheinz did nothing about a countywide sanitation system when Judge. . . . Welch has not been awake during two years on City Council."

A week before election time, polls showed Hofheinz and Welch in front. The Judge decided to have a rally in Welch's own precinct on the north side. "When you have a self-appointed barefoot boy [Welch] in the mayor's race at his own invitation and with 13 headquarters costing thousands, you have a right to wonder about the source of money," the Judge told Welch neighbors. "I won't be a sectional mayor. Your north side will get the same consideration as other parts of the city." Lewis Cutrer, a prominent lawyer who later became mayor, was a popular civic worker. When Welch refused to get out of the race at his request, Cutrer went on the radio eight times to plug for Hofheinz and was a big help. Welch made a last-minute bid for votes with a television appearance in which he promised to give to charity any increase in his personal net wealth while mayor. He also said Hofheinz ran vicious races for county judge and was doing the same thing again.

On October 30, five days before the election, Thomas J. Stovall, Harris County election judge, went to Judge Roy Campbell's State District Court and got him to sign an order requiring Welch and Hofheinz to prove their residence qualifications for the race or be scratched from the ballot. This action brought Hofheinz and Jaworski closer together. "Roy went to several people to discuss

The Hofheinz family following Roy's victorious campaign for mayor in 1952. Photograph courtesy the *Houston Post.*

handling the case in collaboration with City Attorney Will Sears," Jaworski said in 1978. He recalled:

> One of them was the senior John Crooker. I think Crooker said to him, "Why don't you get one or two lawyers from other firms to participate in the case, too?" He got Tom Martin Davis of Baker and Botts. Crooker assigned me to work with Davis, Sears, and Wiley Caldwell, assistant city attorney. We prepared the case and I took the lead. There existed an affidavit made in connection with a loan Roy had with Rice Institute, later University, in which Roy had declared his homestead was "Huckster House" at Bayridge on Galveston Bay. If we had ever gotten into the merits of the affidavit, it would have been a very embarrassing situation. So we went before Judge Campbell, and I

argued that the suit could not be maintained; there would be no way the court could go ahead and declare Roy and Welch ineligible at that late date in the election because it would have disenfranchised those who had cast absentee ballots. This was a sound position, and we had some law to back it up—it wasn't fantasy or theory. After we cited authorities, Judge Campbell threw out the suit. We never got to the issue of whether Roy did or didn't make such an affidavit.

The final City Council count of the election gave Hofheinz 92,681 first, second, and third-choice votes, Welch 85,872, Johnson 39,123, and Reeves 48,627. Elected to City Council were newcomers Dr. Ira Kohler and Jim Heflin. Reelected were Harry Holmes, Jr., George Kesseler, B. Joe Resweber, George Marquette, Matt Wilson, and Clyde Fitzgerald. The *Chronicle* said all were "seasoned, if not hardened, politicians." Mrs. Hofheinz told reporters after the election that the family had great happiness during the eight years the Judge had been out of office, but she was enthusiastic about his new political career. She said the untruths candidates and other people had said about her husband hurt. Oscar Holcombe said, "The people did a fine job in selecting my successor." It was not long, however, before any pretended friendship between the two men would come to a jolting halt. Hofheinz was exhausted after six weeks of campaigning. He hibernated for 48 hours and then began planning to take over the mayor's office on January 1, 1953. He did say, however, that the City Council elected looked like one with which he could work harmoniously. It was wishful thinking.

On January 1, 1953, 2000 attended Hofheinz's oathtaking, including A. E. Amerman, Neal Pickett, R. H. Fonville, and Holcombe, all former mayors. Hofheinz reached his 40th birthday eight months before he became the city's chief executive. His happy marriage of 19 years, his three bright children, his strong financial standing, and his burning desire to build Houston with honest, fair, and progressive leadership as mayor strengthened his belief in himself. He was determined to remain his own man. His friends said his ego carried him to extremes—and ultimate defeat as mayor—but none ever doubted his genius.

19

The Mayor, City Council, and "Palace Guard"

It was dark in the late afternoon of December 31, 1952. In the Houston mayor's office there was sadness because it was the last day of Oscar Holcombe's tenure. He said good-bye to his staff and wished them well, packed his files and mementoes, and left early. "The door to the reception room of the mayor's office suddenly flew open," Mary Frances Gougenheim recalled. "In swept Mayor-elect Hofheinz and two associates, Gould Beech and John Stephen. The Judge said to me, 'Hi, Honey, I'm Roy Hofheinz.' He asked if Mayor Holcombe was in, and I told him that he had gone. He asked if they could look at the offices. I took his party on a tour, and they started making big plans about everything. The vigor of the three men was exciting to me. I secretly hoped, of course, that the Judge would keep me working for him."

Milton Gougenheim, an accountant, came in to help his wife clean out her desk, and Mary Frances introduced her husband to the Judge. Gougenheim said Hofheinz asked him what he and his wife were doing in the office after hours. "I told him," recalled Gougenheim, "that we were getting ready for Mary Frances to move out. He quickly said, 'Leave, hell, she's not going anywhere! I know about Mary Frances. She is the best person for this job and I need her.' Mary Frances and I looked at each other, smiled, and with that became a part of the Judge's people."

Hofheinz planned for Beech and Stephen to be executive assistants—Beech a general administrator and Stephen a specialist to develop the Houston airport. Their appointments would have to be approved by the City Council because a new ordinance was required to have two executive assistants instead of one. He also called in a newspaper reporter, A. Pat Daniels, who had worked in the campaigns, to be executive secretary in charge of relations with the press, radio, and TV. Council approval was not necessary in Daniels' case.

Mary Frances immediately got a new nickname, "Kiddo," from the mayor. She said her new boss worked from early morning until late at night. "Sometimes the mayor would buzz me on the intercom and ask me to get someone on the phone," she recalled. "I would immediately start dialing the number, for I

Gould Beech (left) and John Stephen. Beech photograph courtesy the *Houston Chronicle.*

prided myself on knowing numbers by heart and hardly ever had to stop to look up one. Sometimes after I dialed the first three or four digits, the mayor would buzz again asking if I had the person on the line. He was definitely a man in a hurry. He was the hardest working person I ever encountered. He moved fast and things were like a whirlwind when he was around. His desk always looked like a disaster area, but he seemed to like working from the clutter because when anyone in the office tried to straighten out the mess, he would get upset. He knew exactly what was there—and where."

In his inaugural address, Hofheinz outlined an ambitious program for his two-year term: paving of 456 miles of shelled streets and 156 miles of dirt streets; a time-payment plan to enable the average home owner to pay about one dollar a mont for $8 million in street improvements; use of school grounds during afternoons and summer months for recreational purposes and to strike at juvenile delinquency; an immediate survey of the city purchasing department by the Tax Research Association of Houston and Harris County and seven purchasing executives of large firms to be used as consultants for reorganizing the department; open bidding on all purchases over $1000; appointment of a committee of outstanding citizens to review the most pressing needs of a city which he said was on the threshold of its greatest growth; open meetings of City Council with informal meetings to be held only with members of the press present; and no attempt to usurp the legislative or policy-making powers of City Council. Hofheinz also said the outlook for solving all Houston's drainage problems was bleak, figuring a complete storm sewer system would cost a billion—"obviously beyond our limit."

Preliminary skirmishing in what was to be a three-year battle between the mayor and the City Council concerning the powers of each under the city's "strong mayor" charter began the second day of Hofheinz's administration when he presided at his first meeting with the eight city councilmen. Word had leaked out that Gould Beech had called four department heads before Hofheinz was sworn in and told them that their resignations were expected. An impasse developed at the outset when Council balked at an ordinance creating the two executive assistant positions for Beech and Stephen at $10,000 a year. After lengthy haggling, Hofheinz said he felt certain the council did not object to "my organizing my own executive office as I desire." The ordinance was passed. Both Beech and Stephen had made more than $10,000 as vice-presidents of Hofheinz's radio corporations. Hofheinz said he would not allow them to suffer financially because of the lower salaries at new full-time jobs. He supplemented the difference.

When the question of department head appointments came up, the council reminded Hofheinz it had the power to approve or reject anyone whose name he proposed. "Contrary to any custom I've been able to find in the past," the mayor said, "I have determined to submit my nominations to you for approval." Councilman Joe Resweber quickly asked for a chace to review nominees and moved to delay action until the follwing week. The mayor pointed out that some departments were without heads at the moment and action was needed. After more arguments, Hofheinz stuck his list of appointments in his pocket, but he pulled it out again and said, "Let's trot them out one at a time. Some of them you have already been working with and know." Councilman Holmes commented, "That's a fair thing to do. Let's trot them out." Councilman Marquette broke in, "Councilmen are held responsible for the acts of department heads even though they are appointed by the mayor." Councilman Kesseler explained that in the case of Police Chief L. D. Morrison, whom the mayor had endorsed, "there might be trouble for Council." He cited a hypothetical situation whereby the council "might be embarrassed after approving his appointment should the city become wide open." Hofheinz replied, "I'm ready to assume full responsibility should the city even become partly open." All appointments, however, were held up. During the ensuing weekend, Hofheinz met individually with councilmen. A special meeting was called for Monday. The *Chronicle* reported on January 6: "In honeymoonlike harmony, City Council and Mayor Roy Hofheinz agreed on the bulk of the mayor's list of department head appointments, including Police Chief L. D. Morrison and Fire Chief Homer Lyles."

Two weeks later, councilmen again swiped at the vigorous mayor. He had promised no closed or executive sessions with council as a group, but councilmen charged he actually had been having secret consultations with some council members. At the private sessions, councilmen charged, the mayor carefully avoided having a quorum (four or more) of the councilmen together at a time. He had met with one, two, and as many as three at a time. Councilman George Kesseler, who had been elected mayor pro tem by the council, summed up the device of circumventing closed council sessions this way: "It stinks. It used to be that at least all members of the council knew what went on in executive sessions. Now the mayor talks to one or two or maybe three councilmen about something, and what they discuss is a secret even to the other members of the council. The mayor's policy has caused a state of confusion."

Councilman Harry Holmes, Jr., who crossed swords with the mayor over Hofheinz's announcement that he might get a one-dollar-a-year man to replace Colonel A. W. Snyder as civil defense head, said, "It is impossible to do business by calling in each councilman individually. After he gets a majority to agree to something he wants done, he quits calling the councilmen in." Councilmen Matt Wilson, Joe Resweber, Clyde Fitzgerald, George Marquette, and Ira Kohler also complained in a similar vein. Kohler said the mayor was "a dictatorial tyrant." Councilman Jim Heflin said he was satisfied with the mayor's policy. The councilmen for the most part agreed that Hofheinz was doing a good job. They said they admired the energetic way he was tackling the city's problems, but they thought the mayor was going to have to change his policy—or at least improve liaison between his office and theirs. Hofheinz admitted that this policy, which was one of the major planks in his campaign for election, was a problem, but indicated he was sticking to his guns.

Hofheinz redecorated the private dining room in the mayor's office so that he could do business while eating lunch—and have food available quickly. He also became known as "one of the boys" around City Hall because he took coffee breaks with employees to learn their feelings. Lieutenant Sam H. Clauder and Sergeant "Slim" Kent of the police department became the mayor's chauffeurs and bodyguards. Hofheinz inherited an old Cadillac limousine from the Holcombe administration. It was in bad shape, but while he argued with the council about buying a new one, he made a show of the poor shape of the limousine. Once it stalled on a downtown street, and Hofheinz had to hail associates in another car to get to City Hall. About once a week in the first months of his administration, he called Clauder to drive him around to places where vice might be emerging. He wanted to know first-hand about any effort to open up the city. He did not get a new limousine until the second year of his administration.

No one outside the Hofheinz circle watched the new mayor through his reporters more closely than George Carmack, a six-foot-five, amiable, hard-

R. E. "Bob" Smith

working native Tennessean who had been sent to Houston after World War II by Scripps-Howard as editor to inject new life into the six-day afternoon *Press*. If Hofheinz ever had a rival for long hours and devotion to his work, it was Carmack, who had a habit of saying "Fine! Fine! Fine!" when greeted. People who remembered that the *Press* had supported Louie Welch against Hofheinz were a bit surprised when they read in Carmack's weekly column: "The first two and a half months of Hofheinz's administration were the most fruitful in the city's history. He has brought honor and integrity back to City Hall."

Johnny Goyen, still a city councilman in 1978 after many years of service in that job and in real estate and hotel enterprises, became a confidant of Hofheinz. He recalled being called into Hofheinz's office: "The mayor said: 'I want you to be head clerk of the Corporation [city] Court. I'd like for you to go over there and listen, keep your mouth shut, and not let anybody fix traffic tickets.' I told the mayor I really didn't know anything about Corporation Court business, and he said that's exactly what he wanted—'somebody that didn't know anything but with a free hand to do what is right, and to treat everyone equally.' I found out later that certain elements of the community, when they walked into the court clerk's office, were not allowed or given the opportunity to have a seat." Jack Valenti was appointed chairman of the Houston Library Board, but continued with his private public relations work. He, however, became another advisor to the mayor.

To replace Colonel Snyder in the city's civil defense office, Hofheinz appointed, at one dollar a year, Bob Smith, a millionaire who helped finance and campaigned for his election. The Korean War had not ended in 1953, and fear of a greater conflict was still widespread. Smith had served as civilian defense director for several states under President Roosevelt during World War II and was an outstanding planner. The day-by-day work for the Houston civil defense office, however, required a full-time city employee under Smith, who recommended Welcome Wilson who had worked in his organization. Hofheinz appointed him.

The growing friendship of Bob Smith and Mayor Hofheinz during 1953 led to the ultimate building of the Astrodome. "Mr. Bob," as he had become known to Houstonians in the 1940s, was an amicable, red-haired, muscular six-footer in his youth. Born in Greenville, Texas, on August 28, 1894, he had worked as a roughneck in oil fields in Oklahoma and in Corsicana, Texas. During his wandering, he had been fired five times from various jobs. He had a reputation as a tough amateur heavyweight boxer and semi-pro baseball player. Boxing champion Gene Tunney told Smith, friends said, that he had the skill to make it to the top. He lost two fingers on one hand in an oil field accident.

At 27, in Tonkawa, Oklahoma, after he had joined an oil field supply house as a salesman, he met the owner of two drilling rigs who found the Oklahoma climate too cold and wanted to sell out and go back to Texas. Smith had dreams of making a place for himself in the oil business—it was the "roaring twenties" when oil was becoming one of the country's big industrial giants. The owner told Smith he would sell his rigs for $25,000—a tremendous amount of money then—but the experienced roughneck realized that picking up those two rigs could be a windfall. Smith got in touch with friends in Texas to see if they could help him buy the rigs. They said it would take time to raise the cash; therefore Smith went back to the contractor. The answer he received was no; the contractor wanted to sell quickly and did not want to wait for a group to raise money. Smith then decided on a bold move—he went to the only banker in Tonkawa and said he wanted to borrow $25,000 and had friends who would back him before too long. "The big point," the banker said to him, "is that you have no money to put in the deal yourself. Why come to me?" With characteristic forthrightness, Smith replied, "You're the only man in town who has enough money to buy the rigs." Apparently the banker was sold on Smith's character, and he agreed to lend him the money for an immediate deal.

The banker got his money back with interest when Smith's friends came through with cash in 30 days. Returning to Texas, Smith set up headquarters in

Corsicana and entered the contracting field. He soon found himself spending more time than was profitable in that work. He moved to Houston and became an independent oil and gas finder and producer. He started hitting big fields. Four years later, in 1929, he became a business partner of Claud Hamill, whose father was one of the drillers of the famous Lucas gusher at Spindletop, near Beaumont. This partnership lasted 10 years, and then Smith was on his own again, moving ahead to find more "black gold."

Smith married Vivian Leatherberry, daughter of Mr. and Mrs. L. D. Leatherberry of Houston, in 1935. She was 14 years younger than he, but theirs was a happy marriage. The couple was as devoted and close to each other as were Dene and Roy Hofheinz. Two daughters, Bobby Sue (now Mrs. Morton A. Cohn) and Sandra Ann (now Mrs. Dwight H. Austin), brought great joy to their home.

Smith had developed a love for boxing while in the Army during World War I and attended almost all heavyweight championship fights until his death. He followed baseball news closely and reveled in the feats of great players. He kept on a program of strict physical fitness all his life and did much business while working out in Houston health clubs with groups he invited to join him in "shaping up." After great success in finding and developing oil and gas fields which put him in the Texas millionaire class, Smith began investing in Houston and Harris County real estate. He was 61, 18 years older than Roy Hofheinz, when the two joined hands in developing Houston as an international sports center. By then, Smith had an estimated $500,000 a month income from real estate and was known as the largest single landowner in Harris County. He first bought property in Houston in 1940 when the city totaled 73 square miles. By 1964, the year before the Astrodome was completed, Smith had acquired, according to published reports, 8000 acres in the city, then with a population of 556,000 and 360 square miles of land. Most of the land was undeveloped. Principally an oilman, Smith regarded investment in land as a diversification. He explained it in terms of land value appreciation versus oil property depreciation. "I have a thorough belief in inflation," Smith once told a reporter. "That's why I invest in land. I always took it when I could put my foot on shore." Some he bought was in the Houston Westheimer area where Roy Hofheinz had his homestead. Both benefited handsomely when Houston's "Magic Circle Galleria Area" was developed.

Smith's hair had turned white before he became close to Hofheinz and began financial backing of the energetic mayor, whom he admired as an aggressive poor boy who had fought his way up. Each had the same interests—family, money accumulation, devotion to the idea of building Houston, a desire to keep moving ahead, and a fondness for the outdoors and competitive sports. Hofheinz's ideas always intrigued Smith, and he seldom hesitated to put up money for Roy when he thought them sound.

William W. "Bill" Sherrill also won the mayor's confidence and joined

Hofheinz's team. He recalled in 1978, after he had served as a director of the Federal Reserve Board in Washington and returned to Houston as a business and financial consultant, "Hofheinz's administration was the beginning of social reform in Houston. The racial question at the time was one on which virtually no progress had been made. Mr. Smith backed the principles of social reform. That was a big reason he supported the Judge. Welcome and Jack Wilson, Goyen, Valenti, and I had been in business together and were and are still close friends. I became a fringe member of the group. Roy Hofheinz had a great appreciation of loyalty and I became a full partner in his circle." Gradually formed in 1953 was the mayor's "Palace Guard," as it was termed by the press and Hofheinz's political opponents. It consisted of Gould Beech, John Stephen, Pat Daniels, and Mary Frances Gougenheim on a daily basis, Bill Sherrill, Welcome Wilson, Jack Valenti, and Johnny Goyen on an advisory basis. The advisor closest to Hofheinz, of course, was his wife, Dene, with whom he shared virtually every idea and plan. Next to her was oilman Bob Smith. Hofheinz and Smith later bought property together, hunted and fished together, and were known by the public as an extraordinarily excellent team.

Mary Frances won the confidence of Mayor Hofheinz quickly. She said in 1978:

> Once he told me that he envied the way I could talk to people individually. I told him I knew he must be kidding me because he could speak to thousands with ease. He told me that, yes, he could speak to thousands, but that it was difficult for him to chit-chat with individuals with ease. He was basically very shy. Once someone sent the mayor a watermelon. He opened the refrigerator late one afternoon and saw a whole, huge ice-cold watermelon. He asked me if I wanted any and I said no. He then cut the watermelon in half and ate the entire center of it. He said he had always wanted to do that.
>
> One incident comes to my mind when he was mayor. He had an appointment one day with two men who had a contracting company in Houston. The men entered his office. Several minutes later I heard loud voices coming from the mayor's office. A minute later the door swung open, and the men came out rather hurriedly with the mayor actually kicking the last man in the seat. I found out later the men had offered the mayor a payoff. I guess the biggest problem the Judge had in politics was his honesty. It wasn't enough that he would go about his job as mayor with the utmost honesty—he felt he had to do something about certain councilmen with "their hands in the cookie jar." He openly attacked these councilmen. They fought back and tried to hurt him in many ways.

Hofheinz warned gamblers in Galveston and other surrounding counties to stay out of Houston. He gave Police Chief Morrison and Captain George Seber, vice squad leader, the green light to stamp out once rampant vice. Meanwhile, Mayor Hofheinz worked vigorously for Houston. For example, Police Chief Morrison kept the lid on gambling and vice so tight that at least two councilmen began attacking him, hoping he would ease up. He knew that the mayor wanted a closed town, and he personally rode around the city at night checking on various places where gambling and prostitution had once flourished. A group of ministers heard that gambling actually was going on among employees at City Hall and publicly accused the mayor and Morrison of laxity. The idea was planted by one councilman who wanted to embarrass the administration. When an investigation was made by the mayor, the councilman was found to be a liar and the ministers apologized for falling for the story.

Early in 1953, Southwestern Bell Telephone Company said it planned to raise its rates. Hearings began in June when Hofheinz made it plain he would not go along with increases until he had figures from the company to justify them. He demanded on the first day that the company produce figures on original cost minus depreciation and secured a promise that they would be forthcoming. Preliminary checks on the utility convinced Hofheinz, city auditors, and city attorney Will Sears that Southwestern Bell should cut $18 million from its increase demands. Sears adamantly whacked away at the company's claimed rate base of $85,155,000. In December, when the company sought to have the city tax equalization board cut $704,439 off city and school personal property tax payments, the mayor said home owners would become the big losers if the request was granted. Throughout rate and tax hearings, the company indicated it would go to court to get what it wanted if the city did not go along. Hofheinz was uncompromising. The bitter fight with the utility was to continue for months. Hofheinz's attitude that utilities should be regulated and profits held to reasonable limits had begun when he was a 22-year-old legislator and introduced a bill passed after his term ended which gave cities and other local authorities the right to pass upon utility rates.

Purchasing agent Harling said $100,000 was saved the first few months of the Hofheinz administration by a new system of bidding. When six companies submitted identical bids for shell—an old story to Hofheinz—Harling divided the business among them. It was the first time since 1948 that such bids had been sought by the city. Hofheinz said the identical bids were "peculiar," but he had the satisfaction of knowing that prices were down compared to those of the monopoly he had broken when he was county judge.

Houston's facilities for handling stray, sick, and homeless dogs were grossly inadequate in 1952. One of Hofheinz's first moves was to include in his 1953 budget funds to build a pound with full facilities for cleanliness and comfort of such animals. The city was overrun, some complained, with stray cats. The mayor also talked with cat-lovers and helped start a program to give humane treatment to felines. His affection for dogs since childhood caused him to use every means in his power to see that animals got good treatment. Letters poured into Hofheinz's office thanking him for getting the city out of an almost "don't care" attitude about pets.

Most city employees were underpaid. Hofheinz, after announcing that non-union as well as union employees would get the same consideration, managed to sell Council on payroll increases.

While leisure activities were infrequent parts of the mayor's busy life, he tried to be outdoors whenever possible. Hunting and fishing were particularly favorite pastimes, and recollections by Albert Lopez, maintenance man at all Hofheinz residences, provide glimpses into this fact: The invention of a "plucking machine" by Hofheinz and Stuart Young was the outgrowth of the mayor's enthusiasm for duck hunting. According to Lopez, "It had a lot of rubber teeth sticking out, and it would pick up feathers. . . . I made all the duck blinds myself, and I was the scout who looked for ducks at various places so the Judge would know where to go with his friends." Lopez also recalled that the mayor outfitted a 1955 truck for use on hunting and fishing trips. With a custom-made bed and plenty of hunting equipment, clothes, and boots stored inside, fishing gear on the side, and an aluminum boat on top, the vehicle stood ready for Hofheinz's last-minute departures to out-of-the-way spots. After hunting season, however, the truck stood idle in the driveway of his Yorktown home and was an object of concern for Lopez, who feared that its lack of use would call for otherwise needless repairs. Lopez's warning to the Judge that the clutch might begin to stick was met with the reply, "Don't worry about that. I don't." Later, however, having thought about the situation, the Judge changed his mind and told Lopez to remove the hunting and fishing gear and to take the truck and drive it. The maintenance man says that he drove it until it collapsed.

The mayor's first out-of-the-state pleasure break in 1953 came in May when he accompanied Roy, Jr., to Denver for the National Forensic Tournament. The junior Hofheinz won high honors for his eloquence, and the Judge came home satisfied with his constant insistence that his sons become outstanding speakers; it certainly had paid off with his first-born. Second son Fred later was to win speaking honors, too. Frank Godsoe of the *Press* often spotlighted examples of Hofheinz's leisure activities in his column, following the mayor and his sons to 12 football and a number of baseball games in 1953. Godsoe revealed that Hofheinz practiced his knuckle ball in preparation for the opening of the Houston Buffs' season, and he also reported that once "Roy hit 10 for 10 in a basketball free-throw contest with his friend Leon Green."

The three Houston daily newspapers deplored, during the first half of 1953, the power struggle between the council and Hofheinz, but generally they supported Hofheinz's ideas for great improvements in public works, services, and facilities. Political reporter Everett Collier of the *Chronicle* estimated the needs at a minimum of $500 million shortly after the mayor took office. "While he has been as busy as a squirrel on a hot stove," commented the *Chronicle*, "the mayor has only scratched the surface of dozens of projects needed." Early council dislike of Hofheinz's "I'm going my way" attitude slowed approval of needed projects, but newspapers gave the mayor credit for "whipping up" a balanced budget and launching bond sales for improvement money.

Hofheinz met President Eisenhower at a mayors' conference in Washington and they had a pleasant chat. The president knew of his fellow Texan who had a close relationship with Lyndon Johnson, minority and later majority leader for the senate during a Republican administration. Political observers credited Johnson with saving many of Eisenhower's programs when he became majority leader. Hofheinz appeared on the national *Meet the Press* television program while in the capital. In mid-September, Mayor and Mrs. Hofheinz, accompanied by Councilmen Kohler, Holmes, and Marquette, and their wives, flew to Montreal, Canada, for the International Conference of Mayors in a private plane rented from McCullough Tool Company. Discussing the Montreal meeting, Holmes observed, "Roy went to conferences wearing a bright cowboy yellow shirt, a big 10-gallon hat, boots—in all-out Texas style. George Marquette dressed the same way." When the party returned to Houston, Holmes remembered, "Councilmen who didn't make the trip publicly criticized Hofheinz for his many plane jaunts. When facts showed that Hofheinz paid his own way outside of legal city expenses, the disgruntled councilmen said they were critical of the trips because they just 'didn't feel traveling in private planes was safe for the head of the city.' "

Despite rain, a crowd of 35,000 lined Houston streets on November 18, to see King Paul and Queen Frederika of Greece in a parade of notables. The regal tour was sponsored by the U.S. State Department, which had written Hofheinz asking him to make arrangements. Councilman Holmes said it was one of the greatest shows Hofheinz ever put on. "The thing I recall more than anything else was a plan for a great rodeo he and Bob Smith scheduled at Bob's ranch. The skies opened up that day, and it poured and streets were flooded. We had police escorts on motorcycles who couldn't get through Bellaire on the way to the ranch because water was so deep. I was in the car with the chief of staff of the Greek Army. He said, 'Gee, is it like this all the time?' He couldn't believe we didn't have enough drainage. Our convoy did get to Smith's ranch, but the rodeo had to be called off. A party later at the Hofheinzes' Yorktown home was a brilliant affair." *Press* editor George Carmack and Mrs. Carmack were among those invited to the royal festivities. Recalling the visit of the king and queen in Houston, Carmack said, "My wife, Bonnie, and I found the Hofheinzes great hosts. When we met the king and queen, we found the queen particularly gracious. They could not have had a more interesting visit—nor one more appropriate—than Roy arranged. I remember the wet afternoon at Bob Smith's ranch—a lake in the background, Santa Gertrudis cattle roaming, and a marvelous barbecue. But I particularly remember the buffet supper at the Hofheinz

King Paul and Queen Frederika of Greece with Hofheinz

home. For one thing, it was my first encounter with pheasant—cooked and then put back in its plumage. Everything was done in grand style, but with a simplicity and a naturalness that made it a great occasion."

Joseph W. Reap, state department press officer, said he had accompanied many celebrities on tours, "but never before have I seen such an enthusiastic crowd which put on one of the most remarkable demonstrations in my memory." John Flannagan, president of the Houston Chamber of Commerce, Leopold Meyer, president of the Houston Horse Show, and Ralph Johnson, president of the Houston Fat Stock Show, constituted the mayor's planning committee, but Hofheinz and Bob Smith were the chief entertainers. The mayor led off a customary "popoff" session of the next day's council meeting with a word of praise for just about everybody who had a hand in entertaining the king and queen, including council members, the police department, and public property director Francis Deering. He also included news photographers, who agreed not to photograph the royal couple when requested not to do so. Hofheinz said the king and queen told him that the way their Houston visit was handled was the finest they had ever experienced. Extra police and parade expenses for the king and queen had cost the city $3000, but the tab for entertainment was paid by Smith and Hofheinz.

Dene Hofheinz said there was an abundance of correspondence when she was wife of the mayor, and it took half her day to answer. Telephone calls consumed much of her time, and social life consisted of at least one social function a week. She estimated that dedications filled most weeknights and practically every weekend. Mrs. Hofheinz received many requests for donations, and she was a complimentary member of many civic clubs. She was on the board of the Houston Beautiful Committee, the Visiting Nurses Association, the Public Health Committee, a member-at-large of the Women's Council of Symphony, a member of the English Speaking Union, and a Daughter of Penelope. But Mrs. Hofheinz considered her family her main obligation.

"Little Dene" told a newspaperman: "Every time I see my Dad's picture in the paper, he's smiling. Why do you think he is often a grouch when he comes home?" The reporter, knowing of the mayor's battles in City Hall, smiled and said: "He's just tired, I guess." In September of 1953 Roy, Jr., was a freshman at Rice, Fred a freshman at Lamar High School, and "little Dene" a sixth grader at Grady Elementary School.

Throughout his years as county judge, Hofheinz had worked with the Texas Highway Department to get good roads from all directions in and out of Houston. When he became mayor he led in helping devise plans for better streets, thoroughfares, and freeways. Eugene Maier had graduated in civil engineering at the University of Kansas, majoring in traffic problems. He did postgraduate work there and at Yale University's Bureau of Highway Traffic. He settled in Houston as a registered professional engineer, joined the city's traffic engineering department, and was appointed director in 1952 by Oscar Holcombe. Hofheinz recognized Maier's ability and kept him in the post. They talked at length about what street and freeway programs should be planned. Fully knowledgeable about the traffic problems of the growing city, they understood each other from the beginning.

Looking back in 1978, Maier, now owner of the Flying L Ranch in Bandera, Texas, a resort, said:

> When Hofheinz asked that I stay on as director, although he hadn't known me personally before that, I thought it was a compliment. Right from the start we worked well together. He was one who would give responsibility and authority, and we had a pretty free hand in running our departments, and he supported what we tried to do, so he was an excellent administrator in that regard. Shortly after he was elected, the county decided that it would have a bond election of up to $20 million to improve the roadways in the county. Ralph Ellifrit, director of planning, and I reviewed the county's program, and we noticed that none of the money was to be spent in the city, although most of

the population and certainly the county taxes came from the city, so we went down and met with Hofheinz and called it to his attention. In his usual way, he reacted very quickly and called the county judge and commissioners and told them to come over and talk over the matter. He used a little muscle in saying he wouldn't support their program unless they would go back and provide some funds for the city. They saw that they couldn't get the bonds voted unless they had his support, and so, as I recall, they added $5 or $6 million for city projects. Adding contributions by other sources, the city got about $10 million, the beginning of major improvements on the traffic arteries in the city.

The Texas Highway Department had the responsibility for expressways, but the expressway system works only as you are able to develop a supporting network of major thoroughfares. When the mayor finally saw that he was going to get $10 million, he wanted to spend this where it would be most obvious and would be dramatic and make an impact on transportation in the community. On projects like Memorial Drive and the Elesian elevated structure in the north end of town, it was obvious that these were major traffic ways, and those were the ones which he supported, and it really was the beginning of a network of major thoroughfares that supported the freeway system and actually made it operate.

I wasn't involved in the right-of-way acquisitions for Memorial, but I do recall that there were difficulties because there was very little room between a cemetery and Buffalo Bayou, and rather than build something that was inadequate, it was suggested that four lanes would be enough. But the mayor always wanted to go first class, so he stayed with his concept and our suggestions and we built a six-lane facility. He decided that that's where it ought to be and that's where it was built. That's the determination he always had when he knew that he was doing something right and to be sure that we were getting really what we needed.

Hofheinz had great imagination, and his only real problem was the City Council. He fought with the council, exposed it for what it was. Some members had their hands out. When he caught them doing something wrong, like buying the wrong kind of parking meters, he exposed them in public, and that was embarrassing to them because they'd never had that happen before. Just before Hofheinz came into office, the city had only bought one kind of parking meter, a Karpark. It was furnished by a friend of Oscar Holcombe, Fred Sharp from Austin. They traveled to Europe together. Just before Holcombe left office, he instructed a council committee, who also were all friends of Sharp, to put together specifications for new parking meters which were actually needed. The committee didn't submit the specifications to the council until after Hofheinz was in office. The purchasing director called me and asked me about the specifications, and it was obvious that there was only one meter that could be bought, so we called that to Roy's attention. The way he handled it was, he just walked in to the council and he said, "Your specifications have been rigged." That was embarrassing to the committee, but that's the way he handled any matter like that. In doing such things, he made a lot of people mad with him. He was honest to the fullest degree and never suggested that anything be done, to my knowledge, for anybody whether he was a friend or not; he wanted to do it in the right way.

When Holcombe was mayor, city officials were permitted to give work orders for anything under a thousand dollars to any one of their friends in the contracting business. I would say that during the period that I went with the city in 1947, up until 1953, we did make substantial progress in improving traffic, but we did it by utilizing what we had. That is, we made one-way streets, took off parking, and rearranged bus stops, etc. Those types and regulations would permit improvements, but at no time were we doing the basic development absolutely essential to support a freeway system.

Hofheinz, with the county bond money, gave impetus for demonstrating to the community that the development of these major thoroughfares was important, or more so than the construction of the freeways themselves. There were major arteries all over town where we had just two-lane roadways. With money Hofheinz got for the city, we were able to go in and build four-lane divided roadways and to introduce in the community streets it never had before.

Hofheinz did more during his three years as mayor in terms of transportation which supported the freeway construction and transportation planning than had been done before his time. I'd say that there isn't any city in the country today which has the basic network of freeway major thoroughfares that the City of Houston has. Hofheinz established the basic concept and pattern in support for it.

Maier commented on Hofheinz's abilities:

His great asset, to me, was that I could take a technical problem to him and he would understand it. There wasn't any question about it—he'd see exactly what you were talking about. I can recall in 1953 we were having a transportation study made which was called an "Origin and Destination" study. Specifically, what it did was sound out where people started from and where they went, and those patterns of traffic then indicated where you should build your freeways and your major arteries. This was the first one of those, actually, that had been done in Texas, as I recall. We had gotten along in the study far enough to get some patterns of travel, and they had been plotted on the plastic sheets. I visited Hofheinz one morning and showed him the progress we were making and how the heaviest lines showed where the traffic arteries ought to be. He said, "Oh, I'd like to keep these."

At noon I went to a luncheon meeting of the Chamber of Commerce Highway Committee. There was the mayor. The members asked him to get up and give a talk. He quickly explained all details of the surveys and how they showed where the patterns of travel would be. I hadn't spent 10 minutes with him that morning, but he gave a lucid description of how these surveys were based. He could pick up anything instantly. You can imagine my surprise. He could just grasp anything in the briefest time, and he could separate the politics from it. He was a strong supporter for everything that we did.

I stayed away from council and worked through the mayor. When a problem came up, I wouldn't have to go down and explain it to him and have him go in and explain it to the council. If the problem had any importance at all, he would have me down there talking with the council about it. He expected professionalism all the time, in every department. It didn't matter whether it was engineering or parks or planning or anything else; he thought that the person who was doing the work was a professional and he should do his part in the program. He made many contributions, there's no doubt about that, and he had the imagination to do so.

In September of 1953, Hofheinz unveiled plans for 12 major freeways for Houston—an idea that began when he was county judge. The crowded freeways today are built almost as the young county judge—later mayor—and engineers envisioned them.

Hofheinz attended the White House Conference of Mayors in December of 1953 and returned home to say, "Our War Department said Russia could destroy 65 percent of the total U.S. population with its growing arsenal. Supersecret details which I heard cannot be revealed, but I believe the American people do not like to play tin soldiers. If you give them the facts, you won't have any trouble getting volunteer services needed for civil defense on a local level. We were told that the only defense against the hydrogen bomb—we saw movies of a blast in the South Pacific—is to burrow underground or evacuate the city. Every city is going to be called upon to take care of its own and prepare its defenses. If we in Houston are to be prepared, there must be a tremendous amount of planning and recruiting of volunteers. Houston has made tremendous strides in this direction under the leadership of Bob Smith, but there is still a much greater job to be done." The background Hofheinz gained at that two-day conference loaded his quick mind with information which ultimately led to a bomb-shelter proposal to the Defense Department which got national attention, but was finally vetoed by Washington politicians.

Hofheinz ended the year 1953 with the reins of the city government still in hand despite some extremely rough riding. He managed to pour plenty of concrete and initiate a number of projects in various fields while at the same time keeping a balance in his relations with city councilmen. From the time he took office in January through the summer, one fight after another erupted between the mayor and the councilmen. Suddenly the sniping ceased and the year ended on a peaceful plane. The mayor had made a number of proposals, some of which had been initiated and a number of which had not gotten "off center."

Nineteen fifty-four would be an election year, and Hofheinz let it be known that he was eyeing the governor's chair. When asked if he would be a candidate for reelection as mayor, he did a switch by replying that he would not be a candidate for governor if Governor Shivers ran for reelection. Shivers did run.

Despite difficulties, Hofheinz had made major gains for Houston. Among his impressive accomplishments was what has been termed the introduction of a new era in city-county relations. The mayor sold the idea of earmarking county bond funds for expenditure within the city. Previously, these had been spent outside the city although 80 percent of the county taxpayers lived within Houston. As a result, the city and county initiated plans on three major projects: extension of Memorial Drive into West Capitol, Hardy and Elysian extensions across Buffalo Bayou, and a new 69th Street bridge. New slum clearance laws and a housing rehabilitation program had been passed and a slum clearance committee appointed by the mayor. Hofheinz promised to get this program underway early in 1954.

The mayor also was an enthusiastic supporter of recreation improvements. On his recommendation, the council initiated work on nine small swimming pools. These were completed in time for summer use. An expanded renovation of school playgrounds was coordinated by the mayor with the school district. Hofheinz also pushed a program of park acquisition in neighborhood areas recommended by the city planning commission.

The mayor proposed remodeling the Music Hall to accommodate all the city's cultural activities, air conditioning and new seating in the Coliseum, and the tying in of these buildings, by means of a walkway across the bayou, to new parking areas the city owned. He proposed new recreational facilities and possibly a central health center for the Civic Center. He also proposed that a new recreation center be set up in the Richey Evangelistic Temple, just across the bayou from the Coliseum. In addition, a new purchasing system was introduced by the mayor. It was pelted with criticism by councilmen, some of whom claimed quality had been sacrificed. Hofheinz estimated his plan would save the city $500,000 a year when he took office. An analysis of purchasing by purchasing director Tom Harling showed that $280,000 actually had been saved.

The administration tightened up on traffic court ticket handling with Johnny Goyen the sparkplug. More clerks were put to work to speed up processing parking tickets pending the time when new electronic machines would be installed which would automatically insure that notices were mailed out to ticket holders. Hofheinz also took steps to speed up the right-of-way acquisition necessary for elimination of several of the city's worst street jogs. The mayor speeded up delinquent tax collections with the result that at the end of the year, $1,900,000 had been collected, an all-time record and $1 million more than the previous year. This was aimed at obtaining more revenue and improving Houston's credit rating. The mayor and councilmen approved the creation of a new department of aviation to handle long-range airport planning, as well as to devise methods of squeezing more revenues out of municipal airport facilities. In connection with this, Hofheinz personally initiated a number of changes in the new airport terminal building.

There were council problems and delays on other Hofheinz promises. He planned to set up an inventory system that would keep daily tabs on equipment, office furniture, files, and the like in every department. This was going to be under separate control, independent of the departments. It had not been set up, but the mayor insisted he was working on it. The installation of an information and complaint center to expedite the handling of inquiries and requests from citizens was vetoed by the council. The mayor finally got space set aside for this in the main lobby of City Hall. Appointment of a citizens' committee to study the needs of the city, a bond program to get them under way, and recommendations of new sources of revenue to support those bonds were held up. The mayor said the committee would be in action in 1954. His promise to initiate new laws that could set minimum standards on paving put into subdivisions by private developers was delayed. One of his major promises was to pave every unimproved street within the city in two years. The year ended with less than 100 miles completed, one-fifth of the goal because of fiscal problems.

Christmas at Yorktown in 1953 was not as festive as in previous years. Dene Hofheinz was hospitalized on December 23 in preparation for major surgery after Christmas Day. The family's attention was on her condition, and they were relieved when she came through successfully. All were cheerful at year's end by secret knowledge that a big business deal for the head of the family was planned for January of 1954. The deal involved Hofheinz's becoming a major television stockholder.

20

Reelection as Mayor

Roy Hofheinz's second year as mayor, 1954, brought progress for the city despite his almost continuous battle with city councilmen. Hofheinz remained busy in his duties as mayor. On March 1, 1954, he named a committee to plan Houston's future. It had 50 members and was chaired by Bob Smith. Hofheinz asked the committee to review needed improvements for the entire city in all sections and in all phases during the next 10 years. "Every effort will be made to expedite the committee's recommendations to the mayor and the council," Hofheinz said. Prior to forming the committee, Hofheinz had department heads busy estimating present and future needs to provide data for the civic leaders' deliberations. The committee's study would ultimately provide the basis for a huge bond program for Houston.

The committee's membership constituted a roster of the civic leadership of Houston. Councilman Marquette praised the committee as a good cross-section and a fine selection. Councilman Holmes, an outspoken critic of the committee, observed that if he "were a politician and was going to run for office, that is the lineup I would put up to raise campaign funds." Holmes added, "Roy made a serious mistake in placing Mr. Smith as head of the committee. I have a high regard for Mr. Smith, but it is unfair for the small taxpayer and property owner to put Mr. Smith up to say how and when about unimproved and undeveloped land in the path of future developments. However fair Smith might be, he cannot help being biased. I am speaking specifically of property Mr. Smith owns: 340 acres across from the airport, 60 acres recently purchased off South Main, 560 acres on Westheimer, additional acreage on Sage Road, and other acreage in the vicinity of San Felipe and Westheimer. The committee is not responsible to the taxpayer or anyone else except Roy Hofheinz. In my book, that is bad business, especially since Roy and Bob are partners." Smith replied, "Roy and I are not partners in any effort whatsoever [in 1955]. I definitely would not be biased in my own favor on any question."

Chairman Smith also asserted that the committee "probably is the most representative cross-section of leaders ever assembled for a civic purpose. It will be the committee's job to take a look at the needs of all Houstonians. The committee's success will depend upon whether it truly reflects the views of Houston as a whole and whether the public generally accepts and supports any recommendations it makes."

After many weeks of study, the citizens' committee produced a professional survey of improvements needed beyond ordinary budget considerations. It said that Houston should spend $500 million over a period of 10 years to get the growing metropolis in first-class order. There was little debate about the report, but with a city charter ceiling of two dollars per $1000 in valuations for bond issues, how could the money be raised?

In both the 1953 and 1954 budgets, Hofheinz depended on increased ratios on valuations and equalization to add to the city's coffers. The councilmen as a whole had begrudged every increase sought but, under Hofheinz's persistent demands, had provided for some hikes which provided additional money for some improvements. As county judge, Hofheinz had argued about assessments and the low ratio for tax rates. Some of the same men who served on the citizens' committee were among those who fought Hofheinz's county tax plans. Now, with professional data in their laps and a wide knowledge of actual conditions within the city, they at last agreed on what was needed.

During Oscar Holcombe's 20 years as mayor, no such blueprint had been drawn. Keeping taxes and valuations low was more important than facing up to what bad conditions existed in the once "small town atmosphere." Houston was growing so fast that public improvements were a necessity, not just the wish of a mayor who wanted the city to catch up on improvements for residents and the thousands of newcomers who poured into its confines for better jobs.

The first public threat by the council to throw Hofheinz out of office came in February of 1955, when members told him to "change your ways or we'll impeach you." Hofheinz ignored the threat and went on his way. Debate at council meetings continued to be hot, and when a rabies epidemic threatened, Councilman Holmes remarked, "I'm going to let one of those mad dogs bite me and then I'm going to bite Roy."

Hofheinz also invited problems when controversial Senator Joseph McCarthy was invited by the San Jacinto chapter of the Sons of the Texas Republic, headed by J. Watts, to speak on April 21 at the annual San Jacinto Day Celebration to be held at the monument commemorating the victory over Mexico. McCarthy was at the peak of his power as an anti-Communist crusader. Jerry McAfee, a Republican candidate for Congress, asked Hofheinz and the council to plan an official city welcome for the senator. Hofheinz said the request would have to come from some official of the sponsoring organization. None came. The mayor accepted a speaking engagement at Gainesville that day, and other councilmen also said they had engagements and could not participate. The snub of the senator brought criticism from some who began to fear Communists in every closet, but there was no way to convince the liberal mayor that any Houston welcome was due McCarthy. He did order full police protection for McCarthy, in cooperation with the Harris County sheriff's department, to insure the senator's safety.

The shadow of the "Old Gray Fox" fell across the City Council meeting table again on March 17. Oscar Holcombe, who had served 10 two-year terms as mayor, was not there in person, but he wrote the city that he wanted council action no later than March 24, 1954, on a deal involving some of his property. He was referring to the 2.571 acres, or 111,992 square feet, of land he had turned over to the city when mayor in 1948. It was to be used for the Gulf Freeway right-of-way in the vicinity of Winkler Drive with the understanding that the city would pay him for the tract when he left office.

On March 24, the council instructed the legal department to offer Holcombe the going 1948 price for the Gulf Freeway property. Council said that, in the event Holcombe objected, the legal department should start condemnation proceedings. Councilman Resweber made the motion after hearing a ruling from city attorney Will Sears that the city should pay Holcombe on the basis of a land appraisal of 1948 and not on 1954 prices. Hofheinz said that Holcombe's land had been appraised at 40 cents per square foot in 1948, which would mean that the land would cost the taxpayers about $44,800 on that basis. It would cost the city close to $96,000 at the rate of 85.5 cents a square foot which Holcombe agreed to accept during negotiations with the city land acquisition department. The 85.5 cents was 12.5 cents less than the 1954 appraisal.

Informed of the council's decision, Holcombe said, "Until I get an offer, I prefer not to have anything to say about it. I'm not going to be unreasonable about it." Mayor Pro tem Kesseler, who presided because of the illness of Hofheinz, said that he had talked with Holcombe about the matter and that they both felt the only way to arrive at a fair value for the property would be to determine what the city paid for similar land in the area in 1948. Hofheinz said Holcombe should be treated as any other resident and pointed out that the $50,000 difference could be used for needed improvements. "I've still got shell streets in front of my house, open ditches, no street lights, no bus service, no garbage collection," said the mayor in opposing the 1954 estimate.

Holcombe paid a surprise visit to City Hall on April 28 and castigated Hofheinz and the council in a heated clash. He left with a broad hint that he would run for mayor again. He aimed shafts at Hofheinz in particular, sharply criticized the manner in which the city had handled his land deal, and labeled as "perfectly silly" the remonstrance of the mayor that delay on the land deal was partly the fault of the ex-mayor himself. "The Old Gray Fox," nattily dressed in a brown suit and yellow tie decorated with black cats, pulled no punches as he lashed out at the mayor, city attorney Sears, and the council itself. He demanded quick action in closing the sale of his parcel of land. "I have been kicked around like a football," he said. "I've been treated shamefully. I want this council now to condemn that land, arbitrate the question of payment, or tell me to jump in the creek. I don't care what you do, but do it now." Holcombe said he would take "any price you set on the land in question" and added scathingly to the mayor that "you don't even know how much land is involved."

Hofheinz said the ex-mayor's statement that he would accept payment on 1948 valuations of the land was the first time "you and your representatives have ever told us you would take anything less than the present market value." He added that "with this new information, we can arrive at a settlement quickly." The mayor then said soothingly, "You know of course, that there are many problems connected with city business and many unavoidable delays." That did it.

"No citizen should have to present his problems," Holcombe snapped. "You should know about them. I talked to Will Sears about this. That's the way city business should be handled. I understand Mr. Sears talked to you." Mayor Hofheinz, irked in turn, snapped back, "You're wrong." Before more could be said, several councilmen poured oil on the troubled waters. "You're not really mad, are you Mr. Mayor?" Councilman Holmes asked. Councilman George Marquette added, "We'll get you off the hook today." After the ex-mayor left the room, they referred the matter to Sears with instructions to make a recommendation.

Holcombe opened his fiery talk with the comment that this was his second appearance at City Hall when he was not mayor. The other time had been just prior to his election in 1947, but there was nothing pathetic about that, he added. As he left the council chambers, the former mayor was surrounded by newsmen who demanded to know if he intended to make the mayor's race again in the fall. "I have no plans," Holcombe replied.

"Do you think Mayor Hofheinz is doing a good job?" he was asked.

"I have no plans," he repeated, adding the punch line, "I'm not coming to City Hall again this year." Pressed again for a hint about his possible candidacy, Holcombe jerked a thumb toward the council chamber he had just left and said, "If that's the way the city's business is being run, you can judge for yourself what I'll do."

Holcombe had never lifted a finger from 1949 through 1952 to proceed with condemnation of the land he had turned over for the Gulf Freeway, Hofheinz charged after the meeting. "Just because he was mayor does not mean he should get preferred treatment on his subdivision and land purchasing." Holcombe on May 12 turned down the council's final offer of 40 cents a square foot. "I'm sorry I had to come back here today," he said, "but I want to get the matter closed sometime this year. I think the mayor is under some mis-apprehension what I want City Council to do. After I came here two weeks ago, the mayor said, by innuendo, according to the press, I wanted special favors. I want to call attention to a letter I wrote the mayor and council on March 24. In my last paragraph I said I didn't want any special favors. All I want is some action on my request which has been before City Council for more than a year." Holcombe said he would accept the price the city had paid for adjacent property in 1948, ranging in price from 52 cents to one dollar a foot. He later told a condemnation commission the land was worth two dollars a square foot.

Some councilmen constantly attacked Police Chief Morrison because he kept the city freer from vice than most of his predecessors—because of Hofheinz's orders. They had friends who thought an "open" city would be more attractive than one with "the lid on tight." Morrison suffered from a painful disc ailment. To get relief, he went to a friend, Dr. Julius McBride, a chiropractor, who prescribed codeine in the name of a black man named Billy Jackson. Morrison's condition came to light after George White, a federal narcotics agent, took a room at the William Penn Hotel and began an investigation of a rumored Houston narcotics ring. Mayor Hofheinz told Morrison to let the chips fall where they may, and the chief and his staff cooperated as more federal agents poured into the city to investigate.

The suicide of a vice squad detective outside Morrison's office and federal indictments of a police captain who headed the vice squad, another vice squad detective, and Dr. McBride gave the newspapers big headlines for several weeks. The scandal burst into the open after the home of Earl Boise, a known dope peddler, was raided and heroin and other narcotics were found by the vice squad. A check by federal and police officials showed that from $75,000 to $525,000 in seized dope was missing from a police headquarters storeroom. Grand jury investigations showed that certain vice squad men had taken the dope and sold it to underworld figures. Efforts to link Morrison to the illegal traffic were futile. It was proved he took codeine only for pain, but the pressure on him was so great that he resigned.

Hofheinz always felt that a professional police commissioner chosen by merit was the best answer for leadership in the law enforcement department. City ordinances required that any police chief be selected from the ranks of the police force. The mayor sent a new ordinance to the council to make it possible to hire the best qualified man for the job regardless of residency or service on the force. The police department immediately split over the proposal, and members put pressure on the council to kill the measure. Some members did not like the mayor's candid comment that he could find no one in the department qualified for the commissioner's post. The council killed the ordinance by a vote of six to three. Only Councilmen Heflin and Wilson voted with the mayor.

That defeat caused the mayor and his wife to tell reporters that "the issue for the 1954 election has been set." Dene said, "Roy can't quit with this issue in the air." Hofheinz then asked Arthur Lorton, Jr., former head of the Houston

Bureau of the Federal Bureau of Investigation, to join him as an adviser on the police problem. After long consultation, the mayor offered the council the name of Sergeant Jack Heard. He had been on the force since 1938 and was a lie detector expert. The mayor said Heard was a "very good man, a career-cop-in-a-closed-town man. On August 31 the council approved Heard.

After Oscar Holcombe got back into the news because of his row with the City Council and Hofheinz concerning payment for his land, the *Houston Chronicle* began a popularity poll on possible candidates for mayor in the November election. It printed coupons and urged readers to send in their choices. Hofheinz's associates predicted that the poll would be stacked for Holcombe, who long had the *Chronicle's* support. As the day-by-day count mounted, Holcombe was in front. Gould Beech recalled: "We decided to outstack the Holcombe people, including many who had worked under him at City Hall. We put people on the streets where papers were sold, and when *Chronicle* trucks arrived we would buy bundle after bundle." Beech's home became a clipping bureau. "We dropped about 100 envelopes at a time in different mailboxes," Beech said. "Wives, cousins, and Hofheinz friends made up the mailing crew."

In the beginning, the *Chronicle* poll showed Holcombe with 34.7 percent, Hofheinz 22 percent, Louie Welch eight percent, Frank Gibler six percent, and W. Gail Reeves 5.9 percent. However, following a last-minute mailing blitz by Hofheinz supporters, the final poll showed "Hofheinz 37.5 and 28.9 for Holcombe"; others trailed with less than 10 percent. "The *Chronicle* never caught on to our mailing campaign and had big headlines that Hofheinz had won the poll," Beech continued. "I am sure, however, that Holcombe supporters did just what we did. We just had a better mailing organization." The poll must have had some effect on Holcombe because he announced after it was completed that he would not run in 1954.

On September 23 Hofheinz announced for reelection, saying, "The progress which has been made in the past 20 months is apparent on all sides—expressway extensions, residential topping, water extension, sewers, parks, swimming pools, storm sewers, improvements at the Coliseum and Music Hall; progress as well as tremendous savings in the purchasing department that is concerned only with the price and quality of the product, not the political influence of the seller; and progress in handling of traffic violations and parking tickets and every citizen paying the same penalty." On October 1, Alvin S. Moody, Jr., a virtual political unknown, filed as candidate for mayor after Oscar Holcombe withdrew. Moody, then president of Texas Title Company and an attorney, announced he was entering the race because of a "desire to perform a public service to the city of my birth and a conviction that I can properly perform the duties of the high office of mayor."

Holcombe, who had been hesitating about seeking an 11th term, said he

Oscar Holcombe (left) and Alvin S. Moody, Jr. Photographs courtesy the *Houston Chronicle.*

would vote for Moody and be of whatever assistance he could. Many potential supporters of Louie Welch, who had been considered a likely candidate, were reported to have deserted the former councilman and gone over to Moody following a survey made by real estate developers. This survey, a fairly comprehensive poll of a cross-section of the city, showed that Welch could get only 20 percent of the vote with the rest going to Holcombe or Hofheinz. Moody's title company derived most of its income from builders and subdividers in constant need of city services. Holcombe was probably one of his biggest customers.

Louie Welch, former councilman-at-large who had been defeated two years earlier by Hofheinz, got in the race the next day. He developed his platform "plank-by-plank" and had a program he said would solve many of Houston's problems. One of the first to get his attention was the dope traffic. He flew to Washington to confer with top narcotics officials, he reported, and following that trip outlined a control program he planned to put into effect if elected. The creation of a permanent transit commission to be made up of riders, store owners, business and industrial leaders, and transit company representatives was another proposal. He said he would seek legislation giving this commission power to deal with rates and service. The public health problem was an alarming one, Welch said, and he planned a program to remove the health hazard of poor water and sewage, saying this program would reduce the time necessary to get these improvements. Welch's plans for outdoor recreation included making available top recreational facilities for "all Houstonians," stressing the possibilities presented by Lake Houston. All city parks would be cleaned up, he added. He considered greater cooperation in city government important enough to warrant a separate plank in his platform and said he would accomplish this improvement by serving the people of Houston as a "true public servant with no axes to grind and with no one to please except the citizens."

Shortly after the campaign began, Hofheinz once worked until midnight checking on radio-TV business at the KTHT office. In walked a tall, beautiful woman who was in the radio station's employ. She was wearing a robe. When previously she had told the Judge that she knew intimate secrets about one of his opponents and would be glad to make them public for his campaign, Hofheinz had told her he did not want to get involved. Just as she approached the Judge, the woman opened her robe, revealing her nude body. Hofheinz quickly dialed home for Dene and told her what was happening. Mrs. Hofheinz rushed to the office, took the woman by the arm, and escorted her to Yorktown. Then she called the woman's parents in another city, and the next day she was sent home by plane. Apparently she had wanted to compromise the Judge and hurt his campaign because of his refusal to use her story about one of his opponents, but Dene had come to the rescue as usual.

Washers popped into the political picture as Holcombe spoke over television for Moody. He issued a challenge to Hofheinz, saying he would name a committee composed of *Chronicle* editor M. E. Walter, *Post* managing editor Arthur Laro, and *Press* editor George Carmack to decide the following question: Was Holcombe telling the truth when he said washers distributed by Hofheinz during the campaign were neither washers bought during the Holcombe administration nor washers bought by Hofheinz during the Hofheinz administration? "If this committee of three agree I am wrong, then I will pay $5000 to the United Fund," commented Holcombe.

Hofheinz answered, "I'm delivering the 'Old Gray Fox's' $20 washers and my $3.13 washers—same size, same weight, same thickness—to the Shilstone Testing Laboratory. I hope to have a testing report from them in time for Mr. Holcombe to deliver his $5000 check to the United Fund. The United Fund needs his money and I'm sure the 'Old Gray Fox' won't be Moody or Welch." The mayor was referring to the fiber washers which he said Holcombe had bought at $20 a thousand and which, under the Hofheinz administration, cost only $3.13 a thousand. As might have been expected, after the election washers did not figure in the news any more. Holcombe did not feel he should make the $5000 contribution to the United Fund and Hofheinz did not push the issue further. He had made his point.

Mayor Hofheinz accused wealthy oilman Jim "Silver Dollar" West and a high-ranking police officer of spying on a private party at the mayor's Yorktown home on the night of October 6. Police Chief Heard named West's companion as Lieutenant A. C. Martindale of the burglary and theft division, who had long been a close, personal friend of West's. "The mayor called me Wednesday night and told me about chasing a Cadillac with three radio aerials on it and said Jim West was driving and Martindale was in the car with him," Heard said in a *Chronicle* story. "Martindale, who is on vacation, was found by reporters in the police station Thursday morning and confirmed he was riding with West."

According to the newspaper, after thinking things over, Martindale had consented to meet the press and give his version. He scoffed at the mayor's interpretation that he and West were spying. "We went up there on Yorktown looking for a quiet place where we could get out of the car for a moment. We were not spying on the mayor. It's no secret that West is a friend of mine, and I'm a friend of his. All I want to be sure of is that these politicians spell my name right."

Hofheinz said he had spotted the multimillionaire and his companion parked outside his home in a green or blue Cadillac convertible. "I gave a chase in my son's car, a Ford, and recognized both West and the officer," Hofheinz said. "I gave a party for a group of some 50 to 60 young people, ages in lower 20s. It was a social gathering, not a political strategy meeting." Gould Beech, the mayor's executive assistant, had dropped in later in the evening. When Beech started to leave about 10:30 P.M., he spotted the Cadillac outside and told the mayor. Hofheinz said he had slipped into his son's car and, as he drove out of his driveway, caught West and the police officer in the glare of the headlights. The Cadillac, equipped with three radio aerials, moved out swiftly down Yorktown Drive with the mayor following. "West slowed down three or four times to let me pass," said Hofheinz, "but I slowed up keeping them in my headlights." Hofheinz chuckled: "The officer said he ducked below the seat trying to hide, but he had come up for air, and when he did I definitely recognized him."

The next day, West was reported to be in the room he maintained at Hermann Hospital resting up from his night riding labors and fortifying himself for more of the same. A nurse who answered the telephone on the floor outside West's room told reporters that he could not be disturbed. West, a private citizen, long had made a practice of cruising the city and county at night in his multiple-radio-equipped Cadillac, usually accompanied by a police officer friend and racing to the scene of emergency calls. To end the practice, the former police chief, L. D. Morrison, had issued an order forbidding armed duty police officers to ride with West. As far as was known then, the order was still in effect. Chief Heard said he would talk with Martindale about the affair. Under a new police reorganization plan advanced the previous week by Chief

Heard, Martindale had been listed for promotion to captain in charge of a new robbery detail to be set up, Mayor Hofheinz said. Auto registration records showed 11 Cadillacs listed to various members of the West family. The only convertible in the bunch was registered to Marion West. Hofheinz, early in the year, had leveled a blast at West as the leader of a police faction which opposed his police commissioner plan defeated by City Council.

Three times before the incident, some councilmen demanded that former Chief Morrison be fired by Hofheinz because of the ban on West's "playing cops and robbers," according to the mayor. In discussing the ban, Hofheinz said that he did not want policemen to play around with West; he wanted them instead to pursue the mayor's enemies—"ex-racketeers, hoped-to-be racketeers, and others who would like to see a return of bookie joints and rampant vice of earlier days." Hofheinz said there was "a minority of policemen who would rather play department and city politics and participate in intrigues than to do their jobs properly."

On October 28, the *Chronicle* endorsed Hofheinz, praising his extensive experience in city and county government. The editorial also asserted that the mayor's record in his first administration had been "commendable." It included advances in the municipal water supply, airport, fire stations, park system, sanitation services, and the drainage system, in addition to those in development of the city's highway system. The paper also noted that the mayor had reorganized the purchasing system . . . "saving the city between $600,000 and $1 million in two years." Finally, the select committee to plan for Houston's development was praised, and Hofheinz's "proven ability" was emphasized.

The *Post* endorsed Hofheinz the next day with this terse comment: "In the opinion of the *Post*, Mayor Roy Hofheinz deserves a second term. He has proved himself a good administrator and has kept abreast of modern municipal developments. Hofheinz has made mistakes, but they are far outweighed by his record on the asset side of the ledger." The *Press*, often the object of Hofheinz's ire, endorsed Welch, however. The principle reason cited was the issue of harmony between the mayor and the City Council: "Houston can't go forward with the bickering between the mayor and the City Council that we have had for the past two years. Welch proved, as a councilman-at-large, that he can get along with his fellow councilmen."

Houston *Press* editor George Carmack's enthusiasm for the Hofheinz administration died when the mayor, by mid-year, opened up and continued an assault on the newspaper. He called it a "yellow journal" and particularly attacked Jack Donahue, who moved up from assistant to city editor as Hofheinz took over city government management. Neither Hofheinz nor the fiesty, crusading Donahue, a native of Waco and a graduate of Baylor University, spared the use of "SOB" when referring to people they did not like. Even as late as 1979, neither could refer to the other without such a description although both had excellent command of language. Not even persuasive, peace-making Dene Hofheinz or Leon Jaworski, the *Press* attorney, could get them to agree to be friends. They tried. The Hofheinz-Donahue feud, which flared into headlines during the second Hofheinz-Welch election in 1954, actually began on election day of 1952, when Hofheinz defeated Welch for his first term as mayor.

An author in 1979, after serving as managing editor of the *Houston Post* and *Los Angeles Mirror,* Donahue was interviewed at the request of the author of this book. He did not want anyone to think he volunteered information but recalled: "My first impression of Hofheinz, when I was assistant city editor and he was running the first time against Welch, was that he was a con man. I felt he was a devious person, obviously power hungry. As time passed Roy was in constant conflict with City Council and other elected city officials. There was a bitter fight because Roy had promised not to raise taxes, but tried to raise assessment ratios instead, which amounted to the same thing. I felt he had, in effect, broken his promise. At the same time his arrogance, which bordered on madness, made a shambles of any constructive work at City Hall." Donahue also wrote negative stories about the Hofheinz administration and once referred to "the Hofheinz machine" which, according to Donahue, infuriated the mayor. Hofheinz struck back whenever he could. He threatened, on several occasions to try to "destroy the *Press.*" The feud was bitter and long. Hofheinz's charge of "yellow journalism" plagued the *Press* until it was sold in 1964.

The Hofheinz-Welch-Moody campaign was heated from the beginning. In answer to Moody's call for harmony at City Hall, Hofheinz said he was "unwilling to buy harmony. The city needs so much and I will continue to fight to see that not one dollar will be thrown away or be lost in the form of kickbacks and favoritism." He particularly attacked Councilmen Kesseler, Holmes, and Resweber as "the cookie jar trio" who wanted the characteristics of the long Holcombe administration to be continued. Moody and Welch, he charged, were "Holcombe's boys." Holcombe spoke in behalf of Moody and defended his administrations. Hofheinz in his continuing television talks used graphs to show how much less various items cost under his administration than under that of the former mayor. His demonstrations on the cost of washers caused the greatest comment, and he used them as a campaign symbol.

At one meeting of Young Democrats, Moody walked out, charging that Hofheinz had the session stacked with supporters, thus making pointless his efforts to seek their support. Moody also tried to pin the dope scandal on Hofheinz's shoulders, saying the mayor interfered in police work too much, and he attacked Hofheinz's program of spending, saying he was moving too fast.

With his usual strong labor and black support, Hofheinz won his seventh election November 2. The final official count was Hofheinz 38,379, Welch

28,870, and Moody 28,012. The voters, however, did not give the mayor city councilmen on whom he could depend for support in the progressive program he advocated. Three of his constant critics—Kesseler, Resweber, and Dr. Kohler—were reelected. W. Gail Reeves won on an anti-Hofheinz platform. Shirley Brakefield, who termed himself an independent, was victorious and what course he would follow was unknown. Heflin and Wilson, who often went along with Hofheinz, also won. Lee McLemore, accused as a supporter of the mayor but who denied it from the stump, became the eighth member. He ousted Harry Holmes, Jr., Hofheinz's "friendly enemy" who had often engaged in shouting matches with the mayor when they accused each other of lying during the previous 23 months.

Hofheinz's victory proved that dramatic use of television had outdated stump rallies in attracting voters. Although in neither of his victories for mayor did he win a majority of votes—no runoff election was required—he again felt he had a mandate to go ahead with his program of progress.

Temporary harmony between the mayor and the council prevailed for the rest of the year. When increases of 20 to 25 percent in voters' tax bills were mailed in late November, discontent about the cost of city government in an essentially conservative city grew. Hofheinz strongly felt, however, that his course was the right one, and he made no plans to change.

The mayor took off in December for a goodwill tour of South America to sell the advantages of Houston to businesses and travelers from Latin-American countries. The great Houston Fat Stock Show was scheduled for the following February and the mayor issued special invitations for visits to the growing, magic, bayou city. Hofheinz also bought additions to his collections of antiques and artifacts for his two homes during this pleasant interlude before his stormy second term as mayor.

21

"Old Gray Fox" and "Fat Cats"

The need for increased expenditures—and additional revenues to make these possible—was Hofheinz's theme in his 1955 inaugural address. Speaking to an audience of 1500, the mayor said, "We cannot continue to drift aimlessly and hope that somewhere down the line these needs will be provided by the passage of time." Hofheinz said that a $500 million public works program drafted by a citizens' committee "has no dreams or frills in it, every item listed is needed," adding that one-third of the total was for expressway rights-of-way. "We who are your elected officials," he said "can kid you for a time by promising you everything, and a better quality of what you already have, with no increase in the bill . . . but it just ain't so." The mayor blamed much of the accumulated needs on past city administrations when he commented, "Historically, successful politicians in Houston have not faced . . . harsh realities. The way to get along politically in Houston in the past has been to satisfy a selected group of people with powerful influence, to build a few dramatic improvements which could be spotlighted, and to provide services where the vote was favorable."

As he started his second term, the mayor pledged to promote teamwork on the council and to make every effort to promote economy. He said that Houston would remain a closed town. Hofheinz's call for new revenues set the stage for the bitterest City Hall fight in Houston's history. What happened would end Hofheinz's spectacular political career by year's end.

On January 6, when Hofheinz's administration made public its tentative budget and tax figures calling for a 20-percent increase in property assessment ratios, the long war started. Most councilmen immediately balked. They were led by W. Gail Reeves, a muscular, six-foot-five real estate owner and investor, a man described by the *Chronicle* as "a person with the dignified mien of a Roman senator" or "a Brutus or a Marcellus always ready to mount the political podium." The council newcomer proved to be the biggest thorn in Hofheinz's side. Reeves had won a seat as councilman on an anti-Hofheinz platform, and, according to the *Chronicle*, within a month he and Hofheinz were locked "in mortal combat for supremacy at City Hall."

Councilmen screamed when Hofheinz proposed that the tax assessment ratio be increased from 77 to 94.2 percent. Councilman Heflin said he would quit before he went for any such hike. "Hofheinz," he said, "is on a drunken spending spree." Hofheinz contended the increase would be necessary to provide the same services in 1955 as in 1954 because of the city's growth and its overwhelming needs. The council went to city attorney Sears for an opinion about where tax responsibility rested. He ruled that the council had final authority. The mayor immediately went on TV to ask support for his budget of $42,268,433—an increase of $7,141,011 over 1954—but the council majority was firm in demanding cutbacks which would not require a tax increase. Councilman Reeves said he wanted an investigation into Hofheinz's spending operations and called for reductions in every city department.

As chairman of the city's library board, Jack Valenti often lamented to the mayor that Houston lagged far behind other municipalities in its facilities and number of books. In the contested 1955 budget was money to expand and improve the system because of a study showing Houston ranked last among the cities compared. The mayor used this deplorable condition as one of the reasons for needing additional funds. In one speech, he predicted that Houston in 1975 would be the hub of an area population of 2.4 million people. Estimates of the Houston Chamber of Commerce showed that, as of January 1, 1977, the area population actually was 2,756,000; therefore, Hofheinz's forecast was almost perfect. No man felt the pulse of the growing city and its needs better than he. Councilman Heflin, with Reeves' backing, introduced an ordinance to eliminate three administrative jobs—one of the mayor's executive assistants, Gould Beech or John Stephen, along with Colonel Walter Reid, aviation director, and Robert Watts, office manager of the legal department. They called it an "economy move." Reid and Stephen immediately offered Hofheinz their resignations, but he did not accept them after the council passed the ordinance on first reading, 6-3. Councilman Wilson and newcomer McLemore voted with Hofheinz against the measure.

City law provided that an ordinance could be overruled if petitions were signed by sufficient people to force a "for" or "against" election. Hofheinz quickly figured that it would take 17,000 signatures to force the council to call a referendum on the ordinance or to rescind it. He immediately went on KTRK-TV to say he would circulate across the city petitions protesting the ordinance and accused Reeves of "back door tactics" to usurp the powers of the mayor after having been defeated twice for the position. Reeves responded, "The mayor now has become a cry-baby mayor. I think the people of Houston are fed up with one-man rule at City Hall. I'm going to vote for the ordinance even if Hofheinz threatens to break his oatmeal bowl and run away from home." Hofheinz charged Reeves was behind the ordinance "for political vengeance and hate."

Hofheinz's "Palace Guard" discussed the new controversy and decided that

Stephen's resignation should be withdrawn and that Beech should resign and be made a main target of the ordinance. This was done before the ordinance was passed, and the three men were taken off the city payroll. Beech's annual pay was $12,300, Reid's $8640, and Watts' $6360. Dene again came to the front and led a door-to-door campaign for her husband's aides. Beech recalled, "Within three weeks we had enough signatures to force the council to submit the ordinance to the people. Councilmen saw that they had been licked and so they repealed the ordinance abolishing the jobs." Beech also believed that the ordinance was "a war against reform and decent government. If they couldn't eliminate Hofheinz—they could eliminate me." On March 26, Mrs. Hofheinz arrived at City Hall in an armored car carrying more than 20,500 signatures on petitions. The mayor reminded the council the people had spoken. Comptroller Roy Oakes at first refused to pay the three employees who were targets of the ill-advised ordinance, saying he wanted a court decision on the validity of the petitions. Knowing how efficient Mrs. Hofheinz was in her precinct work, however, the council repealed the ordinance, and Oakes finally paid the three who would have been fired as a slap at the mayor.

The *Chronicle* reported on March 2 that Hofheinz had attacked an ordinance creating a committee of inquiry into city affairs by asserting dramatically that it was drafted by a lawyer as an instrument to open up the town to the policy rackets. These charges were made by Hofheinz on television during the first live telecast of a Houston City Council meeting. The mayor's chief adversary, Councilman Reeves, had introduced the measure as "an instrument of economy." Despite Hofheinz's opposition, the ordinance passed. Following the meeting, Reeves declared, "I think the mayor is seeing things that aren't there. . . . He is fighting windmills and has impugned the integrity of every council member." According to the *Chronicle*, "Hofheinz, with a wide grin, then promised to have all the facts in on the background and legality of the ordinance by next week." Hofheinz, at a press conference after the meeting, promised a full public hearing on the "scope and background of the ordinance. He cracked, 'That sure did calm down the introduction of that ordinance.'"

In the midst of the mayor's struggle with the council, the climax of Hofheinz's long fight with Southwestern Bell came when it began refunding $2.3 million to phone users as a result of court decisions and a compromise agreed to by the council. The company also paid the $1,985,076 in 1954 personal property taxes it previously had sought to have reduced but met with a firm *no* from the mayor and council. The beginning of the great Houston Medical Center of today came when Ben Taub, chairman of an advisory board, County Judge Bob Casey, and Mayor Hofheinz agreed on plans for a $15,600,000 city-county hospital.

Every week council sessions were hot with personal attacks. Hofheinz called Councilman Resweber "a self-admitted Huey Long-type of politician."

Shirley Brakefield   W. Gail Reeves   George Kesseler   Matt Wilson

Lee McLemore   Jim Heflin   Joe Resweber   Ira Kohler

Councilmen who tried to impeach Hofheinz during his second mayoral term. Drawings by Bob Hendrixson, *Memphis Press-Scimitar.*

On another occasion he invited Resweber to meet him outside the council chamber for a fist fight, but the challenge was not accepted. Meanwhile, Hofheinz instructed the tax assessor, Fred Ankenman, to cut the 20 percent assessment ratio increase, since he saw no hope for council approval. Reeves and other councilmen then began meeting behind closed doors to do their own budget-making without Hofheinz present. Reeves said Hofheinz was trying to intimidate city employees to support his budget position. The council cut $2 million from the proposed budget, but that was insufficient. By March the guerrilla war was in full swing. Councilman Kohler proposed charter changes to give the council more power over administration of the government.

In one weekly KTRK-TV "Report to the People," Hofheinz said the policy racketeers would be stormed and attacked out of existence. He exhibited a handful of policy tickets which he said police had confiscated during the last 48 hours. "This confirms what I have said—that they would try to open up the policy rackets here." He said "racketeers, thieves, and scoundrels who are attempting this may be assured that the police chief and vice squad are dedicated to stomping them out." He called the policy game one of the worst rackets. He said that it was most harmful to the community in that it gave back only five cents out of each dollar collected.

The *Chronicle* reported on April 10 that "Mayor Hofheinz's bold 10-year $500 million city improvement program—the major plan in the political platform on which he rode into office—appears to be a dead pigeon." The paper noted that the "knock out punch" to the program had been delivered by the council, who opposed the heavier taxation that would be required.

When the Houston Buffs opened their Texas League baseball season in April, Carl Victor Little, sharp-witted humorist, satirist, and widely read columnist of the *Houston Press,* reported that the "Boy mayor" threw out the first ball, but not in the usual fashion. Instead, "HIZZONER pitched out the first ball and those of you who attended saw him pitch such a curve that the whole game after that was one long dreary anti-climax. . . ." Little concluded, "After Roy had thrown his curve at the stadium we heard—or thought we did, but we can't be positive because of the din—someone behind us say: 'That fellow ought to be able to throw a Grade-A curve. Lord knows he's had plenty of practice.' The voice sounded like that of Gail Reeves. However, we're not sure."

With the *Press* turning against Hofheinz daily, columnist Little's typewriter on May 9 exploded with a long, sarcastic column which on one of the mayor's televised "Reports to the People," commented on "Nephew Roy and his political henchman, Swellionaire Bob Smith." Little asserted that Hofheinz's "head on our set was surrounded by what appeared as a halo. . . ." The columnist then ridiculed the content of the mayor's report.

The City Council, with Hofheinz casting the only dissenting vote, rejected Hofheinz's budget on May 11. After the council session adjourned, Hofheinz called a press conference and told newsmen: "In my judgment there is no longer any authorization for the expenditure of a single penny by the city." City spending would probably come to a halt, the mayor continued, adding that some state highway projects would have to be sacrificed. City comptroller Oakes said he presumed he continued in control of expenditures pending adoption of a budget. However, he said he would ask for a legal opinion as to whether the council inaction restricted all spending. Asked if he intended to submit another budget, the mayor said, "The only way one can be presented is for them to bring it up. This action will pinpoint the philosophy of the 'stop progress' organization headed by Reeves, and of which Resweber is vice-president." Then he tore into Reeves, declaring "Reeves and his dilapidated rooming house crowd have had a victory today. The citizens have lost. Reeves' rent property ought to be protected for the period of delay he accomplished." In the next breath, Hofheinz declared that "what they did today" was not the way the councilmen acted during the election when they "bragged" of improvements.

The motion to reject the mayor's proposed budget of about $42 million was offered by Councilman Heflin. Councilman Kesseler had insisted on the vote following the long hassle over right-of-way bonds. The mayor had proposed that the city on July 1 sell $7.1 million in bonds. The council rejected this proposal, and the mayor countered with an ordinance proposing the sale of $5 million worth. It passed unanimously. It brought to $12,490,000 the total amount of bonds the city would sell on July 1.

Rejection of the budget was interpreted as a rejection of any increase in taxes for 1955. The right-of-way bond sale fight was a key to the whole budget fight. Comptroller Oakes had said he would permit the sale of $12,490,000 worth of bonds without a budget first being passed. Had council agreed to issue $7 million instead of $5 million worth of right-of-way bonds, it in turn would have been forced to vote for the budget if city construction was to go forward.

As various building projects moved ahead after authorization during Hofheinz's first term, he ordered big signs entitled "Program of Progress" erected on each site. Each was signed in big letters, "Roy Hofheinz, Mayor," and below in much smaller letters were the names of city councilmen and Oakes as partners in authorization. The councilmen did not like their names in smaller letters and at one session, when the mayor was ill, voted to have all names removed from the signs. Newspapers had a field day taking pictures of painters wiping out the names.

The ordinance to create a committee of all councilmen "to inquire into city affairs" was ruled illegal, but the council, disregarding the opinion, passed a motion bringing the ordinance up for third and final reading. Again, as he did when the council voted the ordinance on second reading, Hofheinz attacked it as a "plot to open up the town. . . . I don't think you should pass an ordinance drawn up by a law firm which represents the policy rackets," he told the council. Attorney George D. Neal, former city attorney and one-time candidate for mayor, had assisted the councilmen in drawing up the ordinance and apparently was Mayor Hofheinz's target. Neal said that he never had represented "the policy rackets," although he did represent one man whose name has been associated with policy operations in a traffic case.

At a press conference after the council meeting, Hofheinz declared, "I understand the ordinance was to be used 'to put pressure on the police chief to open up the town. But Jack [Chief Jack Heard] isn't buying that one." Councilman Reeves challenged the mayor to start impeachment proceedings against him if he believed he was conspiring to break the law. He also challenged the mayor to reiterate his "preposterous and absurd" charges under oath. "I'll answer the charges under oath," Reeves said. Sears said, in his opinion as city attorney, that the committee "can do nothing that the council cannot do. In essence, it is the council itself, with one significant omission—the mayor. We think there can be no doubt that this ordinance attempts to provide meetings of the council, excluding the mayor and denying him his charter power," Sears ruled. "In our opinion it is invalid."

Hofheinz said he would be glad to join in any investigation of any city department or any reported instances of malfeasance—"a right the council has under the charter. I want the right to join in any inquiries." When Reeves introduced the ordinance, he termed it an "instrument of economy" and announced that one of the first projects under it would be to inquire into operations of the city tax office "to induce more efficiency there."

Meanwhile, Houston department heads, under rigid orders from Hofheinz, started whittling their proposed 1955 budgets a flat seven percent. "I'm tired of being the martyr in this budget fight," the mayor said. "Now I'm going to let the chips fall where they will." It was estimated that the seven-percent cuts, in addition to reductions of nearly $2 million made by councilmen at their lengthy budget sessions, would bring the 1955 budget within the $38,444,167 figure Oakes certified as the available income without a tax increase. Officials who attended the closed session said the mayor appeared sincere in seeking a budget the council would approve. He originally had sought a budget of $42,268,433. Councilman Kesseler said of the mayor's order, "I believe this is the first move of the mayor to get back in step with his council."

The issue of racial integration also caused controversy for Hofheinz. Black community leaders asked him to desegregate libraries in Houston. He agreed, but first he called in representatives of press, radio, and television and asked that they hold off any news about the upcoming change until librarians could determine how the mixing of races in their buildings would work. When word finally got around that black children and adults were going to "white libraries," a woman, prominent in Houston society, complained to the mayor: "I won't let my children sit by black children at the library," she angrily told Hofheinz. "I don't know what they'd catch!" Hofheinz solemnly replied, "Maybe tolerance."

Hofheinz's pledge of fairness and equal opportunity in city government caused him to order police and fire chiefs to seek qualified black applicants for vacancies in the important departments. He was the first Houston mayor to appoint blacks to boards and committees. Hofheinz also ordered removal of all "white" and "colored" signs on public comfort facilities in City Hall and elsewhere. Complaints from delegations of white employees followed. It was not long, said the mayor's aides, before the issue was forgotten and gradually there was little racial unrest evident because whites began using the once "colored" rest rooms. "All that was pioneering in Houston," said Gould Beech.

The mayor also ordered municipal golf courses be opened to blacks. He said, "Blacks paid taxes for golf courses and couldn't play on them. I told them to go to the courses and play and they did so—without trouble." The mayor's racial policies were not calculated to win friends among Houston's fanatical segregationists, but he was compelled by his own conscience to do what he thought right no matter what the consequences.

On May 25, a $38,444,167 city budget went to City Council amid charges that Hofheinz was trying to "institute government by blackmail" of council members. Councilman Reeves made the charges. He referred to Hofheinz's accusation that councilmen were fighting him because he opposed "an open city." Reeves said the mayor's remarks on television that he could rid the city government of squabbling if he made "concessions" were an insinuation that the council wanted an "open city." Reeves said, "I think it is time for him [Hofheinz] to stop his dishonest tactics and cease his efforts to institute government by blackmail. . . . Hofheinz has no equal as a propagandist."

No action was taken on the budget itself. Councilman Heflin moved that it be adopted, but withdrew his motion when several councilmen said they wanted to study it more. The meeting turned into another exchange of sharp words. Hofheinz and Reeves were the principals. Reeves challenged Hofheinz to make public any information he might have on any individual working for an "open city." He made it clear that he thought Hofheinz had no such information. Hofheinz said, "This is not the time nor the place for that." Reeves snapped, "You ought to be man enough to back up your allegations with facts. I challenge you to do it." The budget proposal given to council totaled $3,827,477 more than the budget for 1954. The increase was 11 percent. The budget was seven percent less than the one originally submitted by the mayor after it had been whittled about $2 million by the councilmen. The mayor called the new budget proposal a "crippling one which would severely cut city services to the lowest level in 10 years and would relegate Houston to a second- or third-class city."

To add to the mayor's troubles, a man called the Houston police station on May 27 and told R. G. Reyes, crime prevention officer, that he planned to kidnap Hofheinz's 12-year-old daughter, Dene. The caller said he was broke and desperate and added, "That might be the best way to raise some money, don't you think?" Officer Reyes told the man he would end up behind bars if he tried it and kept him talking for about 10 minutes while other officers tried to trace the call. They were unsuccessful. The man said he had already talked with Mrs. Hofheinz by telephone and warned her he intended to kidnap her daughter. About an hour later a man, presumably the same one, called the city desk of the *Post*, advised a reporter to check on the attempted kidnapping of the mayor's daughter, and hung up. Officer Reyes said no special precautions were taken to guard the mayor's family. "I don't think we have to worry about it," he said. "I think it's just an anonymous crackpot trying to stir up a fuss." But the Hofheinz family was upset and Dene II was guarded.

Hofheinz also was troubled occasionally by scandals involving city workers. When evidence of wrongdoing by city employees came to his attention, Hofheinz always acted quickly if the charges appeared valid. When it was found that three electrical inspectors were taking payments for advance tipoffs on tests for those seeking electrical licenses and also were waiving tests for others they favored, he summarily fired them, telling prosecutors at the same time to present cases to grand juries.

One of his biggest problems as a "reform" mayor was entrenched practices of previous administrations carried on by longtime employees, some protected by civil service. Hofheinz broke up illegal "playhouses" when evidence came to him. Sears, Beech, and others were adept at chasing down tips on irregularities. As a few exposés of wrongdoing were glaringly displayed in newspapers, the effect was a small cloud on the Hofheinz administration. Never, however, was a charge made and sustained that the mayor himself was involved in any dishonest municipal skulduggery.

Word spread on June 24 that the long-standing feud between Hofheinz and the City Council had taken a new turn. Hofheinz was reportedly using a powerful lever to break the City Hall deadlock that stymied city progress—the threat of a new election for all officials. A report went out that the mayor "has his bellyfull and wants an election to clear things up, regardless of whether he wins or loses." No councilman except Reeves wanted an election in 1955. They did not want to campaign; there was too great a possibility that the voters might want to see some new faces at City Hall. Kraus Earhart, chairman of the mayor's charter amendment committee, of which the council did not approve, said, "The only answer is to get the mayor and councilmen out of office . . . call a new election. New faces at City Hall appear to be the only answer to the bickering and fighting impasse. The committee is not opposing any particular city official for reelection. We just think the people should have a chance to decide whether they want a new face for each elective position."

The hub about which the mayor-council contest revolved was proposed charter changes. Eighteen amendments proposed by the councilmen would trim the powers of the mayor and increase those of the council. Those proposed by the mayor's committee would continue and bolster the present strong mayoral government—and call an election of city officials again in November, a year ahead of the regularly scheduled city election. "I don't think," Earhart said, "that there can be a compromise between the mayor and council."

All councilmen said they would put up their amendments for a vote on August 16 unless the mayor agreed to the joint appointment of a charter amendment commission. Hofheinz would not do that. Ultimately the council agreed to a charter vote on 19 amendments, with Hofheinz's committee's plan listed last on the ballot. Hofheinz appointed his charter committee on June 3, and it represented a complete cross-section of the city's population. The principal goal of the committee was to draft an amendment which would move up the election of mayor and councilmen by one year—to the following November—and to get petitions signed so that voters could pass on it while also voting on the 18 amendments already approved by the council for the August 16 referendum. It took only until June 25 for Amendment 19, as it became known in campaigning, to be drafted and petitions signed forcing the council to offer it along with its own ideas for changing the rules of city government.

The Republican Party decided to get into the act, too. It called for another amendment which would set up a legal charter committee to review and draft a new set of city rules and planned to oppose the 19 other amendments. Party members immediately began a drive for signatures on petitions which would have put Amendment 20 on the ballot, but their efforts had not produced the necessary number by the July 17 deadline. Until the last minute Harry Linderman, GOP county chairman, and R. B. Bowen, chairman of the GOP policy committee, felt enough signatures could be obtained; nevertheless, the election ordinance addition would have had to be passed by the council on an emergency basis.

When Mayor Hofheinz said he would not allow the Republican amendment to be introduced on that basis, Linderman and Bowen said jointly: "Republicans will not forget that the mayor found the necessary emergency ordinance on his own amendment, but turned down our plan." The two GOP leaders also said Hofheinz and his friend, Bob Smith, had intimated Republicans had a secret charter slate they wanted to offer city voters. They added, "It was difficult for these two men to conceive of a sincere effort by any other group to create good government without an ulterior motive."

By July 15, differences between Hofheinz and the City Council had become irreconcilable. The council called a special session that day and voted unanimously for charges calling for the mayor's impeachment and his "suspension" from office for 30 days pending a hearing. It overlooked a charter provision that the mayor was also a voting member of the council, and he had been left out of the action which threw the city's political life into greater turmoil. The council told Mayor Pro tem Wilson to take over the city's administrative duties. His first official action was to dismiss Sears from the position of city attorney. Neither Hofheinz nor Sears recognized the moves against them. Hofheinz immediately hired Jack Binion as a special attorney to represent him and told him to go into District Court to try to overturn the council's action. "It will take a court order to get me out of my office!" Hofheinz shouted defiantly. He instructed Mary Frances Gougenheim, administrative aides, and his secretaries to guard the doors of his offices and to carry on with their business and not let Wilson or any councilman enter.

The charges of impeachment were handed to Hofheinz by Councilman Resweber. The mayor smiled as he glanced at the document which was addressed to the City Council and signed by its members. Hofheinz handed the document to Sears who made no comment. Mayor Pro tem Wilson attempted to take over as presiding officer, but Hofheinz said he would not relinquish his position. Wilson then presented an ordinance calling for the mayor's suspension from office, the acceptance of the charges, and the setting of a public hearing for August 4. The mayor pro tem called the roll of councilmen after Hofheinz refused to let Margaret Westerman, the city secretary, read the ordinance. All councilmen voted "Aye," but Sears held that the ordinance was void because it had to be passed on an emergency basis and the mayor had not called that emergency.

A motion by Councilman Reeves to accomplish the same purpose was ruled out of order by Sears and Hofheinz. Another motion to hire George Neal as the council's attorney also was ruled out of order by Hofheinz. Neal seemed nonplussed at the mayor's refusal to yield the chair at the council table. "I thought he would follow the law," Neal said. Asked if he would seek a court order suspending Hofheinz as mayor, Neal said, "I haven't thought of that yet." He said he believed that as soon as the document of impeachment had been offered by the council, the mayor was no longer privileged to act as presiding officer.

Old timers at City Hall said they knew of no impeachment proceedings ever having been instituted against a mayor of Houston before. The mayor called the impeachment proceedings "a blackmail attempt" and said it reminded him of the "inmates of a penitentiary trying to oust the warden." Stripped of legal terminology, the City Council's charges against the mayor were that he (1) permitted city property to be illegally disposed of; (2) ordered city property to be illegally disposed of; (3) ordered various departments not to furnish the city comptroller with necessary information to determine their financial needs; (4) ordered the director of utilities not to collect and dispose of garbage for a certain time; (5) ordered the director of public works to shut down the sewage disposal plant, allowing sewage to back up in homes; and (6) attempted by threat to compel the city comptroller to refuse to issue vouchers for pay to some city employees.

All of the charges, the council said, "constitute misconduct, inability, and the willful neglect of the performance of the duties of mayor of Houston." The eight councilmen added, "We hereby request that the charges of impeachment be filed by the City Council and a copy thereof be served upon the said Roy Hofheinz, that an ordinance be enacted by the City Council of the City of Houston reciting that said charges of impeachment have been presented to the City Council and have been filed with the City Secretary and that a public hearing be set for said charges of impeachment in the City Council chamber, at which time the said Roy Hofheinz shall be given an opportunity to be heard in his defense."

The *Post* reported on July 16 that "Minutes after City Council voted yesterday to impeach Roy Hofheinz, the mayor's third floor City Hall office began to take on the appearance of a citadel under siege. The lock leading to the mayor's inner offices was permanently clamped to be opened only by a buzzer release operated from the desk of the mayor's receptionist, Mrs. Mary Frances Gougenheim. Mrs. Gougenheim herself retreated to the inner office to take over the jangling communications system at her chief's big, private desk as the mayor maneuvered his citywide forces and took reports from scurrying subordinates." The *Post* also observed that "the whole office looked like a beleaguered fortress that didn't quite know the direction or extent of an unexpected attack."

The mayor called a news conference at noon to blast his opponents, calling the impeachment move "an abortive attempt to seize power by revolution and blackmail." He predicted it would fail. "This abortive effort to impeach the mayor and bring on a revolution by seizing the power of the office without holding an election has finally marked the councilmen for what they really are," he said. He also reiterated his charge that the councilmen were attempting to open the city to racketeers. Hofheinz did not go home after the day of the impeachment charges until attorney Binion informed him that State District Judge Spurgeon Bell had issued a temporary injunction restraining the council from suspending the mayor from office with a hearing scheduled the next week.

That the entire City Council had turned against him did not weaken Hofheinz's determination to carry on without compromise or apology. He quickly planned an evening television-radio speech for July 18. He told his audience he was still mayor and hoped "people will toss out the councilmen." He said there would be pandemonium if someone other than the legal mayor himself sought to sign checks and papers. "This is a fight for Houston," he said, "a fight for a clean city. I will not condone graft or corruption. . . . There is not a single word in the [council's] charges that Hofheinz ever took a dishonest penny, much less a dollar. . . . The charges are funny as well as false—funny if it were not for the serious effects on my life as well as on the future of the community." Hofheinz also struck at the 18 charter amendments the council prepared for the August election which, if approved, could weaken the "strong mayor" form of government.

He followed the next night with a rally at the Music Hall attended by 2000 persons, and the entire proceedings were carried on television and radio. The mayor called passage of the impeachment and suspension ordinance "a sneak Pearl Harbor attack." The mayor said 700,000 persons were watching and listening and he would pay for the show out of his pocket, but if people wanted to help, there were barrels in the hall in which they could drop money. He singled out Councilmen Reeves, Kohler, and Kesseler as major targets. Dene, Fred, and Dene II Hofheinz were on the platform. Virtually all of those attending filed up to the mayor to shake hands after he concluded his dramatic talk, illustrated on stage by various charts on the administration's accomplishments.

The hearing of Hofheinz's case against the council's impeachment and suspension action was assigned to State District Judge Ben F. Moorhead on July 20. Attorney Binion argued that the charter provision to remove the mayor by the council was unconstitutional and in violation of "due process" which guarantees a trial by an impartial judge and jury; the councilmen were biased and could not reach an impartial verdict; the mayor was the only person at the meeting, when councilmen took action, who had authority to present an emergency ordinance, and thus Mayor Pro tem Wilson's actions were void; and the mayor was a major state officer and was not subject to suspension or removal in the manner the council attempted. Attorney Neal argued that all council actions followed the charter.

Moorhead ruled the council's action invalid because the city charter said no ordinance could be passed the same day it was introduced except on an emergency basis and then only if the mayor called it that. He left unanswered other arguments by Binion, saying he did not "want to interfere with future actions." Hofheinz had won again, but the council would not give up hounding the city's chief executive. The biggest "City Hall circus," as some disgusted critics termed the administrative-legislative feud, followed.

The campaign for opposing charter amendments began on August 4 when Hofheinz and Reeves glared at each other and shouted their viewpoints before the Houston Police Officers Association. The mayor indicated he would head a slate of eight candidates for the council, drafted by a citizens' committee, if Amendment 19 passed. Reeves walked out during the early stages of Hofheinz's speech, but he returned to ask, "What would be worse than electing an entire legislative body supported by the same financial figures. . . . What would people who backed water bonds, for instance, give to have a slate they put into office voting the way they are told? If you vote for Amendment 19, you will be taking the aspirin of removing an undesirable public official and mixing it with the overdose of cyanide that comes with approving a slate." Of the council's proposed 18 amendments, Hofheinz countered, "You will simply be voting eternal chaos into city government if you allow eight councilmen to take over the administrative powers from the mayor and you will take away open meetings of government and replace them with closed door huddles so that fairness and the public's right to petition will be expelled from government." Reeves concluded that the whole City Hall controversy "is that the council would not approve the mayor's 20 percent tax increase—if we had, there would be harmony."

A total of 124,016 Houstonians were eligible to vote in the election. Newspapers predicted that, because of August vacations, no more than 25,000 to 30,000 would go to the polls. Under the council's last resolution on suspension of the mayor, Matt Wilson was to have taken over the mayor's duties on August 8, but that morning Hofheinz told reporters, "As mayor, I am now going to police headquarters to swear in rookies starting the new training class." Wilson refused to comment when he was asked if he considered Hofheinz's "swearing-in ceremonies" legal. In speaking to the rookies, Hofheinz said, "I can recall when officers were forced to look the other way on orders from the mayor's office. . . . Now we have no payoffs, no rackets, and no policy gambling." At the end of the talk, Lieutenant C. D. Taylor, officer in charge of the training school, said, "Mr. Mayor, I hope you are here to pin the badges on these men 13 weeks from now." Hofheinz replied, "By the grace of eight men on City Council, I'll be here." Before he went to the police function, Hofheinz had arisen at 4:30 A.M. to make speeches to 200 black longshoremen and later to scores at the white longshoremen's quarters on the Ship Channel. "Vote yes on Amendment 19 and restore team play at City Hall," he told the laboring men, usually his strong supporters.

By election eve, the councilmen's support of their 18 amendments had scattered, but Hofheinz did not waver a bit on Amendment 19. He said, "There are just so many gamblers, policy operators, and a few misguided good citizens who want to vote against Amendment 19." Councilmen Brakefield and McLemore went all-out in the campaign opposed to all 19 amendments. Both men said they had a charter commission ordinance ready to be submitted to the council as soon as the fur stopped flying. Councilman Reeves strangely favored only three of the amendments, but was positively opposed to passage of the mayor's amendment. Councilman Resweber took a hands-off attitude. "I voted for the amendments so the people could vote on 'em," Resweber said. However, Resweber said he was telling people to vote against Amendment 19. Councilmen Kohler and Wilson supported all 18 of the council's amendments. Councilman Kesseler said, "Of the council's amendments, I'm in favor of about eight of them, but I'm afraid the mayor's 19th amendment will carry because people who are for him and people who are against him will vote for it. The people who are against him will have too much passion in their eyes to realize that just getting him out of office is not the full intent of 19."

The next regular council meeting began as usual at 9:00 A.M. Hofheinz waved a flag of truce at councilmen, and they took quick advantage of it to conduct some city business for the first time in two weeks. The mayor and councilmen agreed on a compromise which allowed the mayor to preside at the regularly scheduled council meeting. Under the agreement, the fact that councilmen recognized Hofheinz as mayor—although they contended he actually was under suspension—would not have any legal bearing on their future attempts to impeach him. "I think we can transact the city business here in a way that won't jeopardize your legal position, as advised by your attorney, and my position, as advised by my attorney," said Hofheinz. The councilmen, all present except Heflin, perked up and listened attentively. "I have no objection to having joint signatures of myself and Matt Wilson as mayor pro tem on any business transacted here," the mayor said. "Then there would be no question about legality of any action, and it wouldn't jeopardize either side's rights."

"That's beginning to sound all right by me," said Councilman Resweber.

"Yes, but who will preside at the meeting?" Councilman Kesseler asked.

"You'll be voting and, by us having you vote, we'll recognize you as mayor."

Hofheinz explained that he and the councilmen could enter into a written agreement pointing out that they in no way recognized him as mayor by their attendance at the meeting. "And it also will reflect," Hofheinz said, "that in no way do I recognize your suspension." The mayor then dictated the agreement to the city secretary, who entered it into the record as the first order of business. The council then sped through a packed agenda that included most of the items left undone for two weeks. A charter commission ordinance was introduced by Councilman McLemore and was adopted at the first reading. It called for the election of a 25-member charter commission at the next election, November 19. The vote on the charter commission was unanimous. The commission would study the city charter and make recommendations for changes. However, these changes could not be submitted to a vote for two years because the city charter provided that charter amendment elections must be held at least two years apart.

Just prior to the election, 42 Houstonians, well-known in business, labor, and civic affairs, publicly urged approval of Amendment 19. Bob Smith served as spokesman for the group. "We believe it is important that every voter go to the polls Tuesday and vote 'yes' on Amendment No. 19 and 'no' on the other proposals," Smith said in a prepared statement. "We feel that this action will bring order out of chaos at City Hall. Passage of the amendment will give Houston's people an opportunity to select a team of leaders who will have a common purpose and a common desire to serve the city."

The demands of policemen and firemen for salary increases in 1955 were long and loud. Finally, the City Council decided to put the issue to a vote at the same time of the charter amendment election. Voters approved a $1500 annual increase for each fireman and policeman. Hofheinz told the City Council it was unfair for only two groups to receive raises and insisted that similar increases go across the board to all city employees. He won his point when the long-discussed budget was finally enacted.

Warning of "grave dangers," the Harris County Republican executive committee, with its proposed plan for a charter commission defeated, urged on August 10 that all 19 proposed amendments be rejected by voters. "Lawyers who have studied the proposed amendments warn us that their passage would drastically affect the validity of our city government," said R. B. Bowen, chairman of the policy committee. The *Houston Press* likewise called for defeat of all the amendments. The *Chronicle* and *Post* editorialized against the council's amendments and said Number 19 should be approved so that the people could vote again on city leadership.

The impeachment trial began on August 9, with the mayor represented by attorney Jack Binion. Councilman Heflin refused to participate; therefore, Hofheinz would be judged by seven councilmen. It was a stormy proceeding. The council's hearing ended abruptly on August 17 when Binion rested his

Jack Binion. Photograph courtesy the *Houston Chronicle.*

case. Binion, who had been expected to question more witnesses when the hearing reopened that afternoon, told the councilmen, "It is time to get this thing over with and get back to doing city business here. Knowing you as I do and having the faith I do in your integrity, I know you will vote right." None of the councilmen would say when a verdict would be returned.

With the charter election just four days away, the seven councilmen ended the hearing. Hofheinz's defensive tactics—refusal to allow his appointed department heads to testify and refusal of the police chief to serve subpoenas, plus the searching examination of councilmen by attorney Binion—had ruined the council's chance to make an impeachment case—if it ever had one. The people, however, had learned first-hand of Councilman Reeves' machinations in trying to discredit Hofheinz and his assistant, Beech.

Hofheinz went on television again during the council's "impeachment circus" and, surrounded by props to illustrate his points, made a quiet sales pitch for his personal administration and Charter Amendment 19. The mayor calmly recited a "representative list" of savings in the city purchasing department during his reign. He held up cards showing purchasing figures of items at their 1952 costs and at their present costs, which were, in every case, considerably lower. He then pointed out that "by conservative estimate, we have saved $600,000 a year in the purchasing department. That's $600,000 that could have filtered down into the pockets of political friends," he said.

The mayor said that 75 matters on the city agenda were having to go by the boards "because of the monkeyshines of these aldermen who will not even sit down to transact business." He then switched over to the proposed charter amendments at hand. "I need not dwell on the council's 18 amendments," he said. "So avariciously were they drawn up to enable council to raise its salaries, to give them power, to allow them to take the reins of government, that it is impossible for them even to campaign for their own amendments." He strode to a large ballot and voting machine facsimile and, one by one, ticked off "no" votes on the first 18 amendments and an emphatic "yes" on his 19th amendment.

Councilman Brakefield, in a television answer to Hofheinz the next night, warned that Amendment 19 would "furnish 'Honest Roy' Hofheinz—or any other political boss who dreams of dictatorship—with the keys to City Hall and the municipal treasury. They dynamite-laden 19th invites candidates slates picked by the bosses in smoke-filled rooms in a surprise off-year election—a year when thousands of our citizens failed to buy poll taxes because they believed no important elections were scheduled. Moreover, Roy's 'nifty 19th' would eliminate five district councilmen—selected by their neighbors and friends—the people best able to judge their qualifications. If councilmen are forced to seek election on a citywide basis, the costs of campaigning would be prohibitive for the average honest office seeker," Brakefield warned. "Hofheinz's charter committee would eliminate election of some councilmen by districts, ending 'ward heelers.' "

On August 16 voters defeated all of the council's amendments and approved Hofheinz's Number 19 calling for a November election by a vote of 19,265 to 17,679. The mayor was disheveled and subdued when he left his office at 3:00 A.M. on August 17 after hours of watching the tallying of ballots. However, he returned to his office four hours later and told reporters, "The victory of No. 19 was thin, but I won." He carried the box in his own precinct by 374 to 246. At the time he refused to say whether he would be a candidate again in November although he earlier had indicated he would. Newspaper accounts said the 1500-vote margin was smaller than the mayor had expected and his confidence in himself had dwindled. Three councilmen said the mayor received many votes for his amendment from people desiring another ballot crack at him in order to throw him out of office in three months.

The City Council did not vote on Hofheinz's "impeachment" on August 18 because Matt Wilson was absent with illness. Reports, however, circulated in City Hall circles that the verdict would be to "censure," not impeach, the mayor. Hofheinz's "suspension" already had been lifted by the agreement on joint signing of papers by him and Wilson. Newspapers began speculating that a group of prominent citizens were seeking a November candidate for mayor. They had the power and influence to give any candidate strong support, the newspapers said. There was also speculation that Hofheinz would quit city politics and run for governor, but Allan Shivers was still in the saddle in Austin. If Shivers ran for another term, Hofheinz did not plan to oppose him.

After various closed meetings, the seven councilmen, reprimanded by the voters, argued about what verdict they should bring in against Hofheinz. Fearing they would make the mayor a martyr if they impeached him, they decided on August 23 to drop their ouster attempt and voted to "censure and reprimand" Hofheinz for his conduct in office. That completed the mayor's victory—anything short of impeachment, he said, was proof of his proper actions as the administrative head of city government.

The powerful group seeking a candidate for mayor contacted Oscar Holcombe two days after the council's case against Hofheinz was closed. Holcombe reportedly said he did not want to run again if another "suitable candidate could be found." A "touchy peace" then settled over City Hall as various people put up "trial balloons" about candidates. By the end of August, Hofheinz had made up his mind to run again although he did not publicly announce it. Bob Smith confirmed to reporters that he would back Hofheinz again if he did run. "I don't see how Roy can keep from running," said the multimillionaire. "He's going to have to work for it, but I think he can be reelected, and I think he ought to start running pretty soon." Officers of the National Association of Traveling Salesmen awarded the title of "supersalesman" to Mayor Hofheinz on August 29 for his "putting over the 19th Amendment to the Houston Charter." Publicist Steve Alex of the national association said the award had nothing to do with politics. "We didn't want to make anybody mad, including city councilmen," he added. "Even his bitterest opponent will have to agree Hofheinz did a good job of selling the proposition." Those who made the award in the mayor's office were Elmer Wheeler of Dallas, president; Leon Coleman of New York, vice-president; and Howard Stone of Oakland, California; all were members of the national association.

His uncertain political position did not deter Mayor and Mrs. Hofheinz from taking off on September 16 for a tour of Europe and the World Conference of Mayors in Rome. Hofheinz left in Bob Smith's hands any maneuvers for the upcoming November election. Accompanying the Hofheinzes was Dr. John Schwarzwalder, manager of KUHT-TV, the University of Houston station, who reported on the conference and trip for the *Chronicle* and KTRK-TV. The party flew to New York, then London, and visited Frankfurt, Berlin, Paris, Madrid, Rome, Athens, Tel Aviv, Istanbul, and Amsterdam. Their return was scheduled for October 8. They arrived in Rome on September 25 and left there September 30. Hofheinz was the ranking mayor from the United States at the Rome conference by virtue of his being chairman of the board of the United States Conference of Mayors.

Hofheinz's most vivid recollection of his stay in Rome was that of the old Roman Colosseum in ruins. He said, "Mama and I were standing there looking at the large, round facility. I knew that most of the stadiums in the United States were rectangular, built to conform to the shape of the playing fields. I studied the history of the Colosseum. I found out that on hot days they used to have slaves pull a cover over the top made of papyrus, or whatever they used in those days, for cover. I guess they didn't want to spoil the lions' appetite with too much heat. I found out, too, that the emperor and the bigwigs all sat at the top of the Colosseum. Standing there looking back on those ancient days, I figured that a round facility with a cover was what we needed in the United States and that Houston would be the perfect spot for it because of its rainy, humid weather." That was the beginning—although Hofheinz didn't realize it then—of the elaborate plans and the creation of a model of the Astrodome by Stuart Young. At the moment, however, it was just information stored in the mind of the Houston mayor on a holiday.

During the Hofheinzes' absence, Bob Smith organized the United Citizens Association to draft a slate of candidates for mayor and city council. Meanwhile, Oscar Holcombe was busy also, and he received some 25,000 post cards pledging him support. The "kingmakers of Houston," who had voluntarily backed Hofheinz in his first two races for mayor, turned back to Holcombe. They initiated the post card pleas for the "Old Gray Fox" to run and restore harmony at City Hall. Thus Holcombe was organizing, planning for the race, when Hofheinz returned home.

As a preliminary to the mayor's bout, Hofheinz revived the "war of washers" on October 7. In his campaign a year earlier, Hofheinz had used washers, paper clips, etc., to show that he was a better mayor than Holcombe had been; although Alvin Moody was his opponent, Holcombe had backed Moody. He displayed a number of washers which he said he had bought for $3.13 a thousand while Holcombe, he said, had paid $20 a thousand.

Holcombe appeared on television to declare that the only trouble with the argument was that the washers were not the same. He offered to give $5000 to the United Fund if an independent laboratory test showed they were identical. Tests were made. Hofheinz said the tests showed the washers were the same; Holcombe responded that they definitely were not. Fresh from signing a United Fund proclamation, Hofheinz challenged Holcombe to pay the $5000 which the latter had said he did not owe. "Hofheinz is even sicker than I thought," was Holcombe's only comment.

Not until October 20 was the slate for mayor and eight council candidates of the United Citizens Association unveiled; Hofheinz headed the ticket. The UCA's candidates for the council were newcomers to city politics. The slate was announced at a spirited rally attended by about 750 persons, just a short time before the deadline for filing. When the books finally were closed in the mayor's offices at midnight, there were three candidates for mayor, 28 candidates for the City Council, and one candidate, incumbent Roy Oakes, for city comptroller. The make-up of the UCA slate was announced by a secret nominating committee whose members finally were revealed at the rally by Bob Smith.

Smith said he had appointed 10 of the 14 members of the committee. Those 10 then named the other four, he said. Holcombe immediately blasted the hand-picked candidates by "a multimillion-dollar, secret political group."

The council slate was composed of R. R. Royal, former superintendent of mails; Clyde Miller, locomotive engineer; C. A. Chase, insurance executive; Terrel Spencer, a former University of Houston vice-president; E. Pliny Shaw, transport and oil company head; G. W. Hunt, businessman and foreman of the "land scandal" grand jury; Mrs. O. L. Rash, clubwoman; and Leroy Williams, union official. The slate's nine candidates went to City Hall earlier in the day to file their declarations of running as a ticket with Margaret Westerman, the city secretary. Holcombe declared that, "For a group of people secretly appointed by one man to pick in secret, then spring the candidates that they will allow the people to vote for, then completely finance these candidates, is to subsidize your public officials and to make their allegiance to a small group and not to the people of Houston. . . . It is my opinion that the voters of Houston will resent this hand-picking of candidates and will use their own judgment and select our public officials in a democratic way."

George Eddy, a lawyer who earlier had become a candidate for mayor, echoed Holcombe's charges. He said, "Like the Russian parliament, the UCA met for solemn discussion and decision to determine who Bob Smith had decided their free choice would be. I was surprised Hofheinz got along as well as he did with his hand-picked slate, but I suspect that they have by this time fallen into grievous disagreement." The ticket's entry into the political field, plus a few other last minute filings, brought the total number of candidates who would fight it out in the November 19 election to 32.

Hofheinz opened his campaign on November 2 with a slashing personal attack on Holcombe. He said that the former mayor was a "friend of gamblers, a buddy of the honky-tonk operators" and that the "short memory of man" had been his greatest asset. In the verbal assault delivered over KTRK and KTRH, Hofheinz said Holcombe was defeated in four of his mayoralty races. "When his record [in office] has been repulsive, he has been booted out," Hofheinz charged, and he claimed that Holcombe, who had served 10 terms as mayor, had won reelection because the voters did not recall his previous record in office. He mentioned the United Citizens Association candidates running on a ticket with him and said, "I have never been associated with a finer group of people who are sincerely interested in serving their community." Holcombe's charge that the UCA "machine" planned to control that part of the state "is the rankest kind of just plain silliness," Hofheinz said. The mayor claimed that "gamblers and racketeers" comprise the bulk of the "Holcombe machine" and that "graft was pretty rampant" in 1950 during Holcombe's last term as mayor.

Hofheinz and his slate adopted a common platform. Their pledges included no increase in property taxes, a closed city, first priority on any additional revenue to the enlargement of the police force, and top priority on the expenditure of bond funds to those areas which did not have adequate city services. Another UCA pledge was harmony and honesty at City Hall, "which will speed up and simplify every city function." Outlining his own record, Hofheinz noted that, during his fewer than three years in office, a street black-topping program had paved 259.9 miles of streets. Almost $2 million had been either appropriated or expended for the extension of water lines in the North Shepherd and Fidelity areas, Brookwood, Bryker Woods Bay Street Gardens, Whispering Pines, Tulane Terrace, Garden Acres, and other areas. He also pointed out that 10 swimming pools and $8,736,315 worth of storm sewers had been constructed. The mayor added that seven fire stations had been built and 6238 street lights installed, most of them the improved and more brilliant vapor lights. "I have secured from the state highway department allocations of $18,406,157 for the construction of streets and freeways," he said.

At a rally for all mayoral candidates at Shady Park Civic Club forum, Hofheinz spoke for the citizens' ticket. Eddy and Holcombe were present. Both the mayor and Holcombe ignored Eddy in their talks, but Eddy called Hofheinz a "domineering, overbearing intolerant man, utterly incapable of working side by side with his fellow officials." Hofheinz said the "UCA slate is trying to bring order out of chaos. The biggest secret in the campaign is the identity of the backers of Holcombe and the names of the persons who financed the post card poll the former mayor conducted prior to announcing his candidacy." Hofheinz promised to do the greatest good for the greatest number if reelected and recited city improvements carried out during his administration.

On the morning of October 26, Bob Smith got into a heated argument with an oil lease broker. There were reports Smith threatened to punch the other man in the nose. The incident took place in the Esperson Building barber shop. Smith was getting a haircut and shave when the lease broker walked into the shop. He was identified as L. V. R. Townsend, a former Bellaire Republican precinct chairman with offices on the fifth floor of the Esperson Building. Witnesses said Townsend made several statements about Hofheinz. One of them, the witnesses said, was "They ought to give Roy a million dollars and let him go." Smith took particular exception to the remark, interpreting it as an insult to Hofheinz's honesty. Smith jumped out of the barber's chair and asked Townsend, "How would you like a punch in the nose?" Townsend replied, "Go ahead." No punch was thrown, but Townsend walked away from Smith headed out of the shop. Smith followed Townsend to the door and came back inside. Smith's only comment on the altercation was, "Any differences are to be regretted. We should all be above that."

The month-long Hofheinz-Holcombe campaign—candidate Eddy was lightly regarded—was furious and bitter all the way. Holcombe's main theme was expressed in a speech before the Houston Jaycees on October 24 when he said, "The need for harmony is the greatest." He said he had served with more than 30 councilmen over a period of years with no serious disagreements. He pointed out the danger of machine politics and tickets and declared that no matter how good the intentions of those creating such a machine, the peril of its eventually falling into the wrong hands was ever constant. "The mayor of Houston needs a certain amount of dignity," he added. "As an individual, Oscar Holcombe can walk down Main Street in his shirt sleeves or in a sports shirt, but as mayor he should not do this. It is not good for the city." He did not mention anyone by name, but it was known that Hofheinz favored sports attire on many occasions.

The next day a small group of black civic, religious, and labor leaders pledged their support to Holcombe. R. R. Grovey, president of the Third War Civic Club, announced the decision. Grovey declared, "There will be no bloc votes for any candidate." With this group Holcombe was able to break partly into the solid block previously behind Hofheinz.

In one of his first speeches, knowing the "establishment" was leaving him, Hofheinz charged that Jesse Jones "thinks more of money than he does of the welfare of the community. His only interest has been to line a pocket and make a dollar, and I ought to know, because I am his partner in KTRK-TV." The campaign had a whirlwind finish with all candidates in a final vote-getting drive. Hofheinz blanketed the air waves with 24 radio programs and 10 telecasts in three days and called himself the "underdog." He turned attacks on Holcombe into blasts at the three daily newspapers, as well as the publisher of the *Chronicle*. The mayor asserted, "There was collusion between the three newspapers who endorsed Holcombe for their own personal interest and want to bring back an open city. I was refused a full-page ad in the *Chronicle*. Is that the fair way to run a newspaper? Talk about a secret nominating committee," he continued, in reference to charges that the UCA slate was selected in secret. "I was present at such a meeting in 1952 in the Rusk Building. Gus Wortham [president of American General Insurance Company] was there as were Judge J. A. Elkins [chairman of the board of the City National Bank], George and Herman Brown [respectively the executive vice-president and president of Brown & Root], and there was an open telephone line to the *Post* and the *Chronicle*. Herman told Oscar Holcombe then that he was through as mayor and he told me, 'We will support you for mayor and all you have to do is call them down the middle.' But I had to say no to Jesse Jones and I had to say no to Brown and Elkins, and so it was decided that I could not get along with people." Bob Smith appeared on television with Hofheinz to defend the secret method by which the UCA had selected its candidates and praised the members of the nominating committee.

The mayor's fury about Jesse Jones and the newspapers was unabated the last days of the race. He charged that Jesse Jones was trying to lead Holcombe back to the "public trough" with a "phony build-up." He claimed that the "phony build-up" given Holcombe came as the *Chronicle* pulled an "iron curtain of censorship" around Hofheinz's own campaign for reelection. The mayor said in two telecasts, "The truth was completely hidden by the *Chronicle*" when it refused to run as an advertisement an "open letter" to Jones. "This letter revealed the secret committee that has controlled the mayor's office in the past, or has sought to control it," he said. "The *Chronicle* and the *Post* have been parties to the most recent committee meeting in Room 8-F in the Lamar Hotel, which is rented by Brown & Root. . . . The *Chronicle-Post* fat cat committee wants a mayor who will bow and scrape to their group." Referring to the *Chronicle's* endorsement of Holcombe, Hofheinz asserted that "Jones decided in the past 48 to 96 hours that I had failed as mayor after I decided to reveal the fat cats. Should an honest man in politics have to knuckle down to the fat cats? I told Judge Elkins, a partner in the law firm which represents Southwestern Bell Telephone Company, that I could not and would not raise the telephone rates."

Hofheinz argued that the "only bad publicity Houston has had in the past three years" was charges by his opposition that the city was "slipping." "Only Holcombe seems to think that Houston is slipping," Hofheinz said. The mayor claimed that the *Chronicle* "is now using most of its editorial space to castigate me . . . and it has incensed the wrath of the citizens. Is that the way to get Holcombe back to the public trough?" he asked.

Hofheinz launched a costly, last-week radio and television marathon with a campaign directed against Jesse Jones and the three Houston daily newspapers. In one radio broadcast, Hofheinz attacked Jones and claimed that the *Chronicle* had endorsed his opponent because he would not interfere when the city tax bill on "downtown Jones' interest buildings was raised." The mayor maintained that Fred Heyne of the Bankers Mortgage Company and John T. Jones, Jr., president of the *Chronicle*, talked with him "for more than three hours but I refused to interfere."

Heyne said he had never asked the mayor to cut taxes but that the mayor had asked him to favor a tax increase. Jones said the meeting referred to was in Heyne's office and was arranged at the mayor's request. He said the mayor was attempting to get the support of the *Chronicle* for the proposed 20-percent tax increase. "We couldn't see the necessity for the increase," John T. Jones said, "since it would have been in addition to a 19-percent increase made in 1954 on the valuations of downtown business property." George Kesseler, vice-chairman of the city's tax equalization board, pointed out that the alleged meeting occurred in the spring "and at that time Hofheinz would have been powerless to do anything about the assessment, if he had been asked to." The mayor, who served as chairman of the tax equalization board, was invited four times to meet with the board for the hearing on the Jones' property, Kesseler said, but Hofheinz ignored the invitations.

At 8:10 P.M. on Saturday, November 19, Oscar Holcombe jubilantly told workers at his headquarters, "The Boy Wonder has conceded defeat." Hofheinz did so because as the returns came in he knew the trend was against him. Official returns gave Holcombe 38,818, Hofheinz 21,153, and Eddy 7649. Charter Amendment 19 required a runoff if no candidate received a majority, but Holcombe had more than a 10,000 margin over both opponents. Only half of the qualified voters had gone to the polls. Every section in the city went for "harmony." Six of the councilmen who had opposed Hofheinz were reelected— Kesseler, Resweber, McLemore, Wilson, Brakefield, and Reeves. The only newcomers in the 1956 lineup with Mayor Holcombe were Louie Welch and George Marquette, former councilmen who were not political friends of the defeated Hofheinz.

For a while Hofheinz was moody and bitter about the defeat. He conceded that the voters—with "fat cats" and newspapers against him—had decided they wanted "harmony," "cronyism," and "favoritism," as they had existed under Holcombe for 20 years, to return. The only consolation he had in the next two years was that some Holcombe administrators were found guilty of wrongdoing with legal repercussions. Hofheinz never changed his attitude that the voters had "thrown out the warden and turned the city over to inmates."

It was announced December 27 that Hofheinz would head a four-man law firm beginning January 2 in the South Coast Building at Main and Rusk. The three men joining the outgoing mayor in law practice were Will Sears, city attorney, and Robert L. Burns, senior assistant city attorney, both of whom tendered their resignations, and Red James. The new firm was known as Hofheinz, Sears, James, and Burns, and they would specialize in municipal and administrative law. This would include utility rate making, municipal bond issues, condemnation proceedings, and federal administrative agency litigation. A new and creative period in Hofheinz's life was beginning.

22

Television Stockholder

Hofheinz had turned over full management of Radio Station KTHT to Bill Bennett when he was sworn in as mayor. The Judge and Stephen kept their law offices in the radio station and went there occasionally at night. The challenge of mayor was greater to Hofheinz than continuing to be a radio whiz, but his hope of owning a television station was alive. His application, with several financial backers, was still before the FCC. To have more cash available in case he won a TV station, he sold 75 percent of his interest stock in KTHT for $600,000 to a new firm, Texas Radio Corporation, on March 9, 1953. The corporation president was Robert D. Straus, executive vice-president of the Straus-Frank Company, and the secretary was Philip R. Neuhaus, vice-president of Underwood-Neuhaus & Company. Hofheinz was principal stock-holder and chairman of the board. He retained the KTHT property on Travis Street, the station transmitter land near the San Jacinto Monument, and "Huckster House," which he had said operated in connection with his radio dealings. Other stockholders in the new corporation included Colonel W. B. Bates, board chairman of the Second National Bank; William D. Sutherland, president of Henke & Pillot, Incorporated; Stanley Shipnes, Houston general manager of Sears, Roebuck and Company; Corbin J. Robertson, vice-president of Quintana Petroleum; Harry E. Cagle, vice-president of Elmer C. Gardner, Incorporated, contractors; E. P. Parish, Jr., Alfred C. Glassell, Jr., Floyd L. Karsten, and Frank W. Michaux, oil operators; Joseph Rice Neuhaus and Milton Underwood of Underwood-Neuhaus and Company; Robert L. Tilly, investment banker; and Elmer C. Gardner, president of Elmer C. Gardner, Incorporated. "It is with pride I become associated with this outstanding group of citizens," Hofheinz said as he announced the sale. "We promise even bigger and better things in public service."

In 1950 Hofheinz pleaded with Red James in Washington not to go back to Alabama and seek a congressional seat, but to join him in law and radio in Houston. Meanwhile, the two men saw each other often. Their friendship went far beyond the sometimes violent arguments they had over legal and business situations. Finally in 1953, after Hofheinz was elected mayor, James sold his home and went with his family to Houston. He was a member of the bar in the

District of Columbia and Alabama, but had to take a new bar examination in Texas. While he waited for Texas bar approval, he went back and forth to Montgomery to carry on legal business there. "The principal thing for which Roy wanted me in Houston was that he had an application for a VHF television station—Channel 13," James said. "There were five applicants altogether, and all had been called for a consolidated hearing in Washington. We knew what we were up against. Going back to the previous year, Roy asked me if he should apply for Channel 11, then allocated to Galveston, get the grant, and then move the station to Houston. I said no—that would be contrary to FCC rules, and the commission would never permit it to be moved. Paul Taft, today an owner of KODA station in Houston; Jimmy Stewart, the movie actor; and Galveston owners in Sugarland Industries didn't know any better. They applied for Channel 11 and got a grant and began to try to move it to Houston. Ultimately it happened and Channel 11 is now known as a Houston station. Jesse Jones got the same advice about Channel 11 I gave Roy." Time proved that strange things happened in the decisions of the FCC despite legal opinions of lawyers.

Hofheinz's application for a television station was made under the name of TV Broadcasting Company of Houston in which the Judge owned 50 percent of the stock. Vice-presidents of the new corporation included Floyd Karsten, Robert Straus, and Corbin Robertson. The company made a commitment of $1,500,000 to build the station should it receive Channel 13.

On May 29, Hofheinz sold Radio Station KSOX in Harlingen for $225,000. He said he made the sale to the owners of KCBS in Harlingen because they had a permit to operate a television station. "At the time KSOX was developed," said the Judge, "I had no idea that I would ever reenter public life. Being sold on the Valley, I had looked forward to dividing my time between Houston and that area. The demands of my time as mayor of Houston, however, are such that no time is left to develop KSOX or television in the Valley." He had applied for but dropped on May 15 his television application for the Valley. Hofheinz also sold his 49 percent interest in Birmingham's WILD in the fall of 1953. The money he received, his auditors said, did not represent any big capital gain, but rather a return of his investment. Except for his 25 percent interest in Houston's KTHT, Hofheinz was virtually out of radio, but ready for television. He also discontinued his FM station because advertising had dropped off.

Hofheinz informed the FCC that he had bought the 50 percent of the stock formerly owned by a group of 12 Houston businessmen in the TV Broadcasting Company. He announced the purchase in an amendment to the firm's application, filed in Washington just prior to the deadline. The purchase canceled an agreement Hofheinz made in March with the group when he sold them an interest in Station KTHT. Under that arrangement, Hofheinz owned 50 percent of the stock in the television firm, and the group had the remainder. The television stock transaction did not affect the ownership of Radio Station KTHT, in which Mayor Hofheinz had 25 percent and the same group the remaining 75 percent. James filed Hofheinz's amended application and said the first hearings were expected to be held in early 1954.

Hofheinz was able to get 100 percent control of his TV company when his partners hedged about spending more on the application. Bill Bennett said it might cost $2 million more than the money already spent on the application. "These were businessmen and they didn't want to stick their necks out any more on an application which might not be granted." Hofheinz confronted them and said, "You buy me out or I'll buy you out," and added, according to Bennett, "I'm not going to do all the work if you guys don't put up the money." It cost him about a half million dollars to get full control.

Hofheinz was able to buy out his partners' 50 percent interest in the new television corporation because Dick Hooper personally guaranteed the mayor's note to City National Bank for $900,000. Judge Elkins did not advance the money but gave Hofheinz a letter to be used as part of his amended FCC application to show that the mayor had proper financial backing for a station. Hofheinz's four opponents for Channel 13, however, had to give full financial statements, made public when final hearings came in January of 1954. Attorney James was amused that his friend was able to keep his financial status hidden while his opponents had to tell all. Nineteen fifty-four saw fulfillment of the Judge's ambition of nearly 10 years—stock ownership in a television station.

The *Chronicle* reported on January 8, 1954:

> In the biggest merger of television interests yet effected in the United States, Houston's four rivals for a license to operate Channel 13 agreed last night to pool their resources in a single application. The merger agreement brings to an end a rivalry that began February 5, 1948. Hofheinz was joined in the venture by KTRH, of which B. F. Orr is president; Houston Area TV Company, of which Dudley C. Sharp is president; Houston TV Company, with Lloyd Gregory as president. Hofheinz's company, TV Broadcasting of Houston, would hold 16 percent of the stock in the station.
>
> Hofheinz declared that "each of the parties has compromised his individual interest in order that Houston and south Texas might have a great TV station quickly. No other television station in America can boast of a finer cross-section of outstanding local leaders among its owners than those who are my associates in this venture. It is a keen desire of all of us that this station be established quickly and become one of the great community servants in this area in the history of our time."

Wright Morrow was elected chairman of the board and John T. Jones, Jr., president of the Houston Consolidated Television Company at its first organizational meeting in the Rice Hotel. Hofheinz was selected as one of the vice-presidents. John T., nephew of Jesse Jones, said in 1979 that he felt he was the catalyst leading to the consolidated TV application. "I was the only one who could simultaneously talk to Roy Hofheinz on one hand and men like Wright Morrow on the other hand—men who wouldn't go into the same room with

Roy." Jones also recalled that negotiations were difficult, for "everyone started out wanting 50 percent with the other 50 percent being divided among the others."

When Hofheinz joined in discussions for the consolidated television application, he had sold 75 percent of KTHT stock to other people. FCC rules, to prevent duopoly, required that the mayor divest himself of his interest in the radio station to get 16 percent interest in Channel 13. When Red James told him what was necessary, he said Hofheinz agreed. "I told Roy," recalled James, "don't agree yet. Let me review the instruments. Roy shouted at me, 'Don't try to tell me what to do! I know what I'm doing. If I sell my interest in KTHT, I'll sell it for another half million dollars!' The next day I looked at the legal papers and they provided that if Hofheinz ever sold his 25 percent interest in the station, he would first have to offer it to the people who had bought 75 percent—at book value. I inquired from the accountants what book value was and they said $15,000. I went to the mayor's office the next day and told Roy the story. I thought he was going to faint. He asked, 'What can I do?' I barked back, 'You should have listened to me yesterday, but, damn you, you're so butt-headed and so hard-headed, you don't ever pay attention to the people who have your best interests at heart. You think you're smarter, by God, than anybody else. I'm going to let you sweat.'"

James worked out the problem by having Roy resign as director and officer of KTHT and swear he would not again be active in the management of the station. "The FCC ruled with me that this would not be in violation of the duopoly rule," said James. "He did not have to sell for book value. He sold the stock at his leisure and for a high price—his price."

After the FCC's approval on July 7 of the consolidated Channel 13 television application for KTRK-TV, Jones, as president of the new TV corporation, began looking for an experienced man who could operate Houston's third station. Willard Walbridge, affiliated with a Lansing, Michigan, station, was recommended to Jones to become general manager and operating vice-president. "I really didn't have any interest in changing jobs," Walbridge recalled in 1978, "but Jones prevailed upon me and my wife, and I went to Houston in August of 1954. Jones took me around for two days to meet stockholders. I first met Roy Hofheinz when Jones took me to his office. I had been told Roy, as 16 percent stockholder, the largest single individual holding because the Jones' 32 percent interest was tied up in the Jones Foundation, might try to take over management in view of his radio experience. But that wasn't true. He never, under any circumstances, tried to second guess me or give me any kind of a strain. My early wariness about Roy fell away, and we became friends with a good mutual respect for each other."

Walbridge got the approval of the consolidated company's board to bring Bill Bennett from KTHT to be business and sales manager. Bennett was

The Judge and Willard Walbridge

Hofheinz's close friend, but he knew the rules, too, and followed them. Walbridge became a Houston civic leader and during the ensuing years was a figure in the Astrodome-Astrodomain drama with Hofheinz the central individual. "Roy was an interested member of our TV board," said Walbridge in 1978. "Roy was interested in good news coverage and so was I. He always backed me in whatever I did, and he was always there when I called on him. He liked the way I operated. I was invited to all the things he got mixed up in." During 1955, Walbridge was to have a severe test of the FCC fairness doctrine in news coverage and made national history with telecasts involving an attempt by City Council to impeach Mayor Hofheinz.

Said Walbridge in 1978, after he was president of the Houston Chamber of Commerce and a charter organizer of the Houston Visitors Council: "The brilliance of young Mayor Roy Hofheinz was one of the things which lured me to Houston from Michigan. He gave Houston hope in tough years. He had pride. He WAS the mayor. He was a world citizen after he built the Astrodome, bought Ringling Circus, and was involved in other enterprises. He made P. T. Barnum look like 14 miles of bad road. He WAS Houston—with the patina of a rash, exciting future and a kind of spirit which exemplified himself. He made us get off our dime downtown and do something. Now we have two convention centers—one at the Astrodome and one downtown."

23

A Look Back at the Mayor and the Man

Nearly a quarter of a century after Roy Hofheinz's three years as mayor, people who were with him almost daily during his hectic tenure had vivid recollections of Hofheinz the man—father, husband, and friend—and his motives for serving the city he loved. None could completely fathom Hofheinz's sharp, penetrating mind, but all knew he was an uncommon man. They viewed him as a genius marked by quick decisions and unyielding convictions he believed to be right and in the common man's interest.

Looking back as the mayor's administrative assistant, Gould Beech recalled that it fell his lot on the final election night to tell Hofheinz, " 'The jig's up and we lost.' The mayor knew every precinct. He asked, 'What about the black boxes?' I said, 'There are just not enough.' Blacks didn't back us 100 percent as usual. I think we got only 74 percent. There was some attrition of labor, but the story was that the middle class was weary of it all, wanting a change. It was a pretty sad night. In all his campaigns, Roy wouldn't solicit money. Stewart Boyle raised some money in the first campaign and maybe in the second, but most of the money was Hofheinz's. He went out heavily in debt."

Pat Daniels, Hofheinz's assistant who handled relations with newspaper, magazine, and broadcast personalities, always was on a hot spot when he was besieged for information about the mayor. He recalled: "Being mayor of Houston was probably the second hardest job in the nation then, compared to the presidency. The mayor just did not have time enough to see everybody he wanted to see and to answer all telephone calls, even important ones. It was almost impossible to get him to return calls. He'd go through a pile of call notes sometimes and pick out one and make it and then leave the rest of them alone. I had to, among other things, explain for calls not returned."

Daniels said one night he had a call from a real estate investor and was asked to visit his home for a drink and a chat. He said:

> I went. The man told me that he would like for me to take a message to Roy—that he would like for Roy to do the same thing for him that Oscar Holcombe used to do and that was pinpoint a spot in town where a future

development was going so he could buy up the property around it. He said, "I'll take care of Roy and I'll take care of you." I stood up and I said, "I want to tell you something"—I was crying—"I'm leaving now. If Roy Hofheinz knew that I was here and knew what I had just heard, without hitting you, he'd fire me tomorrow." I told Roy that later and he said, "You're exactly right." The mayor was a dedicated, honest man—I don't know of a more honest man alive. You could hear on the street, of course, that he stole the city blind and stole the county blind, but the records don't document this because he sure as hell didn't have any cash at the end of his terms as mayor.

I think Roy could have been a great, great mayor if he could have—and I'm not sure it would have worked—demonstrated a little more tact with councilmen—in a sense, a wheeler-dealer who would make deals on principles. Instead, he would infuriate them. It was just a battle of minds all during the three years we were there. There was never a time that I recall, except right at the very beginning, when the council was ever 100 percent behind him. If Roy had had a little tact, a little patience, a little humility, he would have been not only the greatest mayor in Houston's history, but the greatest president of these United States.

Bill Sherrill said he and others of the "Palace Guard" fully expected the people to throw out council and elect Hofheinz and his council slate in November of 1955. He added:

We thought we'd get a mandate to finish cleaning up the city. It was a great surprise to all of us when the opposite happened. In the course of preparing for that election, the issue almost clarified itself between harmony and honesty. At least that was the feeling of most of us on the side of honesty. The public viewed it, obviously, in a different fashion. They decided that discord at City Hall really needed correction and that it was not good for the city to have constant public controversy in the operation of city affairs.

The campaign tactics against Oscar Holcombe began on the note of trying to display the efficiency and honesty that Roy Hofheinz had brought. One instance, in particular, will give the flavor of the initial thrust of the campaign tactics. Hofheinz had a great flair for the dramatic. One evening I received a call to come to his home at two in the morning. At that stage we all knew we were having difficulty in the campaign. Early polls showed that we were in trouble, so I immediately assumed that he had to come up with some new grand strategy and we had unearthed some information on the opposition that would completely turn this campaign around. I arrived, full of enthusiasm, at his house, along with, again, most of the other trusted and close individuals around him, a group of maybe 20 persons. The purpose of the meeting was to wire tags to flat washers and the tags showed that we were now buying these washers at roughly about—I've forgotten exactly the number—but say a third of the cost the previous administration had been paying, to be an indication of how efficient and honest the purchasing department had become under Roy Hofheinz. We wired washers from two until six in the morning, and they were then distributed as campaign material. It turned out the move was dramatic but ineffective. More and more of this had minimal, if any, effect on the voters.

Hofheinz became more and more upset at the turn of events and became more extreme in the approaches that he wanted to take to paint the opposition the way he saw them, which was as villains. He went into a tactic that caused him a great deal of problems after he left the mayor's office, and in fact followed a number of us who were close to him, for a number of years. He labeled a group of the city's leading civic leaders as "fat cats." They had been important in the growth and formation of Houston for many, many years and formed a loose-knit group of their own. They reacted with huge distaste and, in fact, where they had undoubtedly been opponents of his up to that point, they became exceedingly active opponents and later carried the fight beyond the election itself in displaying their displeasure to Roy Hofheinz and to those around him. Bob Smith was probably the only major individual—in economic circumstances in Houston—who really did stick by him. Smith was completely loyal to Hofheinz and backed him, not only with funds, but personally and in conversations—as far down as arguments in a barber shop—with individuals who were condemning Roy Hofheinz.

City Engineer Eugene Maier, who stayed at City Hall for some time after Hofheinz left, said:

I feel Hofheinz accomplished a great deal. I've always regretted that Roy didn't stay in long enough to establish a strong program and to demonstrate what he could have done if he'd had just a little more time. He often got involved in defending somebody's rights, which was great, but back in those days that didn't mean very much to the average person. Today he'd have a lot of people supporting him. He had, most of the time, blacks, Chicanos, and the working people behind him. He was the first mayor to recognize them properly. I never noticed that Holcombe did anything to help them.

Hofheinz was the first mayor that I ever was associated with who would invite department heads to his home and get acquainted with them socially, as well as professionally. He was always gracious and cordial.

He started a new era in city planning and thinking and open bidding and a lot of stuff. He stuck in the conscience, I believe, of the people of Houston. In my opinion Roy was a genius, one of those people who think when they're right—come hell or high water—they're going to stick to it. He had more new ideas and good thoughts in four minutes than most people would have in days.

Welcome Wilson said:

I was a staunch, avid, and active supporter of Hofheinz, and for that reason I was helpful in whatever way that I could be. Not being on the city payroll, I was in a position to be involved in his personal and political activities to a much larger degree than the average department head could be. When I joined the administration, I immediately was adopted into the inner circle of Hofheinz inasmuch as I represented a close and direct channel with Bob Smith. Our inner circle started off as a relatively small group that included Jim Braniff, insurance man, who was very close to Roy, and others, as well as my brother, Jack, who officed at City Hall, and his responsibility was the security director for the Port of Houston. So a cadre of those people, plus Gould Beech and others, were active with Hofheinz on what you might call a day-to-day basis. My nearly three years at City Hall were among the most exciting of my life. Our inner group—"Young Turks" or "Palace Guard"—was made up largely of men in their 20s. We were in the position—because of the responsibilities we had—to find it rewarding and exciting.

Those years were dominated by one of the most imaginative men I've dealt with in my lifetime—Hofheinz. He had an imaginative approach to practically everything done. He would not accept a city program simply because that's the way it had been done for years. He would not accept the idea that street right-of-way could only be bought at a certain speed; in other words, if the requirements were double that speed, he just wouldn't accept the idea that it could not be doubled. He had the big picture in mind at all times—to his political disfavor—inasmuch as his approach, in my judgment, was "what's best for the long range interest of the city." If somebody didn't agree with that, or took what he considered a backward view, he was candid enough to tell him he thought him stupid. That was not popular. I would have to say that practically everything Roy did was unusual. Let me start off in the early part of the administration to say that Hofheinz gave complete and total support to the civil defense effort. We were able to conduct citywide civil defense drills that, during the Korean War, were something of substantial importance. I recall times when we evacuated the entire downtown area and literally shut it down for the better part of a day in cooperation with President Eisenhower's program. Roy was able, by giving support to such things in a positive and direct way, to get done what most cities in the nation at that time just were not able to manage. Going beyond civil defense, Hofheinz was always campaigning for certain things and fighting to get his way. His way was not always popular, particularly with members of the council. Regrettably, Roy did not have much respect for the members of the council, and it just showed in everything he did and said, so that over a period of time a substantial animosity developed and I would say that the most bizarre year, and perhaps the most bizarre year in Houston's city politics, was his last year in office.

Roy seemed to get along well with people he respected—those he felt were intelligent. Someone could be a substantial adversary, and he could deal with him as long as he felt that his intelligence was good and that his motives were good. But he just had no tolerance whatsoever for anybody who, in his judgment—not always right—was not up with him in dealing with something. One of his great failings was to call some people stupid. It was unnecessary and it certainly didn't help him one bit.

In discussing the Hofheinz impeachment hearing held by City Council, Welcome Wilson said:

Left to right: Matt Wilson, Roy Hofheinz, and Roy Cullen

Mayor Pro tem Matt Wilson was a kindly kind of a fellow. He wore white suits, white hats, white shoes and drove a white Cadillac and was not one I would describe as being the brightest member of the council. He had never presided over anything, much less impeachment proceedings, so it was really somewhat of a comical affair. Some councilmen were colorful speakers and created a circus atmosphere. One particular incident came when the hearing approached the end. Jack Binion was having all kinds of difficulty in his presentation. The meeting adjourned for 30 minutes. Our group went into Hofheinz's office. Hofheinz and Binion were trying to determine exactly what they should do with the rest of us pitching as best we could. After 30 minutes of discussion that seemed to go nowhere, we all marched back with my having the feeling that "My God, we just don't know what we're doing" or "We don't know where we're going" and what have you. When we got back to the proceedings, Binion stood up and just started from nowhere and made an eloquent presentation, with Hofheinz chipping in and supporting him, and made a rout out of the whole proceedings. The next day, the newspapers reported that "Hofheinz forces adjourned for 30 minutes, developed a magnificent strategy and a well-thought-out-plan, and came back in and sprang it on the council." I was amused.

After Hofheinz's forces won the Charter Amendment 19 election, Wilson recalled: "Election was set for the Fall of 1955. We went into the campaign to raise money for the November mayor's election. We found raising money more difficult because, in the previous two and a half years, Hofheinz had made a variety of his backers mad. He was unwilling, under any circumstance, to give any favors to someone who backed him. I felt many people felt it was a burden to be friendly with Hofheinz if they did business with the city for the simple reason that he leaned over backwards and went out of his way to be certain that his friends did not get any favored treatment."

Although the *Chronicle*, seeking "harmony," helped defeat Hofheinz in his third race for mayor, John T. Jones, Jr., said, "I got to know Roy best during the years when he was mayor. I think he made Houston a good mayor. He did, I think, everything within his power to—well, I don't like to say 'clean the city up' because that implies that it was dirty—but let's say, he did everything in his power to regularize city government. Nobody can be completely successful in regularizing a bureaucracy, but he did a very good job of it, and he certainly had extremely good intentions and he was very effective."

When Bill Bennett left KTHT to be with Willard Walbridge at KTRK-TV after Hofheinz became mayor, he occasionally heard the mayor and his law partner, Red James, talk about radio, television, and politics. He recalled: "They were two of the greatest friends I ever saw. We didn't call him Red James for nothing—he had a temper. The Judge sometimes would get kinda carried away and make a statement that he maybe couldn't quite back up, and Red challenged him. I would have bet a nickel they were going to knock each other's heads off. They would cuss each other and raise Cain and in 15 minutes they'd have their arms around each other just like two brothers that had had a big fight. You'd think they were really going to kill each other—the way these two guys could carry on. One wanted to do something one way, the other one another. But they'd finally come to some agreement."

Hofheinz still did business with Judge Elkins, the banker, when he became mayor. Bennett told another story about their relationship:

> Roy could borrow money from Judge Elkins over the telephone and sign notes later. Sometimes, Roy'd get behind with what he owed the bank, and he'd call Elkins up and say about his debt: "There's no use in my worrying, Judge, you're worrying. If we both worry, we're both going to get sick, so you just go

ahead and worry and I'll forget all about it. There's no use in both of us worrying." During the '55 campaign against Oscar Holcombe, he was fighting some of the big brass in town. They were known as "the city fathers." Without them you couldn't get elected mayor. I just figured they expected certain actions. Judge Elkins' wife sure didn't like to be called by Roy the mate of a "fat cat."

One of Hofheinz's favorite sayings used to be when you'd ask him if he knew who someone was: "Oh yeah, I knew him intimately and well." I'd kid him about that sort of a statement. Finally one day I asked him about how well did he know one of the big league ladies in town, and he said, "Oh, I know her intimately and well." With that I really broke out. I said, "Judge, if I were you, I wouldn't say in public I'd known this woman intimately. You could get yourself involved." He never used that word again.

Leon Jaworski discussed Hofheinz's years as mayor:

He became controversial. Roy was no man to give in. Once he made up his mind, he was very obstinate, and everybody else was wrong and he was right. This hurt Roy in the end. I was busy trying lawsuits and had little City Hall business then. Roy did talk to me about the impeachment charges of the council. I thought it was really a very unreasonable thing for City Council to attempt to do, and I saw no way that they were going to be successful in doing it. Jack Binion and Will Sears were in the middle of that and won. . . . Roy's undoing when he lost to Oscar Holcombe was that people were tired of the wrangling at City Hall. It wasn't a question of integrity. I don't think anybody lost belief in Roy's honesty. Roy had a falling out with too many people for no good reason . . . and he was rather ingloriously defeated, which I regretted to see. I thought he was a man with a tremendous political future. I thought Roy was going to step in to higher office, bright as he was, and, having been a state legislator, a county judge, and a mayor, Roy had a background that would have fitted him for governor. Of course, when he was so badly defeated, his political career ended.

Fred Hofheinz, who followed in his father's footsteps as mayor in 1973, recalled:

I was in junior high school when Dad was elected mayor. When you're the Mayor of Houston, as I subsequently found out, it's very difficult also to be in private business. My Dad was completely uninvolved in those days in any of his private businesses, although he still owned 25 percent of the radio station and 16 percent of a television station and considerable property. The amount of time he took to pay attention to his children increased considerably while mayor. There also was a group of City Hall cronies—the "Palace Guard." I was part of it, and mother and the family were part of it. We did an awful lot of hunting and fishing. Dad never has, in his whole life, been able to do anything part way. His thinking—if you're going to have one hunting dog, you're going to have 15—so I ended up at one point with 15 hunting dogs. If you're going to have one hunting rig, or truck or something, you have two, and one of the two that you have has a five- or ten-thousand-dollar attachment to it with compartments and places to carry your hunting dogs and a special compartment for your guns, and for this and for that, all specially made by Stuart Young. I have a son who's a lot like Dad. I call it a big-gimmick syndrome. Dad always liked gimmicks. He always liked little playtoys and little things that were different from the run of the mill. My boy is exactly that way.

The more wealthy Dad became, the more his gimmicks became extravagant. Back in those days, hunting and fishing and outdoors things were on his mind. We had a great time. We had a couple of pickup trucks which were specially rigged—trailers, sleeping trailers, dogs, guns, hunting camps—two hunting camps. He spent a lot of time there, and I was invited to tag along. Those were very happy days, and my Dad and I were closer then than at any time since.

In 1979, when a Hollywood lyricist, Dene II also looked back to her life as the mayor's daughter:

Dad once told me because of my love for music that maybe some day I'd have my own records on the juke box at "Huckster House." It was one of the most important things he ever said to me, because, from the time I was eight years old, the most important thing in the world to me was to bring records to the jukebox. It had been my dream that some day my children would be punching buttons with their friends on the juke box when they spent their summers there, and they'd be hearing songs that their mother had written. I guess the only thing that stands in between a dream and making it a reality is actually believing enough to follow through and make it happen. I have a bit of that Hofheinz spirit in me. Dad gave a lot of it to me, and I'm really grateful for that.

"Huckster House" was the place to be in the mayoralty days. We had the most fun when all of us were together. I used to enjoy gambling with play money called "Huckster Bucks" at the soda fountain in the circus room. Dad was always boisterous. He'd spin that wheel and played like he was the head dude in Vegas. He'd say, "Now it's rolling, where's it going to land, little doll?" He was really an actor. When he was in the mood, he could really get in to the moment. When he was not in the mood, that was another thing. If Daddy didn't want to play, or if Daddy didn't want to be bothered, if he had something on his mind, it was much more important than play or being bothered. He withdrew to himself almost to the point of seeming to be brooding, and he would become very introspective. He would guard himself then, and everything else was shut out. I used to feel a little left out at those times. I know sometimes he would start to fall asleep in his big chair, and his eyes would close and I would say, "No daddy, no. I'm going to miss you."

There were many nights that I'd have bad dreams. I went through a pretty hellacious time. When it was all over the front pages of the newspapers it was pretty difficult to keep news from just the average child, and I was a curious child. It was impossible for my parents to keep things from me. I was one of the first to know that my life had been threatened. I had policemen following me to school every day and waiting for me outside of the classes and driving me home in the limo. I had no moments alone except at night, and then they had someone down the hall from me, watching entrances leading to my room to protect me.

I had my tonsils taken out when I was 10. He was mayor and it was on the front page of the newspaper that "Little Dene" has had her tonsils taken out. I was the Amy Carter of Houston—if that helps put it into perspective—maybe with a little bit more ham thrown in, because there's a little more Hofheinz thrown in; if you're Roy Hofheinz's daughter, there must be a little more ham there somewhere. After that tonsillectomy, I think someone told me that it might hurt your throat if you talked for the first few days, but that's the worst thing that could happen, and, as usual, I made a much bigger deal out of it than it actually was, because for weeks and weeks after that tonsillectomy, I couldn't talk. I whispered. I began talking through my nose because I had been told it was going to hurt my throat. So I was trying to protect my throat and I guess four or five weeks went by and my parents were beginning to get a little worried—I mean mostly worried and partly embarrassed, because all of a sudden their little chatterbox was talking in whispers. They had a conference—like, "how are we going to talk her out of this? What are we going to do with this neurotic child?" because they sat me down in the living room at Yorktown and promised me one of two things—that I could either go to Acapulco where I had been and loved to water ski, or I could go back to New York and see another Broadway play—if I'd start talking right again. They said if I'd get back to my old self and talk well enough, even though it annoyed them, they would be happy to take me on the vacation of my dreams. Well, I think that within 24 hours I was talking quite plainly again, and I think a couple of weekends after that we went to New York and stayed for a week.

I think that Mama had more of a political instinct than even Dad. She had a sensitivity and a perception, an ability to feel which way the tide was going. She had a remarkable quality, too, of just meeting someone and making that person feel like she'd known him or her all her life. She had a graciousness without any pretense whatsoever. I felt her warmth and graciousness and saw her elegance, almost a sense of godliness. Dad and Mama were a magnificent team. As far as I'm concerned, I don't think that any of us in the Hofheinz family realized how strong Mama really was until after her death.

When Mary Frances and Milton Gougenheim met Hofheinz on the eve of his becoming mayor, it was the beginning of a long friendship. Gougenheim said in 1978:

We all celebrated over several bowls of seafood gumbo at Massa's restaurant, a downtown landmark and a favorite of Roy's, after our introduction. Our years at City Hall, despite some of the problems that accompany a mayor's administration, were fun years. It was during this time that I had the opportunity to see Judge Hofheinz operate under the very toughest of circumstances where a little white lie or two meant success or defeat. The Judge never gave in.

Dene Hofheinz during Roy's mayoral years

He stuck to being honest, no matter what, and in politics, quite frankly, it was very costly. I have reason to know that, conservatively, it cost Hofheinz a million dollars of his own money to be mayor.

The Judge's "Huckster House" on the bay made him feel an expert on boating and fishing. One day Mary Frances and I went with Roy and Big Dene to take a boat ride in Roy's speedboat. We were going to ride around the coast line from his pier. Roy read all the maps and swung the boat out into the bay as fast as it would go. It seemed to me that he was too close to shore. I checked the maps and told him to get further out because the bay was full of sand bars. He said, "Hell, what do you know about reading maps?" With that, wham, wham, wham, we hit a monster sand bar in shallow water. I cussed the Judge for all I could think of and he said, "Be quiet, I have an idea to save us." He sure did. He said, "Gougenheim, you and Dene and Mary Frances get out of the boat, get into the water cause it's shallow, and push until we get off the sand bar." I said, "Well, hell, what about you? Get your big ass down in the water and push, too!" Roy's reply was very distinct and yet very priceless. "The captain never leaves his ship," he said.

The Judge did not always tease and kid his friends. There were some times in my life, for instance, that his moral support was priceless and very essential to my welfare. I lost my father, who was in his mid-fifties. I was very close to him. His sudden passing with a heart attack was the first real shock in my life. I retreated to my bedroom and made no effort to leave there, even when friends came to visit. The Judge and Dene came by. He came into my bedroom alone, and we had a chat. He convinced me that I had to get on with life, and I did just that. Years later, when Roy lost Dene suddenly, the blow was immense to him and I remembered his kindness and helped him in whatever way I could to get back on his feet.

Dr. Ed S. Crocker, a 1941 graduate of the University of Texas Medical School at Galveston and a general practitioner, became the Hofheinz family physician in 1950 after he was introduced to Hofheinz by his friend, Stewart Boyle, a Houston oil man. Crocker, still busy in 1978 but trying to slow down in his practice, said the first time he visited the ailing Dene Hofheinz was at her Yorktown home. He recalled:

After seeing her upstairs, Roy and I walked downstairs and he asked me to have a cup of coffee. We discussed Dene's condition. It was obvious to me she had acromegalia—a pituitary gland tumor after puberty. She told me her glove size changed about one a year as her body grew larger. Other than headaches and other minor complaints, she said she constantly lived under tension. I could understand why with the mayor constantly embattled. Subsequently I admitted her to a hospital each year for a checkup. On three occasions I had neurological consultations. I would always X-ray her skull for the pituitary growth follow-up, and there was never any change after I took her case. It was the opinion of my consultant and X-ray people that it had long outgrown itself. It was not active and nothing could be done, but she had headaches and sinus trouble.

I finally determined she needed a hysterectomy. After I did the operation and walked out of her hospital room with a nurse into the sitting room, which was a part of her hospital suite, Roy was leaning against the wall, his bodyguard and two aides with him. I walked up to him and said, "Oh good morning, Your Honor." Nervously he answered, "All right, by God, I've been standing here for at least 25 minutes. Were you in there medicating or fornicating?" That was typical of his humor.

24

New Horizons

Recalling Hofheinz's defeat for a third term as mayor, the then Mary Frances Gougenheim said, "I thought the end of the world had come. It was a crushing blow to his family, friends, me, and his other co-workers. I am sure it was for him." That sad statement about the Judge came from Mary Frances after she had become the second Mrs. Roy Hofheinz. When she was Hofheinz's receptionist in December of 1955, she quickly learned that he was no quitter. At age 43 he could forget political and financial setbacks and move ahead. "Late in December," she recalled, "the mayor invited me into his City Hall office when he was cleaning out his desk getting ready to leave. He asked if I'd like to work for him at his private office in the KTHT radio building, which he had maintained during his years as mayor. He still owned the building. I, of course, said I would because he had become my leader, and where he went, I would follow."

Concerned about the welfare of some 30 city department heads and employees he felt had been close and loyal to him, Hofheinz called the group into his office and asked about their plans if they did not stay with the incoming Holcombe administration. The result was that he put Gould Beech, Johnny Goyen, and Bill Sherrill, along with Mary Frances, on his personal payroll as of January 1, 1956. John Stephen, a key city administrator and Hofheinz's law partner, chose to join the Holcombe administration's legal staff.

The four staying with Hofheinz reported for work every day after the New Year, but had little to do. "We flurried around doing a lot of nothing," said Mary Frances. "I spent most of my time the first six months talking and warding off bill collectors because the Judge's cash had dwindled, and nothing was coming in. It seemed to me he owed everybody in town." Hofheinz's campaign contributions had fallen far short of covering expenses, and his preoccupation with politics had allowed his personal affairs to suffer. "The Judge made a lot of enemies during the campaign—some influential in banking circles," Mary Frances recalled. "Judge Elkins called loans—no doubt because during the campaign the Judge had referred to him as one of a powerful group of 'fat cats.' The irony of it all was that the Judge loved and admired Judge Elkins. He was hurt when Judge Elkins didn't support him against Holcombe. The Judge managed to scrape up enough money to pay Johnny, Bill, and Gould as we went along. I talked the situation over with my husband, and we agreed that I wouldn't take any pay from the Judge until he got on his feet. Then he could catch up. It took him six months to do that."

Hofheinz was not "broke" in the usual sense. He still had radio and television stock, real estate worth millions, and his slag partnership, but his cash flow had stopped. He needed ready money to meet notes and accumulated interest. Bill Sherrill, an accomplished financial analyst, became a key advisor about what Hofheinz should do to clear his debts and have cash to move into new enterprises and investments. "I would analyze a proposal brought to him by someone for investment, and he would take home my appraisal," said Sherrill. "That night he would read several books on the subject. The next morning he would ask me questions, getting more and more detailed and refined until he took me beyond my own depth."

To take his mind off his financial and other problems after he left office, the Judge remodeled "Huckster House." When Hofheinz was worried about something, he would work with his hands—hammer, nail, and decorate. "When the Judge decided on a project," Mary Frances recalled, "he never did it halfway. The remodeling at 'Huckster House' was just as intense as the most important projects of his life." The Judge left his Yorktown home at daybreak to be at his office ahead of his "troops," as he called the group who left City Hall with him. While drinking coffee each morning, he would "hit the ground running," according to Mary Frances. "He would have on his desk long yellow pads of things he wanted each of us to do. Gould, Johnny, Bill, and I always had special tasks—on paper. Halfway down Johnny Goyen's list one day was an item: *swap plane—Sears.* Johnny went to the Sears tool department and asked the salesman for a 'swap plane.' The salesman told Johnny the department was out of them at the moment. Goyen went back to the office and gave the Judge the message. The Judge told Johnny that there was no such thing as a 'swap plane'—that he had intended to exchange one wood plane for another. The Judge reared back and roared in laughter, the most contagious of anyone's I've ever known."

Working with Sherrill and Ed Bruhl, his accountant, Hofheinz knew that he had to consolidate his indebtedness, using his Yorktown home and other properties as collateral. Marshall McDonald, an attorney with a degree in accounting from Wharton Business School in Philadelphia, had worked with Bruhl (and later opened a Houston investment company). He needed business. Walking down Main Street one day, he ran into Bruhl who told him that Hofheinz was a typical Houston "wheeler-dealer," a hustling businessman working hard trying to pay off his indebtedness. McDonald went to Hofheinz and offered his assistance. He found the Judge a man of "uncanny ability with an agile mind always looking for people to finance his ideas." In 1979, when

McDonald was president of Florida Power and Light Company in Miami, he said, "I got up a financial statement for Roy and went to the Sealy and Smith Foundation for the John Sealy Hospital in Galveston, and applied for a loan for $1 million for Hofheinz. The trustees took it under advisement and later approved it. I kept a close check on the deal. Roy paid off every cent ahead of time." Mary Frances said she liked McDonald, not only because he was a "personable man" who did such a good job of getting the loan for the Judge, but also because he brought fresh kolaches (Swedish/Czechoslovakian pastries) for the staff when he visited the offices.

While this loan was pending, Gould Beech thought it would be a good idea to get a favorable feature story about Hofheinz in a newspaper serving the Galveston area where the Sealy trustees lived. When he finished it, he called publicist Jack Valenti and asked him to try to place the story with Fred Hartman, editor of the *Baytown Sun*. Beech told the future aide to President Johnson to use "By Jack Valenti" on the story if Hartman went for it. A feature story with pictures about Hofheinz's incredible career appeared shortly in the *Sun*. "I don't know whether it helped Hofheinz get the loan or not," said Beech, "but it wasn't long after it was published that the million came through."

Hofheinz installed an elaborate office with bar, kitchen, and private bathroom in his new law offices in the South Coast Building, formerly the Second National Bank Building, but he spent little time there. "When we opened the offices," said James, a partner, "Roy, the showman, had a big party for press and friends. But he didn't want to practice law as a total career after he got the political and building-real estate fever. Although he was the senior partner in the new firm, the Judge left his partners to run the new office. He principally advised."

Hofheinz's corner office in the South Coast Building suite attracted much attention. One wall was covered in imported black and white wool tweed. A long custom-made couch along the wall also was covered in the same tweed as was the Judge's executive chair. The desk was made from a magnificent inlaid marble table top which the Judge and Mrs. Hofheinz bought in Rome. On the opposite wall, an alcove housed an exquisite oval antique Florentine Carrara marble plaque showing a lady with a veil. Hidden doors opened to reveal a small cocktail bar. Behind the bar was a lighted plastic panel with mementoes of each phase of the Judge's life, such as a small key to the city.

In April, Hofheinz invested in one of the prettiest tracts of land in Harris County—37.41 acres on Woodway—paying $131,250, about $3500 an acre, to Mrs. Nina J. Cullinan, member of a prominent Houston family. He felt the Woodway region, located near Houston Country Club, would be one of the most promising areas for future residential development. Time again proved him right, for today homesites in the area sell for a dollar per square foot.

Even while mayor, Hofheinz did not stop buying land, although he was careful as the city's chief executive to purchase nothing that would be in conflict with city ethics policies. With Harry Holmes, Jr., as a 50 percent partner, he bought 65 acres on South Main, west of the land where the Astrodome now stands, thinking one day it would be good commercial property. This land was in the Pierce Junction Field, and by the time Hofheinz left City Hall two oil wells were producing there and four more were staked out.

Hofheinz's land philosophy was far-seeing. He told Johnny Goyen, "You add one more family and it affects the price of land just as a rock in a lake. Five hundred thousand people were dumped into Harris County after I bought my Yorktown property. Imagine what it's going to be like when they drop another million people within the next 15 years." Hofheinz's Yorktown farm was near the highest-priced subdivisions in Houston: Tanglewood, Briarcoft, Memorial Drive, Briargrove, Del Monte, and others. In 1958, people who paid less than $500 an acre for land around Yorktown were selling sites for office buildings for two dollars a square foot. Goyen said Hofheinz told him in late 1956 that he should get a real estate license. Goyen found out the rules—a test in Austin one month and another in Houston the next. "I did exactly what the Judge said and reported back to him—he liked to be told," recalled Goyen. "I've been in the real estate business ever since because the Judge originally gave me the idea. He told me Houston was growing fast and I should be in on property development. I still thank him today for leading me."

Goyen also wanted a political career. In mid-1957 he went to the Judge and said, "I'm thinking about running for City Council." He added, "A lot of people thought Hofheinz put me in the race, but when I went to him and told him that I was thinking about it, he said, 'What the hell do you want to get involved in that mess for?' I said, 'Well, Judge I think we need changes. I don't like what's going on.' He said, 'Yes, but you can make a good living by not fooling with that.' This is one time I didn't listen to him and went ahead and ran anyway. The first call I got after the polls closed was from Mary Frances, who said, 'Johnny, you've won by a great number of votes.' I said, 'Mary Frances, are you sure?' She said, 'Yeah, you're going to win this election big. The Judge asked me to check some precincts. I told him the figures, and he says, 'You've won.' The next call I got was from Hofheinz. He said, 'I want to congratulate you on winning.' I said, 'But Judge, the results aren't all in.' He said. 'They're in enough for me to know you've won big.'" Goyen was continuously reelected for 20 years.

Welcome Wilson said that after the mayoral defeat, Hofheinz approached Bob Smith, the largest landowner in Harris County, with the concept that they would team up, with Hofheinz doing the work and planning, to develop the property that he and Smith owned; they also would acquire additional property. Hofheinz was worth several million dollars in his own right, and Smith was worth something in the category of a half a billion dollars. Wilson recalled:

Hofheinz started developing a concept for a regional shopping center in Houston, an idea unknown then in Texas, although there had been one or two around the country. It was a revolutionary idea. Hofheinz felt his Yorktown property, now in the "Magic Circle," was the best piece of real estate in the county. With his million-dollar loan, Hofheinz was able to pay off debts and start planning for the future. Over a 30-year period, Hofheinz lived off the borrowings on that one piece of land.

Hofhcinz hired architects and designed the regional shopping center to be covered and completely air-conditioned. He went around the country to chains to sell the shopping center idea. At the same time, Frank Sharp was trying to get Sharpstown Center off the ground. It was Hofheinz's feeling that there was room in Houston for one or the other, but not both, so he kept saying that if he were unable to get either Federated or Allied to join the center that it wouldn't work, or Frank's wouldn't work, depending on what occurred. Frank Sharp went to Allied Stores [Foley's in Houston] and said if they would build a store on his land, he would give them a 10-acre chunk out of the shopping center. That turned Allied's head. Foley's built there, and when Foley's did, Sharpstown Center was made. Hofheinz's center idea later was abandoned.

Meantime, Hofheinz had bought and sold, along with Bob Smith, tracts of land and made more money. Hofheinz was proud of the fact that almost universally, if he had enough cash to put up 15 percent of the purchase price, he would take 15 percent of the deal. He went out of his way to be sure that he was not leaning on Bob Smith for more cash credit. He was careful to pull his own weight. And so it was a successful relationship.

Remembering how the Roman Colosseum vellarium (tent) had been covered and held up by slaves, Hofheinz explored the idea for the Smith-Hofheinz shopping center on the planning boards. Buckminster Fuller, inventor of the geodesic dome, was called in by the Judge as a consultant. "Buckminster Fuller convinced me that it was possible to cover any size space if you didn't run out of money," Hofheinz said. Mary Frances recalled that Harold Crawford, a bright young architect who worked for the Judge and Bob Smith after serving on the Houston Planning Commission, set up the meeting between Hofheinz and Fuller. "The Judge called Fuller 'Buckie' and they hit it off beautifully," said Mary Frances. "After they talked, the Judge was convinced that, with enough money, any area could be covered with a dome." Hofheinz later would put this conviction to the test.

On June 2, 1958, Hofheinz for $525,000 sold the building which housed Radio Station KTHT and its transmitter site on Miller Cutoff Road at San Jacinto Monument. The buyer was the Texas Radio Corporation, whose president still was Robert D. Straus, executive vice-president of Straus-Frank Company. The Judge, however, still owned 25 percent of the stock in the corporation, the chairman of which was Colonel W. B. Bates, who was also chairman of the Bank of the Southwest. This provided Hofheinz with additional money for investments, including the ill-fated Smith-Hofheinz shopping center.

George Kirksey, a native of Hillsboro, Texas, a journalism graduate of the University of Texas, and an ardent professional baseball fan from the time he was a boy, opened a public relations office in Houston in 1950. He had been a sports writer for United Press and served as a lieutenant colonel in the Army during World War II. His military experience whetted his natural tendency to be blunt, outspoken, and often controversial. Reveling in Houston's growth, he became a one-man propagandist for major league baseball and pushed all sports writers in the Houston area to encourage a civic movement to get the city out of the baseball minor leagues.

In 1957, Kirksey enlisted Craig Cullinan, Jr., Texaco heir, to join his crusade for a major league team. Cullinan, then 26, had attended Houston public schools before graduating from Phillip Exeter Academy in Massachusetts. He joined the U. S. Naval Air Corps as an aviator with the rank of ensign after training at the Naval Air Station in Pensacola, Florida. After leaving the Navy, he entered Yale University and graduated with a bachelor of arts degree. Cullinan joined the *Houston Post* late in 1949 as a cub reporter. He resigned in the summer of 1950 and went into the newspaper business by purchasing a small daily at Angleton, Texas. He remained in the newspaper and publishing business until 1955 when he returned to Houston. He was a director of Fidelity Bank and Trust Company and Review Publishers, Incorporated, and he did civic work with the Houston Speech and Hearing Center. He was married then to Allison Prescott. Cullinan is a handsome, soft-spoken, lanky man, and his enthusiasm for sports, especially baseball, started early in life. He recalled that Houston's major league effort really began to move in 1956 when William A. Kirkland convened a meeting of area men to discuss the prospect of bringing major league baseball to the city. He said:

> While this group agreed on the merits of the idea, nothing came of that meeting for several months until George Kirksey used his considerable powers of persuasion to lead me into forming the Houston Sports Association. Those who joined were committed to nothing more than paying $500 each for the option to examine the merits of investing further in a baseball franchise if one could be established in Houston. From the outset it became obvious that the association was faced with a chicken-and-egg problem of appalling dimensions. HSA had no money to speak of, no major league stadium, and, most important of all, no franchise. The routine became tediously familiar: get a stadium and we will talk to you about a team, Kirksey and I were told on trips to major league cities. Returning to Houston, we were told to find a team and the city might talk about building a stadium. . . .

Busch Stadium, where the Houston team, farm club of the St. Louis Cardinals, played Texas League games, was inadequate for major league baseball, but neither of the major advocates let that bother them. They felt if Houston could get the nod from either major league for a future team, sufficient support could be found in the rich city to build a playing field and to finance entry into big-time baseball.

As a result of growing public demand that Houston become a major league city, the Harris County Parks Commission, legalized by the Texas legislature through a bill introduced by Harris County Senator Searcy Bracewell, was created to submit a revenue bond issue to property owners to build a sports center. Chairman of the commission was civic leader Kirkland, highly respected board chairman of the First City National Bank. The First and City National banks merged in 1956 as financial giants. Kirkland and Hofheinz had known each other for many years.

Kirkland, a native of Houston, had graduated from Phillips Academy, Princeton University, and the law school of the University of Texas, and was a strong force in moving the city toward an adequate sports facility. The legislative act creating a Parks Commission gave Harris County Commissioners Court the right to appoint the commission, which was named February 10, 1958. On the seven-member panel with Kirkland were Archer Romero, chairman of the board of the Houston Fat Stock Show; Herbert Allen, chairman of Cameron Iron Works; Eddie Dyer, well-known sports figure and insurance man; Wilton Roper, vice-president of Citizens National Bank and Trust Company in Baytown; E. B. Mansfield, Pasadena engineer; and Corbin Robertson, oilman and member of the University of Houston board of regents.

The Fat Stock Show was primarily interested because it had outgrown its facilities in the downtown Coliseum. Kirkland said the show's needs had to have prime consideration in the building of any new facility.

In accepting the appointment, Kirkland said, "I accept the appointment, and I think we'll get the job done." Serving then as county judge was Bob Casey. On July 26—just five months after the commission's appointment—voters approved by a margin of three to one a proposal to issue $18 million in revenue bonds for a sports center. Park commission members looked to beautiful Memorial Park as a possible site. Ima Hogg, whose prominent family included a former governor, had sold the park to the city for a low price. When she announced her opposition, consideration ended. Lewis Cutrer, old-time Hofheinz political ally, had just been elected mayor in another ouster of Oscar Holcombe, whose two-year administration after he defeated Hofheinz was beset with "cronyism." Cutrer went to Miss Hogg to seek her support. When he left, he told reporters, "I think the wishes of the Hogg family should be respected. I wouldn't begin to do anything that might jeopardize the city's title to the park." The sale of the land by the Hogg family to the city had been with the understanding that it would be a park and nothing else. The commission had to look elsewhere.

On August 22, 1960, Kirkland said a stadium and exposition center should be built on another site and reported that Houston Fat Stock Show officials liked a 300-acre area near Playland Park in the Main-Knight Road-Old Spanish Trail area. Other park commission members concurred. "Our first job is to satisfy the fat stock people," said Kirkland. The Fat Stock Show already had outgrown its downtown Coliseum quarters.

It was early 1960 when Kirksey and Cullinan, stymied in their efforts to acquire a major league team, went to Bob Smith for advice and help. The millionaire was interested, but he said the two promoters would have to talk to Hofheinz and get his opinion and assistance. Kirksey and Cullinan caught the Judge at the right time at his Brandt Street offices—his promotion of a covered air-conditioned shopping center had hit snags. Mary Frances recalled that when the baseball advocates visited Hofheinz, he listened carefully to their problems. He had known the story of their efforts and, having been a baseball fan for years, was immediately interested in the desire of the two men to enlist Smith and himself in the cause. The Judge made it plain that he did not believe major league baseball would be profitable in Houston if the playing field was uncovered because of the semi-tropical weather. After that meeting, Hofheinz dropped all shopping center work and devoted his time to planning a stadium. He got Smith's promise to join him in a renewed search for a franchise. Cullinan recalled: "The Judge embodied three assets of value to HSA. First, he was Bob Smith's closest associate. Second, he had an unquestionable talent and track record of accomplishment in the field of building municipal facilities. Last, his abilities in sales and promotion would be immensely valuable to the ball club. With Hofheinz on the team, prospects brightened." Until then, the Houston Sports Association was a syndicate of people with risk money.

On September 7, notice was sent to owners of syndicate shares that a meeting for incorporation and stock division would be forthcoming. On November 22, telegrams were sent to all shareholders to be at the official organizational meeting the next day. All who had invested were represented, some by proxy. The minutes show the following as original stockholders in the new corporation and their number of shares: Hofheinz 3300; Smith 3300; Cullinan 1500; K. S. "Bud" Adams 1000; Kirksey 200; and Earl Allen, John Beck, J. S. Cullinan (brother of Craig), A. J. Farfel, Harding S. Frankel, Jack Josey, and Leonard Rauch, 100 each. With each share costing $100, Smith and Hofheinz put up $330,000 each and gained control, which they wanted if they were going to participate. Smith became chairman of the board; Cullinan continued as president, Kirksey executive vice-president, and Hofheinz and Adams vice-presidents. The public did not know details of the structure of the corporation replacing the syndicate, especially that Cullinan and Kirksey had become minority stockholders. Cullinan came to recognize the grave error he committed in failing to subscribe to at least as much stock as Smith and

Hofheinz. The oversight eventually cost him a voice in the operation of the ball club.

Close friend and financial adviser Ben McGuire said that as soon as Hofheinz and Smith decided to take the lead in the Houston Sports Association, the Judge got every book on baseball he could find and sat up for 24 straight hours reading. "He became an authority on the subject quickly," said McGuire, "so that when he went to see National League owners about a franchise he could speak their language. He knew what baseball men were doing and he knew what he wanted to do."

McGuire said he was with Hofheinz at Brandt Street when he first brought up the idea of a covered stadium. He said, "People in Houston aren't going to sit in big numbers in the hot sun and high humidity in the daytime or fight mosquitoes at night to see baseball. We've got to have a covered, air-conditioned playing field." McGuire added, "I told Roy he had lost his marbles, but he was determined. He called architects, and they told him his idea was feasible. At first Roy thought we might finance the project privately. We tried several places, but it was too radical an idea to interest conservative money men. That's when he knew public money would have to be used for building. I was in contact with Roy daily, and he stayed on top of the Dome project for years with only a few hours of sleep now and then."

When Harris County Commissioners realized that authorized revenue bonds for building a sports stadium would not attract investors and, if they did, interest rates would be too high, they turned to tax-supported bonds for financing. Bill Kirkland and the parks board recommended that course. Hofheinz also was greatly influential in the decision. His county judge and mayoral experiences qualified him as a leading expert on public financing. County Judge Bill Elliott, Squatty Lyons, V. V. "Red" Ramsay, Kyle Chapman, and Phil Sayers made up the important Commissioners Court. Lyons recalled, "Roy came to the court and presented his new dream of an air-conditioned, domed stadium, and gave us estimates of costs. . . . Roy's presentation to us was given in such a manner that we could understand it and feel that it was solid. After our decision to go for the covered stadium, I was with Roy frequently as he directed designing of various construction models. Many times he came to the courthouse to discuss the financing and the planning of a bond issue. He sat in with us and discussed methods of procedure.

"All my relationships with the Judge were primarily business," Lyons remembered. "When he had something to discuss about the Dome, he'd always call me. He did it primarily because we were personal friends, and he knew that I didn't have any axe to grind, that I didn't mind bringing up and discussing what might be involved in the Dome. The court had great vision in going along with Roy because I don't know of any publicly owned stadium that cost the taxpayers a little of nothing. Practically every stadium in the nation was subsi-

The old Roman Colosseum after which the Judge modeled his idea for a domed stadium.
Photograph courtesy the Houston Sports Association.

dized by either the city, county, or state. I had utmost confidence in the Judge's integrity and honor. He didn't fail to speak his mind around me on all occasions. We had equal confidence, I would feel, in each other. I know he gloried in the Dome idea."

In the summer and fall of 1960, the liberal wing of the Texas Democratic Party urged Hofheinz to reenter politics either as a candidate for governor or the U. S. senate seat Lyndon Johnson would vacate if he was elected vice-president. Price Daniel was governor, and Hofheinz said he would not run against his friend. The truth, however, was that the Judge was so wrapped up in his plans for major league baseball that he did not want to run for any office. Hofheinz gave support financially, however, to the National Democratic Party and to the Kennedy-Johnson ticket.

Stuart Young's dome model, built quickly after Hofheinz decided to get into the baseball picture, was shown for the first time to National League owners in Chicago on October 17, 1960. Houston and New York were awarded franchises to take effect in April of 1962. Hofheinz said after the award, "I knew with our heat, humidity, and rain that the best chance for success was in the direction of a weather-proof, all-purpose stadium. We had to have a stadium that would be a spectator's paradise, but also one that could be used for events other than sports." Some of the National League owners expressed skepticism that Hofheinz actually could have a stadium built along the lines of the model.

Hofheinz with his model of the Dome, constructed to scale by Stuart Young.

After Houston got the National League franchise, Warren Giles, league president, was the official watchdog of the HSA. He recalled, "After we voted the franchise, I went to see the Judge, and he showed me the stadium site. I went down to see him quite often after that as he worked on the design of the stadium. I was amazed at the details that he had in his models. He had new, yellow pencils sticking up here and there, and they were supposed to represent elevator shafts. He had great details, he showed great foresight, and, well, the more I met him, the more remarkable I came to realize that he was."

Mary Frances enlisted Jack Valenti and others to set up an elaborate welcoming for Cullinan, Kirksey, and Hofheinz of the Houston Sports Association when they arrived at the International Airport late at night on October 18. The HSA officials flew in on a Delta jet with the National League franchise for Houston in their hands. Valenti engaged a Dixieland band to help greet the delegation. Little Leaguers in uniforms were there, too. Said Valenti, "We want to show the National League that we're ready for the big leagues." A big crowd joined the rousing "hurray!" party at the airport. Although the public did not realize it, the real power behind the domed stadium from then on was Hofheinz, with the confidence and financial support of Bob Smith.

Before the Hofheinz "pitch" to the National League directors, Cullinan had been in touch with Gabe Paul, assistant to the president of the Cincinnati Reds, about joining HSA as general manager if a franchise was awarded. He

Welcoming National League baseball to Houston (left to right): Bob Smith, the Judge, Red Ramsay, Johnny Goyen, Bill Elliott, George Kirksey, and Craig Cullinan

attended the meeting of National League directors when the Houston expansion franchise was granted. In 1978, when he was president and chief executive officer of the Cleveland Indians, Paul recalled, "I rode to the airport after the meeting with Craig, Kirksey, and Hofheinz. I decided at the airport to accept the Houston job. We all shook hands. I still thought Cullinan was the big gun. When I and my family moved to Houston, it was very obvious that Hofheinz was clearly in the saddle—to my surprise. I soon gained great respect for the Judge and his intelligence. He's one of the smartest men I've known. The Dome never would have been built without him." Paul also recalled "how well the Judge spearheaded the stadium bond election campaign, even to having sound trucks going around town asking for property owners' support. I had accepted him as a principal stockholder after I learned Craig had minority authority. From a personal standpoint, it wasn't exactly the kind of setup I wanted. Hofheinz was within his rights in policies and things he wanted to do for baseball. The thing which stuck in my mind was that I had thought I was going to work for Cullinan while I really was working for Hofheinz."

In late 1960, Houstonians began to refer to Hofheinz and Smith as the Damon and Pythias of city development. Although the Judge still had other interests, for the most part he was dreaming and planning a domed stadium— and turning dreams and plans into reality just as he had been doing since he was a boy in Beaumont.

In 1978, when he was a judge of the Harris County Court of Domestic Relations, Bill Elliott reminisced about the days when he was county judge and was the presiding officer when commissioners decided to back a domed stadium. He said:

> Roy Hofheinz always was a good Democrat. I considered myself a pretty good Democrat, too. I was in the legislature in '57 when I learned about people looking at bringing major league baseball to Houston. George Kirksey had a film of the Milwaukee baseball stadium and told legislators great things could come to the city if it had major league baseball. Searcy Bracewell was the senator, and he was present when George talked. We agreed to sponsor a bill in the legislature with Searcy taking the lead to get a Harris County Park Commission. With $18 million in revenue bonds voted by the people, we thought the funds would build a stadium. The bond campaign took place in May of 1958 when I was in the race for county judge. I did not envision major league baseball to be as important as my election, but it later became a big part of my political and personal life. After I was elected county judge, Harris County Court and the Park Commission commissioned Si Morris and other architects to do a study in early 1959. One of my early functions was sitting in with the Park Commission. The outstanding people on the Park Commission tried to determine how to get several things—a rodeo, a baseball game, and a football game—in a complex. Roy Hofheinz then came into the picture. I'm not and never have been sure what really motivated him to get involved. Bob Smith was a very outspoken individual in support of Roy, saying he was the greatest mayor the city had ever had and probably the greatest there'd ever be. Bob had a considerable amount of land. Roy and I spent much time going over the potentials of baseball. This was right down his line. He was the greatest huckster that ever came out of this community, probably out of the state, and maybe one of the real great ones in the world. Baseball had a lot of glamour and adventure. Roy was a genius at putting things together. I spent more time than I like to remember in the basement of the Brandt Street house. We talked and planned and thought and kicked around ideas, finally ended up with advice from financial men that the Park Commission could not sell the revenue bonds. There was a division of opinion in the community about a site. Some of the Fat Stock Show folks wanted to build a facility in downtown Houston. Roy was pushing, along with the study commission, Si Morris, and others who had made a study, for a site out on South Main. I never will forget the bitterness generated between different groups over the site. This was not the only time this had

happened. In Houston it happened just about every time things of major consequence came up.

As a result of this, the Fat Stock Show people kind of pulled out and were less than enthusiastic. The first offer of building a domed stadium was really given to the city. The city turned it down. I was a young fellow of about 33 years of age and had just become a county judge and really felt I'd prefer the city or somebody else to have built the stadium. But it was obvious after we got into it, and the research that Roy had done, that the thing would work. We got a program under way in which we started off and also went through the chicken-and-egg proposition. I remember Roy, Cullinan, and Kirksey went to Cincinnati and came back in the middle of a cold night and said they'd gotten a team. They had taken Stuart Young's dome model with them. Young's name ought to be on that stadium because his model contributed to passing tax bond issues and selling of the stadium to the public. Stuart was a great fellow and an unassuming man. In our weeks of planning, everything was done by telegrams from Roy who wanted everything done by tomorrow. I spent a lot of blood, sweat, and tears before that Dome was finally opened. Roy's way was that of a huckster, I guess.

After retiring from Harris politics, V. V. "Red" Ramsay, county commissioner who always supported what was needed for the stadium, recalled in 1978:

When you talk of promoting Houston, you couldn't get around Roy Hofheinz. He was the greatest promoter Houston and Harris County have ever seen; as far as I'm concerned he and Bob Smith were dynamic. Anybody who wanted to do something of magnitude eventually talked to Smith and Roy, especially Roy. George Kirksey and Craig Cullinan were front men first toying with a stadium idea. I talked to Roy about it—Craig's a good friend of mine—because I just believed in Hofheinz. The first time I approached Roy, he told me, he said, "Don't bother me with baseball. . . . My life is too entangled. I don't know anything about baseball." But very shortly he was involved. When he got interested in it, the court was already involved. It wasn't an instant thing that we sold Roy on getting into this thing. Bob Smith was also badly needed because of the financial aid he could give, but Roy was the promoter and the brain that we needed to go forward. Roy got into it fully when talk began of expansion in the National and American leagues. At that time nobody really thought a Dome could be built except Roy, who convinced us. We had a terrible time even talking about a Dome, because it was unheard of to play baseball and football inside a building, but Hofheinz had vision and it paid off.

Indeed, Hofheinz's vision, determination, and ability as a "huckster" would pay rich dividends for Houston and Harris County. He would make the Astrodome a reality.

25

Birth of the
Houston Colt .45s

By January of 1961 the men who were the money backers of the expanded Houston Sports Association were Smith and Hofheinz, who quietly had bought and held controlling stock in 1960; Cullinan and Kirksey; K. S. "Bud" Adams, Jr., president-owner of the Houston Oilers; Earl Allen, president of Foreign Construction Company; John A. Beck, chairman of the board for Boehck Engineering Company; J. S. Cullinan, II, president of Cherokee Mining Company; James A. Elkins, Jr., president of First City National Bank; A. J. Farfel, a certified public accountant; Harding S. Frankel and Jack Josey, independent oil producers; and Leonard Rauch, vice-president of Plumbing Supply Company.

The stockholders elected Smith chairman and Hofheinz vice-chairman of the board, Cullinan president, and Kirksey executive vice-president, Gabe Paul vice-president and general manager, and Farfel treasurer. The *Houston Press* commented on these stockholders: "If the National League team that takes the field in 1962 has as much playing ability as the front office has business know-how, we could have a pennant pretty quick. The stockholders are experienced in every phase of business. With the public vote on a new $20 million tax bond issue coming up, the men behind this move into national sports prominence should be known by the public."

William Y. "Bill" Giles, was hired by Paul as public relations director of the HSA early in 1961 when the new general manager was gearing the Houston team up for its last season in the minors and for the 1962 entrance into the National League. The son of the league president and Paul first knew each other in Cincinnati when they worked in the Reds' office.

In the *Post* of January 18, 1961, Clark Nealon wrote: "Houston's baseball war is a thing of the past. The Houston Sports Association purchased the Houston Buffs for an undisclosed amount and will operate the club in the American Association in 1961, preparatory to play in the National League. The price was believed to be $393,750, give or take a little. It brought to an end the perplexing ownership problem that existed almost two years and will remove the last major obstacle to HSA's qualification for a full National League team."

This acquisition enabled baseball interests in Houston to present a united front in the county vote for general obligation bonds to build a stadium of major league caliber.

HSA stockholders decided the old Houston baseball nickname—"Buffa-loes," or "Buffs"—would not be carried into the National League. A committee of seven citizens, including the three Houston sports editors, conducted a national contest which, in fact, turned almost into a world competition to determine a new team moniker. More than 12,000 entries came from 39 states and five foreign countries: Turkey, France, England, Spain, and Canada. The winning name—Colt .45s—was suggested by William I. Nedes, a Houston shirt salesman and native of Los Angeles who had lived in the Bayou City since 1946. He and his wife won an all-expense-paid trip to the 1961 World Series. The nickname, soon shortened to Colts by writers and fans, came from the .45-calibre revolver of the old Texas Rangers.

Having been an avid and longtime supporter of the Houston Fat Stock Show, which had changed its name to the Houston Livestock Show and Rodeo, Hofheinz knew its distinguished board of directors had sought in various ways to find a location which would accommodate the growing interest and attend-ance in the February gala. The Harris County Parks Board had discussed the show's needs when it first began looking for a site for a sports stadium. Dick Weekley in 1978 was general manager of the show. He summarized how the board of directors decided to build Astrohall, through HSA, next to the domed stadium: "Judge Hofheinz came to the show's officials, who were beset with many problems because the annual event had outgrown the Houston Coliseum where it had been located since its inception in 1932. . . . The Judge made an eloquent presentation to the organization when he was developing plans for the domed stadium. His idea was that the show should build its exposition building adjacent to the Astrodome." The board members voted to build Astrohall in the place Hofheinz suggested. It would prove a wise decision, for by 1978 the Houston Livestock Show and Rodeo was the largest event of its kind in the United States, and Astrohall would be credited with attracting increasing num-bers of national trade shows and conventions to Houston.

The stadium tax bond issue divided the city's "fat cats," who had helped eliminate Hofheinz as mayor, and other property owners. Judge Elkins and his son, James A. Elkins, Jr., already had become HSA stockholders and were in favor of the new bonds, but other wealthy men poured money into the cam-paign of opposition. Robert H. Abercrombie, wealthy civic leader and sports-man, wholeheartedly endorsed the project, saying, "I believe the proposed stadium is one of the finest things that has been suggested for this area in 55 years that I have been living in Houston." *Press* sports editor Bob Rule made a major point on January 21, 1961, when he wrote, "Houston taxpayers will get a better stadium than New York taxpayers. . . . Taxpayer money would never be used to retire the stadium bonds as long as HSA remains a solvent corporation. The New York stadium will cost $1,800,000 more than the Houston stadium, and its playing field would not be covered."

Attorney Leon Jaworski's enthusiasm for Hofheinz's domed stadium idea was so great that he accepted the chairmanship of a citizens' committee to drum up public support for the $22 million, tax-supported bond issue in an election held on March 31, 1961. Named co-chairman was William A. Smith. Mrs. Gus Wortham, wife of a rich Houston civic leader, was an outstanding speaker for the bonds at rallies. Listed jointly on the ballot for a "yes" or "no" decision by property owners were these figures:

- Construction of stadium $15,000,000.
- Purchase of site   3,000,000.
- Access roads   4,000,000.

The Houston Sports Association's contract called for it to pay for construction of the stadium only. For a 40-year lease of the completed stadium, HSA agreed to pay $750,000 annually.

In an appeal to voters to support the stadium bond election, Hofheinz said, "We won't leave any stone unturned in our efforts to make the Harris County Domed Stadium a reality. This is the opportunity of a lifetime, and we can't afford to miss it. This will be the first such stadium in the world with every seat air-conditioned and of such size that you could put the Shamrock Hotel on second base and the glass dome would clear the top of it. The proposed county stadium is the only one in the nation with backers who are willing to guarantee the complete cost. In every other one the city, county or some other governmental agency is bearing a substantial portion of the cost. This means, of course, the taxpayers are paying for them. In our case, HSA is guaranteeing payment of the principal and interest on the stadium bonds at a staggering cost of $1 million a year. We have profound faith that we can make the money to pay this cost because in the planning of the stadium every conceivable combination has been worked out to make it produce revenue. I'm convinced the voters will vote for this; they have everything to gain and nothing to lose."

The *Post* supported approval of the bond issue. Although it said it wanted a stadium built, the *Chronicle* opposed tax-supported bonds. It argued that if revenue bonds were insufficient, as they proved to be, baseball promoters should build their own privately financed stadium. Big advertisements appeared in the newspapers asking Hofheinz and Smith to answer questions about spending tax dollars "for your exclusive use." The opponents' theme was that tax dollars should not be invested in a publicly owned facility to benefit HSA stockholders.

The *Houston Press* was the last to give its opinion on tax-supported bonds. Editor Carmack had had bitter experiences with Hofheinz-the-mayor, and his first inclination was vigorously to oppose taxpayers' coming up with money for any project the Judge promoted. An honest, conscientious man who had developed a great love for Houston, Carmack struggled for a final decision. At last the *Press* came out in support of the bond issue because the editor, with all facts and figures in hand, felt it was his duty to the city. He did not want to be in the position of opposing a far-reaching project because of one man—Hofheinz. After the bonds were approved in a close vote, Hofheinz said that he felt the issue would have been defeated had the *Press,* with its many "middle-lower income customers" who followed its opinions closely, vigorously opposed the project. The vote was 61,568 for and 54,127 against. A shift of 3720 against the bonds would have "doomed the Dome." Hofheinz said support of the *Press* prevented defeat.

When it became apparent on election night that property owners had approved the bond issues, Hofheinz commented, "Dirt will fly on South Main Street immediately, and our motto is going to be 'full speed ahead.' We must get ready for the opening of the National League season in 1962."

Jaworski, co-chairman of the citizens' committee, said "The majority has spoken, and I earnestly hope the decision will be graciously accepted by the minority. Let us all pull together for a still-greater Houston."

On April 27, 1961, after the Buffs changed to the American Association and opened the season in refurbished Busch Stadium, Gabe Paul suddenly quit as general manager. He said that "for personal reasons" he was going to the Cleveland Indians of the American League. "Looking back, I think the Judge was sensational," Paul later said. "He did a tremendous job—a genius, there's no doubt about it. After I left, nothing bothered me except speculative stories about why I left—a lot of crap. I wrote the Judge a letter and told him I was sick and tired of such stories, and I hoped there wouldn't be any more of them. From that point on, the stories stopped. We really never had any personal trouble. I saw the Judge occasionally at baseball meetings. After all, I left of my own accord, and he tried to prevent me from doing it. I took his attitude as a compliment." Paul visited the Dome several times. "I don't know if the Judge was glad to see me or not," he stated, "but he was always very decent although he was a man of strong likes and dislikes. Sometimes his emotions overruled his brilliant mind."

Hofheinz insisted that a successful, big-name baseball man succeed Paul as general manager of the upcoming Colt .45s. Thus on September 2, 1961, Paul Richards formally became general manager. The 52-year-old native Texan accepted the job by telephone in a conversation with Cullinan. His contract was for three years at an undisclosed salary (later revealed to be $60,000 annually plus a big expense account). An experienced baseball man, Richards immediately had the task of naming a new manager and directing the player draft. When Richards arrived in Houston on September 7 with Eddie Robinson, an aide he had chosen, the *Post* carried a picture of Hofheinz greeting them.

Richards acted quickly to put a baseball staff together. Harry Craft, veteran major leaguer, was named field manager and Bobby Bragan, Jimmie Adair, and Jim Busby coaches. Bragan already had been with HSA. Gabe Paul first named him director of player personnel. Bragan and Busby were from Fort Worth and Adair from Carrollton. Luman Harris later became the fifth member of the field staff. He had been a coach in the American League for 11 years.

On Monday, May 9, 1961, architects went back to the drawing board to complete plans and specifications for the county's stadium. A contract for use of the stadium had been signed earlier by Cullinan; Red James, HSA general counsel; County Judge Elliott; and William A. Kirkland, chairman of the Harris County Park Board. Elliott estimated it would be six weeks to two months before architects could submit final plans and specifications. The county sent a letter of intent to the architectural firms of Lloyd & Morgan and Wilson, Morris, Crain and Anderson to notify the architects that they would be hired for the project. The architects did most of the preliminary work on the stadium without cost to the county. Elliott said the letter of intent was in lieu of a signed contract with the architectural firms because the county would not officially have funds for stadium work until the first bonds of the $22 million authorized were sold.

Meanwhile, E. E. Schwenke, county right-of-way engineer, and county auditor S. B. Bruce began the steps necessary to advertise for a contract to build the stadium. They completed the paper work and other steps necessary to place the $4 million in road bonds and $3 million in site bonds on the market. As soon as the contract was approved by the Texas attorney general, the county advertised the bonds for sale in Houston's three daily newspapers and in *Bond Buyer,* a trade publication.

Schwenke began negotiations with the Hilton Hotel interests and individuals who owned the land needed for the stadium site and roads that would give access to the stadium. Landowners, including Hofheinz and Smith, who owned large tracts in the area, pledged to donate $1,536,235 in right-of-way. Schwenke conferred with state and city officials on other off-site improvements pledged by those two agencies. The city voted to spend $720,000 to extend Kirby, Buffalo Speedway, Greenbriar, and Murworth into the stadium area between Main and Old Main, south of Old Spanish Trail, and northeast of Playland Park. The state agreed to build the South Loop from Almeda to Post Oak Road to coincide with completion of the stadium. The Harris County Flood Control District planned to spend $90,000 for a bridge across Brays Bayou on Greenbriar. All these highway and roadway improvements were to have been made whether or not the stadium was built.

Judge Elliott said no contract for stadium construction would be let until the bonds were sold. The contract called for the bonds to be sold by August 1, the land to be acquired by August 16, and construction to be underway by November 1. "I see no difficulties in meeting the deadlines, provided the contract is approved by the attorney general," said Elliott. State approval soon came. On June 14, 1961, a contract for a 33,000-seat auxiliary stadium off South Main—to be completed by February 1, 1962—was awarded by HSA to the Safway Scaffolds Company of Houston. Hofheinz said that between $750,000 and $850,000 would be spent on the project before the end of the year. The stadium was to be built in the northwest part of the 240-acre site selected for the domed stadium. When completed, Hofheinz said, the auxiliary park would seat more spectators than existing major league ball parks in Cincinnati, St. Louis, Minneapolis, Los Angeles, Washington, and Kansas City.

The auxiliary facility would have parking for 12,000 cars and lighting equal to or greater than illumination at the Los Angeles Coliseum, Hofheinz noted. The galvanized steel structure, about 35 feet high, with the field on ground level, would have pressure-treated wooden seats and flooring to accommodate 25,000 spectators, but additional bleachers would be added to bring the total seating capacity to 33,666. As in the county stadium, the seats would be adjustable so that the auxiliary stadium could be used for other sports. Hofheinz observed that the auxiliary stadium would remain in use after the county stadium had been built. He added that the association would have to erect a third stadium at Apache Junction, Arizona, as a spring training camp for the Colt .45s.

President Kennedy on August 12, 1961, announced in Washington that he enthusiastically approved a plan drawn by Hofheinz and accepted by the County Commissioners to build a bomb fallout shelter in the domed stadium. He ordered the defense department to make a study of the proposal and report its findings quickly. Federal officials were told of the proposal by Hofheinz on a rush trip to the capital. The shelter proposal also was backed by Vice-President Johnson, Representatives Bob Casey and Albert Thomas of Houston, Senator Ralph Yarborough, and Assistant Defense Secretary Adam Yarmolinsky. The latter headed the national civil defense program under Defense Secretary Robert S. McNamara. President Kennedy suggested that consideration of the project be given highest priority under a program approved by Congress. The program allowed federal funds to be used in construction of certain types of shelters.

Hofheinz was interested in the bomb shelter idea, in part, because it appeared that the $15 million allotted for actual building of the stadium would not be sufficient. Thus he talked with the County Commissioners, and they decided to seek a federal grant to make a bomb shelter out of the Dome; that would help in costs. Hofheinz, the architects, and the County Commissioners worked for months with civilian defense and the defense department officials on the shelter scheme. The cost of changing plans for the county and HSA was estimated at between $800,000 and $1 million. Full conversion of the Dome into a shelter would cost the federal government about $8 million. On June 26,

1962, a defense department spokesman in Washington announced that no funds would be forthcoming in the next budget for the shelter despite the urging of Vice-President Johnson and Representative Thomas. He said the shelter plan could not be approved because of the cost: $20 per shelter space.

Politics—not the feasibility or value of a bomb sanctuary for 38,000 people—apparently killed the appropriation which was to have been placed in the defense department budget. Under the Kennedy regime, civil defense was shifted to the military department. Defense Secretary Robert McNamara apparently approved the decision to leave the shelter out of the budget. People close to the project, however, said that two or three McNamara aides did not like the unprecedented project, which originally had been considered by civil defense people under Eisenhower's Republican administration as a needed shelter experiment. Democrats around Kennedy and McNamara, other than Texans, were said to argue that Texas got too much federal money, and that the bomb shelter should not be another triumph for Lyndon Johnson and Albert Thomas.

The whole truth never came out publicly. Hofheinz learned the defense department's decision when Philip Baldwin, who had been a liaison man in the White House between the Eisenhower and Kennedy administrations, called and told him the news. Baldwin recalled, "The Judge took the news as he did everything else, saying he really didn't 'give a damn about the federal money. We're building the Dome for bomb protection, if needed. It's going to be here for the people and if the government won't pay its share, okay!' But the Judge really was uptight about it because the potential of federal money, in his mind, would help solve some of his financial problems." Dome architects say today that the Astrodome quickly could become an effective bomb shelter—the plans still exist—if another cold war came along to frighten Americans.

The Colt .45s were only seven months away from beginning season play when, on August 13, 1961, the first shovelful of dirt was turned at the site. Excavation and drainage were started by the Brown and Root Construction firm. Except for the finishing touches, the open-air stadium was planned to be completed by February of 1962, two months before the opening of the Colts' first season. Construction of the galvanized steel stands by Safway Scaffolds of Houston began. The auxiliary 33,000-seat stadium would serve the Colts until the domed stadium was completed. It was designed for both baseball and football.

A major step was taken August 28, 1961, toward construction of the domed stadium when the top officers of HSA—Smith and Hofheinz—bought 494 acres off South Main from the Hilton Hotel Corporation. Hofheinz said 180 acres would be sold to the county as part of the stadium site. Smith already owned the other 70 acres needed for the site and would sell that acreage to the county, said Hofheinz. The Smith-Hofheinz combine paid $10,121.46 per acre to the Hilton Corporation for the 494 acres. Hofheinz said the Smith-Hofheinz acreage and Smith's other land would go to the county for the same price, a total of $2,518,182. County Judge Elliott observed that the county had expected to pay $3 million. Hofheinz noted, however, that the County Commissioners would be asked to pay $70,000 to $80,000 in contract costs for draining 70 acres owned by Smith for a temporary stadium. Hofheinz said the land would be transferred to the county as soon as the Commissioners Court set the alignment for extension of Kirby Drive. That major street was the western boundary of the stadium site. The court already had set the alignment for the extension of Fannin, the eastern boundary of the stadium. The proposed South Loop Freeway would go through the center of the land. The stadium would be south of Old Main and north of the proposed freeway between Knight Road and South Main.

A $430,311 contract for excavation work for the domed stadium was awarded on December 19, 1961, to John Kraak, Incorporated, by the Commissioners Court. The excavation was to be completed in 120 working days. Kraak's bid without sub-drainage installations was below the estimate of stadium architects and engineers. The acceptance of Kraak's bid was recommended to the commissioners by Frank H. Newnam, Jr., spokesman for the architects and engineers. Newnam said a prompt award of the earthwork contract would save several months' time in completing the stadium, and that no other work could be done until the excavation job was finished. He also noted that bidders on the general stadium contract would be able to inspect foundation soils and conditions while the excavation work was being done, with a possibility that their inspections would enable them to submit lower bids on the general contracts.

The contract awarded Kraak was for excavation of a hole 700 feet in diameter with a center depth of 24 feet. Some of the dirt would be banked around the hole and compacted to provide part of the stadium foundation. Hofheinz said the court's award of the contract would get the stadium construction started within a few days. He predicted that events in the sports arena would bring $25 million in new income to Houston business firms each year, this in addition to the amounts paid for admission tickets.

Under the capable guidance of Hofheinz, Stuart Lang, president of the livestock show and rodeo, and Leopold Meyer, the show's building committee chairman, and after months of negotiating and compromising, a contract was signed with HSA for the building of Astrohall at a cost of more than $13 million. It enclosed 23.3 acres of Harris County property. In accordance with an agreement among sports association, livestock show, and county officials, HSA was to have exclusive use of the domed stadium for 40 years from the date of its completion, and the livestock show was to have annual access to designated facilities in the stadium and hall for specified periods of time and without being charged for other than certain reimbursable expenses. Additionally, the live-

Leopold L. Meyer. Photograph by Harold Israel, courtesy Gulf Photo.

stock show was to have space year-round in Astrohall to house its physical and administrative functions, also at no additional charge. In its new, larger facilities, the show expanded its offerings to the public and became an unqualified financial success. Astrodome architects Lloyd, Wilson, Morris, Crain and Anderson detailed plans for Astrohall, and Lockwood, Andrews and Newnam, Incorporated, provided consulting engineers for the project. Attorney Fred Parks, who handled the contract negotiations for the livestock show, displayed the spirit of its backers when he charged only $10 plus out-of-pocket expenses for his participation. Other Houstonians prominent in the continuing development of the livestock show and rodeo were Neill T. Masterson, Jr., G. M. "Bubba" Becker, W. D. Black, Jr., J. A. Gray, Leonard McNeill, W. M. "Bill" Mitchell, W. F. "Bill" Monroe, R. A. "Al" Parker, Louis M. Pearce, Jr., A. G. "Tex" Peden, G. D. "Sonny" Look, Herbert G. Turner, J. S. Abercrombie, Edgar Brown, Jr., James W. Sartwelle, William M. Smith, Lester Goodson, E. J. Gracey, Ralph A. Johnston, Gail Whitcomb, John S. Kuykendall, Woodrow Bailey, Bill Bass, Ray K. Bullock, Rex Cauble, Wade Caves, J. F. "Pat" Corley, Bill Dahlstrom, James C. Epps, Jr., J. R. Ferguson, Vernon Frost, Jack Garrett, Charles G. Heyne, William P. Hobby, Jr., Rex E. Hudson, Frank P. Horlock, Jr., Howell B. Jones, Floyd L. Karsten, Reese B. Lockett, O. J. McCullough, Don F. McMillian, Douglas B. Marshall, John Mecom, Jr., James A. Meredith, Latimer

Fishing from their riverboat at the "Loose Goose" retreat (left to right): the Judge and grandsons Mark Hofheinz Mann and Paul Winfrey Hofheinz.

Munfee, Joe Polichino, John F. Rader, III, Cliff Rampy, Archer Romero, Eddie Scurlock, M. E. Shiflett, R. E. "Bob" Smith, William P. Steven, W. E. Thomasson, Tommie Vaughn, M. E. Walter, Bill Williams, and Gus Wortham.

By the end of 1961, Hofheinz had so many places to which he could retreat and relax from the demands of building that he was hard to find, especially on weekends. In addition to Yorktown and "Huckster House," he had two hunting camps and a "farm," all of which had living quarters furnished, as some said, better than museums. The Yorktown home underwent constant change. By 1962 it had a swimming pool, a soda fountain, a steer-size barbecue pit, nine television sets, a kitchen where a staff could prepare food for large banquets, an assortment of spectacularly decorated rooms downstairs, including a playroom and a circus artifacts room, a guest house, a four-car garage which overflowed with Cadillacs, Fords, and Fiats, a kennel of huge Labradors and Pointers, a stable for four horses, special servants' quarters, and another garage full of trunks and antiques bought on various trips. Of particular note were circus posters on one wall downstairs. Displayed there were large caricatures of the Judge and his family as circus clowns which boldly stood out in white, wooden gingerbread frames. At that time the junior Hofheinz was 25, beginning his climb up the Harvard academic ladder. Fred, 22, was in graduate school at the University of Texas, and Dene II was a sophomore at the University of Texas.

The "Loose Goose," owned jointly with Bob Smith, was on 550 acres west of the Katy Highway. It was full of guns, decoys, fishing rods, goose calls, hunting jackets, waders, and humorous signs collected through the years. The upstairs windows had been built so that guests could lie in bed and shoot ducks or geese through the windows if they were lazy. "Kwik Kwak Klub" was on 250 acres near Danbury, south of Houston. It was decorated with political mementoes and memorabilia of the Judge's long public career, including photographs, newsclippings, cartoons, and awards plaques.

The "Westheimer Farm," on 550 acres near the western Houston city limit, was an antique collector's paradise. Old churns, a Dutch window-washer, bronze cannons from a British warship, old fowling pieces, spinning wheels, and a noodle-slicer were among unusual decorations. A great wooden chest, beautifully carved and compartmented, dominated one room. Hofheinz said it had belonged to a Union general. He like to show it off, said the Judge, because he had trouble with the lock. Talking about the defective lock, Southerner Hofheinz humorously said, "It's a wonder the North didn't lose the Civil War." On the farm lawn was a bell from an old locomotive. Hofheinz said he liked to ring it at 2:00 A.M. (often his time of arrival) "just to let the neighbors know the Hofheinzes were around." In the coming years, Houstonians would know Hofheinz was "around," as he pressed forward with his innovative domed stadium.

26

The Wild West
Comes to Baseball

By February of 1962, nearly $2 million had been spent by the Houston
Sports Association for baseball players, managers, and coaches, and an additional $2 million had gone toward the temporary stadium with no taxpayer
money involved. The original investment by corporation stockholders was $2.5
million with 12 of them pledged to add another $2.5 million. HSA then only
had to pay interest for the first two years of its stadium obligation—$550,000.
There was still $14,500,000 in county bond money unspent. As estimates of
costs mounted, neither the Judge nor members of Commissioners Court felt
the money available would be sufficient to complete the unique stadium.

Hofheinz, nevertheless, continued developing his plans, large and small, to
bring big-time baseball to Houston. For example, Hofheinz's memories of his
knothole club days when he watched baseball in Beaumont caused him to plan a
big "pitch" for youth support of the upcoming Colts. He called in coaches
Bragan and Craft to help him with details for a "Six-Shooter Club." A membership drive, aimed especially at thousands of Little Leaguers, began with a rally at
discarded Busch Stadium. Nothing pleased the Judge more than seeing
youngsters having fun inside a baseball park. He always sought a way for them
to attend games as cheaply as possible, sometimes free.

In Cincinnati, with Warren Giles presiding at a National League meeting
on October 10, 1961, the Colts purchased 23 players at a cost of $1,850,000. At
the same time the New York Mets spent $1,800,000 for 22 players. All came
from a pool furnished by the eight National League clubs. The price tag for Colt
players reflected $125,000 each: infielder Joe Amalfitano, San Francisco; pitch-
er Dick Farrell, Los Angeles; catcher Hal Smith, Pittsburgh; and outfielder Al
Spangler, Milwaukee; $75,000 each: infielder Eddie Bressoud, San Francisco;
infielder Bob Aspromonte, Los Angeles; infielder Bob Lillis, St. Louis; pitcher
Dick Drott, Chicago; outfielder Al Heist, Chicago; outfielder Ramon Mejias,
Pittsburgh; infielder George Williams, Philadelphia; catcher Merritt Ranew,
Milwaukee; outfielder Don Taussig, St. Louis; pitcher Bobby Shantz, Pitts-
burgh; first baseman Norman Larker, Los Angeles; pitcher Sam Jones, San
Francisco; pitcher Paul Rout, Milwaukee; pitcher Ken Johnson, Cincinnati;

infielder-outfielder Dick Gernert, Cincinnati; and pitcher Jesse Hickmon, Philadelphia; $50,000 each: infielder-outfielder Ed Olivares, St. Louis; pitcher Jim Umbricht, Pittsburgh; and pitcher Jim Golden, Los Angeles.

The Colts acquired six players over 30, with Shantz the oldest at 36, six 25 or under, and pitcher Rout, at 19, the youngest. Paul Richards made the actual selections for the club, but consulted with player personnel aides Bobby Mattick, Eddie Robinson, Paul Florence, Bobby Bragan, Tal Smith, and George Kirksey. Craig Cullinan and Roy Hofheinz were in the meeting with other National League officials.

Within a month the names of two bonus rookies signed by Richards flashed in newspaper headlines. They were Daniel "Rusty" Staub, an awkward outfielder-first baseman from New Orleans, and Dave Guisti, a pitcher from Syracuse University. The *Press* asked happily: "Have Colts another Mel Ott in Rusty Staub? Could be, according to Colt .45 officials and other baseball men viewing the Arizona instructional league. The Colts might have come up with their own version of the late great New York Giant slugger in the person of Rusty Staub. Paul Richards said, 'Rusty Staub is for real and it's just hard to believe. Here's a 17-year-old kid, 6'3" and 190, with intelligence, instinct, ambition and ability.' Of German ancestry, Staub is a brown-eyed, red-headed youngster who was named Rusty by his nurses the day he was born because of the little red top of his head. Staub bats left and throws right. He's currently hitting .335 in the Arizona instructional league. This is quite a feat considering he played his first professional game just five weeks ago, and most of the opposition has at least three years of pro experience behind them. 'He has wonderful leverage at the plate,' Richards said, 'and he hits a long ball. He has the instinct at the plate to protect against the bad pitchers and steal hits from good pitchers for distance.' " Pitcher Guisti was signed after Richards saw his high kick, unusual delivery, and assortment of pitches in college games. Both Staub and Guisti were to make many newspaper headlines in the years to come with Houston and later with other clubs when traded by the Astros.

While he was directing the building of Colt Stadium and planning for the domed stadium, Hofheinz hired a staff to set up a radio network for Colt games. Forty-five stations signed. It was announced on April 5 that the opening game also would be carried in Spanish and broadcast by Rene Cardenas of Los Angeles, for five stations in south Texas. Gene Elston was hired as chief announcer, to be assisted by Loel Passe. Cardenas, a native of Managua, Nicaragua, had broadcast Dodger games to Spanish-speaking persons in the Los Angeles area for four years. The Spanish radio network included KCOR, San Antonio; XEO, Brownsville; KOPY, Dallas; XEOR, McAllen; and KVOZ, Laredo. Hofheinz said he expected to add other stations in Mexico, Central America, and the Caribbean.

Maxine Mesinger, a vivacious, popular chit-chat columnist for the *Houston Press*, reported on March 23, 1962, "If you want to know where to locate Roy

The Judge relaxing in the Holster Room at Colt Stadium.

Hofheinz from now on, try suite 18-A at the Shamrock Hilton. Roy is telling pals he is taking it for the rest of the baseball season and that its balcony there gives him a marvelous view of the building progress at the new domed stadium site." Hofheinz kept the suite for years as he entertained associates, baseball clients, financiers, and friends. Many of these people also were guests from time to time at "Huckster House," which grew more charming year by year. A story and pictures about Hofheinz and his career appeared in *Sports Illustrated* on March 26, 1962, just before the opening of the Colts' first season. Although he had been discussed in national publications previously, this was the first to focus on the Judge as a new power in baseball. In the 10 years to follow, few personalities, other than politicians, would get more attention from various national and international publications and radio and television than the Judge.

Hofheinz and Smith bought Radio Station KENS (a CBS affiliate) in San Antonio, on April 9, 1962. KENS radio had been featuring country and western music. The new owners changed the call letters to KBAT.

Hofheinz and his associates opened Colt Stadium to the news media and special guests, including season ticket boxholders, with a cocktail party before opening day. Columnist Mesinger commented, "It's a wonderful, colorful spot depicting the old-time saloons of the gay 90s with bartenders and waitresses in the Fast Draw Club costumed in that period. Bob Smith, like a child with a new toy, burst with pride over the whole scene. He took this reporter on a tour of the temporary stadium. What a thrill to stand on the top tier and look out over what will be the new domed stadium. The whole thing is nothing short of fabulous for our town."

Rocky Renee, the first Miss Colt .45s, and Rene Cardenas, Spanish-speaking announcer for the club, modeling costumes for the Fast Draw Club in Colt Stadium.

The Fast Draw Club was roughly patterned after the Long Branch saloon run by Marshal Matt Dillon and his girlfriend, Kitty, from TV's *Gunsmoke* with one difference: no dirty trail drivers would be able to set dusty boots on the club's gleaming 80-foot brass rail. Texas law then forbade the sale of liquor by the drink except in private clubs. Bartenders sold a Texas-sized schooner of beer for 50 cents and liquor at one dollar a snort. Bartenders wore straw hats, striped shirts, and stiff collars and cuffs. Their fancy vests were copies of those worn by old-time saloon dudes. The club offered a fixed menu at $2.50 a throw: cowboy cuisine, son-of-a-gun stew, bragging beans, Fast Draw salad, cajun rice, black-eyed peas tejano, cow country corn pones, branding iron sourdough bread with wild honey, and cow puncher coffee or iced tea. This chuck wagon grub was served by waitresses dressed in low-cut ruffled gowns, net stockings, and fancy garters into which they tucked toy pistols.

Hofheinz helped devise ingenious ways to serve food quicker at the Fast Draw. It was wheeled out on Wells Fargo-type wagons, with the chef on a platform helped by aides to dish it up. Male employees of the club wore handle bar mustaches. All employees at Colt Stadium wore colorful, specially designed uniforms produced by Evelyn Norton Anderson and Iris Siff, gifted Houstonians. Fast Draw Club membership cost season ticket holders $150 each.

Hofheinz wanted to make a big pitch to attract women. He installed a special press box for newswomen in the hope they would popularize the game among their readers. Virginia Pace, who took a cram course in baseball, presided over the "hen coop," patiently answering such questions as "Why isn't there a fourth baseman?" When the team went on the road, Mrs. Pace doubled at home as a lecturer, explaining the game to women's groups. One such gathering held at a Houston hotel drew an audience of 1300. The stadium had another special box for visiting VIPs, who were whisked to the park with motorcycle escort.

Lorraine George of George Construction Company worked his crews feverishly to get the Colt Stadium parking lot ready for opening day. At 7:00 P.M. of the evening prior to the first day of play, John G. Turney, project director, told George to close down the job because there was insufficient shell to finish the task. As George informed the workers of the problem, Hofheinz appeared and asked why the shutdown. George told him there was no shell base material available and that there was no point in going on. The Judge asked if slag could substitute for shell, and the answer was affirmative. Hofheinz called George Lanier of Houston Slag Materials Company in which he had half ownership. Lanier got his troops together, and they delivered slag all night to workers who operated by automobile lights. The final paving continued up until game time, when the Judge thanked the workers, praised their emergency job, and handed them game tickets. The men got off tractors and marched into the new ball park. It was no wonder some automobile parkers wondered why some of the paving was so soft.

When people poured into Colt Stadium's 13,000 parking spaces on opening day, courtly car directors, gaudily decked out in orange 10-gallon hats, blue neckerchiefs, and white overalls, ushered them into one of several sections. Each section was marked by a towering sign proclaiming it to be "Wyatt Earp Territory," "Matt Dillon Territory," or the domain of some other legendary figure of the West. The signs served as guideposts in a sea of cars. Inside the stadium, pennants of every hue pulsated with recorded pre-game music. Tickets were picked up by turnstile attendants resplendent in 1880-type baseball caps, blue and white blazers, and dazzling orange trousers. Ticket takers were polite and helpful, unlike their counterparts in some major league parks. To those accustomed to baseball's dull green, the seats were a surprise. Like the tickets, they were in four shades: chartreuse, turquoise, burnt orange, and flamingo. A ticket's color indicated the section, an arrangement that simplified finding seats. Usherettes, a corps of 150 picked for their looks and their manners, appropriately were called Triggerettes. The girls wore blouses and skirts fashioned of the same material as the players' uniforms, blue stripes on white with orange piping on the collars. Their caps were blue and orange, the team colors. Along with the recorded music, there was the house Dixieland band, consisting of banjo, clarinet, trumpet, and trombone, which paraded up and down the aisles blasting old favorites. Radio play-by-play of the game was piped through the stadium so that apprentice baseball watchers would know what was going on.

The *New York Daily News* commented that Colt Stadium "is the damndest

Aerial view of Colt Stadium in June of 1962 when the Colt .45s and the Los Angeles Dodgers drew a record crowd of spectators. Photograph by Harold Israel, courtesy Gulf Photo.

you ever saw," declaring "its atmosphere is a blend of Disneyland and the old wild west that made the Houston Park the talk of the majors." There was similar comment by writers in other major league cities.

Thousands of Texas baseball fans were happy to read in the *Post* on April 11, 1962, Clark Nealon's story of the first Colt .45 National League game: "Little Bobby Shantz and Ramon Mejias etched their names deep into a monument for Houston baseball Tuesday afternoon at Colt Stadium. Shantz, the last classic ball player to be developed by legendary Connie Mack, pitched a masterful five-hitter and Mejias, a compact Cuban, blasted a pair of three-run home runs as the Colts beat the Chicago Cubs, 11-2, before 25,271 paying fans. Mejias batted in six and scored three Colt runs. Thus did the Colts at least for a day match the tremendous effort that finally brought major league ball to Houston, Texas and the South for the first time."

On May 28, 1962, Harris County Commissioners were glum when they learned a domed stadium could not be built for $13.4 million still on hand from the original $15 million bond sale. They had a big hole in the ground, called "Elliott's Lake" when rains came down, but no assurance that the unique stadium could be built within the original budget. "There's no use kidding ourselves," Commissioner Sayers said. "This is going to take another bond issue." Sayers' view was seconded by County Judge Elliott. He called another bond issue "the only alternative." These comments came after S. I. Morris, one of the stadium architects, reported on a new study of stadium costs.

The biggest amount of money already spent was for digging a hole 24 feet deep and 700 feet in diameter around which to build the stadium. Morris stunned the commissioners by admitting that the architects could not say exactly how much more the stadium would cost. He proposed that the commissioners get the answer to that question by asking for bids from contractors. Then, he suggested, the commissioners could call a bond election for the money needed. The commissioners had asked Morris a week before to bring back a firm figure on the stadium's cost to the Monday meeting. They gave the architect a rough time on several points including his idea of going ahead with the bids. Commissioner Lyons told him, "I can't conceive of a businessman making this kind of bid when the money is not available." Morris said he was positive that contractors would bid. Although wary of this way out, the commissioners ended the meeting apparently resigned to bid-taking. They had 10 to 12 weeks to mull it over while architects finished drawing up the final plans for bidders.

Morris was asked what sort of stadium could be built with the available $13.4 million. He said that figure would eliminate the dome and the air conditioning, making the stadium unsuitable for conventions and exhibits. The commissioners grumbled because Morris could not arrive at a cost estimate. Sayers noted that the architects previously had been saying that the stadium could be built with the money available. "It looks like after all this time you would have a reasonable figure," he said. Morris said the revolutionary stadium had just too many unknown factors. He said estimates on the dome alone had differed by up to $4 million. "Another example," Morris said, "is that consultants now tell us that we must control the angles of the light coming through the dome precisely in order to make the grass grow properly."

He said advance estimates by out-of-town firms had proved too low. "If I give you an unsafe estimate, we are all going to be in a pickle," Morris said. "If we estimate on the up side or the down side, we could jeopardize the whole project unjustifiably." Sayers estimated that money had been wasted by digging the hole oversize for a federally financed fallout shelter which did not pan out, by delays, and by rising costs.

The commissioners got bids on drainage for the big hole and for topping a parking area. The apparent low bid for permanent drainage was $321,089 by George Consolidated, Incorporated. The county paid $430,311 to get the hole dug. At that time, it turned down a low bid of $664,906 for the combined excavation and drainage. Ned Gill, a businessman who once had blocked the stadium construction with a lawsuit, issued a statement urging the commissioners to cancel all stadium contracts and award no more. He said this was a necessary first step toward salvaging "as much of the taxpayers' money as possible from what is left." Judge Elliott suggested that the county go ahead on building the stadium with the $13.4 million, then ask a bond election for more if needed. He said this would head off any more lawsuits. But Sayers and Lyons opposed that strategy. "We aren't going to kid people by putting in a foundation and then ask them for sufficient money to complete a stadium," Sayers said. "The only thing to do is to get the picture, present it to the people, and follow their dictates. After we get the bids and find out what it costs, it could be submitted to the people at an election. If they want it, fine. If they don't, we've got a nice big hole in the ground."

Hofheinz, the architects, and others closely involved in drawing up plans and specifications for actually building the domed stadium knew that the construction bids which would go to County Commissioners for approval would be too high. Costs had risen while two suits seeking to stop construction had been fought in court. The apparent low bid of $19,440,000 on November 1, 1962, was $6,640,000 more than the first estimated cost. The *Press* commented on November 3, "This means that property owners will have to approve the $6,640,000 extra in bond funds to get the whole job done right unless some other financing device can be found. It also means that any extra bonds needed will have to be paid off with tax money over and above the long-term Houston Sports Association contract to retire the first $15 million. Our feeling in finally getting actual firm bids on the cost of the stadium is one of relief. We now have six contractors hard and fast on the line. Each spent about $50,000 of his own money to estimate cost against the contract requirements and specifications and prepare their bids. The *Press* will support a supplemental bond issue providing it is held to actual stadium extra cost and not involved in anything else. We hope and we believe Harris Countians generally will do likewise."

The *Post* likewise said it would support a supplemental bond issue. The *Chronicle* changed its tune and also supported the additional bonds. It said, "Don't let anyone tell you the stadium will cost the individual citizen any more taxes—it won't." It was found that even more money than the $6,640,000 needed to accept bids should be added to a new bond issue. Commissioners voted for a $9,600,000 additional issue on which voters could decide on December 22, 1962. W. A. "Bill" Smith and Gus Wortham, two civic leaders, were named joint general chairmen of the committee for the additional bonds. County Judge Elliott said, "I am pleased that two men of this stature have joined together to push a project so important to Harris County."

Opponents of tax-supported bonds again put on a vigorous campaign, but the seasoned political troops of Hofheinz again prevailed—narrowly. The vote three days before Christmas was 42,911 for and 36,110 against. The Hofheinzes were never happier than during this holiday season. The money was authorized for the Judge's latest and most dramatic dream. The County Commissioners had warned they would drop the project if the second bond vote failed.

The stadium structure itself ultimately cost $22,000,000, but the overall cost of the entire project was $35,500,000 of which $31,600,000 came from two county bond issues and $3,750,000 from the City of Houston and Texas Highway Department for off-site improvements, including paved streets, bridges, drainage, and storm sewers.

On August 22, 1962, Bud Adams, a 10-percent stock owner in HSA whose Houston Oilers of the new American Football League lost money in two seasons of play at old Jeppeson Stadium, offered to sell the club to the baseball corporation for $2,500,000. The disclosure was made in newspapers after Adams blasted the operation of the baseball club and announced the Oilers would continue to play in Jeppeson instead of Colt Stadium in the fall as originally planned. The HSA answered in a written statement, "In the light of Mr. Adams' disclosures and his own experience in operating the Oilers, we felt that the price is too high." It was estimated Adams had lost between one and two million dollars. This was the beginning of an Adams-Hofheinz "feud," as writers put it.

Hofheinz's grandiose plans and ready spending alarmed some HSA stockholders. The Judge and Bob Smith together owned 66 percent of the corporation, and decisions on what and how to spend money rested primarily with Hofheinz. The result was that on November 28, 1962, the stock owned by Adams, Cullinan, J. S. Cullinan II, A. J. Farfel, Harding Frankel, Jack Josey, and Leonard Rauch was bought by Smith. Retaining their stock were Earl Allen, John A. Beck, and George Kirksey. The outgoing stockholders were paid their total investment as the price of their stock. Smith, as chairman of the HSA board, said, "The faith and confidence which these men demonstrated in investing in the Houston major league baseball effort were major contributions to its success. They were pioneers in a venture which meant more to the community than it could ever have meant to them, and they deserve the appreciation of the community. It has been a pleasure to work with them, and the remaining stockholders in HSA look forward to a continuing warm relationship."

In 1979 Craig Cullinan commented about HSA and his decision to sell out:

> With Bob Smith's financial muscle, Roy Hofheinz's promotional and building talents, contacts in baseball made by Kirksey and me built on several years of studious cultivation, plus Gabe Paul's baseball know-how, it seemed the Houston ball club must succeed in a growing dynamic city poised and hungry for major league sports.
>
> As the 1962 season drew to a close, my concern with Hofheinz's operation, plus a growing realization that the entire venture could fail, prompted me to act. Realizing that Smith owned control of the club and had the right to allow Hofheinz to run it if he chose, I went directly to Smith and offered him my stock at cost, insisting only that Smith buy out any other minority stockholder who wished to sell. After resisting the idea for a short time, Smith eventually acquired the stock of all except Kirksey, Beck, Allen, and, of course, Hofheinz. The selling minority stockholders got their investment back and were released

from their indebtedness to the banks. Not one of us asked for or received one dime in consideration for the years we had stayed with the project. The departure of these stockholders left Hofheinz more firmly entrenched than before.

On December 12, 1962, Smith was reelected chairman of the HSA board, and Hofheinz was elevated to vice-chairman of the board and president. Other officers elected were Kirksey, executive vice-president; Allen, vice-president and treasurer; Beck, vice-president; Red James, secretary and general counsel; and William Brodie, assistant treasurer. Richards continued as general manager for baseball.

Unhappy with the spring training camp at Apache Junction, Arizona, used by the Colt .45s, Hofheinz studied Florida for quarters. Daytona Beach was his first choice, but the city could not meet the Judge's requirements. Cocoa, however, wanted the team, and it agreed to construct an $800,000 facility just nine miles from Cape Kennedy, launching pad for astronauts. Hofheinz signed a 10-year lease for a facility costing $800,000, and it was completed in 1964. The camp included a 5200-seat stadium, a dormitory for 250 players, plus offices for major and minor league operations. An 80 x 50-foot building was added as a recreation room. Two clubhouses were built, one for major league players and visiting teams in spring exhibitions, and one for 300 minor league players who were to come and go for the Colt's Cocoa farm club in the Florida State League.

Hofheinz attracted the attention of New York boxing writers with his announced goal of putting big fights in the domed stadium when it was completed. On March 19, 1963, he was a principal speaker at the writer association's dinner at Gotham. The Judge shared the dias with Senator Alan Bible of Nevada, the first time a Texan had been invited to address the nation's oldest boxing group. Jim Farley (the former postmaster general and boxing commissioner), Julius Helfand (another former New York boxing commissioner), Jackie Fields (the former welterweight champion), Eileen Eaton (a lady promoter from Los Angeles), and Goldie and Aileen Ahern (a husband-and-wife promotional team from Washington, D. C.) were among the honored guests receiving awards. Cassius Clay (Muhammad Ali) and Zora Folley, who were to meet in New York's Madison Square Garden for the world heavyweight title on March 22, also were among the guests.

Hofheinz's lifelong efforts on behalf of Houston were recognized when he and retired Houston businessman Hobart T. Taylor, longtime black supporter of the Judge, were recipients of the E. Pliny Shaw Award, presented at the annual South Central YMCA meeting on May 20, 1963. The two were cited as "symbols of a united effort to build our community as a model of progress, understanding and unity—not only in the South but in the nation at large." The presentation was made by Russell Shaw, son of the late oilman for whom the award was named. Taylor was treasurer of the United Negro College Fund at the time.

Billy Graham and Judge Hofheinz. Photograph courtesy the *Houston Chronicle.*

Another event of major proportions in Hofheinz's life came in the summer of 1963 when Mary Frances and Milton Gougenheim separated. The couple would divorce in October of 1968. Milton and Mary remained friends. He told why their marriage collapsed: "Mary Frances and I had lost the close communication that keeps a marriage together. It was too late and, without either of us knowing it, the damage was done. The demise of our marriage was just as simple as that. No other factor or event brought down the curtain. We just sort of lost each other in our careers." Gougenheim added, "Roy Hofheinz is one of the most compassionate humans that I have ever met when it comes to his immediate family, his friends, and business associates. I've always felt that Roy chased and captured one success after another in life to please these people, his champions, rather than just to please himself."

The great evangelist, Dr. Billy Graham, visited Houston in October of 1963, on Hofheinz's invitation to hold a "Crusade for Christ" in the domed stadium when completed. Ten years earlier Graham had staged a crusade in the Bayou City, calling Houston wicked; he wanted to come back. The newspapers carried pictures of Hofheinz escorting Graham to the uncompleted stadium and explaining details.

The *Chronicle* quoted Graham: "The stadium in truth is one of the great wonders of the world, a magnificent dream coming true before our eyes, the boundless imagination of a man transformed to reality. To be here is a privilege, to see the domed stadium is an inspiration." Thus he—and others—added to publicity that the Astrodome was the "Eighth Wonder of the World."

Graham ended his 4-day visit with a stirring address before one of the largest audiences ever gathered in the Rice Hotel. Flanked by top figures of the religious, business, and civic life of the city, Graham talked before a joint meeting of the Rotary and Kiwanis clubs. People jammed both the Grand and

Crystal ballrooms of the hotel and overflowed onto the old mezzanine. The huge audience made it necessary to set up a special closed circuit television for the benefit of those who could not get to where the speaker stood. Governor John Connally, who described Graham as the greatest force for Christianity in the world, introduced him. Graham accepted an invitation to hold a crusade in the stadium when completed. "It's too bad that we have to wait until 1965," said Graham. "I have been looking forward to the Houston meeting and had high hopes that we would be coming in 1964. Judge Hofheinz tells me that it is impossible to get assurances the stadium will be ready for any large meetings prior to the opening of the 1965 baseball season. We will just have to wait even though it is a disappointment."

A $9.6 million supplemental bond issue to complete the stadium was approved by voters on December 22, 1962. The official vote was 42,911 for the bonds and 36,110 against. Funds from the bond sale supplemented the $22 million in stadium, park, and road bonds approved by an 8 to 7 ratio of voters on January 31, 1961. County Judge Elliott said the public's approval of the bonds was a historic event in the county's history. "The confidence shown by the voters today in the stadium project is a mandate to the Commissioners Court that we move forward with as much speed as good business will determine toward the building and completion of this facility," Elliott said. "It is a mandate to place our name on the convention rolls of the world as the Number 1 city, second to none, with convention, hotel, and restaurant facilities and a dynamic citizenry to welcome and to host the millions of people that will visit our area as a result of the passage of this bond issue today."

Bob Smith said he was happy that the bond proposal was approved by a higher percentage of voters than the 1961 issue: "We recognize that HSA is more than a business venture because of the responsibilities we have assumed under our contract with the county. We will continue to operate HSA with a keen awareness of the civic responsibility we have taken and our obligation to the public. By the time the doors open for the first gathering in the domed stadium, we hope that every person who voted against the bonds today will be glad the stadium was built." Smith commended County Commissioners for work in furtherance of the project and thanked the individuals who had volunteered work for public approval of the supplemental bonds.

Ned Gill, leader of the unorganized opposition to the bonds, said, "The high-pressure, hugely financed Smith-Hofheinz group has won again. Let us hope that this is the last demand of this group for money from the taxpayers. The Commissioners Court should not be allowed to forget repeated promises that taxes and tax assessments will not be increased, the city-county hospital will provide the means to care for the needy ill, regular county services will not be diminished, local labor will be used on the stadium, and that we will get 37 conventions of over 30,000 delegates in the next five years at no expense to the taxpayers." His demands were more than satisfied later.

In 1964 Houston civic leaders wanted taxpayers to build a downtown civic and convention center despite the fact that Hofheinz said the completed domed stadium and addition of Astrohall later would best serve growing convention needs. John T. Jones, Jr., publisher of the *Chronicle* who naturally wanted downtown development to enhance the value of the vast Jesse Jones Foundation properties and a partner of the Judge in a television station, was a leader in the movement for the center. Mayor Louie Welch, longtime Hofheinz political foe, went all-out for voter approval, and he and the City Council approved a bond election for June 27, 1964, to provide $7.3 million for the project. The battle for votes brought Leon Jaworski, prominent attorney who had led the first fight for domed stadium funds, to the front, this time as an opponent of Hofheinz's views.

When voters approved the downtown civic center proposal along with 11 others for water and other needs of a growing city, Hofheinz said, "I bow with good grace to the will of the final arbiter, the public." He said HSA opposed the civic center because of the contract with Harris County to build the domed stadium. "Three years ago, we made a commitment to pay the county $750,000 a year under the assumption that the public wanted this community's convention center to be at the site of the domed stadium," he said. "Had we known that the public was prepared to invest in two convention centers, we would not have been willing to make such a commitment." Hofheinz, nevertheless, asserted that HSA would find other ways to pay off $15 million on domed stadium bonds: "We not only accept the public's decision with good grace; we will go all out to work with all who are interested in promoting Houston as a convention center."

How well Hofheinz could look ahead to the development of Houston, especially around the South Main acreage he had put together for the domed stadium site with Bob Smith's backing, was recorded on April 26, 1964, by Charlie Evans, real estate editor of the *Chronicle*, who wrote, "Real estate and building circles are watching with interest the rapid developments that are making the Uptown Houston district, centering around Fannin-Main-Holcombe intersections, the hottest real estate and construction area in the city. . . . In this district the skyline is constantly changing, and announced plans indicate the building fever hasn't reached its peak as yet. And property values, steadily on the rise for several years, jumped to more than double after the start of construction of the domed stadium."

Although there had been general talk about Hofheinz's three-year hope of having an entertainment and hotel-motel complex on the acreage he and Bob Smith owned next to the domed stadium site, it was not until August 20, 1964, that an official announcement was made. A Disneyland type amusement park was planned on a tract of more than 100 acres south of Astrohall, the Houston Livestock Show and Rodeo Building adjacent to the Astrodome. The hotel-motel complex would be on the 38.1-acre site Hofheinz and Smith owned west of the stadium and across the street from the vast domed stadium parking area.

Hofheinz began talking to the two major leagues in 1964 about playing the 1965 all-star game in the domed stadium, but not until 1968 did baseball's most popular and talented players battle each other under the dome. To carry out his promise to seek big conventions for Houston, he also began work to bring the 1968 nominating conventions of Democrats and Republicans to Houston. It was one of his greatest disappointments that he could not induce the major parties to pick their candidates in Texas.

Meanwhile, the first three seasons of the Houston Colt .45s did not produce a winner. Baseball fans really did not expect the expansion team to win a pennant quickly, but attendance at Colt stadium gradually dwindled during the three seasons in the open-air, temporary Colt stadium. On September 19, 1964, Paul Richards, general manager, fired Harry Craft, field manager, who was 13 games short of his third year as boss of the players. Luman Harris, a veteran coach, took over direction of the team the next day. Said Richards at a press conference, "Obviously we think a change will help the club or we wouldn't have made it. We appreciate the fact that Harry Craft, under circumstances that could not be called favorable, can in some respects be considered to have done a respectable job as manager. We have always tried to appreciate his problems. As far as his replacement is concerned, it should not be considered a reflection on Craft's ability."

The Colts then were in ninth place with a 51-88 record. Houston was picked to finish 10th in the league in 1962 when the National League expanded, but Craft directed the team to a surprising eighth-place finish, beating out both the Mets and the Cubs. The team won 64 games and lost 96 that season. The Colts won two more games than in 1963, but finished ninth, the place they had been assigned in preseason forecasts. Houston again was picked for ninth place in 1964 and ended in that spot. The Colts appeared to have fielded their strongest team as the 1964 season began and by the time half the schedule had been played were only a few games behind the .500 mark. The team ran out of gas at midseason, and since July had won 25 and lost 47. Richards said one reason the change was being made was so that Craft would have a chance to negotiate with other teams in the usual season-end baseball job shufflings.

On October 1, 1964, the name Colt .45s for the Houston Club was doomed—Hofheinz never liked the nickname—when differences with the Colt Firearms Company over use of the name emerged. Colt Firearms had no objection to the baseball team's using its name, but it did object to the baseball club sublicensing to manufacturers the right to use the name on novelties sold at baseball parks. Rather than give up this revenue or share profits with Colt Firearms, Hofheinz decided to change the team name.

Hofheinz announced on October 9, 1964, that the domed stadium would be opened in 1965 with exhibition games with the American League champions, the New York Yankees, and the Baltimore Orioles, the third-place team in 1964. The Houston team would play five games in three days to boost the financing of HSA before regular National League play. The Yankees would play on Friday night, April 9, to open the new entertainment complex and also Saturday night and Sunday afternoon. The Baltimore team would play Saturday afternoon, April 10, and Sunday night, April 11.

On November 17, 1964, Hofheinz announced that the Schlitz Brewing Company had purchased the Houston Colts' radio and television broadcast rights through the 1967 baseball season for $5,310,000. The three-year contract for the new sponsor was equal to the $1,770,000 a year which previous Colts sponsors had paid for the broadcast rights. Robert A. Uihlein, Jr., president of Schlitz, said at Milwaukee that the association with the Houston baseball club stemmed from the company's new role as a resident of Texas. Schlitz had broken ground in Longview in October for a $15 million brewery. Schlitz said it would seek co-sponsors to go along with the company on the radio and TV broadcasts. Officials of the brewery and HSA said efforts would be made to expand the network of 26 radio and eight TV stations which would carry the broadcasts into Texas, Louisiana, Oklahoma, Arkansas, and New Mexico.

Philip Baldwin was visiting Hofheinz in Houston when President Kennedy and Vice-President Johnson came to Texas' largest city on November 21, 1963 for political fence-mending to be climaxed with a joint speaking appearance at the Coliseum, arranged by publicist Jack Valenti, a close friend of Representative Albert Thomas and LBJ. The Coliseum dinner attracted 10,000 people. Valenti did such an outstanding job that the vice-president asked him to fly to Dallas with him late that night for the appearance of the nation's leaders in a parade. Without a change of clothes, Valenti left with the Johnson party. The rest of the story is history. When Kennedy was assassinated and Governor John Connally wounded the next morning in Dallas, Valenti was drafted by Johnson to go with him to Washington—still without a change of clothes—late that afternoon.

Baldwin said he went to the Rice Hotel where the Johnson party was lodged to greet friends there and returned to the Shamrock suite of the Hofheinzes to await their return from the Coliseum. The Judge invited Baldwin to visit with him in the Colt Stadium "Holster Club" the next morning. Baldwin was gabbing with staffers when the blaring radio flashed the news of the Dallas gunman's attack on Kennedy and Connally. Baldwin rushed to Hofheinz and said, "I've got some bad news," and then told of the radio flash. He said Hofheinz paled as he said, "My God! We've got to find out quickly the details." Baldwin told Hofheinz they should get to a place where he could use a two way radio to Washington. They jumped into the Judge's car, which had a two-way radio, and learned that a hot line to the capitol was in County Judge Elliott's office.

"We drove 90 miles an hour to get to Elliott's office," said Baldwin. "When we walked in, Bill hadn't heard the news. I asked about his hot line, and he showed it to me. I got Washington. The Judge was deeply concerned, but he said finally, 'We'll be all right with Lyndon,' but cracked up in tears about the death of the president. When LBJ got back to Washington that night, the Judge talked to him twice, asking what he could do for the Kennedys and the Johnsons. As an original supporter of Johnson for president, the Judge was saddened by how his fellow Texan got the job. He talked and suffered for two days. We went to the 'Loose Goose' after he bought a big load of groceries. 'Why did it have to happen in Texas?' Hofheinz asked me. He knew the state, not the assassin, would get a bad press because of the tragedy."

Meanwhile, Mrs. Hofheinz knew her husband was moving around trying to absorb the Dallas shock. When Hofheinz and Baldwin returned to Yorktown, Mrs. Hofheinz met them at the doorstep. The Judge and Dene hugged and cried, for both were compassionate about people in trouble. Both felt LBJ would help solve the nation's problems.

As he visited time and again with the Hofheinz family, Baldwin said his relationship with the Judge became almost filial. "I think Roy used me as a sounding board for ideas," Baldwin recalled in 1978. "I really never did a damned thing for him except talk. I gained much more from him over 20 years than he did from me. We got along, I think, because we both are dreamers with extravagant imaginations. He could draw the line at the bottom and put dollars where they belonged." Baldwin also observed that the Judge "was humble in his own way and tuned in to the needs and desires of people. As a man of earned wealth, he wanted to let all people, no matter how humble their station in life, have a chance to look at any 'golden staircase' he might build. He was the master entrepreneur."

Mickey Herskowitz, talented *Post* sports editor who had succeeded Clark Nealon as director of the department (Nealon continued as a daily columnist), first told the news that the new name of the Houston baseball club would be Astros. "Out of town writers attending the press conference were somewhat bemused by the new selection," Herskowitz wrote. "The name, they pointed out, isn't one that can be easily shortened and still keep within the boundaries of good taste."

On December 13, 1964, five men, the planned principal tenants of the domed stadium, announced that they had agreed the covered playing field should be named the Astrodome and from that day forward the name stuck. Making the announcement were Hofheinz and Smith of HSA; Adams of the Oilers; Dr. Phillip Hoffman, president of the University of Houston, who had signed the U.H. Cougars to play there; and Stuart Lang, president of the Houston Livestock Show and Rodeo. Harris County Commissioners, representing taxpayers who owned the stadium, did not join the announcement. County

Judge Elliott said, "They can call it what they like, but the official name is still Harris County Domed Stadium. I am confident the name [Astrodome] is not in keeping with the wishes of the people." From then on Elliott was miffed about Astrodome—and is to this day. He and Hofheinz later were to have conflicts, but a majority of the commissioners did not seem to mind the name, which was in keeping with Houston's fame as the new world center for astronauts.

On December 6, 1964, Carroll Martin, general manager of the Houston Oilers, American League football champions, and Hofheinz verbally agreed on a 10-year lease so that the Oilers could switch from old Jeppeson Stadium. The important issue, rent, which was to be determined when the domed stadium was finished, proved a stumbling block to the deal. The HSA felt Adams would sign a final agreement, and a big feature about the Oilers was in the April of 1965 souvenir book of the Astrodome. The Oilers kept their offices, first planned for the stadium, at Ada Petroleum Center while negotiations went on. Adams never moved his headquarters into the Astrodome.

The University of Houston leadership saw in the building of the Dome a great opportunity to put the Cougars in the national spotlight by booking all home games there. Hofheinz already had helped the university in many ways, but in a few years he would become one of its biggest contributors. Cougar football was played in Rice Stadium before a contract was signed in 1964 for domed stadium home games.

On December 23, 1964, Bill Roberts wrote in his *Houston Post* "Town Crier" column: "Party of the night. Houston Astros' bigwigs Bob Smith and Roy Hofheinz's cocktail buffet for a few members of the press in the fantabulous suite on top of the domed stadium. When Hofheinz turned on the lights so that everyone could see the inside of the Dome lighted at night, his partner, Smith, shouted, 'Everybody hold on to pocketbooks, that Hofheinz has all sorts of tricks.' When Mrs. Bob Smith was asked if she would be sitting in one of the plush revolving seats in this penthouse box during games, she said, 'I will be sitting behind home plate, as usual, so that I can fuss at the umpires.' "

Hofheinz had four months left before the grand opening of the Astrodome to change uniforms, the advertising, and countless other projects carrying the Colt .45 name. As usual, he was quick in making decisions and driving his staff to be ready for the 1965 season in the unique stadium.

THE COLOR PORTFOLIO

Wedding portrait of Roy and Mary Frances Hofheinz. Photograph courtesy the *Houston Post.*

Aerial view of "Huckster House" on Galveston Bay. Photograph by Murray Getz.

Harem Room, "Huckster House." Photograph by Harold Israel, courtesy Gulf Photo.

Gay Nineties Room, "Huckster House." Photograph by Harold Israel, courtesy Gulf Photo.

French Room, "Huckster House." Photograph by Harold Israel, courtesy Gulf Photo.

Recreation and Barbecue Room, "Huckster House." Photograph by Harold Israel, courtesy Gulf Photo.

Circus Room, "Huckster House." Photograph by Harold Israel, courtesy Gulf Photo.

South Seas Lounge, "Huckster House." Photograph by Harold Israel, courtesy Gulf Photo.

Buckaneer Room, looking into The Brig, in "Huckster House." Photograph by Harold Israel, courtesy Gulf Photo.

The Astrodome. Photograph by Harold Israel, courtesy Gulf Photo.

First game of baseball played on AstroTurf. Photograph by Harold Israel, courtesy Gulf Photo.

University of Houston football game in the Dome. Photograph by Harold Israel, courtesy Gulf Photo.

Billy Graham Crusade in the Astrodome. Photograph by Harold Israel, courtesy Gulf Photo.

The Judge's office in the Astrodome. Photograph by Harold Israel, courtesy Gulf Photo.

Private dining room in the Judge's office in the Astrodome. Photograph by Harold Israel, courtesy Gulf Photo.

New Orleans Kitchen on the sixth level of the Astrodome. Photograph by Harold Israel, courtesy Gulf Photo.

Crusader Room in the "Celestial Suite," Astroworld Hotel. Photograph by Harold Israel, courtesy Gulf Photo.

Foyer to the "Presidential Suite" in the Astrodome. Photograph by Harold Israel, courtesy Gulf Photo.

Drawing Room in the Astrodome's "Presidential Suite." Photograph by Harold Israel, courtesy Gulf Photo.

Upstairs bedroom in the Astrodome's "Presidential Suite." Photograph by Harold Israel, courtesy Gulf Photo.

Golden Bird Cage Dining Room in the "Celestial Suite," Astroworld Hotel.
Photograph by Harold Israel, courtesy Gulf Photo.

P. T. Barnum Room in the "Celestial Suite," Astroworld Hotel. Photograph by Harold Israel, courtesy Gulf Photo.

Children's Play Room and Astrotots Puppet Theatre in the Astrodome.
Photograph by Harold Israel, courtesy Gulf Photo.

Circus Room in the Astrodome. Photograph by Harold Israel, courtesy Gulf Photo.

Barber Shop in the Astrodome. Photograph by Harold Israel, courtesy Gulf Photo.

27

The Taj Mahal of Sports

Although there had been hundreds of newspaper and magazine stories, radio and television broadcasts and word-of-mouth descriptions by thousands who toured the Astrodome before it was completed, it remained for Hofheinz's aides in the Houston Sports Association—namely George Kirksey, Bill Giles, Earl Johnson, Art Keeney, Al Locke, Tal Smith, Gene Elston, and Wayne Chandler—to put all the facts together for opening-day fans. The story was told in a 260-page book, sold for one dollar and called *Inside the Astrodome*. Today the book is a collector's item.

No individual except Hofheinz could recount correctly the thousands of detailed jobs that building the stadium entailed. He outlined for a staff and photographers working on the book how his dream came true. The result was a story never told completely before, revealing more "world firsts" than any sports and entertainment structure ever built. The information in this chapter must be credited to that book.

The book's introduction said, "Sparkling like a rare jewel on a one-time Houston swamp, the Astrodome is the Taj Mahal of all stadia from Rome's Colosseum on down to this day. Etched 218 feet high against the Texas sky, the Astrodome is tall enough to contain the 18-story Shamrock Hilton Hotel, or the Atlantic City Convention Hall, or the San Francisco Cow Palace with room to spare." In addition, the structure was praised as "the biggest project of its kind ever built, the largest indoor arena in the world, the largest clear-span building ever constructed, the world's largest air-conditioned stadium, the first major league stadium with a roof over it, and the first all-purpose, weather-free combined sports stadium and convention center." Moreover, it was equipped with the "world's largest scoreboard."

The magnitude and comfort of the facility also were extolled:

> The searing Texas sun will still beat down, the angry Gulf winds will still howl, and the tropical rains will still fall, but not on the spectators in the Astrodome. They sit in almost regal splendor in the plush-type opera seats, protected overhead by a permanent translucent roof covered with 4596 sky-

lights of clear "Lucite" plastic and in a temperature of 74 degrees controlled by a $4,500,000 air-conditioning system of 6600 tons. There will never be a game rained out in the Astrodome. . . .

For football . . . the 10,020 seats on the field level are mounted on tracks and move 35 degrees to parallel the football field, making for a perfect football game setting. . . . The Astrodome seats 45,000 for baseball, 52,000 for football, 65,000 for conventions, and 66,000 for boxing matches. There are six tiers of gaily-colored seats—and a seat at a price for everyone from $1.50 for pavilion seat in centerfield to luxurious sky boxes sold at private subscription on a five-year lease at approximately $15,000 for a 24-seat box. Approximately 77 percent of the seats (34,590) are sold for $2.50 (reserved seats) and $3.50 (box seats). The six seating levels are connected by low-level ramps, escalators, and elevators. . . . The Astrodome has parking for 30,000 cars, including 300 buses, by far the largest parking area of any facility in this country.

General contractors for the Dome were H. A. Lott, Incorporated, of Houston and Johnson, Drake and Piper, Incorporated, of. Minneapolis. Lott had built $160,000,000 worth of facilities in Alabama, Arkansas, California, the Canal Zone, Georgia, Kansas, Louisiana, Mississippi, Tennessee, and Texas before he tackled the unprecedented domed stadium. Lott's general superintendent was H. M. "Herb" Eyster, with George Joiner as assistant. The electrical contractor was Fisk Electric Company of Houston, and the mechanical contractor the Sam P. Wallace Company, Incorporated, of Houston. Architects for the Dome were Lloyd and Morgan and Wilson, Morris, Crain and Anderson, two Houston firms with equal association. Structural engineer was Walter P. Moore, and mechanical engineers were an association of I. A. Naman and Dale S. Cooper. All electrical engineering was handled by Lockwood, Andrews, and Newnam. Most of the principals involved were graduates of Rice University. Overall coordination of the project was under the auspices of Harris County engineer Richard P. Doss. Resident architects representing the associated Dome architects were Robert J. Minchew of Wilson, Morris, Crain and Anderson, and James P. Mueller of Lloyd and Morgan.

Special consultants were Praeger, Kavanagh, and Waterbury, engineers and architects of New York City who made the breakthrough in efficiently reconciling football and baseball in one stadium; Roof Structures, Incorporated of St. Louis, designers of the dome frame itself; Bolt, Beranek and Newman of Cambridge, Massachusetts, acoustical consultants and designers of the sound system; John G. Turney of Houston, paving and drainage; Dr. Gerald D. Phillips of Rice University, who analyzed and advised on the problems of light transmission and radiant energy; Dr. Herbert Beckmann, aerodynamicist of Rice, who advised on the characteristics of the Dome as related to high winds; and Dr. William O. Trogden, Dr. Marvin H. Ferguson, and Dr. Ethan Holt, all of Texas A & M, regarding grass growth.

The Astrodome Lucite roof has a 642-foot, clear span dome, the largest in the world. Steel muscles holding up the roof are made of 9000 tons of high strength carbon steels and ultra-strong U. S. Steel Tri-Ten (A-441) and "TI." Skewed framing for the Dome was finally chosen by architects because standard rolled, steel shapes were necessary in order to have competitive bidding required by Texas law. Roof Structures, Incorporated, St. Louis, designed the Dome. The key to the Dome is a 300-ton tension ring, one continuous band of steel which encircles the stadium and rests on 72 steel columns, each capable of supporting 220,000 pounds. The Dome rests on articulated joints consisting of two sets of bearings to allow for movement without stressing the lower structure. Articulated joints are similar to a human's joints at the wrist and elbow. At eight points, Dome columns stand on huge strap footings 11 feet below the playing surface. The Dome had to be designed to permit shrinkage and contraction because of temperature changes. The roof is so designed that it can move five and a half inches in either direction. Winds up to 130 miles an hour, stronger than ever recorded in the Gulf Coast area, could whip the Dome and cause no damage, engineers calculated. The roof of Lucite is about five and a half inches thick.

It took the American Bridge Division of U. S. Steel a little under four months to erect the structural steel for the unprecedented edifice. Although the steel work was termed "a geometric nightmare" by construction men and the jobs posed unusual problems, it was completed on schedule. For the task of erecting the steel across the roof, 37 falsework erection towers, resembling oil field derricks, were used. Removing the towers from inside the Dome turned out to be a delicate job. Each tower was lowered one-sixteenth of an inch simultaneously until all were down. The greatest fear Hofheinz experienced came when the roof lost the support of those towers. However, as architects and engineers figured in advance, it settled on support columns without mishap. The roof actually has three main points: the deck around the outside edge, made of three-inch thick wood-fibre-concrete boards, acoustically corrected and water resistant; steel trusses holding up the Lucite; and 4596 aluminum-framed Lucite skylights. All this meant that the Dome was the most remarkable roof ever put over a stadium.

An idea literally pulled out of the sky brought about the concept of the Astrodome's roof. Architects took the same concept that DuPont scientists had developed for the B-17 "Flying Fortress" aerial gunner's Lucite dome. The Lucite skylights covered approximately 50 percent of the upper portion of the covered stadium and were lightweight and shatter resistant. Patterned panels cast from Lucite effectively eliminated overhead glare while diffusing light evenly throughout the stadium. The steel frames of the Lucite panels, however, proved to be the first big headache at the opening of the stadium. That story appeared in headlines all over the world (and will be told later). The man who solved the problem was Hofheinz himself.

Earthmen vacuuming Astro-Turf in the Astrodome

The covering of the playing field was a direct result of architectural and engineering planning. Tifway Bermuda grass, sodded in December of 1964, was nurtured by sunlight transmitted through the skylights. Experiments at Texas A & M indicated there would be sufficient sun through the Lucite to keep the grass natural—with proper watering. Air conditioning and water were expected to keep the turf in good condition year-round. From the beginning Hofheinz was skeptical of its success. No one really knew if the plan would work. In the back of his mind, the maestro of the Dome looked ahead. If he had not, performing on the field would have been a baseball player's nightmare—as it temporarily was when the Dome opened. That problem was solved with the birth of "AstroTurf" (another story to be told later).

There was a seat in the Astrodome for everyone. Added by Hofheinz at a cost of $1,500,000 to HSA—not the county—were 53 skyboxes built for the elite at the top of the stadium, as were seats in the Roman Colosseum where rulers sat. All boxes of 24 seats were taken before the opening. Of royal blue, they gave a striking view around the upper rim of the playing field. They were sold on a five-year basis for slightly less than $15,000 each. A few boxes with 30 seats sold for $18,600 each. There also were two 54-seat boxes with large adjoining rooms. Each box is joined with a club room, lined with wall-to-wall, thick pile carpeting, and closed circuit TV so that these exclusive fans can get the latest information from the field without watching directly. Special elevators take boxholders from the ground to their elaborate entertainment centers, equipped with a toilet, ice maker, bar, and furniture. An interior decorator designed each box individually with a different motif. Furniture and other appointments were designed especially for each box. Boxholders are entitled to dine in the Skydome Club on the same level, or they can order food for guests in their special spectator quarters.

So that patrons could talk about their acquisition of boxes, Hofheinz gave them names based on the decoration themes: Spanish Provano, Captain's Cabin, Imperial Orient, Western, Las Vegas, Old South, Petroleum Room, Southern Plantation, Dessin Di'or, Summertime, Parthenon, Classical Mediterranea, Roman Holiday, Country Villa, New Yorker, Bangkok, Far Eastern, Baskets and Bows, Spanish Lace, Nordic, Reflections, French Empire, The Aztec, Aragon, Spanish Lady, Before The Dawn, Villa D'Este, Embassy House, Old Mexico, Panium Emerald, French Riviera, Laverne Aloha, Grecian Delight, Spanish Baron, Egyptian Autumn, The Red Dragon, Tahitian Holiday, Palace Gardens, Marbolia, Beauvais, Ramayana, Venetian Holiday, Ivory Tower, Spanish Armada, Old English, Goliwoggs, and River Shannon. Most of the box names resulted from Hofheinz's world travels. He passed them along to designers who spared no expense in making them attractive to corporations and individuals able to pay. The Judge knew "expense account entertainment" would help in selling the boxes, so high that some users took spyglasses for player closeups when they did not want to sit in clubrooms watching television.

Lipstick red, coral, burnt orange, terra cotta, black, purple, gold, and bronze, in addition to the blue of the skyboxes, provided an explosion of color throughout the stadium. These nine colors started with the field level and ascended to the mezzanine, pavilion, club level, loge level, upper level, and box seats. The cost of seats other than the skyboxes in the Astrodome was $929,815. Hofheinz told the American Seating Company he wanted Astrodome patrons to be the "world's most pampered customers." In advertising the seats, HSA publicists said, "Sit down, Sports Fan! Your day is here. A ticket to the Astrodome makes you a king. Since the dawn of history, sports fans have watched events on stone blocks, hard wooden planks and slatted wooden chairs . . . , but for the first time in sports history you can watch a baseball game from deep-cushioned, foam-padded, nylon-upholstered chairs." Equipping the chairs in this manner was so revolutionary that the DuPont Company, which supplied the fabric, called attention to the drastic upgrading with this statement, "Is the new Houston Stadium run by nuts? Upholstered seats for sports fans, radio followers, boxing buffs! Are they crazy? No, they're canny! The Dome people think they're blazing new trails in comfort and pleasure. The seats look luxurious, but they will take the toughest treatment any audience can give them!"

The American Seating Company, commented, "In all the world wherever people sit in large groups—in theatres, music halls, churches, government buildings, auditoriums, or sports arenas, no more comfortable chairs have been provided. The foam-covered, spring-type seats and the foam padding required more than 45,000 square yards of upholstery material. To transport the chairs required enough freight cars to make a train slightly less than a mile long."

Two companies built the $2 million scoreboard, Fair-Play Scoreboard Company of Des Moines, Iowa, and the Federal Sign and Signal Corporation of Dallas and Houston. The scoreboard stretches 474 feet across the centerfield wall behind pavilion seats and measures more than four stories high. Weighing 300 tons, it required 1200 miles of wiring. More than half an acre of the scoreboard display is a virtually solid field of electronically activated lamps providing "the biggest spectacle in lights ever constructed."

The scoreboard is controlled by a 25-foot console board in the press box, operated by a staff of six technicians and a producer. Six main components of the board are the world's largest 100-line television screen covering 1800 square feet in the center of the board, which can produce animated or still pictures or written messages; a home run spectacular covering an area of 360 feet by 36 feet on top of the board using 14,000 lamps (the spectacular is a series of four animated lighting sequences lasting about 45 seconds); a 141- by 21-foot panel left of center on the board to display lineups, umpires, scoring, averages, and other pertinent information, with the right half adaptable for written messages; a 141- by 21-foot matching board right of center board divided in half with the right for scores, innings, and pitchers of other games, and the left half for special messages; two time-of-day clocks; and two 30-foot illuminated disc advertisements.

Long dugouts for players, which Hofheinz used in Colt Stadium, are used in the Astrodome. They are 120 feet long and run along stands and on either side of the catcher's box. Hofheinz said many fans wanted to sit above dugouts so they could see and perhaps talk to players coming on and off the field, and he wanted to meet this demand for "premium seats." No other stadium then incorporated the idea.

"Bomb-sight pictures" of the baseball or football playing field are made possible by a retractable gondola high above and in the center of the playing field. The gondola is 64 feet in diameter and eight feet high. Weighing 27,000 pounds, it is raised on five cables, each five-eighths of an inch thick, by motors weighing a total of 13,000 pounds. Any two of the cables could fail and the gondola still be moved safely with the remaining three cables. Its motor is housed in the cupola on the Dome's roof. The primary purpose of the gondola is to provide a sound system when an event is held with people seated on the field. Then the gondola can be lowered to 36 to 40 feet above the ring. Unusual television, movie, and still photographic shots can be made by cameramen in the gondola. The gondola accommodates 25 persons, most of whom stay in it until an event is concluded. However, an overhead catwalk from it is connected with the rim of the stadium for those who leave early.

Because of Hofheinz's passion for food and the business it generates, the Astrodome was built with extraordinary meal and snack outlets. Final restaurant facilities surpassed anything previously incorporated in any stadium in the world. There are five separate restaurants, exclusive of scores of concession stands, capable of handling 3280 persons at one sitting. Two of the five are private clubs, the other three open to the public.

In his planning, Hofheinz kept in mind the world's press, both TV and radio, which he expected to flock to the "Eighth Wonder." The press box was designed so that all media representatives could see, hear, and work under the most favorable conditions. Two separate press boxes, one for baseball and one for football, are located on the club level. Each box accommodates 58 writers. There also are two auxiliary press boxes, each with a capacity of 58 at peak periods. The working press sits in two rows, with a third row for Western Union operators. There is a room for Western Union operators and TWX keyboards. There are nearly 100 communication outlets in a room immediately behind the press section. Behind the press boxes is a private dining room for the media, a workroom, and individual lockers to store typewriters, record books, and personal belongings. Photographers have special shooting locations. Booths holding six each are at both ends of each dugout on the field. On the press level there are four locations for taking pictures: behind home plate, behind first and third base, and at the 50-yard line on the south side of the press level. One camera location is behind dormitories on the upper and gold level. Six darkrooms, including one for color, are located on the press level, enabling development of pictures for wire services and local newspapers to move directly from the stadium by wire photo.

There also are 15 booths for radio, TV, player scouts, and VIPS. Interview rooms are adjacent to each clubhouse on the second level to permit the press to interview players, coaches, managers, and other personalities before and after any event. Also located on the press level is an elaborate control room for the scoreboard, public address system, and lighting. It requires eight men and a producer to operate these facilities.

Convenience of the customer was always in Hofheinz's mind. Among many novel and new services available were 53 spaces for wheelchairs on the mezzanine level; 30 spaces for the blind on the mezzanine level, with a radio outlet permitting them to listen to any game on the Astro network; and a completely equipped first aid area with a doctor and registered nurses on the mezzanine.

Rocket trains, carrying up to 64 persons each, pick up passengers on the 30,000-place parking lot and transport them to stadium entrances. A heliport on the southwest corner of the parking lot is used by some wealthy customers and visiting government officials. Two train sidings, each located about one mile from the stadium, make it possible for private railroad cars to be parked so owners can attend games with just a short hop to the stadium. All aisles inside the stadium are vertical, insuring that no vendors can move in front of customers to obstruct their view.

To keep at 74 degrees the 41,000,000 cubic feet of unbroken space required centrifugal refrigeration machines supplying 6600 tons of cooling. Engineers said this was approximately the amount of cooling given off by the daily melting of sufficient ice to cover a football field to a depth of nearly five feet. Built to last 40 years, the central air-conditioning plant was designed by the Houston consulting engineering firms of Dale S. Cooper and Associates and I. A. Naman and Associates. Buffalo Forge Company supplied the system, which also controls air-cleansing operations to eliminate haze and smoke and purify the air. Operation of the system is essentially automatic through "The Brain," a central graphic programming-control panel, except for manual temperature starting and stopping of the turbine-powered machines. The Brain is a combination of the most modern system of electronic and electrical gadgets, gauges, scanners, testers, and instruments of a type never before put together for so large an operation. The Brain took the place of 280 men who would have been working continuously to keep the air conditioning working. This control center, manufactured by Minneapolis Honeywell, is located beside the stadium's main mechanical room in an air-conditioned office on the first floor behind center field. It cost $333,000. Honeywell said it spent much more on research and development for the future. The Brain also incorporated an automatic typewriter and an adding-type alarm printer connected to the solid-state logging, scanning, and digitizing computer. At intervals selected by the operator, a log of 180 readings can be typed out for the record at one point per second. The system gives a different alarm in case of internal difficulty. As a result, an hour and a half of normal checking is turned into three minutes, and a three to four hour check in two and one half minutes.

All instruments are of the latest electronic miniature type using solid-state circuitry. Counter-type totalizers compute and display the total amounts of the following: tons of refrigeration output from each water-chilling unit; pounds of steam consumed by each turbine; hours of running time for each electric-driven compressor; cubic feet of gas consumed by each boiler and pounds of steam produced by each boiler.

On the top of the Astrodome is a weather station, the first ever built for a stadium. It is electronically operated to take temperatures at any given moment by pushing a button on a control panel. The station, built by Minneapolis Honeywell, is capable of giving the latest weather information to The Brain faster than any weather station in Texas. Also on the roof is a traffic observation platform used to direct traffic approaching the stadium at key intersections. The director manning the platform relays information to traffic policemen, thus minimizing traffic jams in the stadium's vicinity.

The Astrodome truly deserved the title "Eighth Wonder of the World." A bold engineering feat constructed before the era of inflated building costs, it has proven a magnificent asset to the city of Houston. And it is a monument to the innovative thinking and drive of Roy Hofheinz.

How much did Roy Hofheinz personally have to do with the creation and development of the Dome? First-hand accounts from architects, designers, engineers, contractors, and others not only reveal the entrepreneurial importance of the Judge in the planning and construction, but also show that without his superb salesmanship the Dome might never have gotten on a drawing board, much less off of it. Architect Hermon Lloyd recalled, "The stadium idea had drifted along for about two years until Roy came into the picture. Roy immediately took over the whole thing. He became the leader, and it was a good thing because without Roy we would not have that stadium today. I was real close to the whole project from the beginning," he said. "I know there were no underhand deals of any sort because it was always just a pinch-budget situation. The people of Houston got themselves the best buy in the world, and the only reason was that Roy Hofheinz whipped it and got it done." What Hofheinz "whipped" was a multitude of complex problems that threatened the project from its inception: land acquisition, design snags, bond approval, glare, dying grass, and all the many small and large problems which had to be solved from the Astrodome's inception.

The first problem was where to locate the stadium. Si Morris, whose architectural firm of Wilson, Morris, Crain and Anderson, was asked to make site studies during the 1950s when there was a growing fever in the city for major league baseball, discovered this was not easy:

> What I had to do was to find a place in Houston that had no other development on it because it was going to be a controversial thing, and we sure couldn't move any widows and orphans off property. It also was necessary to avoid the possibility of "entrepreneurial real estate squeezes" while putting together the large parcel of property that fit the requirements. Site after site was painstakingly checked out before being eliminated. When we finally ended studies, our two most likely sites were on Eastex Freeway, which had some flooding problems, and the one where the stadium now stands. It was an undeveloped area close in. Opportunity stared us in the face with what Bob Smith owned and what was available. The county, Roy and Bob—a pillar of propriety and dough and a marvelous partner for Roy—got the acreage required. The wonderful thing about it was Roy's ability to promote and publicize development with Bob's support.

Once the land was acquired, the next question was what kind of structure would be built on it. "Roy decided the stadium should be covered," Hermon Lloyd said. "If he hadn't said, 'Yes, we're going to do it that way or not do it,' it would have gone another way because we'd already prepared sketches before Roy ever came into the planning."

Si Morris, whose architectural firm needed the final approval of Hofheinz before being hired by the county for design studies, remembered the first time he heard the domed structure mentioned. "We went over one day to Roy's Brandt Street basement where he did all his negotiating. The Judge said, 'Now I've been talking about this thing to Buckminster Fuller. He thinks we can build a stadium that will seat 45,000 for baseball and 65,000 for football and have a roof over it, and we can grow grass and it'll be completely air-conditioned. What do you think about that?' "

Morris tried to stall. "Well, why do you ask?"

With the blunt directness that went to the heart of the matter, Hofheinz shot back, "If you don't think you can do it, I'm going to hire Buckminster Fuller." Morris had to make up his mind quickly. "Hell, we'll do it!" And that's the way Morris remembered that "the thing got underway." It was also typical of the way Hofheinz got things moving.

This was hardly underway before there was a snag. Fuller's geodesic dome was discarded. "We investigated it and found it relatively uneconomical," recalled Talbott Wilson, a member of Morris' firm. The geodesic dome was not the only idea to be discarded. Lloyd recalled, "There was some talk in the beginning that the Dome should be sliding. A lot of people wanted to know why we didn't have it like Pittsburgh. I made a trip to Pittsburgh to examine it, but I found out that because of mechanical failures, it was closed three-fourths of the time. When they wanted it open, it was frozen shut. If they wanted it shut, when it started raining, they usually had trouble getting it closed. It was impractical."

Hofheinz clung stubbornly to having a dome. His reason proved long-sighted and practical. "Roy had heard from baseball people that the savings in dollars would be great if you didn't give rain checks," said Lloyd. "Where he got the idea I don't know, but he asked us to talk to Walter O'Malley, head of the Dodger organization in Los Angeles. The Dodgers had planned a covered stadium for Brooklyn. They had taken engineers to Florida and used instruments to determine just how high a fly ball could possibly be hit in a ball game, and they came up with 165 feet. From O'Malley we got calculations on what sort of dome had to be built to handle baseball. Roy picked up a great deal of design ideas from O'Malley, but the Astrodome was purely his own." The way Hofheinz made the Dome his own was literally to mastermind the operation, getting input from everyone concerned and then making final decisions.

From architect Ralph A. Anderson, Jr., of Morris' firm, came a picture of Hofheinz in action: "At planning meetings on the Astrodome, Roy would ask our advice and try out ideas on us. He kept asking and asking and asking and hammering home from there. Then he offered his own analysis."

For those associates such as Lloyd, there was never any question about Hofheinz's ability or right to make the final decisions. "He was pretty well in charge and it was all work," he said. "Roy didn't have to sleep much. He just had endless energy. He was always running on our tails. He was always getting new ideas and saying, 'Let's try this.' Roy not only contributed ideas, but he contributed the energy and the push to bring out things. He was always interesting to work with. He was irritating at times, but not irritating to the point where it wasn't helpful. I've never enjoyed an experience more."

One of Hofheinz's ideas was to have private boxes. This had never been done in a stadium before, and, while it was one of the "irritations" Lloyd as a designer had to put up with, it paid off. "It was an afterthought as far as we were concerned," said Lloyd. "Space at the top we had planned for transverse-travel of our duct work. When Roy saw that space he felt he could sell private boxes for what was then fabulous amounts. We didn't see how he could do it, but we put in the boxes. Ever since, there hasn't been a big stadium built without boxes."

W. R. "Bill" Mackay, formerly president of the American Seating Company in Texas, a wholly owned subsidiary of the American Seating Company of Grand Rapids, Michigan, recalled, "During the latter days of the completion of the Astrodome, the Judge moved his offices out in the center field area in a large glassed area where he and his guests could sit and watch what was going on. He moved exotic furniture to the new location, and used to sit up in the office with a large pair of field glasses and watch all of the workers installing chairs and doing other things to complete the building. This was objected to by many people because everytime the Judge saw someone loafing on the job, he'd get on his radio—walkie talkie type—and get in touch with the contractor's people, or with our people and say, 'Hey, that fellow up there's not doing anything. Get him on the job!' The Judge had to have his hand in every angle of the construction of the Astrodome. The fact that it is one of the most marvelous, magnificent buildings in the world today is partly due to his attention to the smallest detail."

The man who had the most to do with the Dome's roof and because of that, the grass, was one of Morris' partners, architect Ralph Anderson. He said:

> My first responsibility was the roof structure plus grass growing, which was affected by the roof structure because of letting in sunlight. I remember one meeting we had at Brandt Street basement. I was required to give a report on grass growing. After two summers of experiments at Texas A & M, we came to the conclusion that we could grow grass in there and have enough places in the roof for light to come in, but it was going to be very marginal. I said, "Obviously, a system on this roof that could be designed to modulate light from one time of the year to the other is going to cost a lot more money. It will be more difficult to maintain over the years than a system that's just built there solidly and stays unchanged. If you accept a cheaper roof static solution, you've got to accept the possibility that your grass growing efforts are going to be marginal."

It was decided by Hofheinz and the commissioners that we couldn't afford

Warren Giles and Hofheinz inspect the Astrodome during its final stage of construction

the most expensive light. It was after that meeting I began to be worried because what if grass didn't grow and didn't last through the season, where would we be? I talked to Hofheinz in his office on several occasions about it. I said, "Just to be on the safe side, we had better look at something in the way of artificial playing surface that will simulate real grass." He said, "What have you to propose?" I said, "I don't know, I'm still looking." I was asking people to submit some artificial samples to me. He said, "Let me see what you get."

I came back to him one time, and I had some polyurethane chunks with little sprigs of bristles punched through, not unlike the way you'd make a carpet. I threw it on the floor, and Paul Richards looked at it and felt it and stepped on it. Hofheinz asked the general manager what he thought. He said, "These guys aren't used to playing on that kind of thing. It's going to be different from grass, and they could break legs. Baseball players are just like race horses." Finally Hofheinz said, "I think we'd better just close this subject." And I said, "That means you don't want to consider artificial turf any further?" He said, "All things considered, I just don't think it'd be a good idea right now. We will put baseball inside under artificial light and air conditioning under a roof and there's already enough controversy about that." He then didn't want to compound controversy—the artificial grass was just too much, but he actually was laying the groundwork for artificial turf becoming a necessity.

Anderson said he felt Hofheinz did not want the grass to be successful so he would have the excuse to proceed with artificial turf. Hermon Lloyd recalled, "Right from the beginning, Roy kept saying, 'Well, I'm not too worried about that grass. If it doesn't work, I'm sure we can get some firm to develop undertaker's grass used around graves.' I knew what he was talking about." The Dome was designed for natural grass. The thing not counted on was the traffic of playing ball or anything on the grass.

The greatest accolades Hofheinz received came from his associates in the Dome's creation. The designers, architects, contractors, and others who were associated closely during the crucial days with Roy Hofheinz echo the sentiments of Talbott Wilson and Si Morris. "There's no question," said Wilson, "that Roy Hofheinz has been one of the most beneficial forces for Houston. I honestly feel that the Astrodome's impact on the economy and image and stature of Houston is beyond even the usual affirmative assessments. Roy is a man of great integrity, with driving ambition, the love of achieving exciting things, dreaming great dreams, and working terribly hard to bring them to pass. He had a great variety of talents directed in many ways. Of course, he was a helluva salesman, and he used to refer to himself as a huckster. All was not just for the joy of selling but a necessary part of achieving something worthwhile. I don't know whether you can say Roy is an idealist—he certainly is in the better sense of the word, but he is a philanthropist in many ways, too, though he didn't make a fetish of it. He is a very great man."

"There's no doubt," Si Morris said, "that Roy is one of the giants of our community and we've got a helluva community. I'd put him among a half dozen great Houstonians. I knew Jesse Jones. I knew Herman and George Brown fairly well. They're in one category, but as far as I'm concerned, Roy's in a class by himself. Without Roy's showmanship, there wouldn't have been an Astrodome. We can talk about it any way you want to, but Roy did it, and he created a completely new Houston identity by himself. He did it with great elán. He changed baseball. I'd say Roy is one of the great contributors to Houston's history, maybe the greatest."

28

A Dream Comes True

No stadium in history ever received a greater national and international publicity buildup before completion than the Astrodome. Although still second to Bob Smith in stockholding in the HSA, Roy Hofheinz was completely in the saddle, riding all involved toward the grand opening of the stadium, which once was but a dream emerging from his fertile mind. Most people in Houston and Harris County became proud of the edifice on South Main and were anxious as spring came to get inside the strange-looking half-moon in the middle of great acreage. Hofheinz accommodated them—after the Dome opening—with guided tours at one dollar each—which brought in unexpected income to HSA and still does today.

Hofheinz said the happiest and proudest moment of his life, other than family events, came when the first ball was pitched in the opening exhibition game between the Astros and the Yankees. It was the day before he celebrated his 53rd birthday. Despite numerous tasks in overseeing every inch of the massive covered stadium, he found time to see scores of visiting news people who were itchy to find out about the plant in which baseball and football, for the first time, could be played under a roof with fans comforted by air conditioning.

It was February 8, 1965, that baseballs and bats were first introduced to the Astrodome. Hal Lundgren reported in the *Chronicle*: "In the most pompous batting practice session ever held, 200 newsmen from the Southwest looked on as a handful of Houston Astros threw, struck and fielded baseballs for the first time in Harris County Domed Stadium. . . . Singer Anita Bryant threw out the first ball and architect Bob Minchew caught it." The news people were impressed. Lundgren quoted a number of them, and their comments included "it's another world, fabulous, just too much to believe" and "I just can't believe it's real."

Evelyn Norton Anderson and Iris Siff were enlisted by Hofheinz again when he did not like sketches for Astrodome employee uniforms prepared by a New York firm. Mrs. Anderson recalled that Mary Frances telephoned her six weeks before the scheduled opening of the Dome and said the Judge wanted to talk to her. When the designer saw the Judge and looked at the sketches, she asked, "Why didn't you call me in the first place?" She said Hofheinz replied, "I don't know why, but I want you to do it now." Mrs. Anderson asked, "How much time do I have?" and Hofheinz grinned and replied, "six weeks." Mrs. Anderson recalled:

> He was talking about 60,000 pieces of clothing, none of which you could go out and buy ready-made. For instance he wanted space helmets for maintenance men and others—something which had to be made specially. . . . Everything we ordered got to the Astrodome before opening day, including boots, shoes, and hats that had to be specially made and fitted to various sizes. I wouldn't have let Roy down for anything in the world, for I had tremendous respect for his ability. He was humorous as well as brilliant. Most people were scared to death of him, but I never was.
>
> I never will forget one day we were going over sketches and Mrs. Hofheinz came in with one of the grandchildren. He started playing with the baby and the first thing you know, he was on the floor crawling around under tables with the baby—completely forgetting he had business with me. He made an absolute fool of himself over that baby and it tickled me. I thought then: "The Judge is so controversial people love him or hate him. I know that anybody who can do this with a baby can't be bad."

Hofheinz invited President Johnson to attend the opening of the Astrodome. Johnson could give no assurance he would be there on April 9; however, he said he would try to fit a trip into his schedule. Hofheinz felt sure his old friends, Lyndon and Lady Bird, would be coaxed into the visit.

Ben McGuire, who had gone to Washington with the Hofheinz party for the inauguration of President Johnson following his victory over Barry Goldwater, recalled that "Roy and the president were always close, but the Judge never tried to get anything out of Johnson. He didn't use his closeness with the president for his own means. I'm sure that if he had wanted something from Washington, he could have gotten it, but he didn't try. He didn't want to."

Governor John Connally, fully recuperated from Lee Harvey Oswald's gunshots in Dallas, which had killed President Kennedy and wounded him, proclaimed in a letter of Hofheinz and Smith: "The Astrodome is truly one of the great marvels of our time and a wonder of the world. . . . The edifice is a tribute to the imagination, ingenuity, courage and abilities of all who have made it possible. The Astrodome has already become one of the great tourist attractions of the world and will be a tremendous boon in many ways to the State of Texas."

Commenting on the impact of the Dome before its opening, Gail Whitcomb, president of the Houston Chamber of Commerce, said: "The fabulous new Astrodome is a civic and commercial asset of untold importance. From near and far, it will bring massive purchasing power into the community for sports events and for conventions and expositions. It is already a spectacular tourist attraction. It will benefit the economy of the entire Houston-Gulf Coast area and to some extent the entire state and Southwest. . . . All citizens who enjoy professional baseball are indebted to the Houston Sports Association for its vigor and perseverance in building a major league baseball team for Houston as well as this 'wonder of the world' showcase for Houston." The "untold importance" of the Astrodome still could not fully be evaluated in 1979. Billions of dollars in business and international prestige for Houston could be an understatement.

After spring training in Florida, Houston's fourth-season team arrived home on April 6 for the opener with the Yankees. They had won 12 and lost eight in their exhibitions. Astro manager Lum Harris named veteran Dick (Turk) Farrell as his starting pitcher, and Yankee manager Johnny Keane said Mel Stottlemyre would face the Houston ace. Astro players were a little awed by the Dome. As they practiced the first time at night, they had trouble tracking the ball against the grill work of skylights and girders in the roof. The effect was like looking at a boiled marble, the players said. Paul Richards and Luman Harris felt the matter could be corrected without difficulty.

Little Joe Morgan, second baseman, put a touch of history into an intra-squad game by the Astros two nights before opening. Morgan became the first Astro to hit a home run in competition and the first to set off the electrical display on the big scoreboard in center field. Joe blasted a shot about 10 rows deep into the red mezzanine seats in right field. The next afternoon, Astros practiced under sunlight for the first time. Glare conditions for players were terrible, Houston and other sports writers gathered from all over the nation reported.

When Red Smith, nationally syndicated sports columnist of the *New York Herald Tribune*, visited the nearly complete Dome, he was intrigued by the furnishings. He asked Hofheinz, "Are you a fancier of oriental art?" The Judge replied: "No, but I went to visit my son in Tokyo, then went on to Hong Kong and Bangkok. I didn't buy anything until I left Hong Kong. Then I bought 26,000 pounds of junk for this place. Didn't want anybody to come in here and say, 'I saw the very same thing last week in Joe's Bar.'"

Chronicle fashion editor Beverly Maurice got an advance look at the costumes Astrodome employees would wear. She wrote: "Want a job with a future? Try on one of the Astrodome uniforms for size. You can't get much more futuristic than those. Conceived by Judge Roy Hofheinz . . . every one of those new uniforms is strictly out of this world! There are 53 different varieties (only 4 less than Heinz for Hofheinz), and there are thousands of them." For Hofheinz, every element of the Dome's operation featured "show biz" touches, and this was especially evident in the costumes of the employees, all with space themes. Maurice also previewed opening night costumes to be worn by Mrs. Smith, Mrs. Hofheinz, and Mary Frances Gougenheim: Mrs. Smith was to appear in "a stunning white silk-and-wool alaskine suit, white ostrich mid-heel pumps and bag." Her accessories would include a gold pin, watch, and bracelet, and a ripple-brimmed white straw hat with a white silk organza overlay. Mrs. Hofheinz would wear "Brannell's blue 3-piece creation with a print blouse and a turban to match." Her accessories were to be black. Of Mary Frances' ensemble, Maurice reported that her "hat is especially appropriate for the occasion. She will wear Sally Victor's 'open dome' sailor, veiled lightly with daisies on net, above the straw brim. Her silk-and-cotton tweed dress is lime, and she'll wear yellow mid-heel pumps and a French black calf bag with a yellow-toned tapestry on one side. Her gloves are white kid shorties."

"We were all having coffee in the proprietor's box at the Astrodome, Maurice said, "with a gathering of out-of-town newsmen, wives, and secretaries of the Smith-Hofheinz clans. The coffee was served in gold cups and saucers to highlight the gold-leaf decor from Thailand, like the jewel-scaled dragon that adorned one wall. We had just passed the canopied 'throne room' with its regal gold chairs. 'It's really the board of directors' room,' explained Smith, 'but everybody's calling it "Little Versailles." ' Mr. Smith was nattily turned out in a thin-as-paper gray wool suit, a palest-of-pale blue pima cotton shirt, black silk tie and blue pearl cuff links. His shoes were specially made for him in spectator style, with inserts of the suit fabric in the black leather."

Post sports editor Mickey Herskowitz wrote five days before the opening: "Bill Giles is as nervous as a cat in a violin factory. When the domed stadium opens it has fallen to Giles to serve as maestro of the $2 million scoreboard. 'I'm nervous as hell,' said Bill, flexing his button-pushing finger. 'I keep thinking of all the things that can go wrong.' For the benefit of historians the first words to appear on the world's most expensive ball-and-strike indicator will be, 'The Houston Astros Welcome You to the Astrodome—World's First Air-Conditioned All-Purpose Stadium.' For sheer dramatic impact, the message falls somewhere between Samuel Morse's 'What hath God wrought,' and the first command spoken by Alexander Graham Bell over the telephone: 'Mr. Watson, come here; I want you.' The opening game, of course, will be vastly incidental to the structure in which it is held."

On the eve of the opening game, virtually every first-class motel and hotel accommodation within 10 miles of the stadium was rented. Beyond the 10-mile radius, some motels were sold out for the weekend, and several reported advance reservations were more than double those for a normal weekend. The "new" Houston baseball weekend money spent by visitors was estimated by Chester Wilkins, executive vice-president of the Greater Houston Convention and Visitors Council, at more than $500,000, and by other sources at as much as $1 million. Bernard Calkins, president of Rapid Transit Lines, said that more than 100 buses were chartered to transport baseball fans to the Dome. The *Houston Post* estimated the weekend would bring $2 million or more in business to the city.

People came from everywhere, every state in the union plus eight foreign countries, for the opening. Inside the stadium was a tableau of society and fashion, entertainment and prestige, as well as political greats. Men and women manuevered through crowded aisles, stopping again and again to look at a view never seen before.

Governor Connally passed out bouquets to those responsible for building the stadium. The governor gave a short dedication speech, then threw out the first ball officially to open the Dome. "I pass out bouquets to those responsible for this magnificent structure," said Connally. "They are men of vision to whom I pay special tribute. This stadium is a monument to the true faith of Bob Smith and Roy Hofheinz." Connally was introduced by Mayor Louie Welch. The mayor also introduced various dignitaries, including city and county officials and the governor of the Mexico state of Tamaulipas. Welch paid tribute to Smith and Hofheinz. Smith endeared himself to the huge crowd by making the shortest talk of the night. In about 10 well-chosen words, Smith thanked the public for building the stadium. Hofheinz was busy making arrangements for President Johnson and was not at the ceremony.

Mickey Herskowitz's story of the drama surrounding the opening of the Dome was the first to hit the streets. Television carried the game, but Herskowitz outdid announcers with the following descriptions:

> Baseball moved this side of paradise Friday night. Fantasy met reality, and the New York Yankees lost. It was, in short, Domesday. The game was quite incidental to the opening of mankind's first covered ballyard, but the Astros and the Yankees took 12 innings to complete it, as though reluctant to leave their lush environs. Houston won, 2-1, in a delicious finish that saw Nellie Fox—listed as a coach and not even on the playing roster—come off the bench to deliver a two-out, two-strike single that scored Jimmy Wynn from second base. For the second time this gaudy spring night, the scoreboard erupted. Even the players were impressed, which is saying a great deal. The definitive comment came from Mickey Mantle, whose appearance in left field, despite an ailing knee delighted the crowd. "It reminds me," said Mantle, as he stood beside the batting cage, "of what I imagine my first ride would be like in a flying saucer." Later Mickey gave the spectators an exquisite thrill, lofting the first genuine home run—that is, in the presence of paid customers—to be recorded in the domed stadium. In the press box Ken Smith, curator of Baseball's Hall of Fame at Cooperstown, groaned, "I'd like to find that man. Maybe we can persuade him to give up that ball. After all, this is history."
>
> The appearance of President and Mrs. Johnson in Judge Hofheinz's box was not publicized in advance. There was doubt until the day of the game that the President could leave Washington. Hofheinz felt all along, however, that his longtime friend and Lady Bird would show up.
>
> The President's arrival, in the company of Hofheinz, was announced promptly at 8:00 P.M., and the gallery gave Johnson a long and vigorous

welcome. He had been delayed by a phony bomb threat. The applause heightened as the likeness of the nation's chief executive flashed on the television screen in center field, an honor that will later be confined to spot commercials and Houston home run hitters.

The presidential party included R. Sargent Shriver, director of the Office of Economic Opportunity and the Peace Corps, and Mrs. Shriver; Bess Abell, White House social secretary; Lloyd Hand, chief of protocol; and Horace Busby and Jack Valenti, special aides. Mr. and Mrs. Johnson were greeted at the stadium by Hofheinz. They entered the stadium on the Judge's special elevator to his box close to the topmost tier.

The President appeared intent on the game at times and Lady Bird clapped her hands and laughed with pleasure at good plays. Johnson, who made no speech, left just before the ninth inning started. He got out of his car on the stadium parking lot and shook hands with a number of people, the majority of them security guards. He took off from Houston International in a smaller plane—a Jetstar—since the larger one he arrived in was not capable of landing at the LBJ Ranch. He greeted the crowd at the airport again and kissed and handed a ballpoint pen to three-year-old Mike Wood, the son of Rev. and Mrs. Thomas E. Wood, after the boy yelled, "Hi, Mister President Johnson!" The Rev. Mr. Wood was pastor of the Emmanuel Baptist Church. More than 50 newsmen who had landed in a chartered commercial plane more than an hour after the President arrived remained at the airport during his Dome tour. They were reported to be too befuddled by the course of events to go anywhere else.

President Johnson wrote to Hofheinz and Smith on March 3, 1965:

Gentlemen:
    You and the people of Houston and Harris County have shown the world what men can accomplish when imagination, energy and sheer determination are combined to one tremendous project.
    The Astrodome will stand as a deserved tribute to the genius of its planners, to be welcomed by all who respect industry and dedication.
    You have my warmest congratulations in providing this great showplace, not only for this area of Texas, but to be seen and appreciated by visitors from all over the world.
                                    Sincerely,
                                    LYNDON B. JOHNSON

Jack Valenti recalled in 1978 the night he accompanied President Johnson's party to the opening Astrodome game: "I remember that one of Roy's grandest moments came when President Johnson flew to Houston for the game. As the president went into Hofheinz's box, the look of glee and happiness that was spread across the Judge's face as if all of his dreams and struggles and all of his frustrations in bringing this Astrodome into being finally were now at an end, and his great achievement was now flung in full display for all the world to see. It was a moment of rare exhaltation on Hofheinz's part, because I always felt that even in his greatest triumphs he was always looking

Astronaut Gus Grissom (left) and Hofheinz on opening night of the National League season in the Astrodome. Photograph by Al Locke.

toward the next hill to be climbed . . . . His almost Machiavellian plans made it come to pass. The Astrodome is his monument."

Commenting further on the Judge's personality, Valenti observed that Hofheinz "had a resolve that was unremitting. Once he set his mind on a goal, in spite of all costs and difficulties, obstacles, terrorizing, tormenting and frustrating interruptions, he would never stop . . . . He would not accept failure."

More than 200,000 persons saw the five weekend exhibition games. The official National League season opened in the Dome on Monday night, April 12, against the Philadelphia Phillies, who won 2-0 before another capacity crowd. Hofheinz arranged another big sideshow for the fans—the astronauts. Although more entertainment stars, baseball moguls, and celebrities were introduced, the crowd saved its big cheers for astronauts Gus Grissom and John Young. The Gemini twins, along with 21 of their 26 space brothers, strolled out during opening ceremonies to accept lifetime passes to Astrodome games. Before the ceremonies, the astronauts fraternized with their baseball name-sakes in the home dugout.

Warren Giles, president of the National League, presented the passes to the spacemen. "This is a proud day for baseball, for Houston, and for the National League," Giles said. "It took vision, imagination, and courage to complete this stadium." Ford Frick, commissioner of baseball, said he felt "completely insignificant" in the presence of both the Dome and the 23 astronauts. "This opens a completely new field not just to baseball, but to all municipal activities," he said.

Commenting on the difficulty outfielders had seeing fly balls in daylight, he compared the situation to the Yale Bowl, which he said was built without toilets, and Chavez Ravine in Los Angeles, where they neglected to build steps from the dugouts to the field. "That just goes to show you how you can forget little things," Frick said. Those "little things" in the Astrodome would be corrected by Hofheinz, and he would press on to complete new projects.

There were 175 sports writers present for the opening game. Thirteen came from New York alone, and others from such other points as Milwaukee, San Francisco, Chicago, Boston, Baltimore, Montreal, and Toronto. This is what some of them wrote:

Buddy Diliberto, *New Orleans Times-Picayune*: "When the first Astronaut (Uncle Sam's) climbs out of his capsule and sets foot on the moon five, 10 or 20 years from now he won't be any more awed by the sight than you'll be the first time you step inside the Astrodome. The place is unbelievable. Just unbelievable. It takes your breath away on first look. It's like stepping out of the real world into a land of make believe—only it's not make believe. New York World's Fair? It doesn't hold a candle—and this place is about 1,000 miles closer to New Orleans. Lucky for New Orleanians."

John Steadman, *Baltimore News American*: "Not even Jules Verne or Walt Disney, in their most fantastic moments of genius ever conceived anything quite like this unbelievable palace of baseball luxury. This is the new Taj Mahal and it must be seen to be believed. Words and pictures cannot begin to adequately describe the majestic view which overwhelms the visitor. It brought a reaction comparable to the first time we viewed Niagara Falls. Awesome beyond belief. The Houston Astrodome Stadium is like a giant space ship that came from another planet."

Dan Cook, *San Antonio Express-News*: "The most celebrated palace of play since the Romans' Colosseum opened its doors to the public for a first official showing here Friday night and the Domed Stadium's general magnificence made it one of the proudest nights in Texas sports history. At the top of the second inning, members of the New York Yankees and Houston Astros stopped play, doffed their caps and applauded when it was announced that one of those 46,006 fans was Lyndon B. Johnson."

Til Ferdenenzi, *New York Journal American*: "The Astrodome, extravagantly called the eighth wonder of the world by the local citizenry, makes all other stadiums and arenas look like something out of the Stone Age. And that includes such palaces of sport as Shea Stadium, Chavez Ravine and D. C. Stadium. The President of the United States was there, the governor of Texas was there and the rest of the audience, obviously moved by the historic implications of being in attendance at the first major league ball game played under a roof, received the action with noisy enthusiasm."

Lou Maysel, *Austin American*: "Baseball in the Astrodome is an orgy of color. It's as if Roy Hofheinz marched into a paint store, grabbed up the color book and said, 'Give me 500 gallons of each of these colors.' Then you must assume, he went into his favorite fabric shop and bought up every bolt of eye-dazzling material they had and then told the clerk to rush him a few thousand yards of 'this, this and that.'

"If it didn't happen this way, it at least gives you the idea of what to expect when you first take it upon yourself to attend a baseball game in Houston because color reaches out and socks you in the eye from the time you drive in and hand the parking gate attendant a buck and get 50 cents in return."

Dave Campbell, *Waco News Tribune*: "Neither a tardy start nor muffled bats nor a bomb scare directed at the audience's most august member, LBJ, could divert the crowd from the full enjoyment of this red-letter moment in baseball history. Nobody hit the roof but Mickey Mantle hit a home run. They liked that."

Significant comment about the spectacular Dome first games came from the *Post's* Herskowitz on April 11. He wrote:

> There is absolutely no truth to the rumor that Judge Roy Hofheinz is really Goldfinger. Oh, there may be a faint physical resemblance. They do cast shadows of approximately the same shape, on the order of a capital D. And one cannot ignore the fact that the corridors on the fifth level at the Domed Stadium are painted with gold glitter. But they differ in philosophy, and in their mode of operation. Goldfinger, if we remember our James Bond mythology, tried to knock off Fort Knox. Hofheinz has built his own . . . .
>
> The Dome was the start of a revolution, the introduction of baseball under cover. The man who led it, who nurtured the idea and fought it to reality, is Roy Hofheinz. If not for what his critics refer to as his infallible instinct for making people angry, Hofheinz would at this moment be among the most popular men in Houston, a hero to the baseball-daffy masses. Such moves as threatening to sue people who would call their meat patties "Dome-burgers" are calculated to bring the club no sympathy. Even so, this is the Judge's week, and he deserves a volume of credit, though possibly he would prefer cash. The man thrives on crisis and difficulty. Others on his staff wanted only to get this week behind them, like Satan. It was a frightful week, and they asked not to come out ahead, only to break even. But Hofheinz had the zest of a fellow who had just discovered a new card trick. He was at one moment looking over the shoulder of a carpenter, at the next whispering into President Johnson's ear. He seemed to enjoy himself.
>
> Roy Hofheinz is a mover and doer the likes of whom baseball has rarely seen. He burst upon the big league scene four years ago with all the subtlety of a hand grenade. Admirers of action and controversy have hailed him as the most fascinating new personality to invade the sport since Bill Veeck came and went. Everything about the Judge seems to have an extra dimension. His range of knowledge, his drive, his capacity for work, his appetite, his temper. He is a dealer in vast ideas and, like the Internal Revenue Service, he will not take no for an answer.
>
> When the Colt .45s burst into being, more or less, in 1962, Hofheinz designed everything from Colt Stadium to the buttons on the blouses of the girl ushers. Now, a lot of men who don't know buttons from baseball, wind up owning a big league team. But Hofheinz is the sort who, given a week, will beat you at your own game.

29

The Hofheinz-Smith Break

For more than a decade, millionaire civic leader Bob Smith and Roy Hofheinz were a powerful team working to make Houston a greater city. Not even their closest associates thought anything could weaken their confidence in each other. The community and the baseball world were shocked on May 12, 1965, when the two men glumly announced at a press conference that Smith had given Hofheinz an option to buy controlling interest in the Houston Sports Association. Hofheinz, it was later disclosed, had until August 12 to pay Smith $7.5 million in exchange for all but 10 percent of the majority stock his partner held. That would give Hofheinz 86 percent control of HSA. For nearly three months, newspaper and broadcast reports speculated whether Hofheinz could raise the money. The opening of the Astrodome was still the talk of the town, but the Hofheinz-Smith relationship almost equalled it.

A week after Hofheinz obtained an option to buy out Smith, Mickey Herskowitz of the *Houston Post* wrote: "An impeccable source says that in recent weeks Smith grew resentful of what he considered the 'autocratic governing' of the club by Hofheinz. He especially objected to the rising authority of Fred Hofheinz, the Judge's son." The writer also observed that "the next step of the two investment barons, so opposite in style, manner and temper, but so long identified with one another, will be to dissolve their connection in two other enterprises."

Dick Peebles, *Houston Chronicle* sports editor, reported on July 25 that Hofheinz had begun raising the needed funds. He mortgaged his Yorktown home, valued at $3.5 million, as well as other personal property. He also mortgaged the 16 percent interest he owned in Houston television Channel 13, which was said to be worth millions.

Red James, Hofheinz's law partner and attorney for HSA, and Welcome Wilson, a Smith associate whom the oilman befriended by signing his business notes, said in 1978 that they saw signs of the break well before it came. James, who was closer to the situation than Wilson, recalled: "When other HSA stockholders sold out, Bob Smith paid for and owned two-thirds of the stock of HSA. Roy, however, had an option to buy stock so they would have an equal

Judge Hofheinz and Bob Smith. **Photograph by Harold Israel, courtesy Gulf Photo.**

amount. That option began to have an effect on Roy's relationship with Bob and Vivian Smith and me. Roy was my partner and I took his side on anything. The situation became most embarrassing. The relationship just went downhill from then on as Bob called on Roy to surrender the option on the stock. Bob called on me because I was secretary of the corporation. I had the stock in a safe and Bob wanted it. I called Roy and he said, 'Well, hold up until I can talk to him and see if I can buy it.' "

It appeared for a while that the two partners might be getting back together, but about two weeks later Smith wrote James a letter which said: "I want my stock. Let me have it." James said that after several months Hofheinz sent Smith a cashier's check for a down payment on the stock that would give Hofheinz an equal share of stock. James said Smith carried the check around in his pocket for several weeks.

Welcome Wilson said the buy-out period lasted more than a year. During a Gulf of Mexico fishing trip with Smith, Wilson recalled that the millionaire said Hofheinz had developed too many enemies. He quoted Smith as saying: "I am sure getting tired of defending Roy Hofheinz. Everywhere I go, I spend much time trying to defend him." He recalled Smith's relationship with the Judge: "Mr. Smith would never pass over any criticism of his partner. He would jump in and defend whatever the Judge did. He was Roy's complete and absolute supporter. He thought Hofheinz was as honest a man as he knew and he believed Roy intelligent and of high integrity. However, he didn't like, for instance, the fact that Roy wouldn't answer or return telephone calls, and wouldn't answer most letters." Wilson also recalled that when Hofheinz's check for the stock came, Smith folded it and put it in his money clip in his pocket.

Meanwhile, Smith's advisers began to tell the oilman that it was wrong for Hofheinz to exercise his option at such a late date. Wilson recalled:

> Bob Smith's lawyer, Judge Ed Suhr, advised Bob that he didn't think it was appropriate at that late date for Hofheinz simply to give Smith money for purchase of that substantial block of stock. Judge Suhr pointed out that when Mr. Smith bought out the other stockholders the enterprise was a shaky operation. Mr. Smith had written a check for more than $500,000 to buy the stock. Now, 18 months later, the Astrodome was a success, the HSA was in a profitable position, the baseball team was well-received, and Hofheinz wanted to exercise his option which had expired. Mr. Smith's advisors said a successful major league franchise might be worth $10 million or $15 million. The idea of selling a big chunk after it was already proved a success just by giving Mr. Smith his money back didn't seem appropriate to them. Mr. Smith wouldn't say what he was going to do. He just kept pulling that check out of his pocket and looking at it. Mrs. Smith, I felt, was substantially resentful of Hofheinz at that juncture. I believe, in her judgment, the Judge was not giving Mr. Smith adequate credit for his contribution to the Astrodome. I really think all Mr. Smith wanted was some indication from Hofheinz that Roy appreciated what he had done, his support over the years when few people backed the Judge, and recognized Mr. Smith's contribution to the Astrodome.

Red James said that "when national stories about 'Hofheinz, the genius of the Astrodome,' began to flow in newspapers and magazines, he felt they began to have an effect on Mrs. Smith and then on Bob. They felt that the oil millionaire's part in HSA was inadequately told by the writers." James said that he thought "the straw that broke the camel's back between Hofheinz and Smith came when President and Mrs. Lyndon Johnson visited the Dome for the opening game. Roy, apparently in the rush of things, did not tell the Smiths. Bob and Vivian sat in their box right in front of me when, some felt, they should have been sitting in Roy's box in right field to greet Lyndon and Lady Bird. Roy did invite the Smiths to the box in the seventh inning and they went. I overheard Mrs. Smith expressing resentment because of lack of recognition that her husband owned two-thirds of HSA."

When on May 12 Hofheinz told reporters he would exercise the option and would not have partners to back him, he said, "I obviously couldn't exercise the option unless I had the money or knew I had it." On August 3, Hofheinz kept his word. He paid off Smith and told reporters he used Houston Bank and Trust Company as his financing agent in getting the money together. Hofheinz said he didn't plan any personnel changes. "I wouldn't trade our staff for any in baseball today," he said. At that time the Astros were in ninth place.

Bob Smith angrily broke his silence after he received Hofheinz's final check. "Roy is just too autocratic," he told newsmen. He scoffed at earlier reports that they would quit on friendly terms. "All this talk about everything being friendly between us is just not true." He added: "Hofheinz three weeks ago changed all the locks on the stadium and I couldn't get in. That was childish."

Later reports said Hofheinz financed $5.5 million on the Smith payment and put up $2 million cash. Smith said he would keep 10 percent of the stock and would remain on the board of directors. He changed his mind, according to Red James who added, "At the next HSA board meeting Smith resigned as a director and an officer and handed in the lifetime solid 14 karat gold card which Roy had had made up for him. He picked up his marbles and left. It was sad for me. Bob and I had been great friends."

It was shown in a deed filed October 16, but executed August 25, 1965, that Smith and Hofheinz split up their joint real estate holdings in the stadium area. Hofheinz acquired title to 154 acres and Smith 144 acres. Newspapers said some of the real estate first was acquired for as little as $10,000 an acre. Sales in 1965 in the area indicated a value from $2.50 to $3.50 a square foot or from $102,000 to $150,000 an acre. They also sold KBAT radio station in San Antonio.

Bob Smith on a KPRC television interview two weeks after he sold out never referred to Hofheinz as "the Judge" as he formerly had. He said, "I'm not out one nickel after the split." Smith said running a baseball team is a costly operation. "I could have stood on my ear and made more money than I did in baseball," he said. "That's the trouble with some owners. They are so preoccupied with money that the sport suffers." However, he did not hesitate to name Hofheinz as the man who created and sold the Dome idea. "I'll give him credit," Smith told TV viewers. "Of course, give him time and he'd take it anyway." Smith left no doubt during the interview that Houston would never see another Smith-Hofheinz collaboration.

It was considerably in question whether the Judge could raise the money in such a short time. He was able to raise it through what was then Houston Bank and Trust Company. Charles L. Bybee, who was head of the bank, agreed to arrange the loan. His bank was not large enough to handle the loan and took minority interest. Chemical Bank of New York and First National Bank in Dallas put up major funds and serviced the account.

Bybee and his wife, Faith, were great Hofheinz admirers. It was Bybee who kept the Judge afloat during the building of the Astrodome and afterwards. Hofheinz said, "Bybee was a very independent thinker and had faith that I was a good financial risk, and that what his bank was doing was good for Houston."

For nearly 14 years after her husband sold control of the Astrodome to Hofheinz, Mrs. Vivian Smith would not discuss publicly the break between Bob and the Judge. The millionaire himself said little before his death about the breach, although various friends described his "keen disappointment" because he had made the mistake of believing Hofheinz could not raise the money to buy him out.

After declining for a year persistent requests for an interview, Mrs. Smith agreed to break her silence and discuss with the author the Hofheinz-Smith partnership and its eventual breakup. John Leer, former Hofheinz associate and executive in Mrs. Smith's vast organization, tape-recorded the following questions and answers:

Q. What were the social relationships between the Smith and Hofheinz families?

A. There was really no personal relationship between the Smith and the Hofheinz families. Everything was connected with something civic and later with baseball. When the King and Queen of Greece were here, we did entertain them at the ranch, but that was simply a civic event. When Bob was civil defense director, he put much time and effort into his job. Entertaining the King and Queen of Greece was a civic event only.

Q. How close was the relationship that you had with Mrs. Dene Hofheinz?

A. I had great admiration for Dene. I think she was a fine woman and the strongest of the family, really. But we really had no close relations. It was just a casual relationship as a result of being thrown together. Every time we traveled with the Hofheinzes, it was with the ball club or to World Series.

Q. After Hofheinz left the mayor's office in defeat, what business relationships developed between him and Mr. Smith?

A. We had land that adjoined Roy's home and acreage on Yorktown. Roy came up with the idea to put in an air-conditioned shopping center. He came to Mr. Smith and wanted Mr. Smith to go in with him and use our land; that was the main thing. Roy was always trying to get to Bob for something. He did come up with a beautiful concept but he couldn't get it off the ground. He went everywhere and he couldn't sell it.

Q. Mr. Smith did agree to contribute land and possible financing?

A. Yes. I will have to say it was a nice project. It would have been a good project. Frank Sharp got his shopping center off the ground and Roy didn't. You see what Frank Sharp has done at Sharpstown. Roy's plan is still in the mud somewhere.

Q. How many real estate ventures did the two men have together?

A. About three or four. I wouldn't call them ventures. They made land purchases together. Roy would come to Mr. Smith and Mr. Smith had to put up all the money and pay for it. Roy always wanted to come in and have 50 percent. He always poor-mouthed Mr. Smith and said he didn't have any money to pay to buy it, but he would come in for his share whenever he wanted to. Sometimes he did and sometimes he didn't.

Q. Do you recall any stories about the two men fishing and hunting together, visits to "Huckster House," "Loose Goose," or any of Mr. Smith's own retreats?

Mrs. R. E. (Vivian) Smith.
Photograph courtesy the
Houston Chronicle.

A. I never went on the hunting trips. Mr. Smith loved to fish. Surely I got up and fixed breakfast for him whenever he went fishing or whenever he went anywhere. I did that for Mr. Smith and I would have done it for any of his friends or guests he might have. But I don't ever remember Roy coming to my house and going fishing with Mr. Smith. His henchman, Red James, would come, as did Welcome Wilson and Archie Bennett. That's as much as I can remember about fishing trips. We once went to "Huckster House" and happened to be uninvited. One afternoon we dropped by and Bob wanted to see Roy on business. Just as we were leaving, we saw Roy was having a big party for all the baseball club. We hadn't been invited; it just happened that way. I went to the "Loose Goose," when Bob wanted to go one Sunday afternoon to discuss the ball club with Roy.

Q. Did Hofheinz own the "Loose Goose"?

A. Bob paid for building that old house out there. The land was bought 50-50. Roy put in the "Loose Goose." It cost us over $50,000. The "Loose Goose" that we went to was the old "Loose Goose," a little old frame house. We were never at the new building that Roy built on the Katy Freeway.

Q. You mean you paid for it and you were never in the "Loose Goose"?

A. Roy entertained out there all the time, but we didn't have a key to it, and we were never invited. Of course, we weren't interested, really.

Q. How did Craig Cullinan, George Kirksey, and others bring Smith and Hofheinz into the Houston Sports Association?

A. Craig and George came by here one night to visit with Bob because they were soliciting his help in trying to get baseball for Houston. Bob had always been a baseball fan, a sports fan. George and Craig were looking for someone to help them. They laid the ground work for the team. Bob just suggested that they get Roy because he thought that he might have the know-how to get it done.

Q. Didn't Hofheinz have quite a reputation as a promoter from his boyhood on?

A. Yes, he was always promoting something or somebody.

Q. As an ardent baseball fan yourself, how did you feel about the possibilities of this new venture between the two men?

A. As to baseball, we were very eager and excited. I was very naive. I didn't know Roy at that time. I had heard a lot of things, but I never did really know him. The more we got into it, well the less I felt good about it. I always felt that Roy was trying to do things to Bob and didn't keep him advised and keep him informed, and he tried to push him out.

Q. Was the Smith-Hofheinz relationship harmonious, and, as it got under way, were Roy's business practices and methods comparable to Mr. Smith's?

A. No, they weren't comparable to Mr. Smith's. Roy handled all of the money, the deals, the business part of it. In time Bob had to get after him because people would come to him and say Roy was not paying for extra work they had done, materials they had gotten. Bob had to go out there and make him—HSA—pay the bills. Bob just didn't operate like that. There was a policy in the Smith office that when a bill came in, it was to be paid before the close of business the day it arrived.

Q. Did Hofheinz operate that way?

A. Evidently not.

Q. What was the agreement between Smith and Hofheinz on who would do what in the management of the Houston Sports Association in view of the fact Mr. Smith financed much of the operation?

A. Well, that is true about financing. Bob was an executive. He was never one for details. He always passed that on to someone he had confidence in. He always expected everybody to do business as he did. He was really naive about that. At that time, he had confidence in Roy and he thought that he was doing a good job. Roy enjoyed doing detail work and was involved in everything. Bob just didn't like to handle things like that so he passed them to Roy. That is why Roy was managing things.

Q. Did Smith and Hofheinz have an agreement on plans for rehabilitation of old Busch Stadium the last year of minor league baseball and the building of Colt Stadium and the idea or concept of the Astrodome, or was Bob's confidence in Roy's management so great that he left all the details to Roy?

A. I would say Bob financed the building of Colt Stadium before the other stadium could be built because they had to have a place for their ball team to play. He was in accord with that. He approved the idea of the Astrodome, but there never would have been an Astrodome if it hadn't been for Bob because people of Harris County would not have voted for it except for confidence in Bob. Bob carried the election and everybody in Houston at that time will agree.

Q. Was Mr. Smith actually in on the planning and the concept of the Astro-dome?

A. Surely, but not the details of it. He left them to Roy. But Bob approved the overall design.

Q. In the making of decisions, Smith was very much a part of them?

A. Yes. They were subject to his approval.

Q. What prompted Hofheinz and Smith to begin buying out the original stockholders of the Houston Sports Association, especially Craig Cullinan, the first president?

A. All became disenchanted with Roy. I mean, they didn't think he was doing a good job, didn't like the way he was handling things, and they wanted to sell. So, as usual, Roy didn't have any money. He was poor-mouthing, and he said he couldn't, so Bob, always trying to help the other fellow, bought the stock and gave Roy an option to buy half of what he bought, and gave him a year's option. That's what really prompted the break between the two men.

Q. Was there a written option or was it a verbal agreement?

A. I don't know whether it was written—probably it was—but that didn't matter. Mr. Smith would have honored it. He did honor it later on. What prompted the break between them came when he did not take up his option at a specified time. Mr. Smith asked for his stock from HSA, and Roy refused to give it to him. Red James was the HSA attorney and he had the stock in his office. Bob asked Red for it and Red said, "I can't give you your stock." Mr. Smith said, "Well, why not?" He said, "Because Roy said I couldn't give it to you." But it was Mr. Smith's stock and Roy hadn't paid for it and that was six months past the option time.

Q. What are your recollections of opening day at Colt Stadium when the .45s played Chicago?

A. It was real exciting and we were very enthusiastic. Bob always hoped to have a major league team and was very interested in the game and was very pleased. It was like a ball game should be played—outside.

Q. Was Mr. Smith happy during that period of investment with the management by Hofheinz?

A. He was in the beginning. Bob kept confidence in Roy, but all his friends would try to tell him about what Roy was doing to him, but no, he was unaware. The longer Roy ran the show, the less confidence Bob had.

Q. What destroyed that confidence?

A. Roy really didn't keep Bob informed. He took advantage of Bob's friend-ship. Roy brought in business people and he would never have Bob visit with them or anything of that kind. He was trying to keep Bob in the dark about everything.

Q. Did you once find that Roy's expenses were somewhat exorbitant and you had no idea how he was spending money?

A. We had our accountant check, and I think Roy was getting over $300,000 a year, or something like that, paying himself a big salary and having a big expense account, and he was living high on the hog.

Q. During the Colt .45 days, when the three Houston newspapers constantly featured Mr. Smith and you in pictures and copy, was it the plan for Mr. Smith to be out front for the public and Hofheinz do the job of getting the Dome built?

A. No, there was no plan at all for that. I think that Mr. Smith was very friendly with news media, and he respected them and they respected Mr. Smith for all he had done. I think that that was their main interest. It just happened in the normal course of events.

Q. Was Mr. Smith the type of man who sought publicity?

A. Never.

Q. Some people have said that Mr. Smith disliked Hofheinz's operation during the building of the Astrodome and they had confrontations. Do you recall anything about them?

A. I don't know. Roy was not very nice to the public. He would not pay his bills on time. Creditors would come to Mr. Smith to get money. Mr. Smith's name was on everything that Roy had. Bob had to sign for everything. That's the only thing that I recall. Bob didn't like the way Roy operated.

Q. When the Astrodome opened on April 9, 1965, you and Mr. Smith sat in your box until about the seventh inning when you were asked to go to Roy's box on the seventh level and visit with President and Mrs. Johnson. Did you and Mr. Smith feel that on that special occasion of the opening you should have been in Hofheinz's box awaiting President and Mrs. Johnson?

A. We didn't think anything about it because we had invited guests to our box right behind the umpire where Mr. Smith liked to sit. He went to see the ball game, not to see the president of the United States and his wife. We had seen the Johnsons on many occasions. I do remember that we did go up there, but I don't know at what inning or whether it was during the game or afterwards. I had no feeling at all about going up and sitting in that box. They called it Roy's box; I would say it was just a box Smith money paid for. Why should we call it Roy's box? It was supposed to have been the HSA box, but Roy monopolized it all the time. That didn't cause us to feel bad. We didn't care.

Q. Do you remember Mr. Smith making a statement one way or the other about the occasion?

A. Heavens no. He was only interested in seeing the ball game. I would like to say this about the opening when I think we were very rudely treated: We took guests to the Astrodome Club to have dinner. The waiter said "I'm sorry I can't serve you because you don't have a card." Mr. Smith had never been given a membership card. The waiter said, "Well, we can't serve you if you don't have a card." Our guests and we were already seated at the table and had reservations. Bob got the headwaiter and he said, "Go ahead and serve Mr. Smith." Which he did. Two nights later, the following Sunday evening, Mr. Smith called and made reservations for dinner. He said, "I don't want to be embarrassed by asking for my card and a waiter telling me I can't be served because I don't have a card. I don't have a card. I belong, I know, but I just don't have a card." While we were sitting there having dinner, Freddie Boy (Hofheinz) walked up like a smart aleck, pulled his wallet out of his pocket and threw a card in front of Mr. Smith and said, "Here's your card. I've been carrying it in my pocket for three or four days, just haven't had time to give it to you." A friend turned to me and said, "You know, there is such a thing as having too many degrees." He was Albert Johnson, vice-president of the First National Bank of Chicago.

Q. Did you and Mr. Smith feel slighted?

A. Heavens no. We had our plans, our friends, our own box and paid for it, too.

Q. You felt no slight and were not irritated because of the president's visit or by the way you and your guests were treated in the club?

A. We were only embarrassed at the club which HSA owned. Surely it was a lack of consideration.

Q. Did that lead to some of the friction between the Smiths and the Hofheinzes?

A. Yes it did. It irritated me long before it did Mr. Smith. Roy told George Kirksey that if it hadn't been for me, he and Bob would still be together. He blamed me for all of it. I am glad I was there to protect Bob.

Q. Would you have negated the relationship earlier if you could have?

A. Earlier than that, yes.

Q. After the opening, Hofheinz sought to buy and offered a check to become a major stockholder. Mr. Smith kept the check in his pocket for a good while before returning it to Roy. Could you tell about that?

A. Roy didn't offer to buy the stock which goes back to when Bob bought the stock of Kirksey, Cullinan, and others. Roy said that he would like to have half of it, but he didn't have the money to pay for it. Bob bought all the stock and gave Roy an option to buy. There was a time frame to exercise the option. He could buy it for what Bob paid for it. He didn't exercise that option, so six months later Bob began to see the light of day and finally he got tired. He had asked for his stock and Red James wouldn't give it to him. During a Saturday double-header, Bob went to the box to find Roy. I did not go with him. Bob came back mad as all hops. He had told Roy he wanted his stock and he refused to give it to him. Then we went back. I don't remember now whether Roy gave Bob a check then or later. Roy said, "I'll pay for it." It was over six months overdue at that time, so it wasn't a matter of his just offering to buy it, offering him a check for it at that time.

Q. Did Mr. Smith really have to give him the stock?

A. The option had expired for about six months. We went home after the game and Bob said, "Let's go back." Mr. Smith at that time had a key to the back door and to the elevator that led up to the executive offices. We went back and drove up to the back. Bob was going to finish his little tete-a-tete with Roy. When we got there, they had changed the locks so that we couldn't get in. That shows you what kind of a man Roy was.

Q. You think Roy changed the locks because he was afraid of Mr. Smith?

A. I don't know why he changed the locks. He didn't want Bob up there. I understand they moved files and shredded paper all afternoon.

Q. Did Mr. Smith ever have an office at the Astrodome?

A. No. Prior to the opening, my daughter and a friend from New York wanted to see the Dome. I called out and asked if I could bring them out to see. When we got there, Fred showed us all over the Dome in one of those little golf carts. He said, "This is Mr. Smith's office—chairman of the board." I was horrified. I had never seen it. It was one of those garish-looking rooms with red velvet and a woman's breast exposed on the arms of the chairs. I told Fred right then, and I told Mary Frances: "Don't you dare tell anyone that this is Mr. Smith's office. He doesn't go for things like that and I think it's an insult to Mr. Smith to call it his office. Call it whatever you will, but don't you call it Mr. Smith's office."

Q. Do you recall a series of incidents or disagreements which caused the much-publicized quote, "You buy me out or I'll buy you out"?

A. It was certainly a statement, "You buy me out or I'll buy you out," because Bob had become disenchanted, especially when Roy failed to honor his option. The attitude Roy had towards Bob was really the straw that broke the camel's back, so Bob just said, "You buy me out or I'll buy you out."

Q. In other words, Mr. Smith became disenchanted with Roy over a period of time for various reasons, and it was brought to a head when Roy failed to exercise his stock option and wouldn't deliver the stock or pay for it—is that correct?

A. That is correct. He did come up with a check at the last when he saw that Bob wasn't going to give the stock to him.

Q. Did Mr. Smith ever tell you that Hofheinz could not raise the money to buy him out?

A. Sure we talked about that. He didn't believe he could get the money. Why should he? He was always poor-mouthing; Roy never had money to pay for anything. Bob had to put up the money for everything; Roy didn't have any credit without Bob's signature. Nobody would lend him money. Every time they had to borrow money, Bob had to sign on the dotted line.

Q. What was Mr. Smith's reaction when Hofheinz did manage to come up with the money to buy all but 10 percent of Mr. Smith's stock?

A. Well, like everybody else in town, he was shocked. He was disappointed. He felt the ball team would never go anywhere under Roy's management.

Q. Why did Mr. Smith keep 10 percent of the stock in the settlement?

A. Just for meanness.

Q. A news story said Hofheinz paid Mr. Smith $7.5 million for controlling stock. Is this correct? Did the amount represent what Bob had actually spent, and how much was the settlement?

A. I don't know what Roy paid him. I don't think the figure named would cover the cost of the stock or what Mr. Smith actually spent, but, at any rate, he was glad to get out.

Q. Did Mr. Smith or Hofheinz see or communicate with each other after the stock sale giving Roy control—or were their business dealings concluded by then?

A. I don't think they had any relationship at all after that. I am sure all their business dealings concluded then because we were firm believers in that old

Chinese proverb, "Fool me one time, your fault; fool me two times, my fault."

John Easter, controller of HSA, said: "The Smith-Hofheinz partnership was a good one. The Judge was very dedicated to making sure that, even though he was the 'working partner,' he always put up his share of money up front on any deal that he and Mr. Smith had. The Judge never took one cent in salary from HSA or any of their other endeavors during their partnership. On business trips the Judge would spend his personal money on incidentals, taking advertising prospects to dinner, [paying] cab fares, etc., and I never could get him to record or turn in these amounts for reimbursement. Mr. Smith had a very good partner in the Judge."

No one watched the Smith-Hofheinz relationship closer than Mary Frances. She recalled:

> Mr. Smith and the Judge had a very good rapport. They talked on the telephone several times a day and saw each other every day or so during the first years of the baseball club and the construction of the Astrodome. When the team played at Colt Stadium, Mr. Smith never missed a game and nearly always stopped by the Judge's small office to be brought up to date on what was going on. They liked each other and trusted each other. As the Astrodome was nearing completion, all of a sudden the national magazines sent their top reporters in to do in depth stories on "the first air-conditioned, covered stadium" and the two men who had the guts to put it together. The Judge always set up appointments for interviews when Mr. Smith could also be available because, as I heard the Judge say many times, "the Dome never could have been built without Bob Smith." Some of the stories written referred to Mr. Smith as "the money" and the Judge as "the brains."
>
> After one of these national stories, Mr. Smith came to the Astrodome one day and told the Judge that he would like to see him privately. The Judge and Mr. Smith went into the living room section of the seventh level box and pulled the sliding door closed. It was obvious that Mr. Smith was quite upset about something, and was talking very loudly. He said, "Roy, you're fired!" I heard the Judge say, "Aw, come on, Bob; you can't fire me; I'm your partner." The Judge tried to calm Mr. Smith down and find out the problem, but he couldn't. Mr. Smith said, "Well, one of us has got to go." The Judge asked, "Why, haven't we been good partners?" Mr. Smith said, "Yes, but one of us has got to go." Mr. Smith then opened the door to the small elevator and left as abruptly as he had come in. The Judge was stunned. He spent the rest of the day trying to figure out what had set off Mr. Smith.
>
> The next day the Judge worked on a letter which would turn out to be the "buy or sell agreement" between Mr. Smith and himself. Once, while he was working on the letter, he looked up and said, "I don't know why I am doing this. . . . I don't want to split up with Bob." But he thought it was what Mr. Smith wanted, and apparently it was. When the Judge made an appointment and

went down to visit with his partner, Mr. Smith quickly accepted the proposal. The Judge came back to the office and said to me, "Put this letter in the safe. It could be one of the most important letters I have ever signed."

During the weeks to come, the Judge's single thought was to get the money to buy out Mr. Smith. He worked and worried every minute of the day and night. He once almost had a commitment for the money from a Galveston firm, only to have one of the officers of the firm call to tell him that they had decided not to make the loan, that Mr. Smith was one of their good customers and had requested that they not make the loan.

It was truly a sad turn of events when Mr. Smith and the Judge parted. It's really a shame other people interfered in the friendship-partnership. They were really a good combination and it was good for both of them. Mr. Smith was involved, happy, vital as long as he was partner with the Judge. There is no doubt that he loved it all. The Judge also regretted the day he lost his "podnah." Mr. Smith had many millions of dollars, but I believe life didn't seem to be fun for him after his separation from the Judge. The irony of it all is that the Judge was never "mad" with Mr. Smith. He never hated him or even disliked him. He really had a very special love for his good friend. The Judge told me one day: "You'll never convince me that Bob Smith didn't like me. I know he did."

30

Acclaim Abroad,
Criticism at Home

In 1965, while newspaper and magazine writers and broadcast men and women in Texas and in many parts of the nation and world acclaimed Roy Hofheinz for creating the Astrodome, many in Houston and Harris County heaped criticism upon the Judge's tough hide. Partisans of Bob Smith thought it a "shame" and felt angry that Hofheinz could buy out the man who was the financial underpinning of the project. At the same time the Smith-Hofheinz duel raged, another conflict hit the headlines for three months—Bud Adams' refusal to sign a lease for his Oilers to play in the Astrodome that fall as advertised because he said the rental the Judge asked was the "ninth wonder of the world."

Oiler fans already had begun buying tickets for seats in the Astrodome for the season and were upset because they had to change to Rice Stadium when Hofheinz and Adams came to an impasse. They also wanted to watch the Oilers in the comforts of the Astrodome. The *Post* and the *Chronicle* carried almost full pages quoting Adams and Hofheinz on the details of why they could not get together. Adams partisans argued that the Oiler owner ought to get a better lease than Hofheinz offered because the Oiler owner had been an original stockholder in HSA, had helped organize the new American Football League and the Houston team with his own money, had supported bond elections for the county to get the money for the covered stadium, and was due consideration greater than the maestro of the Dome offered. Hofheinz gave figures in support of the rent he wanted to meet the great costs of the sports palace; he adamantly stood his ground.

Adams announced he was withdrawing from the Dome when Hofheinz was in Montreal on a stop before taking off for Europe. When he returned a week later, he said he had been amazed by Adams' announcement because the week before he left the two of them had conferred, and he thought all was in order concerning the lease. Neither newspaper backing of Adams nor public opinion bothered the Judge. Instead, he said he thought the National Football League might want to authorize a team to play in the Dome to compete with the Oilers and that he, himself, would seek a franchise. Pete Rozelle, the National League commissioner, was invited to Houston to discuss a franchise. When he was in Hofheinz's box during an Astro game, he was introduced to the crowd. A loud chorus of boos greeted him along with some applause. Oiler fans in the baseball crowd did not want their team to play in Rice Stadium. National Football League rules, however, provided that no owner could have both a football and a major league baseball franchise, so Hofheinz's bid would come to naught. He did interest the rich John Mecoms of Houston in a Houston franchise in NFL expansion.

Without Oiler participation, Hofheinz had to look to other attractions to keep the Astrodome in constant use for the revenue needed to meet daily costs. Air conditioning, for example, had to remain on continuously to prevent a rain-like moisture from spoiling the inside of the edifice.

Bud Adams talked in 1978 about his early ownership of HSA stock and the break with Hofheinz. "I was more interested in the National Football League than I was in baseball franchises, but nevertheless I was a charter member of HSA and, after it was formed, it was agreed upon that Bob Smith and Roy Hofheinz would come in. The interest that Bob took was actually dollar-wise, but Hofheinz began running the thing. The Astrodome was Hofheinz's creation and his baby. I would say strategy came from Hofheinz and was developed by him. The Astrodome was to be for all purposes. With his legal background, he had all the T's crossed and the I's dotted.

Adams also recalled:

> I had announced the new American Football League in July of 1959. The new Oilers played at old Jeppesen Stadium. In 1965, when the Astrodome opened, people were told the Oilers would play there that fall. I always thought I was making headway and naturally, as the year '65 started progressing and the football training season starting in July approached, I think it was in May, I really woke up to the fact that I still didn't have a signed lease for the Dome. We had a lot of verbal agreements. I remember giving Roy a registered letter asking him to submit the lease because we were fast approaching the oncoming football season, and otherwise I would submit one to him. As it turned out, I believe I did submit a lease to the Judge on terms I thought were what we could agree. His version of the lease came back quite differently. In the final negotiations I had with the Judge, Fred Hofheinz acted as a legal adviser to his father. Thirty days before we were to start football practice, word leaked around town that we weren't coming to a satisfactory agreement. I then received a call asking if I was interested in playing at Rice Stadium. In his suite at Lamar Hotel, Herman Brown, of Brown and Root, and Jess Neely, Rice athletic director, and I got together. Lawyers worked on details all day, and we announced we were going to play in Rice Stadium. In the meantime we'd been selling tickets for playing in the Dome, so we had to announce new plans and redo our manifest to play in Rice. We played there in '65, '66, and '67 and had a five-year lease. The Judge and I finally worked out an arrangement. The Oilers moved into the Dome for the '68 season. Playing in Rice Stadium rains cut crowds, so I looked forward to getting in the Dome.

Regarding the operations of the HSA, Adams revealed that he sold out his interest in HSA because of the amount of money that Roy was spending in the operation. I met with Bob Smith and told him I was unhappy—and thought the Judge was running it for his benefit and not for all stockholders. He said, "Well, I'm happy; I'll buy you out." I asked, "What about the other guys?" He said, "I'll buy you all out for what you've got in it."

Adams continued:

> That's what Bob did; he paid each of us back what we'd put in it. I had refused to put up another $100,000 until I could get a real look at the accounting. I didn't know details so I got out. I was in two major projects, the Oilers and the Colt .45s, so it looked to me like I was going to have to put out too much for both of them each year. It didn't look too good. But Roy and I got along fine. We had no cross words when I sold out.

> After I refused to put the Oilers in the Astrodome, Hofheinz made a presentation to the National Football League for a franchise. A head-to-head battle was going on with the Dallas Texans and the Dallas Cowboys and two teams for Houston didn't seem feasible. I think Roy was serious about getting a club despite there being times when Roy got word to me that we ought to bury the hatchet and come on out to the Dome where we should be—where we wanted to be. I think he would have liked to have seen some additional income. We never had had any real hedonistic sessions—it was all fairly amiable. The disagreement was on terms. In final negotiations, I didn't sit down with the Judge. Associates handled the deal for us to go into the Dome.

> It was to our benefit to go there. It is a great place to play football. I would see the Judge now and then and we had good relations. We buried the hatchet. We never had any problems on a landlord-tenant basis. Our crowds since have been about 96.7 percent capacity.

> I think it fantastic what Roy has accomplished in Houston as far as bringing in conventions and tourist dollars, enabling sports franchises like baseball and football to enjoy—now soccer is getting in—playing in the Astrodome. Roy was ahead of his time. Even if the taxpayers had had to pay for the stadium, the people of Houston really got a bargain. That probably won't happen again anywhere in the world. Seattle taxpayers put out between $50 million and $60 million, and it's not near as elaborate as ours. Neither is the Superdome. The one in Pontiac, an 80,000-seater, was built for about $48,000,000, but again it has a floating roof and is not air-conditioned, so you really can't compare the two, cost-wise. I have the highest respect for Hofheinz and what he has done for the city here.

Skeptical from the beginning that grass would not be satisfactory on the Dome playing field, Hofheinz announced three days after the opening that the next year plastic grass would be used. He did not go into details. As a matter of fact, he hadn't made a deal but felt confident he could, for he had been studying stuff he called "undertaker's grass."

Although writers across the country jibed Hofheinz and architects for daytime glare in the Dome which might cause fielders to be hit in the head trying to catch fly balls, the Judge never lost his cool. By April 14, DuPont technicians constructed test setups in Wilmington, Delaware, to study the problem. They would not guess when they would recommend a cure. "Relax," Hofheinz told questioners about the glare on April 17, eight days after the Yankee opener. "Never fear. I will not be the first man to call a game on account of sunshine." The whole thing, he insisted, would be forgotten by the time the Astros returned for their first regular season day game April 25. Hofheinz added: "We had 1735 people tour the Dome when the Astros were on the road. That's more than we drew last year against the Mets. And this is with no advance promotion. We didn't make the decision to conduct tours until 11:00 A.M. Thursday." The Judge ordered the schedule expanded. The price was one dollar. Four tours a day, at 11:00 A.M., 1:00 P.M., 3:00 P.M. and 5:00 P.M., were conducted seven days a week when they didn't conflict with scheduled events. Fourteen guides described the wonders in both Spanish and English.

Hofheinz was dissatisfied with the pace of DuPont's study of the glare. On April 18, he announced that painting crews would start to apply a translucent acrylic coating on the outside of the Dome's clear Lucite panels. The work would cost $20,000 and would be finished in three days. Hofheinz had received more than 1000 letters recommending solutions to the glare problems. "I don't know when I have been a part of so much sympathy," he said. The acrylic coating, he said, was suggested by the numerous greenhouse owners who offered solutions. The suggestion was adopted by a group of architects and engineers called in by the HSA. The light blue coating worked and no more day fly balls would fall safe because of glare. The effect that the diminution of light would have on the grass growing on the ball field was little discussed then. However, the acrylic coating reduced the daylight coming into the stadium by 25 to 40 percent, according to engineers' estimates, and field lights would have to be used during day games. The grass did become a major problem, but Hofheinz found a solution for that, too, by 1966.

Heavyweight boxing champion Cassius Clay, or Muhammad Ali as he later legally became known, visited the Dome April 17, 1965, and sat behind the Astro dugout. "The only person I've talked to about a championship fight here in this place is the president." There was a pause; then he added, "What's his name?" He was told the president's name was Hofheinz. "Yeah," the visitor smiled, "that's his name." There were those at the Dome who, if their booing when Clay was introduced was an indication, would have called the fighter other than his two names.

"That booing doesn't bother me," said Cassius. "I hope if I ever fight here, the place will be full and they'll all boo me. Then, when Patterson comes in, they can all cheer him. I'll walk out after one round and they can boo me again. That's my game . . . make 'em hate me . . . make 'em pay to see me get beat." He enjoyed a visit with Roy and Fred Hofheinz. He shadow-boxed with the Judge to show his style and without moving a muscle showed the Judge his "phantom punch." The showmanship of Clay impressed the Judge. "He's smart and he knows where the bodies lie in boxing and his business," said Hofheinz. The champion, eventually would be signed later to fight twice in the Dome, first with Cleveland Williams, a Houston resident, and later with Ernie Terrell.

The Clay-Williams fight was, according to *Chronicle* sports editor Dick Peebles at the time, "the biggest evening in Texas ring history." Gate receipts totaled $461,299, and the crowd numbered 35,470 for the event from which Clay emerged the victor. Mutual Radio paid $100,000 for rights to broadcast the fight to 750 stations, and it was carried by closed circuit television to 100 cities in the United States, as well as to Europe by satellite. Sitting at ringside were Bob Smith and John Leer. Of the evening Leer said, "The only time I ever heard Bob Smith say anything derogatory about Roy Hofheinz came when the Astrodome lights were dimmed and the Star Spangled Banner was played. Mr. Smith nudged me and whispered, 'You know, Mr. John, the Judge is as disloyal as a bad puppy, but doesn't he run this place nice?' "

After the Clay-Williams fight, a new promotions group, Astrodome Championship Fights, Incorporated, was licensed by the state of Texas. President of the company, supported by his father as chief financial backer, was Fred Hofheinz, who shortened the name of the corporation to ACE. The first purpose of ACE was to bring Cassius Clay back to the domed stadium the following February to battle with the left-handed guitar strummer, Ernie Terrell.

Comedian Bob Hope was a guest in Hofheinz's box on April 28, 1965, after the Astros had won their seventh game in a row, giving rise to the thought the club might be a pennant contender for the first time. The Judge turned to Hope and said with a grin: "We may have a real problem. If we get in the World Series, whatever will we do with Billy Graham's Crusade planned October 8-17?" When Hofheinz showed Hope the elaborate board of directors room in the Dome, Hope asked, "What time will Basil Rathbone be here?" When they got to the great Thai Temple Dogs in Hofheinz's office, Hope patted one of them and asked: "Have you had your Crest test today?" Neither could recall all the continuous humorous exchanges, but the climax came when Hope referred to the office furnishings as "Early Hofheinz Farouk."

On May 2, 1965, the Astrodome, with Hofheinz a central figure, was featured on a special live show telecast to an estimated 300 million viewers throughout North America and Western Europe via the Early Bird Satellite. It was reported to be the first time that a TV show had been seen by that many viewers. "The main thing the Europeans wanted to see was the Astrodome in Houston," said Av Westin, executive producer of the pool broadcast. Almost half of the one-hour show originated from Houston. ABC, NBC, and CBS

Pictured with the Judge during early visits to the Dome, Muhammad Ali (left) and Bob Hope (right). Ali photograph by Harold Israel, courtesy Gulf Photo; Hope photograph courtesy the *Houston Post*.

networks, Canadian Broadcasting Company, and members of the European Broadcasting union cooperated in producing and relaying the show.

The annual Houston Boy Scout Jamboree held its youth circus in the 9200-seat downtown Coliseum for years before the Dome opened. Hofheinz agreed to let Scouts put on their show in the Dome shortly after the Astros went on the road in May. The Jamboree drew 50,000 inside and a turnaway crowd of thousands outside, angry because tickets had been oversold by Scout leaders. The Scouts had never had any over-flow problem at the Coliseum. Hofheinz adviser Ben McGuire explained: "You'd meet a Boy Scout on the street and you'd buy 10 tickets from him. You didn't intend to go, you just made a donation of five dollars for 10 tickets. That didn't happen. People showed up in droves because they wanted to see the Astrodome. Roy figured he had to have about 300 events a year in the Dome to make it pay off," McGuire said, "but the Scout circus proved he had to be more selective." As the Astrodome opened, Ben McGuire said Hofheinz showed employees quickly he was meticulous about cleanliness. He commented: "Roy would walk through the Dome and if he saw a scrap of paper on the floor, he'd pick up the nearest phone and call the cleaning department and complain. Everything had to be spotlessly clean. We went to several World Series together. He saw how dirty the stadiums were, and he said his stadium was never going to be that way. This, of course, cost money. He had the Dome cleaned up after every game. He said he was going to have the best dressed people in town, in neckties and coats, with air conditioning, and he was right. He got people out to baseball games that wouldn't go in other cities."

NBC's David Brinkley watched Houston and Milwaukee in a Dome skybox May 30, 1965. He said: "It's bigger than the pyramids. It's cooler than the pyramids. It's cleaner than the pyramids. And you don't have to ride a camel to get here. It's a whole new dimension in baseball stadiums. I'm used to thinking in terms of Washington's Griffith Stadium where we had cold hot dogs, warm beer, and dirty seats. When the night haze blew in you couldn't see the outfield. The hucksters in the aisles were short-change artists, and it took an hour to get out of the ball park. Baseball here is almost incidental," added Brinkley.

Brinkley paused to watch the famous scoreboard go into its victory celebration. When it had finished, he sank back in his seat. "That's gorgeous," he said. It was mentioned to Brinkley that the Astrodome had been taking a kidding in the East, including a lot of jokes on Johnny Carson's *Tonight* show, and many other places. Asked for his opinion, Brinkley said: "I liked it before I got here. I've heard the jokes, but I like the idea of a town that is not afraid to be comfortable, that is not afraid to spend its money, that is not afraid of excessive luxury, and that has learned how to enjoy it. I don't see anything wrong with it."

When the 350 performers and 45 acts of Ringling Bros. and Barnum & Bailey Circus came to the Dome for six performances in four days, June 11-14, there was an inch and a half of rubber between the elephants and unicycles and Hofheinz's turf. When "Tuffy" Genders checked over the Dome before opening, he took one look at the 208-foot ceiling ("that's way on up there") and immediately went to New York and began buying special cable—almost half a mile of it—for rigging. The rigging for the trapezes and other aerial paraphernalia was directly from the roof of the Dome. P. T. Barnum never heard of air conditioning, but he was familiar with dollars. Since the 50,000 seats for the circus in the Dome had an average price tag of $2.75, old P. T. would have approved the Houston engagement. The circus drew 156,896 paid admissions. Attendance for the finale was 40,357, the largest single performance attendance in Ringling Bros. and Barnum & Bailey Circus' 95-year history. Pat Valdo, general director of the circus, said he had never seen such circus crowds. The circus, like all other events held there, found the Dome a gold mine, he said.

On June 25, 1965, the Astros soared over the million mark in home attendance, joining the rest of big league society in reaching that exalted figure. A crowd of 27,161 turned out to see the National League's ninth-place team play, lifting Houston's gate for 39 home dates to 1,000,329. Until then, Houston was the only team in either league never to have drawn more than a million fans in a season.

Fred Hofheinz became his father's key assistant in 1965. He agreed to work for one year only. Fred recalled:

> Dad was busy so I didn't spend a lot of time with him in that period.
>
> I took the bar examination and then, in the fall of 1964, while waiting for the bar's okay, I worked on the Lyndon Johnson election. Immediately upon the announcement of my passing the bar examination, I announced to Dad that I wanted to practice law.
>
> He called me at home one night about 10 o'clock. In those days I went to bed early because I had to get up at 4:30 or 5:00 A.M. He woke me and said, "I want to meet you in the morning at my office." We met at the Brandt Street office at 6:30 A.M. and he said, "I want you to go to work for me." I asked, "Doing what?" He said, "I'm not exactly sure, but I need help and you're the only member of my family that looks like he might be interested in being involved in family affairs." I said, "I don't want to do that, but if there is cause for alarm on your part about the critical period coming up in the Astrodome development and all you want me to do is back you up for a year, I'll do it, but I don't think you can afford me." He asked what I wanted to earn. I said I'd have to make something like $20,000 a year. In those days, coming out of school, that was an enormous amount of money. He agreed that it would be for a year. I really didn't want to get involved. I had had to borrow some money to get to the point where I was. I stayed in school so long that I was $10,000 in debt to a bank in Austin. Loyalty to the family was what got me started. That year led on to another, another, and another. It was finally the Humphrey election year of 1968 when I finally broke away. Those four years were exciting and interesting. I became what can only be described as Dad's adjutant—his staff assistant—as opposed to a chain of command. After the purchase of Mr. Smith's majority stock and near the time that my mother passed away on December 1, of 1966, I had a great deal of authority. I was executive vice-president.

Houston was amused in mid-August by "Operation Hot Dog" in the Dome skybox of Astronaut Alan Shepard, Jr. Hot dogs were not sold in the lavish skyboxes. If hosts in the high, private compartments wanted to serve guests hot dogs, they had to send butlers to a lower level to buy them. Shepard and his business associates, Bill McDavid and Jess Hall, installed a machine in their skybox which kept weiners and buns warm. They refused to pay the going rate for hot dogs on the lower levels—15 cents for each weiner and 10 cents for each bun. Each night they brought their own from outside and served them with special trimmings.

The maitre d' heard of the Shepard hot dog bypass and went to the astronaut and told him he no longer could bring his own. "What do you mean?" Shepard asked. "No more weenies," said the maitre d' and departed. Shepard slowly worked himself into a boil and called Hofheinz from his skybox telephone. Mary Frances took the message from Shepard, who told her his guests were "starving to death, like the Armenians." The secretary told Shepard she would get the message to the Judge immediately. She did and he got the ball rolling before he returned the call. He told Frank Keogh, manager of the Astrodome's food operations, to rush to Shepard's suite and find out what was going on. The Judge's return phone call and Keogh hit the Shepard skybox at the same time. Hofheinz told Shepard he could have all the hot dogs he wanted, he could bring them from outside or he could buy them downstairs if he wished. "We don't want you to starve," said the Judge. Keogh then worked it out for Shepard so he could buy hot dogs and buns at the wholesale price. Keogh posed for a picture as Shepard fed him a hot dog he prepared. There was a sequel to the incident: The next night Bill McDavid went to the skybox, but Shepard was absent, out of town. He discovered no hot dogs ready. It was not the fault of the Dome people. The butler for the box, Fred Harris, was in an automobile accident that afternoon and went to the hospital, so nobody prepared for arrival of any occupants of the skybox. Keogh just happened to check on the situation and when he did, he hurriedly made arrangements for the food to be delivered. Mary Frances was told by the Judge to check if Shepard was being properly served. She went to the box in the seventh inning and hinted that the Judge might enjoy a hot dog himself because he had heard a report that Keogh had a good sauce. McDavid prepared a package of the astronauts' baseball specialty and sent a note to the Judge, properly decorated with missile figures and a Gemini capsule. It read: "How much is that doggie in the skybox?" *Post* Columnist Bill Roberts, in detailing the hot dog story, finally reported that the "in thing" at the Astrodome in a few days was for people to buy "Shepard special hot dogs."

Observers believed that when Bob Smith and Hofheinz split, the Judge would not be able to carry out previously announced plans for a new Disney-type amusement park at the Astrodome. Hofheinz, however, who had stretched his resources to buy out the millionaire, said on August 7, 1965, that he planned to go ahead with the idea. Smith had publicly announced he would have "nothing more to do with that project." Land needed for the coming Astroworld was actually owned by Smith. Hofheinz knew he would have to acquire the property to carry out another dream, and his attorneys went to work to see if a deal could be made with Smith. Later in the year, the Judge did buy part of the land, sufficient for his coming venture.

A prostate ailment in September forced Billy Graham to postpone his Astrodome crusade until November 8, 1965. The evangelist attracted about 380,000 persons over a 10-day period. The closing Sunday crowd on November 18 drew 61,000 who overflowed every part of the giant stadium. President and Mrs. Johnson sat in Roy Hofheinz's box for the second time during the year and listened with solemn faces as Dr. Graham preached against racial tension

Dene II

increasing throughout the world. Glancing toward Hofheinz's gold-draped box, Graham remarked, "I told the president a few minutes ago I wished he would come to all our meetings so we would have this big a crowd." While he preached, the evangelist did not forget that President Johnson was the great congressional leader for enactment of civil rights laws and that Judge Hofheinz was a leader in fighting racial discrimination in Houston and Texas.

Abundant criticism of her father for his break with Bob Smith, his feud with Bud Adams, and earlier political controversies with "fat cats" of Houston infuriated Dene Hofheinz Mann who reasoned that people just didn't understand the complex Judge. She felt compelled to speak out and early in 1965 she began to take notes for a book on his career. During the first week of November in 1965, Dene unveiled her 98-page well-illustrated essay, *You Be The Judge*, copyrighted and printed by Premier Printing Company in Houston. It was a loving biographical tribute to her father. Dene said her father was "shy" about her book.

The Judge and Mrs. Hofheinz gave their aspiring author a gold copy of her book inscribed "Doll's first book—11-3-65." Mrs. Mann said the Judge didn't know about his daughter's writing effort until Bill Roberts dropped a note about the upcoming publication in his column, but he did see a final manuscript and made only three slight corrections. Reviews noted that it was not a complete biography and that it was not unbiased. Nevertheless it was read widely.

In one revealing paragraph, Dene wrote: "Daddy is a complex man of much controversy. It takes so many multi-colored adjectives to describe him that I can only venture to begin. He is a dreamer, a big thinker, a doer, and most of all, a finisher. He is both lovable and bold, rude and suave, profane and gentle, shy, yet outspoken, flamboyant, dynamic and charming. He can be or do anything he wants to be or wants to do. He is a tease, a wit, a showman, a politician, a businessman, a family man and a sportsman—all six feet, 220 pounds. He is as colorful and as complex as the stadium with which he is credited."

Paul Richards was fired as general manager of the Astros by Hofheinz Sunday, December 12, 1965. Grady Hatton was named field manager and Tal Smith player personnel director. Lum Harris, who would have been serving the second year of a two-year contract as manager of the Astros in 1965, was offered another job in the organization, as was Eddie Robinson, farm director. Other changes in the organization were left to Hatton, 1964 manager of the Oklahoma City farm club, and Tal Smith, former special assistant to Hofheinz. There would be no general manager as such, with Hatton and Smith sharing responsibility. Hofheinz said, "The move was made without rancor. It was what we thought was best for the club. I don't think reasons would benefit either Paul or the Astros. I'd rather let it stay there."

Richards had an interpretation: "The Judge thinks that Grady and Tal can run the club better than our group. That's 100 percent okay with me. It's his team. He wasn't satisfied with the progress of the team." The 57-year-old Richards had two more years to go on his $60,000-per-year contract as general manager. Hofheinz said: "We'll honor the contract." Hofheinz also said contracts with other members of the Richards staff would be honored in accordance with baseball and legal requirements.

On December 22, 1965, Hofheinz completed the $2.5 million purchase of 147.3 acres on two sides of the stadium which he and former partner Bob Smith had owned jointly. Hofheinz had put up partial payment on the land in September, and the balance became due on the payment date. The acreage was west and south of the domed stadium and part or all of it was the proposed site of the Disneyland-type recreational facility which Hofheinz had been planning for some time. "This will be the site of the Disneyland-type facility if and when it is built," Hofheinz said. Sale of the property by Smith to Hofheinz marked the first of several properties, mostly unimproved real estate, jointly owned by Smith and Hofheinz in which the partnership was dissolved. Real estate sources said the property around the stadium was worth about five times what it was when Smith bought it.

More than four million people paid to get in the Dome from April until the end of 1965. The Astros drew two and a half million and 400,000 took one-dollar tours. University of Houston's Cougars, in six home games, drew 210,106 to set a new attendance for the rising football power. Two disappointments occurred: the National Baptist Convention Musicale drew only 12,500, and, although promoted widely by producer Stan Irwin, Judy Garland was a flop in her appearance which drew only 9500 with the singing Supremes as part of her show. Seats sold for from one dollar to $7.50 each. The stadium was rented 132 nights during its first eight months.

John D. O'Connell, vice-president of HSA in charge of special events, estimated that the stadium had to be rented 125 to 150 nights each year to break even. Hofheinz never gave out financial information about HSA, but there was no doubt at year's end the organization had the know-how to pay its $750,000 annual rent and huge maintenance costs. Many events were already scheduled for 1966 as the new year arrived: a boat show, polo match, the first Houston Livestock Show and Rodeo in the Dome and Astrohall, a homebuilders show, a return of Ringling Bros. and Barnum & Bailey Circus, "bloodless" bullfights, and the possibility of a National Hockey League team and a pro team in the expanding NFL.

Hofheinz relaxed Christmas of 1965 and felt that he was ready to make more dreams come true. The transformation from being thrown out of the mayor's office to Dome maestro in just 10 years brought him great satisfaction.

31

The Birth of AstroTurf

New sights and sounds were offered in the Astrodome in 1966 as Roy Hofheinz continued at an unbelievable pace to make his grandiose ideas come true. With no one to challenge his authority as maestro of Houston's magnificent new tourist attraction, the Judge solved countless problems and set up new entertainment ventures. At the same time, he strengthened a new friendship, begun in 1965, with Irvin Feld, manager of Ringling Bros. and Barnum & Bailey Circus. Feld did not then own any part of the circus. He carried on other show business promotions as sidelines to his Ringling duties.

The biggest problem Hofheinz faced as the year began was finding a substitute for grass on the stadium's playing field. With his usual drive, flair, and confidence, he cajoled and bargained with artificial turf developers so that AstroTurf came on the national market at least four years before the experimenters believed it would be ready. The Judge's "undertaker's grass" idea, born when he was skeptical of live grass in the covered stadium, would become a reality just as he planned—before the 1966 baseball season's opening.

Architect Hermon Lloyd recalled how Hofheinz first experimented with artificial turf: "He asked Monsanto to send experimental grass, about 25 to 30 feet long, and he placed it in old Colt Stadium. He got members of the sheriff's posse to ride their horses across it. He got the University of Houston football team to scrimmage on it. It really was a show. We brought in elephants and had them urinate on it while trampling. Roy even had automobiles run over it. He became convinced that artificial turf was the answer."

Meanwhile, Texas Attorney General Waggoner Carr was urged by animal lovers to bring action to stop the "bloodless" bullfights scheduled the first weekend in February of 1966 in the Dome. He filed before Civil District Judge Wilmer Hunt a plea for an injunction to stop the show. Hunt ruled the plan of the promoter was legal and his decisions brought "olé's" from the crowd in the courtroom. It came just three days before the scheduled opening.

Judge Hunt had heard arguments from Carr that the exhibition would be illegal and rebuttals from attorneys for HSA that the "bloodless" affair was legal with the safeguards for bulls planned. "I have read the pleadings and the affidavit. . . . I conclude this will be an exhibition of skill and grace and daring rather than a fight between a man and a bull," Hunt said. "We're bound by the court's ruling, so we'll have an exhibition of skill, daring, and grace," said Hofheinz. More than 25,000 tickets to the show already had been sold, he said. The event was sponsored by International Bullfights, Incorporated, headed by Irvin Feld.

The *Houston Post* on February 7, 1966, reported on the success of the first "bloodless" bullfights: "Crowds totaling 107,257 paid $409,115 to witness the three programs in Houston. Feld admitted that he had to draw 100,000 persons to break even. 'So we realized a slight profit.' Added Judge Hofheinz, 'We are gratified at the tremendous turnout. You never go into a promotion unless you anticipate it'll be a success. The hazards were great, which we recognized. Attendance was two and one half times greater than at the average National or American League baseball game. So that gives you a pretty good idea of the immediate acceptance of bullfighting in Houston.' "

Hofheinz received from the Houston Sales Executives' Club the "Outstanding Salesman" award for 1965 at the club's 12th annual banquet February 18, 1966, at the Rice Hotel. It was the first big hometown recognition of the Judge's work for the Astrodome.

The long-awaited shift of the Houston Livestock Show and Rodeo from the downtown Coliseum to the Astrodome and the newly completed Astrohall came in mid-February of 1966. For 10 days record crowds turned out and both Hofheinz and livestock show officials felt that their long negotiations had paid off handsomely. Newspapers predicted that the annual winter show of cattle, horses and western performers would become the greatest of its kind in the United States. It did.

Another Robert E. "Bob" Smith came into Hofheinz's life just after the Judge broke with his millionaire partner. Before 1964, the second Bob Smith was vice-president of marketing of the Chemstrand Corporation, a 50 percent owned subsidiary of Monsanto Corporation and the American Viscose Corporation. He continued with Chemstrand until it was taken over by Monsanto in 1964, and stayed with Monsanto. In 1979, he recalled:

> The Chemstrand Corporation had isolated the area of recreation and developing synthetic turf. It was made from a very special nylon-type polyester with an inhibiter to give it maximum properties for sunlight degradation. We had a field installed at the Moses Brown School in Providence, Rhode Island, and had tested the artificial turf for about a year when Judge Hofheinz heard about it. That came almost simultaneously with the big problem they were having with the Dome when the outfielders could not catch fly balls.
>
> The Judge sent several people to the school to see what we were doing, and they became enthusiastic about the potential of the turf. At the same time at Monsanto, we really didn't feel we were ready for any public exposure of the product, early in the experimental phase. The Judge asked for a meeting in late

fall of 1965. He had been successful in painting the portion of the Dome to enable outfielders to have a background to catch the balls. Having done this, enough light did not get into the Astrodome for turf to grow properly. The last two weeks of the season, the field was spray-gunned with green paint.

In our first meeting, the Judge was anxious that we indulge in a research program with him in conjunction with his staff during the winter. He spoke to me and called himself the Astrodome Research Corporation and wanted to make it available at no charge to us. We agreed to work with him with no contractual understanding. At that point we really didn't know how to make AstroTurf, but we did get very serious about it with the objective of having the first installation in the Astrodome. We ultimately agreed in November that we would put in an infield in January of that winter and the Astrodome would be closed to visitors during the time it was done. The Judge said he would call in ball players to work on it. We set up a big engineering effort to figure out how we were going to install it. It was somewhat crude, but about the 17th of January, 1966, we had a full infield installed. At 9 o'clock in the evening there were 10 or 11 Houston ball players called to see it. The infield at that time was quite grainy. When players took infield practice, a ball toward short stop would end over behind third base. A ball would turn at the pitcher's mound almost at right angles. Obviously the turf was not right. Someone had the idea of swinging the infielders around and hitting the ball across the opposite direction of the turf the way it was installed. The original installation had strips of fabric that went from home plate out toward center field. Strangely enough, when the ball was hit across the infield from between home plate and the third base, the ball would perform quite normally, giving a true bounce. We concluded if we installed the infield from the third base line over to the first base line that we probably would have a good chance of success.

Hofheinz said, "That's exactly what we're going to do, and we're going to play our first home exhibition game on it." He shocked those of us from Monsanto. We didn't feel we were ready. The Judge said: "We must try it. I have a season coming up and I can't live with what I've been living with, and I think it will work and that's what we're going to do." Some of us on the scene agreed that we would go along; we would put in that infield. A baseball game was scheduled on March 30, 1966, and that was our target. About 2:30 A.M. the day of the game, we managed to complete the installation of an infield. There was nothing in the outfield at that time. About a week before we put in the installation, Hofheinz called me and he said that he felt that this was such an exciting development that he was personally flying in about 140 sports writers watching exhibition games in Florida to cover an exhibition of the turf.

In the first exhibition game with the Dodgers, I went to the Astrodome in late afternoon for a press conference. Judge Hofheinz, I thought, very cleverly had taken the original diamond that we had put in in January and cut it up in little six-inch squares, packaged them, and was selling them for one dollar each as souvenirs. We had a preliminary meeting in the Judge's office before the press conference. Warren Giles, president of the National League was there along with Paul Runge of Chemstrand-Monsanto. The Judge gave specific instructions. He said he was going to run the press conference, that he would answer practically all of the questions, and that if anything of a technical nature was asked, I should answer. He looked at Giles and he said, "Warren, if anybody asks you a question, don't you answer with more than one word, either *yes* or *no*." Giles said that was fine by him.

We faced the writers sitting in the grandstand between home plate and third base. The Judge indeed answered all of the questions except one very picayune one I handled. Toward the end of the conference, Red Smith, sports ace of the New York *Herald Tribune*, looked up and said, "I'd like to know what Mr. Giles thinks." Giles moved forward and I said to myself he can't answer yes or no. He grabbed the microphone and said, "Great!" We at Monsanto studied the rules of baseball and there was a phrase that worried us which may have involved playing baseball on grass. The dictionary definition of grass didn't quite gibe with what we were doing. We confronted the Judge with this one night. He picked up the phone and he called Mr. Giles in Cincinnati. Roy said, "I don't want anybody like Mr. Wrigley in Chicago who hasn't even gotten modern enough to put lights in his stadium to come around and say that this isn't grass. Just tell me that stuff you saw is grass." Apparently Mr. Giles said it was grass.

On March 30, the first four innings of the first game on our turf was routine baseball. Most of the balls hit were ground balls to the infield. We were amazed and delighted. The next to the last batter in the end of the fourth inning hit a ball that went down the first base line—it just about took the first baseman's arm off. The field was fast. During the course of the game there were several balls that went through between the outfielders at a pretty good clip. After the game we had a meeting on the field of about 12 engineers. One of our engineers said, "We could slow that field down." I remember the Judge looking at him and he said, "Forget about it, son. Give me nothing but three-base hits."

One day when we were working there, tours of the Dome were in progress. The Judge looked at me as we watched: "Bob, I get these people in here and they give you a dollar and they go through those doors and get back on the bus, and I never have a chance to get back in their pockets. You know, I think I'm going to build me a big park and find a way to trap them."

Hofheinz was so positive in his thinking and actions, he gave Monsanto the vehicle to move ahead on AstroTurf. Big companies tend to research things to death, but there was no way we were going to keep that man from putting that turf in. He was really what we needed to get us out of the dream world.

The Judge was terrific. He arranged many things. One of the things that made the first infield difficult he didn't tell us. Suddenly in the middle of our work on how the subsurface had to be compounded and put into shape for the rodeo in the Dome, he brought in about 18 inches of sand for the first Houston Livestock Show and Rodeo in February for the playing field. We had to go back and work that whole thing over again. But he would do anything for us. Because our group had the courage to come in and do it and stand up to our

Standing on AstroTurf in the new Dome (left to right): Bob Smith, the second man of that name to play an important role in Hofheinz's life; the Judge; and Red Smith, sports writer for the New York Herald Tribune.

management, he gave us testimonials. There was one thing which aggravated him tremendously. We were a little smarter than he was—one time only—and without telling him, we registered the name AstroTurf. He thought that was very improper, that anything with the name Astro was his, although he didn't control it. But we just moved faster than he did. I was always impressed with . . . the way he worked with the organization.

To install AstroTurf in a major league playing field required approval of club owners. "How can you have baseball without grass?" "How can AstroTurf be legal in our league?" were questions thrown at Giles. He recalled he said to doubters: "I'll tell you what I'll do. If you show me in the rule book any place where it mentions grass, I'll buy you the best dinner you've ever had." That stopped the questioners. Deep down, I was a little skeptical myself, but it worked out great. It's been a revolution, especially helpful where playing fields were not covered. Roy first showed baseball could be played under cover and could be played on AstroTurf.

Faith, Hope and $5,000, the Story of Monsanto, written by Dan J. Forrestal and published by Simon and Schuster in 1977, records the impressive history of AstroTurf: "In 1966 no one appreciated that the AstroTurf trademark would become the most widely used of all Monsanto trademarks. The big event that brought [it] into being was the erection of the Astrodome in Houston. . . . The only big advantage that was slow in coming to Monsanto was profitability for the inventor. It took seven years for the product to get in the black. A strong assist in achieving profitability came not from baseball or football, but from the lowly doormat. Starting in 1969, millions of AstroTurf doormats were sold, bringing not only profits to Monsanto but also a new, yet relatively risk-free, adventure into the often-troublesome realm of consumer merchandise."

Hofheinz's organization at his constant urging established a Spanish radio network covering 83,000,000 people on 82 radio stations in 13 countries throughout Mexico, Central America, South America, and the Caribbean for the 1966 season. The network was sponsored solely by the Astros with the enthusiastic support of the United States State Department, the Pan American Union, and the commissioner of baseball. The network operated for every Astro Sunday game with Rene Cardenas and Orlando Sanchez Diago at the microphones.

"There are many reasons for the operation of this extensive network," said Hofheinz. "First, it creates tremendous interest in major league baseball in general and the Astros in particular throughout countries that have shown interest in baseball. Second, we feel that it creates a great deal of goodwill for our country, and presents a product that is common to people of all languages. Third, there are many fine young players developing in these countries, and it is our hope that they will come into U. S. baseball through the Astros. We have scouts in these areas who should now have an easier time communicating with the Latin players about the Astros and the Astrodome."

The 11 countries in which the Astros' games were broadcast were Mexico, Guatemala, Honduras, El Salvador, Costa Rica, Panama, Columbia, Venezuela, Puerto Rico, Dominican Republic, Netherland Islands, and the Virgin Islands. "These broadcasts are a great step toward furthering international relations, and the project has my enthusiastic endorsement," said General William Eckert, then commissioner of baseball. "My desire is to promote baseball, not only in our country, but throughout the world. I compliment the Astros' management for their progressive steps in this direction."

George Kirksey sold his two percent interest in HSA to Hofheinz on May 9, 1966, giving the Judge 88 percent of the stock. Bob Smith held on to 10 percent while Earl Allen and John Beck each kept one percent. The exiting executive vice-president, original promoter of major league baseball for Houston, said he would take his first vacation in five years in Europe. The exact amount Kirksey was paid for his stock was not announced; speculation was $200,000, but friends said he could live the rest of his life in ease.

Kirksey said his parting with the HSA was amiable. "I will continue to have a close attachment to the Astros and feel they have a bright future. The only other thing I want to say is that I think the Astrodome is the greatest athletic facility ever built and that there is no second." Hofheinz said, "George made a real contribution to securing major league sports for Houston and to the success of the Astrodome. He leaves the HSA as a good friend and we all wish him well."

The baseball world was saddened May 30, 1971, when Kirksey was killed in an automobile accident in Aix-les-Bains, France, on one of his frequent trips abroad. The administrator of Kirksey's estate set up a scholarship at the University of Houston in memory of the news writer who turned promoter of top baseball in the Bayou City.

Although he had learned in 1965 he could not personally own a National Football League team as long as he owned the Astros, Hofheinz nevertheless seriously sought a team to play in the Dome in competition with the Oilers. Along with representatives for six other cities, he made a presentation in Washington to the directors of the National Football League May 19, 1966, for award of a franchise to Houston with the John Mecoms as owners. Hofheinz and the senior Mecom had several talks with NFL owners. Mecom said: "The NFL wants to go south and is bound to settle on Houston or New Orleans. I'll take a franchise either place." Mecom said he did not think he'd have any trouble getting together with Hofheinz on the Dome rental—the issue which drove Bud Adams to Rice Stadium.

Before the Washington meeting, Pete Rozelle, the NFL commissioner, had visited the Dome during the 1965 baseball season. When Hofheinz introduced him to a baseball crowd, boos of Oiler fans drowned out applause for the commissioner. People were asked to stand if they wanted NFL football in

Houston; about 1000 got up and booing went on. Bob Smith, who had just broken with Hofheinz when Rozelle visited the city, said, "Mecom and his son are nice people. I'd go along if they tried to bring a team here. The Mecoms never do anything in halves." Hofheinz's elaborate presentation to the NFL did not win Houston the franchise. It ultimately went to New Orleans with the rich Mecoms operating it first in Tulane Stadium and later in the Superdome.

Singer Andy Williams and Henry Mancini and his orchestra appeared in the Dome on June 5, 1966. Williams had heard that acoustics in the stadium were not good for Judy Garland's show and he checked the sound on his arrival. He told a press conference: "All my fears about the sound have been dispelled by 10 minutes of singing out there on the mike. I don't know what happened since Judy Garland was here, but it has. I'm really delighted with the sound. It's so different than it was before." He said Mancini wasn't worried about the sound at all. The show was the first of its kind for Williams who found time to visit with Hofheinz and get a grand tour of all the Dome sights. Williams liked the Judge so well that he decided to send him a present from Hollywood . . . a specially gold plated shower head engraved "To the Judge—The man who has everything except a good shower head." Hofheinz has the memento in his home today.

Ringling Bros. and Barnum & Bailey Circus returned to the Dome for six performances June 16-19. Wolcott Fenner, representing the circus, announced in advance a much changed show, including a tiger on horseback, an act which had attracted international notice; the Cosmos, three intrepid fellows riding motorcycles on a wire strung across the Dome; Colonel Seabright, doing a one-hand stand 158 feet up on a swaypole; and Captain Astronaut, who was shot from a cannon across the Dome's expanse. Another featured performer was Celeste in the Moon, whose personal gymnasium was hooked to the Dome's gondola 208 feet high.

Hofheinz had more than baseball on his mind when he hired Stan McIlvaine as a vice-president of HSA in June of 1966. As a former general manager of the minor league Houston Buffs, McIlvaine knew baseball, but for five years since leaving the Bayou City, he had been an executive with the Great Southwest Corporation which controlled the Six Flags Over Texas amusement center near Arlington, between Dallas and Fort Worth. "We feel fortunate to have a man of Stan's experience and know-how in the organization," Hofheinz said. "He will be working in many facets of our ever-expanding organization as my special assistant." Hofheinz gave no hint that McIlvaine would have any key role in the operation of his planned amusement park, but the coming Astroworld was the ultimate reason. There still was much planning before Hofheinz could start construction on the park. McIlvaine was hired to provide the benefit of his experience with Six Flags Over Texas.

When the Chicago Cubs were in last place during 1966, manager Leo "The

Lip" Durocher told Joe Donnelly, *Newsday* sports writer, in anticipation of playing the Astros again in the Dome: "I'm waiting for a big box filled with cherry bombs, torpedoes, firecrackers, sparklers, the works. It's the answer to all that stuff they pull in the Astrodome when the home team hits a homer. Houston is 'bush.' When one of my guys hits a homer against them, we'll make as much noise as their scoreboard. If the umpire complains we're holding up the game, he's gonna have to wait until I get through celebrating." (He changed his attitude when he later was manager of the Astros.)

Total attendance to all events in the Astrodome in 1966 went above the seven million mark on October 15 when the University of Houston played host to Mississippi State in football. The game attracted 45,000 fans. Attendance through October 10 to all events since the Astrodome opened totaled 6,992,191, including nearly five million persons at major league baseball games (more than four million officially paid attendance to regular season games).

At the annual dinner of the Interfaith Charity Bowl, Incorporated, October 11, 1966, at the Sheraton-Lincoln Hotel, Hofheinz was honored as "Mr. Sportsman of 1966." A capacity crowd seated elbow to elbow heard the Judge praised for the leading role he played in making the domed stadium become a reality from a fantastic dream of the modern world. The stadium could not have been built without the cooperation of members of the Commissioners Court and the taxpayers of Harris County and they, too, were honored.

Bullfights returned to the Dome on October 20, 1966, for three performances. Featured were eight different bullfighters. The array of matadors and rejoneadores was headed by Antonio Ordoñez, referred to by the *Encyclopedia of Bullfighting* as the finest toreador of the generation and a favorite of the late famed author Ernest Hemingway. Ordoñez is featured in many of Hemingway's stories on bullfighting. Sharing the spotlight with the Spanish matador was the reckless but colorful Jaime Bravo of Mexico, who delighted Houston's earlier audiences with his daring and devil-may-care courage; Gullermo Carvajal, the champion bullfighter of Mexico and Felipe and Gonzalo Zambrano, the world's leading rejoneadores, or bullfighters on horseback.

On November 18, 1966, officers and directors of Houston Consolidated Television Company, owner of KTRK-TV, Channel 13, recommended sale of controlling stock in the station to New York's Capital Cities Broadcasting Corporation. The purchase agreement stipulated that local management would continue to operate the station and that John T. Jones, Jr., would continue as president and Willard E. Walbridge as executive vice-president and general manager. Chief stockholders were Jones, president of the Rusk Corporation, which held 32.45 percent, and Roy Hofheinz, vice-president of Houston Consolidated with 16 percent.

Capital Cities is a publicly held company listed on the New York Stock Exchange. News commentator Lowell Thomas was listed among the principal stockholders. The New York-based firm owned radio and television properties in Albany and Buffalo, New York; Paterson, New Jersey; Adams, Massachusetts; Durham, North Carolina; Providence, Rhode Island; Huntington, West Virginia; and Detroit, Michigan. Other officers of Houston Consolidated were Wright Morrow, board chairman, and B. F. Orr, secretary. Additional directors besides the officers were Aaron Farfel, Thomas W. Gregory, Jr., Howard T. Tellepsen and Gail Whitcomb; George Bruce was treasurer. The sale price was not announced, but Walbridge said later Hofheinz got about $6 million for his share.

Dr. William B. Cockroft of Memphis, president of United Inns, Incorporated, confirmed on November 26, 1966, that a Holiday Inn was planned for 1967 across from the domed stadium. He said it would have about 500 units. Hofheinz was then dickering with a number of major hotel and motor hotel chains to build facilities on his property. It was understood then the Judge would be included in a percentage of profits.

On December 28, 1966, Hofheinz was awarded a franchise in the new North American Soccer League. He announced that in the summer of 1967, Houston would have a kickball club, imported from some place in Great Britain. The NASL was the only sanctioned, 100 percent league to operate in the U. S. There had been a war of sorts until the NASL crowd got together in the Dome. The league signed a contract with the United States Soccer Football Association which in turn was blessed by the approval of Fédération Internationale De Football Association (FIFA), the largest athletic group in the world.

"This is the greatest day in the history of our sport in the United States," said Jim McGuire, the new commissioner of the NASL. "Within seven years we may be the outstanding professional sport in the country. By 1984 the U. S. may be the soccer power of the world."

Judge Hofheinz said the new league planned a schedule from April through September in 1967 in 12 cities to be represented by a top-ranked foreign team. In 1968 the league would shift to a mixture of American and foreign players under a contract system similar to that of major league baseball. Hofheinz said the league had representatives in Europe and Latin America and the lineup of foreign teams would be announced by January 15.

Thus Judge Hofheinz completed another eventful year in the development of the Astrodome. His pioneering efforts would spawn imitators. However, this year of triumph also brought Hofheinz the most despairing day of his life—December 1, 1966.

32

The Death of
Irene Cafcalas Hofheinz

The brain tumor of "Big Dene" Hofheinz often sent her to bed for extended periods as she suffered from violent headaches. She entered Methodist Hospital in Houston for a checkup early in 1965, and her husband accompanied her. After she took an elevator upstairs, Dr. Ed S. Crocker, long the family physician, saw the Judge and stopped him to say, "Everything will go fine. We'll do our checkup and she ought to be able to go home tomorrow."

The Judge, anxious about the pain of his great love and supporter, said, according to Crocker, "I want you to tell me who is the best brain surgeon in the world." Dr. Crocker recalled: "I answered that we had talked about her condition for 10 years and I felt the tumor was arrested and no surgery was necessary. I told him brain surgery was the most serious operation any human being could have, that in her case of acromegalia, the center of the brain had to be entered." He said Hofheinz replied, "Well, by God, what's causing her headaches?"

"I explained to him," said Crocker, "that Dene had meant much to me and my family and I felt an operation would be too dangerous and it would be better to continue medication. I had her charts and felt strongly her ailment was arrested. That didn't satisfy him."

Mrs. Hofheinz also was not satisfied to continue with her debilitating situation. Her condition was worsening. She went to Mayo Clinic for tests and returned to Houston for treatment at Kelsey-Seybold Clinic, a research unit connected with Mayo. After further extensive tests she was told by her doctors that her only possibility for an extended life was surgery. The Judge and his wife agonized the alternatives. It was she who felt she should take the risk of the delicate operation.

According to Phil Baldwin, friend of the family from Albion, Michigan,

Several weeks before Mrs. H. had her surgery in New York, I spent some time with the Judge and her at the "Loose Goose" hunting camp. The Judge loved to cook and was preparing dinner. Mrs. H. and I took a walk around the lake in front of the camp. She told me about her problem and that the doctors were suggesting an operation. She was trying to decide what to do. She knew

Roy and Dene Hofheinz. **Photograph by Harold Israel, courtesy Gulf Photo.**

the Judge was concerned and had reservations about it, but she didn't want to live her life incapacitated—she wanted to be her full self if she were to live. I told her I had had an uncle who had had the same problem and the same surgery and it had not come out well for him. By the time we finished our walk she had made up her mind to have the operation. She was trying to figure out how to present it to the Judge so that he would understand that it was the only thing to do. She definitely knew the hazards but felt she couldn't live her life as things were. That was the last time I saw Mrs. H. She was an absolutely magnificent person. She had depth beyond comprehension. She had knowledge.

The Judge was desperately fearful of the surgery, but if Dene wanted it, seeking relief from pain, he would agree to it. He made arrangements. Knowing the seriousness of the problem, he asked his son, Fred, and his son-in-law, Scott Mann, to go with Mrs. Hofheinz and him to New York. He also called Roy Hofheinz, Jr., in Boston and asked him to join them. All four men were uneasy but cheerful with Mrs. Hofheinz as they escorted her to a hospital on Saturday for preparation for the surgery on Monday morning.

Mrs. Hofheinz underwent what surgeons called a successful operation. For 36 hours it appeared she might be on the road to recovery. Suddenly, on Wednesday morning her condition became critical. The diagnosis was that her heart was failing. She died at age 54 after opening her eyes and talking to the family men gathered around her bed. It was December 1, 1966, the blackest day in the life of her husband, who immediately began to blame himself because he had agreed to the operation when Dr. Crocker had warned against it.

Spec Richardson was in Columbus, Ohio, at a National League meeting which Hofheinz skipped because of the urgent New York trip. "I was called out of a meeting in the Pittsburgh Hilton and told to telephone the office in Houston," Richardson recalled.

> I got Mary Frances and she said, crying, "I believe Mrs. H. is dead." I went back to the meeting and told Warren Giles and Walter O'Malley. I left for New York and went to the Roosevelt Hotel to join the Judge, his sons, and his son-in-law. We came back on the plane with Dene's body. Dene had left a mink hat in her hotel room. I took it by hand to the plane, not packing it for some reason. As I was going down the aisle with it, the Judge said, "Put that thing away." Many met us at the airport. As we got off the plane, the Judge said to me: "Will you make sure Mama's body gets into the hearse and to the funeral home?" I did as he went home.

Fred, Roy, Jr., and Richardson went to a cemetery, seeking a lot for Mrs. Hofheinz's burial. "The prices asked," said Richardson, "were outrageous, so the children decided to place the body in a mausoleum because they didn't feel their mother would have wanted them to pay $125,000—yes, that's right— $125,000 for a lot. They said they would move the body from the mausoleum later."

Services were held at 11:00 A.M. December 4, at St. Luke's Methodist Church. Dr. Charles Allen, pastor of the First Methodist Church, officiated. Pallbearers were H. B. (Spec) Richardson, Ben McGuire, W. Ervin (Red) James, Waddell Moursund, James J. Braniff, Jr., Gould Beech, Ed Bruhl, Stuart Young, Joe Louis Holiday and Albert Lopez. Survivors included Mrs. Hofheinz's mother, Mrs. Ethel Foster, and two sisters, Mrs. Mary J. Rau of Houston and Mrs. Diana Meek of Dallas.

The *Chronicle* editorially remarked that

> Houston lost one of its most gracious and beloved first ladies in the death in New York of Mrs. Roy Hofheinz. To know Dene Hofheinz was to like her. This applied even to the political opponents of her husband during his long public career as state legislator, county judge, mayor and now owner of the Houston Astros. Her graciousness was extended to all. Thousands who knew her considered her a model wife and mother. No matter how fast the pace of the family's activities, Mrs. Hofheinz kept its members closely knit. Roy Hofheinz many times publicly credited her with being his chief source of inspiration. She was a stabilizing factor in his victories and a comforting rock of loyalty in his defeats. With sorrow Houston will pay its last respects to a great lady.

Bill Roberts, columnist of the *Post* who first gained prominence with the then defunct *Press*, wrote in "The Town Crier" the same day:

> It was with intense grief that we heard of the death of Mrs. Roy Hofheinz yesterday. She was possibly the friendliest, warmest, least pretentious human being we have ever been around. I do not think she ever changed by one fraction during all these years, even when her husband was doing all sorts of great things. . . . She was a lovely, lovely human being. . . . I shall miss her very much. We shall miss her very much.

Dene II said her mother's death left the Hofheinz family "tumbling and crumbling. The family unit lost its strongest link. Dad was greatly despondent, as were we all. I remember setting up a room for Dad at the little house in which Scott and I lived with our two boys. He stayed with us just one night and then went on back to the Astrodome and very rarely left the Astrodome after that."

Richardson and Grady Hatton were with the Judge almost every day for 30 days after the funeral services. "The only antidote to the Judge's grief after a few days," said Richardson, "was for him to go back to work. He was holed up, so to speak, until the end of the year, but he finally realized that couldn't bring Dene back and his very nature dictated that he must move on with the hotel complex and Astroworld he had already announced. Grady and I and others made sure that he was never left alone during his days and nights of deep mourning."

After he attended services for Mrs. Hofheinz, Dr. Crocker said he drove out the Katy Highway toward his own ranch in a bordering county.

> I passed the road to the "Loose Goose" with a feeling that Roy was there. I had not talked with him. I turned around at the next highway cut-off and drove back to the road to the retreat. When I got to the "Loose Goose," I saw a number of people had gathered. As I entered, Roy walked up to me and put his arms around me and his head on my shoulder. I could have later been wrung out with his tears. He didn't say a word, just stood there holding me and sobbing. I finally said, "Roy, I'm sorry. You know what Dene meant to me when I was having troubles with my wife and she was the one who helped with my children." Not uttering a word, Roy turned around and went to his bedroom. I went over and sat down with "Little Dene." She said to me, "Oh, Doctor Crocker, I'm glad to see you." I said, "Honey, this is a difficult thing. I know your Daddy did what he thought was best." She said, "Dad keeps saying you told him of the danger." And I replied, "I did tell him that—unfortunately."
>
> Roy came back into the room and listened as Dene and I talked. I turned to him and said, "You agreed to what you thought was best. Don't look back. Forget it now, or it'll eat you alive." He said, "Thank you," but from that day on until April of 1978, I didn't see him as a physician again. It took him 17 years to return to me as a patient.

Dr. Ed Crocker

The doctor-patient relationship of Dr. Crocker and members of the Hofheinz family went far beyond normal professional association. Dr. Crocker treated "Little Dene" after she had nervous problems and regularly checked the Judge and Mrs. Hofheinz over a long period. It was "Big Dene," however, for whom the physician had a great affection because of her attention to his children when his first wife suffered nervous breakdowns and had to be hospitalized in Galveston.

Dene's sudden death raised financial problems for the Judge also, for as Fred Hofheinz recalled:

> My mother's will (and my father's) were structured in order to fund a major loan to Dad to purchase the Smith stock. In those days before the Tax Reform Act of 1969, it was advisable to form foundations in estates against federal income taxes to take care of children and grandchildren's interests and of interests of creditors. Two trusts were structured in her estate. No one expected her to die, but she did, and that put all of the financial machinations of Roy Hofheinz into a tailspin. Under the Texas community property law, every dollar that my father had and virtually all of his property was community property. With the death of my mother, half of the property he controlled went into probate. It was a terribly confusing period.

Hofheinz made application on January 31, 1967, to Harris County Probate Court to probate the will of his wife. Mrs. Hofheinz left her personal property to her husband, $2 million in real estate and securities to the Hofheinz family Trust Number 2 and the remainder of her estate to charity in Trust Number 1. Hofheinz was named as independent executor in the will. Heirs to the estate were her three children: Roy M. Hofheinz, Jr., then 31; James Fred Hofheinz, then 28, and Dene Hofheinz, then 23. Under provisions of the will, the part of the estate left to charity should be added to the Roy M. Hofheinz Charitable Foundation, which was created by a trust agreement dated August 1, 1965, to be used for religious, educational, or charitable purposes.

It took until May 8, 1968, for appraisers James J. Braniff, Jr., and John P. Sommers to complete and file an inventory of Mrs. Hofheinz's estate in Probate Court. They listed the total value at $8.5 million. The inventory valued her interest in the Hofheinz family real estate at $7.6 million; stock, $2.8 million; checking accounts, $37,000; miscellaneous accounts receivable, $93,000; mineral properties, $4778; and a variety of other assets, $200,000.

Mrs. Hofheinz's estate represented half of the holdings of Roy Hofheinz at the time of her death under the Texas community property law. Financiers figured the other $8.5 million kept in investments and property by her husband had skyrocketed in value during 1967, although debts on new enterprises since her death mounted heavily, too. Beset by grief and financial turmoil, the Judge responded with the only antidote for his situation—landing new enterprises and making dreams come true.

33

New Enterprises

Without his faithful Dene to check on his health and his habits and to give advice, Hofheinz lived most of the rest of his active years in his Astrodome suite. Lavish food always was ready for him. He fought unsuccessful battles against smoking 24 cigars a day, wore horn-rimmed glasses and developed a Santa Claus physique. The weight on his six-foot frame dropped once from 235 to 200 in a "good health splurge," but as he wheeled and dealt at all hours of the day and night, he gained it all back and added more each year. He kept telling friends he would take off weight when he had to do it, but heavy eating was too much a part of his life.

It was in his seventh level box and his main office on the first level of the Dome that the Judge, using telephones constantly, ran Astrodome properties and made deals for new enterprises for his growing complex. Hofheinz's desk in his main office was 12 feet long, shaped like a boomerang and made of rosewood with an inlaid black marble top, carefully designed and crafted by Stuart Young. The desk was flanked by a pair of six-foot oriental "Temple Dogs," their fangs bared, carved of teak and with wide gold collars and curling gilt goatees. The desk was kept clear except for a gleaming gold telephone. A Hofheinz-designed Mondrian-style wall held three television sets which could be on simultaneously and movie and slide projectors behind sliding panels which were controlled by an elaborate system in the Judge's desk. Behind the desk were thinly cut panels of Mexican onyx with rheostat-controlled lighting behind. Beautifully carved 18th century Chinese wood panels, delicate gilded filigrees of people, and plants and animals, decorated the wall. Plush royal blue rugs covered the floor.

Hofheinz called the adjoining board room, "our own little Versailles." The walls were covered with antiqued mirrors divided by gold-leafed, bare-breasted caryatids. In the center of the far wall beneath a suspended red velour ceiling canopy was a great red velvet and solid brass chair. The walls were lined with a fabulous set of ornate brass straight arm chairs and side chairs. In the center of the room was a huge rosewood and gilt conference table surrounded by plush black velvet easy chairs.

Secretary Mary Frances devoted almost every day and many evenings to screening visitors, making appointments, and relaying the Judge's orders to executives. She also kept in close contact with "Little Dene," and saw Fred, the vice-president, almost daily. Her devotion to and admiration of her boss was indispensible to the Judge.

Maxine Mesinger said in the *Chronicle* on January 24, 1967: "If anyone is wondering what the construction is around entrance 13 at the Domed Stadium, Judge Roy Hofheinz, who has a two-story, two-bay wide skybox apartment, is enlarging it to a five-story, four-bay apartment. Word is the Judge will have a private bowling alley, barber shop, beauty salon, and even a baby-sitting room for entertaining VIPs."

The World Boxing Association approved a title fight between Cassius Clay and Ernie Terrell for February 6, 1967, in the Dome, the second appearance of the champion there. Sports writers from all over the world converged on Houston. They reported much jawing between Clay and Terrell. Headlines also revealed that the draft board of Louisville, Kentucky, had announced Clay would be subject to the February draft call and that the champion had responded that he would not go into the armed forces.

A crowd of 37,321 paid $400,145 to see Clay win a unanimous 15-round decision. He received $200,000 from admissions receipts and $400,000 from ancillary earnings (including closed circuit television). Terrell was paid $80,000 and $140,000 out of the two sources of income. Dome rental was $70,000. The promoters earned $50,000 at the gate and $80,000 from ancillary receipts.

Hofheinz announced on February 10, 1967, that Houston's entry into the new North American Soccer League would be known as the Houston Stars and would play in the Dome. He said: "We think the name Stars for a new professional sports entry in Houston, Space City, U. S. A., logically carries our space theme. The Stars should be a compatible tenant with the Astros in the Dome." The soccer team planned to play about eight games at home and eight road games in 1967, beginning in late May. The Stars' insignia was on an olympic-type shield with white lettering and seven white stars on royal blue on the top half of the emblem. A line drawing of the Dome was centered on a field of red and white stripes on the lower half of the shield.

Houston was one of 12 cities in the new league sanctioned by the Fédération Internationale Football Association. FIFA worked with all clubs to select the best teams available from throughout the world. Other cities represented were Boston, Chicago, Cleveland, Dallas, Detroit, Los Angeles, New York, San Francisco, Toronto, Vancouver and Washington, D. C. Teams from Scotland, Stokes City, and Sunderland in Britain, Italy, Ireland, Czechoslovakia, Mexico, Peru, Brazil, Holland, and Portugal were considered to find players to stock the forerunner of soccer popularity in the U. S. in the late 1970s.

Hofheinz hired Geza Henni, Hungarian-born coach of the United States

Olympic soccer team, as coach and director of player personnel. The 40-year-old Henni, formerly was one of the world's best players and considered one of the most knowledgeable soccer men in the world. "Mr. Henni's services were sought by virtually every new professional soccer team," Hofheinz said. "Fortunately for us, he accepted our salary offer to come to Houston. We now feel that the Stars have the best coach available and we will endeavor to have the best team and provide the best entertainment in the Astrodome in the soccer season ahead of us."

Henni did not coach Houston's imported team for the 1967 season but directed an extensive recruiting program in order to organize the Houston club for succeeding years. He was to coach the Stars in competition beginning in 1968. Hofheinz was a leader in getting the league organized. Again, he was years ahead of the public in his belief that soccer would some day become popular in the U. S. as well as other parts of the world.

Asked why he became interested in adding soccer to the Dome, Hofheinz said: "Very simple, I took my family down to Mexico to see a soccer game without telling them why. When it was over, I asked them: 'Number one, did you understand the game?' They nodded yes. 'Number two, could you follow the ball on every play?' No trouble, they told me. It was easier to follow than football or baseball or any other sports. 'Number three, did you see the action of all the players?' Again they all said yes. 'Number four, did you appreciate the niceties of the game as they were shown by the players?' They said it was a great and wonderful thing. I said, 'Fine, you've answered all my questions. We're going into the soccer business.' " The Judge then explained the logic of his reasoning: "In the Astrodome, if an event has special appeal to ladies and children and is of a nature they can understand, without a great deal of education, then those ladies and children will come out. And whenever they come out, the men will follow. The men, of course, pay the bills."

On March 7, 1967, John Wilson, *Chronicle* sports writer, commented that it looked like Houston's sentiment about Hofheinz might be changing to general favor. He wrote:

> A short time ago I was in a conversation with a wealthy and influential Houston businessman, a sometimes foe of Hofheinz. He said, "It would be a sad day for Houston if Roy weren't there to operate the Dome."
>
> This seemed something of a turnabout, or at least an indication that the wind may be shifting on the opinion of Hofheinz held by many Houstonians . . . due to the bonanza in world publicity and local dollars that the revolutionary stadium off South Main has been to the city. . . . They include the taxi drivers, restaurant owners, hotel and motel operators, and a varied collection of other businessmen whose profits benefit directly from the activity stimulated by the stadium.
>
> The public has assumed Hofheinz is driving relentlessly for money. Others have believed it is for power. Some have suspected he just likes to get the

best of a deal. His defenders say he just likes to accomplish things. The money angle is out. Nobody knows for sure, but those with the best educated guesses say he could cash out now for a minimum of $10 million clear and possibly as much as $20 million. Yet, he remains, holding 88 percent of the stock and locked up totally in hock to a venture in which the stadium rental and maintenance alone have burgeoned to an annual cost of $2,700,000. . . .

Power, in the usual sense of the word, isn't the answer either. Hofheinz has refused to compromise—or even adjust—his stand in cases where his instinct and political experience had to tell him were debilitating causes. It has been suggested he wants to leave his mark on Houston—that he will have been a man who was a predominant force in this era that has seen Houston burst from the bounds of provincialism to one of the world's best known cities.

"I think everybody has a little of that in him," Hofheinz answered when asked if he had ever considered the possibility. Turning to something more tangible, Hofheinz said, "If the Dome is a success, if we succeed in this whole thing, and I am sure we will, my family—children and grandchildren—will benefit because we have business interests outside the stadium itself and to which some of the benefits will accrue."

With the enemies he has made, the ill-feeling left in the wake of his own implacable will, the image created by his sometimes disregard for public reaction, Hofheinz may not again hear that big hurrah. It is hard to tell whether he wants it or not. If his goal has been to leave his mark on Houston, he is an unqualified success. Hofheinz recognizes his detractors. Sometimes he is not too generous in his assessment of them. "I started with nothing and when you're climbing the ladder there's no place they can kick you but in the rear."

The additions to Astrodome facilities, first chit-chatted by Maxine, became officially known March 23 when D. M. Dozier, the stadium's maintenance manager, asked Commissioners Court for a permit. Dozier got the permit three months after he had actually started work on office space and recreational facilities in the right-field wall of the Dome. When Dozier ultimately asked approval, some commissioners acted surprised, but County Judge Bill Elliott said: "We heard about the remodeling and asked Dick Doss, the county engineer in January, to look into it. It came out that no building permit had been obtained." Elliott said the county's investigation prompted the Houston Sports Association to get a permit and to seek commissioners' approval. Elliott also said the court had instructed Doss to keep commissioners informed on the remodeling.

Bill Giles confirmed that the recreational facilities to be offered President Johnson and other visiting dignitaries would be a bowling alley, pool table, steam baths, putting green, and "possibly a swimming pool." Giles said the remodeling was 30 to 40 percent complete and would probably be finished by July but would not be open to the public "just as our business offices are not open to the public." He said the area under construction was "blocked off to everyone . . . as of the moment."

Hofheinz told commissioners the remodeling was behind a portion of the scoreboard from the fifth to the ninth level. The permit was to install structural additions, an elevator, and additional space for bleachers on levels five, six, seven, and 10. An observation deck was to be built on level seven and a half. The work was to be done at HSA expense and constituted permanent improvements to the county's property, Hofheinz said, adding: "No stadium seats or services will be affected by the changes. We believe the additions, in keeping with the decor of our offices, will be of great benefit to us in obtaining and servicing conventions and other great events in the structure." Giles described the new facilities as a "place where distinguished guests can stay in unusual and luxurious surroundings."

Millionaire Bob Smith did not exit completely from Hofheinz's life after he sold all but 10 percent of his HSA stock to the Judge and then made deals to separate their jointly owned property. Smith's attorneys filed suit in State District Court to prevent the Houston Sports Association from offering any additional stock for sale unless the former Hofheinz partner had first opportunity to buy it. On April 9, two years to the day after the Dome opened, District Judge Wilmer B. Hunt denied Smith's plea for an injunction, upholding arguments of David Searls, an attorney for HSA, that the association had no plans to issue any stock and had the legal right to deny preemptive rights to present stockholders if and when additional stock was issued. Smith's testimony maintained that denial of such right would tend to dilute the value of stock he held.

With its convention facilities expanding with the decision of the National Association of Home Builders to have its 1969 sessions in the Astrodome and Astrohall, Houston leaders, especially Hofheinz, campaigned during the spring and summer of 1967 to entice Democrats and Republicans to hold their presidential nominating conventions in the Dome the next year. Each party was offered $650,000 to give the Bayou City the nod. With Lyndon Johnson in the White House, Hofheinz had great hope his fellow Texan would influence the Democrats' decision in favor of the state's largest city. Mayor Louie Welch and many other political leaders in Texas and Washington helped apply pressure.

Committees from both parties visited Houston, saw the Astrodome, the hotels being built next to it, and those already in existence. The University of Houston promised Hofheinz its dormitories would be available for delegates if rooms were needed. A major problem developed, however. Both parties announced they wished to hold their conventions in the same city to reduce the costs of communications and national press and TV coverage. Chicago and Miami Beach offered the parties $750,000 each.

The presidential suite Hofheinz ordered built in the right-field wall of the Astrodome was primarily designed to accommodate President Johnson. But the Judge also planned to offer the facility to other political and business leaders who might hold conventions in Houston. The suite consisted of a reception room, a sitting room containing French antique furniture with its original Aubusson tapestry, and a bedroom done in gold and dusty turquoise in addition to the magnificent bath. Between the reception and sitting rooms was a staircase spiraling around an ancient marble statue of the goddess Minerva. The staircase led to another elegant bedroom, this one for the president's daughters. The two parties finally decided to accept Chicago's bid, a great disappointment to the Bayou City, but an especially heartbreaking one for Hofheinz. Lyndon Johnson never slept in his friend's expensive presidential quarters.

Mary Frances Hofheinz recalled that when Judge Hofheinz was given the news in Washington, D. C., just before a dinner honoring President Johnson, that the Democratic site selection committee had chosen Chicago for their 1968 convention, Hofheinz said, "Oh no! I can protect Lyndon in Houston. I have 240 acres behind fences which I can control. They can't give him that protection in Chicago." The Judge was concerned about the unrest regarding the Viet Nam war. No one else in the room truly understood the Judge's remarks at the time.

When the World Boxing Association dethroned Cassius Clay as heavy-weight champion because of his refusal to be drafted, it decreed a round of elimination matches. Hofheinz's ACE bid for some of those bouts. On June 29, 1967, the *Chronicle's* McLaughlin wrote: "The Terrell-Spencer and Ellis-Martin 15-rounders will be run back-to-back (another Domed Stadium first) on Satur-day afternoon of August 5 and will be carried live on the American Broadcast-ing Co.'s 'Wide World of Sports' program. Floyd Patterson and Jerry Quarry are scheduled for a late-summer bout in Los Angeles, while Oscar Bonavena and Karl Mildenberger are scheduled for a September 15 match in New York tentatively."

Ever alert to protect Hofheinz interests, the Judge held a press conference July 31, 1967, and fired a boxing volley heard around the world. Joe Heiling of the *Post* reported:

> Judge Roy Hofheinz slipped on a pair of boxing gloves and fired a stream of well-aimed punches in several directions. A fight billboard would have advertised it this way: Houston's Astrodome vs Madison Square Garden. The portly, cigar-smoking Hofheinz squaring off against the big daddy of prize fighting. He opened first with these assertions: 1) The Astrodome, as repre-sented by Astrodome Championship Enterprises (ACE), is battling Madison Square Garden in New York for the title of fight capital of the world; 2) The Garden, with ex-Houston boxing promoter and manager Lou Viscusi in the picture, is throwing roadblocks into Saturday's opening round of the heavyweight elimination tournament; 3) Local promoter Earl Gilliam is the Garden's representative in the struggle, as evidenced by young heavyweight Joe Frazier's boxing an exhibition on a Dave Zyglewicz-Willi Besmanoff card at the Houston Coliseum.

"The scrap is about which city will be the fight capital," said Hofheinz. "It will either be Houston with the Astrodome or Madison Square Garden in New York. Every roadblock in the world has been thrown up by Madison Square Garden." Hofheinz earlier chose to ignore the rival card to his Saturday production involving Ernie Terrell, Thad Spencer, Jimmy Ellis and Leotis Martin. The whole punching match burst into the open, however, when aging Eddie Machen announced he would not appear on the Coliseum show—that instead of fighting, his mind was more on retirement. Gilliam was unable to accept this explanation from the one-time heavyweight contender who is under suspension in his own state of California since his age is over 35. Speaking out, Gilliam hinted that Machen was paid money—more money than he would have earned fighting here—to stay in California. Only ACE would profit from such an unethical payoff, he insisted.

This was when the Judge's doctor became worried about his patient's blood pressure. "I don't think it's good for anyone to say," protested Hofheinz, "that we tried to buy off a cripple they couldn't get in the ring in the first place. Everyone knew Machen was unacceptable as a fighter even in California." What Hofheinz did resent were the rumors, the innuendos, that something shady was going on. . . . Hofheinz said that his group's efforts are above-board and that noticeable by its absence is the monkey business associated with the underworld characters who run the fight game. "We haven't tried to tie up the world as Mr. (Jim) Norris has in the past," he said, "or as Madison Square Garden would like to do. All we are trying to do is: 1) Elevate boxing to a position never attained by the sport before; prize fighting can be presented to the public as a sport, same as any other; 2) Do a great job for the Astrodome; 3) Do a great job for our city, which has to sustain us all."

On July 27, 1967, Hofheinz took the Astros' paperwork out of Grady Hatton's hands and passed it along to Spec Richardson, saying, "Here, take care of this, will you?" As nonchalantly as he elevated the busy Richardson to the job of general manager of the baseball club, Hofheinz also announced a one-year extension on Hatton's contract as field manager. Previously, Hatton held the dual position of manager and general manager, chores he frankly admitted were too detailed and involved for one man. Relinquishing the title freed Hatton, in his second year as skipper of the Astros, from the business end of things, allowing him to focus his full efforts on molding a winning team on the field.

"When I first hired Grady," Hofheinz remarked at the press conference, "I thought he would be a great manager some day. I still think so. I think he'll prove it in due course." Hofheinz elected to give Hatton, 44, another year to live up to this show of faith. The Judge did not hold the former third baseman of the Cincinnati Reds responsible for the Astro's 10th place station. Instead, he pointed the finger of blame at injuries and the heavy demands of military reserve duty which affected five players each month and which cost the services of prized righthander Larry Dierker for the season.

At the same time, those in attendance were assured that, "We will leave no stone unturned in not only putting an interesting ball club on the field, which we already have, but a winning ball club as well." As general manager, Richardson had the final word on trades and such, but he left no doubt that consultation with Hatton would precede any move. Most of all, however, Richardson had the complete confidence of the Judge, and their closeness continued day after day and year after year.

The Astros were in 10th place in 1967 when Richardson became general manager. In four months, he proved he was a man of action—and tough. He fired field manager Hatton's coaches and assembled a new staff which had ex-relief pitcher Jim Owens as the lone holdover. He levied heavy fines in a get-tough policy with curfew violators on the team and lectured players sternly on behavior and attitudes in a closed-door session near season's end. He became the final word on all trades. Richardson took a strict business approach with the attitude: "If you can't do the job, I'll get someone who can. I've got a job to do and if I have to step on toes, I'll do it." He proved to be a man of his word.

After acquiring land and planning for more than four years, Hofheinz formally announced on September 16, 1967, that a great family entertainment center, Astroworld, would open in the summer of 1968. He did not disclose the possible cost, but investment men said it would represent an investment of $25 million. Hofheinz said 56 acres would be developed and landscaped for rides, a theatre, lagoons and waterways, restaurants, shuttle trains, ice cream parlors, and fruit juice stands. Another 60 acres would be available for future development, he said. Hofheinz would bring to Houston what Walt Disney gave to Anaheim, California—Disneyland. Hofheinz said Astroworld would be "an elaborate, high quality, multimillion-dollar family amusement and entertainment center." And the Barnum in Hofheinz said: "This is destined to become the world's greatest tourist attraction, bringing untold millions of dollars into the Houston area economy." He promised 2000 tons of central air conditioning, "four times that of any other outdoor amusement park," including Six Flags Over Texas. The air conditioning would be blown on all shade areas, including waiting areas, picnic umbrellas, and many of the rides. He said the 240 acres of the stadium parking lot would be used to park more than 30,000 cars in time for Astroworld's opening. Tram trains would transport visitors to the main entrance of the park on a bridge crossing over the South Loop (Interstate 610) connecting the Dome parking area with the park. Brilliant Randall Duell of Randall Duell and Associates of Santa Monica, California, designed Astroworld. He had previously done Six Flags Over Texas. Landscaping the bald prairie site of the park was a major problem, Hofheinz said. The low-lying land needed a fill of 600,000 cubic yards of earth. More than 10,000 trees and thousands of bushes and flowers would be planted, he said.

Stan McIlvaine, former executive with Six Flags Over Texas, was appointed general manager. A staff of 1200 was planned to operate the park.

About 1000 would be college students from the Houston area during the summer months. The park, said Hofheinz, would have a single admission price, about $4.50 for adults, less for children. The park would be able, according to Hofheinz, to accommodate 20,000 persons per hour. He expected the park to draw 1.6 million visitors a year, including 800,000 from outside Harris County. That many visitors, he estimated, would funnel $25 million into Houston's economy.

A Houston investment firm, Ben G. McGuire & Company, handled the financing for the construction through three banks: Houston Bank and Trust, Mercantile Bank of Dallas, and the Chemical Bank of New York City. Three major insurance firms would handle long-term financing, said Hofheinz. They were the New England Mutual Life Insurance Company, Prudential, and Great Southern.

Two weeks after telling of plans for Astroworld, Hofheinz announced details of a motor-hotel complex across from the Astrodome. He had promised it to the National Association of Home Builders for their 1969 Houston convention. Total cost of the complex was reportedly $18 million.

Hofheinz said the project would be developed in two stages. The first phase, to include construction of four motor hotel facilities with a combined total of 982 rooms, was scheduled to be completed in the summer of 1968. Two additional motor hotels were planned later, he said. The first phase included Astroworld Motor Hotel with 444 rooms in three buildings, including an eight-story structure; Holiday Inn-Astroworld with 258 rooms in four buildings, each with two stories; Howard Johnson Motor Lodge-Astroworld with 144 rooms in four two-story buildings; and Sheraton Inn-Astroworld with 136 rooms in five buildings, each with two stories.

Construction work would begin in 30 days. "This is another step in our efforts to make Houston the most attractive convention and tourist center in the world," Hofheinz said. There would be a total of 2800 beds in the complex with all rooms having two queen-sized beds, color TV, separate vanity and dressing room, and intra-room phone service to allow persons to dial any room in the four hotels, Hofheinz said. He added that the motor hotels would be constructed around a central recreation area-playground. The recreation area would have gym equipment and a lake.

Each room was planned for closed-circuit TV, permitting guests to view the playground area, the amusement park, a convention, and other functions (except sporting events) in progress at Astrohall or in the Astrodome. Each hotel also would have two lighted and heated swimming pools, one for adults and the other for small children, and a restaurant and coffee shop. All facilities except Howard Johnson's would have private clubs. A covered walkway between hotels, a large auto service center, and convention rooms were included in the plans. Parking facilities for 1800 cars were charted.

The Houston Sports Association rendered two Astrodome values for tax purposes to Harris County collector Carl S. Smith on October 1, 1967. One was for one dollar for the stadium lease and another for $1.6 million for personal property. Carl Smith insisted that an $11.3 million valuation of the Dome set by his tax office be used to collect from the county's lessee. Because HSA paid the county $750,000 annually for the lease and did maintenance work, its lawyers contended that, for tax purposes, one dollar was proper. During hearings Hofheinz said he would sell the lease for one dollar if someone wanted to take over the rental and maintenance costs, at a total of more than $1 million a year. One group humorously got notices in the papers that it would pay Hofheinz for the lease, but no one came forward with a serious and responsible offer to take up the Judge's challenge. The city also sought to place the same property valuation on the Dome, but, when separate county and equalization board hearings were held, the HSA's figure of one dollar was upheld. Only County Judge Bill Elliott, at odds with Hofheinz, voted for the big valuation. Mayor Louie Welch, longtime Hofheinz opponent, upheld the one dollar value, saying the legality of the situation was far more important than his dislike of Hofheinz.

On December 1, 1967, National League owners agreed at a meeting in Mexico City to expand to 12 teams no later than 1971. Hofheinz, a growing power among baseball owners, was named on a committee to establish ground rules for the expansion. The appointment of the Judge created surprise, for it was widely believed that the Houston club viewed with apprehension the bid of Dallas-Fort Worth for an expansion berth.

How did Dick Butler, who represented the Dallas-Fort Worth ownership of Lamar Hunt and Tommy Mercer, feel about the Judge's being on the expansion committee? Butler said: "We don't mind a bit. As far as I know the Judge has never said that he opposes our application. If it turns out that Dallas-Fort Worth qualifies to be accepted by the National League, I think he'll vote accordingly." San Diego and Dallas-Fort Worth were called by sports writers the front-runners for the two berths.

"I neither propose nor oppose any city," Hofheinz said, carefully dividing the words into two syllables for oratorical emphasis. "I won't make up my mind," he added, "until the blueprint has been established under which the city and ownership will be considered. When we get to that point, we'll know what the complete specifications are, what the tab is going to be, what's involved, what's required on the part of the city, and what will be expected of the owners. I don't think it's any secret that the last time baseball expanded it was done improperly, on our part and theirs. We didn't know what the cost would be or anything about the player-stocking plan. We went in with a hell-roaring application and came out with a franchise, and nine months later we got around to discussing a player plan."

The Judge was asked how he felt about the talk currently making the rounds that he held the fate of Dallas, 275 miles away, in his hands. "There's not much I can do about whatever the talk is," answered the Judge. "It has the same price today that it had yesterday. It's cheap, no matter where it came from." A unanimous vote of all 10 owners was required to approve the National League's expansion, but only seven votes would be needed to accept two more cities.

In trying to assess Houston's position toward the Dallas-Fort Worth cause, baseball experts had to decide how much—if any—the presence of a second major league team in Texas would hurt the Astros. They said it would cut into Houston's attendance, but some of this might be recovered by the natural rivalry that would flower between the cities. A more critical point involved the intrusion on Houston's radio-television territory, which brought a handsome sum into Hofheinz's pockets.

Hofheinz earlier had been appointed on the television committee of the National League. That committee and one from the American League set up agreements for game-of-the-week telecasts. The first color telecast of a game was offered the nation from the Dome by NBC.

34

Two Hucksters
Buy Ringling

Roy Hofheinz and Irvin Feld had two things in common—each was a huckster from teenage days, and each was a promoter who wanted to offer high quality entertainment better than the paying public expected. Each was successful in various enterprises before the friendship started in 1964. It was inevitable that their fertile show business brains would bring them together in huckstering the public and also that their strong individualism would clash and ultimately end their association. The story of how they bought Ringling Bros. and Barnum & Bailey Combined Circus, Incorporated, from John Ringling North in Rome on November 11, 1967, was typical of the drama each relished. Hofheinz and his three children and Feld and his family formed the Hoffeld Corporation in Delaware as the vehicle to buy the circus. Everything about the new corporation and negotiations with North was "hush-hush" except for hints in *Variety* that the ailing 97-year-old "Greatest Show on Earth" was for sale, probably to Feld who was the salaried operating manager.

Feld, a native of Hagerstown, Maryland, born May 9, 1918, was six years younger than Hofheinz. As a high school student, he worked with his older brother, Israel, in selling a "snake oil" liniment at various carnivals. One summer at the bottom of the Depression, they were reported to have made $500. That led them to producing an imitation vanilla and lemon extract product which they later sold along with the "snake oil." Irvin graduated and, by age 22, owned a drug store in a black section of Washington, D. C. He produced all sorts of advertising signs and gimmicks to entice a flow of customers. The store had a circus atmosphere, and the great talker and seller of products within it was Irvin. Feld loved music and musicmakers, and records blared as he thrived with the variety drug store. By 1940 his flair for selling led him to form Super Music City, a record corporation of which he was president through 1956. In 1954 he became producer for Super Attractions Incorporated and booked singing stars and other performers in cities throughout the nation. On March 5, 1946, he married Adele Schwartz, and their union brought two children, Karen and Kenneth. From 1954 through 1974, Irvin produced, as a sideline, the annual Summer Series of entertainment for the Department of the Interior in Washington. He also produced and presented a number of top show business attractions, including Frank Sinatra, Harry Bellafonte, Andy Williams, and the Beatles, and he was personal manager of pop singer Paul Anka from 1957 through 1964. He ran the circus and other enterprises from his Washington office.

When Hofheinz persuaded Feld in 1964 to change the 1965 schedule of the circus to include Astrodome appearances just after its opening, the Judge and his family and Irvin Feld and his son, Kenneth, found they had much in common when they were together in Houston. The Judge had called Feld in to promote the Dome's "bloodless" bullfights. He and the Houston Sports Association took gambles in unprecedented Astrodome attractions—and made money.

Feld said that, when he first began managing the circus, it was in bad shape. John Ringling North left the United States forever after his deal with Feld in 1956 and went to Switzerland to live. He had a second home in Rome. The next few years were horrendous for Feld, he told reporters. The circus was bedeviled by various heirs suing for control. John and Henry Ringling North and their sister owned 51 percent of the stock, but John's interest was controlling. Other heirs were called "the 49ers" and went into Florida courts seeking to oust the Norths.

Feld went to the Excelsior Hotel in Rome for a conference with North early in 1966. He offered to buy the circus, Feld said, and North told him that if he could get together $8 million in cash and bring it to Europe with him, he would sell out. Feld said he made it clear to North he wanted 100 percent of the circus stock.

Feld recalled that he had a telephone call from Hofheinz who said: "You're one hell of a guy. You forget your friends. You are going to buy the circus and you didn't even call me. You know I love the circus." Hofheinz had resources and credit—millions more than Feld. As usual, Hofheinz wanted controlling stock if he invested in the circus. In the formation of Hoffeld, the Judge became chairman of the board with 55 percent of the stock jointly owned by his three children and himself, and Feld, president and chief operating officer, with 45 percent of the stock, partly owned by members of his family. Feld had an equal voting voice and was secure as president, but actually the Judge and family trust owned a majority of the capital stock and options.

Waddell Moursund, who was with Houston Bank and Trust Company at the time, said, after searching the money market, that he was able to set up a meeting for Hofheinz and Feld to see officials of Wells Fargo Bank in San Francisco, the president, Richard Cooley, and John F. Holman. The meeting went on for hours, and the bank officials asked pertinent questions, Moursund said. Irvin Feld became upset and things got tense, and the bank officials asked Feld to leave the meeting. They then worked out the financing arrangements with Hofheinz, the man on whose credit and reputation they were basing the loan.

There was a whirlwind of trips, conferences, legal technicalities, and agreements to be made for the $8 million—all with great secrecy. Both Hofheinz and Feld feared Florida suits by Ringling heirs might stop North's decision to sell out.

In 1978, Bill Giles told the most vivid story of Hofheinz's trip to Rome to buy the circus. He said:

> It was the most exciting and unusual event in my life. The Judge called me into his office on a Tuesday and said, "Do you and your wife, Nancy, have passports?" I said, "No, Sir." He said, "Well, you have to have a couple, one for each of you, by 9:00 A.M. Thursday." Mary Frances made arrangements with the passport people, and we got packed.
>
> The Judge told me: "I can't tell you where we're going, but pack for about 10 days and meet me at the Houston airport." We didn't know what we were doing, but we got somebody to take care of the kids and we were at the airport on time. The Judge handed us a Pan American leather folder in which were plane tickets for around the world. He said: "All I can tell you is you're going to all those places. I can't tell you why." We flew to New York, changed planes, and took off for Rome. Halfway across the Atlantic, the Judge explained to our group that we were on our way to Rome to buy the circus from John Ringling North. He said we were going to check into the Excelsior Hotel under assumed names because there were other groups trying to buy the circus and we had to move fast and without letting the other groups know what we were doing.
>
> On the flight, the Judge asked me, because I was the publicity and promotion man for the Astrodome, to work with Lee Solters, who was also on the flight and joined us in New York. Solters is a New York public relations man. The two of us, the Judge said, were to work together on publicity of the event. I decided that, in order to make real national news, we needed a good prop or two for the picture we were to take in the signing of the papers. It would be a great idea to have a lion as a decorative part of the signing, for that would have a better shot in making national magazines. I went down to the bell captain's desk and asked if anyone knew where I could rent a lion. It kind of threw them, but they pointed me in the direction of the Rome zoo. At the front entrance to the zoo there was a photographer with a little lion cub. After trying to negotiate with his speaking only Italian and I English, we finally negotiated a deal where he would rent me the cub for $85. We got to the Colosseum just in time to meet the Judge, Feld, and John Ringling North. It was there, with the lion cub in the background, that Hofheinz, Feld, and North completed the signing for the purchase of the circus.

Commenting on Hofheinz's trip to the Italian city, Morris Frank of the *Chronicle* cited the adage " 'See Rome before you die.' Well, [Hofheinz] saw Rome. And to make it even, Rome saw him. No doubt both were impressed. The builders of the Colosseum must have envisioned someday you would make

Rented lion cub looks on as signing for the purchase of the circus is completed. Left to right in the Roman Colosseum: Irvin Feld, the Judge, and John Ringling North. Photograph courtesy the Houston Sports Association.

your appearance there, Roy." Of rumors that Hofheinz had purchased Ringling Circus while in Rome, Frank wrote that the "guy who could write a supplement to Webster's dictionary without dangers of plagiarism," answered his questions about whether or not the reports were true with a chuckle, saying "Every man has to have his props, you know." In summary, Frank said that "This circus is known as the Greatest Show on Earth—and that's a fitting place for the Greatest Showman."

Asked about the price of the circus sale, HSA attorney Bill Dwyer said that newspapers reported about $10 million. He added:

> My recollection is it was more like—actual investment money put up—$8 million. In arriving at that $10 million figure, they added the value of some employment contracts with the Norths and things of that nature. When the circus later merged into Mattel, I believe the value was about $48 million, of which about $28 million to $30 million in stock went to Hofheinz interest.

After Dene Hofheinz's death, the Judge made arrangements so that the family trust, the three children, would have an equal interest with him in all of the basic assets. He even sold them part of his interest in order to equalize it so that they would own a half interest through the trust and he would own a half interest. He was an extremely dedicated family man, in spite of some of the problems that occurred later between him and the children. He wanted to do the best he possibly could for the children. That attitude never waivered.

When Hofheinz bought majority stock in Ringling, he called Milton Gougenheim, Mary Frances' estranged husband and said, according to Gougenheim:

"We have just bought Ringling and I need for you to get down to Sarasota as quickly as possible and get a handle on that outfit and find out what we've bought and get the job done as you see fit. You are the boss as to how you are to audit the circus." Weeks later, after the Judge had made a few trips to Sarasota and the circus left for its annual tour, we all met in the Judge's office high in the Astrodome and began discussing the various assets the circus had and what kind of valuations we might have. The Judge pinned me to the wall with his questions. He asked: "Gougenheim, what do you think our gorilla, Gargantua the Second, is worth?" I replied, "Judge, it's going to be tough placing a value on him; he only cost $600 as a baby." With that, the Judge raised his voice and said, "Gougenheim, that damned gorilla is worth at least $1 million, you dumb ass." I told him he was off his rocker, and he quickly hung me out to dry with his second question: "Would you please tell me where I could find in captivity another healthy 850-pound gorilla named Gargantua the Second? Can you tell me that?" The Judge was right again.

Attorney Dwyer recalled:

The first time the relationship of Feld and Hofheinz became strained was the first year the circus came to the Astrodome after the two men bought control. The Judge was convinced that the circus would do well if it would play in the Astrodome area for as long as six weeks. In the past it had never played anywhere longer than a week except six weeks at Madison Square Garden where it was always a sell-out. The Judge thought the circus would do as well in Houston. In order to get the circus to stay six weeks, the Judge had to guarantee the circus a minimum income. The Judge did everything within his capacity to try to keep attendance up, but the booking was too long. Hofheinz was required to honor his guarantee. The Judge felt Irvin should have adjusted somewhat on the terms of the guaranty agreement, but he did not. The loss was about $100,000.

Later there were situations where the Judge wanted to use his circus stock as loan security. There were concessions he wanted from Irvin Feld to make his stock more attractive for borrowing purposes, and Feld was pretty unrelenting. He was concerned about his own stock and maintaining his position in the voting trust as president. He was not willing to make any concession at all that would in any way tend to jeopardize that. That's when relationships started getting more strained.

Did the Judge himself contribute any ideas to the circus? Dwyer answered:

> Yes, not much in the acts, but in some of their plans. For example, they were going to make contracts with toy manufacturers to pattern toys after circus clowns and animals. The Judge and Feld talked at great length about things of that nature.
>
> The Judge went to Florida during circus training. He loved to watch the performers and animals. The Judge and Feld continued to own the circus until after I left as resident attorney in June of 1970. Even after I left, the Judge kept me on the board of directors of the circus, HSA, and Astroworld Corporation. I was with them once a month. When I left, the Judge told me my last assignment was to find my own successor. I talked to Bill McDonald and he took over when I left. I escorted Bill to "Huckster House" to meet the Judge, and they seemed to hit it off pretty well. The Judge hired him. I accepted my new assignment.

On February 12, 1969, the Securities and Exchange Commission announced in Washington that the owners of Ringling Bros. and Barnum & Bailey Circus had decided to open the famous 98-year-old operation to public ownership. New shareholders would, in effect, have the opportunity of being part owners of more than one circus, for, as stated in the prospectus, Hofheinz and Feld had elected to split the original into two units, thus touring twice as many cities in 1969 as the single operation had reached in the past.

Ben McGuire recalled that the Judge was adamant about the design for the Ringling stock certificate. He wanted circus wagons, clowns, and the like to appear on what would be "the most beautiful stock certificate in the world." Harper Goff was chosen as the designer, and his creation prompted many people to buy a single share simply for framing. The document was so attractive, according to McGuire, that, when the circus merged with Mattel, the Ringling certificates were returned to stockholders marked "cancelled" so that they would be kept as mementoes.

With the division of the circus into two units came the need for additional clowns. Hofheinz and Feld, therefore, hired 42-year-old Fred Miller, himself a former clown and curator of the state-operated Ringling Museum in Sarasota, to train new funnymen—the backbone and trademark of any circus. As dean of the Ringling Bros. and Barnum & Bailey Circus College of Clowns in Venice, Florida, Miller hired a professor from Florida State University to teach the elements of comedy, and he called on some of the world's greatest clowns to pass on their secrets. After eight weeks, 30 clowns—selected from more than 1000 applicants—graduated and were assigned to the two circus units. Miller, who would do anything he could to preserve the circus he loved, stood ready to train more clowns for the future.

The Judge as a clown. Photograph by Harold Israel, courtesy Gulf Photo.

Mr. and Mrs. Ben McGuire were with the Hofheinzes on a trip to Germany during a circus talent hunt. McGuire recalled: "We drove from Frankfurt to a little town to see Gunther Gebel-Williams. Williams Brothers Circus was performing there. It was Gunther's birthday. After the show, Williams' adoptive mother had a party for him at the circus. We were invited and it was an interesting occasion. Irvin Feld made deals for talent—but the Judge came up with all kinds of circus ideas. Hofheinz and Feld worked out a deal for Ringling Bros. to buy the entire Williams Brothers Circus including star Gunther Gebel-Williams, all performers, tigers, elephants, horses, etc., to be intermingled with the present Ringling Bros. and moved lock, stock, and barrel to the U. S. A. Hofheinz said then that at the end of five years the circus would be worth between 30 and 40 million dollars. He was right. The Mattel deal proved that."

35

Tales of Hofheinz

From the time he became interested in major league baseball until he retired, Roy Hofheinz kept a constant watch for talented people to whom he could delegate the hundreds of tasks his fertile mind created. No organization as large as the Houston Sports Association could have functioned well without a variety of intelligent people in whom the Judge had confidence. The general public was not aware of the Judge's aides because the media concentrated mainly on Smith and Hofheinz.

Spec Richardson in 1978 recalled his early days in baseball when he was general manager of Houston's Triple A franchise, the Buffs, and an opponent of Hofheinz. Hofheinz needed to buy the Triple A territory as a condition to operate his baseball franchise, and Richardson represented the Buffs owners during the negotiation stages of the deal. As it turned out, Richardson and Hofheinz were tough bargainers, and the squabbles between the two men often reached heated dimensions. This was when Richardson said he learned that Hofheinz "was the man who made final decisions, and the price of the Buffs was going to be in his lap." And so it was. The Buffs' territory was sold to Hofheinz at "his" price. Hofheinz had his franchise and Richardson was out of a job. The day after the Buffs deal was set, Hofheinz offered to make Richardson business manager of his new club. "In hiring me, Hofheinz said, 'All I want you to do for me is to represent me as you did the people you've been working for. Every time I turned around in trying to buy the Buffs, you have had a log in the road for me to fall over.' "

Hofheinz's demand that he have things his way never ceased. He wanted a new facility to house his baseball club, and nothing short of that goal would suit him. Associates quoted Hofheinz as saying there were three ways to do jobs—the right way, the wrong way, and the Hofheinz way. Some associates of Hofheinz felt differently. Spending millions of dollars on a new stadium for a major league club would be too grandiose, too big for the Houston Sports Association and its stockholders to face, some felt. The old Busch Stadium when remodeled would suffice, they argued. That was not good enough for the

Judge, Richardson remembered. "I'd like you to meet me at the Colt Stadium site tomorrow morning at seven. We're going to turn the first spade of dirt for the stadium, and I want you there," Hofheinz demanded of Richardson. In Florida at the time, Richardson managed to get back to Houston for the groundbreaking and the days of building the temporary stadium.

In typical Hofheinz fashion, the Judge had given construction workers only about seven months to have Colt Stadium completed before the 1962 major league season began. "We worked 20 hours a day. Sometimes we'd go out and measure by flashlight something he wanted built," Richardson said. "Those were hectic months, but he got the job done through sheer determination, imagination, and his great knowledge of building."

Talbot "Tal" Smith arrived in Houston in 1960 to work for the HSA when Roy Hofheinz was little more than a distant name to him. Initially his role with the HSA was in player personnel. Smith, recalling his early years with the HSA and when he was farm director in charge of the team's development program under the general managership of Paul Richards, said, "On my first day I went to Brandt Street house. That office was quite a departure from what I had been exposed to previously in baseball because the Judge's personality and his flamboyance were expressed in it. He was in his 'working kitchen' where he used to stand, walk, and keep many devices and closed circuit television at his fingertips."

Smith said he and Paul Richards were not compatible. In 1978 he recalled the day in early 1963 that he learned Richards was going to fire him. Smith said it was then he decided to accept a position with the Cleveland Indians. "I told the Judge I was going," he recalled. "He thought for a minute and said, 'You know, we have broken ground on the construction of the Dome.' He asked me to reconsider and stay in Houston as his personal assistant with much more responsibility and to coordinate the construction of the Dome with the engineers and the contractors and everybody else involved. The Judge fully realized that I didn't particularly have any background for that work, but I guess his offer was a result of my two and one-half years of employment." Smith accepted the position and from that time until December of 1965 he and Hofheinz had a close relationship.

Smith said 1965 was the toughest, but happiest, year for the Judge. He added: "I worked for him directly until December of 1965, when he terminated Richards. We grouped again, the so-called triumvirate of Spec Richardson, Grady Hatton, and me. Spec became virtually the only person in that organization to whom the Judge gave a lot of time. Spec made most of the major baseball decisions from that time on. Grady was named vice-president and director of player personnel. Spec was business manager, really the strong voice in the operation."

Smith remained with the HSA, but disenchantment with his position

grew. "For one reason or another, my relationship with the Judge deterio-
rated," he said. "The Judge's time became limited. He began to isolate himself
more, became more of a man in the ivory tower, very little communication with
a lot of the staff. He depended on Spec almost exclusively. I felt that Spec was
his principal confidant, perhaps even more than Fred, his son, who was still
there."

Smith observed Hofheinz's two wives closely during his long tenure at the
Dome. He said:

> Dene Hofheinz, in the early years of the baseball team, went to spring
> training in Apache Junction and Cocoa. During construction of the Dome, I
> spent many hours with the Judge at "Huckster House" and his other retreats.
> During hot, muggy Houston summers, we'd go down to Galveston Bay and the
> Judge would recharge his batteries. My wife and I had two small children, and
> the kids really loved that place. Mrs. H. and Mary Frances and other folks often
> were there. The Judge would spend half the day sleeping and then he'd get up.
> Somebody would be out crabbing off the pier and bring the crabs in and he'd
> prepare his own concoctions and boiled crab. He loved chili and eggs ranchero
> with all the spices you can imagine. Sometimes a lot of employees would be
> down there, and they all felt they had to eat what the boss cooked. If you like
> hot, spicy food, it was delightful. This was when the Judge was at his best
> because people in those days would have done anything for him. He was warm,
> and even though he was demanding, you felt a bond with him. Mrs. H. was the
> most charming and gracious woman I've ever met. I'm very fond of Mary
> Frances, who is just completely devoted to the Judge. With the Judge's illness,
> she carried on as if it were no burden.

Smith and Fred Hofheinz had offices next to each other in the heyday of
the Dome. Smith recalled: "When Fred was still at the University of Texas and
we were at Colt Stadium was my first exposure to him. He worked some in our
radio and television station network. He began to learn about the intricacies of
the business. Fred became more or less counsel. There was much legal work in
conjunction with the Astrodome, what with our contracts and our leases to
other users of the facility. He was actively involved in the negotiations and the
drafting of agreements and the protection of the club's interests." When asked
if he felt Fred became his father's right arm after he finished his education,
Smith answered, "By that time Spec was undoubtedly the Judge's right arm to
the exclusion of almost anybody else."

Tal Smith said Hofheinz and the controversial Charlie Finley "had more
impact in the last 20 years on the marketing and merchandising of baseball than
anybody else," although he added that the 1979 Oakland owner was not an
equal to the Dome creator in promotional ability. He added:

> The Judge's principal love, I used to hear him say, was the circus. He
> would gladly have traded places with Barnum. I'm sure that he was a Barnum

Paul Richards

in his own right. I saw his love of building, designing, and decorating. That's where he made his mark, from that standpoint of taking baseball out of something that was just a game with drab uniforms and drab surroundings and completely revolutionizing it with comfort and color. He was a master promoter. The Judge was always at his best when he could be selling, putting together a pitch. The Judge created in the minds of other baseball owners and administrators new ideas—playing fields and the ancillary things that could be done for increased attendance and patronage. I think he's the only man who could have fought his way through all the obstacles, political and public sentiment, to pull it out. The Astrodome and Hofheinz will always be synonymous.

Living in semi-retirement in his old home at Waxahachie, Texas, in 1978, Paul Richards reflected on his four years as general manager of HSA. "The big reason I went to Houston from Baltimore was the strength of Bob Smith. I would not have gone to Houston had not I thought that Smith was the dominant force. I never, in my wildest expectations, even felt that Bob would get out of the picture. As long as Smith stayed with HSA, I had no interference."

Richards' assignment with the HSA was to build an expansion club. He said:

The most important thing about an expansion club is building an organization and fortifying it with good scouts, which we did. The Judge did not realize what an expansion club needed. We did.

When I arrived, the Judge was working on the domed stadium. He took an interest, of course, in the ball club, but not enough. There was no doubt about Roy Hofheinz being a very brilliant man, but I've got to say he made a lot of childish mistakes that just surprised me completely. One was that he surrounded himself with people who were prone to flatter him.

He gave a little too much authority and took a little too much advice from people who were not exactly friendly or cooperative with the baseball program. That was a bad situation.

Richards saw the conflict between Hofheinz and Bob Smith develop and watched the day arrive when Hofheinz bought control of the club from Smith. Richards remained with the HSA until Hofheinz made Grady Hatton his general manager. When Richards was fired, he was bitter but that did not interfere with his respect for Hofheinz. "The Astrodome could not have become a reality without him," said Richards. "Roy did for Houston something that no other person ever did. You can't deny that Hofheinz has been a great asset to Houston. If it ever came up that I had some kind of problem, if I had my choice, I'd rather have Roy Hofheinz on my side."

For almost 10 years Bill Giles was the public relations and promotions director and vice-president of the Houston Sports Association. In 1978, as executive vice-president of the Philadelphia Phillies, Giles recalled that the first two persons hired by the HSA were himself and Gabe Paul. Giles said:

I thought the Judge unique when I first met him. There were many trying days, both on the baseball front and the stadium front. Hofheinz was much more involved with getting the domed stadium built with the proper bond issues. I can remember riding on a sound truck in the black district telling the people to vote for the bond issue. We had recorded voices of Hank Aaron, Ernie Banks and said on the speaker, "If you don't have transportation to the polls, turn your porch light on and somebody will pick you up and take you to the polls so you can vote." The Judge's political experience was a big plus in getting bond issues passed.

I guess that was one of the greatest victories he had ever won in his life. Without the passage of bond issues, I question whether the Astrodome would have been built and become successful.

As time passed, Giles recalled, the Judge became more powerful and, in the process, developed problems with individuals. "The sad thing was to see the Smith-Hofheinz relationship break up," he said. "I guess there were many reasons on both sides why that relationship didn't last. But soon after the opening of the Astrodome, it was strictly a Hofheinz show." Giles also said that

Hofheinz was a real stickler for details. One time, about four hours before the opening day of the Astrodome, Giles and Hofheinz drove a golf cart around the various floors of the dome. Hofheinz went into every rest room and made sure there was toilet paper.

"I'll never forget one of the few times he ever chewed me out. I had hired a trick golf shot artist, a one-armed man named Hahn. Little did I know that he was going to hit golf balls off our $2 million scoreboard. The Judge, I guess, felt the golfer was going to destroy it. He called me on the hot line and told me to get that 'SOB' off the field before he broke down the whole stadium. We shortened the act."

Giles said that one time he had saved $2000 and, knowing Hofheinz had been successful in investments, he went to the Judge for advice. "Do you know a piece of land I could buy for $2000?" I asked. Hofheinz said, 'Bill, the first thing you've got to learn in investing is if you have, say $2000, you don't want to buy a piece of land worth $2000. You buy a piece of land that would sell for, say $20 thousand or $30 thousand and put $2000 down and borrow the rest. That's the way to make your way through life as far as investing is concerned.' "

Giles remembered, "He never did like the name 'Colt .45s.' The Judge felt that was building in the image of the past and guns and was not in the best interest, and he had the vision of calling the team the Astros. When he announced 'Astros' without telling anybody in advance, it was quite a shock and was mocked quite a bit in the newspapers, particularly nationally. We were going to call our farm club the 'Half Astros,' some said. There were a lot of funny jokes about it but as it turned out, the Judge knew what he was doing and we named the domed stadium the Astrodome."

Since 1956, John Easter was one of Hofheinz's closest business associates. Mary Frances described the quiet, efficient accountant as the man who had the greatest ability of anyone to ward off bill collectors from the Judge. "He deserves a star in Heaven for his help in our financial difficulties," she said. In 1978, when he had his office in a huge Houston warehouse where Hofheinz's collection of treasures was stored when he left the Astrodome, Easter still handled affairs of Hofheinz Interests, after years with the Houston Sports Association. Shortly after Hofheinz left the mayor's office, Easter's firm, Masquelette-Bruhl, assigned him to handle the Judge's account. "He [Hofheinz] was so busy being mayor that he did not spend the time he should have with his personal matters, and it cost him dearly," said Easter. "That's contrary to what a lot of people thought about politicians. From a personal financial standpoint, he had to start a new career after being mayor to replenish his fortune."

Easter knew about Hofheinz's many loans, but he was not a front man for them. When time to pay came, he was in the middle. He recalled:

> The Judge sometimes interrupted his 24-hour-a-day, seven-day work week with sleep. It was always one of the Judge's traits that it was pretty hard for

John Easter

one to get through to him, but—he'd track you down to the end of the earth if he wanted to talk with you. Time meant nothing. He's a man who loves good food, but he would go maybe all day long without eating anything, and maybe at midnight or two or three o'clock in the morning he'd have his first meal. He would eat, go to bed, and sleep a few hours and get up and start the next day.

A lot of people really think the Judge is a gruff, hard fellow. That's one of the fallacies. He has a heart the size of the domed stadium and was an easy touch for his old friends. Many of them touched.

The year 1965 after the Dome opened was fantastic. Just about every event was a sellout. It was wonderful to be a part of it. The Judge had scaled a mountain, and he wanted one in the distance to be even higher. Before the Dome opened, Bob Smith at intervals would inquire of the Judge, "Roy, when are we going to build our amusement park?" It was on the drawing board—an amusement park and a hotel complex.

But the Judge and Smith parted before they were built, and Easter played a bigger role on Hofheinz's team after the Judge bought Smith's stock.

In 1978, when he was president of the marketing division of Pace Management in Houston, Hugh Cohn looked back on his five years with Hofheinz. In 1960 Cohn was vice-president and head of the radio and television division of the Lawrence G. Gumbinner Agency in New York, which represented the American Tobacco Company for national and local advertising. The news that

Houston had been awarded a National League franchise attracted his attention because his agency dealt with many major league clubs. Looking ahead to 1962 when the Colt .45s would begin National League play, Cohn made arrangements for American Tobacco to sponsor radio broadcasts of the 1961 Houston Buffs. Cohn said he dealt with Hofheinz on the telephone in late 1960 and set up agreements for the Triple A league broadcasts. Cohn recalled:

> I went to Houston in July of 1961 when the Buffs were playing, to meet Hofheinz. I wanted to discuss contracts for the 1962 Colt .45 season. Roy met our party of three—our sports director, Dick Blue, and an accountant accompanying me—at the Hobby Airport. He took us immediately to the Brandt Street office basement. Roy could follow Mary Frances by closed circuit television. She actually cooked our lunch as Roy made his presentation with the model of the Astrodome which, at that point, was just a figment of his imagination. Roy commented as he'd watch her walk across the TV screen, "There goes Houston's highest paid waitress and lowest paid secretary."
>
> We had already done our study of Houston and what sponsorship should cost. We were, at that time, in nine other baseball packages. We had a pretty good base to decide what was the value of the Houston advertising package. When we got around to that part in the conversation, we said, "We'll pay you $300,000 for your rights, and then we will go out and set up the network."
>
> Hofheinz just turned a deaf ear. He wanted a million dollars and a 10-year deal. We told him he was crazy. He ignored what we said and kept selling. This went on, non-stop, until time to go to the "Old Timers' Night" for former Buff players. Roy did not stop selling throughout the game. After the game we went into the press lounge. There Roy kept selling. Finally, at two o'clock in the morning, we had not eaten. We were starving. We weren't smart enough to eat hot dogs when available. Finally he took us to the Shamrock. He came up to the room and did not stop talking until 4:00 A.M. Typical of Hofheinz, he had sent up, during the day, an enormous basket of fruit with a bottle of booze. He had set up these arrangements, the best suite that the Shamrock had, really laying the wood to us.
>
> We subtly broke the cellophane over the fruit and began eating grapes and cheese while he continued to talk. Finally he left and said he'd be back at 7:30 in the morning to get us. He came back at exactly 7:30. He took us to breakfast and at 10:00 A.M. he took us to the airport. We got on the plane and went back to New York, and he was still talking as we left. He had never once acknowledged the fact that we had said the package was not worth more than $300,000.
>
> The usual practice in those days was that an agency, on behalf of the sponsor, bought advertising rights from ball clubs. You'd buy the rights and then you'd go out and put it together for the advertiser. Each club got a different amount of money. Roy patterned his demand for a million dollars after Walter O'Malley had helped build his Los Angeles stadium by making a 10-year, million-dollar-a-year deal, with Union Oil. The Judge said, "If Walter O'Malley can get a million dollars a year, I'm going to get it, too."

We went back to New York and recommended against Roy's proposal. The Southwest was growing and had potential. It was at that time called "R. J. Reynolds country," and we wanted to crack it for American Tobacco, but we said a million dollars was outlandish. The agency followed our recommendation. Because Al Stevens, the ad manager, wanted to buy it, we bought half the rights for $500,000 on a one-year basis. That still left half unsold. Also left open were pre- and post-game programs.

In October of 1961, Dick Blue, our sports director, and I went to see the Judge, who knew we had recommended against the whole million package. We spent six weeks setting up the original radio and television networks in Texas, Louisiana, and Oklahoma for 1962. We lived with Hofheinz—I mean that literally.

At night we'd go to the Judge, tell him what we'd accomplished and talk about baseball. He was a fun guy. We seldom slept at the Shamrock—just had our meetings there and spent nights at one of his places. We'd go out to the "Loose Goose," and he'd cook.

After Cohn and Blue set up the broadcast network, Hofheinz still had to seek $500,000 in advertising to get a million. Cohn recalled:

Roy did not sell the other half of sponsorship until about three weeks before spring training in 1962. Pearl Beer of San Antonio bought it. Roy got Frank Horlock, Bob Durden, and Buddy Bray, the three Houston Pearl distributors, around the neck, and he took them to the brewery in San Antonio and made the deal. He did it with his own salesmanship.

With all play-by-play time contracted, the Judge got Phillips Petroleum signed for the pre- and post-game shows. We handled all the billing for HSA. We did most of this work in New York. Just after the Judge sold Pearl Beer, he called me in New York and said: "You and Dick get your asses down here. I just sold Pearl Beer, and you've got to get them into the package, help get their spot done, and all that other stuff." I said, "Well, Judge, we can't just come down and do that. We've got our jobs up here." He said, "I want you down here." I said, "Well you just call Al Stevens and tell him you need us, and if he instructs the agency, we'll be on our way." He did, and we went to Houston. I got in about 2:00 A.M. and I took a cab to the Shamrock. I was sleepy as I walked in and said to the guy behind the desk, "You probably remember me, I've got a reservation." He replied, "Oh, yes?" He called the bellman over and said, "Take Mr. Cohn up." On the elevator, I asked the bellman, "What room—what floor?" He said, "Eighteen, the penthouse." I didn't say anything. We got off on 18, and I started to sense something was different. We opened the door at 18A. I looked and felt that I was in the opening of a Fred Astaire movie. Double doors open up and the camera sweeps in and music comes up, and you see the panoramic scene—well, that's what you do when you walk into this suite. There was no one in it. I was starved. There was no place to eat in Houston at that hour. I called my wife to tell her that I had arrived safely. I started describing the suite and told her I couldn't believe it. She asked, "How big is it?" I said, "Wait a minute, I'll look." I put the phone down and counted nine rooms—two living rooms, one enormous kitchen, and a massive dining room. Whenever we were trying to use it to impress people, we'd say, "Come on, we'll take you up to the broom closet." People wouldn't pay any attention and then, when they'd get there, it was a juxtaposition of what we'd said, and it was so dramatic it was very impressive to them. I learned Roy had leased it for a long period.

Dick Blue came in the next day, as did people from Tracey Locke, the Dallas agency for Pearl Beer. Bob Jarnorvaz was the Pearl advertising manager. Larry Dupont, head of Locke's radio and television division and Tracey Locke himself, delightful guy, also arrived. I was there four days. When I was ready to leave, I knew damn well I wasn't paying for that suite. Roy hadn't said anything. He'd just keep quiet about things like that. I knew how Hofheinz worked by that time. So I figured when I was leaving, I should at least check out and pay my incidentals. I went over to the cashier and said, "I don't know how you're handling the billing for 18A, but I've been in there and I've got some charges and I'd like to pay them." The clerk asked my name and I told him. "Here's your bill," he said. I was the first one in there and everything was charged in my name, including the room rate which was several hundred dollars a day. The bill for four days—we had several "state" dinners—was about $4200. I said, "I think there's been a mistake made." I looked at the bill and saw where everything was being charged to my name. The clerk finally said, "Oh, here's the note that the whole thing is to be billed to the Houston Sports Association." I said, "Thank you very much," and left. That's how 18A became the central place for a lot of selling in the coming years.

There was an incident during that time. One night about 11 o'clock, the Judge, Mary Frances, Red James, and Blue and I were having steak dinners. Red mentioned to the Judge that he'd been trying to get him for several days. The Judge said, "Well, I've been busy. I've got M.F. You're supposed to tell her what you want." Red said, "When I call you to talk to you, I don't want to talk to M.F., I want to talk to you." Red was his law partner. "I have something to talk to you about—very important." Roy replied, "Well, you just tell M.F." Red said, "Well, when I've got something important, you've got to talk to me." Roy asked, "What is it?" Red said, "Well, KENS Radio in San Antonio is for sale." The Judge became interested. Roy told Red, "You get on the phone first thing in the morning and you buy that station." Red told him how much they wanted— $700,000—a helluva buy. Roy said, "You buy that station or I'll get myself a new law partner." That's the way he handled Red. Red didn't like that at all, and I didn't like it for Red. I realized later Red was used to it. Red did get on the phone and Roy and Bob Smith did buy the station. I later ran that station in 1964 and 1965, commuting from Houston. We renamed the station KBAT.

Cohn and Dick Blue eventually were lured by the Judge to positions with the HSA. "Roy never let you know one damned thing about his business," Cohn recalled, "and you weren't aware of it. He could dig in; no matter what your professions and what you did, he'd learn enough from you, know everything you knew, and you'd know nothing of what he knew when you finished the conversation." Cohn said he and Blue were put on the baseball team's payroll "temporarily" until a company which Hofheinz had envisioned was established. The company, separate from the HSA, would be responsible for packaging sports and working in broadcasting. But the company never was established. Three years after joining Hofheinz, Cohn left. "I was treated well in my area, but I had no opportunity to grow, no equity. I just walked out."

In 1979, when he was advertising and marketing director of the Tampa Bay Buccaneers of the National Football League, Dick Blue said he and Hofheinz had similar thoughts when they first discussed the Colt .45 advertising program. "The Judge told me to be in charge of a radio-TV network and to get the job done. He wanted the whole program under a single setup—radio, TV, ads on buses, newspaper promotion, and other advertising." Blue's association with HSA reflected a different story from Cohn's. Blue worked for the HSA almost 13 years as executive director for broadcast operations. He always was an admirer and business crony of the Judge but, at the same time, an ardent critic of the man he called boss.

According to Blue, "Once you got your part of the operation going, Hofheinz would never bother you. You stayed there. He'd never give anyone a raise. Some stole him blind, and he knew it. Everyone moonlighted, including me. Finally, I was making more from my moonlighting than I was on the job. He was the dumbest genius I ever met. He was like a Napoleon. He'd never cover his flanks or rear. He just kept stretching his financial burdens. Someone would do a topnotch job on some phase of the Dome, but he wouldn't keep him for a subsequent project."

Blue recalled an incident reflecting Hofheinz's power base in Houston:

> At my suggestion, we stole Rene Cardenas from the Dodgers for our Spanish baseball network. He spoke a Spanish that was understood by all Latins. We needed a color man and Rene suggested Orlando Sanchez Diago, the Red Barber of Cuba, who had sneaked out of Cuba when Castro took over. I spent six months trying to locate him, and finally one of our scouts located him in Venezuela. He had no papers. I had sent him money and tickets, and now, 48 hours before we started our first game, there was no color man. I went to the Judge. The Judge called his secretary and said, "Get me Lyndon." He soon had Lyndon Johnson on the line. He explained the problem to the then-U.S. Senator. Johnson asked, "What's that man's name?" Roy replied, "Orlando Sanchez Diago . . . in Venezuela, and he ain't got no pants or nothing. Can you do something to help me get him here? . . . Well I appreciate that. . . . Say hello to Lady Bird." Twelve hours later, the guy was sitting in his office.

Blue said that he always felt Hofheinz was smart:

> Some people went the booze and broads route to influence clients. Not Roy. He would invite the individual agency owners, but he'd also invite their mamas, papas, and children. He'd never talk business around them. He took them to "Huckster House" for entertainment. When they'd get back to New

York, the mamas would tell their husbands to give the business to Hofheinz. Roy Hofheinz could sell you a look at the moon. Being a politician and a Texas politician—they play rough down here—he had lots of opposition on one of the stadium bond drives. They were what he called "aginners," who rounded up a big bunch of volunteers to distribute anti-bond pamphlets. Guess who were the volunteers? We Hofheinz people were. We picked the "anti" stuff up and put it in the city dump.

Roy could recharge his energy quickly, surprising for a person weighing well over 200 pounds and always looking like he'd swallowed nine bowling balls. All his offices had kitchens and that is where he did his work. He collected things constantly. Roy was a great believer in color. He felt color had a lot to do to set the mood of a listener. If he had a dramatic idea to sell, he'd use lighting that was dramatic and add proper mood music. His sales presentation included slides, movies, and music which he'd punch up on a panel at his desk.

John D. O'Connell left Chicago in 1964 as manager of McCormick Place to become vice-president of HSA, responsible for putting events other than baseball and football in the Astrodome. He also had the responsibility of overseeing the building of Astrohall for the Houston Livestock Show and Rodeo Association. The time came, O'Connell recalled, when the HSA had to enter the hotel business. He said:

> We were getting a lot of criticism for not only not having enough hotels, but also because they were spread out. We couldn't accommodate conventions like the Homebuilders with 50,000 delegates. The Judge knew something about the Homebuilders. We made a very dramatic effort and finally got the Homebuilders to Houston. We worked on it a long time in terms of hotel rooms. One night as I was leaving the Brandt Street office, the Judge said, "You're working late, what's the trouble?" I said, "Hell, I need some more hotel rooms." He asked, "How many?" I told him at least a thousand. He said, "Well if you really need that, tell the Homebuilders you'll build them a thousand rooms across the street from Astrohall." And so I did.
>
> At that point the Judge's credibility was great with everybody; the Homebuilders loved him. That's about all it took—his word that he'd build hotels. They bought it. The next hurdle Homebuilders presented was, "We can decide to hold the convention in Houston and our membership will come 50,000 strong, but if our exhibitors don't come because of the added distance from point of supply, and the added expense and all the rest of it, we're going to be in bad shape." They depended on the profit that they made off exhibits to subsidize the whole Homebuilders convention program each year. Roy asked them: "How much do you make out of the exhibits?" They said, "Our best year we made $750,000." He said, "All right, I'll guarantee that." That's about where it rested.
>
> After nearly two years of efforts at untold meetings in Washington and Chicago, we got up a pitch for the convention and exposition committee. It voted against us, but we got a minority report filed and it was adopted unanimously. Roy is a frustrated showman. His hotels were his own creation. He put

together three motels and a hotel. It was the only place in the world that any one owner held competitive franchises in the same place.

The first couple of years, 65 percent of the overall Astrodome attendance was from outside Harris County. Our problem was to figure out how to keep these people for more than a baseball game. That's what sort of stimulated the development of Astroworld. "Bring your family. Stay three or four days. See the Astrodome" was our pitch. All that stuff. The hotels were completed just in time for the Homebuilders. They still talk about it because we were still moving in beds and mattresses as the guests were checking in.

O'Connell recalled the beginning of Hofheinz's relationship with Irvin Feld of Ringling Bros. and Barnum & Bailey Circus. He said:

In December of 1964, we had the major league baseball meetings in Houston. At the same time I went to Chicago to the Homebuilders convention to lay ground work for our bid. When I came back, the Judge asked: "Did you get the Homebuilders?" I said, "It's going to take a long time." He said, "While you were screwing around with your kinfolk up in Chicago, I got Ringling Brothers down here. The circus is going to be here next summer." He had invited Irvin Feld, who owned the company called Super Shows, Incorporated. Feld is an egocentric guy and was very impressed that the Judge would drop the whole baseball organization and take time to take him to the Astrodome, which was under construction, to talk about the circus and entertain him. Feld was impressed and they reportedly made some kind of a deal so the Judge told me to "mark these dates in your book." I did. After lengthy negotiations, an agreement was reached, and Feld cancelled a series of towns and moved the circus on the longest train trip that ever was made in its history—from Toronto to Houston.

Hofheinz and Feld got along beautifully. Hofheinz told Feld: "You would have made more money had you taken my original deal." Feld said he was happy he had done well. They called John Ringling North at three o'clock in the morning in London to give him results. Everybody was very happy about everything. There's nothing like a winner to make friends. Feld and Hofheinz became close. As time went on, we began to do other things. We'd hear about some crazy deal, and the Judge would call up Feld and ask him what he thought. Feld is a perceptive box office guy, having pioneered tours for Frank Sinatra and Andy Williams. He really was the premier concert guy in the United States for live shows. For instance, somewhere along the way, a friend of Ted Kennedy called me, wanted to bring bullfights into the United States for the first time. So, as it turned out we had them all together out at the "Loose Goose." The Judge called Feld and asked him to come down. Feld said, "I can't, it's my son's 18th birthday." Roy said: "Bring him, we'll have a birthday party." So we had the Armenian, Irvin Feld, and his son at the retreat. The Judge cooked for everybody for a weekend.

We decided jointly to venture bullfights in the Dome, the first time in the United States. We had a million problems, including lawsuits, which we won.

O'Connell said that after Bob Smith left HSA, things went well until the death of Dene Hofheinz. "As far as the overall HSA operation was concerned, it did well through 1966."

In 1979 John Leer was an associate in massive R. E. Smith interests in Houston, headed by the widow of the financial giant who backed HSA. From 1954 to 1964, he was director of marketing and sales development for the American Tobacco Company in New York. He became director of marketing for the Houston Sports Association and continued until late 1966. "One day in 1961 I had a telelphone call from Bob Smith in Houston to my New York office," he recalled. "He told me that a man by the name of Judge Roy Hofheinz was coming to New York and he would appreciate anything I could do for him. The Judge proved a very interesting person—flamboyant, outgoing, different, charming, and entertaining. Subsequently, American Tobacco sponsored the Colt .45s the first year."

Leer said: "I got to know Hofheinz from 1961 to 1964 in New York. . . . I was responsible for bringing Roy together with the executives of the Colgate-Palmolive Company who did participate, thinking that the Astrodome would become a reality."

For a variety of reasons Leer got Astrodome fever. He resigned his post in New York and moved to Houston. He continued:

> Roy's concept of the massive scoreboard was that there could be only one sign in the stadium. The logo on the $2 million scoreboard was sold for $200,000 a year for a five-year contract, first purchased by Gulf Oil Corporation.
>
> For marketing, Roy developed what he called the green area—Astrodome territory. It covered Texas and ran all the way into Oklahoma, Louisiana, and parts of Mexico. He did that in order to put together figures that would come close to justifying his prices and the million-dollar profit he was shooting for. That would match the profit that Walter O'Malley was getting for the rights of Dodger broadcasts.

Leer said Hofheinz's experience in advertising was entirely different from his when they got together:

> I had been a buyer. I had always called myself an investor in advertising. I approached things on a little different basis from Roy. I was experienced on a national level. There's one thing I often thought about—if Roy would only price this package halfway reasonably, I'd have no trouble selling it. At that time he had at least three or four beer companies trying to talk him into selling them one half of the broadcast package, but that's all they would take. None would go for 100 percent for three years. At first I wondered why he didn't put the price realistically for a new club. I woke up one day and realized he had been very smart because there was no question he could sell 50 percent of it—and he was really asking about twice what it was worth as an advertising

John Leer

buy—so the worst thing that was going to happen to him was he was going to sell 50 percent and that 50 percent would return as much as it would be if he had priced it realistically and sold 100 percent. He had everything to gain and nothing to lose. Once I realized that, I was satisfied.

Leer recalled that Pat Gorman was advertising manager of Schlitz Brewing Company:

Roy told me it had just never occurred to him to call on the Schlitz Brewing Company. I guess the reason was that he had Budweiser and Lone Star and any number of beers that would buy 50 percent and was satisfied with the brewing contacts that he had made. He felt that if a brewer was going to buy, one of them would spring for the whole thing. Schlitz had never been contacted and, by coincidence, the advertising manager was an old friend of mine. I had telephone conversations with Pat and he promised me that he would bring Bob Martin, vice-president of marketing, to Houston in the future. I finally got a call from Pat and he said that he'd be in town. I went to Roy and said, "Pat Gorman, the advertising manager of Schlitz, and Bob Martin are coming to Houston next week to look at the package and I'd like very much for you to meet them and set a time that you'll be available."

He said, typical of Roy, "Well, can Pat Gorman make the decision to buy this package?" I said, "No, he can't." He said, "Well, can Bob Martin make the decision to buy this package?" I said, "No, he can't." He asked: "What are you having them come down here for?" I said, "Roy, it just doesn't work that way. They may not be able to make the decision to buy the package, but I'll tell you one thing: Mr. Vihlein of the Schlitz Brewing Company will not make the decision to buy it without them." Roy only wanted to talk to the president, but the president of a major corporation doesn't have the time nor the desire to get involved in these things. Roy had difficulty appreciating or understanding it, but nevertheless he agreed to meet with Pat and Bob. Bob and Pat and the Judge hit it off right away.

The Schlitz men's visit worked out well. As I was getting ready to take them to the airport, I'll never forget I caught three fingers of Pat Gorman's hand in the trunk as I slammed it down. He screamed and as I lifted the trunk said: "Boy, you'll do anything to sell this package, won't you?"

As he left, Pat said, "John, I'll try to get you a quick answer." This happened to be a Wednesday and on Thursday he called me at my home, from Milwaukee. He said, "John, Bob and I had an opportunity to talk coming back on the plane last night, and I thought about it and I got up early this morning—I didn't sleep too well thinking about a deal. I have only one question to ask you—can you believe what Hofheinz says?" I said, "I don't think you should worry about that, Pat."

Later that day I had a meeting with Buck Black, then manager of the Houston office of the Glenn Advertising agency of Dallas. We were going to meet Ward Wilcox, chairman of the board and owner of the agency who was coming in with Harry Mackeldowning, vice-president of Lone Star Beer. They were due roughly at 1:30 P.M. Buck and I wanted to be sure and be there when the plane arrived. We went out to the Mediterranean Room at the hotel across the street from Hobby Airport and had lunch. I was paged for a telephone call. Mary Frances was on the telephone and said, "The Judge wants to talk to you, Mr. Leer, he's got wonderful news." The Judge said, "You can come home, we're all sold out." He couldn't have been happier. That baseball package was sold for $6 million for three years. I sat down with Buck Black and we finished our lunch and then I notified Buck that it was too bad, but the package had been sold to a competitive brewer and Lone Star wouldn't be able to participate. The least we could do was go over and meet with Mr. Wilcox. Mr. Wilcox was one of those people whose bark was louder than his bite; he was actually a charming guy and had a heart of gold, but I think he went out of his way to give people the other impression. He got off the airplane and had a big cigar in his mouth and gruffly said, "Let's go somewhere and talk." I said, "Well, I'm sorry, Mr. Wilcox, but you're about 45 minutes late. I don't think there's anything left to talk about." He asked: "What do you mean?" I said, "Well, I just had a phone call about 30 minutes ago and a competitive brewery has purchased the whole package for three years."

He said, "You can't do that. I have a million-dollar check in my briefcase and we have a right of first refusal and I came down here to close the deal." I said, "No you don't have the right of first refusal; nobody ever had a right of first refusal on this package." In any event, he was very upset.

The challenge of selling the first advertising package for the Dome provided great days in my life. Mr. Smith was very supportive of Hofheinz—without reservation. He used to say to me, "You've got a wonderful opportunity here and all you have to do is just go along with the Judge because he's going to do great things. He has done great things and he's going to do them in the future, and you'll just go right along with him." I should add that the day that baseball package sold twice on the same day I went back to Brandt house. I had to clean up some things and I had other appointments. It got to be dark. Roy called me every 10 minutes—he wanted me to come out to the Astrodome and have a drink with him and celebrate the sale. I got out there about 6:30 P.M. Mary Frances was there and the Astrodome was dark. We had a drink and we were both on cloud nine. I felt like, finally, I had justified my being there. To me, that was the turning point; I had made the right decision in coming to Houston. I was in the Hofheinz Yorktown home on numerous occasions for dinner. Dene Hofheinz was a lovely person and I had great respect for her.

Leer said:

The break between Smith and Hofheinz put him in a difficult position because Roy knew—and we talked about it frankly—I had great loyalty and affection for the Smiths. So it was—you might say I was placed in the isolation ward during the period when a lot of people were sitting around wondering whether Roy would or would not get the money to buy out Mr. Smith. I was always inclined to think that he would, but hoped he couldn't, frankly. Mr. Smith would say to me during that period: "I don't think he will get the money. If he doesn't, I'm just going to hand you the keys and let you run it." Later he said: "Roy may get the money, we'll just wait and see." The Judge did get the money and paid Mr. Smith. The next day I went to see the Judge in his box. I asked him, "Where do we stand?" He tried to assure me that there were not going to be any changes and said, "I know that you're disappointed. Frankly, I'm sorry about Mr. Smith, too, but you know, it's one of those things that had to be."

No new agreement was reached by Leer and Hofheinz. Leer resigned to become vice-president for sales with Braniff Airlines in Dallas.

Robert A. (Bob) Martin was another associate of Hofheinz who developed a close friendship with the Houston magnate through an advertising deal when Jos. Schlitz Brewing Company bought advertising rights. "The Judge is certainly one of the most unforgettable characters I've ever known and certainly one of the world's great entrepreneurs," he said in 1979.

Martin remembered Hofheinz as the most persistent salesman he ever had encountered. The Judge, he said, never took "no" for an answer, and Martin related this story to describe what he meant:

I recall the first year of the Astro-Bluebonnet Bowl, which was to be played on New Year's Eve. A lot of people thought that might not be the best time for a bowl game, but the Judge was interested in getting people into the stadium and also making some money for the radio and TV rights. I was at home on New Year's Eve, and I recall the phone ringing and it was the Judge. He said, "Turn your TV set on." So I turned the set on and the players were coming out on the field and bands were playing and there were quite a few people in the stands. I said, "What the hell's this all about?" I hadn't even heard about the Astro-Bluebonnet Bowl. Not many people had. He said, "This is the Bluebonnet Bowl and it's the first time anybody's had the guts to schedule a bowl game on New Year's Eve. It's gonna be a big hit . . . and I've got half the game unsold so I thought I'd call you and tell you that you have a great opportunity to become a sponsor on the inaugural or first Bluebonnet game." I said, "You gotta be out of your tree, Judge . . . . you can't call me five minutes before a football game and expect to get some sponsorship. Besides, we don't have a lot of money left over right now just because you're not sold out." Well, he went into a long, ten-minute, dissertation on all the merits of the Bluebonnet Bowl and I told him, "No," that that was that, and hung up. I couldn't believe that a little over an hour later the phone rings again and it's halftime and it's the Judge again. He said, "You know, I went over and talked to the guys and we've got some of your commercials and I strung one of them up for the second half." He says, "You're the only one in America who has an opportunity to be a sponsor in the second half. . . . All you gotta do is give me the go ahead." I never heard of anybody still trying to sell commercials at halftime, but the Judge didn't think there was anything abnormal about that at all.

He also recalled one evening when Hofheinz regaled a group with stories.

The phone would ring, and one of the Judge's minions would answer it. It was always the same long distance operator asking for Judge Roy Hofheinz and calling for a gentleman whose name I forget. Let's call him Joe Blow. The telephone calls were interrupting the party, and the Judge did not want to talk to Joe Blow, so he would instruct his aide-de-camp to tell the operator he wasn't there. The fourth time the phone rang, I was a little upset, and I said, "Hey, wait a minute. . . . I'm the one that's registered in this room. Let me answer my own phone and I'll get rid of this turkey for you, Judge." So I picked up the phone. The long distance operator said, "Judge Roy Hofheinz, please," I said with a wink, "Whom shall I say is calling?" expecting to get rid of Mr. Blow in no time at all. But the operator said, "The White House." It turned out that the Judge's close friend, Jack Valenti, was calling to finalize arrangements for a presidential visit to the Astrodome. I was very embarrassed as I put the Judge on to talk to him. After he hung up, he turned around and gave me one of those looks that only he can give you, and I said, "Well, from now on why don't you answer your own damned phone?"

Several years after Schlitz became involved in Astro broadcasts, I was sitting at home one Saturday at 4:00 P.M. The phone rang. It was the Judge. He said he really had a problem and he didn't know where to turn. He said that he had a rather complicated financial structure with a lot of loans between insurance companies and some local banks and there was one son-of-a-bitch at one of the local banks that he owed a real small amount of money, but he was calling a note on him and it could cause the whole financial structure to crumble and, in fact, he felt he might be in serious jeopardy as far as his entire holdings were concerned. I talked to him for a few minutes and said, "What the hell did you call me for?" He said, "Well, I thought maybe you'd have an idea." I said, "How much money's involved?" He said, I forget the exact figure, but it was something like about a quarter of a million dollars, $225,000 to $250,000. I said, "Well, Judge, it really isn't all that much money." After we talked about it awhile, I suggested that we owed him more than that on our radio-TV package for the rights and that it seemed to me that it would be perfectly legitimate for us to advance payments to him if he would be willing to sign a note and pay us interest on the advance payment and that certainly should solve his problem. He said, "You know, that's a good idea; I think it'll work. Do you think you can make that happen?" I said, "Oh sure, it shouldn't be any problem at all. How much time do I have?" He said, "Well, I have to have the money by noon Monday." I said, "Noon, Monday! Do you realize it's Saturday afternoon? Thanks for all the warning and all the time, but I'll see what I can do." Monday morning I went into the office early, and I arranged to send him the money after he had agreed to pay interest on it. I found out to my horror that this very simple little plan, which obviously would work, had one little problem in that Monday was a holiday—Washington's birthday—and all but one Federal Reserve Bank was closed. Fortunately, the one Federal Reserve Bank open happened to be the one that Schlitz used so we were able to transfer the money to him, but it wasn't easy because I had wasted quite a bit of time finding out that it was a holiday, and that we were going to have some difficulty locating an easy way to transfer the money in time. I was sitting in my office Monday about 11:10 A.M. when the phone rang and I picked it up. The Judge didn't even say "hello." His exact words were, "The baby has arrived and is doing nicely," and he hung up. He was, of course, very appreciative for the help and as a matter of fact, when he promptly sent back a signed note agreeing to the interest rate that we had talked about, it was the first time that I had ever seen his signature. One of the hardest things in the world was to get the Judge to sign anything. We had been a sponsor of his and had his radio and TV package for years and years, but he never signed any of the contracts. This was kind of strange, but apparently he doesn't sign anything unless it's absolutely necessary. I kidded him about it and said, "You know, I never did know what your signature looked like." But it's also interesting that in all those years without a signed contract, the Judge never bent or changed or failed to comply with one condition of a contract that we ever had with him. He was always good for his word.

Evelyn Norton Anderson gained a reputation in Houston during the 1950s as an expert designer of fashions. Blessed with great imagination and skill, she took the leading role in designing costumes for employees of Colt Stadium for the 1962 major league baseball opening and for the colorfully dressed figures who worked in the Astrodome in 1965. In 1978 Mrs. Anderson was well-established nationally as a designer for major league baseball. She recalled:

I first encountered Judge Hofheinz after a call from Mary Frances to visit the temporary Colt Stadium offices to talk about uniforms. I had never done uniforms, but I thought it might be fun to try. To encounter the Judge is a happening. He is not an ordinary person by any means. He asked me to make sketches, based on early baseball, of things with period connotation like old-fashioned baseball suits for the various people who would work at the open stadium. I thought it would be grand for us to have a fabric uniquely ours. I designed a fabric of white and had on it about an inch and a half baseball stitch done in royal blue. The Judge thought it was grand. I didn't show him the fabric, just the sketch. He said go ahead and have it done. So I called Mission Valley Mills and I got the fabric. I talked to A. B. Knox and we felt it would be impossible to do the job before season opening. The Judge never gave you enough time. In fact, he doesn't give you any time. I came back to the Judge and said: "It looks like we will not be able to get our baseball fabric."

"Why not?"

I said: "The only mill I know that can do this kind of thing is Mission Valley and they simply do not have the time to do it." I said I talked to Irvin Boarnet.

He said: "Hell, I've known him all my life."

I said, "I wonder if it would do any good for you to call him." He picked up the phone and called him and then said, "Yes, they'll do it." I mean, in five minutes it was done. By the next Friday I had the fabric in my hands to start work. I told the Judge: "The opening is close at hand. I'm going to have to have some help. I said I knew Iris Siff who was good at coordinating. I needed her to help me. We were then talking about shoes specially made, everything you could think of specially made—every kind of company in the world. He said: "Okay, that will be fine." I said, "You'll have to pay for her services." He said, "That's okay."

We made it on time. Everything was lovely. He was crazy about our costumes. Oh, we even had baseball buttons made by OBC (Original Button Company) and had a gold die made. I still have one of them. They looked like a little baseball mounted in brass. There were costumes for usherettes, gate ticket takers, venders, parking attendants—I mean everybody in any capacity—grounds keepers, too. We even went so far as to do a uniform—a beautiful western—with a western hat and everything. The team didn't like them at all—refused to wear them. He was furious about it, but he didn't win that one.

There came a time when we got ready to settle bills. I went to the Judge and said: "Judge, now remember, we talked about Iris Siff. Here's a bill for her."

He perked up. "I don't remember saying that."

I said, "But you did."

He said, "I don't recall it at all." He refused to pay. So I wasn't too happy about it. I went home. The next afternoon he called me on the phone. He said, "Now Evelyn, I really don't remember ever saying that. I'm not kidding."

I said, "But Judge, you did."

He said, "Well, I don't want you to be mad at me."

I said, "Well, pay me my money."

He said, "Well, I don't think I can do that, I don't have a recollection of doing it."

I said, "Okay, what do you think I'm going to do—sue you, Judge?" So we left it at that.

He said, "Well, don't be mad at me because I want to get back to you in the future."

I said, "Okay, probably so, we'll worry about that later."

There was to be a later deal between Mrs. Anderson and Hofheinz.

Iris Siff, working for the Alley Theatre in 1979, said: "When Evelyn got the costume job, I knew she didn't have time to get the work done by herself—it would have killed her. She knew I was addicted to baseball. I thought probably the best thing, entertainment-wise, that may have ever happened to me in my life was when we got a major league baseball team." She continued:

When Evelyn and I met with the Judge and found out how many weeks there were available to do the job he had in mind, I got hysterical and started laughing. Evelyn became concerned, but I thought it funny that he thought the job could be done. The thing that really stuck with me—concerned me, however, was that if we didn't do it, he would have probably done it himself and could have. We had six weeks. He wanted specially fabricated material for the uniforms and buttons to go on them. I know one thing that I didn't say and some inner or Higher Being advised me not to do it—was to say anything that might suggest the job couldn't be done in the length of time. My pride prevented it. That brief encounter with the Judge was especially nice for me because I didn't really need anything from him, but after we talked, I began to wonder why I was so enchanted with him, aside from the fact that anybody with any degree of intelligence would have to be fascinated with the gentleman. He's just a mixture of so many things—mind-boggling. The challenge that he presented to people, I'm sure, on his payroll would sometimes be kind of a tremendous burden, ulcer-making. On the other hand, there was something in working with him that was a sort of honor. If he asked you to do something, on the assumption that you could do it, you felt honored.

That is how he got a whole lot of things done in less time and sometimes maybe even with less money, although that wasn't a factor, at least with us. Evelyn got into some conflict with him over that, and the best time we ever had in our lives was trying to collect our money. I just loved it. I hated it when it was paid off because we didn't have that fun anymore. He would battle over something like our bill and turn around and spend a million and a half dollars without batting an eyelash. I just loved it.

Colt .45 uniforms were sharp, but the baseball buttons the Judge wanted didn't exist. I called all over the U.S. I knew most resources for women's wear and if I didn't, I knew who to call to find out. Many laughed at me about buttons. It would not be a big order. Buttons are produced in the millions of grosses. It was the one aspect we couldn't accomplish. I will never forget the day when we had to go in and tell the Judge we couldn't find the buttons, that we'd have to make them. He picked up the telephone and in one call to somebody in Rhode Island, he got the buttons. We paid a fortune for them. In my investigation, I just couldn't get anybody to make them. Our fabric came out of New Braunfels. In Colt .45 Stadium, the Judge wanted the usherettes to look like cocktail waitresses, or hostesses in a fine night club. That was the atmosphere he wanted to create. We went through quite a number of showings before we came up with what he really liked—and to be very honest—I never did. He proved right and we were wrong.

After he served as executive vice-president of the National Association of Homebuilders from 1965 through 1976, Nathaniel H. Rogg continued in 1978 to exert influence for the vast organization in a Washington office. Rogg recalled Roy Hofheinz as a salesman, host, and keeper of promises:

I first encountered—the phrase is accurately used—Hofheinz in 1966. We had taken a group of NAHB leaders to a number of cities, including Houston, for a review of the potential and the facilities as convention towns. Chicago had the convention for a quarter century. We went to the Astrodome to meet Roy. I had been warned by Pat Harness that I was about to encounter what he called the "Eighth Wonder of the World." I collected myself from looking at the many wonders of the domed stadium area to see a rather husky, heavy-set man—hair combed straight back—who began confidently talking of the facilities and of the operation. It was a striking meeting. Nothing Pat had told me prepared me for the actual presence of Hofheinz who then seemed to me to be larger than life. He was a spellbinder from the start as he described the facilities, obviously in terms larger than life. He talked about what they would do in order to make the convention a success, convincingly. We had some social chit-chat with him afterwards and returned to Washington.

My next encounter with him was at the board meeting in May of 1966 when he flew up in a National Guard plane with John Connally and Mayor Louie Welch. When Roy got up to speak, he said, "The Astrodome and everything around it is a private facility; I control it. You will not have to deal with government. You will make your deal with me. I will make commitments and promises to you and I will keep them." He described in glowing terms the prospects for the homebuilders in Houston. It was a splendid speech and quite persuasive.

We made a number of trips to Houston and stayed in Roy's apartment at the Shamrock. Problems about the contract came up. I was in Houston dealing with Fred Hofheinz, Roy's son, then vice-president of HSA, who had been designated by Roy to develop a contract. In the course of Roy's speech to the board of directors, he had made an offer to assure us that we would make at least as much net profit from the convention as we had ever made in Chicago. This proved to be something of a stumbling block in negotiations over the contract because it was an open-end offer since it had no limits on expenditures and had nothing to do with total gross receipts. Fred said, as I recall at the time, "I guess my father has been somewhat reckless."

There were some amusing consequences to the negotiations over this deal because Roy was unable to find a security or fidelity bond firm that would or could issue a guarantee on something which, to tell the truth, was as nebulous as this. Roy offered to guarantee $750,000 profit for us, but would not guarantee it personally since he said he did not wish contingent liabilities which might affect other business operations he was in. The thing nearly came to a breaking point one day in Houston when I was down there with Lloyd Clark, then the NAHB national vice-president-treasurer. Clark had been discussing the matter in Roy's box at the Astrodome while we watched a baseball game. Roy was not in a good mood; the Astros were losing and Lloyd had made a number of suggestions to him which did not sit well. Among them was that we get a copy of Roy's financial statement or his income tax return. As I recall it, Roy snapped at him and said, "There is no way I am going to make my income tax returns and financial data available to a two-bit builder from Iowa." Lloyd had to leave for the airport. I took him there and went back to the ball game. I told Roy that he had probably overstepped the bounds of propriety with Lloyd. He was not convinced, at least he would not admit being convinced, though I think he realized he had made something of a gaff. We agreed on a unique approach. Roy would send his banker to Washington to our banker and would then explain details—only the bankers could—of Roy's financial status. No documents were to be used. Roy expressed a fear of the Xerox. Our banker would be asked whether on the basis of the statement that Roy's banker made to him, he would make a loan of approximately three-quarters of a million dollars to Roy. If our banker gave the answer in the affirmative, then that was all the assurance we needed, and Roy's signature as chairman of the HSA would be adequate. When the deal was explained to him, our banker, Ed Riggs, was somewhat reluctant to take care of the matter, but finally agreed. The Houston banker came up and visited with him and we, meanwhile, had gone to Las Vegas for the fall board meeting. I received a telegram from our banker in the affirmative about making the loan, which is all we needed to get the matter straightened out with our executive committee and our board.

Roy came to Las Vegas with his first wife, Dene, and his secretary, Mary Frances. We had a good meeting in his room in Roy's suite with Lloyd Clark. Roy made gracious amends for his crack about "a two-bit builder from Iowa." We were Roy's guests at an Andy Williams show. I remember Roy paying for everything with a big wad of bills, which he had stuffed in his pocket. That fascinated me since most people I knew paid their bills with credit cards. From that point on all seemed to be smooth sailing in preparation for the conventions, but this was merely surface. We moved into the next year still without a contract. We had signed a contract; Roy had not. He came to Washington to visit me and Leon Wiener, then president of the Homebuilders. He had never visited our building before and had no concept, really, of what kind of a national organization we were. As he saw the building which was our headquarters and wholly owned by us, he made the remark, "I guess you're here to stay." We ironed out what I thought were the final details of the contract and then drove him to the Baltimore airport with no time to spare. Leon, who was never the most careful of drivers, exceeded himself on the trip. Anyway, we got Roy on to the plane on time, still no contract signature.

Later I could not reach Roy. I wanted to have the signature in hand before our spring board meeting. I finally called Jack O'Connell and said I was asking Chicago whether they could keep dates open for us because I was not sure—in view of the lack of a signed contract—that we had a deal with Roy. Ten minutes later, the elusive Roy Hofheinz was on the phone wanting to know why I was so "antsie." I said that I was trying to protect our flanks because of his difficulties in signing the contract which simply were not understandable to me. He said, "Well, I tell you, we have a problem here." He said, "I want the people of the livestock show, which owns the Astrohall, to put in improvements you fellows said you needed. We still haven't gotten their agreement, and I've been telling them you don't want to sign because of that." So I said, "Roy, why don't you sign the contract, send it up to us, and we'll come down there and talk to those people and try to help to get them to make the commitments." He said, "All right." Leon Wiener and I then went to Houston and were guests at a dinner at the Shamrock. We met what amounted to the Houston establishment. Roy explained to them that we had some reservations about facilities—particularly the sanitary facilities and the availability of certain utility outlets in Astrohall. We also thought it necessary, he said, to have the large air conditioners which were scattered throughout the hall raised about the floor and out of sight. Furthermore, he pointed out, we wanted adequate meeting rooms and the meeting rooms were not then available at Astrohall. By the time we were through, there was a group of highly convinced Houstonians. They decided to put up the money to improve the facility to do what Roy Hofheinz had promised.

One of the interesting things about our dealings with Roy was that, in the end, his word was good and every promise he made—whether in writing or not—was kept. I can't ignore the great efforts made by the city, the convention bureau, the Junior Chamber of Commerce, and by Houston in general to prepare for our convention. I would like to say that they were really splendid hosts and went the last mile to try to help. Our first convention in Houston was a rip-snorting success. A couple of items I remember were the problem we had with the ballroom just prior to the convention opening. Apparently Roy wanted to have the largest chandelier in any hotel in the country and decided to add several rows of glass—I forget what they are called—to the chandelier so that it would be slightly larger than the one at the Waldorf. This was finally completed the day before we were due to use the ballroom.

The National Sporting Goods Association was one of the first large organizations to have a convention in the Astrodome complex. G. Marvin Shutt, executive director with offices in Chicago, became a member of the "Roy Hofheinz Admiration Society" as he dealt with the Judge. He said in 1978,

After meeting Roy at a farewell party we gave in Chicago when John O'Connell decided to leave McCormick Place to become a vice-president of the

Houston Sports Association, I went to Houston in 1966 to check out the possibility of holding our annual convention and trades show in Houston. The hallmark of working with Judge Hofheinz was that you didn't need to have a signed contract, all you had to do was say "yes." If you agreed, everything was fine, and you had no problems because each person accepted the other one's word. If there were difficulties that arose, as there always are in the case of putting on a large show or convention, Hofheinz was willing and could help solve problems and make decisions rapidly and fairly. This is a very rare trait in the business world—to be able to do business for millions of dollars just by a handshake. That is the way that I personally like to do business, and Judge Hofheinz was one in a million. He has had an effect on everyone with whom he came in contact. One could not help but have a feeling that he would give extra inspiration to do a little bit more for what is necessary for a real success. If you measure success by the people who have loved him and known him, he's a success. If you measure him by the people who may not like him, he is also a success.

Shutt recalled that his wife, Margaret, and he were escorted through the "Celestial Suite" atop Astroworld Hotel. Mrs. Shutt noticed a large figure, "Justice with Scales." She turned to Hofheinz and said, "The scales of justice are seldom in balance." The telephone rang and interrupted the exchange. Hofheinz answered and returned to say, "It's my banker. He's more interested in my good health than anything else, because I owe him and others so much money."

Shutt said that after Hofheinz suffered a stroke, an incident in O'Hare airport involving the Judge was always fresh in his mind. He recalled:

Roy, Mary Frances, and his grandchildren were on their way to the all-star game in Milwaukee. My wife and I were returning from a trip. In the luggage area at O'Hare, I saw the Judge and Mary Frances at the far end waiting for their luggage. He was in his wheelchair. Roy saw me and said, "Mary Frances, there's Marvin, go get him." She came running and I held open my arms. When a staff member asked, "Who's that Marvin is hugging and kissing?" Margaret answered, "That's Judge Hofheinz's wife." Mary Frances and I walked over to the Judge and we had a great visit. I think that shows the personal nature of the man—he never forgot friends.

At our convention in Houston in 1975, the Judge came to a dance we put on and we presented him with the first NSGA Sportsmatic Seth Thomas watch, duly engraved. That was in recognition of what he had done to help us make the show and develop the growth of our convention in Houston in 1969, 1973, and 1975. The growth of the association has been tremendous and we got the first big spurt when we went to Houston in 1969. In 1978 when we met in Houston again, we had 8000 members. About 45,000 attended that convention and trade show. We had almost 1700 exhibitors, twice as many as in 1969. We've outgrown the Astrodome complex and unless more facilities are added, I don't think we can return again.

Robert E. Smithwick in 1979 was general manager of Texaco with offices in Harrison, New York. He recalled his warm business relationship with Hofheinz:

> I first met the Judge in 1964 when Texaco transferred me to Houston. He was in the beginning stages of masterminding the Astrodome. He was running the Colt .45s. The Astrodome was under construction. Hofheinz spent a great deal of his time attempting package arrangements which would benefit both the purchaser and the HSA. He was first and foremost looking for a radio and television sponsor of his baseball schedule for the 1964 and subsequent seasons. In my role as one of the marketing managers for Texaco, I had an objective that dealt with attempting to increase profitably our sales through our retail and wholesale outlets in Texas. Hofheinz had innumerable ways that he felt that this could be done. I knew him intimately up until my transfer to Denver in late 1968, and up through my transfer from Denver, Colorado, to our headquarters in New York City in 1970.
>
> I had many wonderful experiences with Hofheinz. The one that stands out most in my mind occurred one evening when my telephone rang in my northern New Jersey suburban home. It was Mary Frances. She said, "Bob, the Judge plans to be in New York on Sunday night at his suite in the Waldorf Towers and would like very much for you to meet him there at seven o'clock. Come prepared to spend the night. He has some things he'd like to discuss with you and then you can go direct to your office from the hotel on Monday morning." I said, "M.F., I don't see how I can do that. Why don't you ask the Judge to call me when he comes in and then we'll see if we can't make arrangements to get together." Mary Frances' response was, "Bob, you know the Judge thinks a great deal of you and he would like to see you." It was pretty much left that I would be there at seven o'clock in the Judge's suite. I went to his suite just a few minutes before seven o'clock. The Judge was not there and neither was anyone else. The huge three-bedroom suite with living room, dining room, and resplendent with all its great trappings, was standing idle and was obviously awaiting Hofheinz's triumphant entrance. He never went anywhere except with great pomp and circumstance befitting his character and the role of respect that he garnered from everyone with whom he came in contact, at least, those people who had the privilege of knowing him well.
>
> About 8:30 the Judge came in with others in the party and greeted me warmly as he always did—big cigar clinched between his teeth and said, "Bob, we have a lot to talk about." All of this came on the heels of our having made a business arrangement between Texaco and the Judge where we would be one of the principal sponsors of the radio-television baseball broadcasts, a participant in the Astroworld park, and the advertiser on the scoreboard in the Dome, and in addition to that, the lessee of a service station that was built to mini-dome specifications on the loop outside the Astrodomain complex. We had dinner delivered to the room which had been pre-arranged by someone in the Judge's party. About 1:00 A.M., after much conversation about all sorts of things, the Judge decided that we should all retire. There were four other people in the

party and the Judge turned to me and said, "Bob, you and I will share a bedroom." We went into the bedroom with two big beds. We proceeded to get ready to go to sleep. I lay my head on the pillow and as usual in about six seconds I was asleep. I had been asleep for some undetermined period of time when all of a sudden I awoke with a start to the noise of what sounded like a freight train coming—only to find that it was the Judge lying on his back in his bright red, silk pajamas, snoring away, cigar lit and lying in the ash tray on the table between the beds, and all the lights on. It appeared, "Well, I'm awake for the night." I rolled over on the side and tried desperately to close my eyes and return to the land of sleep. Suddenly I was awakened again with what sounded like the gondolier on top of the Astrodome bouncing off second base. It was the Judge jumping up out of bed grabbing his cigar, clinching it between his teeth, walking over to the dresser, taking pencil in hand and paper that was lying in a ready position, and beginning to make some notes.

I didn't say anything because I didn't want to get into a business conversation at that hour of the morning. A quick glance at my watch told me it was after 2:00 A.M. Roy got back in bed, put the cigar back on the night stand and both of us proceeded to fall asleep. I did, only to be awakened a short time later with a tremendous roar. It was his snoring again, and the huge midriff was rising up and down which each breath he took. The noise sounded not unlike a 747 taking off from an airport. The Judge awakened again, bounced out of bed, repeated the same procedure, grasping his cigar between his teeth, going over to the dresser, making notes, coming back, replacing the cigar in the ash tray, and going back to bed. This continued until about 5:10 when I awoke with a start at what I later determined was absolute silence. There wasn't a sound anywhere; the lights were off. I looked over, as I turned the light on, to find that the Judge's bed was empty. I staggered out of bed after having had an interrupted evening's sleep of short duration, put on my robe, and walked out down the hall into the living room where I found the Judge sitting in a chair surrounded by newspapers from all over the world, delivered by one of the hotel service men who was pouring coffee into the Judge's cup—at shortly after five o'clock in the morning. The Judge said, "Good morning, Bob, I hope you slept well. I sure had a productive night. I had several great ideas during the evening." To me, this described Roy Hofheinz to a T. Even when he was asleep, his mind worked wonders to produce results that would have made P. T. Barnum look like a newsboy.

I was saddened when I learned of Roy's stroke later that year because I knew that this would slow down a great man. I heard him say one time when we were talking about a mutual friend of ours who was in charge of a corporate entity dealing with forward planning: "He's a good man, but for forward planning, he should really be in charge of hindsight observation." It wasn't that he didn't like the person, it was just that he had such a unique ability to size up the capability of a man as it regarded the contributions that that person might make to the Judge's overall effort. Roy Hofheinz is one of the greatest men I've ever known. I enjoyed his sense of humor, his charm, his wit, but most of all he came as close to being a genius as anyone whom I'd ever met.

O. Kelley Anderson

O. Kelley Anderson, former president and chairman of the board of New England Mutual Life Insurance Company in Boston, after he retired talked in 1979 of his relationship with Hofheinz. He said:

> I can remember very distinctly meeting the Hofheinzes in 1960. One of my senior officers of the investment department called me and he said he had a Judge Hofheinz with him and wanted my presence for lunch. Even I had heard a little bit about Hofheinz by then and one of the things I knew was he had a baseball team coming up and I was quite a baseball fan. We had a special dining room. Roy was a genial, heavy-set fellow and obviously enthusiastic. We got along fine right away.
>
> We had a good time. We subsequently did business with the Judge. Every time I saw him there was never anything dull or conventional about him. I saw him in New York, Boston, and California. My associates were more active with him, saw him in Texas and various other places. I had a good personal friend, Ben McGuire. McGuire, his mother, and my mother were friends many years ago. It was he, I believe, who brought the Judge to our company. Roy's son, Fred, used to drop in and see me from time to time, before he was mayor.
>
> The Judge was really serious about this air-conditioned baseball stadium . . . which I thought was nuts. Sherman Badger was my financial vice-president. He didn't think much of the Dome idea either. He told Hofheinz if he had any idea of building a covered, air-conditioned stadium, he ought to get it financed by the city or county. We told him the government unit could borrow the

money, tax free, and he could lease it. I didn't know anything more until about 1962 that Harris County had voted bonds. I felt, since he had accomplished that, he was one of the greatest salesmen that this generation had had.

Right after that, Hofheinz called me and wanted me to come down and see a mockup of the Astrodome. I wasn't available to go down. Later he called and asked Mrs. Anderson and me to come to the World Series in New York in 1960. He brought along his wife, Dene, and Bob Smith and his wife, Vivian, who were delightful. Roy and Smith had the Prince of Wales suite in the Waldorf. He had the model of the Astrodome installed in the suite. Talk about snake oil! He sure had it. We had a pleasant time. The next spring, Roy invited me down to the Dome opening. I couldn't be there April 9, but I went down about 10 days before that. I'll never forget that dream come true. Our mortgage department loaned Roy money to develop some of the land surrounding the Astrodome. I'm a baseball nut and I'd never seen anything like the Astrodome in all my life. The first time I went they were still putting down seats and training usherettes. I walked in and, by gosh, out on the center field they had fireworks going. I then went to his office and soon, by God, he practically had my biography on the scoreboard. I went to the playing field and told him I'd never been in a dugout and I wanted to do it. The dugout went from first base way out to right field, way out to left field. This showed me what a salesman he was. He said, "You know, people from all over the country are going to come to the Astrodome here and they're going to see a ballgame and everyone will ask, 'Where did you sit?' They can say, 'Right behind the dugout.' " He said he had 25,000 seats behind the dugout. Normally, at Fenway Park in Boston, we've got about a 1000. He really made an impression on me; he just knew how to do everything.

A couple of years later, he came up to Boston for the World Series. We've got a nifty little stadium there. When there's a big crowd, nobody can go out in the street. Roy got a great big car there. The governor couldn't get in there and the mayor couldn't get in there. I think he told them Johnson was coming, or something. He never bragged about things, but they happened. I remember the time he had a nice party at his hotel. A lot were there. There was no music and by God, he had Spec Richardson to go out and buy a piano so we could have music. I don't know where Spec got it.

Two of my associates, John Storey and Stokes Gaither, were in my financial department. They used to go shooting and fishing with Roy some place south of Houston. I went with Roy and Storey to Disneyland when the Judge was planning Astroworld. We flew to Los Angeles, first to see an all-star game and then to see Disneyland. I flew back from Los Angeles to Houston and went out to Astroworld. He had my name on one display, either in wigs or a barber of some kind. He did that, not just with me, but for a lot of other people.

I never will forget the time we were down in Houston and Mrs. Anderson was with me. We went over to the "Celestial Suite" and felt there was nothing left in Asia for him to buy and put in there. He showed me pictures of who had been in the Dome, an aerial picture of the Astrodome and pointed me to a little spot on it. He said, "That's the Astrodome, 40 miles up." That evening, Roy took a group of us around. I showed one young man this picure. I said, "Roy said this is a picture of the Astrodome taken 40 miles up." He said, "No, it was taken 60 miles up." I said, "No, I think it was 40." Well, after he got through, Hofheinz said, "I see you got along pretty well with my friend." I said, "Yes, we had a little argument—I said this picture was taken 40 miles up and he said no it was 60." He said, "Well, he ought to know; he's Alan Shepard."

Once my associate, Stokes Gaither, told me, "Roy wants you to come down, but don't go." He said, "I don't want to be unkind to him because he's a heck of a nice guy, but don't go, he'll snow you." I feel Roy was a combination of old P. T. Barnum and an international banker. He was astute and I liked him very much. He had to do everything himself, and he had everything under control. He was a promoter. He wanted to do things with other people's money, and he was perfectly willing to pay a good rate of interest. Sometimes he got a little over-extended, but as far as I'm concerned, with us he came out with flying colors. There were some squeaky times. I know he had some pretty close calls. I'm aware that he had some opportunities to sell out at a fantastic price which he wouldn't do. Roy certainly put Houston on the map by just being the promoter of the Astrodome. That's about like the hanging gardens of Babylon, and other places around the world. I remember when he bought Ringling. I thought he was crazy, but, you know, I think he wished he had been in the circus all his life.

I'll never forget one time when he was abroad. He bought up stuff in the Balkan states. I got a cable that said he was having a hard time shipping three elephants over and he was shipping them to me in Boston and asked if I would get them on to Houston. You know, he had a marvelous sense of humor. He was almost a Will Rogers. I don't know how he got motivated, but he had the stuff to move ahead.

36

Designing and Collecting

In his long career of building, Roy Hofheinz had assistance in designing, decorating, and furnishing his creations. Stuart Young was his chief craftsman in making models and carving exquisite furniture. Harper Goff, a nationally known Oscar-winning Hollywood designer, and Sam Daidone, Houston expert whose main hobby was collecting antiques and artifacts with help from tipsters scattered around the nation, were key figures with Young in three of the Judge's unusual ventures—the unique rooms and apartments in the right-field wall of the Astrodome, "Celestial Suite" in Astroworld Hotel, and various decorations and attractions in the Astroworld amusement park.

Hofheinz was no amateur in designing and collecting himself, starting early as an adult, but he needed the expertise of others, usually in a hurry, to help him carry out his fantastic ideas. Frank Arnold and Raymond Rogers of Houston were among the early contributors to the decor of "Huckster House," Yorktown, and the various offices the Judge occupied. In the late 1960s and early 1970s, however, Goff and Daidone combined to put extra dimensions to the projects of the growing Astrodomain.

In 1979 Goff was project engineer for Disneyworld's newly announced EXCOT Center project and specialized in planning international pavilions for World Showcase, permanent international exposition, expected to be completed at the big Florida resort in 1982. He was employed by Entyniss, Incorporated, Disney's master-planning firm, key designer of the great expansion planned for the fun center just west of Orlando. Goff shuttled between Los Angeles and Houston for years in working for Hofheinz.

The Judge's railroad car brainstorm brought the two together initially. Goff recalled that he was contacted in 1966 by Harpour Locomotive Works of San Pedro who asked him to "design some cars for a railroad to be built in Houston at an amusement park adjacent to the Astrodome for a man whom I later learned was Judge Hofheinz." An invitation for Goff to visit him in Houston came soon after the designer's preliminary sketches reached the Judge. During the years that followed, respect which from the outset each had for the other's creative ability was to develop into a valued friendship.

Harper Goff

Hofheinz told Goff about the railroad he had in mind. When he learned Goff had an affiliation with Minibus, Incorporated, designers and makers of minibuses and trams, he discussed "two four-car circus-carnival-type trams with big engines, two four-car stage-coach-type trams, and two four-car covered-wagon types. I want a personal VIP-type car like a San Francisco trolley car, only I want it fixed up with a bar. That'll be kind of a sales car when I am taking people around in order to sell them convention space in the Dome or the hotels that I intend to build. We won't have to ride with the crowd but can go across in a private car." Fred Hofheinz was present during the conversation, and when he protested that his father should order only one of each tram before deciding on the others, the Judge looked at Goff and said, "I don't have to look twice at a four-leaf clover to know it's lucky."

The Judge always knew what he wanted. Also, he insisted that it be top quality. "When he inspected samples of things for trains," Goff continued, "the Judge would look at me real hard and say, 'It is the best of the lot, isn't it? I want the best.' " Goff designed a special VIP railroad car with a beautiful art glass dome. His plans called for it to be supported by marble-like columns. He recommended a Californian for the job, telling the Judge the man could "take a wood turning and paint it and grain it so it looks just like finest marble." Hofheinz vetoed the idea, however, for he wanted the columns to be authentic, not imitation marble. Goff was astonished; the painted columns he had in mind would have been expensive enough, but the Judge always wanted the best. His taste for hot peppers was no exception. Once, while on a Sunday afternoon drive with Harper and Flossie Goff, Hofheinz spotted "the best hot peppers [he had] ever seen" at a roadside vegetable stand. He bought the stunned proprietor's entire stock and, "with a great deal of joy, industry, and enthusiasm," washed and preserved the peppers himself. His pride in his product was evident from his gifts of peppers to friends in years to come.

Goff said the VIP section he designed was in the right-field section of the Astrodome. Behind center field at a certain level was the scoreboard. It was on that level the Judge decided that he wanted five floors of VIP apartments and guest rooms.

"He assigned me to fill these five floors of about 200 feet long by approximately 14 feet wide with suitable rooms and private areas," Goff recalled. "In doing this, we first started on the seventh level and provided an elaborate and a suitably secure presidential suite. This took up the equivalent of two floors. The presidential living room was two floors high with great chandeliers hanging down, elegant carpets, and genuine Louis XIV and XV furniture, tapestries, and fine paintings. There was a presidential bedroom and an elaborate presidential bath as well as an anteroom, communications office where the red telephone would be located, and guest rooms. He was always thinking of Lyndon Johnson and his family. The two Johnson girls had elaborate princess-type suites. The Judge had a handmade circular rug with the Seal of the President of the United States of America to adorn an entry. Permission for use of the seal was given by President Johnson. This room had a library and all the Judge's books that he collected over the years. The entry room connected with the Judge's private suite, or box, where the president came for the first game in the stadium. The presidential suite, of course, could be used by any future president, or people like Billy Graham and Frank Sinatra." Randall "Randy" Duell, formerly an award-winning Hollywood set designer specializing in period French, selected the furnishings and decor for the presidential suite. Duell now is a planner and designer of theme parks such as Astroworld and Six Flags Over Texas.

Goff continued to describe his work:

> I designed a miniature golf course and a small billiard parlor, all in the period of the 1870s, 1880s, and 1890s. We roamed the country for antiques to fill these. I was allowed to develop an idea I'd always had: the "Tipsy Tavern." The bar would be tilted about 20 degrees so that when you walked across the floor it would seem like you had had too much to drink, because you couldn't keep your balance. We had a trick spittoon which would make a loud noise and splash and spin-a-round on itself and finally come to rest. We had a special elevator. If you had to go to the restroom, the Judge would tell you to take that

elevator and go down to the restroom on a different floor. You would get in this elevator, press a button, the door would close and then you would seemingly go down an interminable distance into what seemed like the bowels of the earth, when actually you didn't leave the area where you were. The elevator would vibrate and the floor would seem to drop out from under you and you would look out a tiny window and see the brick walls of the elevator shaft going by for what seemed like hours. Finally you'd make a jolting landing at the bottom of this elevator shaft and another door would open up and let you move into a dank, dirty, dark, ill-conceived restroom which consisted of nothing more than a barrel with a five-gallon can of water and a hose with a clamp on it, and a sign saying, "When finished using toilet, please release a small amount of water." There were cobwebs in the disastrous-looking place. Many was the time I saw a lady guest who had been on this imaginative trip come back and say to her escort, "Don't bother to go down to that toilet if you don't have to because it is ghastly." The Judge loved this because right around the corner was a lovely restroom.

Another amusing thing in the "Tipsy Tavern" was at the end of the bar where a guest would sit. We had implanted under the bar top a 60-pound electromagnet. In the base of one of our big beer steins, we had a steel cylinder set up in the hollow part. When someone sitting on that end seat ordered a beer, the bartender, who was always in on it—most of the time it was the Judge himself—would choose this special mug, fill it up to the rim with beer and then send it sliding down the bar at a great rate of speed. You just knew it was going to come right off in the guest's lap, but then the bartender would put his foot on a pedal to activate the magnet under the bar, and the beer would come right up within two inches of the edge of the bar—after the guest had gotten off the stool trying to get out of the way of this flying beer stein—and stop dead in its tracks. We had an unexpected humorous event once. A man stepped back to take the stein to drink. The Judge was a little late in deactivating the magnet and the visitor was tugging at the stein, trying to lift it off the bar, and, when the Judge belatedly deactivated the magnet, beer flew all over the visitor.

Goff also designed a beauty parlor, a children's library and playgrounds, and a chapel in the Dome. Also fashioned were a New Orleans dining room, an elaborate board room, an early American barber shop, a South Seas Polynesian dining room, and numerous private suites.

Goff related that when "the Judge began building hotels, most of them were designed by Brodnax and Phenix. However, shortly after beginning construction of Astroworld Hotel, the Judge got an idea that he wanted to redesign the upper two floors and make them into the finest penthouse in the world. I was brought back from California especially for this project." Goff recalled:

We decided to put the circus motif in all Astroworld Hotel public rooms. The Judge intended to live there, moving out of his quarters in the Dome. Inasmuch as the Judge traveled a lot, he thought he would make the penthouse so that it would have a lot of guest rooms for his own friends when he was there and could turn it over to the hotel when he was out of town. I was given a year to design and get the penthouse built. It was one of the most interesting jobs I ever had. I spent two months on designs. We made simple plans. There wasn't time to go further. I started construction almost in a manner of drawing out on the floor a plan of the building and designing the surface texture right off the top of my head. I don't suppose any other man in the world would have ever given anybody the go-ahead on that basis. All the Judge said to me was, "I want a penthouse so designed that when people come to visit me they will have never seen anything like it. I want nobody ever to be able to top me, or top this penthouse." So it was a great challenge.

The next year was one of the most exciting and entertaining that I ever had. The Judge, Mary Frances, my wife, and I toured up and down Texas and Louisiana to buy antique furniture. Instead of building a house totally, we designed the penthouse and the different rooms to accommodate the furniture the Judge had bought. I came up with the idea that we name each of the individual suites after great names in history, literature or legend.

We started off by designing the Judge's private quarters and I gave him a kind of baronial, crusader-type suite with a great stone fireplace, huge carved mantle, great size. Stuart Young made an eight by eight foot, four-poster bed like a royal bed, with a huge canopy over the top. Up in the canopy was hidden a 21-inch television set. You could lie in bed and see television with remote controls. You could control the drapes and all the curtains from the Judge's bed. At the side of the bed, as you came into the bedroom, up a couple of steps with marble pilasters was a fireplace. On one side of the fireplace was a little breakfast nook. A huge private bath area included the Judge's wash basin, settled in the cap of a big actual Corinthian capital from a Roman column. There was an extravagant brass swan's neck water faucet and hot and cold water taps, gold plated, and a beautiful antique oval mirror which swung out from a medicine cabinet. It was a great room with a tub about 20 feet long. At the entrance to the tub was a large oval tub about seven feet long, a jacuzzi-type for heat therapy. Big Roman columns surrounded it. In back was a special little alcove that included Roman urns and beautiful imported Italian tile and a vast shower. That went into a long Roman pool backed up against a stone wall; about 12 feet up on the wall was an antique bronze lion's head. You could pre-program the kind of water you wanted. The swimming pool was 20 feet long. You could swim, shower, or go into the jacuzzi.

There was a door in the wall which you could unlock and find a private dressing room, small shower, wash basin, wardrobe room, a sewing room, and a balcony. On a different level was a cold storage room for furs. This could be locked off from the rest of the suite so that when the Judge was out of town he could lock one particular door and the suite could be used without having to move personal possessions.

The second thing designed was a night club called the "Mini-dome." It was an accurate replica of the Astrodome. This was where you could have big private parties. The "Mini-dome" looked from the inside and the outside almost exactly like the Astrodome. You could see out of the 16-foot high tempered glass windows which surrounded the whole area. In this area were two bars, a kitchen, a catering facility and many of the Judge's band organs and automatic musical equipment.

On the second floor was a pool room with a billiard table, band organs, and a balcony. You could look down on a green linoleum baseball diamond below. On this baseball diamond we had a kind of shuffleboard game you could play by using the rules of baseball. There was a scoreboard which was an exact replica of that which was in the Dome.

A large television screen was in the center of the "Mini-dome." You could see whatever game happened to be at the Astrodome at the time, and VIPs didn't have to bestir themselves to go to the Astrodome. The replica of the information on the scoreboard in the Dome was repeated in the miniature in the penthouse.

Next to the Judge's suite was "The Marble Library." This was a replica of part of the royal palace in Madrid and had an elaborate, carved, gold leaf ceiling, and book cases were built up to the elaborate gold leaf cornice around the room. The marble was fine imported Italian with lovely stripings. We installed a fabulous mantelpiece brought from a French chateau. The fire screen was from Queen Wilhelmina's winter palace outside of Amsterdam. A specially designed large Spanish conversation grouping of high back chairs was placed around the fireplace. Windows opened on a balcony overlooking the city. Antique stained glass graced the upper part of the window. Beautiful antique furniture and statuary lamps made up the rest of this room. This room had a door to a corridor and also went into a dining room in the form of a gold bird cage. It had controlled lighting which could run the gamut of colors for whatever kind of party you wanted.

A tremendous antique chandelier hung down above a beautiful table which was based on a gorgeous lion's head pool table base from a turn-of-the-century New Orleans poolroom. We had dining table top leaves that could go over the pool table so that when one was having a dinner party this could be a dining room with its dozens of gold chairs. After the dinner, the dining table top was removed and there was one of the most elegant pool tables that you could possibly conceive.

There were china cabinets for the Judge's collection of beautiful English china. Through two antique swinging, stained-glass doors, you went into a modern kitchen, a copy of a Mexican kitchen south of the border. The kitchen had a center cooking island, and over it was a decorated tile chimney to take the cooking fumes out of the room. An antique circular pot hanger accommodated the Judge's collection of antique cooking utensils which were both decorative and practical. There was a lovely little breakfast alcove where you could sit and eat off Spanish dishes on a Spanish tile tabletop and look out of a window to see Houston.

There was a tiled corridor that connected with the private elevator, key operated, that would take you from the ground floor on the outside up the side of the hotel, giving you a view of the Astrodome and the rest of the four hotels.

You would arrive up at the top and come out on this special little landing area with one of the most beautiful antique mirrors, about 16 feet tall, that I've ever seen, and special chandeliers.

Then you came around into the general entry area where the regular elevator stopped. Two fountains were there and you could either go to the "Mini-dome" or you could turn the other way and go down a long corridor which had a green house roof over the top that opened to the sky. Poodle trees grew along the walk. To the right and left of this corridor you could enter the Judge's suite, "The Marble Library," "The Golden Bird Cage Dining Room," or "The Monterrey Kitchen." On the other side you would find small private suites named after such people as Sadie Thompson, with South Pacific-type bamboo and missionary South Pacific architecture. Artificial rain fell alongside the window on the balcony all night long.

Next to the "Sadie Thompson Room" was the "Lillian Russell Room" in which there was an elaborate, vast enamel bedstead and a beautiful, elaborate stove. The bed had a canopy and was all the colors that were in the taste of Lillian Russell. All the bathrooms were almost as large as the suites and had special step-down step-in tubs, all themed to the room itself. The "Lillian Russell" was antique with chain-pull toilets and an old fashioned pedestal wash basin. Passing the "Lillian Russell Room" you came to a semi-circular patio which was reminiscent of much of small European patios with the sky showing through skylights from above and a huge fountain.

There was a choice of two larger individual suites. One was "The P. T. Barnum Suite" and the other was "The Adventurer Suite." "The P. T. Barnum Suite" had one room which was called the "Bandwagon Room" in which the king-sized bed was based on a famous Ringling bandwagon, complete with carvings of trumpeting angels on the headboard. There was a peacock on it, and it had red velvet upholstery and special lamps. Instead of being on casters or legs, the bed was set on elaborate circus wheels. All beds had special covers. This suite's ceilings were carved in gold leaf ornaments on the sides. There was a special fireplace. The bathroom was themed toward the circus and was highly decorative. Part of the circus suite was the "Big Top," which could be a suite itself if you wanted to break it up into small parties. The "Big Top" part had no bed, but a huge couch nine feet long could be folded into a tremendous bed. This was decorated with memorabilia from the life of Barnum. The wallpaper and paintings that I had painted myself commemorated the highlights of Barnum's life.

We had an original statue of Tom Thumb, one of Barnum's most widely acclaimed attractions. The other half was "The Adventurer Suite." Here we took from literature. The outer suite with the permanent bed in it was the "Fu Manchu." It was in high Chinese style and elaborate with Chinese antiques, lamps, bedspreads, and carvings. That joined with the "Tarzan Suite," a duplication of a forest complete with trees and branches and hammocks clearing the floor and decorative wall paper. The suite had a fabulous bath. It seemed like you were taking a bath in a pool in the middle of a tropical forest. This suite was for anyone who had a lot of children. They could use the "Fu Manchu Suite" and then pile all of their children in the "Tarzan Suite" where there were ropes to hang on and balconies and trees to climb.

The penthouse represented the way the Judge thought. It was my good fortune to have many hours with him, planning and chewing the fat over ideas. The Judge gave me a free hand. Nobody second-guessed me. The final product was unparalleled.

In summary of Hofheinz, Goff said:

> Although I spent a great deal of the Judge's money in my work, I never felt any anxiety or nervousness. For example, this job that I now have on the Disney project in Florida keeps me awake nights and is very wearing and tiring, and a lot of nervous energy is spent and very little reward. I don't mean monetary reward, but satisfaction, because everything is so far away and long in the future. But working with the Judge, at the end of every hard day's work there was the reward of companionship and talking to each other about the day's accomplishments, and that special show biz atmosphere and life and humor and talk about fun we had today and what fun we're going to have tomorrow. I consider myself one of the luckiest men in the world to have met this man and to have been a part of his accomplishments. I first sensed, then knew his greatness—the man with the vision to come up with the first domed stadium. He had this ability to put things together at the right time and be a pioneer. Although I was a longtime associate of Walt Disney and undoubtedly he was the great man that everybody felt he was, I will always have a warm place in my heart for Roy Hofheinz, the Hofheinz family, and for his wonderful Astrodomain.

Following completion of plans and drawings of the impressive "Celestial Suite" for the Astroworld Hotel, millionaire hotel enthusiast John D. MacArthur of Florida visited Hofheinz who showed him blueprints and plans for the hotel's $2500-a-night luxury quarters. MacArthur expressed particular interest in specifications for the master bedroom, which had been dubbed the "Crusader Room." Shortly before MacArthur called the Judge and laughingly confessed having "borrowed" one page from the suite's plans, Hofheinz had discovered the loss. MacArthur, whom Mary Frances described as "a good guy," had decided he had to have a replica of Astroworld's "Crusader Room" in his Colonnades Hotel at Palm Beach, Florida. Hofheinz understood.

Antique hobbyist Sam Daidone of Houston recalled his personal and business relationship with the Judge:

> Owning many antique and fancy cars, I was called on to furnish three cars for a parade from the Gulf Freeway to the University of Houston. Mayor Hofheinz rode in a 1912 Model T. Hugh Roy Cullen and I rode in a 1908 Sears, a two-cylinder, high-wheeler outer buggy, and city and university officials rode in a 1912 Overland touring car. It was 12 years later that the Judge's path and mine crossed again. After I had collected many antiques, a hobby begun in

1950, I had stored in three buildings and rented houses antique cars, furniture, music boxes, cigar store Indians, steam operated peanut roasters, tractors, and so on. When Hofheinz announced plans for an amusement park near the Dome, I contacted him about my antique collection, and he and his son, Fred, came over and checked out the antiques. I remember the Judge asking me not to turn on the music box or any mechanically operated antiques, or elaborate on any of them. He just wanted to look at them without comment. When he was through, he told me that he was ready to buy and to meet him at the Dome to close the deal. We did. I found out that the Judge was an older antique collector than I. Of course he collected more rare and expensive items that I did not. Many people thought the Judge was foolish in buying a large collection of junk, as they called my collection, but the Judge was years ahead of them because today, two of the 20 cars in the collection would pay for the entire collection. A complete antiquated drug store that I bought—Bill Huston's store—with the collection, one item in the store alone now is worth around $5000. I sold one car for $25 which is now worth $60,000 to $65,000. The Judge was years ahead of expert antique collectors.

A few years later, after our deal, the Judge's antiques were still stored in my care when someone noticed an old bicycle hanging from the ceiling of one building. He wanted me to ask the Judge if he could use that bicycle for reproduction and selling. When I asked the Judge about this matter, he remarked, "Oh yes, you mean the bicycle hanging near a window that had no chains on it?" I said, "Yes sir." There were about 10 bicycles hanging from the ceiling, but the Judge remembered this one especially and probably the others, too. The Judge then asked me to retire from my business and join him in the department of antiques at Astrodomain.

The Judge was versatile in his choice of antiques. It just depended on what he needed and he even bought when he didn't need things. My headquarters for a time were in the amusement park. The Judge and Goff called on me to find everything from gunny sacks to old furniture, everything needed at the park. The Judge wanted stained glass. I went down and bought a big van load at $1600. I made good deals for him. I bought a whole drug store at Damon's Mound, 60 miles from Houston, for $500. We got a juke box, about 15 wall cases, a marble soda fountain and a lot of old drugs.

On occasion, the Judge would call and say he wanted to go antique hunting. I was always ready to go. We started out one morning and I said, "Let's go to Galveston. I know somebody there who has got an awfully big collection, especially Wooten desks, not rolltops." Each of those had a mail box and two wide doors about a foot and a half thick which would open and had chutes for incoming and outgoing mail. The Judge had a big time looking over music boxes and furniture, but especially the Wooten desks. The Judge quickly bought one. I had to make arrangements to have it picked up later. We drove to Houston. It being Saturday, a lot of the shops were closed. We went out on Westheimer and stopped at a country store owned by a fellow named Sowell. We bought a few items there. As we headed towards the Dome, we stopped by a place called Richard's. I think the Judge bought at least $50,000 worth of stuff before he left the place. He looked at a unique piece of furniture, about nine feet high and about 15 feet long. It was built for a baron, general and banker in France. The common name for it today is "breakfront." That piece is magnificent. As we were going out, the Judge said, "Wait a minute. What about the breakfront?" Mary Frances and I said we didn't think he wanted it for $65,000. He said, "I want it." So we had to clear a lot of furniture away so he could wheel his chair up to it. He wanted to see it again. He looked again and said, "I still want it." He asked if I could get the seller to come down in price. "All right," I said, "I'll do my best." I got Richard aside and said, "Listen, I know about antiques and I know value of a lot of things and I know you can afford to reduce your price. I think the Judge is interested." I said, "If he thinks you're too high and won't work with him on it, he'll just say keep it." He thought a while and said he'd cut $5000. I told the Judge. He told the owner to put a sold tag on it. That wasn't all. We stopped at Samuel Hart Galleries, on Main Street. My gosh, when they got through there, I can't remember exactly, but it was a bundle he spent.

I had a friend in Shawnee, Oklahoma, Bill Stewart. He passed away and he left a collection of about 40 cars—collectors' items. Word got to me so I talked to the Judge and said, "Judge, there are 40 cars there and my advice to you is not to collect any more cars—you have 30 now." He said: "I want to go up there." The Judge, Mary Frances, and I flew by commercial flight to Shawnee and went to the Stewart home. There we met Jimmie Leake, a big operator in Muskogee. He had a lot of cars and was a big auctioneer. He wanted to show the Judge his collection, too. We investigated all of the cars and the Judge said, "Well, what do you think?" I said, "Judge, I want to point out two cars to you, just two out of the 40. See that Mercer Raceabout and that 1935 Dusenberg?" I said, "Judge, you could sell those two cars on today's market for everything you might pay for the whole 40. You'll wind up with 38 cars free, outside of transportation to Houston on them." I added that my friend, Lister Sander, of San Antonio, and antique dealers from elsewhere would be in Shawnee to buy. "If I were you, I'd tie this deal up right now." We tied up the deal. Later we heard that Sander, while we were going home, flew to Shawnee to buy. I think the Stewarts wanted the Judge to have them because he was talking about a museum at this time.

To bolster his financial position, Hofheinz had to auction part of his collection of antique cars on June 8, 1974. Elizabeth Bennett of the *Post* reported May 31: "Houston's flamboyant Roy Hofheinz has never done things on a small scale. And now, the mastermind behind the $100 million Astrodomain complex has a new project. He's selling his cars—those rare antique automobiles he started collecting as a boy in the '20s. And like in his colorful career, the sale promises to be A Big Event, complete with auctioneer in black tie and tails, candelabra and crystal chandeliers, and collectors and celebrities on hand from all across the country." Officials from the New York auction house that conducted the sale said Hofheinz netted $545,820.

The Judge and Bernard Calkins at antique automobile auction in Astrohall. **Photograph** by Harold Israel, courtesy Gulf Photo.

The public was not informed, but the sale of Hofheinz's antique cars was not of his own volition. Creditors had a lien on the valuable holdings and were anxious for quick cash. In fact, collector Daidone felt the auctioneers hired actually got less money than the sale could have brought. "When I saw the brochure advertising the cars," said Daidone, "I had a fit. I called the Judge and said: 'These people should have asked your opinion on the highs and lows of the cars. I think they're virtually giving away some of the cars. For instance, there's a two-engine, two-cylinder Rambler 1905, single chain drive, open front seats, wood and metal. They've listed that at $1500. They ought to start it from $8000 or more as a minimum. There's a Mercer which ought to start at about $75,000 and work up from there.'" Daidone said he and the Judge had a meeting with T. H. Neyland, then operating chief for the lenders, and complained about the brochure. He added: "I fought about the minimum prices from 10 in the morning until 5 in the afternoon. It seemed to me all interests except the Judge's were at stake. They tried to convince me that even if the minimum price on the Rambler was $1500, it would go for a much higher price at the auction." Daidone said he cited other examples, but got no results—except assurances the minimum prices listed would bring much more.

After the auction, Daidone said his warnings proved correct. Daidone said the Mercer went for $65,000. After the sale, Daidone received a brochure from the man who bought it and it was listed for $150,000 after it had been refurbished. "I went to Mr. Neyland and showed him the brochure to prove I had been right in warning him about the minimum prices. But it was too late. The cars were gone, except for a few the Judge purchased himself to start a new collection." Hofheinz still had some antique cars in 1979 and would not sell. Each year after his retirement, he bought a new Cadillac. He would not trade. He could not get over the feeling that the money received at the forced auction was far less than it should have been, and he bided his time waiting for the opportune moment to sell again. The antique car field boomed in the late 1970s, and the opportunity could present itself to capitalize on what he has left.

Many urged Hofheinz after retirement to sell at auction some of the hundreds of valuable items in a warehouse. Daidone did arrange two small sales—of valuable old music machines and antique furniture—which brought the Judge thousands during 1978 and 1979. But these sales hardly dented the vast collection. It is possible in the future that he may decide to part with more of the treasures he accumulated over more than a quarter of a century.

37

Astroworld—
A Delight for the Family

Roy Hofheinz found it easy to borrow more money and build anew in 1968. John Easter, comptroller of HSA, said it did not take the Judge long to look at financial statements at board meetings. Bankers and insurance companies, which already had made millions in interest by advancing the Judge money for his projects on short-term notes, had confidence the Hofheinz magic in making money would continue. Interest rates for the time were about normal. It wasn't until the turn of the 1970s, when a recession hit, that they went sky high to the detriment of Hofheinz's holdings.

The Judge's majority ownership of stock in the Ringling Bros. and Barnum & Bailey Circus added to his financial prestige. Irvin Feld was a tight operator of the big show and turned it into a profit-maker. Everything appeared rosy for the future of Hofheinz interests. Work, work, work—build, build, build—to sell, sell, sell entertainment to customers and advertising to big companies were the Judge's prime orders to his executives, but he set the pace as usual and grew physically heavier as he did it.

In January Hofheinz reorganized and expanded HSA's public relations, publicity, and promotional staff. Bill Giles, who earlier had become vice-president, directed the public relations staff in all phases of the HSA operation and began coordinating plans for promotion of Astroworld and the motor hotel complex under construction. Wayne Chandler took over the publicity for Astroworld. Fred J. Duckett, formerly assistant director of admissions at Rice University, and Orland Sims, the assistant sports information director at the University of Texas, joined the public relations staff.

The largest crowd in the history of college basketball attended the spectacular game between the University of Houston and the University of California at Los Angeles in the Dome January 20, 1968. It was the first time the vast stadium was tried for the cage sport. Pre-game publicity abounded on the nation's sports pages.

Harry Fouke, Houston's great athletic director, already was an admirer, friend, and sports counselor for Hofheinz and his Astrodome assistants before the basketball game. His football teams began playing in the Dome the first year it opened and had gained national attention. According to Fouke, the idea for what was to be the Dome's premier basketball game was first discussed in 1966 by the Houston athletic director and J. D. Morgan, who later was to direct the athletic program at UCLA. Morgan, then tennis coach for the Bruins, visited Houston with his team en route to the national tennis championships in Miami, and while in Houston he and Fouke talked about the possibility of the Dome's being the site of a Cougar-Bruin basketball contest in 1967-1968. The two men envisioned the court which, when added to the giant stadium, would increase the Dome's already versatile offerings.

"UCLA had a great freshman named Lew Alcindor," Fouke recalled, "and we had a great player named Elvin Hayes. We thought we could draw at least 25,000 people, setting a new basketball record. By the time game night came, we had sold 52,693 tickets. NBC contracted to televise the game to a vast audience and that, of course, gave our Cougars, never before ranked in UCLA's class, the opportunity for national exposure. All the time the Judge was just as interested in the promotion as were the two universities. We were not only tenants of the Dome, but guests. Even though we paid a rental for every game, word went to all executives in the Dome to do whatever was needed for the University of Houston to conduct athletic events there. Newspaper people in the city in 1978 voted that the outstanding athletic event ever conducted in Houston was that game."

Written by Jerry Wizig, a story of the Cougar-Bruin classic carried the Chronicle's headline "UH Stuns Mighty UCLA." It read, "They said it would never happen, but it did—the king is dead. Elvin Hayes built the coffin and the University of Houston barely nudged UCLA's fantastic Bruins into a grave beneath the Domed Stadium, 71-69. Binoculars were the equipment of the night. Before the game, much was made of a possible noise problem. However, from courtside the noise, like the crowd itself, was a distant rumble, swirling around the stadium, then exploding with each Cougar score. The crowd was faceless and a little frightening, but it was a happy crowd—happy when it came, happier when it left. So basketball's first venture under the Dome was a success."

The success of the Houston-UCLA basketball game caused Hofheinz to announce quickly he would try to get the NCAA basketball tournament finals in the Dome. He ultimately won his plea. "The game proved to the world what we contended all along—seating is a matter of relativity and that, presented correctly, any type of sport or form of entertainment can be enthusiastically enjoyed at the Astrodome," Hofheinz said. "We are proceeding full speed ahead to host such great sports attractions as the NCAA finals, indoor track meets, championship tennis, an invitational basketball tourney, major league hockey, and many others," he continued. He said the Dome provided good seats for those in the field boxes on the first level and for everyone up to the skyboxes on the ninth level, 350 feet from the court.

On February 11, the Houston Oilers signed to play 1968 games in the Dome. Bud Adams announced he had signed a contract with the Houston Sports Association to play in the Dome for 10 years. The move to the Dome by the AFL Eastern Division champions apparently was made without settlement with Rice University, which had a five-year contract for the Oilers to play in Rice Stadium. The contract had two years to run. H. Malcolm Lovett, chairman of the board of trustees of Rice, said, "We can only assume that he (Adams) expects to fulfill all of his obligations to Rice University."

Adams said the move to the Dome opened the possibility that Houston might land the 1970 Super Bowl game. "Much has been made of a so-called feud between Judge Hofheinz and me." Adams added, "I would be remiss if I did not dispel such rumors—for they are exactly that, rumors. We are both businessmen and naturally seek the best terms we each can obtain." Adams continued: "It is no secret the Oilers have suffered a declining attendance. The hard facts of business economics dictate remedial measures. In addition, a qualified survey of public opinion, as reflected in editorial form by all media, indicated an overwhelming desire for the Oilers to play in the Dome."

Hofheinz said on March 28 that the Houston Sports Association had realized a net profit of $217,000 for the first seven years of its extensive and diversified operations. "For housekeeping chores alone," Hofheinz said, "we spent $328,500 annually, and overall it has cost us approximately $3,200,000 to run the Dome itself."

Hofheinz cited the need for larger turnouts at Houston baseball games as the key to the financial success of the HSA enterprise. "The increased number of conventions at the Astrohall and the soon-to-be-opened Astroworld will certainly help," the Judge said, "but baseball attendance remains the most important single factor for our success. More than 60 percent of the attendance at Astro games last season came from people who live outside Harris County. That has to change."

"The Greatest Show on Earth," a new show under new ownership, opened April 2 at the new Madison Square Garden in New York. Hofheinz and a party attended. The beginning of the circus' 98th season, its first under the ownership of Hofheinz and the Feld brothers was troublesome. The sideshow had to be eliminated and the menagerie curtailed because the new Garden complex had no area comparable to the old Madison Square Garden's dingy but huge basement. The escalators did not work and those who walked up them to the menagerie found such a jam that only tall men could see the animals. The circus owners hoped by the 1970 season, marking the 100th anniversary of the combined circus, the Garden would be ready to accommodate the show as it previously did.

The Ringling Bros. and Barnum & Bailey Circus did not appear in Houston in 1968 because of contracted performances with the great HemisFair in San Antonio. Hofheinz announced, however, that in 1969 the show would try an experiment in Astrohall to run 13 weeks from Memorial Day to Labor Day. He and his operating partner, Irvin Feld, decided a long stand of a circus unit next to Astroworld might be profitable.

When Hofheinz decided to try midget car racing in 1968 in the Astrodome, friend and money arranger Ben McGuire, a devotee of the Indianapolis 500 which he attended each year, asked the Judge to go with him as his guest. McGuire recalled:

> Unfortunately it rained after 20 laps of the 500. That was another time the Judge prepared food. He went to a shopping center near our Ramada Inn and bought cheese, beef steak, and other goodies and made sandwiches for about 20 people on the trip. At the 500 you have to take your own lunch. We ate it in the rain.
>
> After that the Judge thought of putting a racetrack in Houston with all kinds of crazy ideas like running competitors through the middle of the Dome so everybody could sit in the Dome and watch them as they came through. That didn't work out, but the Judge did arrange for midget car racing. Now they have the motorcycle racing and auto destruction derbies. It was his idea that eventually the Dome would be used at least 300 days out of the year.

Hofheinz always sought new ideas for his ventures before he opened them to the general public. Six weeks before the June 1 opening of the family amusement center, Astroworld, he took his grandchild, Mark Mann, 4, on a best-by-boy-test jet trip to Disneyland and Six Flags. He wanted to watch his reactions to various rides and scenes. Mark put the hex on pirates. He got scared in Disneyland's watery dark canyons filled with one-eyed swashbucklers.

The scouting trip also prepared Mark for showing the wonders of Astroworld to a group of playmates at a preview party two weeks before the opening. Mark and his brother, Dinn, like the children whose grandfather owns the candy store, took their friends to a preview because their grandfather had the keys to the gates. Mark and Dinn dressed alike in orange jumper suits with pink elephant appliques and yellow knee socks. Their mother, "Little Dene," engineered the party.

The National League's 10 owners voted the night of May 27, 1968, to expand to San Diego and Montreal in 1969, thus matching a similar move to Seattle and Kansas City by the American League. The National League's expansion committee, composed of Hofheinz, John Galbreath of the Pittsburgh Pirates, and Walter O'Malley of the Los Angeles Dodgers, approved five cities in the running for the two expansion franchises. Losers in the balloting were Buffalo, Milwaukee, and Dallas-Fort Worth.

Montreal became the first major league baseball franchise outside of the

United States—a fact which pleased Hofheinz and dismayed Tommy Mercer, one of the prime movers in Dallas-Fort Worth's arduous struggle for a big league team. "I think it was a wise move by the owners to go into Montreal," said the Judge shortly after the 120-hour session in Chicago concluded. "It's a fertile territory with a lot of people, a suitable playing site, and ample financial backing. I wouldn't call Montreal a compromise selection," he added, "because our expansion committee unanimously approved all five of the cities being considered, and then the league owners unanimously agreed on both cities. I'm delighted with the entire situation, and I think baseball will benefit from it."

Mercer, who along with Lamar Hunt had pleaded Dallas-Fort Worth's case for several years, was distressed and dismayed by the decision to expand outside the territorial limits of the U.S. "I think baseball has moved unwisely," Mercer said in a mournful tone. "I'm certain that it will suffer in the long run because of it. The National League turned its back on the people of the United States who have supported the game so well for so many years," he said. "I think they did it to compromise with Hofheinz, too. Everybody knows that he was very much against us. He wouldn't vote for us because, as he put it, 'it would make me (Hofheinz) go bankrupt.' " Dallas and Fort Worth newspapers editorially castigated Hofheinz for "turning his back" on another Texas city, blaming him for all sorts of things. The Judge, as usual, shrugged off the accusations.

Preceded by national and international publicity buildups, Astroworld opened June 1, 1968, as planned. The story of opening day was well told by Frank Davis, *Post* reporter:

> Astroworld, the wonderful world of thrills and creature comforts, opened Saturday. The Astrowizard himself, Judge Hofheinz, impatiently unlocked the gates 15 minutes ahead of schedule. "It was a typical Hofheinz product," commented Wayne Chandler, the publicity director. Hofheinz graciously welcomed the throngs of visitors who had been gathering since early morning at the entrance to the 57-acre park south of the Astrodome. . . . The Hofheinz grandchildren had the honor of officially opening Astroworld. They pressed a switch, unleasing 2000 balloons. Then the Astroworld Band, 14 members strong, guided Hofheinz, his children and six grandchildren and a procession of 500 VIPs into "Wonderful World of Fun!" Chandler said that 23,456 persons attended the first day of operations and that Judge Hofheinz was "tremendously pleased." Astroworld can accommodate 20,000 persons an hour on more than 50 rides and attractions.

> It costs 50 cents to park at Astroworld and $4.50 for adults and $3.50 for children to get into the park. Other than that, it's a free ride all the way—from delightful trams which pick up visitors at convenient stops on the parking lot and deposit them at the main entrance to the scary Black Dragon and invigorating Astroway rides. Visitors wait in air-conditioned comfort to board the rides. A total of 2000 tons of central air-conditioning in any area of the park leads the list of creature comforts on a hot day. All except one of the rides operated smoothly.

Aerial view of Astrodomain complex against background of downtown Houston. In the foreground is the Astroworld Hotel, and behind it is the Astrodome. To the right of the Dome is Astrohall (striped roof). The Astroworld amusement park (not pictured) is situated to the right of these facilities. Photograph by Harold Israel, courtesy Gulf Photo.

The *Chronicle,* often a Hofheinz critic but never a newspaper to underestimate his abilities, said in an editorial on June 2:

> Astroworld, a colorful and imaginative family amusement and entertainment center, enraptured thousands of young and old alike when it opened. Congratulations are in order for Roy Hofheinz, whose dream of a giant sports, recreation and entertainment "Astrodomain" based upon the space theme, became one step nearer to reality.
>
> Astroworld, like the domed stadium, defies description. Actually, it will take considerable eyeball inspection fully to appreciate it. There is no doubt that Astroworld will prove to be of inestimable value to Houston in attracting tourists and conventions. Besides the financial return, spread through a large number of retail businesses, this city is rapidly moving into the national and world spotlight as a sports and convention center.

On June 6, Louisiana Governor John McKeithen attacked Houstonians, particularly Hofheinz, with a charge that they were trying to make New Orleans' proposed domed stadium a doomed stadium even before it was built. McKeithen appeared before the Louisiana legislature for his blast and to beat down an attempt to force a vote by Louisianians to repeal or retain the Louisiana Stadium and Exposition District, created to build a New Orleans dome. McKeithen accused Astrodome officials of flooding the legislature with "pessimistic propaganda" about the possible Superdome income. "If you kill it, it will be a black day for Louisiana; Houston will stay up at night celebrating," McKeithen said. He called Hofheinz "the slickest thing they ever produced in east Texas." Hofheinz once had said he did not believe a stadium could pay its way on football alone without a major league baseball franchise. Hofheinz was stunned by the attack by McKeithen because he had entertained and given VIP treatment to a group of 28 to 30 planners headed by Governor McKeithen just the week before. The Judge had instructed all HSA staff to assist the group in any way possible.

On December 31, 1968, Mark Lee, real estate investor and contractor, and his associates acquired 50 acres on Yorktown in Houston's "Magic Circle Galleria Area" as the site of an apartment and commercial complex that would represent an investment of about $40 million. The property was part of the Hofheinz estate and extended from the former Hofheinz home northward along Yorktown to San Felipe. It was acquired from the Hofheinz Foundation. Yorktown extends from Westheimer Road to San Felipe. The property fronts 2000 feet on Yorktown and 1200 feet on San Felipe. Purchase price was not disclosed, but sources said it was at least $3 million.

Lee said a major portion of the property would be devoted to developing a low-rise and mini-rise apartment community, being planned as Houston's finest such development. The Mark Lee organization built many structures in the Houston area, including the Finger Furniture Center, the Marriott Hotel, Hallmark Apartments, and the Junior League Building.

The Hofheinz Foundation in mid-1968 also sold about 16 acres of the original Hofheinz estate to a group of investors. In December of 1968, the Finger Group, real estate investors, and apartment builders, signed an agreement to purchase another 17 acres of the Hofheinz property. The sale of the tract to Mark Lee and Associates completed the disposition of all of the Hofheinz Yorktown property, including his former home and acreage surrounding it.

The 1968 National-American League all-star game was played July 10 in the Dome before an over-capacity crowd of 50,000 and an international television audience. Rusty Staub, the great first baseman of the Astros who was picked to play for the Nationals, suited up and shared with Hofheinz pre-game pictures and interviews for the vast television audience. The Nationals had won five straight games in the mid-season baseball classic, and they did it again in the Dome with a 1-0 pitching battle. Hofheinz had given a stag party the previous evening at the Astrodome Club for notables who would attend the game. Joseph E. (Joe) Cronin, president of the American League, was repeatedly asked by Houstonians attending if he was Red James, Hofheinz's law partner. The two men looked enough alike to cause more than a few double takes. Guests also included Baseball Commissioner Eckert, National League president Warren Giles and O. Kelley Anderson, chairman of the board of New England Mutual, and a Hofheinz financial backer. News media representatives from all over the nation and baseball guests were agog over the great variety of buffet food Hofheinz had chefs prepare. Most had been guests at such all-star affairs in other cities but had never been to a party with such a king-like display of all kinds of delicacies. In short, the party resulted in more conversation than did the next day's game.

As Lyndon Johnson's two daughters, Luci and Lynda Bird, grew up, they became friends of "Little Dene" and often visited Houston, usually to enjoy "Huckster House." Luci, who was closer to "Little Dene," married Pat Nugent. Luci's first child was Lyn, who became the world's most publicized child while his grandfather was in the White House. Luci took Lyn with her on a tour of Central America, but cut short the trip to attend the all-star game with her friends, Dene and Scott Mann. Little Lyn got his first glimpse of big league baseball from the sky-high Tahitian Room at the Astrodome. Cameras followed the one-year-old tyke as he, boy-like, crawled up and down the stadium seats and watched with wonder when the stadium's million-dollar scoreboard flashed its technicolor show. Luci and Lyn spent the next day touring the wonderful child's world of fantasy—Astroworld. Five secret service men guarded the Nugents and Mrs. Mann. The exuberant Lyn got a glimpse of glaciers, snow storms, waterfalls, and even the abominable snowman as he hurtled through the chilly tunnels of "Der Hofheinzberg." The animated world adventure unfolded below as the VIP guests rode 340 feet up in the "Astroneedle." They also watched the fast-paced vaudeville show at the Crystal Palace and then the party moved on to the "Lost World Ride" where the lazy trip down the jungle swamps lulled the littlest member of the party promptly to sleep. His mother and the grown-ups had a late lunch when little Lyn was fast asleep in his playpen in the VIP lounge. For a little boy it had already been a big day.

On July 31, 1967, Hofheinz announced the HSA had purchased the Houston Apollos ice hockey team from the Montreal Canadians. The Apollos, he said, would continue to operate as the Canadians' number one farm club under the agreement. Thus hockey joined the umbrella of HSA.

For the time being, and probably the next three seasons, the Apollos would continue to play their home games at Sam Houston Coliseum, Hofheinz said. The team's contract with the city for the rental of that facility had that much time remaining before expiration. The HSA was willing to honor the agreement. The reluctance of the Judge to put his newest team into the Astrodome was unexpected. He said: "We're going to get our feet wet in the hockey business before we bring it to the Dome. We must first find out whether or not fan support warrants such a move. We are anxious, though, to learn about the operation of a hockey franchise and then use that knowledge to convert the Apollos into a major league franchise. We hope to be included in the next major league hockey expansion movement," the Judge continued, "but for the present the Apollos will remain in the Central Hockey League."

For nine years Houston's NCAA-sanctioned Bluebonnet Bowl post-season college football game struggled against December weather conditions as teams played in Rice Stadium. Hofheinz wanted the game switched to the Astrodome, but it was not until August 3, 1968, that he and Bluebonnet officials reached an agreement. Joe Kelly Butler, prominent civic leader, was Bluebonnet president.

The game usually was scheduled the Saturday before Christmas so it would not conflict with any other bowls. In the television war for bowl games, American Broadcasting Company signed a contract with Bluebonnet. In 1967, it paid Bluebonnet $175,000 for the rights. Butler announced an agreement with Hofheinz to shift the game to the Astrodome on New Year's Eve, 1968, and to call the event the Astro-Bluebonnet Bowl. Hofheinz purchased the television contract with ABC in the deal. He felt he could make the Bowl extra money by selling additional commercials. His contract with Bluebonnet would run five years.

When bowl bids were out on November 17, Astro-Bluebonnet invited Southern Methodist and Oklahoma to play as the highlight of a big weekend entertainment extravaganza Hofheinz arranged. Working with the University of Houston, Hofheinz arranged an Astro-Bluebonnet basketball classic for December 27-28 preceding the football game. Portland, San Francisco, and Utah State accepted invitations to compete with Houston's Cougars to decide the championship. Houston had basketball fever, and the opening game of the tournament would be the second time the cage sport had been played in the Dome.

Hofheinz signed four bands for a New Year's Eve Astrohall party to follow the football bowl game. He featured orchestras led by Duke Ellington, Les Brown, and Joe Tex along with the Firehouse Five Plus Two. Each ticket cost $12.50, but Hofheinz included free champagne. The Judge's early life experiences with dance promotions were vividly recalled by some of the elders in the great crowd which jammed the hall. As food and beverage director of Astroworld, Astrohall, and the Judge's motels, Jim Volpe was swamped with details before the New Year's Eve gala. He ordered 30,000 hats, noisemakers, horns, and festive paper gadgets. He also ordered 600,000 serpentines, long thin streams of paper. About 100,000 balloons were filled the day before the gala for ceiling decorations, and Volpe scoured the state to rent 30,000 folding chairs. He ordered 8000 magnums, or about 110,000 glassfuls of champagne. Volpe figured Hofheinz's investment totaled about $120,000.

The British Broadcasting Corporation decided in the summer of 1968 as Astroworld opened to send a crew to Texas to do a film for empire television viewers on Texas multimillionaires about whom much had been written in the press. BBC picked four men who agreed to appear in the production of "The Plutocrats." They were H. L. Hunt, David Harold Byrd, Stanley Marcus, and Roy Hofheinz. The Judge was described by the BBC: "Hofheinz likes taking on the impossible. He was interested once in buying London Bridge and two Cunard liners, but he wanted both the Queens or none at all. He also some day would like to buy the leaning tower of Pisa, but only if they can guarantee re-erecting it in the Texas sub-soil at exactly the same angle as in Italy! In short, he is Texas' brashest, most flamboyant plutocrat."

Hundreds of letters poured into Hofheinz's offices from British subjects after the first showing from London. One person offered Hofheinz, easily the big star of the documentary because of his natural showmanship, a half mile of a Roman road in England. "I don't know what you will do with it,"said the writer, "but I'll be glad to sell it to you." Another had built a small gas-fired engine and wanted the Judge to buy and market it. A ballet enthusiast wrote from London that his daughter was developing as a dancer and asked Hofheinz to pay her way to the United States for advanced training. A sculptor wanted the Judge to be his sponsor. A music teacher asked him to endow her music school. Another man wanted a million to form a corporation for a venture without saying what it was. "Please invest in my Greek Island tours," wrote a travel agent. A case of ship models was offered by a collector. A young man wanted money to sponsor a young soccer team. A boys' school also wrote asking for money. A woman who had a house on the Isle of Wight offered it for sale. It had six bedrooms and only two commodes. A builder asked information on how to build an Astrodome. Pipe caddies were offered the Judge—for a price—by another collector.

The drawing power of the Dome made Bud Adams—and Hofheinz—happy August 2, 1968, when 42,000 packed the sports palace to see an inter-league football exhibition match between the Oilers and the Washington Redskins. Adams' American League eastern-division champions defeated the National Football League team 9-3. But even a defeat would have been far less distasteful to Adams than comparing that crowd under the Dome with the much smaller ones which paid to watch his team play in the open air at Rice Stadium for three seasons. Hofheinz's love of young people, especially children, caused him to join in two programs to give them incentive for learning and recreation. In August of 1968 he extended his congratulations to the more than 8000 straight "A" students in 12 counties in the Houston area and gave each six tickets to Astro games in the program sponsored by the HSA and the *Chronicle*. He sent each this letter: "You are all to be sincerely congratulated on your outstanding scholastic achievement and we hope that you all enjoy your visits to the ballgames as much as we enjoy having you with us. Your presence at the games adds much enthusiasm to the crowd, and is greatly appreciated by the players. We wish you continued success in your educational endeavors."

Hofheinz also participated in a project launched to expand Houston's progressive anti-poverty program. Through joint efforts of the city, Astroworld, and various business firms and civic organizations, the program provided for group tours of Astroworld by underprivileged children. The program was more proof of concerted efforts in Houston toward handling its own campaign to aid the poor. It was typical of the numerous projects being conducted in the city. Houston's newspapers and broadcast outlets commended Mayor Welch and Hofheinz and the firms and organizations which sponsored the tours. Under the program, sponsors purchased tickets at reduced cost which gave needy children the same opportunity of enjoying Astroworld as those more fortunate.

Mrs. Robert Vernon (Joanne) King, Houston socialite, headed a committee formed to entertain Princess Grace (Kelly), the former great movie queen from Philadelphia, and Prince Paul Ranier of Monaco when it was announced the royal couple would visit Houston after going to the HemisFair in San Antonio. The Ranier party of 30 would arrive in Houston early Friday, September 27, 1968, and leave the following afternoon in a private plane. Mrs. King called Judge Hofheinz and asked if he would give a luncheon for the royal pair and its entourage in the Astrodome at noon Saturday before the Raniers' planned takeoff for Yucatan, Mexico. She invited the Judge and Mary Frances to be guests at a dance she and her husband and the H. H. Coffields of Rockdale would give Friday night at the Kings' "Grecian Palace" on Houston's Rivercrest Drive.

The party lasted from late evening until early in the morning. Mrs. King called Hofheinz mid-morning Saturday and said he would have to cancel his luncheon because the schedule of the Raniers and their guests was so tight they could not get to the Dome. Hofheinz's chefs had prepared his specially cut steaks and other delicacies for 50 people. He was greatly disappointed because he wanted to meet and talk with the royal couple, also rulers of a special entertainment retreat. "The Judge shook it off," said secretary Mary Frances, "and immediately had me round up people in the Dome to come in and have a feast of a luncheon—fit for royalty."

Shortly after 2:00 P.M. a guard at the Astrodome gate called Mary Frances and told her he had just seen the Raniers come through and buy one dollar tickets to go on the tour. The prince and princess had read and heard much about the "Eighth Wonder of the World," and it was one of the reasons they visited Houston. When their hostess told them the luncheon with Hofheinz had been cancelled, they decided to leave their hosts and guests and taxi to the Dome. It took a couple of minutes for the Judge and Mary Frances to race to the gate guard to ask where the Raniers were. He pointed to the crowd entering the stadium. They raced to find the "just plain tourists" and take them away from the crowd. Hofheinz gave them his own spiel about the giant structure as they walked around and then took them to the Astrodome Club where the chef and waiters had been putting together last-minute refreshments.

Princess Grace and Prince Ranier, visiting Houston on a trip from their kingdom in Monaco, were impressed with Hofheinz's own little kingdom.

When the Raniers sat down with Hofheinz and Mary Frances at a table, the visitors were asked if they would like cocktails. Princess Grace called for a beer—but the Prince ordered a cocktail. The event was so exciting for Mary Frances that she could not recall too much of the conversation, but she did remember that the Judge had brushed up on his history of Monaco the day before. The little pleasure resort on the southern tip of Europe next to the Mediterranean, where the royal couple reigned and legal gambling flourished, is an area of only 368 acres with a population of 20,000. The Astrodome and parking areas covered about the same acreage. As the two men talked of their entertainment "Kingdoms," waiters brought the best food they could find the royal couple who had not taken time for lunch. Mary Frances said the two men were most compatible, and Princess Grace joined in with interesting comments.

"The prince and princess told the Judge they would not leave Houston without seeing the wonders of the Dome, and that's why they slipped away from their entourage," said Mary Frances. "They stayed in the Dome for nearly two hours and finally had to rush to get to the airport so that they could take off for Yucatan." In 1978, Princess Grace was asked for her recollections of the Astrodome visit, but she said, in the middle of a lecture tour, that she could only recall that she and the Prince had a "lovely and interesting visit with Judge Hofheinz."

At a meeting in Chicago, November 2, 1968, the North American Soccer League suspended play for at least three years. Hofheinz returned his franchise to the league in Chicago. During their two years, he lost close to $500,000 despite great promotion efforts. As usual, Hofheinz felt the sport would develop in the United States and it cost him dearly this time to be ahead of soccer's time. The sport began flourishing in the nation after 1975.

Hofheinz never lost his interest in the Democratic Party. He regretted the decision of Lyndon Johnson not to seek reelection and was unhappy when he did not get the party's 1968 convention for the Dome. He still wanted the Dome in the political spotlight and invited Vice-President Hubert H. Humphrey, the

Democratic nominee, and Richard Nixon, the Republican candidate, to debate free in the Astrodome at 3:00 on Sunday, November 3. Humphrey immediately accepted. If Nixon declined, Humphrey said he would be most happy to appear alone.

Nixon had avoided a debate—as front-runners traditionally do—saying he did not want to give third-party candidate George Wallace any free forum. Under federal equal time provisions, any free time given by television stations to a presidential candidate had to be matched by an equal amount of time given to the other candidates. "Well, I'm not bound by the equal time provisions," said Hofheinz, "and I haven't invited George Wallace." He said Wallace was excluded because "we felt a debate is appropriate between the candidates of the two major parties." If Nixon turned down the invitation to debate, the Astrodome would have, said the Judge, "an empty chair to stand for Nixon."

Nixon declined to debate, apparently believing he would be at a disadvantage in a big seat of Democratic support. Herb Klein, press secretary of the GOP National Committee, told Hofheinz that the debate would be "a waste of Mr. Nixon's time." Humphrey's Harris County campaign was managed by Fred Hofheinz, warming up for his own political career. Fifty thousand heard Humphrey at his best at the rally. The absence of Nixon did not spoil the Democrats' enthusiasm for the Minnesotan they hoped would follow Texan Johnson into the White House.

Fred Hofheinz gave his resignation as vice-president of HSA to his father on December 4, 1968. "I regret having to leave an enterprise with the interest and potential of Astrodomain, but there are opportunities available to me which require that I be independent of my father's ventures," Fred said. The younger Hofheinz continued as president of Astrodome Championship Enterprises, Incorporated, the Dome's boxing promotion organization, and as a major partner in Astroworld and a complex of four hotels and motels across from the Dome.

Rumors spread that father and son had had strenuous disagreements about the Judge's expensive operations and that Fred left because he had no assurances he would ultimately be in line to run the complex. In 1978 he went beyond the paragraph explanation of his resignation carried in the media. He said:

> Dad and I had a major disagreement in which we were both right and both wrong. It was with respect to the settlement of Mother's estate. That was not as important in the dispute as the second element—the investment policy. It was my opinion that we were investing money too rapidly. The budget of the amusement park overran from what we originally started some $3 million. There was an exceptionally large amount of money being placed in VIP rooms in the Astrodome that I thought was excessive. I felt the same with respect to the Astroworld Hotel, which had been my special project until it came to developing it. We were overcapitalized. I had no influence over that. Maybe if I had been made a part of the decision-making at that point, I would have been

more cooperative. That was just the basic business dispute. When the number two guy in a family venture left, bankers were interested. But the truth is my motive was to get out on my own. It was more an ambition on my part to be able to be in control of my own fate than any disagreement I had with Dad.

In retrospect, the few complaints I had about overcapitalization of Astrodomain were small in comparison to the chips with which Dad dealt. In that aspect of it, he was right and I was wrong. It was Roy Hofheinz's game, not mine. That was the key point in our argument. It was not my game, and it was unfair of my father to call upon me under those circumstances when he was playing a game I didn't like, to stay in the family business and dedicate the rest of my life to this effort. I was 31 years old, and I didn't want to spend the rest of my life living someone else's life. That was the essential point. Dad couldn't see that. There was a family discussion, shall we say, at that period of my life. It didn't last long.

Fred was told that some suggested in that argument period the son wanted to be the president and let his father be the chairman of the board. He replied: "That was not true. Titles were unimportant to me, but influence over policy of the company and the long-range role that I would play in the family venture were [important]. I reasoned: Is manager of the family venture to be my life role? Am I merely an investor in the family matter? I felt if I merely was an investor, then I really didn't want to be a manager. If I were to be manager, then I wanted to be THE manager. That was the discussion, not an argument, that ended my active career in the Astrodome. I didn't want to continue as the alter ego of somebody else."

Spec Richardson was and is an admirer of Fred Hofheinz. He said the Judge was upset when Roy Hofheinz, Jr., refused to work with HSA, but Fred "did a fine job as long as he stayed at the Dome." He added that the Judge sometimes was "very hard on Fred when he was involved in legal matters and doing a good job. I told the Judge he shouldn't be too tough with his son. I could say anything I wanted because our relationship was such that I could do so." Richardson said he guessed the Judge didn't think his son had had enough experience when he was rough on him, often in Spec's presence. Fred Hofheinz and Richardson developed such a close friendship Spec named the young attorney administrator of the wills of his wife and himself.

Hofheinz announced on December 10, 1968, that the Astro Grand Prix would be a two-day, $50,000 event May 8-9, 1969. The race, co-sponsored by HSA and PACE Management Corporation of Houston, was sanctioned by the United States Auto Club, officiating body of most major automotive competition in the nation, and would feature the cars of the popular midget division of USAC, driven by the world's top racing drivers.

The two days of racing on a quarter-mile dirt track in the Astrodome would pay a $20,000 purse for each day's event with the remaining $10,000 purse being divided by the top 10 overall point winners from both events. Leading international and American drivers were expected to be attracted by the $50,000 purse, ranking among the highest USAC purses for 1969.

One of the drivers who entered was A. J. Foyt, Jr., favorite son of Houston, reigning United States Auto Club national champion and the driver with the most wins in history. He helped the HSA and PACE Management Corporation with plans. Foyt was asked to compare midgets to other race cars. "Midgets are my first love," Foyt said. "They are very quick and tricky to handle." He said they were as dangerous and perhaps more dangerous than some of the bigger cars.

Hofheinz sought to impress upon the representatives of the news media that the race would be the biggest of big-league. "This is going to be the race of races in midgets," he said. "It is to be the Indianapolis of midget racing." As the explanations of plans continued, it developed that the Astro Grand Prix would not only add a page to the annals of racing history, but would be a monumental engineering feat. The quarter-mile clay track was to be constructed on the floor of the Dome in six 24-hour days. The track builders would have to put in 13,000 cubic yards of clay fill and get it in good enough condition for the fiesty little cars to lap at an average speed of above 60 miles an hour. The track would cost $50,000—the most to be spent to build a track for one event. A sturdy steel guard rail would encircle the track to keep the cars out of the laps of the spectators. J. C. Agajanian, a member of the USAC board of directors and one of racing's most colorful figures, would be the grand marshal of the race, Hofheinz said.

Dick Blue's observation that certain people in the Judge's employ "stole him blind" was true, according to associates who tried to protect Hofheinz's interests during building of the Astrodome, Astroworld, and the hotels. Projects were so vast that building materials, tickets to baseball games, and other athletic events, and expense accounts of executives could not be closely checked. Under-the-counter deals for personal gain by some sub-executives of the complex sometimes occurred. According to Blue, "There were so many events and so many opportunities for graft that he couldn't check everybody out personally. He trusted them and, sadly, a couple of them let him down." From time to time, Hofheinz did admit feelings of being cheated. Hofheinz trusted his "people"—so much so that one of the men who was involved in millions of dollars of purchasing shattered some of the Judge's faith. When it was proved this man was building a beautiful home and a lake in another county with materials worth up to one-half million dollars from Hofheinz's construction projects, the Judge was crushed but so fond of the man that he did not prosecute. He was deeply hurt that a "friend" would do this to him. He did, however, recuperate some of his losses through the help of insurance companies and sale of the property on which the man was building. Jim Braniff, Richardson, and designer Goff were among those who uncovered the thefts. Every time Hofheinz had to fire a dishonest employee, executive or department head, he was disturbed, not as much because of the monetary loss, but because people he trusted had let him down.

38

"Kiddo" Becomes
Mrs. Roy Hofheinz

Mary Frances McMurtry was "Best All-Around Senior Girl" in the 1945 graduating class of Houston's Stephen F. Austin High School. Her quick mind, amazing energy, lovely figure, and happy disposition endeared her to classmates. She was runner-up as "Sophomore Beauty" and winner as "Junior Beauty." Her academic work brought her membership in the National Honor Society, composed only of students in the upper 15 percent scholastically. She was elected to the Senior Council, student advisory body to the school administration. She climaxed three years with the Scottish Brigade, drill team which wore Scottish uniforms, as captain of the drum corps. As a member of Quill and Scroll, the international organization formed to encourage students to become journalists, she was feature and finally page one editor of *The Austin Roundup*, student newspaper sponsored by the organization.

Petite Mary Frances also was a member of Lambda Sigma Alpha, composed of students who had won American Legion awards at the end of their first year in high school. She was interested in the stage and joined the Green Masque Players. The Mustang Boosters supported all athletic teams, and Mary Frances as a member helped in promotions when she was not on the football field with the drum corps. She was recognized for her charm by being tapped into the Sub-Deb Club, organized to improve the school's cultural and social activities—dances, teas, and home parties. Her mother and two sisters helped her to make and buy attractive clothes. She was a dazzler, especially in evening gowns. She was also vice-president for two years of the Aloha Club, which planned each year's graduation gala.

Young Miss McMurtry could not afford college, took a secretarial course, landed a job at City Hall, and married Milton Gougenheim. Her roles as the Judge's receptionist (when he dubbed her "Kiddo"), as private secretary, and as an intimate friend of Dene Hofheinz and her daughter already have been outlined in this book up to April 9, 1969, when she married her boss. Hofheinz's 57th birthday was the day after the marriage. Mary Frances was 40.

Roy Hofheinz's first marriage in Beaumont had been spur-of-the-moment. His second in Austin was almost like it. Only an intimate few guessed

Marge Crumbaker

that 28 months after the death of Dene Hofheinz, the Judge would wed his faithful and adoring secretary.

Ben McGuire, who had known Mary Frances from her first days at City Hall, said Hofheinz talked with him first about marrying his secretary. He recalled: "Mary Frances called and told me the Judge wanted to talk to me. I talked to him and he said he was lonesome. The Judge never liked to be alone, always wanted people around him. He said he was going crazy being alone and was not eating and wanted to marry Mary Frances. I told him I thought it was a wonderful idea."

Dene II talked of her father's second marriage:

> Dad called me to come to the Astrodome. Mary Frances had gone to the beauty parlor. Dad sat me in a big gold chair and he asked me what I thought about his marrying his secretary. I was really excited about it. He said, "You go on up to the Dome Beauty Parlor and you tell her." He actually had me propose to her in a sense. I went darting to the elevator, into the beauty salon and said, "Daddy's going to marry you." She claims that that really was the first time she had heard about it. I think my only concern in the drive from the Astrodome to the house was that Mama had tried to tell me it would happen if she passed on. Many things went through my head about how Mary Frances was going to make the transition from secretary, my best friend, to step-mother. That's really about all that was on my mind. My brothers were concerned about the

trust situation after the marriage, which is something that, even to this day, I don't really totally understand. There were a few weeks of family discussions after the marriage that needn't have taken place. With the Hofheinz family as dramatic as I think it is, it was rather gruelling. I moved out of Houston when Scott and I got divorced. Dad didn't at first understand why I was moving. Now he understands, now that I have become so successful at what I do with songs. Unless I was rubbing elbows with people that were making songs happen, writing all the good songs in the world was not going to do me a bit of good if I were sitting in Houston. I chose Los Angeles. The boys and I set up a new life in L.A. Dad was reluctant to let me go, but as time went on, I think he grew to understand why I had gone and I think he even respected my having left.

Marge Crumbaker, vivacious *Post* reporter, wrote the most interesting story about the marriage of Mary Frances and the Judge more than five weeks after the ceremony. Her interviews with the two, entitled "Home, Home in the Dome," were published May 18.

The Judge's proposal wasn't made humbly, down on one knee, nothing like that. It was more in the manner of the king addressing his most loyal subject. There he sat in his great throne room-office, the decor of which was once described by comedian Bob Hope as Early King Farouk. His feet, encased in expensive shoes, rested on the top of his elaborate desk. One shoe was tapping the gold telephone. "Kiddo," the monarch said, "how would you like to consider yourself engaged to be married?" The attractive size 8, most loyal subject smiled. "To whom?" she asked. "To me, Kiddo."

She replied promptly and firmly, with just the right touch of adoration, "I would like that very much."

"OK, Baby," a grin spreading over his round, often-photographed face, "you've got it. We are going to get married."

Mary Frances asked, "Anytime soon?"

The Judge answered, "As soon as I have a couple of minutes. OK?" Happy Mary Frances echoed the "OK."

And that, kiddies, is how Astrobrain Roy Hofheinz, boy wonder-lawyer-judge-mayor-showman-genius, asked for and won the hand of his vivacious secretary. Big Roy didn't find those important two minutes until two days after the proposal. In the meantime, in typical Hofheinz fashion, he got the show on the road, as they say in show biz: "Let's get blood tests," he instructed, and they did. "Let's get the license," he said. "Out of town," he decided a moment later. He phoned a judge, an old friend, in Columbus and asked for assistance. On the second morning of their engagement, he summoned his secretary and said, "Today—right after I make my speech in Austin to the House of Representatives. Call Robert and ask him to do the honors."

"Whee!" exclaimed Mary Frances, whom Hofheinz refers to variously as Baby, Kiddo or M.F.

With M.F. behind the wheel, and the Judge sitting beside her, puffing on a big, black cigar, they drove to Columbus to pick up the license. They were off to Austin where Robert Calvert, Chief Justice of the Texas Supreme Court, was to perform the ceremony immediately after Hofheinz's talk. After the speech—and it was a fabulous one in M.F.'s eyes—the Judge raced out into the halls and grabbed his bride-to-be, who was carrying his briefcase, "You didn't forget to bring it?" he quizzed sternly. "No," she answered. "It's right in here." She patted the briefcase. Arm-in-arm they entered Judge Calvert's office.

"Now, Roy," Calvert said, almost as nervous as the pair he was to unite, "I've never performed a marriage ceremony before. I figure if you wanted the long complete ceremony, you'd be in a church. So I am going to read the short version, if that's all right." Hofheinz said: "That's fine." Calvert said, "We will have 'I will's' instead of 'I do's.' Is that all right?" Hofheinz said "Fine" again. He opened the briefcase and took out a small pearl-encrusted Bible. Billy Graham had once written in it, "The Astrodome is Truly the Eighth Wonder of the World," and a few months later added a second inscription, "The Astrodome is Not the Eighth Wonder of the World, It is the First." Roy Hofheinz, called gruff by some, ruthless by some, a wonder by others, and brainy by almost everyone, held that tiny Bible while Judge Calvert conducted the ceremony.

"Baby," Hofheinz said at the conclusion of the ceremony, "I'm sorry you didn't have a chance to change into the dress you wanted to wear."

"That's all right," Mary Frances replied. I'll wear it for something special later." The plain gold band on her finger was a perfect fit. Only an hour before, while the Judge stayed by the car because it was in a no-parking zone, she had dashed into an Austin jewelry store to buy the ring. "We wanted M.F. to have a simple one," Hofheinz said. "I thought that made a little better sense." Looking around his board of directors room, he laughed and said, "Lord Almighty, we have enough of the grandiose and grotesque around here!"

Mr. and Mrs. Hofheinz, undecided at first where they should spend their wedding night, agreed it should be in Houston. They stopped briefly at LaGrange to send telegrams to Roy, Jr., Fred, and Dene Hofheinz Mann, his children by his wife of 33 years who died of a heart attack after an operation. For the time being the Hofheinz home is in the Dome, light housekeeping in the right field section, far above the ball diamond. The private quarters include a large bedroom, a sitting room and two large baths. Adjacent to the Skyboxes, M.F. and Big Roy can entertain a couple of hundred people in their private bar where the decor is colorful, casual, and heavy on rattan. On the same floor are two suites for visiting pals, with names like Nancy Sinatra and her daddy, Frank . . . .

Roy and M. F. Hofheinz don't really know where they will finally settle down. "Right now," he said, leading the way to the French Kitchen, a breath of New Orleans with a picture window overlooking the interior of the Dome, "we are living here at the Dome. Soon as I get around to it, I am going to get us a place, probably a house, maybe build one. In the meantime, I'm fixing us a little suite over at the Astroworld Hotel." It is to be just a plain little spot, Hofheinz discloses, but with some fun things—like a waterfall in the bathtub. And the bathtub will be 17 feet long. Looking fondly at his wife, Hofheinz laughed and said, "I sure didn't marry her for her cooking. Hell, Kiddo can't even boil water. I cook for her!" And she will eat, he disclosed delicately, anything which doesn't

*Roy and Mary Frances Hofheinz following nuptials at which Judge Robert Calvert (center)
officiated.* Photograph by Harold Israel, courtesy Gulf Photo.

eat her first. "Now if I were to fix him a meal," M.F. said grining, "it would consist of. . . ." He broke in with a hearty laugh. "I know what it would be," he chided. "It would be, in this order, a TV dinner and something frozen which you prepare by simply immersing it in hot water until hot." She responded: "Sweetheart, you don't need a lot to eat. Could you button your coat?" Roy looked down at the white shirt bulging slightly through the front of his jacket and replied, "No way, Baby."

The dinner plates in the French Kitchen have black centers. Glancing at the dish before him Roy got in another dig. "This looks like something you'd prepare. About the entire extent of it. Burned black." She leaned over and gave him a kiss. He touched her hair. "Listen Baby, that's some hairdo you've got there."

"Sorry about that," she replied gaily. "I didn't mean to get it so poofed up."

"That's OK," he said, examining some curls which normally were not there. "But what I got here is a girl with something borrowed, something blue. Borrowed hair, teeth. . . ." She laughed with him. "I just had to take her as she came."

"The first two years," she commented on their friendship which has extended across 17 years, "he didn't even know my name. That's why he calls me Kiddo." They met when he was making his bid for mayor of Houston in 1952. . . . The boss-secretary relationship went from City Hall to a radio station, a law office, and then the Astrodome. "I am a follower and he is the leader," M.F. said. When did their friendship turn to love? She answered straightforwardly, "After his wife died, he turned more to me, I believe."

"Marrying M.F. has made me very content," Hofheinz said. "You don't know it until, well. . . . Dene, my first wife, and I were very devoted. We were together every night. I'm a stay-at-home type guy. I don't think I've ever been in a nightclub since I've been grown. I can take 16 hours a day, but the nights . . . well, they get kind of lonesome. Now, I'm contented and happy."

But just when did love begin to bloom? "It was last August 1," M.F. said. "The Judge was honored that evening by the Lions Club in Beaumont, his hometown. That day he told me to get his mail together and make the ride to Beaumont and read the mail to him. Well, we didn't read much mail, but we laughed and talked. The Lions seated me at the head table, and I never was happier. That night, returning to Houston, he said he wouldn't mind having me at the head table on every occasion. That is when I believe it really turned from friendship to love."

Roy Hofheinz was thinking of a special photograph. "My Mother and Daddy posed for their wedding portrait with Mother standing in back with her hand on Daddy's shoulder. Could you take a picture of us like that, a tintype shot?"

"Yessir. You bet."

M.F. changed from the blue dress she had intended to wear on her wedding day to a soft black cotton embossed with tiny figures. "Right here," the Judge decided. "Right here in front of this painting called 'The First Christian of the Day Being Thrown Out to the Lions.' " He sat down and folded his

Harold Israel

hands. "That's the way Daddy has his hands." M.F. placed her hand on his shoulder and said, "This is the way your Mother was standing." These photographs would be their official wedding portraits, the Judge announced.

"The good thing about marrying my secretary," he said, patting her hand, "is that we don't have to be re-introduced. She has a pretty good idea of my frailties, and I have a good idea of hers, and it makes it a lot easier. I'd hate to start over at the age of 57 with a Floradora Gottrocks and try and get going."

So love and romance are here to stay? "I think so," M.F. said. What do you say, Judge? He replied: "I say it has sure progressed a hell of a long way and I'm damned glad to know the world now recognizes me as an authority on love and romance. Anytime you want expert advice on love and romance for your readers, just let me know." The Judge took his Kiddo's arm and led her down a corridor. As they passed his private barber shop, he patted her head and said, "Kiddo, I'm going to teach you how to cut hair so you can help us make some money around here."

"Great," she replied. "You're the boss."

He said, "No, not anymore. You're the boss. Hell, I'm working for you now."

Photographer Harold Israel found himself an unexpected witness to the wedding. He recalled that the Judge called him at home on the evening prior to the nuptials asking him to be in the capitol building at Austin around noon the next day. He needed him to photograph a legislative hearing, Hofheinz said. Israel agreed and made the trip to Austin. When, however, during the course of the hearing, he repeatedly asked the Judge what shots he wanted, the answer was always the same: "I'll let you know." Finally the Judge beckoned Israel to "get one of those cameras and follow me." It was not until they met Mary Frances at a law office and began to proceed to the Supreme Court Building that the photographer realized what was happening: the Judge and Mary Frances were getting married, and he had been chosen to photograph the event! During his long years of dealing with Hofheinz, Israel made more than 15,000 negatives for the Judge—the number of prints is anyone's guess.

Fred Hofheinz was asked if the marriage of Mary Frances to his father added to any estrangement he and his brother, Roy, Jr., had with their sire. He said: "To say we were upset probably goes too far. To say that we wanted to be sure that he understood the implications is true. We weren't given the chance to say yes or no because he married Mary Frances without conferring with my brother and me. Subsequent to the marriage, we did point out to him all the problems that it created." Community property laws would be involved in the second marriage, too.

Roy Hofheinz, Jr., said: "I was not opposed to it and I thought Dad should have remarried. It was perfectly natural that he did that. I congratulated him when he called me. I was a little bit anxious at that point about him and I appreciated his calling me, but I wasn't surprised by it. All in the family recognize that without Mary Frances, Dad's life would have been very miserable."

The new Mrs. Hofheinz, a vivacious lady in red, received men close to the Judge and their wives at a party in the Caribbean Room in the Astrodome April 13, the night the Astros opened the 1969 season against the Los Angeles Dodgers. The Astros lost 9-3, but that did not dampen the spirits of the newlyweds or their guests, most of whom had not seen the Hofheinzes since their wedding ceremony. Spec Richardson was busy with game duties and could not join the party, but auditor Ed Bruhl, financial adviser Ben McGuire, bankers Waddell Moursund and Charles Bybee, attorney Red James and television executives Jack Harris and Willard Walbridge, and their spouses, joined in congratulations during the evening. All had known Mary Frances during her long tenure as the Judge's secretary and were happy that she would fill the void in Hofheinz's life caused by Dene's death. In the words of Beverly Maurice, feature and fashion editor of the *Chronicle*, "No man is an island. Not even a man like Roy Hofheinz. Somewhere there must be that loyalty that one can depend on, one who spins security, who weaves the pattern of encouragement, of enthusiasm, of love. For the Judge, it's Mary Frances, his 'Kiddo.' "

39

One-Man
Chamber of Commerce

Roy Hofheinz's hectic business, building, and civic pace in 1969 was interrupted only briefly by his marriage. It was a year of general contentment with more of his dreams coming true; the city was growing as a convention and tourist attraction, and his loneliness was ending with the constant companionship of his second wife.

In characteristic showmanship style, Hofheinz on January 14 told newsmen attending the 25th annual convention and exposition of the National Association of Homebuilders, the first in the Magic City, that the best was yet to come. Outlining improvements already on the drawing board for the second Houston NAHB meeting in 1970, he said conventioneers would find 3000 additional beds available in the Astrodomain complex and from 2000 to 4500 more elsewhere in the city, plus a few surprises. He again was a one-man chamber of commerce. He called Houston the best planned city in the nation and attributed this favorable condition to the city's refusal to adopt restrictive zoning ordinances. Houston was then the largest U.S. metropolis without zoning—and still is. Voters had turned down every referendum proposing such property control.

Exhibitors expended more than $3 million to display and try to sell their products during the Homebuilders' convention. New products and improvements on old ones were shown by 459 firms, most nationwide in scope, in the Astrohall. The exhibitors brought 12,000 employees (more than the total attendance at most Houston conventions) to erect, maintain, and staff exhibits, to sell products and entertain prospective buyers, and finally to dismantle exhibits and ship products displayed back to factories. Total attendance at what was termed the biggest convention-exposition in the world topped the 40,000 mark. Visitors also spent a bundle for entertainment, special brochures, and giveaways for the convention, and for shipment of products for display from plant to Houston.

Firms with building materials, carpets, and a maze of floor coverings, tiles, paints, and appliances that go into homes and apartments contracted with NAHB for more than 160,000 square feet of exhibit space. Exhibitors paid in excess of $1.5 million for this display space to show more than $3 million worth of products. Space in the exposition hall was contracted for from $800 for the smallest booth to the $18,960 General Electric paid to show and sell its products. That was just for the space. Erection of the exhibit, decoration, and installation of products came extra.

GE brought in 150 trained employees to staff, maintain, and sell products as well as to set up open houses and other entertainment for prospective customers. The big corporation also picked up the tab for hotels, meals, and other expenses incurred by these employees during their stay—plus, of course, transportation to Houston and return to their home base. This example was just for one of the exhibitors, albeit one of the largest. Considering that 12,000 of the visitors were associated in some way with the exhibit end of the meet, it was easy to see that the exhibitor tab for transportation, lodging, meals, and other incidentals was enormous.

The financial backbone of the NAHB convention, not unlike many others, was the cash flow from exhibit space contracted for with officials of the convention. In its first year in Houston, NAHB convention chairman Stanley Waranch, Norfolk, Virginia, said a record number of exhibitors contracted for space at the exposition. A convention official said Hofheinz was "off the hook" in his cash guarantee. Hofheinz said Houston proved it could handle the largest conventions in America. NAHB was committed to return to Houston for two more years. "I think we have a wedding that will last a long time," said the Judge.

Hofheinz and the prominent, rich Finger brothers, Sammy and Aaron, were honored for "long and meritorious service to baseball" by the Houston Professional Baseball Association at its annual banquet January 18 at Pine Forest Country Club. The Fingers long had been active in Houston and Gulf Coast area amateur baseball. Their Houston Baseball Museum was located in the Finger Furniture Center on the Gulf Freeway. Plaques commemorating the honor were presented to the three recipients. Fred Nahas was the master of ceremonies. Ray Dabek, and Buster Hackney, friend of Hofheinz since high school days, made arrangements for the gala banquet where baseball stories abounded.

At the Houston baseball writers' annual awards dinner at the Shamrock on February 1, Hofheinz said in the main address that a number of cities at one time or another had announced they either were going to build domed stadiums or were going to look into the possibility. Seattle, Montreal, Cleveland, New Orleans, Buffalo, New York, Chicago, Boston, Atlanta, Dallas, Kansas City, San Francisco, and probably others discussed domes, some even announcing plans and others authorizing surveys, appointing committees, calling for bond votes, or merely batting the subject around. He said: "Not a shovelful of dirt has yet been moved toward the construction of the world's second domed

Awards presentation in January of 1969 during which the Judge, Sammy and Aaron Finger were honored by the Houston Professional Baseball Association. Left to right: Walter F. "Buster" Hackney, the Judge, Clark Nealon, Fred Nahas, Sammy Finger, and Ray Dabeck. (Aaron Finger was unable to attend.) Photograph courtesy the *Houston Post.*

stadium. The next domed stadium that is constructed will cost four times what it cost Harris County to build the Astrodome. The rising costs of land, construction, and borrowed money now make it impossible to build a domed stadium that can pay for itself out of its own revenue. The city that builds one will be undertaking a huge public subsidy of six or seven million dollars annually. Every passing year establishes the wisdom of the decision made by Harris County voters and the public officials who stuck their necks out. The Astrodome will be the only public facility built in this country in the last 68 years from bond money that will be paid for out of its own revenue. This is a new era for Houston, the beginning of the hour of opportunity for every business in the city."

The National Basketball Association professional San Diego Rockets played the Boston Celtics, and the Detroit Pistons battled the Cincinnati Royals in a doubleheader in the Dome on February 14 to increase Houston's growing enthusiasm for basketball touched off by the Houston-UCLA sellout. The Rockets later were to be transferred to Houston and become a power in the NBA.

On March 2, Stan McIlvaine resigned as general manager of Astroworld. Hofheinz expressed regret at McIlvaine's leaving, for he had headed the planning, design, and development of the amusement and recreation center since its inception two years earlier.

The Astro Grand Prix midget auto race March 8-9 attracted a vast crowd of thrill-seekers. There were bumps and turns and twists, but no big casualties which some had feared might result.

The Judge was honored March 26, by the Houston Chapter of the American Marketing Association as the "Marketing Man of the Year for 1969." Ceremonies and the official presentation were held in the Houston Club at a dinner. P. Mitchell Clark, marketing officer of the Southern National Bank and the association president, presented the award.

Dene Hofheinz Mann joined Edwin Morris and Company in New York as a songwriter in June. She had recorded for the Astrodome. In late 1965, she had joined the Astrodome payroll as official hostess.

Construction began July 28 on a 25,000-square-foot ballroom next to the Astroworld Hotel. Spaw-Glass Incorporated was the contractor, and Phenix and Brodnax design architects—both were Houston companies. The ballroom would have a capacity of 2000 for banquets and 3000 for meetings. Completion was expected by January of 1970, in time for the second home-builders' convention.

When Bill Giles left the Houston Sports Association in July of 1969 to become executive vice-president of the Philadelphia Phillies, Warren, his father, recalled Hofheinz's reaction to the resignation of his longtime publicist: "Roy showed his good sense of humor. Houston newspapers had a streamer on page one: 'Giles Leaves Astros.' I asked Roy, 'Did Bill talk to you about this?' He said, 'Yes,' and added: 'You know, Warren, I've been here. I built this stadium and I've done this and that. I've been mayor of this town and have never seen more than a one-column head on any front page about me. Here Bill leaves and he's got his name emblazoned on a streamer across the front page. How do you account for that?' He was kidding because during his many years as a Houston leader, the name Hofheinz was often blazoned across the top of front pages."

Paul Haney, one-time radio and TV "Voice of the Astronauts" who during their early flights into space was heard by millions throughout the world, succeeded Bill Giles as public affairs chief. In August of 1978 he told stories of Hofheinz and the astronauts and of his own relationship with the Judge. After he settled in Charleston, South Carolina, to write books, he said:

> The first thing that struck me about Roy Hofheinz was his voice. It was bigger than the man who weighed a not-inconsequential 350 pounds. I studied his pronunciation, projection, volume, even the sentence structure. Like seasoned television hands—the Cronkites and the Huntleys and the Brinkleys—Hofheinz gave me the feeling he was reading a teleprompter just over my shoulder when I first met him while being shown around the Dome a few nights before it opened officially in 1965.

As public affairs officer for the NASA Manned Spacecraft Center in the early '60s, I was constantly reminded that Houston was growing—the arrival of both NASA and the major league baseball franchise. NASA moved into its permanent quarters at Clear Lake during the spring and summer of '64. The Colt .45s, now the Astros—a name change that was cleared in a phone call from Roy to Alan Shepard who in turn called me—moved into their new Dome home in April, 1965. During that period, I used to poke some fun at the Dome builders in speeches around the city and the state. Houston was determined to build a roof over part of the city, I used to say, while the other part, NASA, holds roofs in contempt. In space, the sky is only the beginning and certainly not the limit.

We finished the Mercury program in May, 1963, but we had a long way to go in space sophistication in order to do all the things we wanted to do in Gemini and Apollo. The Russians were pushing us pretty hard. We flew the first manned Gemini in March, 1965. A month later, 27 of the 28 astronauts lined the first and third base paths for introductions the night the Dome opened for the first official National League game. They received lifetime gold passes to all major league ball parks. Just before the ceremony, Bill Giles realized that no one present knew each of the pilots by rank and full name—except me. So he handed me a mike down on the field and I did the honors.

I got so carried away with the job, I also introduced George Low, NASA's deputy director, and Chris Kraft, then director of flight operations and now director of the center, who were seated up in the stands. From that day forward, we at NASA got VIP treatment at the Dome. Baseball, football, bullfighting, you name it. At first, my office was the central clearinghouse for free tickets. After 1965, the Dome and NASA became must-see items on every Houston tourist itinerary. People by the thousands shuttled between the two points. I fought one of my bigger battles within NASA to get an open-door tour policy. When we opened in '64, none of NASA's 14 centers was open daily or weekly to casual tourists, all because of rinky-dinky security. From day one, I fought for an open-gate policy and finally got it because the people of Houston turned out to tour NASA in great numbers—65,000 the first weekend we opened in September, 1965. Millions have toured it free.

With Hofheinz, it was different. The tour element was one fact he overlooked in his original planning, but he adjusted quickly to capitalize on one of the biggest moneymakers the Dome ever had. "Look at all those people," I said to him five years later when I worked for him. One of the five daily tours was trundling through. "Yeah," Hofheinz said with a grin, "just look at them: walking dollars!" He charged one dollar a head for the tours which attracted about one million persons a year for at least the first 10 years of the Dome's life. He didn't have to split any of this with the county although it took several spirited discussions with Commissioners Court and lawsuits to make the point.

Haney said his deal with Hofheinz was a salary of $20,000 a year, plus a new car for private uses with all repairs covered and unrestricted Texaco gasoline credit card—"All of which meant I earned twice as much for my outside, part-time jobs as I did from the full-time job at the Dome."

Haney said Alan Shepard, a promoter first and a baseball enthusiast second, signed a launch picture of his Redstone booster for Roy "in hopes you'll have the same good luck in getting off the ground." Hofheinz kept it in his ceremonial office in the Dome. Haney added:

> When I left NASA in the summer of '69, rather than take a nothing job in Washington, I looked around. I wanted to hang my hat, hopefully in Houston. When Bill Giles left, I called Mary Frances. The Judge asked that I meet him the next morning. We made a deal in something like five minutes. I became vice-president for public affairs, including all stadium-type promotions, the amusement park, the hotels, the ball club, even the circus. I didn't realize at the time just how fragile the whole empire was, but it sure as hell looked good that morning from the "Mini-dome"—a re-creation of the Dome itself, atop the then brand new Astroworld Hotel. The Judge emphasized he wanted me to do more than the baseball job. He also said I was free to follow my outside pursuits just so they didn't conflict and I kept him aware of where I was and what I was doing. We sealed it with a handshake and a drink of Scotch. Four or five days later he introduced me to the press at a conference in a posh Dome Club. That afternoon we left for the World Series in New York.
>
> When we got to the Waldorf, Hofheinz threw a snit fit in the lobby. It seemed he had reserved the Gold Suite—the most expensive in the house—but the hotel was holding it for Jordan's King Hussein. In a matter of minutes, however, we were esconced in the Gold Suite—which I hadn't seen since February of 1962 during the Glenn post-flight ticker tape parade. For years the hotel had reserved the suite for visiting heroes and royalty. Hofheinz qualified both ways for my money.
>
> The next day when we went to Shea Stadium, I met Roy, Jr., the Harvard professor. The junior Hofheinz was then head of Harvard's Far Eastern department, and spoke many dialects of Chinese. We wound up sitting next to each other at the game—the first World Series game for both of us. Along about the fifth inning, I noticed Butch had given up on the game and was reading a history book in Chinese. Meanwhile his old man was wheeling and dealing among the baseball-owning families.
>
> That fall, I got to know the Judge fairly well. I found him available, knowledgeable, and incredibly decisive. Around the Dome, a legend grew up about him that he encouraged—that he only worked on one problem or project at a time. That fall, winter, and spring, I would say that he spent six out of any given eight hours on the phone. I have no idea to whom he talked, but I do know he would get locked up on things like trying to find a television sponsor for the Bluebonnet Bowl. When other avenues failed, he would start digging on the phone. He had one obsession: Get to the head man because he's the one who can make decisions—or stated another way, don't screw around with the underlings, they just waste your time.
>
> The Judge asked me in late December, 1969, if I knew anyone with authority at any of the auto companies. I told him I had met Henry Ford as a seatmate at a Washington gridiron dinner and that I'd had some dealings with

Lynn Townsend who ran Chrylser in those days. "Call Townsend and see if he'd like to sponsor the Bluebonnet game," he said. I did, but he wasn't interested—said he left those decisions to his advertising people. Another time when the Judge apparently needed a financial transfusion, he asked me if I knew anyone with $25 million. I said "Sure, Bob Hope." The Judge said, "Call him and see if he'd lend me $25 million for a half interest in the whole shebang." I had gotten to know Hope fairly well the year before when he did a 90-minute special at the Spacecraft Center which I helped arrange.

I reached Hope at home and put the question to him. He laughed and said, "Hell, Paul, the only person I know with that kind of money is Howard Hughes." According to news accounts, Hope is worth in excess of $500 million. After the special at Clear Lake, Hope gave me and a dozen people closely involved with the show individual wrist watches of the finest Swiss make, worth $3000 each and each inscribed on the back, "Thanks for the memories, Bob Hope." A few months later, we worked again when he came into the Dome with half of Hollywood and raised $400,000, playing to 40,000 people, to set up a charity for the three astronauts killed in the 1967 fire. But Hope still wasn't interested in buying into the place.

During that winter, Hofheinz sidled up to me one day going into Astrohall. "I want you to plan on going to Europe next week. I'm not sure that I can make it. It's to promote next year's Supermarket Association convention here." He didn't make the trip, but I did with two weeks of . . . promotion. It was all well laid on, organized to the gnat's eyebrows—by the Judge himself. We covered something like 12 major cities in 14 days. It paid off. The Europeans came to the convention in April, 1970 in record numbers.

I recall riding downtown with Hofheinz one day as he went to a city planner to make sure some plans didn't come to grief. All the way down Travis Street, he chatted about the buildings. "You see that one," he'd say, "I sold it four times, and that one—Oh, wow." I don't think I ever saw him more animated. Downtown Houston real estate was his thing. Next to real estate, I think he liked promotion best—or pulling something off with a little flair, class.

The Judge particularly liked one little thing I did. In the fall of '69, the Russians were getting very friendly all of a sudden with American space types. Whole boat loads of cosmonauts began showing up at the Spacecraft Center, a precursor to the joint mission which was finally flown in 1975.

Frank Borman called me one day and said he'd like to bring a couple of Russian pilots by the Dome. We worked out the gate routine and where to meet. Just for the hell of it, I called Adie Marks, the Dome's ad man, and asked him to do a slide for the big scoreboard screen that would welcome the cosmonauts in Russian. Marks had a helluva time getting it together, but he did it. The result was page one art in both the local papers. The Judge congratulated me for that job. We planned a lot of other stunts. For instance, we had the first ball of the 1970 baseball season launched in the Dome on a small rocket, complete with parachute.

One day Bob Altman, the movie man, called me. We'd known each other slightly from the space days; he'd worked for ABC News. His film MASH—the one that made him famous—was not yet released, but he'd finished work on it, and he was ready to start a new one. He said it was a fantasy about a guy who wanted to learn to fly. The script had the hero practicing by jumping off the Golden Gate Bridge, but Altman said they could rewrite it to have him learning nights in the Astrodome. I told the Judge about it and he pooh-poohed the idea. "Might give us a bad name," he said. "We'll have to have script review rights." Then I gave him the clincher. "They're planning to pay rent for the use of the place," I told him. Whoosh! He lit up like a Christmas tree. A few weeks later *MASH* appeared, and Altman was proclaimed the new genius of motion pictures. That's open to some question. As it turned out, the turkey Altman made in the Dome was no *MASH*, but it was, like most other Altman pictures, different. It was called *Brewster McCloud.* When the hero is not ushering at the Dome, he slips in after hours to try out a set of bird-like wings, and he learns to fly—until the Houston police literally shoot him down. Anyway the picture premiered in the Dome in 1970 to a paid audience of 28,000, the largest crowd ever to see a movie indoors. Even nicer from the Judge's point of view was a check from the producer in excess of $100,000 for rental of the Dome and adjacent structures for a period of about three weeks during the shooting. In addition to all the free publicity about the Dome, we earned $100,000-plus for the effort. I doubt if MGM did as well. They released it.

One of the things I admired about Hofheinz was his analytical gift. I have never seen anyone who could look at a large undertaking, examine it from dozens of different facets, and then make a decision. I'm talking particularly of show-biz-type acts for the Dome. In a matter of minutes he could gauge the house, ticket costs, audience reception, critical reception, promotional vehicles, ad costs, and on and on. I asked him one day what the toughest undertaking of his life had been. Without a blink, he said it was when he took over all but 10 percent of Bob Smith's stock in the Dome. He said he didn't sleep all week. He said it was one of the few things he ever undertook where he really knew fear of failure and what it would mean to his family, to him. Of course he made it with a few hours to spare.

During the first six months I worked in the Dome, the Judge did at least one major refinancing. As I understood it, it was bill-consolidation-type loan. I managed to get a check for Adie Marks in the amount of $182,000 for billing Marks said went back to the early '60s. Jack O'Connell told me once that Astrodomain had to make $12,000 every day just to cover debt service.

When the chips were down—and they were frequently—Roy had an imposing array of good friends to count on, Red James and Leon Jaworski in particular.

On December 31, Bob Smith announced the sale of his 10 percent interest in the Houston Sports Association to The Timewealth Corporation, a Houston-based leisure-time firm. Officials of Timewealth had long been known as "The Bob Smith Boys," for he had given them financial backing since the late 1940s. Sale price of the stock was not disclosed. "I've known the purchasers for 20 years," Hofheinz said. "Most of them worked for me when I was Houston's mayor. I am sure the relationship will be harmonious."

Officials of Timewealth included Welcome Wilson, Jack Wilson, Johnny Goyen, Eugene Maier, and Sherwood Crane. The firm owned and operated six resort communities in the West Galveston area and a 2800-acre subdivision near Lake Bastrop. "This (HSA) investment fits in perfectly with our corporate philosophy," said Welcome Wilson, Timewealth board chairman. "The Astrodome complex is the greatest structure in the history of mankind. We are proud to be associated." All Timewealth principles except Maier were alumni of the University of Houston. (Goyen was a city councilman then and was continuing in that role when this book was written.)

40

A Crippling Stroke

From January to May 8, 1970, Roy Hofheinz worked feverishly with his associates to get his financial house in order. The debts of his corporation, short-term notes, had mounted with each new building enterprise, a recession had set in, interest rates mounted, and lenders pushed him for long-term financing which the receding cash flow could meet. The Judge never lost confidence, however, that the assets of the Astrodome complex, his majority ownership of the circus, his personal nest egg in Houston Slag Materials Company, his real estate, and investments in antiques and other properties would pull him through. Although there were rumors, the public knew little about his financial problems.

Meanwhile, in January the Houston baseball writers held their 1970 annual awards dinner, and five baseball stars toured the new "Celestial Suite." Joe Heiling, *Chronicle* reporter, recorded part of their conversation:

> Slugger Reggie Jackson (then with the Oakland Athletics) spotted the Judge and said, groping for words: "Nice pad you got here. What else can I say? Nice pad." Wandering in and out of the various rooms, the 47-homer hitting athletic was bug-eyed by it all. Not a Sam McDowell fastball nor the sight of one of his own mighty wallops made a deeper impression on the 23-year-old with the muscular swing than the plush surroundings. Reggie, along with Johnny Bench, Harmon Killebrew, Steve Carlton and Larry Dierker (dinner honorees) termed just walking through the plush layout "an experience."
>
> "Do you actually live in this place, Judge?" Killebrew asked, incredulously. The Judge took a puff on his long cigar, paused for effect and replied, "I do when I don't rent it out. This is home." Carlton, the tall St. Louis Cardinal lefthander, asked the next question. "What do you rent this place for anyway?"
>
> Answered Hofheinz: "Twenty-five hundred a night." Gulping once, Steve fished a handful of coins out of his trouser pocket and said, "I think I just might have the price in some loose change." The Judge laughed, "If you do," he said, "just name your date."

County Judge Elliott, in another slap at Hofheinz, proposed to limit smoking in the stadium February 10, 1970. It did not get past the suggestion stage with commissioners. Elliott's resolution would ask "the Houston Sports Association to ban the smoking of tobacco except in designated areas in the stadium," although he was a cigarette smoker himself. Commissioner Chapman, a nonsmoker, said he would vote against any such resolution. Commissioner Lvons, a pipe-smoker, and Commissioner Ramsay, also a nonsmoker, passed the buck to Hofheinz who ignored the idea.

The second Astro Grand Prix was run March 14. Hofheinz and Sidney Shlenker, president, and Allen Becker, vice-president of PACE Management Corporation, were co-sponsors. Speaking on behalf of the co-sponsors, the Judge said: "Following last year's inaugural which drew over 55,000 racing fans, we decided to make the USAC (United States Auto Club) race an annual affair. It is with a great deal of pleasure that we announce we have obtained a sanction for a one-day event." The top 50 car owners of the USAC midget division in the 1969 final point standings received invitations to 1970s race, and 10 others participated.

On March 10, 1970, ARA Services contracted with Hofheinz to operate all food and beverage concessions in the Astrodome and Astrohall, replacing Harry Martin Catering Company. ARA began service just before the Astros' first home pre-season game March 31. The food service firm, with annual sales of more than $600 million, then had 20,000 clients, including 275 colleges and 180 hospitals; it served more than 8,000,000 persons daily.

Jack O'Connell explained the ARA deal while looking back at some of Hofheinz's financial maneuvers. He said in 1978:

> The Judge was a resourceful guy relative to bankers. He didn't really look to me or any of the other officers for help. The Judge did all borrowing on 90-day notes. He just rolled it over all the time. He'd never pay anything down on the principal, but paid interest or borrowed the interest and extended his note. With interest rates going up, it became pretty tough. We were carrying a lot of raw land on our books. Part of the concept of building the hotels and the amusement park was to shelter the income for HSA which, to the best of my knowledge, always was pretty profitable. In any case, the income generated by HSA could be sheltered by the depreciation of the hotels, the amusement park, and improvements.
>
> The Judge began to open up some of these problems to me. In January of 1970, when we desperately needed $5 million, a friend, Don Greenway, called me. Greenway had founded a hotel-restaurant school at the University of Houston. He asked me if I would meet a former student of his, saying, "I don't want to get into business dealings, but you and he should know each other." His name was Bill Segal. I took Segal through the Dome. He was with ARA, and he said he would like to have the concession contract at the Astrodome. I talked to him about what could be done with the right kind of operator.
>
> Although Harry Martin and the Judge had a great personal relationship, the Astrodome was really too big a deal for him. He sold out to another

corporation with the Judge's agreement. Martin still had the key, however. The understanding was that Martin was the Texas manager for that company, and as far as we were concerned we were going to deal with him the way we always had. Eventually that company sold out to Ogden Corporation, a much bigger company, but Martin stayed. Harry did everything the Judge wanted him to do within the limits of his ability.

The Judge said he'd rather stick with Martin. I told Segal, "Just forget it, there's no way the Judge is going to divorce himself from Harry Martin." We parted as friends. That night I was talking to the Judge again about the $5 million problem in his suite in the Astrodome. I asked him, "Do you want to change concessionaires? I think we could get a sizeable chunk of money just for consideration of ARA buying the contract, percentages the same, and everything else the same, but a bonus of significance."

He asked, "Five million?"

I said, "I don't think we could get that much."

He said, "Call them up and ask."

I said, "Judge, the guy just left here a couple of hours ago for Philadelphia."

He said, "Ask him anyway; try to call him." So I called him at his Philadelphia home. I'd just met the guy that day and he'd just left. He wasn't in yet, his wife said, but he had just called from the airport; he'd be home soon. I asked her to have him call me. He called me and I said, "Bill, the situation has changed since I talked to you this afternoon. We might consider making a switch, but you've got to talk about sizeable dollars."

He said, "What do you mean, sizeable?"

I said, "We're talking about seven-figure numbers." The Judge was listening on an extension. Segal said, "You mean like a million or two?"

I said, "We wouldn't throw that out completely, but we are now talking about more than that."

He said, "I'll discuss it with our people."

I said, "No, Bill, you don't understand, I'm talking about we have to do this quickly or not do it at all."

He said, "All right, I'll talk to my associates and I'll be there Monday."

I said, "No, I'm talking about tomorrow morning."

He said, "All right, I'll be back there by noon tomorrow."

He came back and we hammered out a deal. Where we were getting 38 percent of gross from Martin, or a minimum of $750,000 a year, we got 40 percent from Segal with a million-dollar-a-year guarantee and a million-dollar consideration for just switching the contract. The Judge called Bob Martin, vice-president of marketing for Schlitz, and arranged to get a half million dollars. These two deals gave us a million and a half.

We were worried about Houston Bank and Trust notes. Joe Allbritton had bought the bank. We didn't have the money wired to that bank for fear the funds would be used to offset delinquent interest. We decided to go to Citizens Bank at the foot of Main Street and open an account. At that time, the Battelstein family controlled the bank. Roy's friend, promoter Sidney Shlenk-

Sidney Shlenker

er, was in Miami then, but his father was president of Citizens. The Judge knew him well. Schlitz wired funds, and we deposited them with Citizens. A subsequent irony—the Citizens Bank was merged with Houston Bank and Trust. Joe Allbritton bought Citizens; that's how Houston Bank and Trust became Houston Citizens Bank and Trust, so Allbritton knew what was going on. At the end of February, banks agreed to lend Roy another 3.5 million, but required that he put all of his assets into one corporation and that they, the creditors, control the board of that corporation. Many papers had to be drawn.

O'Connell said there was much debate about who the directors of Astrodomain would be because the Houston Bank, Chemical Bank in New York, Wells Fargo in San Francisco, and Mercantile in Dallas all had financial interests at stake. One other creditor, New England Mutual Life Insurance Company, had a lien on the land and the first lien on the Astroworld Hotel. Prudential had other liens. It took time to devise the new structure demanded by the lenders.

Debts incurred by Astroworld, the hotel complex, additions of the fabulous penthouse, and a ballroom in the Astroworld Hotel caused various lenders to force the formation of an umbrella corporation which could supervise all entities and make way for refinancing over a long period. Astrodomain Corporation resulted in March of 1970. There was a five-member board: Hofheinz was chairman; Joe L. Allbritton of Houston Citizens Bank and Trust Company and J. D. Francis of Mercantile National Bank of Dallas represented short-term lenders; Leon Jaworski, president-elect of the American Bar Association, represented the public interest; and Bill Dwyer, Hofheinz's longtime house attorney. Assets of Hofheinz and his children were lumped together in Astrodomain. Not included in the corporation then were the Judge's and his children's majority interest in Ringling Bros. and Barnum & Bailey Circus, the undeveloped land in the domed stadium area, and other holdings, including undeveloped property off Westheimer.

When he became a director of Astrodomain Corporation at age 45, Joe Lewis Allbritton was chairman and director of the Houston Citizens Bank and Trust Company, successor to banks which had been Hofheinz lenders and holder of notes given by the Judge. His operations reached from Houston to California, and he was known as a rich man when he moved into leadership of the consolidated bank. It was he, speaking for major bank lenders, who insisted that Hofheinz's various corporations be put under one holding firm. He knew Jack O'Connell well and had great respect for Hofheinz's right-hand financial man. As a member of Astrodomain's board, he felt he could help Hofheinz and O'Connell get long-term financing. At least, he would know fully about the corporation's operations and problems.

Fred Hofheinz said financial planning for his father's ventures "had been, of necessity, haphazard because they had grown topsy-turvy and the result was that at the time of my mother's death there was a confused financial situation. Dad concentrated on investments more and more—building things. I had to try to make sense out of the things that he had built and some of the operational details. I think that this period, however, was when Dad's real brilliance came to the fore. He built from nothing in a short period of time one of the great entertainment complexes in the country. If it had not been for the death of my mother and the resulting financial burden, it would have been a success far in excess of what is recognized today. Financial problems could only be solved and were only solved after my departure by some rather extreme steps that had to be taken because interest rates rose to 14 percent or 15 prime plus four. That interest range was prevalent on most projects from the period of 1968 to 1973. It was a crippling, awful situation."

After he became general manager of HSA, Spec Richardson wore many hats. He was responsible for all of the activities inside the Astrodome, including stadium operations, personnel, maintenance, hiring, and firing. He had to deal with rodeos, bullfights, and grand prix races, not to mention looking out for stray elephants. With all this responsibility, there were occasions when Richardson was forced to ignore the baseball end of things when more pressing problems emerged. To ease pressure on Richardson, Hofheinz announced March 30 that his valuable right-hand man would be concentrating fully on his baseball duties in the future.

"We're going to let Spec devote more attention to minor league personnel and spend more time on baseball," said the Judge, "now that we've developed personnel in other aspects of operation." Many of Richardson's former duties fell on Owen Martinez, one of the most versatile men in the Houston Sports Association, as director of stadium operations.

Hofheinz was appointed chairman of the 1970 fundraising dinner for the National Jewish Hospital and Research Center held on April 29. A thousand persons, paying $125 a couple, responded to the salesmanship of Hofheinz, working with Irvin M. Shlenker, general chairman. The non-sectarian Jewish hospital in Denver, Colorado, specializes in the treatment of respiratory diseases and does research on the effects of air pollution to breathing mechanisms. The hospital does not charge patients for treatment.

In 1978, Mary Frances Hofheinz sadly recalled: "In April of 1970, banks pushed the Judge hard to get long-term financing so they could get out. The Judge was concerned about how he was going to work it out. Money was really tight and interest rates were soaring. The Judge made 'Huckster House' our residence for several weeks to get away from his problems. He was doing some redecorating, which is one of the things he does when worried. He was very irritable and on edge. I had never seen him quite like that in the 17 years I had known him. We had to go into town to the Astrodome now and then to take care of business matters."

On May 8, the Judge had a meeting with John Easter and Spec Richardson, Mary Frances continued:

> As they were leaving his office, he walked to the door of his office with them. Halfway there, he suddenly had a weakness on the left side of his body. It was so bad that they had to help him to a chair. They helped him get up to his suite. By this time they had gotten me there and we called Dr. Hatch Cummings, the Astros' team doctor. He came quickly, examined the Judge, and suggested he enter a hospital then, but my husband asked if he could go to "Huckster House" for the weekend. The doctor agreed.
>
> The Judge entered Methodist Hospital on May 10. He told me he wanted me to stay with him, which I was planning to do anyway. The next few days were spent going through tests. Dr. John Stirling Meyer was called in as the Judge's neurologist. On the evening of May 13, Dr. Meyer came by the hospital room and told the Judge he needed to do an arteriogram. The Judge asked quite a few questions about this test. He specifically asked questions about whether there were ever any complications. For some reason, the Judge was concerned about taking this test—maybe because he was going to have to be put to sleep for it. Anyway, he was very anxious.
>
> The next morning the Judge was wide awake about 5:00 A.M. He woke me and we were talking about everything in general. I was worried and so was he, but we never mentioned it to one another. He gave me a list of things he wanted me to do that morning. At the top of list—an order for swings for the grandkids for "Huckster House." Hospital personnel came in starting about 7:00 A.M. to

sedate him. Shortly after that they came and took him downstairs for the arteriogram. I threw on my clothes and went downstairs and sat outside the room where he was having his test. About noon, Dr. Cummings came out and told me that it looked bad—that part of the blood vessels in the Judge's brain were blocked off. I didn't know anything about strokes and I took that to mean that the damage done was what the Judge had experienced when he had the weakness of his side. I sat there several hours more. Late in the afternoon a nice lady receptionist on the floor told me that they had taken the Judge to recovery and I might as well go on up to our room. I went. The more time went by, the more frightened I was. Around 5:00 P.M. the telephone in the room rang. I grabbed it. The voice was that of Larry Rasco with Channel 2 television station. He said he understood the Judge was in real bad condition. My heart started pounding and I thought to myself, "He knows something that they're not telling me." They hadn't told me anything.

Somehow I came up with a very calm voice and told Larry, "Oh no, Larry, the Judge is just in for a test, nothing serious at all." He said that he must have gotten wrong information and we said our goodbyes. I put the telephone down and started sobbing. I was so scared I thought I was going to die. I called Joe Louis Holiday and asked him to come to the hospital and sit with me until I found out something. I was afraid to ask anybody anything because I was afraid of the worst. Joe arrived quickly and sat with me until attendants finally let me in to see the Judge in intensive care. I couldn't believe what I saw when I entered his booth. The Judge was gasping for breath and had a tube in his throat so that he could breathe. He was unconscious. I stayed with him as long as nurses allowed. On the way out from intensive care, I saw Dr. Cummings. I begged him to stay with the Judge. He promised he would. I went to our hospital room. I was freezing cold and in a state of stupor. I guess I must have been close to shock.

I remember that "Little Dene" and one of her friends came bubbling into the room thinking that they could see the Judge. I said something to her that scared her, but for the life of me I can't remember what it was. That night was the only night in my life that I ever took a sleeping pill because of the agony of worrying. The next day I spent as much time as they would allow me to visit the Judge and the rest of the day praying. I went to the beautiful little chapel at the hospital several times and prayed with all my heart: "God, please let the Judge live." As a matter of fact, I still am trying to repay my debt to God. I made some promises to God that day and hope that I am living up to them and that I will continue to carry them out.

The first day the Judge was awake enough so that I could talk to him I remember saying to him, "I love you." He couldn't talk to me, but motioned for me to get a pencil. He scrawled on a piece of paper, "Me, too." That's one of the nicest love letters I ever got in my life. As the Judge improved, I am sure the intensive care unit never had a patient quite like the Judge before. He was unbelievably loud when he was hungry and he was always hungry. Gradually, I gained confidence the Judge would live.

Houston newspapers did not know the full extent of the Judge's stroke. The hospital superintendent issued brief statements that Hofheinz had suffered a stroke, but was recuperating. Hofheinz's illness compounded fears of his lenders that the genius who had made deals with them might not survive.

Attorney Bill McDonald was affiliated with Hofheinz in various legal matters after the Judge suffered the stroke. He recalled: "I knew of the Judge for some time but it was May 9, a Sunday, when I first met him. I had been talking with his then counsel, Bill Dwyer, a former associate of mine, and Gus Elkins, about the possibility of going to work in place of Dwyer, for the Judge and for the Astrodome complex. We met at 'Huckster House' the day before he was taken to the hospital. The Judge wasn't feeling well, but we made a deal for me to go to the Dome. . . . Billy Dwyer went into the real estate business, but agreed to remain on the Astrodomain board. I told my partner that I was going with the Judge."

County Judge Elliott continued his vendetta against Hofheinz by proposing June 11, when the Judge was recuperating, that the Houston Sports Association's 40-year lease on the domed stadium be terminated unless the corporation complied with the contract and furnished a required annual financial report. County auditor Grady Fullerton had written a letter to the Commissioners Court saying that the papers due in his office on or before April 1 had not been received. "We have advised Houston Sports Association of its failure to comply with the terms of the contract with Harris County," Fullerton said in the letter. Copies of the letter were forwarded to Hofheinz and Joe Resweber, county attorney. "All we can do is file it," said Commissioner Squatty Lyons of the Fullerton letter. HSA was often late in filing reports, but never failed to pay its big annual rental. Elliott's demands about the contract were constantly brushed off by commissioners.

While Hofheinz was going through therapy, rumors floated that Howard Hughes or some other millionaire might buy Astrodomain. Jack O'Connell quickly denied them. He told the *Post*: "The rumors are ridiculous. However, I think the Judge would consider selling anything he owns at the right price. I think he would consider it because he's a reasonable man, but he is certainly fond of some of the holdings." Asked if reports were true that Astrodomain Corporation was having trouble meeting its bills, O'Connell replied: "I think some of the rumors have been from player trades; let's face it, we had a hard winter. We got behind. But now we're caught up. Everyone is paid off." O'Connell acknowledged another possible reason for financial headaches. "The last two things added to the complex were the Astroworld penthouse and the ballroom," he said. "They put a little strain on the operation. We are having to pay the price of expanding at the Judge's pace. We are well satisfied now." The penthouse and the ballroom were estimated to have cost $1 million each, or more.

"That stimulated the Astrodomain Corporation organization," O'Connell continued, "in a search for the healthiest economic climate. That brought about the need of additional financing, provisions for a tax shelter, generally a more intelligent position. For the first time in three years, the ball club, amusement park, and hotels are in the black, including coverage of operating costs, principal and interest payments. This is the first year that all of these are earning profits based on everything including debt retirement."

O'Connell said that every firm had start-up investment problems. He described a vacant 302-acre dome area tract as an albatross. He pointed out that the holding of undeveloped land with such high market value was expensive. He said the ideal solution for the land would be to sell it or develop it through a joint venture with Hofheinz furnishing the ideas and someone else furnishing the capital. O'Connell confirmed that there had been discussions regarding possible sales of Astrodomain entities including the land. He termed these preliminary in nature. "The Judge is the kind of guy who never sells anything." O'Connell said. "Doesn't want to part with anything. He never sells a car even, just keeps them."

The Astrodomain Corporation, according to O'Connell, then had these assets: Hofheinz's 88 percent interest in the Houston Sports Association, including the leasehold on the domed stadium and Astrohall, the country's largest convention center, and the Astros baseball team and farm system teams; four motor hotels, Astroworld, Holiday Inn-Astroworld, Howard Johnson-Astroworld, and Sheraton Inn-Astroworld; a service station constructed in the form of a miniature dome and the 57-acre amusement park, Astroworld.

Bill McDonald's first day as counsel for the Astrodomain Corporation was June 1, when the Judge was still going through intensive therapy at the hospital.

> My job as counsel included the Houston Sports Association, all affiliated corporations, and personal counsel to the Judge. The fact that the Judge was out of action necessitated some shifting around. Rather than being purely house counsel, I was pressed more into a management than a legal role. Jack O'Connell was chief operating officer. The Judge used to laugh about an organizational chart. In any organization, his concept, we felt, was a circle with a dot in the middle and he, of course, was the dot. Fortunately for the Judge in the entities of the new Astrodomain Corporation was the fact that it had structures under which we could operate. Otherwise, if all was in his name and he was not able during this short period of time to do anything, no one would have had authority to move. Ownership of all properties, however, was in Judge Hofheinz, individually for one half and as trustee of the Hofheinz children one half.
>
> As I got into Astrodomain affairs, I often felt—and I expressed it to the Judge and Mrs. Hofheinz more than once—that I bet he hated to see me coming. I never was able to have a relationship with the Judge that many of the people around him previously had. He was not available for chit-chat and for a

lot of brainstorming because his health, his physical endurance, wouldn't allow it. As a consequence, most of the time when I was with the Judge I had some sort of problem that needed an answer. Basically, there were routine types of things I prepared and then got with the Judge for his signature. I got more into management then just for the sole reason that he used to be in the center of that circle and had his finger on everything throughout the perimeter of that circle, and he was no longer able to put his finger on everything and some of the rest of us had to fill in that void.

O'Connell, John Easter, (Spec Richardson had the baseball end of it), and I had the responsibility for operation of the entire complex. The three of us would bounce things around and come up with ideas and then present them to the Judge for decisions. We were the ones who were dealing on a daily basis with outsiders, whether they were bankers or suppliers or people who wanted to put on some sort of event in the Dome or rent Astroworld park for something.

In a major financial development, Ringling Bros. and Barnum & Bailey Combined Shows, Incorporated, agreed to merge with Mattel, Incorporated, of Hawthorne, California, on December 21, 1970. The value of the transaction was estimated at $47,650,000, of which Hofheinz interest as board chairman was $27 million. Announcement of the plan, whereby Ringling became a subsidiary of Mattel, was made by Elliot Handler, chairman and chief executive officer of Mattel, and Irvin Feld, president of the Washington-based circus. Feld and Hofheinz retained their positions with the circus. The Hofheinz and Feld families privately held 1,560,000 shares. In addition, Hofheinz had a warrant for 1,554,000 shares at $1.41-⅔ per share.

In June of 1969, the circus had its initial public offering of 346,000 shares at $14 a share. The merger announcement said Mattel would issue 1,250,000 shares of its stock in exchange for 3,460,000 shares of circus stock. Mattel opened that day on the New York Stock Exchange at $38.25 a share. Ringling began trading in the over-the-counter market at $11.25 bid, $11.25 asked. Mattel closed at $67.62 a share. The California firm is the world's largest toy manufacturer. Mattel, formed by a partnership in 1945, fashioned talking dolls, costumes, and accessories which accounted for a large part of sales. Major diversification included wheel goods, bicycles, tricycles, toy trucks, and children's clothing. Mattel is the parent of "Barbie" dolls.

For its fiscal year ending January 31, 1970, Mattel said its sales totaled $228,575,000, and its net earnings were $12,069,000, or 91 cents a share. For the first nine months of 1970, the company reported sales of $263,857,000 and net earnings of $13,395,000, or 93 cents per share. For its fiscal year ending December 31, 1969, Ringling Bros. and Barnum & Bailey had gross revenues of $15,728,230 and a net income of $823,414, or 28 cents a share. For the nine months ending September 30, 1970, gross revenues were $16,618,242, and net income was $1,293,967, or 37 cents a share. The Greatest Show on Earth celebrated its 100th anniversary all during the year, having been founded in 1870 by P. T. Barnum.

The Judge's physical condition worried sons Fred and Roy and his daughter, "Little Dene," not only because he was their father, but because he was trustee of the trust their mother left them. The junior Hofheinz flew down from Boston to see his brother and father after the Judge was able to talk about financial affairs. Attorney McDonald, new on his job as Astrodomain counsel, recalled: "With Fred present, we had a meeting trying to convince the Judge to sell something to meet short-term notes. As we were leaving, Fred said, 'You know, Dad has never sold anything in his life. He buys everything, but sells nothing.' He was talking about a piece of farm equipment, to use as an example, that he had bought years ago, and it was lying out in the field some place rusting and going to waste. Fred added: 'The reason is that Dad thinks anything anyone else has isn't worth anything, but everything he has is the best.' He's that way about people, too. If you're in the employ of Judge Hofheinz, for example, you are the best, in his judgment."

Navy Captain Eugene A. Cernan was spokesman for all astronauts at the National Aeronautical and Space Agency outside Houston who were guests at a 1970 Christmas party in the Astroworld's "Celestial Suite." Said Cernan: "It was probably the best party we ever had and will long be remembered." He thanked Hofheinz for his "gracious generosity" in agreeing to allow Wes Hooper and Erik Worscheh to be hosts for "super hospitality" in the suite. The Judge and Mary Frances were in Venice, Florida, that holiday season for the signing of the Mattel merger. They believed the merger had ended his financial woes and were extremely happy, despite the Judge's crippled condition.

41

"Snitch," "Pixie," Leslie, and M.F.

Under doctor's orders, four women played vital roles in the recuperation of Roy Hofheinz from the stroke which paralyzed his left side. Two, Peggy Woods and Jewell Williams, were registered nurses. The third was Leslie Brothers (later Mrs. William Ritchie), occupational therapist. The fourth was Mary Frances, generally known as M.F.

It was Peggy Woods—dubbed "Snitch" by Hofheinz because she held back nothing in reporting the Judge's behavior to his doctors—who led in getting the patient back on his feet despite his constant opposition and often crafty means of thwarting her orders, especially about food. She was a 1946 graduate of Allegheny General Hospital School of Nursing in Pittsburgh. She married John (Jack) Woods and went with him to Houston when his company, Jessup Steel, transferred him to Texas' largest city as a base for nationwide traveling. Peggy did private duty nursing in all Houston hospitals before she became Hofheinz's chief nurse after he was moved from Methodist Hospital's intensive care unit into a private room. Tall, trim, strong, patient, and dedicated to her profession, "Snitch" was at the Judge's side from early morning until late evening for almost a year.

Five-foot-one Jewell Williams, a charming 110-pound native Floridian who graduated from the Medical College of Virginia in 1960, became, in 1969, physical therapist at Methodist Hospital. She specialized in cardiovascular and orthopedic rehabilitation. It was not long after the Judge went to a private room that she coaxed him into doing some helpful exercises. Later she resigned her hospital position to go on the Judge's private payroll. He called her "Pixie."

Vivacious Leslie Brothers trained for occupational therapy for five years at Texas Women's University. Two days after her internship at Methodist Hospital, she became staff therapist and helped develop the then new department for a year and a half before Hofheinz became a patient.

"Snitch," "Pixie," and Leslie knew from the beginning that the Judge was an unusual patient. Each did her part in teaching Mrs. Hofheinz to become an expert medical aide to her husband, although she perhaps proved in the long run too loving of her husband.

Left to right: "Snitch" (Peggy Woods), "Pixie" (Jewell Williams), and Leslie Brothers Ritchie.

In 1978 when she was assistant to Ted Bowen, Methodist Hospital administrator, Peggy Woods relaxed for a long interview as her husband listened and often commented to refresh her memory. By then they had a grown son. "Snitch" said, "My introduction to the Judge was to see him pounding with a spoon on the siderail of his bed, put up at night, and yelling at the top of his voice that he wanted food. He had had his breakfast, but didn't think it adequate. I quickly learned he was obsessed with food. One of the biggest problems in rehabilitating a stroke patient is keeping weight down so that weakened muscles can support the body. With him it was a terrible and increasing problem because every day he missed food more than the day before."

The Judge kept Mary Frances and Joe Louis Holiday near him as much as possible. "The most difficult thing for Joe and me," said Mary Frances, "was that we were not allowed to let the Judge have any food other than that which came on his hospital tray. It wasn't very much or very good because he was also on a low sodium diet. He would plead for food constantly. Sometimes he would give me such a bad time I just couldn't take it and I would very quietly leave his room, go up the hall to the restroom, lock the door, and start blubbering. I would stay there until I got it all out of my system. Then I would fix my face and go back to the Judge's room. Dr. Lew Leavitt, the Judge's physical medicine doctor, who was a tower of strength to me because he understood what the Judge was going through, had told me that if I ever felt like crying, not to do it in front of the Judge . . . that he had enough problems trying to overcome the aftermath of the stroke."

"Snitch" said that Mary Frances and Joe Louis Holiday loved the Judge so much that it was difficult for them to deny him the rich foods he loved so much. Mary Frances explained: "For several months after we left the hopsital, the Judge stuck to his diet, because we all wouldn't let him get near anything he shouldn't eat. But one morning, I was helping the Judge get out of bed, which by this time I had learned to do. He sat on the side of the bed and smiled a big good morning smile at me and said, 'I think I'll have three eggs, sunnyside up, six slices of bacon, four pieces of buttered toast, a large glass of orange juice, and black coffee.' I looked him right in the eye and said, 'Judge, why do you torture yourself like this? You know you can't have all that for breakfast.' He gave me the most serious look I'd ever seen on his face and said, 'M.F., I'd rather be dead than to have to live like this. This isn't living . . . . This is death.' With that, he won. . . . I decided he had to live his own life. He wasn't a child. He was a very brilliant human being capable of making decisions for himself, even if they weren't necessarily to his advantage. I truly believe that if we had continued treating him like a child he would have given up completely . . . and I don't like to think of the consequences."

After spending a week in intensive care, the Judge had a hard time getting his nights and days straightened out. Doctors decided nurses needed to get him back on a regular schedule. Mary Frances recalled: "Peggy kept him awake during the day; the evening nurse kept him awake in the evening; and the night nurse kept him awake all night. I just assumed that everyone was doing what they had been ordered to do by the doctor. I don't recall the name of the night nurse, but the Judge had nicknamed her 'Hitler' because he said she tortured him just like he knew the prisoners in German prisoner of war camps must have been. For about four days I watched, then I asked Peggy why all three nurses were keeping him awake. It didn't seem fair to me not to let him sleep sometime. Peggy said, 'You mean the night nurse is keeping him awake too?' I told her yes. She said, 'My God, she is supposed to let him sleep.' She got that straightened out."

Bob Young was a daily visitor in the Judge's room. He knew what it was like to be confined to a hospital for he had spent seven months in one after he was burned when his boat caught fire. The longtime friend of the Hofheinzes had severe burns and after living through excruciating pain and long days of rehabilitation and therapy, he understood what a patient had to go through.

"Each time Bob came in," said Mary Frances, "he would bring or do something which would brighten the Judge's day. Some of the things were insane, but all were fun. Once, he printed up book matches which read 'Stalag 891,' which was the Judge's room number. The Judge had a ball handing them out. He also brought the Judge a loud horn for his wheelchair, which the Judge had a wonderful time honking until other patients complained. Bob was in the upholstery business and would take parts of the Judge's wheelchair and do special work adding padding or whatever trying to make the Judge more comfortable."

"Snitch" said that during the Judge's hospital confinement she had not learned to love the patient and added:

> I was the only one around him who constantly could say "NO!" I could shake my finger in his face and say, "NO, there isn't any more food! That's it." He had a way of putting people off by his gruffness and ill temper which wasn't

doing anything but hiding his true nature because he is not ill-tempered. He has a wonderful sense of humor. Few people stayed around him long enough to discover this.

The Judge presented a challenge to me—one, because he had a stroke, and two, his tremendous weight. I, his doctors, and his therapists knew we had a tough job. He weighed 275 pounds and this presented a problem of an overweight body being supported by weakened muscles. Until we could get those muscles strengthened, we had to try to make the two meet—strengthen his muscles and reduce weight so that the weak muscles would hold up that weight.

In the beginning the Judge was determined. At that time, people who knew him well told me he had always been an amazing man physically. He figured he was stricken and wouldn't be able to use his body anymore and he'd find a mechanical way. That's exactly what he did. I went off duty one afternoon and came back next morning and there was a mechanical lift in the room. He had asked for it the night before so that he wouldn't have to work to get himself out of bed and was going to use the lift. I walked over to the telephone and called building services and told them to remove the lift. While I was talking on the telephone, he yelled at the top of his voice, "Don't you dare move that out!" I ordered them to get it out of there and, furthermore, nothing mechanical was to come into that room unless it had my signature and personal approval. The Judge yelled bloody murder the whole time. The lift left the room and he asked: "How am I going to get up out of this bed?" The Judge called me his school teacher partner. I shook my finger at him and looked him in the eye and said, "You are going to get yourself out of bed on your own two legs." He said that was impossible. I said, "You stick with me and I will show you that it is possible and you will stand upon these two legs again." Finally he did. After a while it became a game we played. I had to figure every night when I went to bed what ploy I was going to use the next day to get him to do what I wanted him to do because, once he figured out my plan of action, I had to go to another one.

In another room of the hospital during the Judge's confinement was Judge J. A. Elkins, Hofheinz's banking friend won during and after his county judge days and lost in his third campaign for mayor when "fat cats" were attacked. Mary Frances recalled that Judge Elkins' brother, William (Bill), daily stopped at her husband's room door to inquire about his condition so that he could relay it to his ailing kinsman. Judge Elkins was in his 87th year and could look back on a distinguished career.

Mary Frances recalled, "I'll never forget the Judge's first trip out of the hospital. Bob Young brought his van to the hospital. The Judge had one wheelchair which could be folded back to make a bed. Peggy and Bob figured out how to get the wheelchair into the van, but there wasn't room to have it sitting completely up. So here we were, the Judge with his head just barely up, Peggy, Bob, and I stuffed into the van. Bob turned around and asked the Judge where he'd like to go. The Judge said he'd like to go see the Astrodome, so Bob headed out that way. When we got there, the Judge looked out the window and said, 'Isn't it beautiful?' We made a circle around the stadium, then headed back to the hospital. It was a successful day."

"Snitch" said the Judge's next excursion out of the hospital was to Astro-world Hotel. She recalled:

That was the day former President Johnson went to the hospital to see the Judge. By that time the Judge had accepted me. He also labeled me his coordinator. Before we went anywhere or did anything, I would case the joint to find out if he could make it. Then I'd lay out the plan of action for him before we would go on any venture. Before this outing, he asked me if I thought that he should go back to the Astrodome or if he should go back to the hotel to live. I questioned him about the hotel and Dome. I'd never seen either place. I felt the hotel sounded like the most likely place to go because he could move to a suite on the first floor and it just sounded like there would be fewer problems there. I told him I'd have to see it and he—we were in physical therapy at the time—said, "Well, you want to case the joint?" I said, "Yes, I think that's what we're going to have to do before we make any final arrangements where you're going to go. We're going to have to find out where we can put ourselves operational with the least amount of trouble." So he said, "Well, when are we going to go?" I asked: "When do you want to go?" He said, "Now!" So I agreed.

We put on his brace. He was then in a long-legged brace. If you've never seen anyone who's had a stroke, the first improvement that he must make is with the hip muscles, the strongest. Using hip muscles, one can swing a whole leg around. The lower part of the leg is harder to manipulate because it's weaker and it swings by the knees. He had not been out of the hospital with that brace on for any length of time. We knew we could get him out of a car and that was just about as far as it went. I told him when we went to the hotel he was going to have to walk or we'd never know how much he could. He asked: "Well, do you think I can?" I said, "Yes, I'm sure you can." So we didn't even take a wheelchair with us.

I called the nursing station to report I was taking the Judge out of the hospital to the hotel. They were used to our doing crazy things. You must have a doctor's permission before you can leave the hospital with a patient. I had an unusual patient and unusual privileges in taking care of him. The doctors gave me carte blanc to do whatever I felt was necessary. My goal was to try to restore him to as normal a life as possible within his physical limitations. I felt that any time we could do anything without the wheelchair it was to his benefit.

We went to the hotel. The Judge had not at that time negotiated any kind of steps; it was all he could do to drag that leg with complete support and with Joe Louis holding his belt in the front to steady him and my holding his belt in the back. The two of us supported him while he dragged his left leg, or tried to swing it out from the waist using his hip muscles. I wish I had had a movie camera with me. I wish someone had taken pictures of the three of us maneuvering him up over the curb into that hotel. We had called the hotel and alerted employees that we were coming. They had the door open, but by the time we got to the hotel door from the car, the Judge no longer could lift his leg. His physical capacity was limited so I had, with each step he took, to lift his leg myself and move it for him; then he would bring his right one up even with it and I'd move his left one. That's how we made our way into the hotel room. He ordered lunch while I started casing the joint.

We had been there about an hour and a half when we got a call that the hospital was looking for us. I called the hospital and asked what was going on. Soon after we left there, the hospital got a call that Lyndon Johnson was on his way there to see the Judge. LBJ had security men around him always. The news about LBJ was a big thing at the hospital. Everybody just about came unglued. They wanted everything to be perfect. Mr. Bowen, administrator, had stationed aides at the front door to meet the former president after having gone to the nursing floor to make sure that everything was copasetic and was shipshape for the visit. LBJ arrived and hospital administrators met him and accompanied him with his security guards to the eighth floor. They got off the elevator; security men stationed themselves; others went up the hallway to the Judge's door, knocked, and with no response finally they pushed open the door. The room was empty. All this scenario had been played for nothing. Administrators came tearing back out, asking the nurses where the Judge was. They began a systematic search. They didn't know where he was—he had just flatly disappeared.

Mary Frances recalled, "I had been to a luncheon honoring Lady Bird Johnson at the River Oaks Country Club. When I returned to the hospital, the place was in utter turmoil. The head nurse told me that President Johnson had come to visit Judge Hofheinz but that the hospital had been unable to locate the patient. Things were getting panicky until Peggy Woods called in to tell the nurses' station that they were at the Astroworld Hotel. At that point President Johnson and the Judge got on the phone. They decided it would be easier for the President to go to the hotel than for the Judge to rush back to the hospital." Johnson, with sirens screaming from the caravan of cars, arrived at the hotel quickly and the two old friends had a lovely visit, talking for 30 to 40 minutes.

Peggy said:

During this time the Judge's mind was quick and alert. Now I had no way of comparing his mind with what it was like before the stroke, but during the time that I was with him, his only problem was the physical disability because of his paralyzed leg and arm. His mind was totally clear. When he began again attending and running Astrodomain board meetings, I did not stay in the board room with him. At the first board meeting he attended, I made him walk. Board members were expecting him in a wheelchair. I told him he couldn't go to the meeting unless he walked in. If he really wanted to do something, he knew there was no point in arguing with me because he could not physically get up without my help and get into the wheelchair. So it was my choice, always, whether he was going to walk or ride. He proudly walked into the meeting, and the surprised board members applauded.

We decided the hotel suite was probably going to be the best place for the Hofheinzes to set up housekeeping. When he left the hospital, he was homesick for the Dome, his love. He wanted to move back there first, so Joe, Mary Frances, and I made a visit one day to figure out if we could take care of him there. We had a ramp put up beside his bed so that we could move the wheelchair up to the bed. When we moved there, he was happier and a little more cooperative, sometimes, except that there it was easier for him to get food. When he lived in the hotel and the kitchen was closed, it was hard for him to get food. In the Astrodome it was easy because there was a kitchen downstairs and he could get Mary Frances out of bed any hour, or if Joe Louis was there, send either downstairs to get him something to eat. God bless their everloving hearts, they never did learn to say "No!" to him.

The Astro baseball season was going on when the Judge was taken to his Dome suite. Nurse Woods said the Judge wanted to go to see a game one night from his box. They were alone. She recalled:

I said, "Okay, I'll get you dressed and we'll go down to the ballgame." I got him dressed and put on his brace. His suite had an elevator and steps, but you had to walk approximately the length of a room to get from his bed to the elevator, and then an equal distance to his chair in the box. I got him up on the side of the bed. He looked around for the wheelchair and said, "The wheelchair is not here. Where is it?" I said, "I have it downstairs." He demanded, "Go get it." I said, "No, I'm not going to get it. If you want to go to the ballgame, you can walk." He said, "That's too far." I said, "No, it isn't too far. Come on." I got him off the bed and he started walking. He made it. He could do it easily. He got on and off the elevator. His box led to a ledge where his and other chairs were lined up. From there you can see all in the baseball audience. He walked to his chair from the elevator. I was beside him, but I did not help him. I pulled his chair up and helped him to stand by it. Just as he was getting ready to sit down, some of the fans noticed his walking. We heard a little clap, just a little bitty clap down below his box, and then applause started spreading all over the Astrodome. Fans had been sitting there watching the Judge. It gave me goose bumps. He cried and I cried. It was a beautiful, great night.

At this time, the Judge was thinking again about making a trip to Europe. As majority stockholder in Ringling Bros. and Barnum & Bailey Circus, he wanted to go on a talent search, which circus officials did every year, and he wanted to be involved. He knew he couldn't go without medical help, so he began arranging for many to go with him.

By January of 1971, the Judge was in a short-legged brace. He worked very hard in therapy. He strengthened his muscles. I had told the Judge he couldn't make the trip until he was in a short-legged brace because it was too physically exhausting for me and also for him to handle long-legged hardware. He had to be slim enough to handle the short-legged brace and then we could start trips. We had him down to 232 pounds and he was rather trim. He was—believe it or not—walking alone. Most of the time he thought my finger was holding him by the belt, but if it was, I was just putting the pressure of my finger against him so he could feel it. He walked alone with no help whatsoever from anybody. Whatever we did, he wanted to practice ahead of time. I'd case the joint; then we'd practice.

He came up with the idea of a short trip to Mexico and I couldn't figure out why he wanted to go since he had talked only of going to Europe. He invited Jack to go with us for a week and he agreed. Later I discovered the reason he chose Mexico was he figured the Mexican Airline would have the closest we'd get to European aircraft so we could practice. He figured if we went to Puerto Vallarto—he knew there were cobblestone streets there—we could practice work with his wheelchair and with walking on those cobblestone streets in a foreign environment. We'd know from experience pretty much how we could plan for any obstacles we might be up against when we got to Europe.

Peggy Woods added: "We had a game we played when we'd go to the Astroworld Hotel to eat meals while he was living at the Dome. The waiters were all intimidated by him because he was the boss. We'd go in and sit down in the dining room and he'd start ordering many things. I'd sit there indicating to them 'No!' The waiters were just scared to death because they didn't want him to fire them, but they faced a stern-looking woman sitting there signaling to them and threatening to have them fired if they brought what he ordered. It was a terrible time for the help. They minded me, because if they didn't, if they brought anything he shouldn't have, I'd just reach over and take it away from him and put it on a table behind him. There wasn't any way he could get up and get the food without me. He enjoyed a certain amount of this. It was a contest with him, to test my will."

Ringling Bros. and Barnum & Bailey Circus and the Astrodomain seemed at a peak of success when the ailing Hofheinz decided to go to Europe after he could walk some again. He wanted to thank those who had helped save his life and mind in the months after his stroke with a group tour at his personal expense. He planned for weeks. His invitation list was much longer than the list of those who finally accepted to be his guests on a trip beginning in February of 1971. The Judge told the circus president Irvin Feld what he planned to do. Feld said he and his son would join the party after it reached Europe. Hofheinz specified in the beginning, his wife said, that the costs of taking his guests would be borne by the Judge personally. In his files today is a cancelled check for $35,721.95 made out to Ringling Bros. and Barnum & Bailey Circus as reimbursement for the "thank you" to friends. Airline fares cost $25,779.

Those who accepted invitations were two of Hofheinz's doctors—Dr. Lewis Leavitt and his wife, Lorraine, and Dr. John Stirling Meyer and his wife, known as Wendy. Peggy and Jack Woods were automatically on the list. Sten Martinssen, a male nurse, completed the medical team. Others who accepted were Joe Louis Holiday and his wife, Velma, because Hofheinz insisted he could not get along with his wheelchair without Joe and principally because he had a great affection for his "Man Friday"; Red James and his wife, Martha, because

Hofheinz party prior to boarding Pan American's 747 Jet Clipper for the Iron Curtain Countries, left to right, seated: Velma Holiday, Alita Young, Judge Hofheinz, Marti Shlenker, Lorraine Leavitt, Nancy Young, Bob Young, and Mary Frances Hofheinz; standing: Red James, Stuart Young, Erik Worscheh, Martha James, Dr. John Meyer, Joe Holiday, Sidney Shlenker, Sten Martinsson, tour coordinators Mr. and Mrs. James Demezas, Dr. Lewis Leavitt, Mary Worscheh, Wendy Meyer, Peggy Woods, and John Woods. Photograph courtesy Pan American Airways.

Hofheinz could not overlook his best friend who watched over legal affairs of Astrodomain; Robert B. Young and his wife, Nancy; Stuart B. Young, the great building artist who continually was at the Judge's side, and his wife, Alita; John O'Connell, who had taken over operation of Astrodomain when Hofheinz was stricken, and his wife, Carol Ann; William B. McDonald, a new house attorney for Astrodomain Corporation, and his wife, Gayle; John Easter, treasurer of the Houston Sports Association, and his wife, Betty; Erik J. Worscheh, head of food services for Astroworld Complex who had menus to satisfy the Judge's appetite, and his wife, Mary; and Sidney Shlenker, who became chief operator of the Houston Sports Association when O'Connell suffered multiple injuries in an automobile accident after he took charge of Hofheinz's affairs at the Astrodome, and his wife, Marti.

On the trip to Europe, Peggy Woods said Hofheinz walked on and off every plane. She recalled:

Our first stop was New York; then we flew to Sofia, Bulgaria, where we were guests of the government which furnished transportation and guides. Red James and Bill McDonald were interested in the judiciary of Bulgaria. They asked permission from our woman guide to visit a courthouse or court-room. She told them there was no way any American would ever be allowed in a Bulgarian courtroom—"Nyet." Red James kept pushing. He went to the Amer-ican Embassy and finally received permission for six of us to visit a courthouse. It was very cold with snow and ice. I put on a pantsuit. Underneath the suit I wore a pair of black stretch pantyhose. Once you get them on, they fit skin tight and over your feet and everything up to your neck. When you have one on, you don't need an extra shirt because—it's like a turtle neck shirt underneath your pants. I must admit it was quite a bit sexier than anything the Judge was used to seeing me in. I went to get him up that morning and ordinarily I would have had my jacket on, but I had to get dressed first because I was the one who got him up in the morning and bathed him and got him ready for the day. I went in to get the Judge and I had on the body stocking. He nearly lost his eyeballs. He teased me all morning. Unbeknownst to me, he arranged with Red James to try that afternoon, while we were in court, to get me arrested. He told Red James he wanted some kind of a piece of paper stating that I was arrested and my offense was to be "no visible means of support." Red James had quite a time trying to get a Bulgarian lawyer, who was our guide and spoke little English, to understand what it was he wanted. Red James asked: "What do you call people who don't work?" He said, "We don't have anything like that here, everybody works." Then Red James asked: "What do you call people who don't have a job but obviously are eating well and have a place to live?" He said, "A thief. He'd have to be a thief because everybody works, even the old ladies that sweep the streets. If you don't work, you don't eat." Finally Red got through to him asking: "What would you call somebody without support—not a thief but with no obvious, visible means of support?" he said, "That would be—Oh! Oh!" He pointed at me and said, "Oh, you are a very bad person." Red James asked: "What would you call her?" He said, "A skitinick," Bulgarian name for a prostitute.

The guide couldn't get us a paper of any kind for the Judge, but we did get the name for what I was to be called. We went back to the hotel with that and the Judge immediately shortened it to "shitnik."

Jack Woods told a story about a poker game in Sofia: "We were in the Grand Hotel in the evening and there was nothing much to do so somebody came up with the idea to play poker in a semi-boardroom which was part of the Judge's suite. We found a deck of cards. Nobody had enough matches for chips so we took a roll of toilet paper and tore little pieces and gave each man the same number for chips. The Judge didn't win and his pile of chips gradually was depleted. Nonchalantly, coolly, he said to Joe Louis: 'Take me to the bathroom.' We didn't think too much about it and continued the game. In a little bit, the Judge came out of the bathroom and sat down. I was dealing and I saw Hofheinz with a big pile of paper chips. I knew what he did—in the bathroom he made his own chips. The next morning the Judge came to breakfast and reached in his pocket and pulled out a hand full of paper chips and said: 'Jack, I want to cash these in.' I said: 'In a pig's eye you're going to get those cashed. I know you manufactured them.' He accused me of being a deadbeat. He said: 'You are a helluva banker—you won't even make good your chips.' He had a great sense of humor."

Circus manager Irvin Feld and his son joined the party in Bulgaria. Once a year the government arranged for circus managers from all over the world to see the best performers in the country. To be hired by Ringling Bros. and Barnum & Bailey was the biggest plum any performer could get. Feld negotiated with government agents for talent.

At every European stop, the Judge and Mary Frances bought antiques and other expensive items. When he liked something, the price didn't matter to the Judge. When he was lukewarm about buying, he used all his bargaining power to get prices he'd pay. He loved to bargain, but in Bulgaria he was at a disadvantage because prices were fixed by government rules.

Next stop of the Hofheinz party was Athens, Greece. Mary Frances said:

> Bob Young had an interest in a cattle business in Greece and good friends in Athens. One of them was Haris Grymanis of Olympic Airways who had visited us at the "Celestial Suite" in Houston. Bob called Haris and asked him to set up some crazy and fun things for the Judge while in Athens. When our plane landed, we were greeted at the airport with photographers flashing pictures and each lady in our party was handed a bouquet of long-stemmed roses as she came down the ramp. There were limousines waiting to whisk us off to our hotel. It was definitely the "royal treatment." The next day in all newspapers were big pictures of the Judge and me and our party arriving. Underneath the pictures was a caption and a long story which none us could read. Our telephone starting ringing off the wall with people talking to us in Greek. Letters were being personally delivered to us by the dozens. We couldn't figure out what it was all about. We asked one of the waiters, who could speak a little English, to tell us what the newspapers said. He translated, "Rich Texan Comes to Buy Greek Islands." We never were sure, but something tells me that Bob Young spread that little rumor. Anyway, it was hilarious trying to be nice to all the people and to thank them for calling and bringing information about islands for sale. Some had beautiful pictures of scenery and houses enclosed. Bob had also talked to Haris before we arrived. Haris had carpenters build a "Pharoah's Chair" so the Judge could be carried up the Acropolis to see the Parthenon. Later in the week the Boutari Wine families and Samaras family (cattle people) honored Judge Hofheinz at their ranch in Thessalonica, Greece, with a glorious Greek barbeque.

"Snitch" recalled:

> In every country we went, I tried in flight to teach myself to say "yes," "no," "thank you," "good night," and "good morning" in the native language. Everywhere we went, litter bearers awaited the plane to carry the Judge. I wouldn't

let them do it. If he wanted to get off the plane, he had to walk off. If he wanted to get on the plane, he had to walk on. That was an understanding that we had. In spite of that, the Judge had someone arrange for people to be at every stop to carry him off. They would come rushing up the steps and I had to say, "No, no. He's going to walk off." The Judge would get a big charge out of that.

Jack and I slept in a room in the Judge's suite as always so that I could be close to the patient. A living room separated our bedrooms. I had the Judge almost ready for bed one night and the telephone rang in our bedroom. When I answered, it was a woman's voice and she spoke Greek. I couldn't understand her so I just kept saying "nai," meaning, I thought, "no." In between her Greek words I could catch, occasionally, "Hofheinz." I assumed that she was asking about an island so I just kept saying "nai, nai," and hung up. A few minutes later she called back to the living room on the other line and I told her the same thing. I thought I was saying "no" in Greek. Greek "no" was "okhi" I later learned. The Judge wanted to know where all the phone calls were coming from and asked, "What are you getting so aggravated about?" I said, "Some woman keeps calling, speaking Greek. I don't know what she's saying or what she wants and I keep trying to tell her 'no.' " After she had called five or six times, I called the operator and asked her to stop the woman from calling.

The next afternoon we were packing bags getting ready to leave. A knock came on the door. Joe Louis went to the door. Jack and the Judge were sitting in the living room exchanging jokes. At the door Joe looked at me and said: "General, I think you'd better come here and see what this is all about." I went to the door and here was a woman—a movie picture of a floozy with a feather boa. She was made up like you wouldn't believe and wore a long dress and a fur coat. She demanded to see Judge Hofheinz. I wouldn't let her in. She went back downstairs and brought back the bellhop. The bellhop said, "She has an appointment with Mr. Hofheinz." I said, "I or Mrs. Hofheinz make all of Mr. Hofheinz's appointments. She does not have an appointment. Mr. Hofheinz is in bed taking a nap." She said, "I know, I know." I said, "No, you cannot see anyone. He's in bed taking a nap." Everytime I said that, she'd go to the bellboy and say, "Ya, ya." So finally I said, "Get her out of here. She's not going to see the Judge." So he said, "All right, let me take care of it." So I went back in the living room and told the Judge this floozy was after him and he got the biggest kick out of it. He said, "Well, I can't take advantage of her, but maybe Jack can." So he sent Jack out to look the girl over. We laughed about it.

The next day as we were leaving the hotel and I pulled the Judge's wheelchair to get him into the car, here came little hands, urchins, to help. It was confusing to the Judge because my little finger was all it took for him to walk. The more hands trying to help him, the more confused he would get. I pushed everybody away saying, "Nai, nai, nai!" One little boy, in spite of all my efforts to push him away, kept coming back. The driver finally came up and said something to the boy who backed away. I asked: "What did you say to him?" He said, "I told him no." I said, "Well, what have I been saying to him?" He started laughing. He said, "You have been telling him yes." The Judge was halfway up out of his wheelchair, sat back down and looked up at me and at the driver and said, "What is the word for 'yes'?" I guessed it was "okhi." The driver said, "Okhi, okhi is 'no'." I'd been using "okhi" for "yes" thinking I was very smart. I had it reversed so we had spent a whole evening the night before trying to figure out how the floozy girl was so positive that she had an appointment with the Judge. The Judge said, "Guess who made the appointment for me with the chippie?" He pointed to me.

A trip up the Acropolis, the upper fortified part of the ancient Athena, to the peak to see the ruins of the Parthenon, celebrated Doric temple built in the Fifth Century, BC, was a must for the Hofheinz party. It was decided that Jack Woods and Bill McDonald would help two Greek men carry the Judge in the Pharaoh's chair. "It was a chore," both Jack and Bill recalled later. Jack said, "The Judge was in his glory—the king of the party being carried on a litter. He had on a beautiful sealskin coat and hat Houston furrier Samuel W. Spritzer made for him. He was Mohammed going to the mountain. We carriers had to rest now and then for it was treacherous going up. I would guess we carried the Judge a total of two miles, but it seemed farther to me. Every time we'd stop to take a rest, we'd have to lower the Judge and get the chair to stay level. Those Greeks were shorter than Bill and I. We were up in the front and we had to compensate for their shortness by lowering the litter. Everybody in our party kidded by calling out, 'The King, here comes the King! Look at the King.' They had fun and onlookers were interested."

One evening in Athens, most of the Hofheinz party was in the hotel dining room where there was a band. They had a good time eating, drinking, and dancing. Jack Woods said, "The Judge asked Peggy: 'Snitch, why don't you and Jack go up and join the crowd and have some fun and just put me in bed for the evening?' Peg got him tucked in and made sure he was comfortable, and she and I went upstairs and joined the festivities. Soon Peg said to me, 'Something tells me I ought to go down and check on the Judge one time.' I said, 'Oh, he's okay.' She said, 'No, I have a hunch something is going on,' because it wasn't like the Judge to say, 'Why don't you go and dance?' He always wanted her there by his side when awake. I told Peg again: 'No, heck, he's all right, he's probably sound asleep.' She said, 'Well, it'll only take me a minute to go down and go in the room and check on him.' She went down and walked in the bedroom. That son of a gun—as soon as he got rid of us—got on the telephone to room service and had quickly two chocolate sundaes sitting by his bed. Peg said, 'Give me those sundaes!' It proved to be a Mexican stand-off; neither won."

Nurse Woods said that after the trip to Europe:

> The Judge knew I wasn't going to spend the rest of my life attending him. He was tired. He had proved to himself and everybody else that he could make it if he really wanted to do so. We went to the Cocoa training camp of the Astros in March. I made a deal with the Judge—any morning that he would walk to breakfast from his room in the Astro Motel to the dining room, a long haul, I

The Judge being carried down the Acropolis in Athens, Greece. To his left are Bill McDonald and Sidney Shlenker. Photograph courtesy Union News-Photos Agency, Athens.

would sit at another table and pretend I wouldn't see what he ate and he could have anything he wanted. At first he kept his word. He lost weight like mad because he was walking well by himself.

Near the end of March I was mentally, physically, and emotionally exhausted. The trouble was that I was starting to love the Judge as everybody around him did. It was getting more and more difficult for me to push him and to insist that he not eat, do his exercises, and walk. I was finding it easier to look in those soulful eyes that he'd give you and say, "Oh, the poor man. Let's push him in the wheelchair today." That's the effect he had on me as I grew weary. I did not have any life of my own since the beginning of my job with him because, with the Judge, you don't see any of your own friends, you see his. I hadn't had a chance to spend a lot of time with Jack and my son. Jack came home when I was ready to leave for the spring training camp. We met at the airport. The stewardess had arranged for us to have five minutes together in the VIP lounge. So in Cocoa I felt a little badly, thinking I was neglecting my family.

Spring training for the Judge was a place for total relaxation. The food he approved for players and others was unbelievable. He wanted relaxation. The Judge gradually quit what was good for him. He ate as I had never seen him eat before. He was beginning to know that I was weakening because we were very close at this time. We had lived in each other's pocket for nearly 11 months. We had hardly been out of each other's sight.

I had told him, after we came back from Europe, between Europe and spring training, that I thought it was now time for me to get on with other jobs, that I had done for him all I could professionally do. He was walking, could throw the wheelchair away; he didn't need the wheelchair again. I had trained Johnny Powell and Joe Louis Holiday to take care of him. The Judge listened to my conclusion and was subdued. It made him sad because he had gotten used to my being around. He wanted me to stay with him and be, not only his medical coordinator, but just be part of his organization, not just his nurse to oversee his medical treatment. I told him I couldn't do that, that I needed to go on to other people. I had done everything I could do for him and from now on I told him it could be just smooth sailing; all he had to do was to keep up the program with men attendants. He said, "I don't understand why you think I should have men taking care of me." I said, "Judge, you are a respected member of this community, and as such you deserve a man to go into the bathroom with you; you deserve a man to go into the shower with you." He sat back in his chair and said, "The hell you say. If I had my choice, I'd take a good looking broad any day." He asked: "Do you mean to tell me that those who shower together, stay together?" I said, "No, I have to be thinking now about making other plans." At Cocoa, all he really wanted to do was lie in the bed all day and, as soon as the dinner bell rang, have Joe Louis push him to the dining room. He got so he wouldn't wait for me to get up in the morning. He awakened Joe who would get him out of bed, push him to the table. I previously had him walking to all his meals. I discovered one morning when I got up that he and the wheelchair were gone and found him in the dining room gorging himself. He was getting heavier, his legs were getting weaker.

I told Mary Frances I was going to have to leave him because I couldn't help him any more. By then I was too fond of him and he knew it. He felt he could manipulate me just as he did everyone else. I was no longer the "no" person. I was turning into a "yes man." When they cleared the dining room out after noon that day, the Judge and I were the only ones there. He was stuffing himself with food. I went to him and pulled a chair up closely. He wouldn't look at me. I said, "Judge, I have to talk to you; this is very serious." He hung his head and he wouldn't look at me. I chucked him under the chin and held his head up and I said, "I want you to look me right in the eye because I want you to hear me clearly. I've made plane reservations and I'm going home." The Judge didn't say anything. I said, "You've made your choice. I've helped you get rid of the wheelchair. Now, if you've changed your mind and if you've decided that you want to spend the rest of your life in a wheelchair, then you're going to have to find someone else to teach you how to do that because I don't teach people how to live in wheelchairs. I teach them how to throw them away." He cried and

I cried. I said, "If you change your mind and if you decide you want to try again, you call me and I'll come back. But if I come back, there's no wheelchair in your future. I can promise you that. I will not spend one day of my time teaching you how to be comfortable in a wheelchair." I got up and left. I flew to Houston.

Mary Frances called me in a couple of days and said, "Peggy, he walked to breakfast this morning. He's really trying." I said, "Well, I'm not going to come back now. You're going to be there two more weeks and you let me know how he does and call me when you get home." She called me when they got home. She said, "Oh, Peggy, he's trying so hard. He's walking everywhere." I said, "Beautiful, it worked." I added: "That's the only way I could help him—to get away from him." She said, "Well, the only reason he did it was so you'd come back." I said, "But he doesn't know that I know that, you see. He's doing the right thing, he's walking." She said, "You know he'll never call you, never ask you to come back." I said, "I know that and I will never give in until he walks up to my door." So I did not go back and for a while he progressed well.

I didn't see the Judge for a long time. I felt that I had done the best thing for him and I didn't regret leaving because I didn't know at the time that he was to regress as he did. It was over a period of time that he finally settled back in his wheelchair.

In 1979 when she was in Panama City, Florida, continuing her therapy career, Jewell Williams looked back happily at the months she also worked diligently in helping the Judge to get on his feet. She said:

My introduction to the Judge at Methodist came when he was in a wheelchair, gnawing on a cigar, sizing me up and asking questions. He wanted to know what I planned to do for him in therapy and why. I told him what I had to offer and why it needed to be done in a particular way. If treatment made sense to him, he accepted it and cooperated. The Judge liked to be the last one in the department for therapy. He didn't care about other people seeing him exercise. Occasionally there would be other patients still there when he arrived. He had a real compassion for them. Some were stroke victims, too. I think they encouraged him to see how well they were doing. He was able to see their accomplishments and know he could do it, too. He had a real compassion for the children he saw. I remember one small child with paralysis of both legs. The Judge was very concerned. The next time he came for therapy, he gave the little boy a baseball cap and an Astro ball autographed by all players. There was another little child with a hand paralyzed, and he brought him a baseball cap. One day the Judge said to Joe Louis: "Remind me to get a bunch of caps and a bunch of baseballs." Joe brought them and the Judge passed them out to all children in the hospital "Compliments of Judge Hofheinz."

I will never forget my first trip to treat the Judge at the Astrodome. I went to the west gate which was manned by a security guard. He asked who I was and asked my business, then called at the Judge's office to verify what I said and to see if the Judge was expecting me. Then he directed me around to a private door into the Astrodome. I knocked on the door and Wesley Thompson (later wife of Dr. Charles Boyd) answered the door. Wesley, the Judge's secretary, was a sweet, amiable person, efficient, always happy and smiling. She asked me to have a seat—it would be just a little while. Well, I asked if there was a restroom I could use. She told me to go on through the next room. The next room was the Astrodomain board room, the most fabulously decorated place I had ever seen. When I walked from this room into the bathroom, I stood in awe. I wasn't sure if I was supposed to use it or if it was just for show. Shortly I was called and went up the elevator to his quarters. We had many therapy sessions.

In May of 1971, Jewell Williams quit Methodist Hospital and became the Judge's fulltime therapist. She said "Huckster House" proved an excellent place for the Judge to recuperate. She added:

Usually just the Judge and M.F. were there. Joe and I would come and go. Sometimes I would stay overnight if we were late finishing therapy. This was when I got to know the Hofheinzes well. They were thoughtful and considerate and treated me like one of the family. We did a lot of therapy out on the porch. The Judge would ride a stationary bike. Sometimes he would say, "Let's not do therapy now; let's just sit and talk." He would explain to me about the ships we saw in the channel, where they were going, and their nationality. This was usually when he would talk more about his children. He was concerned about their happiness; he worried about their problems. He did some bragging about them. He enjoyed his grandchildren. Dene's two sons were there often. He and M.F. enjoyed them. He never mentioned concern over material or financial accomplishments or failures. He wanted them just to be happy.

When a baseball game was on the air, we would listen. If the game was in Houston, we would go to the Astrodome. I remember one time the Judge was listening to a ballgame. I walked into the room after checking crab traps at the dock and asked, "Judge, how many touchdowns have they made?" The Judge turned and looked at me and said, "Pixie, you had better just stick to therapy. Baseball is evidently not your field. You would never make any money at that." He laughed a lot and was more relaxed at "Huckster House." At the Dome, there seemed to be too many pressures.

One day the Judge decided to take up golf—a fun way to do therapy. So he got golf clubs for himself, M.F., Leslie Brothers, and me. We went to the golf course and drove some balls. The Judge did the best of all. Then we decided we would start on the golf course. The Judge hit the ball well. He found the hardest part was getting in and out of the golf cart so the best thing to do was for Joe to drive the cart up by the ball and the Judge would lean over and hit the ball. He didn't have to get in and out of the cart. We all got some laughs and had good times, but we certainly got some exercise for his arms and legs.

Mary Frances was the real asset for the Judge. He relied very heavily on her. She had been a super secretary and was a sharp businesswoman. After his stroke, she was everything a helpmate could possibly be. She was always by his side, smiling, encouraging him and those around him. Even when things were not going well, Mary Frances could smooth things over and she stayed optimistic even when things were discouraging. The Judge was never gushy with words, and he only said exactly what he meant. On different occasions he expressed to me how fortunate he was to have Mary Frances as his wife. He appreciated her understanding and reassurance and her constant love and encouragement when crises occurred. He said, "Pixie, you know I am a very lucky man to have M.F. I don't know what I would do without her. She is really good to me." She contributed a great deal to his rehabilitation then and constantly encourages him to do better.

Greatly improved in late 1970, Hofheinz went to Venice, Florida, to close out a merger of Ringling with Mattel, Incorporated, maker of toys. Nurse Williams said:

> One of the most memorable events happened outside Venice in a small supper club after we had seen a circus performance. There were seven people in our group. Two men came to the table and asked Leslie Brothers and me to dance to the music from the juke box. We did. A woman sitting across the room kept her eyes on the Judge. Finally, she came and asked him to dance. "No thank you," he said. M.F. chimed in: "The Judge used to enjoy dancing. We danced together many times, but he doesn't think he can do it now." Peggy Woods spoke up, "Come on Judge, we are almost the only people left here and you should try." M.F. looked at the Judge and asked him if he would. Finally he said "Okay" when a slow tune rang out. Joe Louis walked with the Judge to the middle of the dance floor and M.F. joined him. When she went into his arms, M.F. was as happy as I've ever seen her. She seemed to melt into his arms as they slowly started dancing. Leslie, Peggy, Joe, and others watching felt their hearts swell with pride and happiness. The Judge and M.F. on that dance floor to us were a beautiful couple. I looked closely and saw blissful joy and tears streaming down M.F.'s cheeks. We all cried with happiness that the Judge was walking and dancing. It was a memorable occasion for all of us. It was moments like this which made all our work and efforts worthwhile.

The Hofheinzes wanted to spend Christmas in Venice. Fred, "Mac," and their two children, Paul and Tracey, and Dene II and her two sons joined them. The Judge told Peggy, Joe and "Pixie"to go home for Christmas with families. Peggy and Joe planned to fly back to assist the Hofheinz entourage in returning to Houston.

Nurse Williams recalled:

> The night before the Judge's aides were to leave, we had a Christmas party. Judge and M.F. had a lovely live orange tree decorated with oranges and candy in their suite. It was hard to know what to get for the Hofheinzes who had everything money could buy. The Judge and I had some real fun therapy sessions at Methodist. During them, the Judge didn't talk but he would make some humorous remarks unique to the situation and occasion. Leslie and Peggy and I decided to give the Judge a tape recorder and a tape made during his therapy when Leslie and Peggy were working with him. We placed the recorder so that he was not aware of it, nor did M.F. know about it. When we

unwrapped gifts, the Judge and M.F. opened the recorder and we had a note instructing them to turn it on. They were completely surprised. The Judge enjoyed the sound effects of his therapy. He and M.F. really enjoyed the tape. The Judge and M.F. gave me a gold Astrodome charm and gold charm bracelet engraved. I think they gave Peggy and Leslie the same. It was a beautiful pre-Christmas party.

In April of 1971 after the jaunt to spring training at Cocoa, Hofheinz suddenly decided on a trip to Frankfurt, Germany. Samuel J. Spritzer, internationally know Houston furrier, for months had urged the Judge to join him to establish an import-export fur company and suggested that if Hofheinz really wanted to get into the business, he should go to the International Fur Fair on the German Rhine.

Hofheinz invited nurses "Pixie" and Leslie Brothers, Joe Louis Holiday, and a young man named Kenneth Browning to help Joe with wheelchair duties, to accompany Spritzer, Mrs. Hofheinz, and himself on the trip. "Pixie" recounted her experiences:

> During the day we went to the festival. There was every kind of fur available in the world. One day Judge and M.F. bought a mink bikini for Dene II. All of us enjoyed trying on the furs. The Judge bought a fur coat and hat which he wore the rest of the trip. One day Leslie and I told the Judge we wanted to go shopping. He asked what I was going to buy. I said that I really wanted a cuckoo clock made in Germany. He laughed and said: "Pixie, you can get a cuckoo clock a dime a dozen back home." I said, "Maybe so, but I want one from Germany." He said, "Okay, go downstairs and get the driver to take you." I went shopping in the chauffeured rented Mercedes.
>
> I believe the Judge enjoyed our activities as much as he did the festival. After the festival ended, M.F. wanted to go to Paris, although the Judge wasn't enthusiastic about it. He told her, "We'll go, but you all will be disappointed." M.F. made reservations for the presidential suite at the Inter-Continental Hotel.
>
> Our Paris arrival turned out to be a unique experience. Mary Frances had confirmation on the hotel rooms so we were not concerned about late arrival. Around midnight we arrived, tired and sleepy. On the trip we had VIP service and never waited. People rolled out the red carpet when they heard the Judge's name. This time was different. M.F. went to the desk clerk and told him who she was. The man looked at her and said, "I'm sorry, but you did not get here earlier and we gave your rooms to someone else." Mary Frances looked at him in complete shock and said, "You couldn't have; we had guaranteed reservations. We had the presidential suite reserved." He said, "I'm sorry but someone else has those rooms and we do not have any available." M.F. said, "I'm sure you don't understand. Judge Hofheinz does a lot of business with this hotel and the French Airlines." He was nonchalant and said, "I'm sorry." All this time the Judge sat just listening, gnawing on his cigar. Not saying a word, he rose from

his wheelchair; everybody watched. There was silence as the Judge reached for his cane. He walked over to the desk, reached into his pocket, pulled out a card, firmly laid it before the desk clerk and said, "I'm sure you can find something." I don't know what card that was, but the desk clerk began to turn pale and began to apologize. "I am so sorry. I do not know how such a horrible mistake could be made. The guy on the other shift is the one that did this. I am sure we can come up with something. Have you had dinner? Have a seat and let me get you all a drink while we are getting the dining room opened to serve you."

We were served drinks and in a few minutes the dining room was ready to serve us. It was a delicious meal. Then they told us our rooms were ready. On the mezzanine, hotel maids and porters converted the banquet and party rooms into bedrooms. M.F. and the Judge slept in one banquet room, Leslie and I had one room, and the men had one room. We had to use the public bathrooms. The next morning, M.F., Leslie, and I went to brush our teeth and put on our makeup. While we were in there wearing housecoats, a couple of sophisticated American women came in. They thought we were French. They began to talk about us in English. One said, "Do you see that? Surely you don't suppose they have rooms in the hotel without baths." We decided that we had better not say anything but we laughed about it. They served us pancakes on a silver cart with all the fine crystal, china, and silver in our banquet rooms amid roll-away beds. It wasn't long before they had our rooms ready and our things moved in.

We went from Paris to London. The Judge was interested in the double-decker buses. We saw an amusement park similar to Astroworld. The Hofheinzes had some friends connected with the Astrodome soccer team. We were guests at the soccer game. We stayed at a very old, quaint little hotel in a town near London.

In August of 1971, Jewell Williams decided to return to Florida and work in Pensacola. She said: "About 100 of my friends gave me a surprise going-away party. The theme was 'This is your life, Jewell Pearl.' A friend introduced Judge Hofheinz, saying he had meant the most to me professionally because I had worked with and traveled with him. The Judge then walked across the stage and gave me a gold St. Christopher's medal as a going away gift from himself and M.F. Mary Frances later told me that she asked the Judge if he wanted Joe to push his wheelchair and he said, 'No, what Jewell wants more than anything else is for me to walk. I am going to walk up there to her.' That was his real going away present to me. I'll always love him for that. He and M.F. walked on the stage and hugged me and gave me the medal. There will always be a very special place in my heart for the Judge and Mary Frances. In May of 1978, they stopped in Panama City and had lunch with me before going on to Houston. The Judge likes oysters. We had just shucked out some fresh oysters and ate many. I prepared some on ice for the Judge to take on the trip for a snack later."

Occupational therapist Leslie Brothers did not resign her hospital position. She went on the Judge's payroll in the beginning only on an after-hours basis and later took leaves of absence to go on trips with his parties. In 1979 she was acting director of physical therapy at St. Luke's and Texas Children's Hospital in Houston. She reminisced:

> One of the Judge's doctors called me out into the hall at Methodist and asked if I would see his patient and give him intensive rehabilitation therapy. I saw him for the first time when he was on the tilt table in the physical therapy department. Peggy already had the job of caring for the Judge daily and Jewell's job, primarily, was to get him on his feet to walk (gait training) and muscle reeducation. My occupational therapy was primarily concerned with the paralysis of the Judge's upper left extremities. I worked diligently with muscle reeducation on that left side and most of all, initially, I had to make him aware of that side. When it was time for the Judge to leave the hospital, I was asked if I would continue seeing him. Often, in the hospital he was sleepy and it was difficult to arouse and keep him going. He really didn't want to be bothered with my program, but he finally accepted me. When he went back to the Astrodome, it was extremely difficult for me to get to him. I often had to wait two or three hours while he finished with business talks. It was rather frustrating to me but I carried on.
>
> I went on many trips with the Hofheinz party, but I didn't go to Mexico or the famous junket behind the Iron Curtain. The hospital decided it wouldn't be proper for me to go on either trip. I did get to go to Frankfurt. We had a great time but I wasn't able to get in much therapy work with the Judge. We really were kind of a family then and the rules were relaxed.
>
> When we were in London after our stay in Paris, the Judge decided he wanted to see a couple involved with English soccer in Blackpool. The Judge and Mary Frances had showed the couple, Mr. and Mrs. Alan Hardaker, a fine time in Houston when they came there to help begin soccer in the Astrodome and he wanted to go to Blackpool, hell or high water. The next morning we went to my first soccer game after driving to the little country town in a black Rolls Royce as the guests of the Hardakers.
>
> I was invited on other trips after that. My first World Series experience was in Cincinnati with the Reds playing Baltimore. He kidded me that he had wasted his money taking me to the series when I had never seen live professional baseball, but I found it exciting there and in Baltimore. The Judge simply loved baseball, and he often would get perturbed with his female medical aides for their real lack of interest.
>
> On these trips I don't know how Mary Frances and Joe had the energy to care for him day and night. He kept up his spirits, however, and always made fun of those trying to help him—and we'd just laugh at his remarks and carry on. In my therapy treatment, I said things to prompt him to move his arm and elbow and wrist. He took different things out of context and would make them sound strange in talking with me, but I could challenge him.

Leslie said she worked with the Judge longer than needed. "It reached a point," she said, "where he couldn't progress anymore." On a trip to Curacao with the Judge's party, Leslie was told by her patient that things there were inexpensive and it was fun to shop there. "After we had done a lot of shopping,"

At the urging of Samuel Spritzer (right foreground), members of the Hofheinz party visited the International Fur Fair in Germany.

the therapist recalled, "the Judge asked me if there was anything I wanted and hadn't bought. I said I had wanted a watch which was unique but not a bargain and I didn't buy it. Several minutes later, he had Joe on the telephone ordering watches. Apparently he was familiar with what I wanted. Within 30 minutes. watches arrived for M.F. and me—just what I had talked about."

Hofheinz trusted no one outside the family more than Joe Louis Holiday. When the Judge was in Methodist, Joe went to the hospital every day to see what the Judge wanted and needed. "Sometimes," Joe said, "the Judge would want to go out and I'd take him out in his wheelchair with Peggy Woods' help. He knew I was tight-lipped and wouldn't tell newspaper people or others about his condition and what he was doing. People would ask me where the Judge was and how he was doing, but I'd tell white lies like I hadn't seen him or didn't know where he was. There was great speculation then about whether the Judge would get well. Some felt his entertainment empire would be in danger if he could not run it."

Hofheinz was disappointed that Ben McGuire was too ill to make the "thank you" trip during which cold, freezing, and snowy weather was constant, but the Judge did not forget his friend who had stood by him in mayoral elections and in his many money adventures. He bought McGuire a beautiful gold-plated on sterling silver ship model. McGuire asked Hofheinz what it cost because he wanted to insure it. "Well, I paid $1600," McGuire said the Judge replied. Just before Christmas of 1978, McGuire had the beautiful keepsake on a mantle at his home appraised and the value had grown to $6000.

42

The Judge
Back in the Saddle

Newspapers told the public in January of 1971 that both from a physical and financial standpoint Roy Hofheinz seemed improved. Jack Gallagher of the *Post* wrote:

> After spending an entire afternoon in meetings, the Judge taped a 15-minute message to employees kicking off an Astro season ticket drive, then caught an early evening flight to Florida to attend a circus opening. Ringling Bros. recent merger with Mattel, Inc. stabilized the Judge's economic position, removing a management load and stock worry. The transaction enabled Mattel, world's largest toy manufacturer, to use the circus as a marketing tool, and was a wonderful marriage for both parties.

> While the Astrodome continues to be a moneymaker, Astroworld showed a 25 percent attendance increase in the amusement park's second year of operation. This week the Judge's hotels will be filled with NCAA convention visitors. Then comes the National Association of Homebuilders'convention, the Houston Livestock Show and Rodeo, the NCAA basketball tournament finals and 10 million other tourist attractions that mean money for the city as well as for the Judge.

> Oh, the Judge isn't out of debt by any means. Who is? But, says a business associate mindful of both Roy's health and his financial condition: "He's going to make it, he really is." He is indeed a remarkable man, one of the few people I know with a love of sports who has never competed at the lowest level of any sport. "I guess about the most exercise I ever got," the Judge reflected the other day, "was shooting craps." For the crapshooter who took the biggest gamble, a monument of steel and glass emerged out of the South Main prairie. It will stand long after Roy's petty critics are dead.

On January 9, 1971, the Touchdown Club in Washington, D.C., presented Hofheinz "The Timmie," a special award for the "Sportsman of the Year." Among other things, Hofheinz was cited as the "father" of the Astrodome. The presentation was made at the club's 36th annual awards banquet, attended by scores of sports greats and 2000 fans. Making the presentation, Housing and Urban Development Secretary George Romney said Hofheinz was responsible for a "unique housing and urban development complex called the Astrodomain." Romney added that Hofheinz had actually developed "a new concept in sports" in the multi-purpose indoor stadium. Curt Gowdy, a television sportscaster acting as emcee of the dinner, paid special tribute to the Judge for attending the dinner despite having been seriously ill. Gowdy called Hofheinz's recovery "by far the finest performance in the sports world for the year."

In his acceptance speech, Hofheinz gave credit to modern medicine which he said had accelerated his recovery. He said that had the stroke occurred 15 years earlier, with the limited medical knowledge available then, he would not only have been unable to attend the dinner but would have been "just a casualty statistic." Also, noting the Touchdown Club's emphasis on football, Hofheinz urged members not to neglect other sports. He called sports the "one vehicle" capable of "bringing our people together" and said professional baseball had assisted in achieving a peaceful racial integration of hotel and restaurant facilities in Houston. The Judge also urged the Touchdown Club members to come to Houston and visit the Astrodomain.

Hofheinz shared the black-tie dinner dais with four Supreme Court justices and three Cabinet members. One reminded the Judge that the year before Richard Nixon was the recipient of the same special award. When asked if he would like another drink, Hofheinz displayed his usual sense of humor. "How about that," he replied, "I'm already paralyzed, and he's asking me if I want another drink."

When Vice-President Spiro Agnew visited Houston in February of 1971, Hofheinz did not let his role as a liberal Democrat curb his hospitality for top elected public officials. Agnew accepted the Judge's invitation to use the "Celestial Suite," as a special guest. Agnew wrote the Judge from Washington: "It was very generous of you to allow me to use your apartment. The 'Celestial Suite' is a masterprice. You must have had a great deal of fun putting it together."

Jack O'Connell now was the man in the "bullpen" to step forward after consultation with Hofheinz to handle Astrodomain's finances. He had an excellent team working with him—Don Vaughn as convention manager, George W. Lanier, Jr., as general manager of Astroworld, James J. Spring, Jr., as general manager of hotels, Spec Richardson as general manager of the Astros, Owen Martinez as director of Dome operations, Bill McDonald as legal counsel, John Easter as controller, and Sidney Shlenker as the new director of sales and marketing.

On April 10, 1971, nearly a year after Hofheinz's stroke, O'Connell publicly recounted some of the financial problems faced by himself and his nine-man managerial team. He said: "We never have had any solvency problem. We have only liquidity problems. The Judge's strength in Mattel toys changed our picture. He had $35 million in Mattel stock, depending upon market fluctuations. If Mattel stock could have been sold then—SEC rules allowed only the sale of small portions of the holdings at given periods—Hofheinz could have paid off all corporation debts."

Fred Hofheinz campaigning for mayor of Houston. Photograph courtesy the *Houston Chronicle.*

After he resigned from Astrodomain, Fred Hofheinz's political fever rose. As a boy, he loved working in his father's political campaigns. After managing Hubert Humphrey's bid for the presidency in Harris County, Fred, at 33, decided he would run for mayor to dislodge incumbent Louie Welch, twice defeated by Roy Hofheinz. As he opened his campaign in September of 1971, he gave the public a personal financial statement showing his net worth to be $107,252; he challenged other city candidates to do the same.

A new state law required all candidates in the city election of November 20 to submit financial statements to the Texas Secretary of State by November 4. Fred said he believed the law was vague, particularly regarding real estate. "The people deserve to know the addresses of properties," he said, "so they can drive by and see for themselves if there is a candidate's conflict of interest." The real estate business should be "highly suspect" when city officials take part, he said, because it is so easy to have a conflict of interest in that field. As for himself, Fred said he saw no conflict between his being elected mayor and his father's holdings because he did not then have benefit of the holdings.

"I think the whole city benefits from the city's Albert Thomas Hall," Fred Hofheinz said. "I think the whole city benefits from the Astrodome." He said even though he had no direct interest in the Astrodome, he would treat it as a conflict of interest. His financial benefits from his father's holdings, he said, would come at some time in the future. For people who thought his father would run the city if he were elected, Fred had a terse comment: "These are the people who don't know me."

The Judge tried to talk Fred out of running for mayor when they first discussed the idea, the younger Hofheinz said. He told reporters he was talking about "the family matter" because Welch was insinuating in his advertising that Fred was "a front" for his father. When they discussed the idea, Fred said his father told him, "Son, they'll crucify you just because your name is Hofheinz." Fred was well aware that his father was a controversial figure as mayor in the 1950s and earlier as county judge. "He is not a candidate in this race," said Fred, "nor is he running my campaign." When Fred filed a campaign expense and contribution report, the only contribution listed from his father was the use of a billboard on the Southwest Freeway. Hofheinz said he had tried during the campaign to discuss the problems and issues facing Houston, but that Welch had used a "wide variety" of innuendoes and insinuations. "No matter how much pressure Louie Welch puts on me," he said, "I am not going to change my name to win this race." Welch won reelection, but Fred Hofheinz established himself as a liberal political leader who in two years would reach his goal of mayor.

Despite accrued indebtedness for Astrodomain Corporation, Hofheinz would not quit planning more developments. He announced from his wheel-chair on September 30, 1971, that he had begun a master plan program on some 300 acres of undeveloped land near the domed stadium as possible sites for office buildings, entertainment facilities, and other operations. The land was estimated by realty experts to be worth about $13.5 million. Jack O'Connell said Bovay Engineers, Incorporated, had begun a land use study to determine building sites, traffic flow, relationship between the land and city street plans, and utilities.

"The study has just begun," the Judge's chief financial officer said. "We have some very valuable land, and it is only logical that there be a master plan for it. We will be more positive about it shortly." O'Connell said that Hofheinz would probably be the developer of the project, "depending upon his health." O'Connell earlier had pointed out that the holding of undeveloped land with such high market value was expensive and that the ideal solution would be to sell or develop the tract through a joint venture.

On September 27, 1971, Hofheinz left no doubt that he was still boss at the Astrodome. Ignoring the feelings of fans and the advice of some of his trusted employees, Hofheinz rehired baseball manager Harry Walker and his coaching staff for 1972. Hofheinz also announced that general manager Richardson would be retained. Until Hofheinz made his announcement, the press and fans generally took it for granted that Walker, who barely escaped being axed at the end of the 1970 season, would not be back. There were many who believed that

Richardson also would be a victim of a general house cleaning. "I made up my mind over the weekend to retain both Richardson and Walker," Hofheinz said. Asked what he thought the reaction of the season ticket holders would be, Hofheinz replied, "They are very understanding." In pointing out his faith in the management, Hofheinz said, "Compared with the progress of other clubs, the Astros' progress has been greater. We've made steady improvement. Some of the kids this year showed their capabilities. I'm really encouraged. The club is on the upgrade, not on the downgrade." The Astros finished the 1972 season in second place in the National League, the highest in their history, and for the first time Astros management was given the go-ahead to print World Series tickets.

After a long series of hearings, Hofheinz won state approval to open a bank in the Astrodomain complex. On October 26, 1971, Astro Bank became the 113th bank facility in Harris County. Hofheinz was chairman and Waddell Moursund became president and chief executive officer. The bank recently had received approval from the Federal Deposit Insurance Corporation to establish a drive-in facility about 40 feet from the main office.

From the time the Houston Sports Association raised cash in 1961 to buy out the city's franchise in the American Association to make way for major league baseball, Waddell Moursund had been one of Hofheinz's closest banking friends and admirers. It was no surprise that he was the Judge's choice to head the new Astro Bank. Moursund was an associate of Charles Bybee of Houston Bank and Trust Company and handled many negotiations for the Judge as he secured loans. Bybee and Moursund accompanied Hofheinz on trips across the nation seeking the help of other financial institutions when Houston Bank and Trust had gone as far as law allowed in giving credit to the Judge.

When Moursund left Houston Citizens Bank and Trust after a long tenure to become Astro Bank president, he said there was a plan to develop the area around the bank into another business plaza. "We had a letter of intent from a major company," he recalled, "for a large building and a bank was to go on the ground floor. About that time, the Judge suffered a stroke; the project began to fall apart. The public picked up information Astrodomain was getting into financial problems and deposits in the bank dropped from $9 million to $6 million in 60 days—basically on rumors."

On October 17, 1975, Texas Banking Commissioner Robert Stewart closed Hofheinz's Astro Bank, after finding "losses in excess of the bank's remaining capital structure." The closing coincided with the last-minute chances for Hofheinz to regain control of his troubled Astrodomain empire. A spokesman for the Astrodomain Corporation said that there was "no connection" between the company and the bank which was licensed to use the name "Astro." Stewart said the bank was "under water more than just a little." Deposits at the close of business on September 30 were $5.3 million, and Stewart said he had unverified information that the bank had about 1900 depositors.

In August of 1976, the Federal Deposit Insurance Corporation (FDIC) filed a $1 million damage suit against the former directors of Astro Bank: Harry E. Bovay, Jr., James J. Braniff, Jr., Roy M. Hofheinz, George W. Lanier, Ben G. McGuire, and Waddell Moursund were the defendants named. The suit held that the directors, operating in violation of banking laws and regulations, had engaged in liberal and hazardous loan practices, failed to adopt effective collection methods, and operated with inadequate liquidity and capital funds. When the FDIC took over as liquidator of Astro Bank, it claimed that the directors' negligence had resulted in a loss to the bank and its receivers of $1 million. In answer to the allegations and seeking to minimize their effects, McGuire stated that the FDIC's action against Astro Bank was standard and similar to that taken whenever a lending institution closed. "There were no wrongful acts that I know of," he said.

As of December 30, 1978, FDIC reported that Astro Bank still owed it $231,000, plus interest, but assets still on hand totaled $371,000. A final settlement of 100 percent thus appeared to financiers a possibility. When the bank closed, it was immediately sold to Commonwealth Bank which was allowed to move its location. Original Astro Bank stockholders recalled that Roy Hofheinz asked permission to move the bank's location before it was closed, but permission was refused. The Astro Bank should never have been closed, according to top Houston financial men who still wonder today why the purchasing bank was allowed by examiners to change locations. Said one of the bank's stockholders, who did not want to be identified until final settlement, "Pressures on Roy Hofheinz at Astrodomain and at Astro Bank came about the same time. It seemed to me an unfair situation developed and the bank examiners acted too hastily."

In a November of 1971 deal which was never fully explained in newspapers, Hofheinz bought from Timewealth, headed by Welcome Wilson, the 10 percent of HSA stock Bob Smith had vowed the Judge would not get. Speculation about the matter was triggered by a business story in the *Post* November 4 that Astrodomain had conveyed its half interest in a 480-acre tract of land on Interstate 10 about a mile east of Katy to the Timewealth Corporation. A $400,000 debt on the property was assumed by Timewealth in return for the conveyance. No other consideration was listed. Realty circles estimated value of the property at about $4000 an acre or a total of $1.9 million. The speculation on the deal centered around the possibility that Timewealth had included its 10 percent ownership of HSA in the deal for the choice acreage. The other half interest in the "Loose Goose" property, which included a farmhouse, a barn, and a rice farm, was owned by Bob Smith. It later became known that this was the transaction which gave Hofheinz 98 percent of the stock in HSA, a part of

Astrodomain Corporation. Astrodomain said the transaction was completed before Timewealth filed a petition on October 4 for reorganization under Chapter 11 of the Bankruptcy Act.

Regarding the 10 percent HSA stock transaction, Mrs. R. E. (Vivian) Smith answered these questions:

Q. Did Mr. Smith sell the 10 percent of the stock in HSA to Welcome Wilson?

A. Yes.

Q. Did Mr. Smith personally ever negotiate with Hofheinz for the final 10 percent?

A. Welcome came to Bob and wanted him to buy his Timewealth Company. He (Mr. Smith) called Roy and told him that he was going to sell to Welcome. Roy called and offered—I don't know how much—to buy it, but Bob wouldn't sell it to him because he didn't want Roy to have it. He sold it to Welcome. He let Welcome have it with the understanding that he would never let Roy have the 10 percent, but Welcome did. We didn't find out until after Bob was sick and unable to speak. I never did reveal it to Bob what Welcome had done to him.

Q. Was Mr. Smith fond of Wilson?

A. Yes, he liked Welcome.

Q. Did he have any other business deals with Wilson?

A. No, he really didn't. Welcome and others liked to make the impression that Bob was interested in their projects, but Mr. Smith never went in with them. He went on their notes once or twice, but Bob saw that they paid the notes. He never did have any interest in any of their business dealings. It was his way of helping young people get started—by helping them to get financing. The last deal was this 10 percent he let Welcome have. He sold it to Welcome, and he sold him some land at Jamaica Beach.

Q. What was the price of the stock?

A. I don't know. It was less than what Roy offered. He let Welcome have it with the understanding that he was not to let Roy have it. After Mr. Smith was unable to speak, why it came out in the paper that he had an interest in the Katy property which Bob and Roy had bought—the "Loose Goose." Welcome let Roy have the stock for his half interest. I don't know what the arrangements were. Anyway, he got the title to the land out at Katy, unbeknownst to us. He never said one word about it. I told Welcome what I thought about it.

Q. Welcome Wilson then took the 10 percent of the HSA stock and traded it to Hofheinz for the undivided one-half interest in the 160 acres out on Katy Freeway?

A. Yes, that's what he did. Welcome got the Katy Freeway property and Roy got the stock.

Q. That left you owning an undivided one-half interest and Mr. Smith and Welcome Wilson owning an undivided one-half interest in this property. Subsequently, you got all of the property. How did you accomplish this?

A. Bought it. I don't know just what the details were, but I remember we bought it through a trustee. Welcome came to our house, but I would not let him talk to Mr. Smith because I was afraid Bob might be soft-hearted. Welcome made his bed, and I let him lie in it. I never quite felt the same about Welcome.

While working on various plans for long-term financing for Astrodomain with the advice of the new board and particularly Joe Allbritton, Jack O'Connell was hit by an automobile leaving the Astrodome on December 17. His body was badly crushed, and he was rushed to a hospital. For weeks, long-term financing completion for Astrodomain was delayed because the chief executive officer was unavailable. Before the accident, O'Connell had worked with attorneys and financiers on several plans for long-term financing. He said he favored a plan whereby Allbritton would become chairman of the Astrodomain board, would handle debt refinancing, and he, O'Connell, would continue as chief executive officer. O'Connell, Ben McGuire, and attorneys also developed a plan whereby General Electric and Ford Motor Credit Corporation and HNC Realtors, a trust set up by Hartford (Connecticut) National Bank, would make the long-term loan.

O'Connell recalled:

> I suppose the two extremes with whom we attempted to get a mortgage were the Southeastern Teamsters Pension Fund and a colorful group in Zurich, Switzerland, and everybody in between. I worked my ass off between trying to stay on top of operating businesses. Personally, the most significant thing to me in the fall of 1971 was Fred Hofheinz's race for mayor. The banks were patient on overdue notes because they were not going to let this crisis be a factor in Fred's election. Fred got into a runoff. Banks hadn't counted on being patient that long. We weren't making any progress on long-term financing. Ben McGuire's plan with Ford and GE and HNC division of Hartford National Bank for $38 million had been offered earlier that year, but to me, to fund the deal just required excessive work. One question we'd answer for financiers would prompt three others. We just had truckloads of papers and questions. So that loan hadn't been closed. The bankers were itchy. They weren't too thrilled with it to begin with because it would be a very expensive loan, in terms of interest rate—the floating rate—four above prime. But when you need money, you can't be too choosy.
>
> Roy was in on the deal when it was started, but the burden of going from signing the commitment letter, for which we had put up about $375,000 earnest money, to closing the loan took me ultimately a total of 14 months, so all but three or so of those months, the Judge was out of the picture. Bankers were leaning on me pretty much to get the job done one way or another. The likelihood of the deal closing was questionable because the Judge, meantime, was not happy with the loan plan either. He was not active, was going to therapy everyday. He knew what was going on. After Fred's runoff election, I knew the world was going to come to an end one way or another. And as a matter of fact,

election night at "Little Dene's" house, as we watched the election returns, we knew what was going to happen. I told Jim Braniff and Red James, two close Hofheinz friends, "We have to act." I recited the status quo.

With the family seated around a kitchen table, I said I had reason to believe that Allbritton would take another course if the Judge wanted him to. If the Judge would let Joe be the chairman of the board or call the shots and hold him personally harmless, Allbritton would depend on me to run the show. To put that into focus required some kind of an expression from the Judge to Allbritton, endorsed by his children. Joe was not looking for the job—but was willing to do it, he inferred, if he was asked. Nobody wanted to force himself on the Judge.

O'Connell drafted on December 8, 1971, two letters he wanted Hofheinz to approve and sign. One was from the Judge to Allbritton in which Hofheinz asked Allbritton to become chairman of the board of directors of Astrodomain Corporation. The letter drafted for Hofheinz to send members of the executive committees had Hofheinz resigning as chairman of the board.

O'Connell said, "The letters were delivered December 9 to Allbritton by Fred and Roy, Jr., but upon receipt, Allbritton wanted to give them thought, so nothing was done immediately. From my perspective, the next significant thing that happened was my accident. The financing plan became rather academic. There was debate about whether I'd live and what kind of shape I'd be in if I did live. It was a bad situation. Therefore, others began considering alternatives."

When the Judge received O'Connell's two letters requiring his signature, he conferred with Mary Frances and his children. The year ended with no decision on long-term financing. All the Hofheinzes knew that would have to come in 1972. Obligations of Astrodomain to lenders were not being met. Mattel stock, dwindling in value on the New York Stock Exchange, could not be sold fast enough to meet notes coming due.

Astrodomain board member Bill Dwyer commented:

> Joe Allbritton was an extremely capable banker and businessman, but he suffered, I observed, somewhat with braggadocio. I heard comments to the effect that he guessed he was going to take over and run the Astrodome and things of that nature. The Judge began to be afraid that he meant that literally, that he eventually not only would take over and run Astrodomain, but would end up owning it. That caused a definite problem, I think, between the two. Even though Allbritton tried to do a number of things to convince the Judge he really had his best interests at heart, I believe he was always suspect in the Judge's mind. It was uncanny when the Judge was having problems with financial arrangements how lenders' representatives at board meetings acted. They would get together before meetings and talk like they were going to lay down some final rules the Judge would have to follow. When the Judge came in, you'd think that he was their absolute A-number-one best borrower and

acted perfectly happy. They had much respect for the man—obviously there was some sympathy because of his health—but it was mainly respect.

At year's end, Hofheinz was asked by a reporter why he did not sit back and take it easy after all his accomplishments. He replied: "I'm not made that way; I have always worked; I love it; it's my life. I would like to think that I have contributed something to my city and the people who live here."

43

Askanase, G E, and Ford

The beginning of the end of Roy Hofheinz's control of Astrodomain came in 1972. The Judge's apparent apprehension about turning over the board chairmanship to Houston banker Joe Allbritton, plus son Fred's desire for an alternative deal, brought a family decision to find an able financial man to head Astrodomain.

When publisher of the Washington, D.C. *Star* in 1978, Albritton was asked for an interview to recount his part in Astrodomain affairs. He replied: "I would like very much to assist you, for certainly my association with Judge Hofheinz was a most interesting part of my life. I have, for personal reasons, declined such interviews in the past and I do not think I should make an exception. I hope the Judge is doing well. Please give him my regards." It was Allbritton who handled the 1974 financing of the Lazy Lane residence in River Oaks which was to become the Judge's retirement home.

When Jack O'Connell left the hospital in January still in bad shape, breathing into machines because his lungs had been crushed, he became aware that Fred Hofheinz had induced his friend, Reuben Askanase, to come out of virtual retirement and take over Astrodomain management with approval finally given by the Judge. This was not, of course, the plan O'Connell wanted, but he could not do anything about it.

On January 30, Roy Hofheinz removed himself from minute-by-minute duties of Astrodomain Corporation and named Askanase as president and chairman of the board. The Judge took the title of senior board chairman. Newspapers speculated there was little significance in the title changes. "All it amounts to is the Hofheinz family is asking Askanase to move in and help with finances," said the *Post*.

Askanase, 63, had been a consultant and director of Questor Corporation. He was board chairman and chief executive officer of the company when it was known as Dunhill International, Incorporated. A former top official with the Spaulding Sporting Goods Company, Askanase served as a director of Rice Food Markets and Houston National Bank. He had not been associated with any of the Astrodomain enterprises previously, but he was a supporter of Fred

Reuben W. Askanase.
Photograph by Harold
Israel, courtesy Gulf
Photo.

Hofheinz in his unsuccessful campaign for mayor. He had donated, records showed, $11,000 to Fred's vote organization.

The changes were made at the corporation's annual board meeting. Allbritton and J. Darrell Francis, bankers, said they "did not wish to stand" for reelection and resigned, along with attorney Leon Jaworski. Bill Dwyer, the other board member, was reelected. Allbritton and Francis said the corporation was not in financial trouble. They said they had banking jobs on which to concentrate and the Astrodomain Corporation needed a full-time leader.

The new board consisted of Askanase, Dwyer, and Hofheinz. Newspapers asked if the board changes meant that Askanase was heading an investor group with an option to acquire all or part of Hofheinz's stock in Astrodomain. "No," Askanase said. "Astrodomain would not be here today if it were not for Roy Hofheinz. I am in this alone at the request of the Judge." Askanase said he was honored to accept the position. He also said there would be no changes in management responsibilities. Askanase said he joined Astrodomain to assist Hofheinz in financial arrangements, including possible new long-term notes totaling $38 million. He said that three major lenders were involved in the negotiations and the loans might be closed within several weeks. With the closing of the loans getting close, and with O'Connell out, the Judge said he needed someone to come in and assist. "Naming Askanase to help run Astrodomain should be healthy for the organization," said the *Post*. The Judge called Askanase a "strong, two-fisted businessman, widely and favorably known in financial circles." Askanase said Hofheinz "has done tremendous things for Houston." O'Connell was to continue as senior vice-president, the new board decided.

O'Connell recalled after he returned to the Dome in better health:

> The condition of the GE and Ford loan from the very beginning of loan negotiations was that they were to have a new chief financial officer. They also wanted me to be the general manager, whatever the title might be, of the operating things. Everybody realized the Judge was not physically in a condition to be the general manager. So those conditions were to a degree satisfied. Askanase was knowledgeable in a variety of financial fields. When I returned, he insisted on a contract with me. I had great difficulty with Rube. I didn't ask him for any more money. I wanted clarification of my responsibilities because, frankly, I had a close personal relationship with the Judge. I didn't need that kind of clarification with the Judge or with the board, but with Rube you need everything spelled out in blood. He wouldn't clarify my job. As a matter of fact, I finally said to him, "We just can't conclude the GE-Ford deal. That's all there is to it." He said, "I'm going to sue you for the $375,000 earnest money we've put up if this loan doesn't close because you won't sign the contract." I said to him: "Slavery is over. I don't have to do this. And if you can get it done some other way, have at it. But frankly I don't want that to happen, not because I give a s--- about you, but because of the Judge and his family for whom I've worked a long time, I don't want anything to happen. They need the GE-Ford loan. It's the only proposition left." I talked to Fred and Roy, Jr., in Askanase's office. They would not clarify my position, either. I decided, "The hell with it." I signed the damned loan contract because there was no other out for them.
>
> During this period I talked to the Judge and Mary Frances and filled them in. She was unbelievable in her energy and devotion to the Judge. I didn't like Askanase. Rube's contract was like $175,000 a year for five years and if he died, his wife was to get 50 percent of it. He was well-covered and had the authority, but he could seldom convince the Judge to go along with him. He was afraid to go against the Judge because the Judge still had the big equity as chairman of the board. Their relations got more and more strained. It became a battle. Meantime, operations were going down.

O'Connell said that during Askanase's leadership "the chemistry of Fred and his father was involved. They're both capable, brilliant guys who are very individualistic. I don't want to say domineering, but self-confident, and the mixture was not going to work for both. The Judge wouldn't work for anybody when he was Fred's age and earlier. If Fred and his brother were different from what they are, the Judge would have been disappointed. He was proud of them, but he would run his own show."

Astrodomain Corporation on March 15 completed a $38 million long-range financing program. Hofheinz and Askanase said that the new program would give the entertainment complex the financial program it had been seeking. Participating in the funding were HNC Realty Company of Westport, Connecticut; General Electric Credit Corporation of Stanford, Connecticut; Ford Motor Credit Corporation of Dearborn, Michigan; and a group of participating banks led by Houston Citizens Bank and Trust Company. The bank group included Chemical Bank of New York, Wells Fargo Bank of North America in San Francisco, and the Mercantile Bank of Dallas. The banks participated in the new financing to the extent of $10 million.

Hofheinz said, "With our long-term financing future secure, we can set about our business—continuing to build the most imaginative, creative entertainment complex in the world." The loan, he said, was expected to enable Astrodomain to operate from substantial working capital for new projects and for "more efficient fiscal operations for the Astrodome, Astroworld, Astrohall, and Astroworld hotels."

Allbritton, spokesman for the participating banks, said in press releases that Askanase's success "in helping Judge Hofheinz obtain vitally needed long-range financing assures a far brighter future" for Astrodomain. Allbritton said it was no secret the participating banks had been undergoing pressure to demand retirement of the short-term loans. "We are bankers—but we are also citizens—and we are proud of our Astrodome, our growing Astroworld Park, and our great baseball club," he said. Allbritton said the bankers were proud to have "walked that extra mile" for Hofheinz.

Attorney Bill McDonald recalled:

> The new lenders had confidence in Mr. Askanase. In the deal, there was a requirement that all of the family assets be put into Astrodomain Corporation, including the Judge's stock in Mattel Corporation. One of the things that we had to have before we could close the loan was proof that the lease on the Astrodome premises was not in default. There had been wrangling between the Judge and the county about various things, including the leaking Dome roof.
>
> Judge Bill Elliott was not Roy Hofheinz's biggest fan. Elliott proved a big thorn in our sides. I believe he wanted the stadium to be named Elliott Stadium. He wanted credit for having been around and supporting the building. He said the only damned thing he got was a picture on the front page of the *Press* with "Elliott's Lake" underneath. He certainly was not supportive for what we were trying to do and I felt he didn't give a hoot if the whole place fell down. There was then pending a lawsuit involving the leaking roof. We had to get that matter resolved in order to get the loan. As a consequence, HSA took on the responsibility of putting on the new roof which had been done and it was a super job. It cost more than $3 million. HSA paid. We ultimately got a judgment, but it just about paid attorneys' fees. We could have appealed it and probably should have appealed it, but didn't have the financial wherewithal to

Joe L. Allbritton. Photograph courtesy the *Houston Chronicle.*

do so at the time. The creditors were intimately involved and they didn't want to fool with it, so we didn't.

When Mr. Askanase came on board, Hofheinz was still the chief and there's one thing about him that is consistent. When the Judge is boss, he's boss. That was the source of problems through the years between him and Fred. That characteristic of the Judge created problems with Mr. Askanase almost from the outset. The Judge became increasingly more disenchanted with the situation. He had been booted upstairs, so to speak, to senior chairman of the board. I think the creditors were trying to hem him into a corner with Mr. Askanase running it. This was degrading to the Judge. It hurt those of us who saw it happen—not the least of whom was Mary Frances. It was tough on her.

Jack O'Connell, then 41, announced on November 1 that he would resign his position as senior vice-president and chief operations officer of Astrodomain. O'Connell said the resignation would be effective soon. He said no date was set because he would stay with the holding company for a period of time until his departure would not be inopportune for the organization. Askanase accepted O'Connell's resignation and said he would move into the Astrodome, where Astrodomain offices were located, to supervise operations with O'Connell.

Bill McDonald observed: "Askanase developed a great rapport with new lenders. I don't know what was said by anybody and I'm not making any accusations, but the upshot of it all was that the lenders had confidence in Mr. Askanase and no confidence in Judge Hofheinz. The lenders, I think, had instilled in Askanase a fear that the Judge was going to spend $2 or $3 million dollars of the corporate funds to do something, buy something, or start another program, or whatever, and they didn't want him involved in that way. That fire, I think, was kindled and fueled by Mr. Askanase—my personal opinion."

When O'Connell left in 1972, Sidney Shlenker was elected to his position. Bill McDonald recalled: "After the new loan was made, revenues started declining. Part of the reason was that the baseball team didn't have good years. It was the hub around which the wheel turned. The baseball club, as a whole, never lost money, but it had to support much of the rest of the operation."

A beautiful 4.5-acre tract in River Oaks was sold in August of 1972 by oilman Nick Morrow to Mr. and Mrs. Hofheinz. The sales price was not revealed but the going price of real estate, experts said, was anywhere from two to seven dollars a foot. Huntingdon was then the hottest street in River Oaks. A tiny strip needed by a lot owner went for $10 a foot, a bit over the price of large parcels. The Hofheinz purchase bore out reports that the Judge and Mary Frances wanted to build themselves a mansion designed by Harper Goff and to enjoy life to its fullest. Mary Frances said the Judge already was at work on some fun ideas he had for the home. Financial problems prevented the Hofheinzes from building their "dream home." In the summer of 1978, they sold the property.

On October 25, 1972, Hofheinz sued the Internal Revenue Service for more than $2.3 million in estate taxes he said were overpaid. Hofheinz, executor of the estate of his wife, said that after her death he filed and paid $1,293,061 in taxes in March of 1968. In June of 1971, the suit said, the IRS asked for $2,177,051 more in federal estate taxes which Hofheinz paid March 1, 1972. The next month he filed for refund of the taxes and had no reply—either allowing or disallowing the application—and that caused him to seek relief in federal court.

"Little Dene" married Joseph Robert Bolker on December 12, 1972. Bolker first married Barbara Tabor, daughter of a savings and loan executive and they had four children. He was divorced and married again to Christina Onassis over objections of her father, Aristotle Onassis, the Greek millionaire who married Jacqueline Kennedy, widow of the president. Dene II recalled: "As I sought my own life in Los Angeles and Hollywood, my only mistake was in marrying Bolker. Dad did not try to stop me. He allowed me to make my own mistake. I was married to Joe for about 11 weeks. When I married Joe, I think I felt that I needed a man to help me accomplish the things that I wanted. I certainly chose the wrong man. Joe had swept me off my feet. That came during a confused period in my life. After Dad's stroke, there were Mary, Frances and Dad on one side of the fence and there were my two brothers on the other, whether it was a small issue or a big issue involving the business. I always seemed to be the fifth and deciding vote and in months to come I found I really could not take that kind of pressure. I felt like a ping-pong ball. I made a decision in 1973 to take myself out of that position."

44

A Fire and A Firing

A fire in the Astroworld Hotel at 4:45 A.M., extinguished at 6:00 A.M. on New Year's Day in 1973, virtually erased any desire Roy and Mary Frances Hofheinz had to live in the "Celestial Suite" when unoccupied by renters. The fear of smoke and flames rising to the ninth-floor penthouse caused them to avoid in the future, when possible, any hotel accommodations which were above the second floor.

Mary Frances recalled what happened:

> "Little Dene" and Joe Bolker, her husband of three weeks, were in Houston for the holidays. About 5:00 A.M. I heard a light, but rather urgent, knocking on our bedroom door. I jumped up and opened the door and there stood Dene in her gown. She said, "M.F., don't get excited, but the hotel operator called and said there is a fire downstairs and we need to get out right away . . . nothing serious . . . but we just need to get out." Darwin Roberts was the Judge's aide on duty. I told Darwin to start getting the Judge up. I grabbed my robe, but didn't get the belt and didn't think about putting on my slippers. All I could think about was that we had to get the Judge out. I dashed out to call the inside elevator and hold it for the Judge, then I remembered that the night before the hotel had been 100 percent full for the Astro-Bluebonnet Bowl game and I was sure most of those people were still in the hotel. I decided it wouldn't be fair to hold one of the two inside elevators. I ran out to call the glass elevator which goes from the ground floor to the "Celestial Suite" only. As I rounded the corner to the foyer of the glass elevator, I could see through the huge glass windows that one end of the building was engulfed in flames and that the flames were leaping up over the top of the hotel. I remember wondering if all the floors below were gone. It ran through my head, "My God, are we going to die in a fire?"
>
> I rushed back into our bedroom and Darwin had one sock on the Judge. It seemed like an eternity had gone by, but I'm sure it was just a minute. I said, "Darwin, get the Judge up." I put one shoe on the Judge while he put on the other. Darwin lifted the Judge to a sitting postion on the side of the bed with sheer strength (usually the Judge helps push up with his right arm). Also, usually, we count one . . . two . . . three . . . and the Judge stands up, but this

time he stood right up, took his cane and made the quick steps to his wheel-chair. By this time, the bedroom was filled with smoke. Dene came running in again and said the operator called back to tell us not to go down on the elevator, but to go down the stairs. I thought to myself, "Oh, no, how are we going to get the Judge down nine flights of stairs?" About this time, the hotel security man, Roxie Simmons, came into the bedroom. He asked if he could help. I grabbed the sheet off the bed and put it around the Judge since all he had on was his shoes and socks and a T-shirt. Darwin started rolling the Judge in his wheel-chair toward the ramp of the split-level bedroom. At this moment, the Judge's wonderful wit came shining through. He said, "Hold it, let me get a cigar." He reached for one on top of a heavily carved breakfront. The Judge said, "I don't think I'm going to need my lighter." The room was so thick with smoke that we couldn't see more than six or eight feet in front of us. Darwin rolled the Judge's wheelchair down the small ramp and out to the tile hallway swiftly. As we were going down the hallway, I remember telling the Judge, "Don't worry, we're going to get you out of here even if we break some bones doing it." I don't know what the others had on their minds, but I was planning to put the Judge on a mattress or some blankets and pull him down the stairs.

We went through the P. T. Barnum Suite and out the glass sliding door to the balcony outside. It was sleeting and freezing cold. Dene took off her mink coat and put it around the Judge. I looked toward the other end of the building where the fire was and saw that the outside glass elevator was coming up. I said, "If that baby can come up, it can go down one more time." So we all ran back through the smoke to the glass elevator. Just as we got there, the elevator door opened and there stood Jim Spring, manager of our hotels. He had come to see if he could help us since we were the last people left in upper floors. I could have kissed him. We boarded the elevator and descended to the ground floor with flames lapping all around the elevator on the way down. Thank God for Jim Spring!

The fire started on the seventh floor, moved up to the eighth floor, and the only reason it didn't demolish the ninth was that it was set in from the outside with a balcony all around. All hotel guests were sitting around the lobby and restaurant in various stages of dress. From the sixth floor down, the hotel was unharmed. After about an hour, we were told that it would be impossible to return to the ninth floor to sleep so we went to the Astrodome. Channel 13 had a camera man outside the hotel and he was zooming in on the Judge like the eyes of the world. I knew we had to unwrap the Judge from Dene's fur coat and the sheet before he could stand up to get into our limousine. I didn't know what to do with the camera pointing at the Judge. I leaned over to the cameraman and explained that we had to unwrap the Judge and that he didn't have anything on underneath. He was dear. He put his camera down on the hood of the car and held one side of the sheet as a screen for the Judge. After checking, we found that the seventh and eighth floors were burned out. It is absolutely amazing that no one was hurt. The operator on duty that night should be given a medal of honor for getting everyone out safely.

James J. Spring. Photograph courtesy the *Houston Chronicle*.

Hotel director Spring confirmed his part in rescuing the Hofheinzes and said: "The Judge was very quiet all during the scare, but he was pretty well shaken up. Several times after that he went out of his way to thank me and Simmons because it could have been serious. The fire wouldn't have burned up there, but the smoke was bad." What caused the fire? Spring said, "We can only assume that somebody left a cigarette smoldering and a sofa caught fire in the parlor of a seventh-floor room."

In 1972, a 511-acre property on the north side of Alief Road, just west of Farm Road 1960 or State Highway 6 and south of Westheimer Road, was sold to Morris-Glenney and Company by Hofheinz interests. Realty circles estimated the price at $3 million. The property is bounded on the west by the 12,000-acre Barker Reservoir and is just west of the proposed Shell Oil Company Research and Development Center and north of the Chelford City development planned by Pan American Land Company and Houston First Savings Association. It was to be bisected by a future extension of Richmond Avenue and Westpark Drive and by the proposed Addicks-Clodine Road. The area was considered for annexation by the City of Houston.

Morris-Glenney is a real estate investment, development, and sales firm which has been in business in Houston since 1958. J. Franklin Morris, partner in the firm, which also includes Daniel Glenney III, said the property was purchased as an investment.

Fred Hofheinz was sworn in as mayor of Houston the day of the fire, January 1, 1973. After defeating the younger Hofheinz son for mayor in 1971, with 53 percent of the vote to overcome the heavy support by minorities for Fred, Louie Welch stepped down two years later to become president of the Houston Chamber of Commerce. City Councilman Dick Gottlieb felt he was heir apparent for the mayor's job and announced his candidacy. Fred Hofheinz, at age 35, decided to try again. He won in a runoff with Gottlieb and thus fulfilled his ambition to follow his father in the powerful job as the chief executive of the "Magic City." After he took office, he, like his father, worked hard for Houston's progress, while keeping in touch with Astrodomain affairs.

By the opening of the 1973 baseball season, the Judge made up his mind that he wanted Askanase out of the Astrodomain management. Fred and his brother did not, but they needed the vote of their sister to prevent Askanase's removal. The Judge had 50 percent and his children 50 percent of the ownership's voting power. A tie vote would keep Askanase in control. Hofheinz wanted to be sure his daughter would stand with him in any showdown. He asked Mary Frances to fly to Los Angeles to get her proxy. She got it.

"Little Dene" explained: "I turned my vote over to Dad's side of the fence because I felt he had made it and he had the right to break it. I felt it was his right to continue to run his own affairs. I felt that if he were to be taken away from his position of power, it would strip him of whatever dignity had been left since his stroke. I certainly didn't want to be one to contribute to that. In order not to choose between blood, as family oriented as I have been all my life, I asked that Mary Frances cast my vote, feeling full well that her loyalty would be to Dad and that she was sensitive to his desires. In retrospect, it may seem to have been a mistake. There was a bit of family conflict as a result of my decision."

As a result of "Little Dene's" position, Askanase, 64, resigned on July 10 at the regular meeting of the corporation's board of directors, who elected Hofheinz as chairman but did not fill the top positions in the subsidiaries. "When Judge Hofheinz asked me to take this position in January, 1972, I agreed to do so for a year's time and it has now been 18 months," Askanase said to newspapermen. "We have successfully completed a long-term finance program and built a strong and aggressive organization. I have enjoyed my tenure with the corporation and feel a very strong friendship for the Hofheinz family."

Fred Hofheinz said a rumor he and his brother sought to remove their Dad from Astrodomain at that time was not true. "It apparently resulted from our desire to secure Mr. Askanase's postion. Votes had been taken on the issues that Mr. Askanase was interested in. Decisions were made against Mr. Askanase because Dene gave her proxy to Dad. Mr. Askanase could not run the company and would not if the guy who controlled the stock objected. It was that simple."

Attorney Dwyer observed: "Askanase had ideas, particularly about selling assets. Hofheinz always resisted selling assets. He wasn't too opposed to selling some, but he did not want to sell such things as his railroad car and his antique car collection. He had a number of things like that he just did not want to lose. If the Judge agreed to sell Astroworld or the hotels, he wanted pretty high prices. Askanase's idea was to liquidate some of the assets, get the debt to a more manageable situation. It was inevitable that they eventually would not agree. When the Judge finally got Rube's resignation, Askanase received a fair cash settlement."

Dwyer also discussed the relationship of the Judge, his sons, and daughter during the trying financial period. He said: "Although there was talk about the sons trying to ease out the ailing Judge, I don't remember anything about it and I was on the board until June of 1975. The sons certainly tried to get together where they could at least block anything the Judge wanted to do in which they didn't believe. I was in a pretty ticklish situation in that the Judge always had my 100 percent loyalty, but at the same time I had the confidence of Fred and his brother. With the Judge's full knowledge, I would meet with them and try to allay their fears. I could never, of course, side against the Judge. Fred, Roy, and 'Little Dene' didn't have any individual ownership in the assets. Theirs was all in the family trust for their benefit, but the Judge was joint trustee with Houston Citizens Bank and Trust."

When he was managing Johnson and Loggins Real Estate and Development Company in Houston in 1978, Askanase commented about his Astrodomain tenure:

> The Judge promised to turn me free, but he never turned anybody free. This is the history of the man and I knew it when I agreed to be of help, the result of my close association with Fred. My stumbling block with the Judge was he had other advisers to whom he had been close for years. When a crisis came, they were never present. Once we began to get on the right road, their presence became pretty obvious, not on the corporate level but on a personal level which, of course, was difficult to separate from the corporate level. The Judge was very loyal to many people. While we were resolving problems and setting up programs, the Judge cooperated one thousand percent. It was only after the program appeared successful that I felt he was influenced by them. The big problem was that the Judge was one of the most imaginative men I'd ever met in my life. The imagination was not coupled with conservatism. After a year of work, it became obvious to me that I could not be permitted by the Judge to carry through the program necessary to restore the whole Astrodomain complex to health without selling some of the assets, or at least leasing them off. I had an irrevocable proxy, not only to handle Astrodomain, but to try to straighten out the Judge's personal affairs. Fred was an invaluable help to me because of his tremendous background, although he didn't work in the Dome. He always stood up for what he thought was right. I had a tremendous job to do with the inability of the cash flow to pay bills. I had no time for humor or fun.

My function was to keep Astrodomain moving. I left after 18 months because the job was not the job I hired out to do. The climate under which I was to work—and which the Judge had agreed to permit me to work—changed and it was just not worth my effort. I had already retired and the job was not necessary for my livelihood.

Bill McDonald said: "When Mr. Askanase got out of the picture, the lenders were very upset. In my judgment they didn't have all the facts. They didn't talk, for example, with John Easter, or they didn't talk with me. They were listening to Mr. Askanase's side of the story and every story has two sides to it. Perhaps Mr. Askanase was not getting the proper information about the Judge's involvement. The Judge never interferred, never went down and said, 'You go do so and so,' or 'You go buy X.' Not at all. The Judge was there to counsel and advise and to help, but the Judge was virtually out of operation, but this was his life. He was very proud of it and justifiably. But here was an outsider dabbling in his business. When Mr. Askanase's job was open for some time, lenders were communicating with me and chewing my fanny out on a daily basis, asking, 'What's the Judge trying to do?' We tried to satisfy them that the Judge was not trying to interfere or operate; he just didn't like the way things were going and for a number of reasons felt it was necessary to make a change and by golly he made a change!"

Chairman of the board Hofheinz had a new group of directors for Astrodomain by October of 1973. They were Carter B. Christie, managing partner of Christie Investments, Incorporated; Bill Dwyer, president, Charter Associates, Incorporated; Roy Hofheinz, Jr., professor at Harvard; Dr. Lewis A. Leavitt, chairman of the department of physical medicine at Baylor University's College of Medicine; Bill McDonald, Astrodomain Corporation secretary and general counsel; Dan Monroe, retired general sales manager for the southwest region of Texaco; and Willard E. Walbridge, senior vice-president for corporate affairs of Capital Cities Broadcasting Corporation. Thus, with the Judge still technically in control of Astrodomain, he faced a family division which kept his sons away from him except on a strictly business basis.

On November 29, 1973, at age 79 and after a long and debilitating illness which confined him to a wheelchair, the Judge's former partner, Bob Smith, died. Several months before Smith's death, friends of the two men sought to have a big dinner in their honor, hoping the affair would prompt a reconciliation, but, because both were in ill health at the time, the idea had to be dropped. Although Hofheinz planned to attend funeral services to pay his last respects to the civic leader whose friendship he had always regretted losing, his own physical condition prevented it.

45

Losing Control
of Astrodomain

After Reuben Askanase's resignation, the powerful Astrodomain lenders hired a firm to find an experienced financial man to take his place. In 1974 they decided to employ T. Herbert Neyland of Houston. A certified public accountant, he had been with a big accounting firm as chief financial officer. It was a local concern that decided to transfer its offices to New York. Because Neyland did not want to go to New York, he resigned from the firm and was thus available for Astrodomain leadership. He, Sidney Shlenker, and Hofheinz became the team for Astrodomain. Shlenker had been in the banking business with his father but withdrew from that to go into promotions. He became Dome promotions manager with a contract to supplement what the Judge and Jack O'Connell were doing. Then the Judge suffered his stroke, and O'Connell became chief operating officer; Shlenker was trained to do work previously done by O'Connell. He was sales oriented, had the contacts, and with O'Connell's assistance was able to perform. He was made a vice-president. The lenders decided Shlenker would be a good man to protect their interests in cooperation with Neyland.

Neyland and Shlenker thus became the powers of Astrodomain although Bill Dwyer and other Houstonians stayed on the board. It was obvious to insiders that Shlenker, because of his banking background, would support the financial backers. He knew lenders did not want to push Hofheinz too much because of his achievements and great contributions to the city's growth and felt they did not want to force a takeover. Operating Astrodomain was a difficult job.

Behind the Astrodomain scene, the financial picture did not improve. Bill Dwyer said, "When Hofheinz creditors were paid off by the $38 million loan, the interest rate was four percent above prime. By 1974 the prime went to 12 percent. The Judge was trying to pay 16 percent interest on that huge indebtedness and there just was not enough income to take care of that kind of debt. Any lesser man than the Judge would never have gotten anywhere near as far as he did without being shut down by his creditors."

Dwyer added: "There were times when we'd have one to two million dollars in past due bills. Because people had so much confidence that the Judge would succeed, that he would come out of it, nobody would take him to task. They wouldn't file suits or wouldn't file liens. John Easter did a tremendous job of keeping creditors happy. I don't know why it didn't drive him crazy. I can remember on at least two occasions, when he had been stalling creditors for months, the Judge got some new financing and John and his staff would stay up all night, if necessary, writing checks. While I was there until 1975, I don't remember anybody who ever actually lost money doing business with the Judge. All eventually got paid. Sometimes they had to be patient."

Working closely with his brother while commuting from Boston to Houston about once a month, Roy Hofheinz, Jr., kept a look into Astrodomain affairs. He said: "The problem with Astrodomain was not mismanagement, not overexpansion, not misinvestment. It was a rug being pulled out from Dad. We had perfectly good collateral for our loans and he'd still be in the catbird seat had it not been for Mattel stock's decline. Dad had no control over the biggest financial blow he suffered. He always had a certain mistrust of the people controlling his financial fortunes, but the Mattel deal that was offered by the Handler family (I was not in on it) was a swap of stock for Ringling Bros. and Barnum & Bailey. It was such a good deal that he simply couldn't turn it down. The problem was that he was unable to do anything about the terms of that deal, which were quite restrictive. He couldn't divert the stock into cash. If the stock had not gradually collapsed, Dad would very likely still be in charge of the Dome today."

On April 6, 1975, as a preliminary to the 10th anniversary of the Astrodome on April 9, TV Channel 2 carried a salute to a decade of "wonderful and wild fun" in the stadium. Geoff Winnington, teacher and photographer at Rice University's Media Center, carried on a romance with the Astrodome and documented the things that happened there to be able to show what the giant structure had meant to Harris County. The show also provided a rare opportunity for the younger generation to see and hear the man who was the genius who dreamed and developed the great center of entertainment.

The *Chronicle's* Ann Hodges wrote in her "TV Scene" column: "Roy Hofheinz in a poignant and uniquely personal interview with Ron Stone, and looking remarkably like another onetime boy wonder, Orson Welles, recalled his victory, and the memory was sweet. It was the first extensive Hofheinz interview since he suffered a stroke five years ago, and it's a tribute to Stone's ability as a TV interviewer that Hofheinz appeared at all."

Hofheinz celebrated the 10th anniversary of the Astrodome by cutting a gigantic cake on the baseball field. The cake bore likenesses of the Dome and a baseball diamond with miniature players in action. Mary Frances stood at his side to help because he could use only his right hand. His condition kept him from the public eye most of the time, but he saw reporters on April 11 and Herb Holland of the *Chronicle* wrote:

> Roy Hofheinz sat in his wheelchair and looked at the Houston Astros' game program for opening night 1975. In appearance, Hofheinz is an invalid, a shell of the man who promoted major league baseball and a domed stadium for Houston, and the city of Houston itself for so many years before that. His words, though slow and forced through semi-paralyzed lips, left no doubt his crippling stroke has done little to dim the flares of his inventive mind. He lit a cigar.
>
> "I don't know that I'm keeping up with everything like I used to," he said. "But I've always had a pace—go as fast and as long as I have to to get the job done—and my stroke hasn't altered that. The board of Astrodomain always liked to be the best at whatever we did. I wanted Houston to have the best ball club and the best place for the ball club to play." Hofheinz extinguished his cigar. "You know, this is going to be one hell of a town—if we ever get it built."

In the fall of 1974 and spring of 1975, rumors circulated that another shakeup of Hofheinz's Astrodomain was brewing and that the Judge might lose what control he had left to lenders. John Wilson and Harry Shattuck of the *Chronicle* reported in a copyrighted story on June 24, 1975:

> Roy Hofheinz, the onetime boy wonder Harris County Judge, mayor of Houston and entrepreneur, has lost control of his Astrodomain empire because of crushing debts. Ford Credit Corp., General Electric Credit Corp., and HNC Realty have been assigned authority to run the entertainment complex. Astroworld lenders now have a three-man board to run the operation: Hofheinz, T. H. Neyland, earlier named president of Astrodomain Corp. and its subsidiaries, and Sidney L. Shlenker, who has been Astrodomain first vice-president. For the first time, Hofheinz, or the Hofheinz family, does not have majority control. Neyland and Shlenker must be responsible to lenders' wishes, *Chronicle* sources said.
>
> The Hofheinz children, Roy, Jr., a professor at Harvard; Dene, who lives in Los Angeles; and Fred, mayor of Houston; met in family council more than a week ago and agreed to relinquish control of their holdings. There have been divisions at times in the Hofheinz family. Hofheinz's biggest financial problem was the tremendous debt service to Ford, G.E. and HNC. The $38 million which consolidated previous loans was at a floating interest of 4 percent above the prime rate, with a payment due every 90 days.
>
> Financial sources have estimated the total value of Hofheinz's Astrodomain holdings up to $100 million, but all agree there has been no way to generate enough cash flow to keep payments current, particularly with a sharp drop in attendance at baseball games. Speculation is that the new setup will sell some of the properties. Besides the ball club and hotels, the holdings include undeveloped land in the Astrodome area.
>
> The new organization will likely make changes in the Astrodomain operation, including the ball team. Bill McDonald, secretary and general counsel of

the organization, has resigned and plans to return to private law practice.

The total operational costs of the Dome now come to about $5 million a year, sources say. Many possibilities have been discussed within the Astrodomain councils to keep the entity afloat. If Six Flags had purchased Astroworld instead of leasing it on the long-term basis, it might have given Hofheinz the capital to remain in control. Sale of the ball club has been discussed. Although H.S.A. must put a ball team in the Dome to retain its lease, it might be possible to sell the Astros and secure a long-term lease that would satisfy the contractual obligation to the county.

The *Chronicle's* story brought an immediate comment by Shlenker: "As far as the Judge losing control of the company, that is not completely true. The Judge retains his title as board chairman and, I would say, would continue his activity with the company similar to that the last couple of years." Hofheinz would not comment publicly.

Shlenker and Neyland fired Spec Richardson July 6 and hired Tal Smith from the New York Yankees to become HSA general manager despite Hofheinz's protests. It developed that Hofheinz actually had until October 15, 1975, to regain control of the corporation. Neither of the lenders, they said, really wanted the Judge out. They told him if he would sell some of his personal holdings and raise more than $19 million, he could run his big empire again. Hofheinz worked doggedly to secure funds. The odds were against him. When he did not find the cash, Shlenker and Neyland had authority to do as creditors wished with the corporation's operations.

Shlenker on October 16 told newsmen: "There is no question that over a period of time there is going to have to be some sale, but there will be no hasty sale or one made on a fire-sale basis. Nothing is going to be done to the detriment of Hofheinz or without his full knowledge and consent. Hofheinz is still board chairman." Shlenker denied to reporters that he represented the Astrodomain's creditors. "My only objective is to see that the place operates properly and the creditors get paid and the Judge continues in any position he wants," Shlenker said.

Shlenker was elected president of the Houston Sports Association by its board on July 9. He replaced Neyland, formerly president of HSA and Astrodomain Corporation, in what Hofheinz called "a move to simplify the management structure." Neyland remained president of Astrodomain and Hofheinz remained chairman of the HSA board.

Lew Harpold joined the law firm of Hofheinz and Red James, previously known as Hofheinz, Sears, James and Burns, in 1965. Sears and Burns had left the law practice. The new firm then basically became a law practice with James and Carl Hendricks and Harpold. It went on like that until the firm was changed to Hofheinz, James and Harpold. When James became a district judge, the firm became Hofheinz and Harpold.

Harpold recalled:

I saw Judge Hofheinz from time to time at the Dome because Red was the secretary of the Houston Sports Association and general counsel. We did most of the legal work for the Astrodomain complex. Red, at first, did most of Hofheinz's work, although being Red's associate and later his junior partner, I ended up doing a lot of the work. Judge Hofheinz was satisfied with it and indicated his pleasure with me.

After Dene's death and the Judge married Mary Frances, I saw more of him in meetings. I was made advisory director of the board at Astro Bank. Those were trying years—the period right after the big loan he made with GE and Ford. Things were tight and tense, and the bank was not doing well, and the Judge was not doing well, health-wise. His enthusiasm was subdued, I think, controlled, more or less, by his health. At the board meetings at the bank, he didn't have a lot to say. He wasn't the normal Hofheinz, of course.

We had a number of meetings with the Judge and his sons and "Little Dene." Those meetings were rather interesting because it was the first time I had been around his family and him since the sons had drifted away from him. I never heard him say anything abusive to his children. In fact, I don't recall ever seeing the Judge abusive of anybody. He always handled himself well. He would make a statement of his position and sometimes, particularly during these meetings with his family, one of the children would disagree with him and he wouldn't get into an argument. It was almost either he didn't care to argue or he was not up to arguing. I think he realized after his stroke his limitations.

When the Judge was dealing with his children then, I had the feeling they thought he ought to get out of Astrodomain completely. Votes of the children were necessary to keep him in control. His daughter voted with him, and he carried on for a while.

I think one of the saddest things that I've observed, just being on the periphery of his life, was the disappointing conduct of those that surrounded him during his hey day. It seemed like a number of his so-called confidants and close friends who were probably nothing more than synchophants, faded away and almost, in some cases, turned against him. He suffered a lot in that regard. I handled all the closing out deals with Astrodomain creditors.

The Judge always should be known as an outstanding Texan and outstanding contributor to the growth of Houston—a legend in his own time. I remember I was in New Zealand working for a client there to drill oil wells. I was there about three months. BBC put on a program entitled: *The Plutocrats*. I saw it and it made me proud. Every place I've been outside Houston, Judge Hofheinz is respected and recognized as an outstanding man. I think unfortunately only 50 percent of the people in Houston feel that way. But there's no way that you can overlook Judge Hofheinz when you report the history of Houston, or the history of Texas and, in reference to the Astrodome, the history of the United States. He was a genius that caused things to happen. He was a doer.

Mary Frances Hofheinz proved to be one of the most unusual and in some respects outstanding women I've come across. She has been in a very difficult situation since the Judge's stroke. Constantly a person of happiness and joy, she has given loving care and attention to the Judge. I think if he'd been married to anybody else, he probably wouldn't be alive today. She has a capacity of being cheerful in the midst of trying circumstances that I've not seen equaled anywhere.

Despite disagreements with his sons, Hofheinz was happy in November of 1975 with the reelection of Fred as mayor. He defeated former Harris County District Attorney Frank Briscoe, 137,698 to 104,599. Fred was able to make a broader pitch to voters after two years in office. Young people and minorities gave him the push for his first victory. In his second campaign, he told voters he had created a budget surplus of millions and had helped make Houston's unemployment figure decline. Ads said Fred had improved mass transit, cut taxes, kept the crime rate down, improved the sewage systems, increased city services, and brought about a healthy economy with a well-managed city government. The pitch worked for a big majority vote.

As 1975 ended and the Astros and Houston Cougar football team had completed 11 seasons of play in the covered stadium, Mary Frances Hofheinz, who had seen most events there, said the Astrodome had a

personality of its own—the Judge's hidden personality. It is like a giant puppet reflecting the man who created it. The magnificent scoreboard has had witty remarks for all occasions. Some were planned in advance and some were spontaneous. During the early years, the Judge and Bill Giles worked closely with the scoreboard. The Astrodome defended itself against Johnny Carson, Leo Durocher, and many others. It bragged of being the "Eighth Wonder of the World" and the world's largest room. It quipped, it razzed, it jabbed at the umpires and once had to say it had talked out of turn and had washed its mouth out with soap.

The scoreboard welcomed and praised the Judge's bankers and lenders and courted sponsors and prospective sponsors for baseball broadcasts, and different sponsors for the rides at Astroworld. It ballyhooed the Astrodome and helped to do its own selling for one-minute commercials between innings. It said the things the Judge was embarrassed to say, for he had a basic shyness only his intimates realized. The scoreboard also had glowing congratulations for his daughter, Dene, when her second son, Dinn, was born. It wished his family and friends "Happy Birthday" and "Happy Anniversary." It even wished the Judge and me "Congratulations" when we were married.

46

Selling Astrodomain

Early 1976 was a frustrating time for Hofheinz. He was out of control of his empire and he had to face rumors that his beloved Astros might be sold and moved from Houston. That brought back fully his old fighting spirit. On January 8, 1976, he admitted publicly for the first time that he was no longer Astrodomain boss, but he said he would wage war with anyone who tried to sell the Astros and move them from Houston. Commented the *Chronicle* the next day: "So far Hofheinz can't find anyone to battle, least of all HSA's Sidney Shlenker or Houston millionaire John Mecom, Jr."

A series of events started with a report from New Orleans that Shlenker was negotiating with Mecom, who owns the National Football League New Orleans Saints, to buy the Astros. Both Shlenker and Mecom issued statements denying the report, but Hofheinz, in a style reminiscent of the days when he carved the multimillion-dollar Astrodomain complex out of flat prairie land, issued his own statement. "I frankly don't know what the people running Astrodomain at the present time are working on," Hofheinz said, "but I will fight with everything I have any move of the Astros from Houston and the Astrodome. I will fight it by vote, I will fight it in the courts, I will buy time on television and radio, and I will do everything in my power to organize the people of Houston to join me. The Astros belong in the Astrodome."

Shlenker said he couldn't agree more. "Our attitude is exactly the same," he said. "There is no intention of moving out of Houston. We don't have anything to fight about." Although Hofheinz was still listed as chairman of the board of Astrodomain Corporation, the parent firm, Shlenker ran day-to-day HSA functions. Shlenker said: "There is no way the Houston Astros are going to move out of Houston. There are three votes on the board of directors and any such proposal would not just get one no vote; it would get three." Shlenker, Hofheinz, and T. H. Neyland made up the board with Shlenker and Neyland responsible to the creditors. Shlenker said even if the Astro creditors wanted to move the team, the problems would be insurmountable. Creditors then were Ford Motor Credit Corporation, General Electric Credit Corporation, and

Left to right: John Mecom and son, John Mecom, Jr. **Photographs courtesy the** *Houston Chronicle.*

Hartford National Credit Realty. "The National League would never give such permission," Shlenker said.

After the story broke in New Orleans, Shlenker talked to Mecom who said the report apparently came from something he said while host of a cocktail party for an Astro promotion caravan that included Astro manager Bill Virdon and several Astro players. The New Orleans media also was at the party. "John said he didn't remember exactly what he said, but that he had made some jokes about buying the Astros," said Shlenker. Apparently he had also discussed moving the team out of Houston, causing the rumors. He added, emphatically, that there had been no discussion with Mecom about his buying the Astros.

However, it was not just talk that Mecom was interested in buying the Astros. Behind the public view, he talked with Hofheinz, Shlenker, and Neyland, who finally said in mid-February that in three weeks a deal might be made with the rich Houstonian to buy the National League team and its Dome lease. Neyland said warranties, indemnities, and other legal complications were delaying negotiations on a transaction whereby the baseball team would be sold to the senior Mecom and the Dome lease to the junior Mecom. Neyland said the proposed transaction would have to be approved by Harris County officials and by team owners of major league baseball and the National Football League.

He added that football owners would need to approve because the junior Mecom held an NFL franchise, the New Orleans Saints. Neyland neither confirmed nor denied a report that $25 million in financing to prevent the proposed transaction was being sought by Hofheinz. "I hope the Judge can raise the money if that is his intention," Neyland said. "My work with the corporation would then be at an end." Neyland denied that the Judge opposed the sale of assets to pay creditors. "We have very fine relations with the creditors and with the Judge and other shareholders," he said.

Neyland said the debt owed by the Astrodomain Corporation was originally $38 million and was reduced by selling the Astroworld Hotel complex to Servico Incorporated and leasing the Astroworld amusement park to the Six Flags Corporation. Forty percent of the debt was reportedly owed to four banks—Houston Citizens National Bank, Mercantile Bank of Dallas, Wells Fargo Bank of San Francisco, and Chemical National Bank of New York City—and 30 percent each to the General Electric Credit Corporation and the Ford Motor Credit Corporation.

Jack O'Connell interrupted his private business in an effort to get the Mecoms, neighbors of the Judge, and Hofheinz to agree on purchase of the Astros. He recalled:

> There were various efforts to sell the ball club, but the Judge never really wanted to sell. He wanted it maintained as a big part of his life. He enjoyed identification with it. There were various people who wanted to buy—the creditors, Reuben Askanase, and Fred Hofheinz—at bargain prices or at bargain terms. Creditors could never get the Judge to agree to any of these sales. I remember the closest thing to a sale came when Astrodomain Corporation brought me in to work out a deal between the two Mecoms to buy HSA. The hotels and the amusement park were gone. We got close to a deal, but it got hung up. I think the Mecoms felt that they needed more and stronger warranties and representations from the sellers then either General Electric, Ford, or Hofheinz was willing to give. We were down to contract signing. Leon Jaworski prepared the contract. It was important to the Mecoms that the Judge feel good about it. I got them to come across the street to the Judge's residence and talk about it. Fred was there. The Hofheinzes took the position that "If we have to get rid of our stock, we'd rather the Mecoms have it than somebody from out of town or somebody we don't know." It was a compatible, pleasant relationship, but ultimately it went by the board. Creditors didn't want to foreclose—they wanted to avoid any lawsuits that the Judge would bring against them, feeling he probably would tie them up in court. But what else was Roy to do? I don't know the details of the final settlement. . . .

When the Mecoms bowed out, the Astros stayed under the domination of the creditors. Hofheinz still wanted to regain control, and the creditors could not collect the prime-plus-four percent interest rates they had charged Hofheinz for themsleves because of declining revenues. As the season ended with the Astros showing progress with young players, Hofheinz and his three children finally agreed to sell their Astrodomain stock to the principal creditors, General Electric and Ford. Neyland made the announcement on September 23, 1976. He told newspapers: "General Electric Credit and Ford Credit recognize the company's need for financial stability and they will fulfill those needs as required." Neyland also said the sale involved an exclusive option for Hofheinz to repurchase certain assets, including the Houston Sports Association.

"It is a personal matter between Astrodomain and the Hofheinz family," Neyland continued, "so we do not feel at liberty to disclose the purchase price or the length of the option given to the Hofheinzes for repurchase. But I will say that the option is not very long." This meant that until the Hofheinz option expired, Astrodomain was no longer for sale on the open market. "If, after the Judge has used his alloted time, interested parties with a burning desire to become owners of a major league baseball team will contact me, I'll be happy to talk with them," Neyland said.

Neyland also announced the promotion of Tal Smith, general manager of the Astros, to president of the Houston Sports Association. He succeeded Shlenker who resigned as executive vice-president and chief operating officer. Neyland emphasized that Shlenker's departure was of his own choosing. "I have been trying to for five months," Shlenker said, "and it's time I returned to my own business interests." Martin Kelly, who joined Astrodomain in 1975 as assistant to the president, was elected vice-president and chief operating officer. He was a former financial executive with General Electric.

The action by the Ford and General Electric credit corporations freed Hofheinz from all financial claims by them, as well as the several lesser credit organizations that held notes against Astrodomain. Neyland said that all creditors were invited to share in purchase of the Hofheinz stock, but the others declined. He said that the debts outstanding held by the other creditors would not be retired at the time.

Hofheinz was not present at the news conference on the sale. The Judge's friends still were confident that his option would be exercised. The amount Hofheinz received for his equity was not disclosed, but it was apparent from his lifestyle that he was still in the millionaire class personally.

Neyland described the Astrodomain Corporation as it stood as a holding company with principal assets consisting of the Astroworld amusement park's being operated by Six Flags, around 300 acres of undeveloped land in south Houston, and the Astros. The portion covered under Hofheinz's option included the Houston Sports Association and the Stadium Corporation, which held the Astrodome lease and also operated Astrohall and Astroarena.

One of the essential problems in the Hofheinz family's sell-out of Astrodomain, Fred Hofheinz said, was the Judge's refusal to sell some assets. "Astrodomain values were tremendous, and they still are tremendous," Fred continued. "The point was, without selling assets, the cash flow was incapable of paying the amortization, interest, and principal on the debt. Lenders, under those circumstances, were wondering, 'How are you going to pay?' Without sale of assets, there was no other way to pay them. Lenders discussed selling assets, and that led ultimately to agreement with these lenders that we would merely sell to them certain assets and we would take certain assets based upon values. That transaction was an arm's length sale and it involved the separation of the assets of the Astrodomain Corporation along with the liens of a carefully negotiated sale. But it by no means was creditors taking over, as some may have thought."

Neyland was not misleading in his statement that Hofheinz's option would not last long. It expired October 6, 1976, with the ailing Judge unable to raise repurchase cash. The new owners expressed intentions of pumping new money into the operation, including funds to repair the club's spring training facility in Cocoa, Florida, and stronger promotional efforts to improve sagging baseball attendance.

In his deal with GE and Ford, Hofheinz kept most of the fabulous furnishings of the Astrodome which he personally had bought over a long period of years. Forty-eight big vans were filled with the treasures and moved during a week's time to a giant warehouse on North Post Oak Road. Longtime comptroller John Easter moved out of his Astrodome office and established one in the warehouse where he would continue as financial watchdog of Hofheinz Interests which still controlled considerable property, plus most of the treasures—some of all descriptions which had brought favorable and unusual comment when they were seen at the Astrodome, Astroworld, and in the "Celestial Suite."

When he settled down in his Lazy Lane home, Hofheinz felt he ought to show his continuing support of the Astros by renting a skybox. After Mary Frances called Tal Smith's office seeking the reservation for the 1977 season, she received no return call. GE and Ford officials made it plain, she said, that they did not want the Judge around. Warren Genee, Astrodomain vice-president, said in a 1978 interview that he and others in control felt the Judge's presence in the Dome at any time could be upsetting for officials and employees working to straighten out the organization's problems.

Hofheinz could have gone to games—he occasionally did—and sat in the box rented by Houston Slag Materials Company. His love of the Astros continued despite his bitterness toward the "prime-plus-four percenters." He watched televised games and listened to radio when games were not on the tube.

On November 1, 1978, Ford announced purchase of General Electric's half interest in Astrodomain. Genee was spokesman and said Tal Smith, Astro president, and Bill Virdon, field manager, would be retained. Genee became chief operations officer. Ford sent W. E. Odom to the Astrodome to become president in December of 1978.

On March 26, 1979, two weeks before the Astrodome was to observe its 14th anniversary, Jack Gallagher reviewed what critics called the "doomed stadium" before its completion. He wrote:

It seems only yesterday when that most creative man, Roy Hofheinz, invited the Texas press to a preview showing of his spectator's paradise and imported Anita Bryant to entertain. But opponents knocked the project when it was proposed, claiming only filling stations and hotel owners would benefit. Instead its effect has been profound and far-reaching while enriching every aspect of the community.

We've seen some embarrassing consequences—orange baseballs, brown grass and a leak-prone roof. But we've also seen the National League all-star game, AstroTurf surfaces, heavyweight championship fights, the Bluebonnet Bowl, NBA basketball, plus the presence of Joe Namath, Roger Stauback, Dick Butkus, Lance Alworth, Fran Tarkenton, Franco Harris, Ken Stabler, Bob Lilly, O.J. Simpson and Earl Campbell. Visitors from all over the world marveled at the facility, and as well-known lawyer Leon Jaworski says, "Having NASA and the space program gave us a boost, but there has not been a single event as great as the Astrodome."

They said it would be an eyesore, a disgrace, Hofheinz's folly, a white elephant. However, it has become a source of community pride while the land on which the complex is built is already worth as much as it cost to build the stadium. Roy, a city salutes you!

On May 11, 1979, Astrodomain president Odom announced that agreement had been reached with John J. McMullen of New York for purchase of Astrodomain stock in the Houston Sports Association. No sale price was then announced. The purchase included the long-term lease on the Astrodome and the convention and entertainment operations in the Astrodome, Astrohall, and Astroarena. McMullen requested and got approval of the sale from the National League owners at a Chicago meeting. McMullen, a limited partner in the syndicate owning the New York Yankees, kept negotiations secret until the sale was announced. Tal Smith, whose experience with the Yankees and friendship with McMullen, undoubtedly was the key in making the deal. He said the sale was "a positive step for the ball club and the community."

After secret visits to Houston, McMullen was reported to have visited, in the company of Christopher O'Neill, son of House Speaker Thomas "Tip" O'Neill, two Texas political leaders in the nation's capital. U.S. Representative Jim Wright, Democrat from Fort Worth, and Representative Charles Wilson, Democrat from Lufkin, did not disclose the substance of the meeting, but a New York source said: "McMullen talked to Wright and Wilson because he wanted some political clout from Texas in the deal." Wilson had influenial friends in Houston although it was not his home district. McMullen, a native of Jersey City, had just reached his 61st birthday when he bought Astro control. A graduate of the U.S. Naval Academy, he became known early as a naval architect and transportation expert. He owns 16 companies or corporations and works out of the World Trade Center in New York.

On July 12, 1979, McMullen announced he had 25 "limited" partners in his purchase. Most prominent among the Houstonians investing was Vivian Smith, widow of the club's once majority owner bought out by Hofheinz. Auto racing tycoon A. J. Foyt, who had cooperated with Hofheinz in developing midget car racing in the Dome, was a "surprise investor." Twenty of the 25 (non-voting) partners included 18 other Houstonians, four members of McMullen's family, and one of his neighbors from Montclair, New Jersey.

Houston's 1979 baseball success "made it easier [to sell partnerships in the organization]," McMullen said, but he added, "I don't think it changed anything. All the economic data we gave people was based on attendance of 1.3 million," which the 1979 Astros easily passed. The "limited" partners own 56 percent of HSA. Percentage of ownership varies. New Yorker Dave LeFevre owns 10 percent and, McMullen said, "some are close to that." At the other extreme, Mary Mochary, a neighbor of the McMullen family, owns one percent.

"The limited partnership has invested about $6 million," said McMullen, who paid more than $19 million to Astrodomain. "We have an excellent cross-section of ownership. I will have to say, however, it took A. J. Foyt's participation to convince my 10-year-old son that this was a good investment." Four members of Rotan Mosle, Incorporated, the Houston investment firm which handled the purchase agreement, were included in the new partnership. McMullen met his new players for the first time just before the sale announcement. "I told them the reason I hadn't shown up before (in the clubhouse) was that I wanted to wait until the transaction was consummated," he said.

47

"Hatchet Man Spec"
and the Astros

No decision about any of his many enterprises was made by Roy Hofheinz without his consulting Spec Richardson. Early in the close relationship of the two men, Houston Sports Association personnel called Richardson the Judge's "hatchet man." Generally speaking, Spec's job as general manager was to handle baseball finances and to sign players and make trades believed advantageous to the major league team. He seldom acted without consulting the Judge. At no time during his tenure did the Astro club, as such, lose money, but when no division pennants came along after several years of enthusiastic support by fans, profits were not sufficient to help finance other ventures in the Astrodomain complex.

Reviewing his relationship with the Judge, Richardson in 1978 recalled that he "would be on the road and sometimes at three o'clock in the morning my phone would ring. The Judge had a favorite expression: 'Sit up on the side of the bed and get the girls out of the room; I've got something I want to talk to you about. Wake up.' " This was particularly humorous because Richardson was known to be a devoted and faithful husband.

"The Judge would take me on trips with little notice," Richardson related. "One was to Miami Springs, Florida. A restaurant there, Miami Beach Villas, had grills he liked. The Japanese restaurant in the Skydome Club now has those grills. We were constantly looking at stuff for the Astrodome. My boss was always fair in his negotiations. If he sold somebody radio and TV packages or signs, he didn't walk off and leave them. His staff was instructed to take care of those people. If he was involved in radio and TV packages at the Astrodome, he had a special gate for clients. He gave them tickets to games, the number depending upon how big a package was bought. If you bought half of it, then you got something like 112 tickets to a game. He fed his clients well. In other words, after they bought, he took care of them to be sure they were happy. If there was a job to be done, the Judge would stay with it until it was done. He wouldn't say, 'You got to do this, I'm going home and go to bed.' He'd stay. . . ."

Richardson also remembered that "the Judge, Fred, and I went to New York for the last night of the World's Fair. The Judge was thinking about making a bid on the fair's Monorail to run between the Astrodome, the hotel complex, and the Astroworld convention facility. We took a trip on the last run of the tram. We later went to a party. The next morning, Fred and I got up, but the Judge wasn't there. We didn't know until two days later where he was. He'd gone to O'Hare Airport in Chicago for a secret television meeting when a baseball committee put together the first game-of-the-week package. We found out finally where the Judge was when the first TV game-of-the-week package was announced. Meanwhile, Fred and I were in Waldorf Towers worrying."

Criticized for many of the trades he had made and the fact that the Astros had failed to win a pennant, Richardson asserted that he would operate in the same manner if he had another chance under the same circumstances. His regard for Hofheinz had grown stronger through the years. When he was fired, Richardson was concerned about ever becoming a general manager again. But he knew he could always find a job in baseball and, in fact, he turned down a job as assistant to the president of a major league team to become co-general manager (and later general manager) of the San Francisco Giants, whose operations the National League had taken over from Horace Stoneham. Within 48 hours of the time Bob Lurie and Bud Herseth bought the team, Richardson was offered the chance to stay on and started the process of changing his baseball image. He was honored as the National League's "Manager of the Year" in 1978.

Richardson said, "I don't have a contract. I could get one from Lurie today, but it's not important. If they don't want me, I don't want to work for them. You may think I'm crazy, but I can go to sleep anywhere. I haven't missed a payday in baseball since 1946. I don't worry about what people write, what people say. I never had anything to prove."

"Man Friday" Joe Louis Holiday, who spent more time in the Judge's presence during 30 years service than any other individual, did not like Richardson's baseball judgment. He openly criticized choices of baseball managers, but was most vociferous about various trades made by the general manager. One night at a party in the "Celestial Suite," Holiday, attending the Judge in his wheelchair, sounded off to guests about Richardson's having made bad trades to help other clubs to the detriment of the Astros. Richardson overheard and called Holiday aside. "I told him," Richardson recalled, "that if I ever heard him speaking about me that way again, I would fire him. I had the authority because he was on the HSA payroll. I felt the Judge, although ailing and accustomed to Joe Louis as his most trusted physical aide and messenger, would back me up."

Time proved Richardson right. One day in the spring of 1973, Holiday was with the Judge in his Astrodome office and felt it was the time for a showdown about Richardson and his firing threat. He said that if the Judge kept Richardson as general manager, he was going to quit. Holiday had keys to every important door in the Astrodome, and he pulled them out of his pocket. Mary

H. B. "Spec" Richardson.
Photograph courtesy
Houston Sports Associa-
tion.

Frances recalled that she walked into the office as the Judge took the keys from
Holiday and handed them to her. It took the Judge only a few moments to make
up his mind. He did not like ultimatums. There were no harsh words. Holiday
walked out, unhappily ending his long stand on the HSA payroll, in good
financial condition because of Hofheinz's help and advice. In 1978, the former
aide was a church and civic leader in Houston's black community. He continued
his friendship with Hofheinz and often visited and reminisced with him. The
Judge regretted he had to make a choice between two of his most trusted
friends.

Houston has been traditionally loyal in its support of winning teams, and
attendance figures at 1978-1979 sporting events brought this fact into focus. In
1978 the Oilers reached the semi-finals of the NFL playoffs, losing in Pittsburgh in horrible weather, and in 1979 the Astros posted their best record ever,
finishing one and one-half games behind a victorious Cincinnati team for the
western division title. The 1979 *Media Guide of the Houston Sports Association*
recounts the Astros' earlier performances:

> In their first year under the Dome, the Astros were 65-97 under manager
> Luman Harris who was replaced by Grady Hatton in December. The high
> point of the '65 season was the performance of rookie second baseman Joe
> Morgan. Morgan set club records for the most at-bats, runs scored, hits and
> triples in his first major league year. In 1966, Morgan continued his fine play

and was selected to start at second in the All-Star game. However, an injury prevented him from participating. Left-hander Mike Cuellar compiled a .222 earned run average that year, a record that still stands. Another record set in 1966 was the crowd of 50,908 that squeezed into the Astrodome to see Sandy Koufax and the Dodgers defeat the Astros, 5-2, on June 22. It stands as the largest crowd ever to watch the Astros play.

The Astros had many stars in 1967, but none shone more brightly than right-hander Don Wilson. On June 18, Wilson struck out the formidable Hank Aaron for the final out as he recorded the third no-hitter in Houston baseball history. In the 2-0 game, Wilson allowed only three base runners, all on walks, and struck out 15. Along with Wilson's brilliant performance, Jim Wynn smacked 37 home runs and drove in 1075 runs in 1967, both of which were club records. Rusty Staub batted .333 and, along with Cuellar, represented the Astros on the National League All-Star team.

In 1968, Grady Hatton was replaced as manager by Harry "The Hat" Walker in June. Wilson fanned eight straight Cincinnati Reds on his way to an 18-strikeout performance and a 6-1 win on July 14. Wilson, a 13-game winner, was one of four Astros pitchers to win 10 or more games in 1968. The others were Larry Dierker (12), Dave Giusti (11) and Denny LeMaster (10).

The Astros were involved in back-to-back no-hitters in 1969. On April 30, Cincinnati's Jim Maloney no-hit the Astros, 10-0. The following night, Wilson walked six and struck out 13 in no-hitting the Reds, 4-0. The Astros also had their first 20-game winner in 1969, when Dierker completed 20 games on his way to a 20-13 mark. One game that even Dierker wouldn't have been able to complete, even if he had pitched in it, was the 24-inning marathon against the Mets in the Astrodome on April 15, 1968. The Astros finally won 1-0 on an unearned run in the bottom of the 24th. It still stands as the longest game in Houston baseball history.

Following rather quiet 1970 and 1971 seasons, the Astros shocked baseball with one of the game's biggest deals of the 1971 winter baseball meetings. They traded Joe Morgan, Jack Billingham, Denis Menke, Cesar Geronimo and Ed Armbrister to the Reds for Lee May, Tommy Helms and Jimmy Stewart. The blockbuster trade, coupled with the performances of Cesar Cedeno, Jerry Reuss, Doug Rader and Bob Watson in 1972, gave the Astros enough strength to propel them to their best finish ever, an 84-69 record. It was also the year that Leo Durocher replaced Walker at the helm in mid-August. Cedeno and May were the bright spots in 1973, as the Astros finished 82-80. Cedeno batted .320, stole 56 bases and hit 25 home runs to become the first player in baseball history to steal 50 or more bases and hit 20 or more home runs in back-to-back seasons. May drove in 105 runs in the year, third highest in Astros' history. After Durocher retired at the end of the 1973 season, Preston Gomez was named manager and led Houston to an 81-81 finish. Included in the Astros' 81 wins were three one-hitters by Houston pitchers (Tom Griffin vs Pittsburgh, Dave Roberts vs Philadelphia and Don Wilson and Mike Cosgrove vs Cincinnati). In that third one-hitter on September 4, Wilson had pitched eight innings of no-hit baseball, but trailed in the game, 2-0. Gomez opted to use a pinch-hitter for Wilson in the bottom of the eighth and Wilson was deprived of a shot at his third no-hitter. Cosgrove came on in the ninth and surrendered a single as the Astros lost 2-1.

The Astros underwent a major facelift in 1975. Tal Smith, who had been with the Houston organization for 13 years before leaving to take a position with the New York Yankees in 1973, returned to become general manager, replacing Spec Richardson on August 7. Less than two weeks later, Smith named former Pittsburgh and Yankees manager Bill Virdon as skipper on August 19.

In 1976, his first full year as manager, Virdon led the Astros to an 80-82 record, one of the wins coming on Dierker's no-hitter against Montreal on July 19. James Rodney Richard became the second 20-game winner in Astros' history by posting a 20-15 mark. He also finished second in the National League in strikeouts with 214, a club and personal high for J.R. He also led all Astros' pitchers in complete games, innings pitched and ERA. Cedeno stole 58 bases in 1978, a club record. He also won his fifth consecutive Gold Glove.

In 1977, the Astros finished with an 81-81 record with Virdon. They were the only team in baseball to have three players with 40 or more stolen bases (Cedeno 61, Cruz 44, Cabell 42). The Astros' pitching staff led the NL with 37 complete games. Richard tied his own club record of 214 strikeouts, 14 of which came against the Dodgers on the final day of the season. Bob Watson set a club RBI mark with 110 and Jose Cruz was named Astros' most valuable player by Houston Baseball Writers Association, as the Astros finished third behind Los Angeles and Cincinnati.

In 1978, the Astros finished 74-88 and in fifth place. J. R. Richard struck out 303 batters to become the tenth pitcher, third National Leaguer and first NL right-hander in history to fan 300 hitters in a season. Enos Cabell finished tenth in the league in hitting and set club records for games played in a season (162), at-bats (660) and hits (195). Jose Cruz hit .315 to finish third in the league in batting. Astro pitchers, led by Richard, led the league in shutouts and strikeouts.

Clark Nealon, sports editor of the *Post,* was an admirer of Spec Richardson and did not castigate him for player trades. Regarding Hofheinz, he asserted, "I was not a Hofheinz man, but I think Houston owes him a tremendous debt for the Astrodome, among other things." Nealon noted the striking similarities in aspirations shared by Glenn McCarthy, builder of the Shamrock, and Hofheinz. McCarthy, he recalled, first conceived the idea of a covered stadium late in the 1940s, but, because "Glenn was a quarter century ahead of football thinkers," his proposal was considered impractical at the time and his idea abandoned. Nealon further paralleled the McCarthy-Hofheinz personalities, remembering that McCarthy also wanted "Houston to be the center of everything." The Judge, however, was the one who persevered. "The Dome was Roy's dream and he made it come true. One of [his] drawbacks, to me, was that he never had any patience with people who couldn't keep up with his thinking. That worked to his detriment because he didn't make any half-way enemies. When he made enemies, they were gut enemies. I told him once during one of our debates: 'Dammit Roy, you could have been president if you had given anybody else a license to think.' To me, Roy brought baseball to grand opera."

Nealon said he and Dene Hofheinz were good friends and often discussed the Judge. "She wondered about some things he did," the journalist said, "but had great patience. She impressed me as the great balance and steady guide for her husband." Of the second Mrs. Hofheinz, he said: "Mary Frances always fascinated me with her ability to handle people. She was always bright, cheerful, and a great buffer. She was a master at being noncommittal. When people asked about or wanted to see the Judge, she would charm them, wouldn't tell them what the Judge didn't want them to know."

Close observer of Hofheinz for more than a decade was Dick Peebles, sports editor of the *Chronicle*. In 1978 he said:

> Judge Hofheinz is the most remarkable, brilliant man that I ever met. He had expertise in many fields. He was a lawyer, knew a lot about architecture, about buildings, people, and how to sell. He had a great vision. I was introduced to him in the late 50s when Houston was pursuing a major league franchise. I was immediately taken over by the man and, as time progressed, even more so. The Judge was tremendously loyal to the people who worked for him. I remember that, in the first year of the Colt .45s, radio announcer Loel Passe was a controversial figure. One night after a game, I was sitting in the Judge's office. He picked brains. He wanted to know what I thought about his situation. I suggested he might get rid of Passe. He said, "Let me tell you one thing, Dick. Loel Passe will be with this baseball team as long as I'm with it." He said it with such finality that I never broached the subject again. I felt Passe didn't fit the major league image as a broadcaster. (Passe stayed with H.S.A. until late 1978.)
>
> When the Judge first came into the baseball picture, a standing question was, "How long will it be before the Judge believes he knows as much about baseball as Paul Richards?" The concensus was five years. As it turned out, it was only four. When Richards was dismissed—it was a Sunday afternoon in December, and I was putting Christmas tree lights up outside my home—Bill Giles called and said, "We're having a press conference in an hour in the Astrodome and need you to be there, very important." Richards was dismissed, the Judge announced. After that session was over, Mickey Herskowitz, then the baseball writer for the *Post*, and I went over to the Shamrock with Richards. Richards was very embittered. Herskowitz tried to calm him down a little bit and said: "Paul, the Judge is his own worst enemy." Richards looked at him with those steel grey eyes and said, "Not as long as I have a breath in my body."
>
> I didn't agree with the Judge in some things, but I think proof of the pudding is the Astrodome which stands as a great monument to him and to his vision. I remember the weekend that the Dome opened when he was standing

on the press level looking out on the field, he made the statement that the Dome would never be duplicated again. I asked him why. He said, "Cost."

The Dome presented such a challenge to the people in Louisiana and in the state of Washington that they couldn't turn down building covered fields. One of the big reasons that the outrageously expensive Superdome was built was that surveys the Judge ran on the cars in the Dome parking lot showed that as many Louisiana as Texas cars were in the parking lot. Early year attendance figures showed out-of-town Dome visitors outnumbered those locally.

Peebles, who has seen most of the major league stadiums, said Hofheinz's "firsts," outside of building the Astrodome, were followed and copied in places throughout the nation. He added that he felt the Judge's accomplishments in the sports building field far outstripped his knowledge of baseball, the game, itself. He said: "One thing the Judge always insisted upon was the fan be treated fairly. He insisted the stadium be kept clean and fans be comfortable. The foresight the Judge showed in the Astrodome is remarkable because you know that there have been few changes made in it over the years. After they built the new Madison Square Garden in New York, opening night was a farce; the toilets didn't work, the sight lines weren't right from the press box for hockey games—you couldn't see the goals. It was an example of bad planning and how well the Judge charted his course."

Peebles concluded: "My feeling about the Judge is that it is almost like reading a book and you never get a chance to finish it because you keep wondering what would have happened if Roy had kept his health. I think he never went into anything so blind that he did not see the light at the end of the tunnel when he went in. He knew there was a way out. He knew it was going to be tough getting there but I always thought that he knew where he was going."

48

Exposing the
Mattel Securities Scandal

In the mid-1970's, when—it was thought—his days of major accomplishment were behind him, Roy Hofheinz managed to record still another remarkable achievement. He personally outstripped the Securities and Exchange Commission and scores of expert attorneys and accountants by proving what none of them had been able to discover—that the stunning financial success of the Mattel toy company in 1969 through 1971 and its equally stunning failure thereafter were both produced by fraudulent accounting practices. In fact, as Roy Hofheinz learned, Mattel had misstated earnings by millions of dollars to enhance its "success" and then wiped out those phantom earnings in later years thus exaggerating the company's financial downfall.

Hofheinz was a major shareholder in Mattel during its last glory-year when Ringling Bros. and Barnum & Bailey Circus was acquired by Mattel and the circus shareholders, including Roy and his family, who received Mattel common stock for their circus stock. In 1967, Hofheinz and Irvin Feld, together with their families, had jointly purchased the circus from the estate of John Ringling North. They proceeded to modernize and revitalize it and to set it on the successful path which it still enjoys today. In 1969 the company which they had formed to own the circus, Ringling Bros. and Barnum & Bailey Combined Shows, Incorporated, sold approximately 20 percent of its stock to the investing public. As a result of this sale, Hofheinz and the family trust of which he was sole trustee owned 54 percent of the circus. From the time the circus stock was offered to the public until January of 1971, it was traded over the counter at prices ranging from a high of $14 to a low of $4.50. In December of 1970 the stock was trading in the range of $9 to $10 a share, at which time the proposed merger with Mattel was announced.

Mattel seemed to be an ideal merger partner. Under the leadership of Ruth and Elliot Handler, it had become preeminent in the toy field. In 1959, the year Mattel went public with its stock, Mattel had introduced "Barbie Doll," one of the most successful toy products ever marketed. Thereafter, Mattel began developing numerous innovative new toys, including the extremely popular "Hot Wheels" car and track game, and became known throughout the world for the many toys it manufactured and marketed. By 1967 Mattel had made a well-recognized record of consistent earnings and increasing sales. In fact, Mattel had become the largest toy manufacturer in the world, with sales in excess of $100 million.

By 1968 Mattel was actively courting investment analysts, many of whom liked what they saw in Mattel. Numerous reports and letters were distributed by analysts recommending Mattel stock for investment purposes. As a result, it became one of the darlings of the market and one of the most actively traded stocks on the New York Stock Exchange. Having traded in 1968 at a low of $10.125, by late 1970, it had grown to $40 a share.

In the late fall of 1970, Mattel and Irvin Feld began discussions which looked towards a possible acquisition by Mattel of the Circus. Those discussions led to an agreement, and on December 10, 1970, an announcement was made that the two companies were going to merge.

The merger appeared to be a highly favorable one for the Circus shareholders. It would permit shareholders to obtain the stock of an actively traded growth company trading on the New York Stock Exchange for their holdings in a small company with its stock thinly traded in the over-the-counter market. In addition, the value of the Mattel stock which each Circus shareholder would receive represented a substantial premium over the 1969 initial offering price of the Circus stock. From the perspective of Roy Hofheinz and his family, the merger would give more than 670,000 shares of Mattel common stock carrying a market value of more than $26 million.

In connection with the proposed merger, the Circus was required to submit a proxy statement to its shareholders describing the transaction. Because the merger anticipated the exchange of Mattel stock for circus stock, the proxy statement included consolidated financial statements of Mattel which were supplied by Mattel. They showed that for the fiscal year ending January 31, 1970, Mattel had net sales of approximately $300 million, and they showed net sales for the nine months ended on October 31, 1970, of $263 million. Mattel's financial statements also showed shareholders' equity of $77 million as of January 31, 1970, and $90 million as of October 31, 1970. Based on information contained in the proxy statement on February 23, 1971, the merger was overwhelmingly approved by Circus shareholders.

These Circus shareholders, such as Hofheinz who approved the merger, had every reason to believe that Mattel's fortunes would continue to be good. Mattel had a consistent growth record and was being actively touted by many stock market experts. Unfortunately the experts, and Mattel's shareholders, were in for a rude awakening.

During the first quarter following the merger, ending May 1, 1971, Mattel reported continued success. However, on September 7, 1971, the company's consolidated statement of income for the six-month period ending July 31,

1971, disclosed a decline in sales and net income. Then Mattel reported an after-tax loss of $4 million for the nine months ending October 30, 1971. The bad news culminated with the report for the fiscal year ending January 29, 1972, when Mattel reported an after-tax loss of almost $30 million.

Hard times for Mattel continued through much of 1972, but, during early 1973, Mattel issued several press releases which ultimately became the subject of litigation. The gist of these press releases was that a turnaround had occurred. The first press release was issued on February 5, 1973, when Mattel announced that "preliminary estimates" indicated "a definite turnaround" from the prior year's loss. On February 23, 1973, just 18 days later, Mattel announced that it "now expects a substantial operating loss . . . rather than a profit as previously anticipated." When the financial statements for the fiscal year ending on January 1, 1973, were announced, Mattel reported another substantial loss.

These optimistic press releases, followed by the continuing financial failure, resulted in attention from the Securities and Exchange Commission. Too, a lawsuit against Mattel commenced, captioned *Greenfield* v. *Mattel*. The *Greenfield* action was filed on March 31, 1973, on behalf of all persons who had made market purchases of Mattel stock after January 1, 1972. It charged in substance that Mattel had made false statements with respect to its financial operations during its period of decline, culminating in the misleading press releases of February of 1973. The Securities and Exchange Commission's investigation also focused on this period.

By mid-1974, a settlement had been agreed upon in the *Greenfield* action, and the appropriate court-supervised procedures had been set in motion to approve that settlement. The Security and Exchange Commission's investigation also was winding down, and in August of 1974 a consent decree was entered by which Mattel agreed not to engage in further violations of the securities laws. Although extensive investigations were made in both of these cases, Mattel's financial statements were not shown to be false in either of them. All that was shown was that Mattel had issued public statements after it was already in financial decline that falsely suggested that its performance was improving. Neither the Securities and Exchange Commission nor the *Greenfield* plaintiffs found any fault with Mattel's practices durings its days of success, and neither offered solace to circus shareholders like the Hofheinz family.

During the period in which the Security and Exchange Commission and *Greenfield* actions were pending, Mattel's fortunes continued to decline. As a result, in February of 1974, Mattel's stock was trading at less than five dollars per share, representing a loss of almost $40 a share from the giddy heights which existed at the time of the circus merger.

Roy Hofheinz had by this time personally become convinced that he had been the victim of fraud. He simply would not accept Mattel's public position

Month-End Closing Prices For Mattel, Incorporated 1970-1979

	1970	1971	1972	1973	1974	1975	1976	1977	1978	1979
January		41½	28	10⅛	4	No Trading	No Trading	5⅜	7⅝	7½
February		46½	30¾	6⅛	3½	No Trading	No Trading	5¼	7	6⅝
March		43⅝	28⅝	6½	2¾	No Trading	No Trading	5⅜	8	9⅜
April		46	25¾	6	2¾	No Trading	No Trading	5¼	8¼	9½
May	28¾	42¼	24¾	4¾	2½	No Trading	No Trading	6¾	9⅞	8
June		35⅞	23¾	4½	2⅝	No Trading	7½	8¾	10	
July	30½	31	21⅜	5	2⅛	No Trading	6½	8	10¼	10½
August	32¾	28⅜	14⅜	4⅜	2	No Trading	5⅞	9⅞	13	
September	37⅞	27¾	13⅞	4⅛	No Bid	No Trading	6	9½	10¾	
October	37⅛	22⅛	11⅝	4⅞	Trading Halted	No Trading	3½	9¼	6⅞	
November	38	21⅝	14¾	3½	Trading Halted	No Trading	6	9¾	7½	
December	36⅝	16¼	14¼	2½	Trading Halted	No Trading	5¾	8½	7½	

that the fortunes of the company in fact had declined so suddenly and dramatically. Proving a fraud, however, was another matter. The cost alone would be enormous. Counsel and accountants would have to be engaged to investigate in detail the entire workings of the huge and complex Mattel operations. Moreover, for that investigation to be successful it would have to disclose fraudulent practices which has escaped notice by the Securities and Exchange Commission and by the *Greenfield* plaintiffs. Finally, real doubt existed as to Mattel's ability to pay damages of the size that could be proved even if fraud were demonstrated.

Despite these obstacles, Roy Hofheinz decided to proceed against Mattel. In January of 1974 he attended a meeting in New York of the board of directors of the circus, of which he still served as chairman. Located in the same building as the site of the board meeting was the law firm of Willkie Farr and Gallagher, which represented the baseball industry of which Roy's Houston Astros were a part. After the board meeting, Roy, his wife, and Bill McDonald, who was house counsel for Astrodomain, went to the law offices to discuss the Mattel matter with Louis M. Hoynes, Jr., who handled the baseball account for the firm, and his colleague, Bob Kheel. At that meeting and in subsequent telephone conferences, Hofheinz described the history of Mattel's problems and gave the green light for a full-scale assault. He authorized Hoynes to retain counsel in the Los Angeles area to assist in the prosecution of the action, and Bill Shea and Frank Wilson of the firm of McCutchen, Black, Verleger and Shea were engaged. Realizing that investigative accounting expertise was required, Hofheinz also directed the hiring of an accounting firm, Kenneth Leventhal and Company, to assist in the massive effort which he was commencing.

The Judge also insisted that the lawsuit take the form of a class action brought for the benefit of all former circus shareholders. Whatever he achieved for himself and his family, he wanted to share with all of his fellow shareholders. But he was prepared to run the risks himself!

In February of 1974, an action was commenced in Los Angeles in the United States District Court for the Central District of California under the title *Easter* v. *Mattel*. The named plaintiffs, rather than the Judge himself, were John K. Easter, a business associate of Hofheinz, and the Judge's brother-in-law Charles Semands of Houston. They were named in order to reduce the publicity and adverse impact that the lawsuit might have on Mattel, a company which at that time was in extreme difficulty. A month later, when the initial publicity concerning the *Easter* action had subsided, an Amended Complaint was filed naming Hofheinz an additional party plaintiff.

The complaint in the *Easter* action alleged in substance that the financial statements prepared by Mattel and submitted to the shareholders of the circus were false and misleading. In response to these allegations, Mattel rose vigorously to defend itself. Despite its business difficulties, Mattel was still a large public company able to commit virtually unlimited resources to its defense. On the other side, Hofheinz had much more limited resources—but he was determined to battle Mattel to prove that he and thousands of other investors had been victimized.

After weeks of intense efforts and thousands of dollars of expense, the legal and accounting team prepared a plan for the unraveling of Mattel's financial affairs. The first step of this plan took the form of an extensive set of carefully drafted interrogatories, or detailed written questions, dealing with Mattel's accounting records and practices. These interrogatories, which were presented to Mattel in June of 1974, covered more than 125 pages of text and contained almost 300 detailed questions, many with numerous subsections. Each question was designed to elicit specific information about how Mattel operated and, in particular, how it prepared its financial statements.

This enormous investigative effort, going far beyond that of the Securities and Exchange Commission or the other parties engaged in litigation with Mattel, was absolutely necessary to come to grips with the task that Hofheinz had undertaken. Like David's slingshot, Hofheinz's interrogatories aimed at Mattel, the giant, hit true, but it would be weeks before Hofheinz would know how successful he had been. Mattel had just weathered the Securities and Exchange Commission investigation. Also, even though it had withdrawn from the proposed *Greenfield* settlement as a result of the filing of the *Easter* case, it also had weathered the investigative efforts of the *Greenfield* plaintiffs. Accordingly, Mattel was prepared to join battle again, and it set out to deal with the extensive Hofheinz interrogatories.

Mattel filed countless objections to the penetrating interrogatories and made it plain that Hofheinz would have to fight every step of the way to get any meaningful information. While this conflict raged and appeared to promise months of continuous court procedures, a startling event occurred. Without any warning, and with no reference to the Hofheinz claims, on September 6, 1974, Mattel issued the following press release:

> Mattel Inc. announced today that it has discovered information which, if verified, indicates that its financial statements for the years ending January 30, 1971 and January 29, 1972 inaccurately reflected in material respects the financial conditions and results of operations as, at and for the periods covered thereby. Such information, if verified, may also affect the financial statements of the Company for prior and subsequent years. Accordingly, pending verification of this information and an assessment of the effect thereof, the board of directors of the Company has requested a suspension of trading in its common stock.

After this announcement, trading of Mattel stock on the New York Stock Exchange was halted at 2:45 P.M. This bombshell, which reduced the value of Mattel common stock effectively to zero, caused the Securities and Exchange Commission again to grapple with the Mattel problem. A special counsel,

Louis L. Hoynes, Jr.

prominent Los Angeles attorney Seth Hufstedler, and a special auditor, Price Waterhouse and Company, were appointed to make a full investigation and to report to the SEC.

Despite all of this, Mattel continued to fight the Hofheinz litigation. It demanded that all procedural issues dealing with the class action aspects of the Hofheinz claim be dealt with before it had to confront the interrogatories, and it filed a set of its own interrogatories dealing with Hofheinz's finances, his circus acquisition, and other personal matters unrelated to the claim against it. Mattel also argued that the investigative efforts of Hofheinz should be put aside for months until the special auditor and special counsel completed their report.

Hofheinz simply would not give up. On December 9, 1974, he sent Lou Hoynes to court in Los Angeles before U. S. District Court Judge Malcolm M. Lucas, who was hearing all of the Mattel cases, to argue that Hofheinz should not be delayed or sidetracked in his pursuit of Mattel.

As Hoynes put it in his argument to Judge Lucas:

> There is a difference between our case and the other [Mattel] cases . . . .

We really have a plaintiff [Roy Hofheinz]. This isn't a type of class case in which there are lawyers with many, many, many, thousands and thousands, of small shareholders, which dictates a certain handling of the case. We have a plaintiff [Hofheinz] who was the majority shareholder of Ringling and who is prepared to go ahead with this case, to finance all of the discovery required, to pay for the lawyers and accountants, as he is on a current basis, to see to it that this case is pressed home. . . .

Shortly after this hearing, Judge Lucas issued an order permitting Hofheinz to proceed with his investigation. Before this probe could get in motion again, however, counsel for Hofheinz received a telephone call from a representative of Mattel suggesting that Hofheinz, as the largest single claimant against Mattel, should lend his assistance and lead the way in trying to negotiate an overall resolution of the complex claims against Mattel, which by now had multiplied far beyond the original *Greenfield* and Hofheinz claims. Following this approach, a dialogue was opened among Mattel's counsel; the firm of Irell & Manella, counsel for Hofheinz; and counsel for the *Greenfield* class, David Gold. In discussing the basis for an overall settlement, Hofheinz finally discovered what his investigation had accomplished—and what had not been admitted in any of the press releases issued by Mattel dealing with its inaccurate financial statements. Hofheinz learned that his interrogatories had so specifically inquired about the fraudulent accounting practices of Mattel that Mattel's employees had been compelled to come forward with the truth:

The formal report of the special counsel and special auditor put it quite plainly:

An Irell & Manella partner with no previous exposure to these class actions was brought in to conduct the factual investigation necessary to gather the information required to answer the *Easter* interrogatories. Toward the end of July, 1974, the partner requested the assistance of certain employees of the Toy Company to answer some of the interrogatories, one of which inquired whether any conditional sales were booked in January, 1971. Those present were admonished that they had an obligation to answer all the questions truthfully and that the Company did not want to be surprised in court by an inaccurate answer.

Two staff personnel present at the meeting said they wanted to talk to someone. The Company's general counsel directed them to the Irell & Manella partner. The two individuals told the partner, among other things, that they were aware that Mattel had recorded $15 million of "bill and hold" sales in January, 1971; that the merchandise represented by the bill and hold orders had not been shipped to the customers; and that the bill and hold merchandise had not been physically segregated in the company's warehouse facilities. As a result of further conversations with the two individuals and a member of accounting management in August, 1974, the partner concluded that the bill and hold sales had produced irregularities in certain prior years' financial statements.

Upon being apprised of counsel's discoveries, the company decided to conduct a further limited and somewhat hasty investigation. That investigation was conducted just after the Labor Day holiday in September, 1974. As a result, the Company's board of directors was informed that there were probably irregularities in past financial statements of the Company.

So it had been Roy Hofheinz's investigation which caused the dramatic announcement about irregularities in Mattel's financial statements and which had led to the suspension of trading in Mattel stock. And it was Roy Hofheinz who was being asked to provide leadership in working out a settlement which would aid those who had been victimized by Mattel and which would ultimately permit Mattel to put its troubles behind and seek to return to its former prosperity.

By April of 1975 the framework for an overall settlement had been agreed upon, and on November 1, 1975, a settlement was entered into. At the time it was signed, the settlement was perhaps the largest settlement under the federal security laws in history. It provided for the payment to a broad class of former and present Mattel shareholders of $7 million in cash, $18 million in debentures, and five million warrants entitling the holders to purchase Mattel stock within the next 10 years at four dollars per share. The aggregate stated value of the settlement at the time was $30 million. But, after the settlement, Mattel's fortunes began to rise and the warrants were soon trading at prices in excess of four dollars, thus increasing the real value of the settlement to more than $45 million. Also, in June of 1976, Arthur Andersen and Company, the former Mattel auditors, settled as well, and an additional $1,800,000 in cash and $2,200,000 in debentures were contributed, making the aggregate settlement fund approach $50 million in value.

Of course, even this immense settlement could not satisfy the claims—totaling more than $200 million—of those who had suffered loss in Mattel stock transactions. A tremendous victory had been won, however, and a greater recovery obtained than anyone had thought possible. In the final analysis, it was one man—stubborn, proud, and determined—who had made the difference: Roy Hofheinz!

For Roy and his family, the recovery came too late, and was too little, to save the Astrodomain empire. The millions which were lost when the value of the Mattel stock plummeted put more strain on the Hofheinz financial structure than it could bear, and control of most of the Hofheinz enterprises passed on to financial institutions. But Roy had made another unique mark in history with the Mattel litigation, and thousands of persons throughout the country are in his debt for what he accomplished for them.

Irwin Feld personally did not participate in the lawsuit. Neither did Astrodomain leaders. As circus president, Feld apparently felt he would jeopardize his position. Astrodomain leaders apparently felt participation would be too costly. Neither gained from the suit settlement. (Feld repeatedly refused to be interviewed by the author.)

49

Retirement Years

From the time Roy Hofheinz suffered a stroke in 1970 until the fall of 1979, Mary Frances spent only five nights away from her husband—two when she flew to Los Angeles to get a voting proxy from "Dene II," and three when she had influenza and stayed home when the Judge was in a hospital for therapy and diet. She always stayed with him in hospitals which he entered occasionally for treatment of his left side.

Hofheinz had around-the-clock attendants, each on an eight-hour shift, seven days a week. Occasionally when one of the men failed to show up for work, Mary Frances took over care of her husband as she learned to do the first year of his affliction. Other than Johnny Powell, the most faithful attendant was muscular Sammie Lee Drain, who first joined HSA in 1964 as a stadium construction worker and later was a costumed "Earth Man" in maintenance of the Astrodome. Drain changed to attendant in 1970, and a day seldom passed that he was not at the Judge's beck and call. It was he who drove and cared for Hofheinz's luxurious bus on trips out of Houston. A native of Louisiana with knowledge of Cajun cooking, he also cooked well the bean and rice dishes which the Judge relished.

Housekeeper for the Hofheinzes in their home was Mrs. Mary (Pete) Ibarra, native of the Rio Grande Valley. She was of Mexican descent. She did housekeeping work in the Astrodome suites before the Hofheinzes moved to Lazy Lane and agreed to leave there for the Judge's personal payroll. Mrs. Ibarra saw to it that the spacious mansion was kept in order. She kept eight dogs fed and watched their health. She also made from time to time what the Judge referred to as "the most delicious tamales in the world." She said that, as a child, she became grateful to Hofheinz because of the public education debates he had with R. C. Hoiles. It was Hoiles' "Freedom Newspapers" in three Valley cities which sought to close public schools as unconstitutional, and it was Hofheinz who, as the Valley's radio voice, knocked the publisher's arguments into oblivion.

Mrs. Ibarra engaged her sister, Petra Cabellero, to help her with multitudinous tasks as Mrs. Hofheinz carried on business for her husband. Two of Mrs.

Hofheinz attendants, left to right, Mary Ibarra, Sammie Drain, Richard Nico, and Johnny Powell

Ibarra's daughters, Debbie and Barbara, occasionally helped. Mrs. Ibarra gave birth to a third daughter, Rebecca, in 1977. The housekeeper took only a short time off for the birth. She brought the child to work with her every day. Becky, crawling and later toddling in diapers, became the household darling and often climbed into the Judge's wheelchair seeking hugs and kisses. He obliged.

Mary Frances' sister, Sally Sullivan, became her almost daily companion and adviser. The Judge's wife needed assistance as she handled, under his direction, continuing business affairs and investments.

Richard Nico, once a young and kindly hospital trainee in New Smyrna Beach, Florida, joined the attendants in 1978 when the Hofheinzes vacationed there. There was an emergency need for his help, and he moved his family, lovely wife and two children, to Houston.

Visits of the six Hofheinz grandchildren often enlivened the mansion and pleased the Judge. Mary Frances gave her step-grandchildren almost undivided attention whenever they were in the house. Mary Frances and Sally arranged parties, especially at Christmas, for the wives, husbands, and children of all on the household payroll. They were a part of the big "family." The Hofheinzes treated them with kindness, gifts and encouragement, and they helped them solve problems.

Trips to New Orleans, where the Judge could get a variety of food he loved, and to Florida, California, and Arizona in 1977, 1978, and 1979 broke the household routine. The bus, Cadillacs, and a luggage truck usually made up the traveling caravan. The Judge stayed off airlines because of his growing fear of them and his physical needs. Airplane toilets became almost too much for him and his attendants.

The Judge's home in River Oaks always bustled with activity. Hofheinz kept his inventive brain active by discussing projects with friends, Ben McGuire and Red James. He began new building schemes after he had won back from

Mattel money which put him in the best cash financial position of his life. He talked frequently with his stockbroker, Leland Fruhman of Bache, Halsey, Stuart and Shields, Incorporated. He pondered real estate proposals almost daily with John Easter and Mary Frances. He invested in property in an adjoining county and worked on plans for a new venture. He also sold some of his warehouse treasures, antiques and furnishings, through Mr. and Mrs. Donald Mudd, auctioneers and parents of six girls.

Mary Frances said:

> One day in 1972, I happened to mention to Barby Allbritton, wife of Joe Allbritton, chairman of the board of Houston Citizens Bank and Trust Company, that we were thinking about buying a home. She said she would give me the name of a great real estate man, George L. Murray. George is a young, personable man who has the "patience of Job." We looked at house after house. We would look awhile, then stop. Then when something new would come on the market, George would call again and we looked some more. We finally bought a four-acre lot that backed up to the River Oaks Country Club. We commissioned Harper Goff of Hollywood and Palm Springs, California, to work with our architects, John R. Phenix and A. Carroll Brodnax. Before long, we had the most beautiful house ever designed. At that time, interest rates were astronomical and the price of building materials had zoomed out of sight. Everyone advised us to wait awhile to build, that surely costs of materials would come down.
>
> We started looking for a house to buy in the interim. Over a period of two years George showed us every available house. One day he was in the car with us and we were riding down Lazy Lane. The Judge looked up and saw the white colonial house that was the home of D. E. Hughes and his beautiful blond wife, Louise. The Judge said to George, "Now, that's the house I'd like to buy." George said to the Judge, "Judge, it's not on the market, but if you want me to, I'll check to see if there's any possibility of buying it." The Judge said, "Yes, I'd like for you to do that."
>
> In a few days, George called and said that the Hughes house was not on the market, but they would be happy for us to come over and see the house if we would like. We accepted their invitation and went to see the house. The Judge loved it. We made an offer, which at first they declined, then later decided to accept. We have been happily settled in the house, thanks to Joe Allbritton, whose bank handled the financing.

It took Harper Goff, the designer, two months to pick furniture from warehouses and to decorate the first home the Judge and Mary Frances had away from Astrodomain. Covering three-and-a-half acres, it became a special stopping point for tourist sightseeing buses. Mary Frances was always curious about the tourist buses and wanted to know what speakers said. Maidee Ray suggested in 1978 that she and Mary Frances take a tour to find out. Mrs. Ray bought the tickets to make sure the bus company would not know Mrs. Hofheinz would be aboard. Mrs. Ray recalled:

After we boarded the bus, the driver was going about 45 miles-an-hour down South Main and cutting in and out of traffic in rain. Mary Frances said, "Sir, could you slow down a bit?" He replied, "Madam, the speed limit is 35 in Houston and that's what I'm doing!" When we reached bus headquarters downtown, Mary Frances asked who would be the tour guide. The driver came back and said that he was the guide and that she could get out and get her money back. Mary Frances and another couple got out. The driver did slow down after that. I had on a tape recorder. As we drove out Allen Parkway, he started his spiel. We turned on to Kirby and he said we would see the "poor" part of town as we came south on Kirby. He told us to watch for a security guard. There was a policeman parked on Lazy Lane checking traffic on Kirby. The guide said he was the security guard for the Hofheinzes. We pulled up in front, and the guide went into detail about how the Hofheinzes had built the home in a circle just like the Astrodome. (They had bought it.) It did look impressive with cars and station wagons parked in the circle because men were there working on the Hofheinz swimming pool. I did not tell the guide until it was over that the lady he invited off the bus was Mrs. Hofheinz. He looked blank and did not even connect the name, but he did say we could report him. He had fantastic stories about other people in River Oaks, including John Connally, Alan Shepard, the Mecoms, and Candace Mossler. I knew some were tall tales, but the other people aboard from Saudi Arabia, Iran, and South America swallowed it all.

The *Post* reported on April 1, 1977: "Locking horns with city councils seems to be a Hofheinz family trait. Like son Fred, former Houston Mayor Roy Hofheinz faced a hostile City Council as did Fred in his fourth term in office." The newspaper recounted the Judge's hectic three years at City Hall. By June of 1977, Fred decided that he had had enough of the bickering with the council over issues he felt were progressive and announced he would not run for reelection. As he left office January 1, 1978, Fred still had powerful political support despite potential "dirty tricks" of opponents who sought to smear his character. He returned to law practice and began trips to Europe to interest investors in Houston. In 1979 some figured that James Fred Hofheinz might enter the political field again.

On April 15, 1977, Roy Hofheinz reached an agreement with the U.S. Internal Revenue Service in his suit asking the return of $2.3 million in taxes he had paid on the estate of his first wife. Details of the settlement were not announced when U.S. District Judge James Noel dismissed the suit filed in 1972. Later it was learned that the IRS had refunded $1,137,500 to the Hofheinz Foundation and $1,457,870 to the Hofheinz trust.

David Casstevens reported in the *Post* on January 22, 1978:

No one even seemed to notice as he was brought inside through a back door of the Astroarena and wheeled up to within view of one end of the indoor court. With his horn-rim glasses, wintry mane, that full graying beard and great

Hofheinz retirement home, 2929 Lazy Lane in Houston's River Oaks

girth, Judge Roy Hofheinz looked from afar like an aging Orson Welles as he sat somberly and silently and almost motionless in the wheelchair that has confined him since a paralyzing stroke he suffered eight years ago. Clutching a lit cigar in his right hand, he said little, either to his wife Mary Frances or to an aide. Both sat dutifully at his side.

The one-time Houston political figure and prominent business tycoon had arrived unannounced moments after the start of the third singles match of the night at the Virginia Slims tennis tournament. Curiously, as soon as that particular match ended, Hofheinz was silently wheeled away. No one turned a head, no one even seemed to notice, as he was ushered away and out the same back door to a waiting car. And so ended an inconspicuous and rare public appearance by the man who was once one of the nation's most aggressive, widely acclaimed sports magnates as reigning czar over the Astrodomain empire.

Obviously, Hofheinz had braved the chilling subfreezing night for some reason. No one stopped to ask him. But perhaps, like so many others who vividly remember the Battle of the Sexes tennis match in the Astrodome more than four years ago, Hofheinz had come either out of curiosity or appreciation—or both—to see, once more, Billie Jean King, an overwhelmingly popular figure in Houston with people of all ages.

Photographer Harold Israel recalled an incident involving Judge Hofheinz during the 1978 baseball season:

I was going from one level to another with my camera. An elevator operator told me the Judge had just rolled in and was on the ninth level. I put my camera in my darkroom and went there. I got out of the elevator and found the Judge sitting as close as he could get to look at the field. I went up to him and said, "Judge, I know what you're thinking; you're looking out there and you did it all." My heart just went out for him because here was the man sitting in a wheelchair looking at what wouldn't have come about if it weren't for him.

I'm an old-time baseball fan. I came to Houston from New York 42 years ago. When baseball and the Dome arrived, it was one of the greatest things, second to the ship channel, for Houston. Anytime anybody says anything that is not a compliment to the Judge, I really get on my high horse. They think that they're paying for the Dome, don't realize that they had to put out little for it. I've got a reputation now. People say, "If you can't say something nice about the Judge around Harold, you'd better not say it." That's just the way I feel about him.

"Dene II" introduced to her family in Houston during Christmas of 1978, Ron Anton, head of Broadcast Music, Incorporated, of Hollywood. She said: "I was a member of the ASCAP (American Society of Composers, Authors and Producers) when I met Ron at an awards party in Nashville for my hit song, *Saying Hello, Saying I Love You, Saying Goodby.* Ron told me that he would like to see me about joining BMI. I accepted my ASCAP award that night. I became Mrs. Ron Anton in May of 1979." After she went to Nashville to accept her second award from ASCAP, she said: "It'll be the first time in the history of the music business that the head of BMI attended an ASCAP awards dinner. Going to Nashville was important to me. I have the Hofheinz spirit for achievement."

Although the Judge had business discussions with his sons before and after he retired from the Astrodome, he did not have the opportunity to have them and their families and "Dene II" and her sons for a family reunion until Christmas of 1977. Mary Frances made arrangements for gala days. Lavish gifts were exchanged and differences of the past forgotten. The Judge was proud of his childrens' accomplishments. Dene II, the mother of Mark Hofheinz Mann, born March 13, 1968, and Denie Hofheinz Mann, born March 27, 1965, had moved up the Hollywood lyric ladder. His sons also had distinguished themselves in their respective careers.

Roy, Jr., who at the time was director of Harvard's East Asian Research Center, received a bachelor of arts degree from Rice University, where he served as a Union Carbide Fellow, in 1957; a masters degree as a Rhodes scholar at Oxford University's Exeter College in 1959; and a Ph.D. from Harvard, where he was a National Defense Foreign Language Fellow and later succeeded Henry Kissinger as professor of government at the institution. Roy, Jr., is the author of *Broken Wave: the Chinese Communist Peasant Movement,* as well as of many articles. He and his wife, the former Harriet Parker of Boston, are the parents of two children: Fredrick Haven Hofheinz, born May 17, 1967, and Irene Patricia Hofheinz, born October 12, 1969.

Fred, the Judge's second son, was completing his second successful term as mayor of Houston. He had received his bachelor of arts degree in 1960, his masters degree in 1961, and a Ph.D. in 1965, all from the University of Texas. He was awarded his law degree from the University of Houston in 1964. Fred and Elizabeth "Mac" Winfrey Hofheinz, a Houston native, are the parents of Paul Winfrey Hofheinz, born July 14, 1962, and Tracy Virginia Hofheinz, born November 23, 1964. All three offspring of the Judge recognized that their pioneering father in his suit against Mattel had enhanced the fortunes their mother had left them, and they were grateful.

As 1979 came to a close, the Judge was looking forward to opening a new suite of offices in the popular Galleria Towers, built by his longtime friend, Gerald D. Hines. Dominating the suite would be his famous desk from the Astrodome, built by Stuart Young, which had been stored away.

50

Lasting Monuments

As of May 31, 1979, the Roy M. Hofheinz Foundation had a net worth of $4,327,385.21 in blue chip investments handled by the First International Bank of Houston as joint trustee with the Judge as co-trustee. Created before the death of Dene Hofheinz to ease tax burdens, the foundation earned $2,810,900 over 15 years, which was given to educational, health, and charitable organizations and was so well administered that benefits to institutions and worthy causes will continue for an unlimited time. Every cent involved represented money made by Hofheinz with the advice of his first and second wives and financial experts.

Prime beneficiary until 1979 was the University of Houston, which had received $2,150,000. The Lyndon Baines Johnson Library Endowment Fund at Austin received $250,000, its largest contribution, and the Houston Museum of Fine Arts the same amount. Other grants included Easter Seal Society for Crippled Children and Adults of Harris County, $60,000; Retina Research Foundation, $54,900; Alley Theatre, $15,000; Muscular Dystrophy Association, $50,000; Texas Southern University Law School, $7500; Houston Educational Foundation, $7500; and Harris County Heritage Society, $6000.

Harry Fouke, University of Houston athletic director, recalled the sequence of events which led to the foundation's first gift of $1,500,000 for his long-planned basketball pavilion on the campus. He said, "Every time I saw the Judge he asked how we were coming along with financing the facility. He offered help in whatever way he could in funding. He suggested people I should see. One day he called and asked, 'How's the money coming along?' I said the project was at a standstill because we needed additional pledges to get it off center. 'How much is that, Harry?' he asked. When I told him, he said, 'Well, I think maybe I've got an answer to that.' I naturally was anxious to find out the answer. The Judge said, 'It just might be possible that the Hofheinz Foundation, honoring my late wife and members of my family who have been close to the University, would be interested in giving the money necessary.' I said: 'Great! Let me talk quickly to Dr. Hoffman [university president] and tell him of this conversation and we'll be in touch with you shortly.' Both Dr. Hoffman and

Hofheinz Pavilion. **Photograph courtesy the University of Houston.**

I didn't hesitate. We called the Judge back and said we'd be greatly appreciative of a gift. The Judge immediately pledged $1,500,000 needed for the start of construction—to be spread out over 10 years. The cash flow of the foundation made that plan necessary, but we knew the pledge was as good as gold."

Trustees of the university voted to name the 15,000-seat building "Hofheinz Pavilion" for the man who actually opened the construction door. In it later were played many exciting basketball games, including one regional NCAA tournament. Giving the name Hofheinz to the building did not please a few immature students who did not understand the situation. They put on a campaign, publicized by newspapers, radio, and television, to have the trustees change it to "Elvin Hayes Pavilion" in honor of the great Cougar basketball player who fascinated the nation in the Houston-UCLA game televised from the Dome. Dr. Hoffman called in eight leaders of the small group to give them the facts. Six of them came out saying the trustees and Dr. Hoffman were right in naming the building after Hofheinz. They had let their feeling for Hayes, who became a great professional star, sway their judgment. "The issue is dead," said Bob Ulmer, student president. "Dr. Hoffman taught us the facts of fund-raising," he said. Dr. Hoffman and Fouke emphasized that the Judge had definitely not asked or even suggested that the pavilion—which cost $10 million—be named for him. "We decided on that because the Judge made another university dream come true," said Fouke.

Fouke added a sequel to the original gift.

As a result again of the initiative of the Judge and Mary Frances, as intermediary, we later got another gift, pledged for an office building for coaches and a dressing room facility next to the pavilion. We had a small building which housed trophies, but it was inadequate. We had to add to it to put ourselves in a position of being reasonably competitive with Southwest Conference schools. We were looking for $650,000 to do the job and weren't sure where it was coming from. The Judge was then confined to his wheelchair, but he still wanted to see football games, which required planning for him to do so comfortably. He went to most of our big games whether home or away. He went to Texas University and the Cotton Bowl when we played in Austin and Dallas. He was in the University skybox during one game. I enjoyed visiting and gossiping with him about the past. Mary Frances joined the conversation and mentioned the foundation was looking for a project and asked if the UH athletics had any need. We had a desperate need. One thing led to another in an informal way. We visited again with the Hofheinzes, described our need, and within a short period of time, we were informed that the foundation had committed an additional gift of $650,000 toward the enlargement of the facility for coaches' and players' dressing rooms.

The University of Houston's brass band, part of the Cougar marching unit, made certain that the Judge was at his River Oaks home one night before Christmas of 1978. Quietly the members assembled in front of the mansion for a Hofheinz serenade. They played and sang carols. The Judge listened in his wheelchair with joy—and grateful tears. The event resulted when Louie Gavrel, ardent Cougar booster, informed Hofheinz about the needs of the university's band. He told Hofheinz it was a pity the University did not have funds to send the band to the Cotton Bowl in Dallas when the Cougars won the Southwest Conference title. Mary Frances called Dr. Bill Moffitt, band director, and confirmed the need for band funds. The Judge's foundation paid for expenses for two trips—$30,000 each. The Christmas caroling was a thank you for the band's first-class trips to the Cotton Bowl.

Lady Bird Johnson and Hofheinz had a reunion on December 11, 1977, when "Friends of the LBJ Library" gave a gala in Austin—"A Tribute to Lady Bird." When the former First Lady saw the Judge, immaculately dressed for the formal occasion and accompanied by Mary Frances and an attendant, in the crowd of notables raising money for the library, she rushed to him and gave him a hug and a kiss. She did not know until after the gala that the Judge's foundation had pledged the most substantial gift to the library's educational endowment. It was one of the happiest evenings Hofheinz had spent since his stroke. Mrs. Johnson twice had the Hofheinzes as her guests at the LBJ ranch after the gala.

On January 1, 1979, the research division of the Houston Chamber of Commerce issued its annual "Houston Facts," the best instrument for up-to-the-minute data on the Houston area. Pending the 1980 census, the chamber showed that Houston was the nation's fifth largest city with the incorporated

Lady Bird Johnson and the Judge. **Photograph by Frank Wolfe.**

area showing a population of 1,232,802, Harris County 1,741,912, and the Houston-Galveston metropolitan area 2,979,000. From the 1920s, when Hofheinz was a teenage scholar and promoter, until 1979, the City of Houston had grown by 1,154,002, Harris County by 1,553,255, and the metropolitan area by 2,653,374 residents. No other metropolitan area in the United States could match the growth in a 50-year period.

Dale Young, director of visitor development for the Houston Convention and Visitors' Council, observed that "since the inception of the Astrodome in 1965, there has been an ongoing growth pattern in the convention and visitor industries of this city. The Astrodome was the catalyst in the truest sense of the word and became the springboard for other developments which all augmented the Houston scene in both convention and visitor circles." He also recognized the establishment of Astrohall as another result of the Judge's astute thinking and planning and applauded the unfolding of Astrodomain.

"The Astrodome surely put Houston on the map as the new convention city," Young continued, "and with this bright focus, the city fathers then decided we needed still another hall so that we might even expect to host two conventions simultaneously. With that came Albert Thomas Convention & Exhibit Center in 1968, making Houston truly a unique convention city with two major convention complexes. One might gather that the Dome was indeed the big chicken that laid the golden egg, for not only did it put Houston on the convention and visitor map, but [it] led other developers, both civic and private, to building a wide variety of facilities and attractions. The year of 1968 brought nearly 400 million new dollars to Houston via delegate and visitor expenditures. In truth, we cannot say this is all directly attributable to the existence of the Astrodome, but surely we can concur that it all began with the Dome.".

Harris County Commissioners on July 9, 1975, accepted the donation by the Hofheinz Foundation of the Brandt Street house where Houston major league baseball was born. The historic two-and-a-half story house now is used to shelter youths in difficulty. In addition the foundation donated $5000 to Concerned Teens, Incorporated, as the beginning of a fund to help renovate the building. It became the Hofheinz Sand Dollar House for Youth. Judge Frank G. Evans, associate justice of the First Court of Civil Appeals, a special consultant to the project, planned the emergency shelter and counseling for 250 to 300 youths a year. The program provides a method whereby young people who have committed no crime may be diverted from the juvenile justice system.

Houston visitors seldom fail to visit the famous "Magic Circle Galleria Area" of buildings on and around Westheimer Road. Although Hofheinz did not participate in the erection of the magnificent shopping centers, office buildings, townhouses, homes, and other attractions, it was he who realized as a young county judge that this area was ripe for development. His Yorktown acreage purchase was one of his greatest investments. He urged Bob Smith to buy land near his. His plan of a covered, air-conditioned shopping center on land he and Smith owned near his home did not materialize, but the idea that "out Westheimer" was a great growth area resulted in billions of investments by others.

Although it was Glenn McCarthy who built the Shamrock Hotel far from downtown Houston to start business development of South Main, it was the Astrodome which skyrocketed land values and new buildings in the area. Thus two major areas of the Bayou City's growth were greatly enhanced by the visions of Roy Hofheinz. Oldtimers in Houston radio and television say today that the ideas and promotions of Hofheinz in both broadcast fields gave the city leadership in the air communications field.

Martin Kelly, vice-president and chief operating officer of Astrodomain Corporation in 1978, said that from its inception in 1965 to the Astrodome's 13th birthday anniversary, the South Main complex produced $1.5 billion in cash that would not have ordinarily flowed into Houston's economy. In addition to the $15 million in Harris County bonds it agreed to pay off over 40 years, Houston Sports Association spent $6 million of its own money in improving the Astrodome. The total cost of the site and stadium documented by general obligation bonds issued, including access streets, was $32,230,000. Interest rates averaged about 3.5 percent. The $17,230,000 Harris County property owners invested directly in the Astrodome would cost each over the life of the bonds less than one dollar a year, according to one financial expert. Benefits from increasing property values around the stadium actually would more than wipe out the cost to taxpayers for the mammouth structure. It was Hofheinz's financial thinking and planning and his building genius which made the Astrodome "an entertainment plum for taxpayers," as one writer called it.

That description was attested by published reports of what it cost other governmental agencies to build covered stadiums. The Superdome in New Orleans cost $163 million when completed in 1975. It has suffered huge deficits ever since. In 1976 Louisiana general tax funds totaling $6.4 million were voted by the legislature to keep the Superdome running. Even when a private firm took over operation of the biggest covered stadium in 1977, the state had to allocate $4.7 million the first year of the new operation.

The Pontiac Silverdome, built in 1975 as home for the Detroit Lions at a cost of $55.7 million, required in 1979 an annual subsidy of $800,000 from the state. In 1977 the Silverdome was $2 million in the red and Pontiac taxpayers had to foot the deficit.

Seattle's Kingdome cost $59.8 million, financed by a property-tax assessment and a tax on hotel and motel room occupancy. With three major teams as tenants, the football Seahawks, the baseball Mariners, and the soccer Sounders, plus other events, the Kingdome ran a poor second to the Astrodome in low taxpayer costs.

With one possible exception, all other major sports facilities built by public money during a 15-year span have been termed "taxpayer white elephants." New Yorkers complained about the $115 million spent to refurbish Yankee Stadium and its surroundings. In the first year after the overhaul, the Yankees paid only $147,267 in rent compared to the Astrodome's annual rent of $750,000. Rich Stadium built for the Buffalo Bills football team after Hofheinz's proposed domed stadium there went by the boards, proved a money loser. The Bills left War Memorial Stadium to play in Rich leaving taxpayers with the abandoned field on their hands, too.

A congressional committee figured taxpayers in Arlington, Texas—between Dallas and Fort Worth—would be taxed nearly $22 million over 30 years for the stadium and other costs of luring the Washington Senators of the American League to the Lone Star State. Three Rivers Stadium in Pittsburgh, Robert F. Kennedy Stadium in Washington, Riverfront Stadium in Cincinnati, Atlanta-Fulton County Stadium in Atlanta, and Kansas City's Truman Sports

Complex all fall far short of covering the costs that taxpayers underwrote. One financial expert computed that the cost to the average homeowner in Kansas City for the Truman Complex is about $14.40 a year. Philadelphia's round Veterans' Stadium was reportedly making a little money in 1978 after five years in the red. Apparently this uncovered stadium, the Astrodome, and the Kingdome would be the only big, modern sports facilities which could not be classified as "white elephants."

Monuments for outstanding civic, business, and political leaders normally are erected after their deaths. In 1979, when he was 67 years old and had been confined to a wheelchair for nine years, Roy Hofheinz said little about his accomplishments, but his monuments were in Houston for all to see. The Astrodome was his greatest pride and joy and monument. With the "prime plus four percenters" out of the operational picture, the Judge planned to rent a skybox so that he could again regularly see baseball, football, and other events in the stadium in 1980.

Hofheinz was on vacation in Florida when John J. McMullen bought control of HSA. When the Judge returned to Houston, it was time for him to undergo therapy and diet again at a hospital. Appreciating Hofheinz's genius in building the Astrodome, the New York millionaire arranged a visit with him in the hospital. For more than an hour, they talked of the surge of the Astros, growing attendance, and, of course, money lenders with whom both had varied experiences. McMullen learned then that GE and Ford had never publicly recognized Hofheinz's contribution to baseball and the city. For three years the officials of the "prime plus four percenters" running Astrodomain had tried to ignore the Judge.

McMullen made up his mind during the hospital conference that he would honor Hofheinz in the Dome before the end of the 1979 season. He sent telegrams to hundreds of former associates of the Judge to attend a reception with a social hour and dinner in the Astrodome Club. Afterward guests would watch Hofheinz throw out the first pitch of the Houston-Atlanta game on Thursday night, September 20. Newspapers, television, and radio announced that "Roy Hofheinz Night" was upcoming and that as a special feature all prices at concession stands and restaurants in the Dome would be reduced to what they had been on the night of April 9, 1965, when the Dome opened.

A crowd of 25,000 applauded loudly as the Judge was helped from his wheelchair to throw out with his good right arm the first ball; afterward it was given to him as a souvenir. It was not the knuckle ball of his youth, but the Judge said to his aide, Johnny Powell, "Get out of the way—I'm going to throw a screwball." Loudspeakers emphasized what Hofheinz had done for the Dome, for baseball, and for Houston. The scoreboard flashed his picture. Mary Frances was given a big bouquet of red roses. Both had to fight back tears because never before had the Judge been asked to throw out the first pitch or

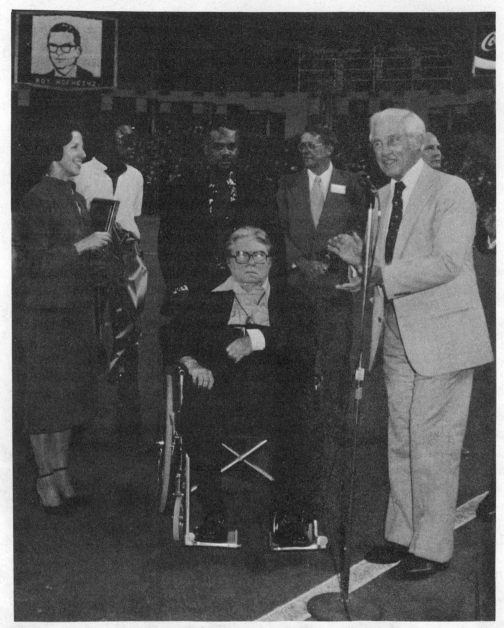

Tribute to Judge Roy Hofheinz held September 20, 1979, in the Astrodome. Left to right: Mary Frances Hofheinz, John Mills, Johnny Powell, the Judge, R. Y. Eckels, and John J. McMullen. Photograph by Harold Israel, courtesy Gulf Photo.

been the honoree in the first domed stadium in the world. McMullen and his new associates in HSA's operation graciously greeted all former Hofheinz associates and undoubtedly received a multitude of thanks for his quick gesture of friendship toward the Judge. What he did for Hofheinz was long overdue.

The Judge went back to the hospital that night glowing with happiness and respect for the new chief of the Dome. The tribute to Hofheinz, carried by radio and television, and reported with pictures and stories in newspapers, gave him, at age 67, new determination to carry on. Some thought the days of the "Genius of the Astrodome" would be short after his stroke, but more than nine years later his mind was alert for opportunities and his bank accounts in shape to back them. Writing in the *Chronicle* the next day, John Wilson said:

> It was a nice gesture on the part of the present Houston Astros' management to honor Judge Roy Hofheinz Thursday night. The Judge was due the plaudits he received. I remember a baseball dinner in 1964 and Hofheinz described the then-being-constructed stadium as it would be when finished. He told about a lot of the things that were only on the blueprint and had not been revealed before—the theater-type seats, the color, the scoreboard, the sky-boxes. It is hard to realize now the novelty, the innovation that went into this stadium. The reason those things do not seem like novelties now is because this stadium—which perhaps had borrowed from Dodger Stadium which opened in 1962 more than from any other—set the trend that has been followed by all the stadiums built since 1965. And most of those innovations came from Hofheinz, whose foresight into the future of entertainment was phenomenal. That was his genius, thinking big, creativity, foresight and then driving to bring his vision into being. He could make some bloopers, but nobody who thinks big and does things can always be right. Hofheinz never was the beloved figure to the people that many men of his stature have achieved in other cities. One reason was that he never had the time nor the inclination to work at creating such an image. In fact, his personality wasn't all that sweet. He wanted to do things and he wanted people around him to do things. He was impatient with those who couldn't grasp his visions and he was even more impatient with employees and associates who were not pressing to make his visions reality. Hofheinz is a man who will have left his mark on his city, will have helped create the positive side of Houston's image as seen by the world. [His] achievements have been immense. Our countries, our cities, our civilization always have been spurred forward, when forward movement has been made, by men who were bigger than life.

APPENDIX A

COMMENTS ABOUT JUDGE ROY MARK HOFHEINZ

EVELYN NORTON ANDERSON, Houston designer who quickly sketched outstanding costumes for Astrodome employees and who later was employed by other major league clubs to design their outfits: "Roy is one of the most fantastic persons I've ever seen. One thing I learned about him—he will drive you crazy if he doesn't have confidence in you."

Evelyn Norton
Anderson

Ralph Anderson

RALPH ANDERSON, member of the Houston architectural team which, with Hofheinz, designed the Astrodome: "There have been many stories about where Hofheinz got the idea for the Dome. There are those who attribute the idea to his having seen the Colosseum in Rome or to some kind of brain washing he was given by Buckminster Fuller on the geodesic dome. There has been enough legend connected with the genesis of the Astrodome so that to this day it is referred to as the geodesic dome by an awful lot of people—when it's no more geodesic than I am. I think Hofheinz will have to be the final authority on the real genesis."
Photograph courtesy the *Houston Chronicle*.

REUBEN ASKANASE, retired executive of chain stores who was chairman of the executive committee of the Houston Sports Association after Hofheinz suffered a stroke. The Astrodome gave the city that glamour which you get as a result of worldwide publicity—that you do not achieve by building another building, by bringing in another industry, or erecting a historical monument. Only Roy Hofheinz's brilliance could have done it."

Vernon Bain

VERNON BAIN, Houston CPA who handled finances and auditing for Hofheinz in the Judge's early radio and television ownership days: "John Stephen, an attorney and aide to Roy, came to me one afternoon and said, 'The Judge is really off on a limb now.' I asked what he meant. He answered, 'He's going to try to put a $100,000 package together and sell it to the unions. The unions have never gone for radio advertising. The Judge is away off base.' Stuart Young was called to make an advertising presentation for baseball broadcasts. It wasn't long before the union men showed up in Roy's office. A couple of days later, the word came to me that the Judge had sold the unions on something new for them. ... I think Hofheinz was a man of vision. The most provoked I believe I've ever seen him was when he talked to people and they couldn't see what he could see for the future. He had confidence in Houston and staked his whole life to make his dreams come true."

PHILIP C. BALDWIN, an attorney of Albion, Michigan, who was general counsel at the White House during the Eisenhower and Kennedy administrations: "I went to Houston on government business. Urged by R. E. 'Bob' Smith, I went to the Judge's downtown office. I wasn't easily impressed as a young lawyer who had been around Washington and worked with President Eisenhower. The first thing I saw was a brilliant carpet. It went a long way across the floor and up the walls—all walls—and it was the first time I had seen such a furnishing. This made a tremendous impression upon me, and I thought whoever thought that up must be something special and unusual. . . . Pretty soon Roy Hofheinz showed up. I quickly found him to be an aggressive man. He was a dynamo, full of speed and boundless energy. You could perceive this instantly. As I left him that time, I felt he had impressed me more than any person I had met except Lyndon Johnson with whom I had dealt in the Congress. The Judge has been my close friend and advisor ever since."

Philip Baldwin

Dick Blue

DICK BLUE, longtime director of marketing for the Astros and later for the Tampa Bay Buccaneers: "There is no doubt in my mind that Roy Hofheinz could have been president of the United States. I think the only reason he didn't pursue that goal was that he was a good friend of Lyndon Johnson. When Lyndon took that avenue, the Judge decided he would stay at home and build an empire. I heard that in one county judge race Roy was called a 'fuehrer.' I never heard it said in my presence, but I can't help comparing him with Hitler in many ways, not from a derogatory standpoint, but from an oratory standpoint. There were three men that I have heard in my lifetime that I thought were the greatest orators—Franklin D. Roosevelt, Hitler, and—by far the best—Hofheinz. I listened to Hitler on the radio, and, although I didn't speak German, I could feel the tension as he built his speeches. Hofheinz followed the same pattern of speech. It was incredible."

GEORGE CARMACK, associate editor of the *San Antonio Express and News* following his retirement from service as editor over the years of three Scripps-Howard newspapers: "As editor of the *Houston Press,* I particularly remember when the King and Queen of Greece came to Houston while Roy was mayor. . . . They could not have had a more interesting visit—nor one more appropriate—than Roy arranged. One event was at Bob Smith's ranch with a lake in the background, Santa Gertrudis cattle roaming, and marvelous barbecue served. But I particularly remember the buffet at the Hofheinz home where I had my first encounter with pheasant—cooked and put back in its plumage. Everything was done in grand style, but with a simplicity and a naturalness that made it a great occasion."

George Carmack

Hugh Cohn

HUGH COHN, former Hofheinz marketing director and now president of the marketing division of PACE Management Corporation: "Roy was a unilateral genius. I never knew anyone stronger than he was the first few times out. I never met anyone who could sell stronger. He lost some of his credibility after he didn't deliver some of the things he talked about. He was a grand huckster and that's what he claimed to be. He made no pretense of being anything else."

EVERETT COLLIER, editor of the *Houston Chronicle:* "I do not know another human being who could have made the Astrodome the success that it became and is. He's worse than a bull in a china closet; he's like a herd of stampeding buffalo. When he gets started and he is convinced that he is right, he will stop at nothing."
Photograph courtesy the *Houston Chronicle.*

Everett Collier

WILLIAM DWYER, Houston attorney who served as counsel for Astrodomain Corporation: "I rank Hofheinz in Houston at the top with Judge Elkins, Jesse Jones, and others. He didn't control the amount of money many others had, but he made a tremendous contribution to the city. He had such tremendous imagination and showmanship; he just excited people. He promoted the Astrodome. When we were traveling in Europe, people there weren't anywhere nearly as interested in the circus, for instance, as the fact that we worked at the Astrodome. That was the most important thing. He built a real monument for his city and county. I think it will never be surpassed. . . . I was fascinated by the Judge's ability to put together colors and color schemes which, if I hadn't seen them together, I would never have guessed would go together. He just had a fantastic ability to put together exciting arrangements and have it all come out in good taste."

JOHN EASTER, Houston certified public accountant, longtime treasurer of the Houston Sports Association, and now financial advisor and purser for Hofheinz Interests, Incorporated: "I don't know any better promoter who ever came down the pass than Judge Hofheinz. He to me is a brilliant man. I always enjoyed working with him even though he was and is very, very demanding. Anytime you went in to meet with him or discuss a matter with him, you knew going in he was going to be 10 strides ahead of you in his thinking."

BILL ELLIOTT, former county judge who also voted to subject the domed stadium financing to the voters, but who later became an outspoken critic of Roy Hofheinz: "Everybody either loved or hated Roy Hofehinz, and he liked it that way. I don't disagree with that kind of approach to a public figure. . . . You know he's going to kick you in the ass to make sure you're climbing that ladder."

HARRY FOUKE, athletic director of the University of Houston: "Greatness is reserved for just a few, and Roy Hofheinz is one of those great people, not only in his relationship with the city of Houston, but in the athletic growth of the United States. I'd say he was one of the greatest people I ever met."

Harry Fouke

Photograph courtesy the *Houston Chronicle*.

JOHN W. GALBREATH, chairman of the board of the Pittsburgh baseball club of the National League: "Let me say that in Roy Hofheinz's early days, when he was completely well, it was a pleasure to sit in a National League board meeting with him and benefit by his judgment and wisdom. It has been very sad the last few years to see the Judge physically handicapped. However, his mind was always alert and, despite his adversities, he always kept the issues clear and made constructive remarks about important matters."

William Y. "Bill" Giles

WILLIAM Y. "BILL" GILES, for nearly six years executive vice-president of the Philadelphia Phillies, who was Astrodome publicist until he moved up the baseball ladder: "More than anything else, the Astrodome has made the world realize that Houston is a major city. Before it opened, Houston was regarded as another big, lazy town in Texas. The Astrodome is perhaps the greatest monument to a city since the Romans built the Colosseum."

WARREN GILES, president emeritus of the National Baseball League: "Roy Hofheinz had great vision and courage to attempt what to many of us old-line baseball operators were ideas that didn't fit into baseball but developed into projects that were very helpful to the whole game. He was very cooperative with me as league president, and I became fond of him personally. I remember him first when he made a great pitch to get Houston an expansion baseball franchise in the league. . . . When we had our first meeting of league directors in Houston, he had one of the greatest displays—vulgar, it seemed at first—of food in the Shamrock Hotel I had ever seen. It was at a luncheon—gorgeous and just great!"

JOHNNY GOYEN, longtime Houston city councilman, appointed by Hofheinz as a young man to be judge of City Court with orders to stop any ticket fixing: "Roy Hofheinz outwardly appeared to be a real tough, aggressive man whom nothing bothered. But I think deep down he was a rather shy person. He had, I think, an inferiority complex in many areas and tried to cover it by being tough and boisterous, and he really was not. Basically he is a kind man."

WALTER F. "BUSTER" HACKNEY, writer and former president of the Professional Baseball Players' Association of Houston: "I was a Hofheinz classmate and marveled at his ability to promote dances—when he wasn't working to clean up the dance hall for the owner and selling future events through placards he himself printed and painted. Our baseball association honored him in 1968 for bringing major league baseball to Houston and for the many contributions he made to sandlot and college baseball."

LEW HARPOLD, one of Hofheinz's Houston law partners: "The Judge is an outstanding Texan, as well as an outstanding contributor to the growth of Houston. He is a legend in his own time."

FRED HARTMAN, editor of Texas' *Baytown Sun*: "Roy's credibility and integrity were always just absolutely unquestioned. Of people who impressed me most in this Greater Houston area, he'd be right up there at the top."

Fred Hartman

FRED HOFHEINZ, mayor of Houston for four years, lawyer, and once assistant to his father in the Astrodome: "Dad had a wealth of different professional experiences, and in each one he excelled. He was a politician—and an excellent politician. He was a radio station owner, announcer, and promoter—hence his 'Huckster House' on Galveston Bay—and the best in the country. There was no one who could sell, on a one-to-one basis, better than my Dad. He was a great public speaker, with no peer in this part of the United States. There are men who are great in finances, who make a lot of money. There are men who are good politicians, and they make great political records. There are great sports innovators, as was Dad. But usually when you find one in any category, you learn it's about all the guy has done. In Dad's case, he did all of them and did them well."

ROY HOFHEINZ, JR: "My Dad always had a great determination. He was the sort of a man who, once he made up his mind, nothing could stop him from going through with the plan he had in mind. He had the ability. Occasionally, those close to him saw him as an exceptionally stubborn and hard-headed person and sometimes hard to get along with. I know many other members of my family felt that about him. But in retrospect, I think we all realized that was one of the qualities that made him such a formidable person to deal with, one who could persuade others to go along his way. His sense of being right was perhaps stronger than that of people around him. It makes a big difference to have that internal conviction about your

Roy Hofheinz, Jr.

Photograph courtesy Harvard University.

own rightness. To bring other people along makes a man a leader. Dad was that way, a born leader, and he could pull his weight in whatever field that he entered. He always said to me, 'I could have gone into your field and been a great teacher, a great professor, or a great journalist. I decided to do the kind of business that I do because it's what I found interesting, but I could have done many other things. I could write.' "

Dr. Phillip Hoffman

DR. PHILLIP HOFFMAN, president of the University of Houston: "The Judge learned about the basketball facility the university had planned. He called one day and asked, 'How's it coming along?' When I said it was at a standstill because we needed 'x' amount of money in order to get it off center, he came back with 'How much is that?' When I told him $1.5 million, he said, 'Well, I think maybe I've got an answer to that.' The result was Hofheinz Pavilion."

JOE LOUIS HOLIDAY, "Man Friday" to Hofheinz from 1948 until the Judge's retirement, who spent more time with him perhaps during that period than any other individual: "I was an assistant to the Judge in his first radio days. He didn't want 'no' for any answer. He couldn't work without his 'pitch-kit.' I was the quick-change man for his selling presentation. The Judge was a perfectionist." Photograph by Sam Siegel, Metropolitan Photo Service, Incorporated.

Joe Louis Holiday

JUDGE W. ERVIN "RED" JAMES, Houston attorney and Hofheinz partner in one law firm, who helped the Judge win a radio station license and was considered by many to be the closest to a brother Hofheinz ever had: "In Philadelphia at the 1948 Democratic National Convention, Roy and I and his son Roy, Jr., about 15 then and called 'Butch,' had lunch together. A beautiful young woman came in and sat down in a booth by herself. I told Roy: 'I bet you five dollars that I can go over and introduce myself and have lunch with the girl.' He accepted. I leaned over and said: 'Pardon me, ma'am. I'm a stranger here. Would you mind giving me some information?' I trumped up more to say and eased into the seat beside her, continued talking, and ordered my lunch. I had won the five-dollar bet, but what did Hofheinz do to me? He sent Roy, Jr., over to catch me by the coat and say, 'Come on, Daddy. Mama's waiting for us.' The girl looked up at me and I gave up. I don't think he ever paid me the five dollars."

Leon Jaworski

LEON JAWORSKI, Houston attorney and Watergate prosecutor: "Roy sort of reminds me of Benjamin Franklin or even of Thomas Jefferson. He always found a way of providing whatever was needed or always coming forth with something that was brand new. He was a very gifted speaker. He was a dreamer up to a certain point, but his weren't idle dreams. They were dreams that had substance. Houston and Texas owe Roy Hofheinz much. He is a good, if sometimes difficult, and great man."
Photograph by Fabian Bachrach.

LADY BIRD JOHNSON, widow of the late President Lyndon B. Johnson: "Roy is dynamic, just a volcano of energy. He is a very special human being with enormous vitality. He would, as Lyndon would have said, 'charge hell with a bucket of water.' An innovator with a passionate belief in his philosophy, he is a great American."

E. A. "SQUATTY" LYONS, longtime Harris County commissioner, friend of Hofheinz from high school days, and one who voted to call referenda so that voters could decide on financing the Astrodome with public money to be repaid by rentals: "I always had utmost confidence in the Judge and his integrity and honor. He didn't mind speaking his mind around me on all occasions. Hofheinz was an innovator in the radio business. 'Way back yonder, it was supposed to be bad politically to be called a 'liberal.' Roy qualified for that label, for he always has felt that a human being is a human being."

E. A. "Squatty" Lyons

S. I. Morris

S. I. MORRIS, member of the Houston architectural team which designed the Astrodome: "Roy's a great showman and one of the great giants of our community. He is in a class by himself. I'd say that he is one of the great-great contributors to Houston's history, maybe the greatest."

BEN McGUIRE, Houston banker and investment broker: "This is the only city in the world that has a facility like the Astrodome that really doesn't cost the taxpayers 10 cents. Taxpayers should be grateful to Hofheinz for what he did for this city. Too few know and too few realize that if it hadn't been for his foresight, his genius, that the Dome would never have been possible in Houston. In his political life, Roy was one of the first to come out for racial minority rights. The Judge, I am sorry to say, didn't make a lot of friends along the way because he bucked the 'establishment.' In his last race for mayor, he called them 'fat cats' on the radio and the stump."

Ben McGuire

CLARK NEALON, retired sports editor of the *Houston Chronicle:* "Roy Hofheinz was in baseball to make money, not for the love of the game. . . . He produced baseball as the grand opera . . . with all the trimmings, the comforts, for fans. The Dome makes every other baseball stadium look like a ladies' toilet. Poor old Casey Stengel, bless his memory, was impressed most about the Dome by its comforts. He gave voice to the fact that if all the toilets in the Dome were flushed at the same time there would be another Johnstown flood."

JOHN O'CONNELL, Houston investment expert hired by Hofheinz from Chicago to bring big conventions to the Astrodome, president of the Houston Sports Association, and operator of the Astrodome when the Judge suffered his stroke: "I believe the Judge is the greatest salesman I ever met, the most imaginative leader in this part of the country. He was both difficult and great to work with. I belive he made as great a contribution to this community as any single person ever."

John O'Connell

Loel Passe

LOEL PASSE, radio and television announcer for Astro baseball who worked for Hofheinz for a quarter of a century: "The Judge picked me when I was announcing in Birmingham, and I was with him until he retired. He was and is the Astrodome. He was great in many fields, and I learned much from his ideas and enthusiasm. Roy Hofheinz had great faith and belief in the growth potential of Houston, and he gave part of his life—physical and mental—to the development of this city."
Photograph by Braeswood Vazquez Photographers.

DICK PEEBLES, sports editor of the *Houston Chronicle:* "We didn't always agree with the Judge on many things, but I think the proof of the pudding is the Astrodome which stands as a great monument to him and his vision."
Photograph courtesy Houston Sports Association.

Dick Peebles

V. V. "RED" RAMSAY, former Harris County commissioner who voted to submit to the voters the question of financing the Astrodome: "Judge Hofheinz was the greatest promoter that Houston or Harris County has ever seen."

PAUL RICHARDS, baseball great and former general manager of the Houston Astros of the National League, who was fired by Hofheinz in 1965: "Hofheinz has been a great asset to Houston and baseball. The Astrodome is not through; it hasn't even started being what it will be in the future. If I had my choice, I'd rather have Roy Hofheinz on my side."

MATT ROGG, executive of the National Association of Homebuilders: "Getting to know Roy Hofheinz was an important fringe benefit of my role with the Homebuilders. I would have hated to have had Roy as an enemy. He was tough. I think sometimes he said more than he meant. I think he was a brilliant, innovative human being. I marveled constantly at the many sides to his nature, including not only his creativity but the kind of canny business skills he had."

William Sherrill

WILLIAM SHERRILL, aide to Hofheinz as mayor, appointed to the Federal Reserve Board by President Johnson, and later financial advisor to businesses in Houston: "When Roy Hofheinz took office as mayor, none of the current civil rights laws had been passed. One of his first moves was to have removed signs over water fountains on city property which said 'White' and 'Colored.' City employees threatened to strike so we put back the 'White' signs but not the 'Colored.' The result was interesting. The white employees began to use the unmarked fountains, and you began to be able to identify which employees were sympathetic and which were not. In another six or eight months, we simply removed the 'White' signs, and nothing was ever said of it again. That was one of the very early and very small steps toward social justice in Houston."
Photograph by Fabian Bachrach.

IRIS SIFF, managing director of Houston's Alley Theatre: "The Judge is one of the most fascinating men of this, or any, generation."
Photograph courtesy the *Houston Chronicle*.

Iris Siff

JAMES J. SPRING, former manager of the famous Shamrock Hotel in Houston and later manager of Astrodomain hotels: "People sometimes say to me that they felt Roy built the Dome and other things for self-aggrandizement. That isn't true. He built the Dome because he felt that it would be good for the city and good for Roy Hofheinz. I think the man is a genius, and I think that's the opinion of most people who have known him well. When I first saw his plans back in 1959, I said, 'This man's got something I haven't seen before.' It was a chain of circumstances he couldn't foresee—and nobody could—that really resulted in his losing that empire. When he sold his share of Ringling Circus and took stock, it was worth a sum of money in the neighborhood of $35 million. Who could foresee that the bottom would drop out? If the stock had maintained its value, or if it had been stock that he could have sold, he probably would still control that empire."

JACK VALENTI, president of the Motion Picture Association of America and former aide to both Johnson and Hofheinz: "Hofheinz and Johnson were in many ways remarkably similar men in their drive, ambitions, absorption of facts, and in their massive and almost occult powers over those with whom they came in contact. Roy was probably, next to Hubert Humphrey, the finest platform speaker I've ever heard. Building the Astrodome was one of the most daring financial coups I ever saw a man put together. Once he set his mind on a goal, Hofheinz would never stop. He would not accept failure. Even in his greatest triumphs, he was always looking toward the next hill to be climbed and the next height to be scaled."

Jack Valenti

Louie Welch

LOUIE WELCH, president of the Greater Houston Chamber of Commerce, former mayor defeated in two bids for the office by Hofheinz, and constant political foe of the Hofheinz family; "The Astrodome, NASA Space Center, and Houston's medical center made Houston better known than its great port, or all the contributions by Jesse Jones. . . . Roy's monument out there is going to be there for a long, long time, and I think his name will be associated with it in the minds of the public for as long as anyone in Houston today. The three things I mentioned made Houston come through to the world quickly and almost simultaneously."
Photograph by Gittings of Houston.

TALBOT WILSON, member of the architectural team which designed the Astrodome: "Roy showed a British visitor through. He said later the visitor was a little supercilious about what he viewed, and commented on Hofheinz's private suite: 'I don't quite identify the style here.' Roy said he answered: 'This is early Hofheinz Farouk.' "

Talbot Wilson

Welcome Wilson

WELCOME WILSON, aide to Hofheinz when mayor; close friend of Hofheinz's partner, Bob Smith, in promoting, selling, and constructing the Astrodome; small stockholder on the Houston Sports Association board in the early 1970s; and now a developer: "I found Roy Hofheinz to be an extremely intelligent man, very creative. He may have been the most articulate man I've ever known. In Houston he was the originator of television for political campaigning. I found him completely honest . . . a man of his word. On the down side, he could be extremely overbearing, unable to mask even temporarily his bad feelings toward someone. As a result he was forever creating unnecessary, hard feelings."

PEGGY WOODS, assistant supervisor of nurses at Houston Methodist Hospital, who served as Hofheinz's private nurse following his stroke: "Judge Roy Hofheinz had to have the imaginative, volatile mind of a genius before his illness. After he suffered a stroke, his physical stamina diminished, but that creative mind was active and alert. The gradual demise of mental activity which we have watched during the last couple of years would seem to be the result of the inability of that mind to cope with the lack of stimulation, the lack of daily purpose if you will. The Judge, in spite of a legion of friends and acquaintances, is essentially a very private person. Many people call him friend, but few are afforded the same title by the Judge. Only a handful have been allowed to know his gentle, sentimental, fun-loving side. Less than a handful know of his deep dependence upon his second wife, Mary Frances. He is a difficult man to know and an even more difficult man to deal with, but once the deal is made, his word is his bond. The people of Houston will not again see his match because there could be only one Judge Hofheinz."

APPENDIX B

COMMENTS BY THE JUDGE

"I started on the wrong side of the tracks, but they must have replaced the location of the railroad."

"I've picked up people who don't like me—and for justifiable reasons—and a few who do. I've picked up an elephant skin in the process."

"They're only snapping at your heels when you're on the way up the ladder."

Defending his elaborately decorated offices which he felt helped him make sales: "It doesn't make any difference if they like it or not—as long as they remember it."

Concerning trying to get things done: "The squeaking wheel gets the grease."

Regarding entertainment of prospective sponsors: "When you bow, bow low."

About duck hunting: "They never ask you how many shells you shot. They ask you how many ducks you got."

Concerning the Astrodome when it opened in 1965: "It'll be at least 10 years before anyone builds another covered stadium—and the next one will never pay for itself like this one."

About cleanliness in the Dome: "If you look like a tobacco-spitting venture, it won't work. You're in show business."

APPENDIX C

ASTRODOMAIN FACTS AND FIGURES

A month before the Dome opened, Hofheinz was making plans for approximately 2000 employees to operate the stadium for each baseball game: 35 daytime maintenance men; 100 post-game cleaning men; 30 restroom matrons; 22 restroom porters; 15 section supervisors; 4 wardrobe room employees; 43 parking cashiers; 70 parking lot attendants; 10 parking lot checkers; 90 gatemen and ticket takers; 15 deputy sheriffs; 15 city policemen; 16 firemen; 2 nurses; 1 doctor; 10 first aid and rescue squad members; 8 elevator operators; 1 press gate attendant; 1 pass gate attendant; 1 umpire's room attendant; 3 batboys; 1 ballboy; 1 press box attendant; 7 press runners; 5 ground crewmen; 9 scoreboard operators; 226 girl ushers; 47 ticket sellers; 500 concession vendors; 70 concession commissary workers; 275 concession stand workers; 40 loading dock and concession clean-up workers; 300 cooks, waiters, and cashiers in restaurants; 3 gift shop workers; 9 operational engineers; 4 refrigeration men; 3 electricians; 6 general maintenance specialists, plumbers, and carpenters; and 4 security guards. In addition to these stadium employees, plans were made to include 68 Houston Sports Association employees: executives, scouts, publicity men, etc.; 36 roster ball players; as well as managers, coaches, clubhouse personnel, trainers, etc.

In 1975 milestones in the 10-year history of the Astrodomain, other than the ups and downs (usually downs) of the Astros, were recounted by newspapers as tribute to the genius of the disabled Judge Hofheinz. Highlights cited included June 10, 1965: Ringling Bros. and Barnum & Bailey Circus makes first appearance; September 11, 1965: University of Houston and Tulsa play first indoor football game; November 19-28, 1965: Billy Graham Crusade; December 17, 1965: Judy Garland in first musical concert; January 29, 1966: polo debut in the United States; February 4-6, 1966: first "bloodless bullfights"; February 23, 1966: Houston Livestock Show and Rodeo moves to Astrohall and the Dome; November 14, 1966: Cassius Clay knocks out Cleveland Williams in third round to retain his world heavyweight boxing title; January 21, 1967: first Auto Thrill Show; February 6, 1967: world indoor boxing crowd record set when 37,321 fans see Clay successfully defend his title by defeating Ernie Terrell in 15 rounds; April 19, 1967: first international soccer game indoors, Real Madrid vs. West Ham United of Britain; January 20, 1968: University of Houston defeats UCLA, 71-69, before a record basketball crowd of 52,693; February 10, 1968: record crowd of 31,372 watches the National Indoor Motorcycle championships; June 1, 1968: Astroworld opens; August 1, 1968: Houston Oilers meet the Washington Redskins in the Astrodome debut of the American Football League's Oilers; November 3, 1968: "Hubert Humphrey for president" political rally is attended by 51,753; December 31, 1968: SMU defeats Oklahoma, 28-27, in the first Bluebonnet Bowl held in the Astrodome. (The post-season college football game was then renamed the Astro-Bluebonnet Bowl); February 14, 1969: Astrodome hosts Houston's first National Basketball Association double-header, the San Diego Rockets (who later move to Houston) playing the Boston Celtics and the Detroit Pistons playing the Cincinnati Royals; March 8, 1969: Astro Grand Prix midget auto races; January 17, 1970: American Football League holds its final all-star game; May 16, 1970: the "Bob Hope Extra Special" is presented before 48,857 fans, raising funds for the Ed White Memorial Youth Center near the Manned Spacecraft Center; December 5, 1970: a crowd of 15,780 attends the movie premiere of *Brewster McCloud*, filmed in the Astrodome; January 9, 1971: Evel Knievel sets world record for indoor motorcycle jump before 41,857 spectators; March 25, 1971: National Collegiate Basketball Association tournament is held; May 28, 1971: American Basketball Association and NBA all-star game is the first meeting of the rival leagues; September 30, 1971: Houston Rockets make debut in Astrodome against the Milwaukee Bucks; December 31, 1971: Houston and Colorado play in Astro-Bluebonnet Bowl before a record number of 54,720 football fans: March 10, 1973: Russian gymnast Olga Korbut appears with Russian gymnastics team; September 20, 1973: Billie Jean King defeats Bobby Riggs in $100,000 Battle of the Sexes tennis match before a world record tennis audience of 30,472; November 8-10, 1973: Elvis Presley entertains 88,149 fans at two performances of the Houston Livestock Show and Rodeo, a one-day attendance record; December 20-21, 1974: Astrodome hosts the Women's Superstars competition, featuring America's top women athletes; February 1, 1974: a crowd of 40,012 sees the Yamaha Gold Cup Short Track motorcycle championships to set an indoor attendance record; February 18, 1975: Astroarena opens. In October of 1976, Roy Hofheinz and his family sold Astrodomain.

INDEX